Er. D.C. Gupta

Ray & Wave Optics

for JEE Main & Advanced

(Study Package for Physics)

Fully Solved

Includes Past JEE & KVPY Questions

Useful for Class 12, KVPY & Olympiads

- **Head Office :** B-32, Shivalik Main Road, Malviya Nagar, New Delhi-110017

- **Sales Office :** B-48, Shivalik Main Road, Malviya Nagar, New Delhi-110017

  Tel. : 011-26691021 / 26691713

Page Layout : Prakash Chandra Sahoo

Typeset by Disha DTP Team

Printed at : **Repro Knowledgecast Limited, Thane**

DISHA PUBLICATION

ALL RIGHTS RESERVED

© Copyright Author

For further information about the books from DISHA,

Log on to **www.dishapublication.com** or email to **info@dishapublication.com**

Contents

Contents

Reflection of Light

(1- 44)

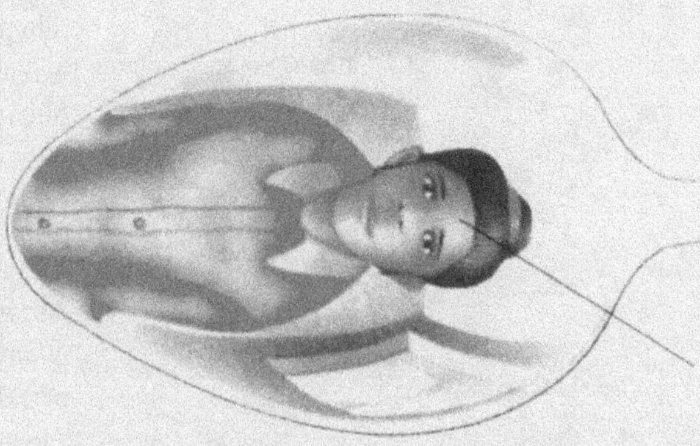

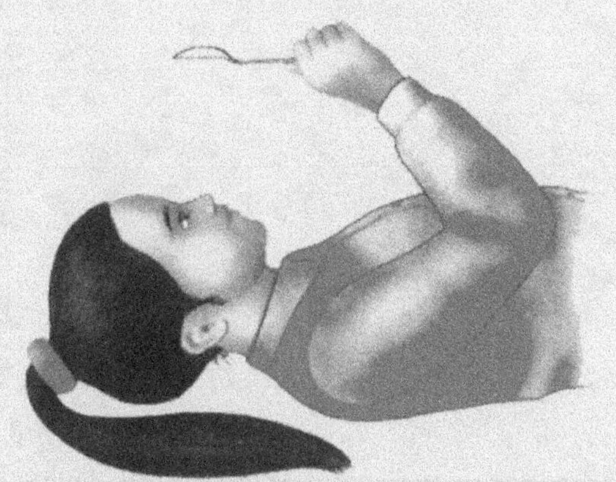

1.1 WHAT IS LIGHT?

The curiosity about the nature of light; whether it is particle or wave has a very interesting and long history. In the last more than three hundreds of years, scientists discovered numerous facts regarding with the light. These are : rectilinear propagation of light, double refraction, diffraction, interference, polarisation and photoelectric effect etc. On the basis of these observed phenomenon, many theories about nature of light have been proposed. These are :

(i) Corpuscular theory

Newton and many other scientists of the day supported this theory. According to this theory, the light consists of small weightless particles called corpuscles; which come out from the source at a very high speed. This theory was able to explain the rectilinear propagation and reflection, but could not explain the phenomenon of diffraction, which was discovered by Grimaldi as early as 1665.

(ii) The wave theory

Huygens proposed the wave theory of light. According to him light is a wave form, which travels from the source to the surroundings in all directions through a hypothetical medium, called ether. The experiments of Fresnel and Thomas Young on interference and diffraction showed that there are many optical phenomenon that can be understood on the basis of the wave theory but not by corpuscular theory.

(iii) Maxwell's EM-wave theory

The next great forward step in the theory of light was the Maxwell in 1873. According to him the light was considered to be electromagnetic waves composed of electric and magnetic fields oscillating mutually perpendicular and also perpendicular to the direction of propagation. The presence of ether is not needed. This theory however failed to explain the phenomenon of photoelectric effect and Compton's effect.

(iv) The quantum theory

This theory was proposed by Max Plank in 1900. According to this theory light was considered in the form of small packets of energy called photons. Photoelectric effect was explained by Einstein in 1905 on the basis of this theory, but this theory could not explain the phenomenon like interference, diffraction. Scientists today consider the light to have dual nature i.e., wave as well as particle. The phenomenon of light propagation may be best described by the electromagnetic wave theory, while the interaction of light with matter is a particle phenomenon.

1.2 SOURCES OF LIGHT

All bodies emit a mixture of electromagnetic waves as a result of thermal motion of their molecules. About 800°C a body emits enough visible radiation to be self-luminous and appears red hot. At 3000°C, the radiant energy contains the visible wavelengths, between 4000Å to 7000Å, and the body appears white hot. The light which consists of mixture of wavelengths is called polychromatic light. Light of single wavelength (roughly a single colour), is called **monochromatic light**. Laser light is more nearly monochromatic, than any other light source. The object which gives out light energy by itself, is called **luminous object**. The object which does not give energy by itself, but reflect light falling on it is called **non-luminous object**.

The speed of light

The speed of light in vacuum is one of the fundamental constants of nature. The first successful determination of the speed of light was made by the French scientist Fizeau in 1849. Fizeau's measurements were not of high precision. He calculated the speed of light as 3.15×10^8 m/s. By the precise measurements, the speed of light is found nearly 3×10^8 m/s as obtained by Michelson.

1.3 THE ELECTROMAGNETIC SPECTRUM

It is now well established that light is in the form of electromagnetic waves, which is a small part of electromagnetic spectrum. Each part of the spectrum has general characteristics. The relation $f\lambda = c$ holds for each, where f and λ are frequency and wavelength respectively. The wavelengths of visible light are found to lie in the range 4×10^{-7} m to 7×10^{-7} m. The corresponding range of frequencies is about 7.5×10^{14} to 4.3×10^{14} Hz. Different parts of the visible spectrum give the sensations of different colours. Wavelengths for colours in the visible spectrum are as follows :

400 nm to 450 nm	Violet
450 nm to 500 nm	Blue
500 nm to 550 nm	Green
550 nm to 600 nm	Yellow
600 nm to 650 nm	Orange
650 nm to 700 nm	Red

Wavefront, ray, and beam

A wavefront is defined as the locus of all points at which the phase of vibration of a physical quantity like pressure or electric field is the same. The electromagnetic waves radiated by a point source is represented by concentric spheres (see figure). At a very large distance from the source, the spheres can be considered planes and so plane wavefront will be obtained.

In geometric optics, it is convenient to represent a light wave by rays rather than by wavefronts. From the wave viewpoint, a ray is an imaginary line drawn in the direction in which the wave is travelling. In a particle nature of light, rays are merely the paths of photons. In general, the path along which light energy travels in a given direction is called a **ray** of light. A collection of number of rays of light is called **beam** of light.

Some definitions

1. **Optical medium :** Anything, through which light energy can pass is called optical medium.

2. **Homogeneous medium:** If an optical medium has a uniform composition throughout, it is called homogeneous medium. Ex. vacuum, glass, distilled water etc.

3. **Hetrogeneous medium:** If an optical medium has different composition at different points, then it is called hetrogeneous medium. Ex. air, dirty water etc.

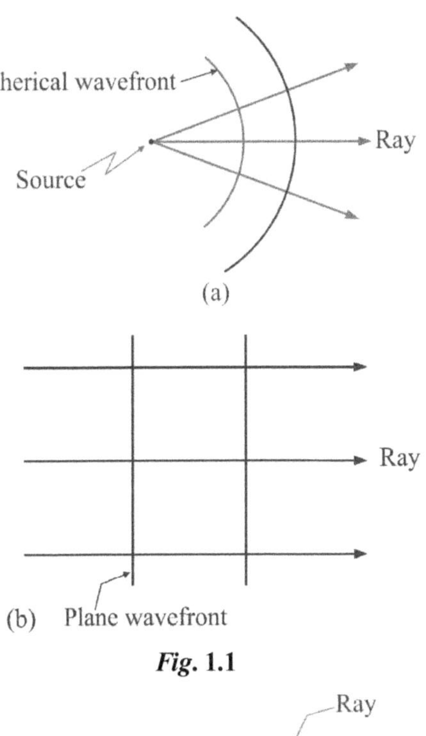

Fig. **1.1**

Fig. **1.2**

4. **Transparent medium:** A medium which allows most of the light energy to pass through it, is called transparent medium. In such a medium we can see through clearly. Ex. air, glass, plastics etc.

5. **Translucent medium:** A medium which allows only small part of light energy through it, is called translucent medium. In such a medium we can not see through clearly. Ex. frosted glass, greased paper, dirty water etc.

6. **Opaque object:** The object which does not allow the light energy to pass through it is called opaque object. This type of object either absorb or reflect the light energy. Ex. bricks, wood, stones etc.

1.4 REFLECTION OF LIGHT

When a beam of light is incident on the interface between two media, three situations can happen. These are :

(i) Some part of incident light is sent back into the first medium. It is called reflection.

(ii) A part of light gets transmitted through the interface. It is called refraction.

(iii) Rest part of the light, gets absorbed by the medium. It is called absorption.

Two types of reflection

(i) **Regular reflection:**

In case of highly polished surface, all the incident parallel rays are reflected to the same new direction. This is called regular reflection.

(ii) **Diffused reflection:**

Most of the surfaces, even if they seem flat, are really quite rough. This page may look very rough under a microscope. Each small piece of the surface is angled differently. Parallel light rays falling onto the surface still obey the laws of reflection, and so are reflected to all sorts of new directions. The reflected light is scattered. This is called diffused reflection.

Mirror

A smooth and polished reflecting surface is called a mirror. There are two types of mirrors.

(i) **Plane mirror:** A highly polished plane surface is called a plane mirror.

(ii) **Curved mirror:** The reflecting surface may be spherical or parabolic.

Laws of reflection

1. The incident ray, the reflected ray and the normal at the point of incident lie in the same plane.

2. Angle of incidence is always equal to the angle of reflection. If i and r are the angle of incident and angle of reflection respectively, then

$$\angle i = \angle r.$$

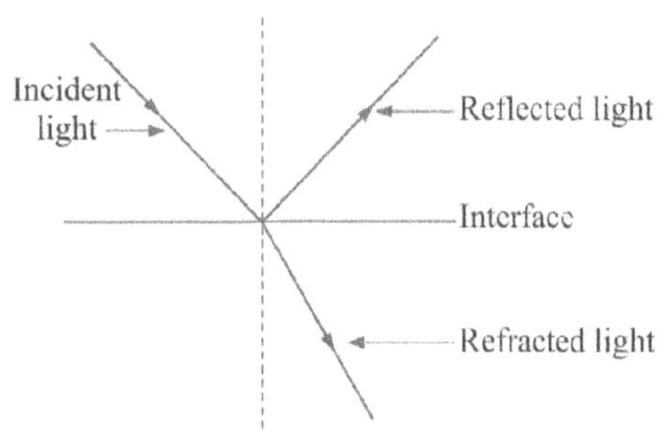

Fig. 1.3

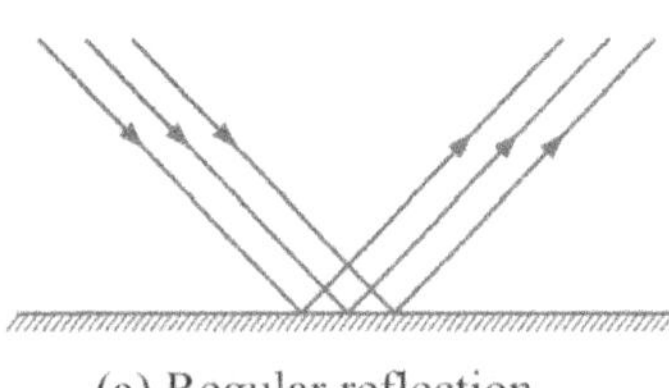
(a) Regular reflection

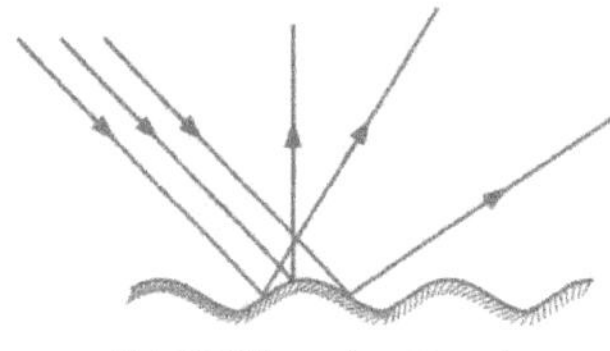
(h) Diffused reflection

Fig. 1.4

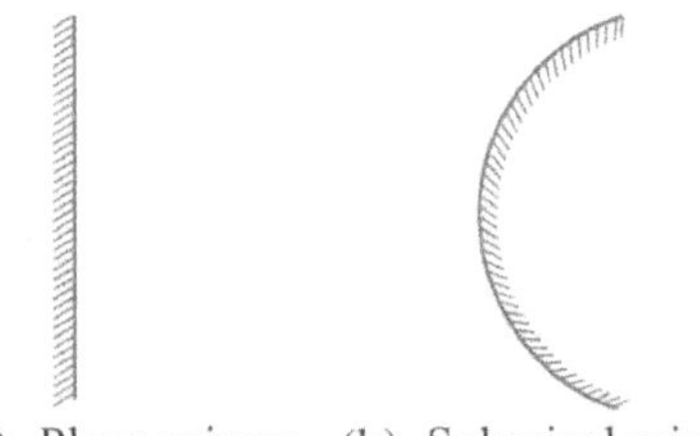
(a) Plane mirror   (b) Spherical mirror

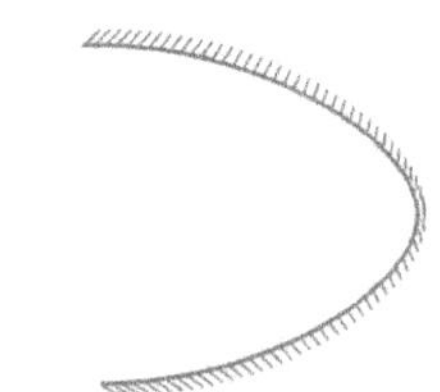
(c) Parabolic mirror

Fig. 1.5

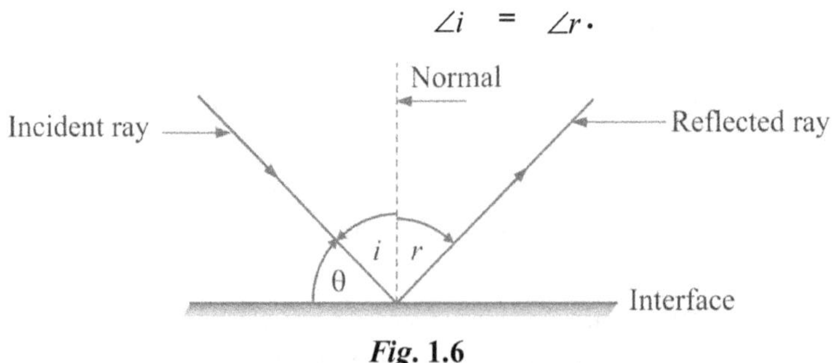

Fig. 1.6

In figure $\angle\theta$ is called glance angle of incident

For ray 1, $\angle i = \angle r = 0$

For ray 2, $\angle i = \angle r = \theta$

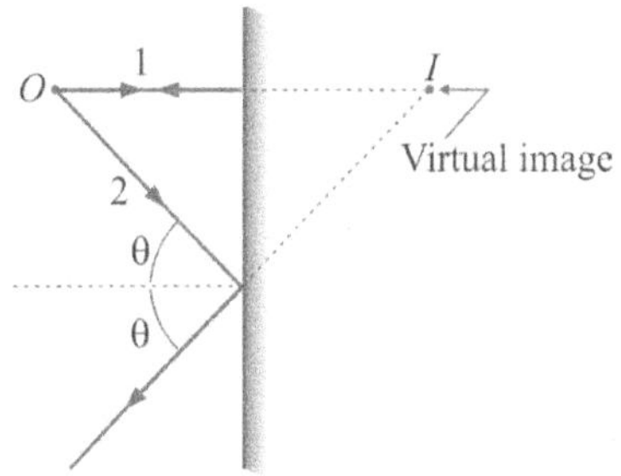

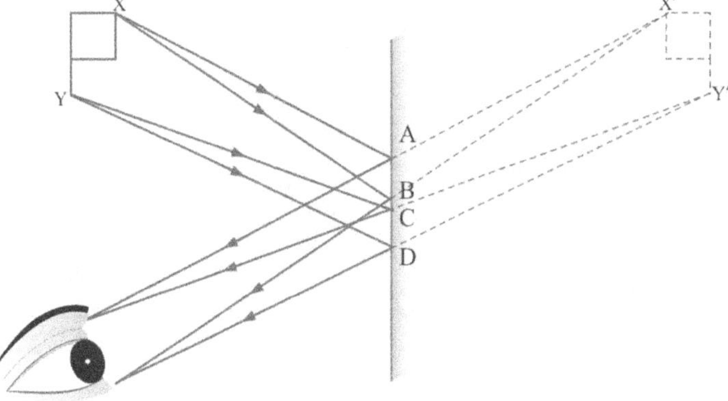

Fig. **1.7**

1.5 THE IMAGE

The central concept in the study of optics is the image. We will see, the rays after reflection or refraction are passed through some common point, which we call the image point. In some cases the emerging rays really meet at a common point and then diverge again after passing it; such an image is called a **real image**. In other cases the rays diverge as through they had passed through such a point, which is then called a **virtual image.**

Difference between real image and virtual image

Real image	Virtual image
1. The rays after reflection or refraction actually meet at some point.	1. The rays after reflection or refraction appear to meet at some point.
2. It can be taken on the screen.	2. It can not be taken on the screen.
3. It is always inverted.	3. It is always erect.
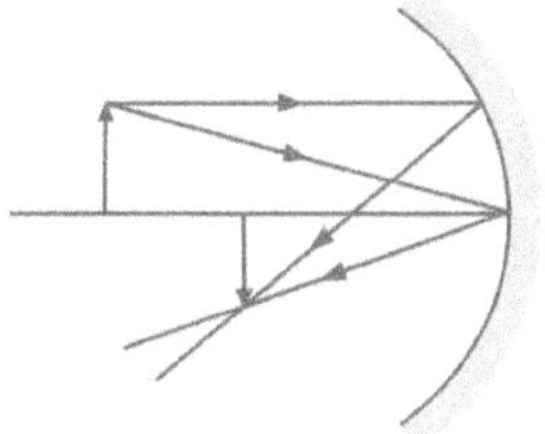 Real and inverted image *Fig.* **1.8**	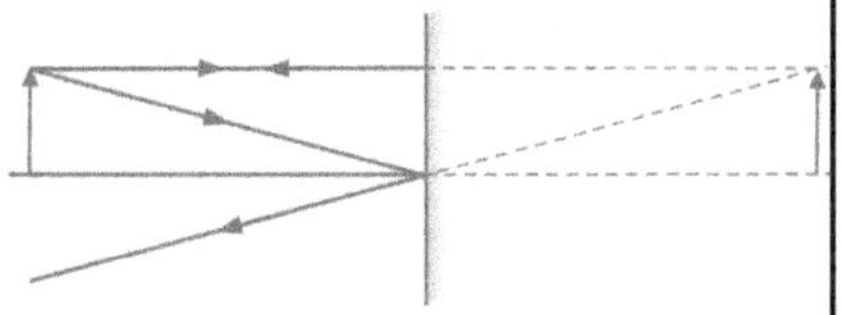 Virtual and erect image *Fig.* **1.9**

Formation of image by plane mirror

The image forms by a plane mirror has following characteristics :

(i) it is visual and erect,

(ii) of the same size as the object,

(iii) laterally inverted

(iv) as far behind the mirror as the object in front.

Consider an extended object of shape P placed in front of a plane mirror. To make its image, take rays from its turning points X and Y. In locating the position of the image keep in mind that image formed in plane mirror is as far behind the mirror as the object is in front of the mirror. To make the image of X, take at least two rays XA and XB, which after reflection forms the image at X'. Similarly take two rays YC and YD from Y, which after reflection forms image at Y'.

Fig. **1.10**

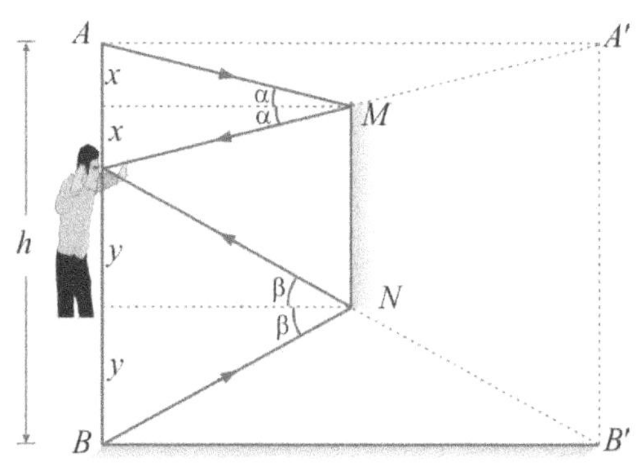

Fig. 1.11

Minimum size of the plane mirror required to see the full height of the observer himself

Consider a person AB of height h. The person will be able to see every part of his body if he can see the points A(head) and B(feet). Let MN is the minimum size of the mirror, such that rays AM and BN, after reflection, reach the eyes of the person, thereby forming image $A'B'$, when produced backward. From the geometry of the figure the size of the mirror $= MN = x + y$.

Also
$$2x + 2y = h$$

$$\therefore \qquad x + y = \frac{h}{2}.$$

Thus in order to see the full height, a person requires a plane mirror of half its own height. This relation is true for any distance of observer from plane mirror. Also the lower edge of the mirror should be kept at half of the eye level i.e., at a height y from the feet level.

Note:

1. It should be noted that a person can see his full height, by turning his head or eyes even in a small mirror.

2. An observer can see the image of a tall building in a very small mirror by keeping mirror at a large distance from the building (see *fig.* 1.12).

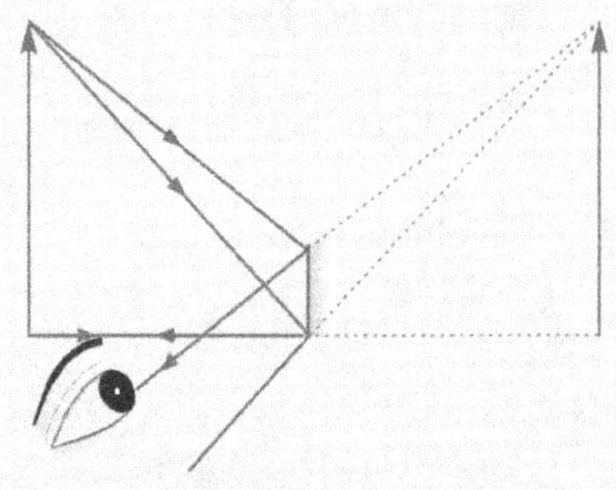

Fig. 1.12

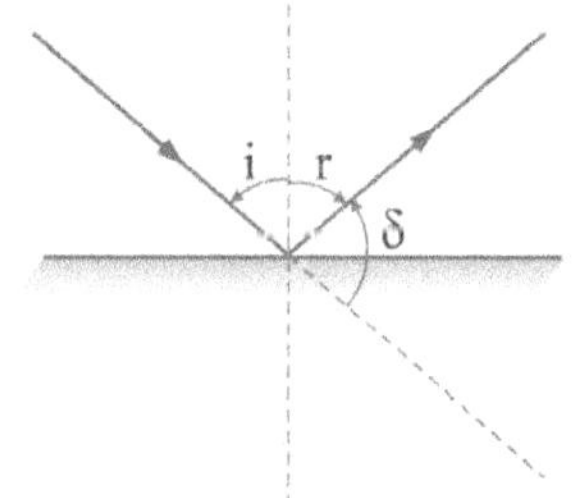

Fig. 1.13

Deviation produced by a mirror

It is the angle between the reflected and the incident rays. If i is the angle of incident, then angle of deviation

$$\delta = 180° - \left(\angle i + \angle r\right)$$

$$= 180° - \left(i + i\right)$$

or $\qquad \delta = 180° - 2i.$

Effect of rotation of mirror on reflected ray

Consider a ray of light AB, incident on plane mirror in position M, such that BC is the reflected ray and BN is the normal. Thus

$$\angle ABN = \angle CBN = i$$

$$\therefore \qquad \angle ABC = 2i$$

Let the mirror be rotated through an angle θ about point B, such that M' is the new position and BN' is the new normal. As the position of the incident ray remain the same, so the angle of incident becomes $(i + \theta)$. Let BD be the reflected ray, which also makes $(i + \theta)$ from BN'.

$$\therefore \qquad \angle ABD = (i + \theta) + (i + \theta)$$

$$= 2i + 2\theta.$$

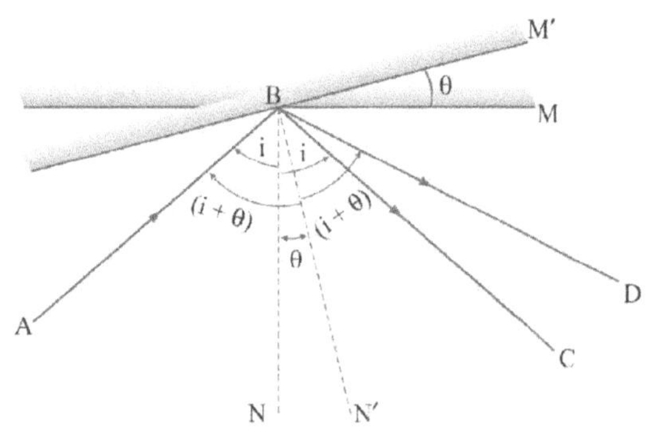

Fig. 1.14

The angle $\quad CBD \quad = \quad \angle ABD - \angle ABC$
$$= (2i + 2\theta) - 2i$$
$$= 2\theta.$$

Thus for a given incident ray, if plane mirror is rotated through an angle θ, then the reflected ray will rotate through an angle 2θ.

Image formed by two mirrors in contact

Suppose θ is the angle between the mirrors.

(i) If $\dfrac{360°}{\theta}$ is even integer, then number of images

$$n = \left(\dfrac{360°}{\theta} - 1\right) \text{ for all positions of the object.}$$

(ii) If $\dfrac{360°}{\theta}$ is odd integer, then number of images formed $n = \dfrac{360°}{\theta}$, if the object is placed off the bisector of the mirror, and $\dfrac{360°}{\theta} - 1$ when object is placed on the bisector of the mirrors.

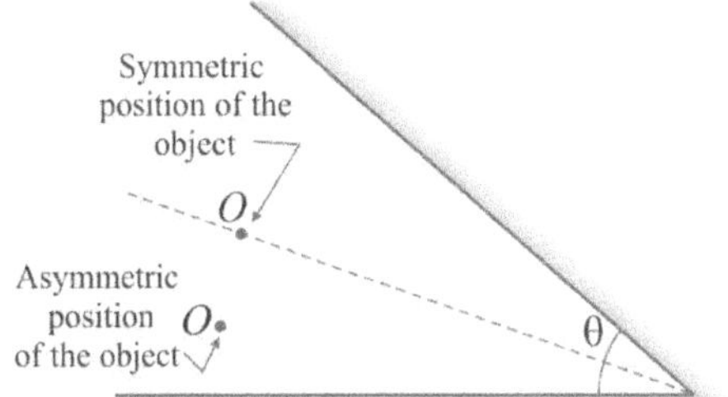

Fig. 1.15

(iii) If $\dfrac{360°}{\theta}$ is a fraction, the number of images formed will be equal to its integral part.

$\dfrac{\theta}{\text{(degree)}}$	$\dfrac{360°}{\theta}$	No. of images	
		asymmetric position	**symmetric position**
0	∞	∞	∞
30	12	11	11
45	8	7	7
60	6	5	5
72	5	5	4
75	4.8	4	4
90	4	3	3

Images formed by mirrors placed mutually perpendicular

'O' is an object placed between two mirrors M_1 and M_2. The distances of the object from the mirrors M_1 and M_2 are a and b respectively. I_1 and I_2 are the images form by the two mirrors at the distances a and b from the mirrors. The image I_1 acts as the virtual object for mirror M_2, which forms its image I_3. Similarly image I_2 acts as virtual object for mirror M_1, which forms its image I_4. Both the images I_3 and I_4 overlap to form a very bright image. Thus an observer can see three images. All the three images and object are situated symmetrically about P, and so they will lie on the circle, with P as the centre.

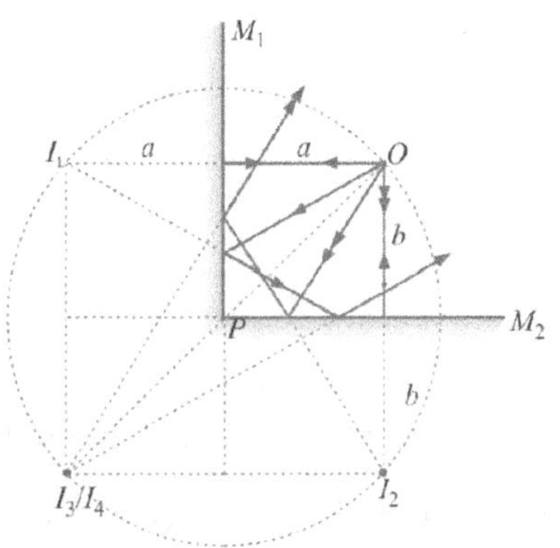

Fig. 1.16

Ex. 1 Why diffused reflection is more important than regular reflection ?

Sol.

During diffused reflection, light on striking the rough surface, gets scattered in all possible directions and hence visibility in surroundings increases whereas glare decreases. However in regular reflection, light is reflected in a particular direction, with the result the surrounding region remains dark. Moreover, there is a lot of glare in the direction of reflected light.

Ex. 2 Can plane mirror form real image ?

Sol.
Yes. If virtual object is obstructed by the plane mirror. In the figure O is the virtual object and I is its real image.

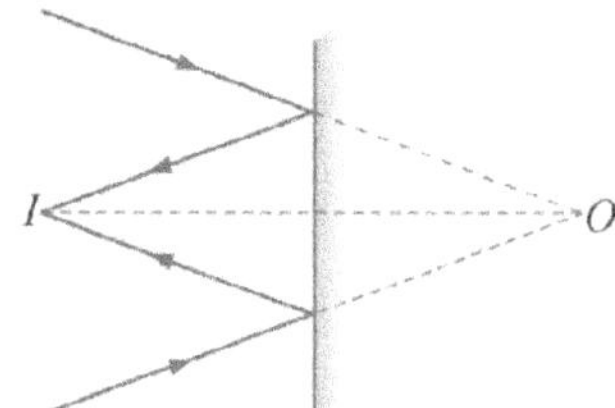

Fig. 1.17

Ex. 3 A ray of light is incident on a plane mirror along a vector $\left(\hat{i} + \hat{j} - \hat{k}\right)$. The normal on incident point is along $\left(\hat{i} + \hat{j}\right)$. Find the unit vector along the reflected ray.

Sol.

The component of incident ray along the normal to the mirror will reverse, while component of ray parallel to the mirror remains unchanged. The component of $\left(\hat{i} + \hat{j} - \hat{k}\right)$ along normal is $\left(\hat{i} + \hat{j}\right)$, and parallel to the mirror is $-\hat{k}$. Thus the reflected component normal to the mirror becomes $-\left(\hat{i} + \hat{j}\right)$. Therefore the vector along reflected ray is $\vec{R} = -\left(\hat{i} + \hat{j} + \hat{k}\right)$, and $\hat{R} = -\dfrac{1}{\sqrt{3}}\left(\hat{i} + \hat{j} + \hat{k}\right)$.

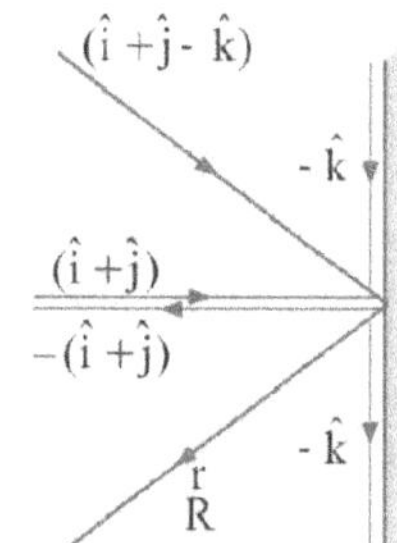

Fig. 1.18

Ex. 4 An ant is moving towards a plane mirror with a velocity $\left(4\hat{i} + 3\hat{j}\right)$ m/s as shown in *fig.* 1.19. What will be its image velocity with respect to the mirror?

Sol.

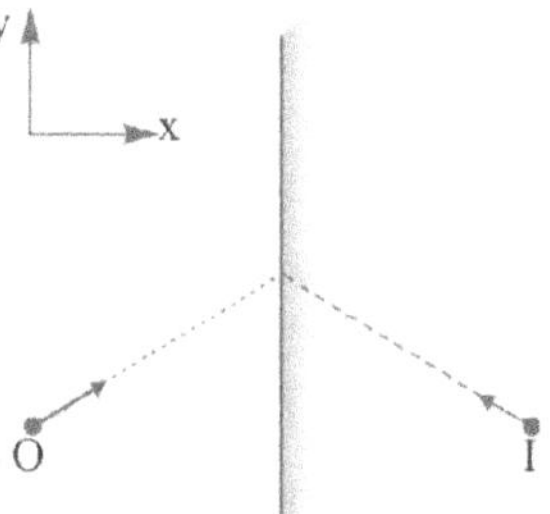

Fig. 1.19

The component of velocity of image perpendicular to mirror is $-4\hat{i}$ m/s and parallel to mirror is $3\hat{j}$ m/s, and so velocity of image will be $-4\hat{i} + 3\hat{j}$ m/s.

Ex. 5 An ant is moving along the normal of a plane mirror with speed of 1 m/s. At some instant it is at a distance of 5 m from the mirror. What will be distance between ant and its image after 1 second ?

Sol.

The distance moved by the object in 1 second = $1 \times 1 = 1$m. The distance of ant from the mirror after 1s is 4m, so the image distance is 4m. The distance between ant and its image after 1s is 8 m.

> **Note :**
>
> If an object moves towards a plane mirror at a speed v relative to the mirror, then the speed of the image relative to mirror will be v, and relative to object will be $2v$.

Ex. 6 Two mirrors are placed at an angle θ between them. Prove that angle of deviation produced by mirrors together is independent of angle of incident.

Sol.

Consider a ray incident on first mirror at an angle α. The deviation produced by first mirror will be $\delta_1 = 180° - 2\alpha$. The ray after reflection from first mirror, incidents on the second mirror at an angle β, and so angle of deviation produced by second mirror will be $\delta_2 = 180° - 2\beta$.

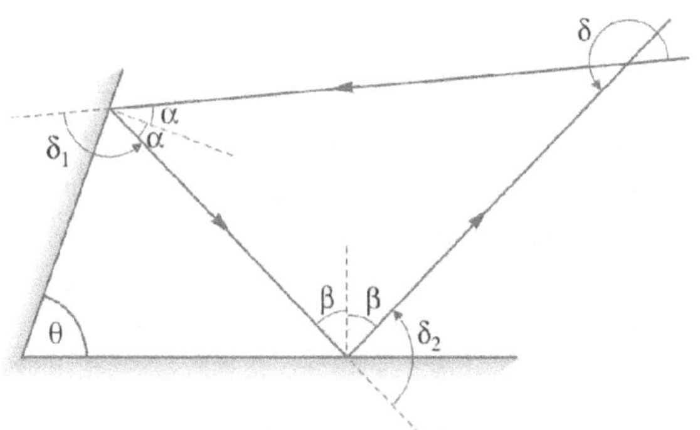

Fig. 1.20

The total deviation produced by mirrors together

$$\delta = \delta_1 + \delta_2$$
$$= (180^\circ - 2\alpha) + (180^\circ - 2\beta)$$
$$= 360^\circ - 2(\alpha + \beta)$$

From the geometry $\theta = \alpha + \beta$,

$$\therefore \quad \delta = 360^\circ - 2\theta. \quad \textit{Proved}$$

Ex. 7
A man is standing exactly at the centre of the hall. He wants to see the image of his back wall in a mirror hanging on front wall. Find the minimum size of the mirror required.

Sol.

Suppose the height of the wall be h and required height of the mirror be y. The position of man, wall and its image are shown in figure. For getting simple geometric relations, here we have drawn single ray diagram of the image.

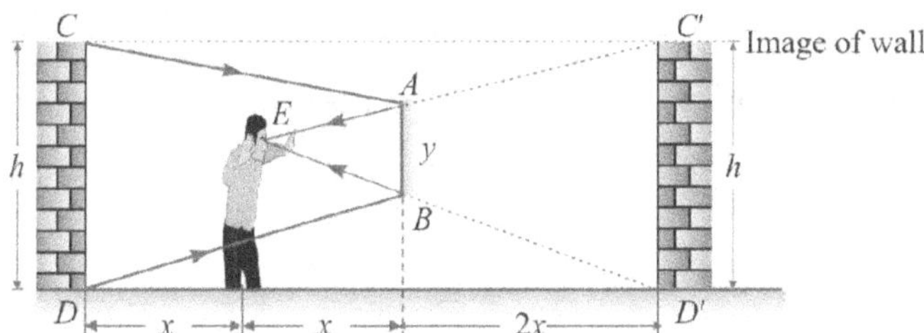

Fig. 1.21

In the similar triangles EAB and EC′D′, we have

$$\frac{y}{x} = \frac{h}{3x}$$

$$\therefore \quad y = \frac{h}{3}. \quad \textit{Ans.}$$

Ex. 8
A point source of light S is placed at a distance L in front of the centre of a mirror of width d, hangs vertically on a wall. A man walks in front of the mirror along a line parallel to the mirror at a distance 2L from it as shown in figure. Find the distance over which he can see the image.

Sol.

Suppose O is the object and I is its virtual image. The rays after reflecting from the mirror diverges as shown in figure. A man at a distance 2L from the mirror can see the image from A' to B'. In the similar triangles IAB and $IA'B'$, we have

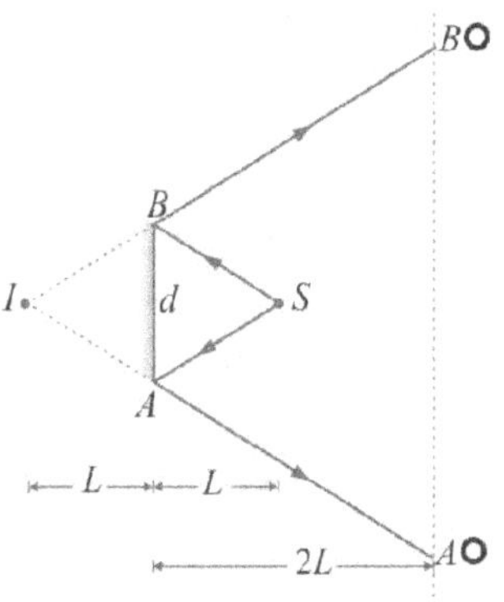

Fig. 1.22

$$\frac{d}{A'B'} = \frac{L}{3L}$$

$$\therefore \quad A'B' = 3d. \quad \textit{Ans.}$$

Ex. 9
A child is standing in front of a straight plane mirror. His father is standing behind him as shown in figure. The height of father is double the height of child. What is the minimum length of mirror required so that

(a) the child can completely see his father image in the mirror ?

(b) if father wishes to see his child image completely in the mirror ?

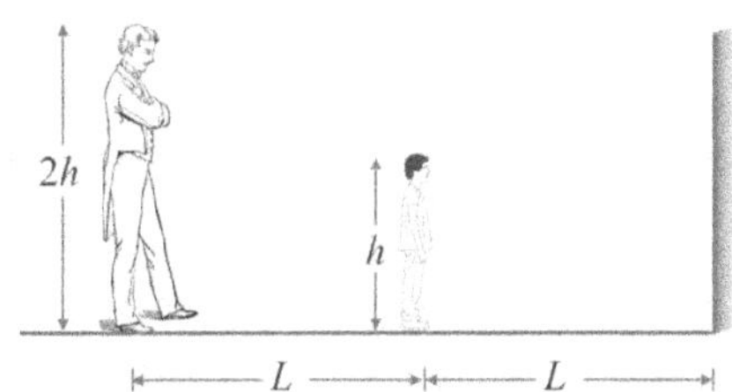

Fig. 1.23

Sol.

(i) To see the full image of his father the rays from head and feet of the father after reflection from mirror must be reached at the child's eyes. The situation is shown in the figure. The required size of the mirror is y. So from similar triangles,

$$\frac{y}{L} = \frac{2h}{3L}$$

$$y = \frac{2h}{3}.$$

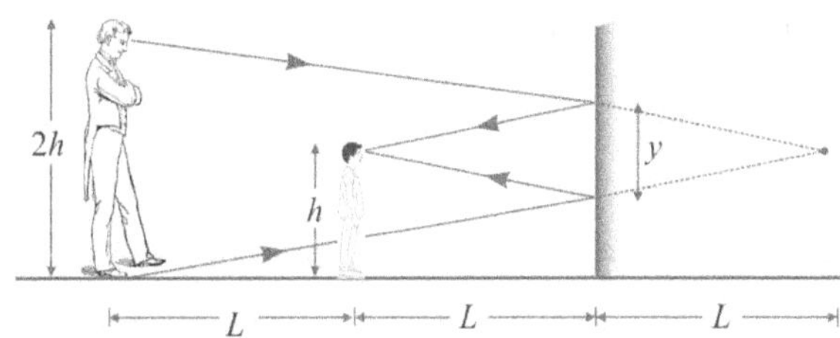

Fig. 1.24

(ii) The situation is shown in figure. From similar triangles, we have

$$\frac{y}{2L} = \frac{h}{3L}$$

$$\therefore \quad y = \frac{2h}{3}$$

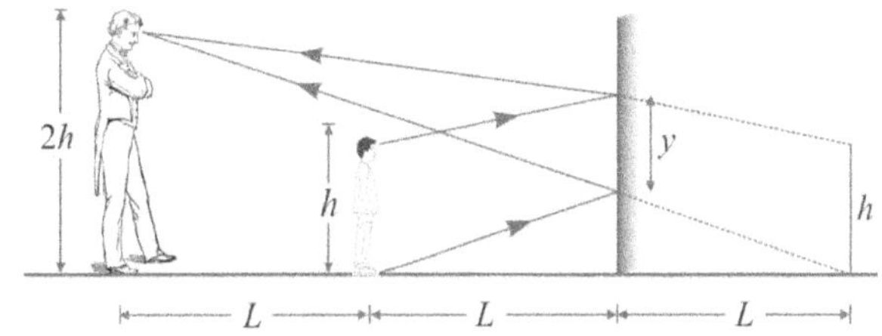

Fig. 1.25

Ex. 10 An object O and mirror M are moving with the velocities shown in the figure. Find the velocity of the image of the object in the mirror.

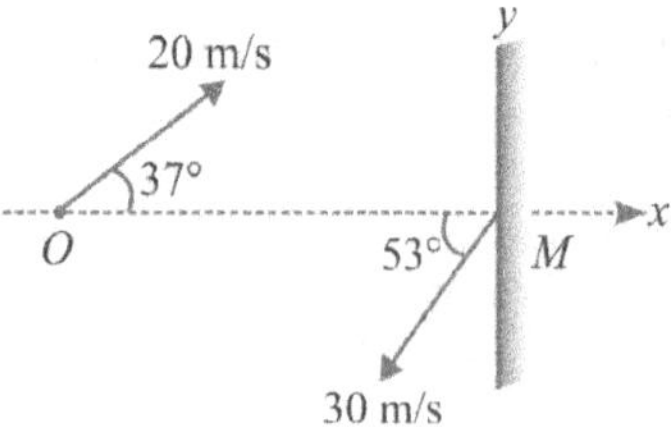

Fig. **1.26**

Sol.

Velocity components normal to mirror and parallel to mirror are shown in figure.

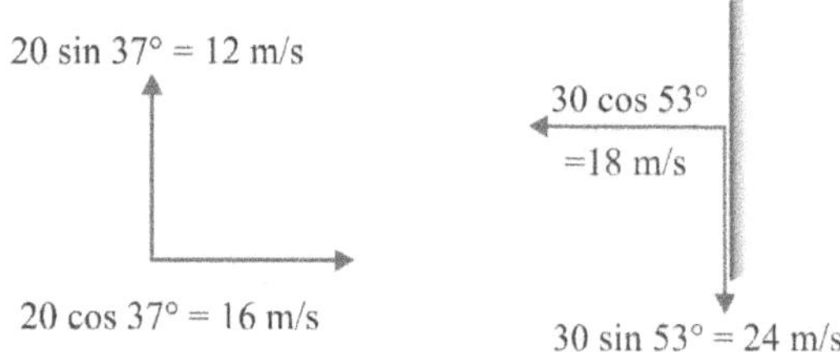

Fig. **1.27**

Velocity of object relative to mirror

$$\left[\vec{v}_{om}\right]_{\perp} = 16\hat{i} - (-18\hat{i}) = +34\hat{i} \text{ m/s}$$

Velocity of its image

$$\left[\vec{v}_{im}\right]_{\perp} = -34\hat{i} \text{ m/s}$$

Now velocity of image w.r.t. ground observer

$$\left[\vec{v}_{ig}\right]_{\perp} = \left[\vec{v}_{im}\right]_{\perp} + \left[\vec{v}_{m}\right]_{\perp}$$

$$= -34\hat{i} - 18\hat{i} = -52\hat{i} \text{ m/s}$$

The velocity component parallel to mirror remains same and so

$$\vec{v}_{image} = v_x\hat{i} + v_y\hat{j}$$

$$= (-52\hat{i} + 12\hat{j}) \text{ m/s} . \quad \textit{Ans.}$$

Ex. 11 A light ray is incidenting on a plane mirror M. The mirror is rotated in the anticlockwise direction as shown in the figure by an angular velocity 18 rad/s. The light reflected by the mirror is received on the wall W that is at a distance of 10 m from the axis of rotation. When the angle of incidence becomes $i = 37°$, find the speed of the spot on the wall.

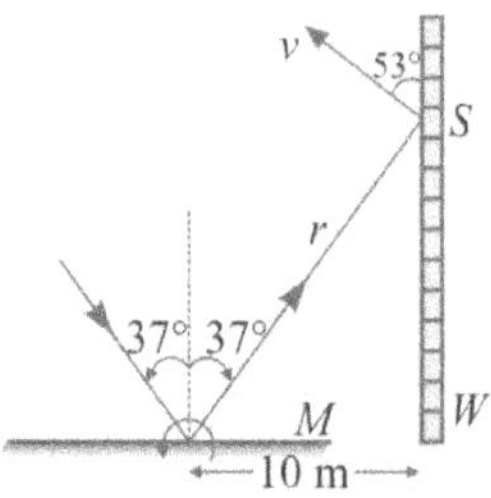

Fig. **1.28**

Sol.

From the geometry $r = \dfrac{10}{\cos 53°}$ or $r = \dfrac{50}{3}$ m

The angular velocity of rotation of the reflected ray,

$$\omega' = 2\omega = 2\times 18 = 36 \text{ rad/s}.$$

If v_s is the velocity of spot, then

$$v_s \cos 53° = v$$

$$= \omega' r = 2\omega r$$

or
$$v_s = \frac{2\omega r}{\cos 53°} = \frac{2\times 18 \times 50/3}{3/5} = 1000 \text{ m/s}.$$

Ans.

Ex. 12 A boy of height 1.5 m with his eye level at 1.4 m stands before a plane mirror of length 0.75 m fixed on the wall. The height of the lower edge of the mirror above the feet level is 0.8 m. Find the length of his image that he can see in the mirror.

Sol. The situation is shown in figure.

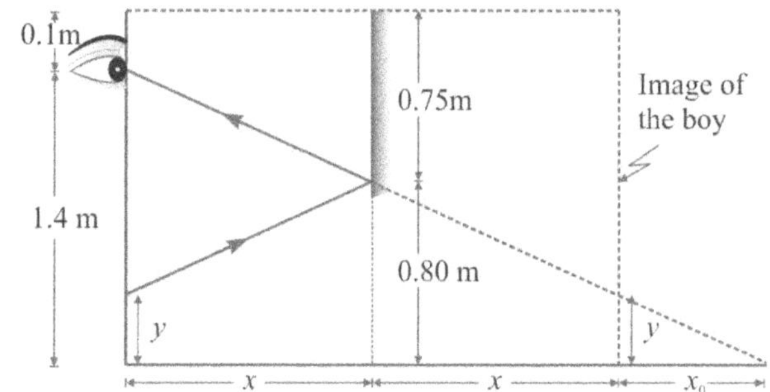

Fig. **1.29**

From similar triangles, we have

$$\frac{1.4}{2x + x_0} = \frac{0.8}{x + x_0}$$

or
$$x_0 = \frac{x}{3}$$

Now
$$\frac{0.8}{x + x_0} = \frac{y}{x_0}$$

or
$$\frac{0.8}{3x_0 + x_0} = \frac{y}{x_0}$$

$$\therefore \quad y = 0.02 \text{ m}$$

Thus the length of the image he can see in the mirror

$$= 1.5 - (0.02)$$

$$= 1.48 \text{ m}. \quad \textit{Ans.}$$

Ex. 13 An object O is placed in between two parallel mirrors as shown in *fig.* 1.30. Find the separation between n^{th} order images.

Sol. The ray diagram of the images is shown in figure.

Separation between I order images $= 2a + 2b = 2(a + b)$

Separation between II order images $= (a + 2b) + (b + 2a) + (a + b)$

$$= 4(a + b) = 2[2(a + b)]$$

Separation between n^{th} order images $= n[2(a + b)]$

$$= 2n(a + b).$$

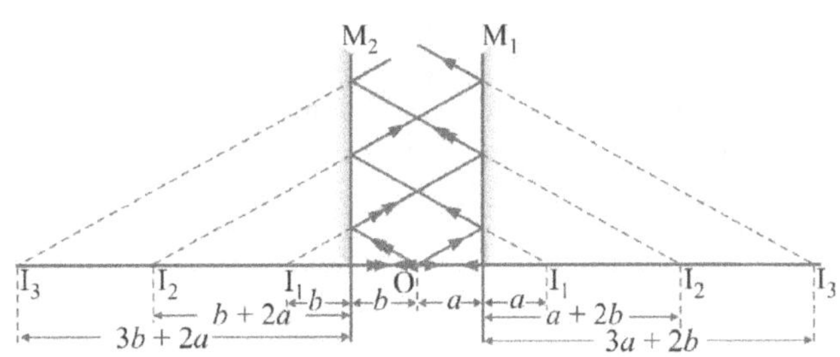

Fig. **1.30**

1.6 PERVERTED IMAGE

1. See the image of a three dimensional object in the plane mirror. The image formed by a plane mirror is the same size as the object in both its lateral and transverse dimensions. However, the image and object are not identical in all respect but are related in the same way as are a right hand and a left hand. When an object and its image are related in this way the image is said to be **perverted.**

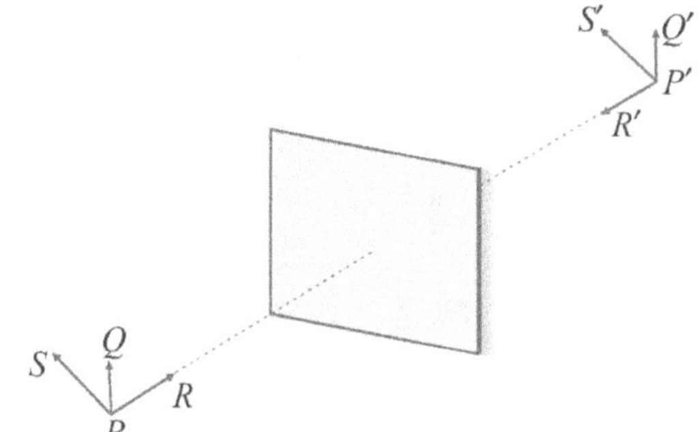

Fig. **1.31**

2. If one looks at his own face in the plane mirror, the image observed is technically described as perverted. The image is the same as though the face were reproduced as a rubber mask and the mask turned inside out and viewed from the new front. The right ear of one becomes the left ear of the image, and vice-versa. To see one's face as others see it, two front mirrors should be placed mutually perpendicular in contact as shown in figure. The observer's left ear will then be seen, because of two reflections as the left ear of his image etc. This experiment can be performed in case when many people's faces are, unknowingly, slightly unsymmetric seen in perpendicular mirrors, all such irregularities are reversed; they therefore appear double in magnitude and are very noticeable.

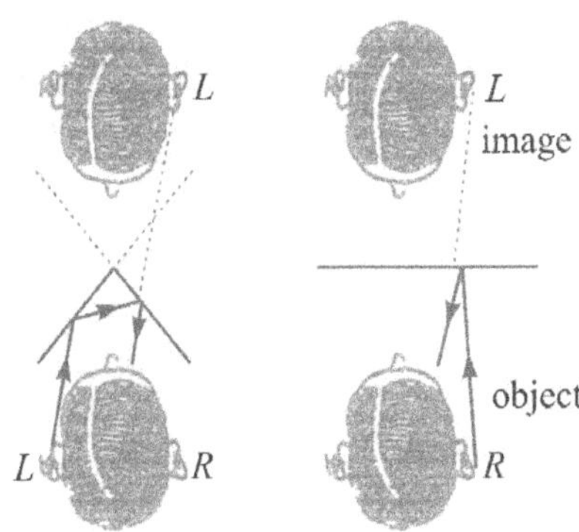

Fig. **1.32**
One's own image seen in 90°
mirrors is normal, that seen in a
plane mirror is perverted

Reflecting periscope

It is used to see the object, if the vision gets obstructed. It consists of a wooden or card board tube as shown in *fig.* 1.33. Two plane mirror are fixed at the turnings at an angle 45° each, such that the mirrors face each other.

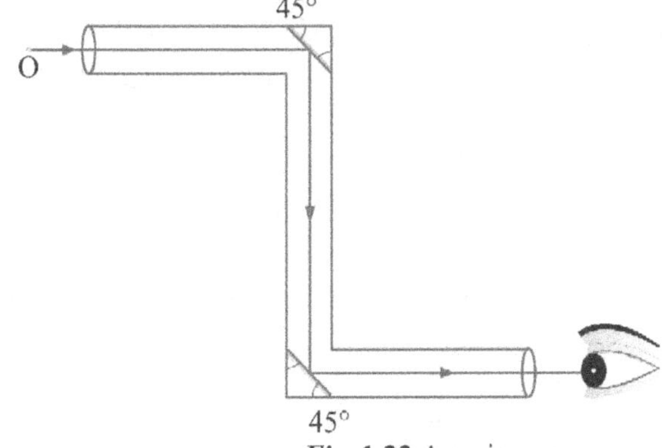

Fig. **1.33** A periscope.

Ex. 14 Two pins A and B arranged as shown in figure are struck in front of a mirror. What arrangement of the images of these pins will be seen by an observer in different view positions? In what position of the eye will the image of the pins be superimposed on each other ?

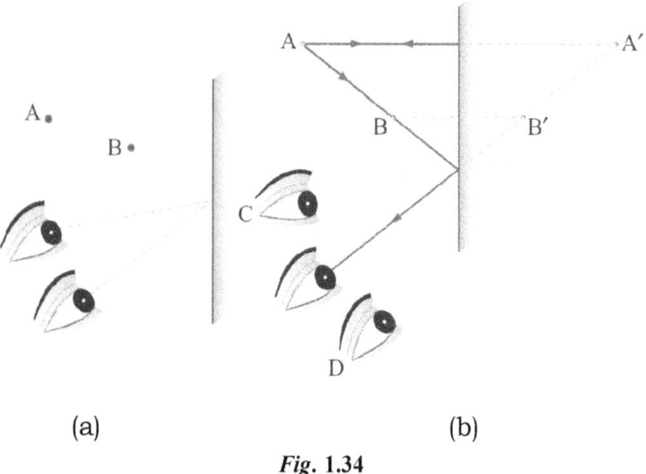

(a)

(b)

Fig. 1.34

Sol.

The ray diagram of the image is shown in figure. If the observer looks along the line passing through the images A' and B' of the pins in the mirror, he will see these images superimposed on each other. In the position C or D observer can not see the two images in a line.

Ex. 15 An object $O'O$ and a mirror AC are placed as shown in figure. Construct the image of this object in the mirror. Where should the eye be placed to observe the image of the entire object ?

Sol. See *fig.* 1.35. The rays coming from the point O' will be propagated inside the band restricted by the straight lines AD and CB after reflection from the mirror. The rays coming from all the points on the object will only arrive at each point in space between the straight lines AF and CB. The eye can see only the entire image of the object if it is at one of the points enclosed between the rays, AF and CB.

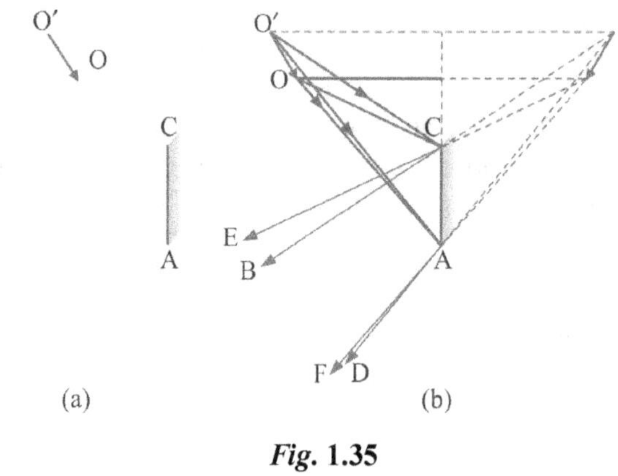

(a)

(b)

Fig. 1.35

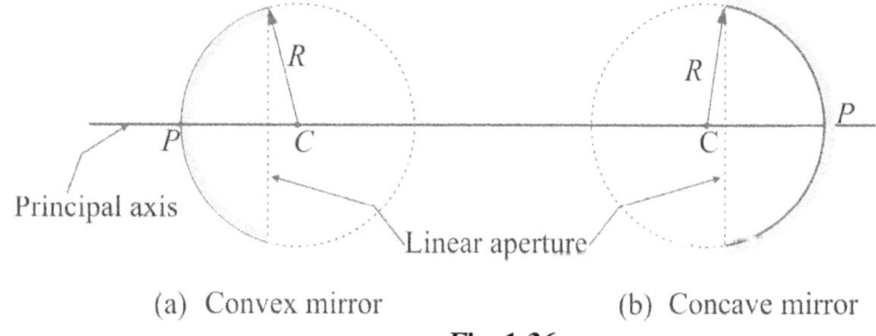

(a) Convex mirror

(b) Concave mirror

Fig. 1.36

1.7
SPHERICAL MIRRORS

It is a small part of hollow sphere whose one face is polished. If its inner face is polished, then its outer face becomes reflecting, and it is called **convex mirror.** If its outer face is silvered, then its inner face becomes reflecting, then it is called **concave mirror.**

Some definitions

(i)   **The centre of curvature C :** It is the centre of the sphere of which the mirror's surface is a part. Centre of curvature of plane mirror is at infinity.

(ii)   **Pole P :** The mid point of a spherical mirror is called pole.

(iii)   **Principal axis :** The imaginary line which passes through the pole and centre of curvature is called principal axis. Principal axis divides the mirror into two equal halves.

(iv)   **Linear aperture :** The diameter of the spherical mirror is called linear aperture.

(v)   **Principal focus F :** It is a point on the principal axis at which a beam of light, after reflection, either actually meet or appears to meet.

(vi)   **Focal length f :** The linear distance between pole and principal focus, is called focal length.

(vii)   **Radius of curvature R :** The linear distance between pole and centre of curvature is called radius of curvature.

Concave mirror as converging and convex mirror as diverging mirror

In concave mirror all the rays, coming parallel to principal axis meet at the focus F. In this way the rays converge at a single point. Thus concave mirror acts as converging mirror. In case of convex mirror all the rays coming parallel to the principal axis, after reflection appear to meet at focus F. In other words, the reflected rays appear to diverge out from F. Hence convex mirror is called diverging mirror.

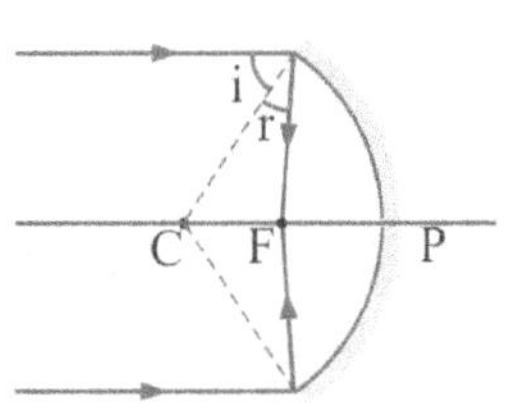
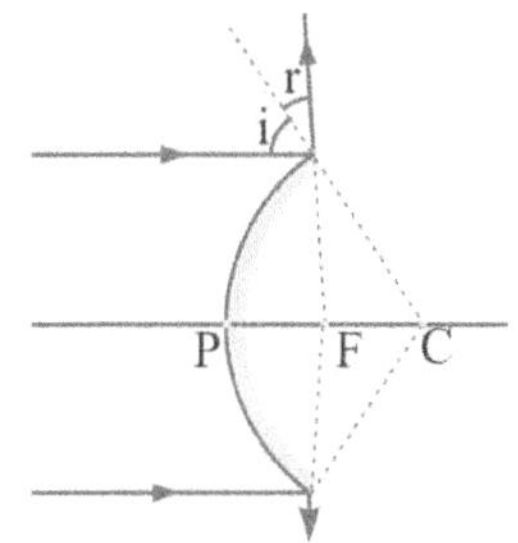

(a) Reflection of parallel rays in concave mirror

(b) Reflection of parallel rays in convex mirror.

Fig. 1.37

On the bases of laws of reflection, it can be concluded that

1. Any ray of light travelling parallel to principal axis, after reflection, it will pass or appears to pass through focus and vice-versa (according to principle of reversibility of path of light).

2. Any ray of light which travels along centre of curvature, after reflection it will retrace the path.

Sign conventions

1. All the distances should be measured from pole of the mirror along and perpendicular to the principal axis.

2. Distance measured in the direction of incident rays, can be taken as positive and opposite of incident rays, is negative.

3. Distance measured above principal axis is taken as positive and negative below the axis.

   According to our sign conventions, the focal length of the concave mirror becomes negative and that of convex mirror becomes positive. (see *fig.* 1.38).

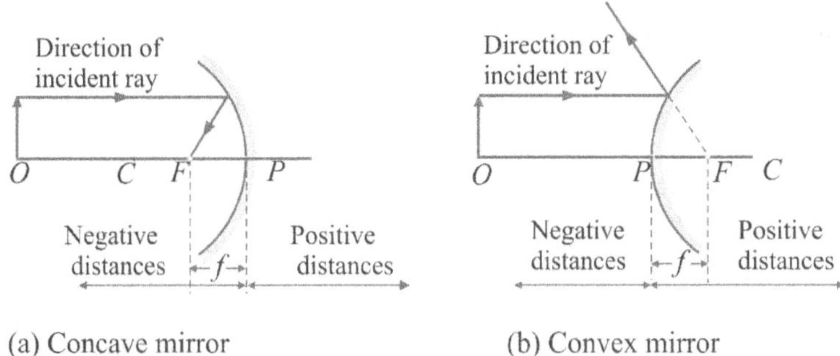

(a) Concave mirror

(b) Convex mirror

Fig.1.38 Sign conventions for spherical mirrors illustrated.

Relationship between f and R

For getting relationship we can take any of the spherical mirrors. Consider a concave mirror of radius of curvature R. Let AB is the incident ray; the angle of incident is i. After reflection it will pass through focus F; making angle r (see *fig.* 1.39).

If C is the COC, then

$$\angle BCF = i$$

Also

$$\angle i = \angle r.$$

$$\therefore \quad BF = FC$$

If point B is closed to P, then

$$BF = PF$$

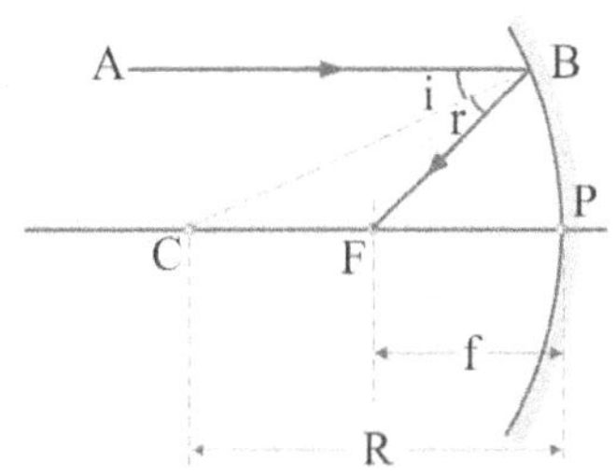

Fig. 1.39

$$\therefore \qquad PF = FC = f$$

Since
$$PC = PF + FC$$

$$\therefore \qquad R = f + f$$

or
$$f = \frac{R}{2}. \qquad \qquad ...(1)$$

1.8 MIRROR FORMULA

Consider a concave spherical mirror of radius of curvature R. Let O is the object placed at a distance u from the pole P of the mirror. Take two rays OB and OP, which on reflection makes an image at I. Suppose ray OB makes small angle α with the principal axis. CB and IB make angles β and γ respectively. Then :

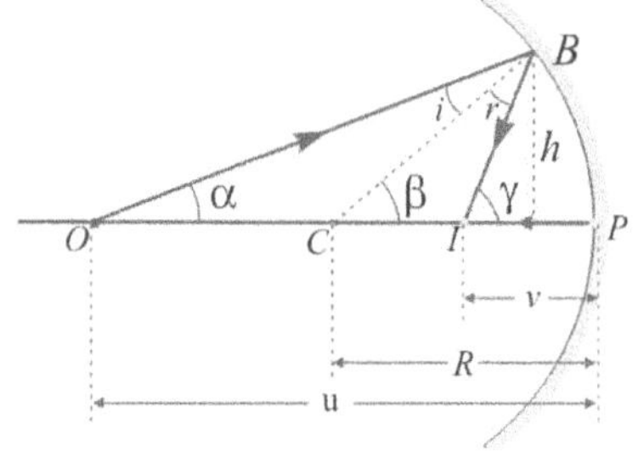

Fig. **1.40**

In $\triangle OBC$, $\qquad \beta = \alpha + i$

$\therefore \qquad i = \beta - \alpha \qquad ...(i)$

In $\triangle CBI$, $\qquad \gamma = \beta + r$

$\therefore \qquad r = \gamma - \beta \qquad ...(ii)$

Since $\qquad \angle i = \angle r$

or $\qquad \beta - \alpha = \gamma - \beta$

or $\qquad \alpha + \gamma = 2\beta \qquad ...(iii)$

For small angles, we can have

$$\alpha \simeq \tan\alpha = \frac{h}{-u},$$

$$\beta \simeq \tan\beta = \frac{h}{-R},$$

and
$$\gamma \simeq \tan\gamma = \frac{h}{-v}.$$

On substituting these values in equation (iii), we get

$$\frac{h}{-u} + \frac{h}{-v} = \frac{2h}{-R}$$

or
$$\frac{1}{u} + \frac{1}{v} = \frac{2}{R}. \qquad \qquad ...(1)$$

As $\dfrac{R}{2} = f,$

$\therefore$
$$\frac{1}{u} + \frac{1}{v} = \frac{1}{f}. \qquad \qquad ...(2)$$

Note :

1. It must be remembered that the equations (1) and (2), as well as many similar relations to be derived later, are the result of a calculation containing approximations and is valid for paraxial rays (the rays nearly parallel to the axis).

2. If $R = \infty$, ... the mirror becomes plane and $u = v$.

3. The above derived formula can be used for convex mirror also.

4. In using these formulas, the signs are given only to known values.

Graph between $\dfrac{1}{u}$ **vs** $\dfrac{1}{v}$ **:**

We have derived the mirror formula

$$\frac{1}{u}+\frac{1}{v} = \frac{1}{f}$$

or

$$\frac{1}{v} = -\frac{1}{u}+\frac{1}{f}$$

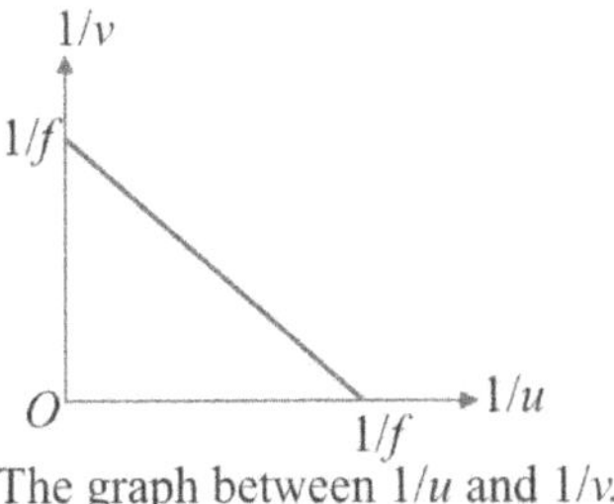

The graph between $1/u$ and $1/v$.

Comparing this equation with $y = mx + c$, we have $m = -1$ and $c = \dfrac{1}{f}$. Thus the given equation represents a straight line with negative slope ($\theta = 135°$ with x-axis). The graph between $\dfrac{1}{u}$ and $\dfrac{1}{v}$ is shown in the figure.

The graph between u and v is a hyperbola. For

$$u = \infty, v = f.$$
$$u = f, v = \infty.$$

The graph between u and v is shown in figure.

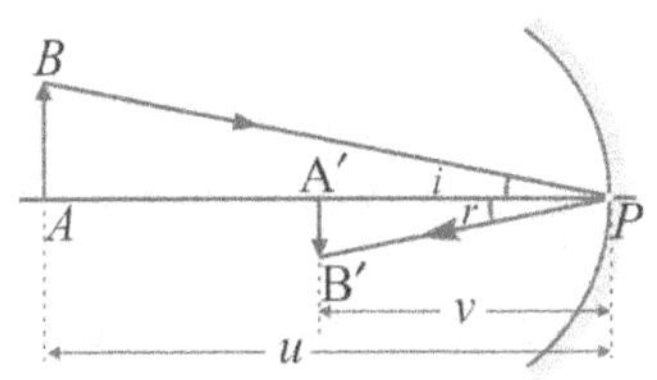

The graph between u and v.

***Fig.** 1.41*

1.9 MAGNIFICATION

In spherical mirrors, the size of image can be greater or less than the object. The relative size of the image can be understand by magnification. Thus magnification m can be defined as :

$$m = \frac{\text{size of image}}{\text{size of object}}.$$

Depending on the height, length and area of the object, there are three types of magnification. These are :

(i) **Lateral magnification** When the object is placed perpendicular to the principal axis, its image will also perpendicular to the principal axis. Thus lateral magnification:

$$m = \frac{\text{height of image }(I)}{\text{height of object }(O)}$$

For getting lateral magnification consider an object AB of height O, placed perpendicular to principal axis, at a distance u from the pole of the mirror. A'B' is the image formed by the concave mirror at a distance v from the pole of the mirror. In similar triangles ABP and A'B'P, we have

$$\frac{AB}{A'B'} = \frac{PA}{PA'}$$

According to the sign conventions, we have

$$AB = O, \qquad A'B' = -I,$$
$$PA = -u \quad \text{and} \quad PA' = -v.$$

Thus we can write

$$\frac{O}{-I} = \frac{-u}{-v}$$

or

$$\frac{I}{O} = -\frac{v}{u}.$$

$$\therefore \qquad m = \frac{I}{O} = -\frac{v}{u}. \qquad \qquad ...(3)$$

***Fig.** 1.42*

Negative value of m indicates that the image is inverted relative to the object m may be either positive or negative, a positive value always corresponds to an erect image, a negative value to an inverted one.

The value of m

The value of m may be from zero to infinity.

When $u = f$, $v = \infty$ and so $m = -\infty$. It means a very large inverted image will form at a very large distance. When object is placed at pole of the mirror, its image is also at the same position, and so in this case $m = 1$.

Note :

1. Normal eye can see any large distance between 25 cm to infinity, provided there is no obstruction in between.

2. In practice, distance of few kilometer (say 10 km) can be taken as infinite in comparison to focal length of the optical system.

3. Focal length of spherical mirrors does not depend on the medium in which it placed.

(ii) **Longitudinal magnification :** When a thin object is placed parallel to principal axis of the mirror, its image will also parallel to principal axis. Thus longitudinal magnification :

$$m_L = \frac{\text{length of the image}}{\text{length of the object}}.$$

Here two cases arises.

(a) **For short object :** If du and dv are the lengths of object and image respectively, then

$$m_L = \frac{dv}{du}$$

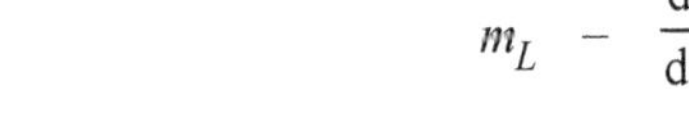

Fig. 1.43

From the mirror formula

$$\frac{1}{u} + \frac{1}{v} = \frac{1}{f},$$

After differentiation, we get

$$-\frac{du}{u^2} - \frac{dv}{v^2} = 0.$$

Or we can write

$$\frac{dv}{du} = -\frac{v^2}{u^2}.$$

Thus

$$m_L = -\frac{v^2}{u^2}. \qquad ...(4)$$

As lateral magnification $\quad m = \dfrac{v}{u}$,

$$\therefore \qquad m_L = -m^2.$$

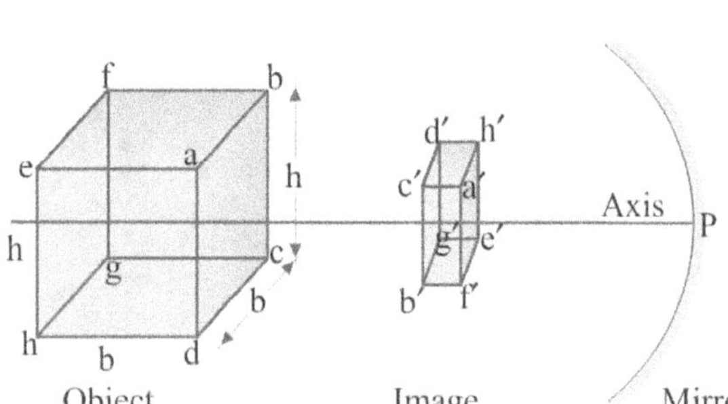

Fig. 1.44

In particular, if m is a small fraction, then m^2 is very small and the three-dimensional image of a three-dimensional object is reduced longitudinally much more than it is reduced transversely. Figure represents this effect. The image formed by a spherical mirror is also perverted.

(b) **For long object :** The positions of two ends of the object is taken as u_1 and u_2. Then by using mirror formula find v_1 and v_2. Thus lengths of the object and image are $(u_1 \sim u_2)$ and $(v_1 \sim v_2)$ respectively. By the definition

$$m_L = -\left[\frac{v_1 \sim v_2}{u_1 \sim u_2}\right]. \qquad ...(5)$$

(iii) **Magnification of area :** Suppose an object of width b and height h is placed perpendicular to the principal axis. The area of the object $A_o = bh$.

By the definition of the lateral magnification, the width of the image

$$b' = \frac{v}{u}b,$$

and height of the image $\qquad h' = \frac{v}{u}h.$

The area of the image $\qquad A_i = b'h' = \left(\frac{v}{u}b\right)\left(\frac{v}{u}h\right)$

$$= \frac{v^2}{u^2}(bh) = \frac{v^2}{u^2}A_o$$

Or we can write $\qquad \dfrac{A_i}{A_O} = \dfrac{v^2}{u^2}.$

Thus the magnification of area

$$m_{\text{area}} = \frac{A_i}{A_O} = -\frac{v^2}{u^2}. \qquad ...(6)$$

Velocity of image

For the moving object, the velocity of the image in spherical mirrors depends on the object velocity as well as on its distance from the mirror. The image velocity can be obtained by differentiating mirror formula with respect to time. Thus we have

$$\frac{d}{dt}\left[\frac{1}{u}+\frac{1}{v}\right] = \frac{d}{dt}\left(\frac{1}{f}\right)$$

or $\qquad -\dfrac{1}{u^2}\dfrac{du}{dt} - \dfrac{1}{v^2}\dfrac{dv}{dt} = 0 \qquad ...(i)$

Here $\dfrac{du}{dt}$, is the rate of change of position of the object, which is v_o, and $\dfrac{dv}{dt}$ is the rate of change of position of the image, which is v_i. On putting these values in equation (i), we get

$$-\frac{v_o}{u^2} - \frac{v_i}{v^2} = 0$$

or $\qquad v_i = -\dfrac{v^2}{u^2}v_o. \qquad ...(7)$

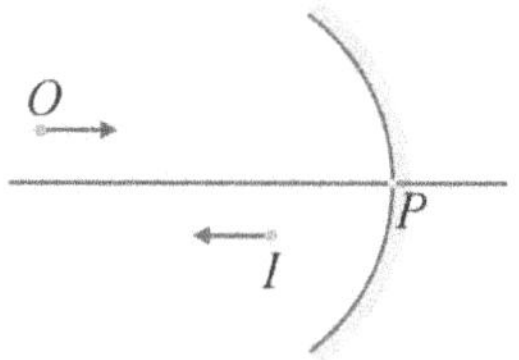

Fig. 1.45

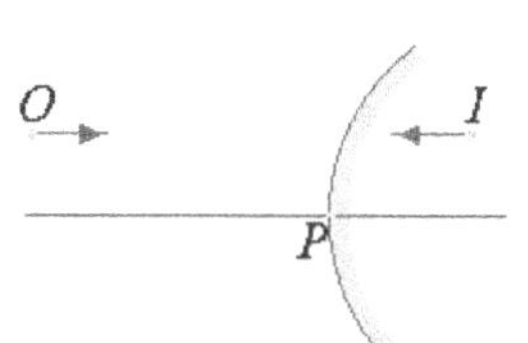

Fig. 1.46

Special cases

1.   In concave mirror, the real image always moves opposite to the object and so if v_o is positive, then v_i will be negative.

2.   In convex mirror, the image always moves in the direction opposite of object and so both v_o and v_i are opposite. Image velocity in convex mirror is always less than the object velocity.

Note:

It should be remembered that both v_o and v_i are to the measured with respect to the mirror.

Image formation in concave mirror

S. No.	Position of object	Ray diagram	About image
1.	At ∞		Real and inverted image, $m \ll 1$.
2.	Between C and ∞		Real and inverted image, $m < 1$.
3.	At C		Real and inverted, $m = 1$.
4.	Between F and C		Real and inverted, $m > 1$.
5.	At F		Real and inverted, $m \gg 1$
6.	Between F and P		Virtual and erect, $m > 1$

Image formation in convex mirror

S. No.	Position of object	Ray diagram	About image
1.	At ∞		Virtual and erect, $m << 1$.
2.	Any where between ∞ and P		Virtual and erect, $m < 1$.

1.10 Uses of spherical mirrors

1. **Convex mirrors :** On being very large field of view, these mirrors are used in automobiles to see the traffic behind him without turning his head. Plane mirror is not useful for this purpose because its field of view is small.

2. **Concave mirror :** We know that when a source of light is placed at the focal point of the concave parabolic mirror, it produces parallel beam of light. Thus it is used as a reflector in automobiles head lights and in search lights.

1.11 Spherical aberration in mirrors

In practice spherical mirrors are capable of forming reasonably sharp images if their apertures are small in comparision to the focal length. In case of large mirror, the rays reflected from the outer edges cross the axis at different distances as shown in figure. This inability to focus all the incident rays at a single point is called spherical aberration. A parabolic mirror, however, brings all rays to a focus at one point. A small source of light located at the focal point of a parabolic reflector becomes a parallel beam after reflection, which is used in automobiles headlights and in search lights.

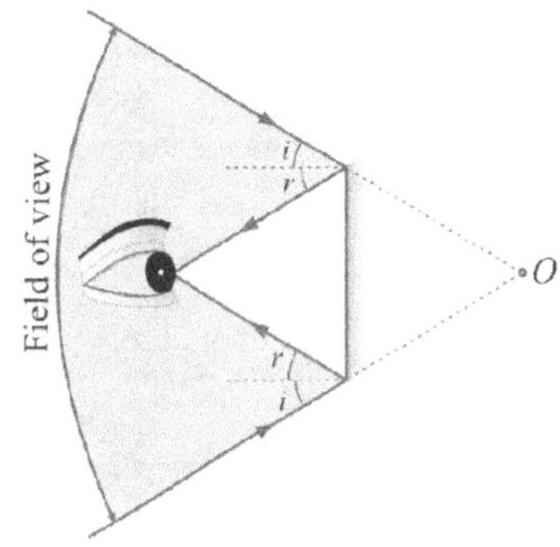

(a) Field of view of plane mirror.

Fig. 1.47(a)

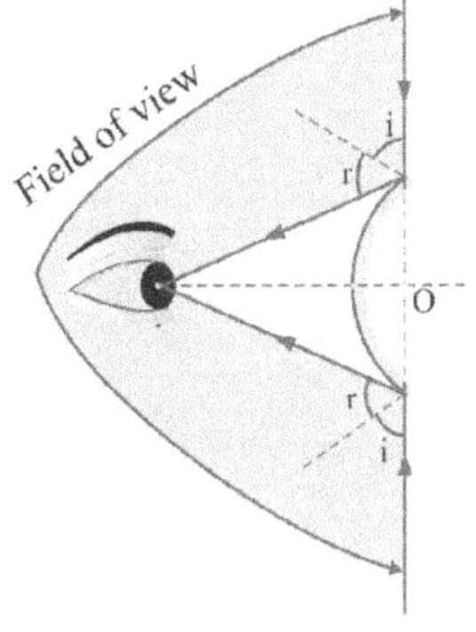

(b) Field of view of convex mirror.

Fig. 1.47(b)

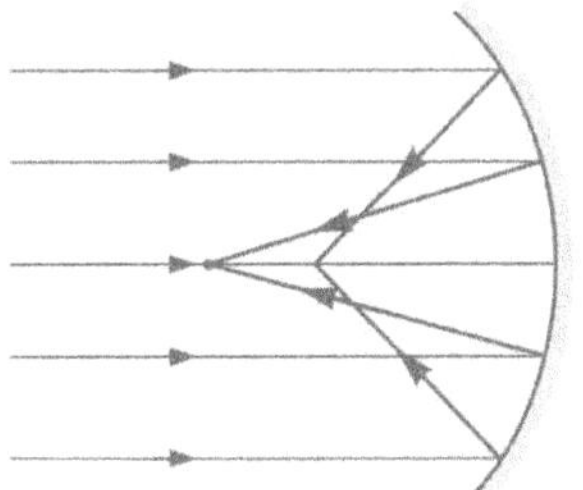

(a) Spherical aberration in concave mirror.

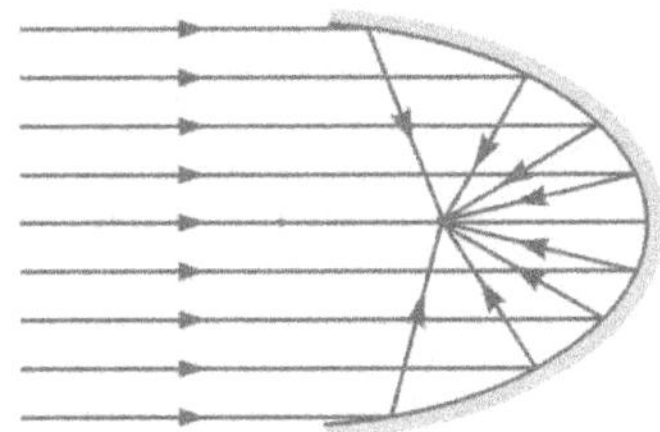

(b) No spherical aberration.

Fig. 1.48

Ex. 16 Find the distance of object from a concave mirror of focal length 10 cm so that image is four times the size of the object.

Sol. **Case I :** When image is real. Suppose object distance is x from the mirror, then

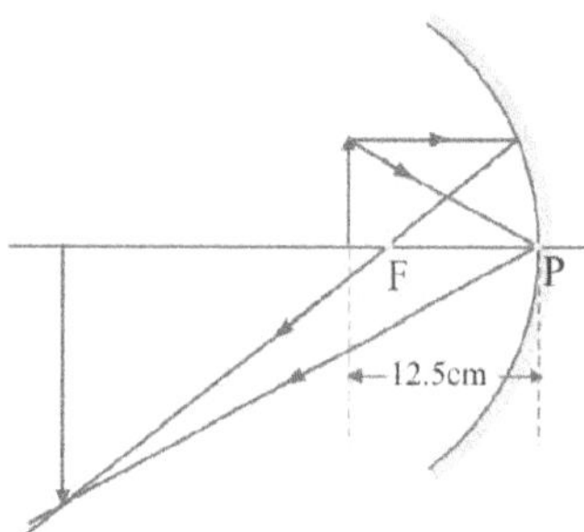

Fig. 1.49

$$u = -x$$
$$m = -4$$

We know that,
$$m = -\frac{v}{u}$$

or
$$-4 = -\frac{v}{(-x)}$$

$\therefore$
$$v = -4x$$

Now using mirror formula
$$\frac{1}{u} + \frac{1}{v} = \frac{1}{f}$$

or
$$\frac{1}{-x} + \frac{1}{-4x} = \frac{1}{-10}$$

which gives $\qquad x = 12.5$ cm **Ans.**

Thus in this case, object is to be placed between focus and coc.

Case II :   When image is virtual.

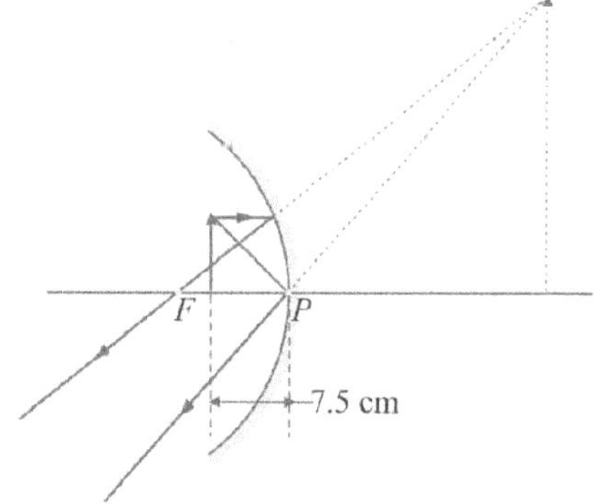

Fig. 1.50

$$m = +4$$

$\therefore$
$$4 = -\frac{v}{-x}$$

or $\qquad v = 4x.$

Now by mirror formula
$$\frac{1}{u} + \frac{1}{v} = \frac{1}{f}$$

or
$$\frac{1}{-x} + \frac{1}{4x} = \frac{1}{-10}$$

which gives $\qquad x = 7.5$ cm **Ans.**

Thus object is to be placed between focus and pole of the mirror.

Ex. 17 A point source S is placed midway between two converging mirrors having equal focal length f as shown in figure. Find the values of d for which only one image is formed.

Sol.

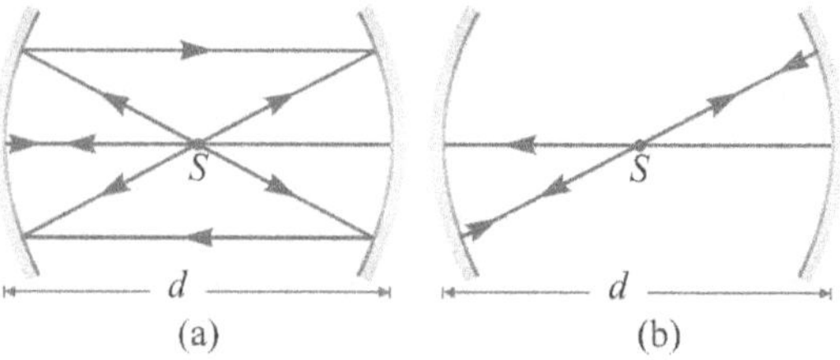

Fig. 1.51

In the situation when S is placed at the common focus of mirrors, the rays after reflection from one mirror incident parallel on to the second mirror, which finally intersect at focus of the mirror. Thus there will be only one image. In this case the value of d will be $2f$. In the other case when S is placed at the centre of curvature, the image will form at the same point, so in this case the value of d will be $2f + 2f = 4f$ (see figure).

Ex. 18 A thin rod of length $\dfrac{f}{3}$ is placed along the optic axis of a concave mirror of focal length f such that its image which is real and elongated just touches the object. Calculate the magnification produced by the mirror.

Sol.

The elongated image will be formed when object is to be placed beyond coc. The one end of the image will touch the rod when it is placed at coc. Thus AB is the right position of the rod. Thus for the end B, we have

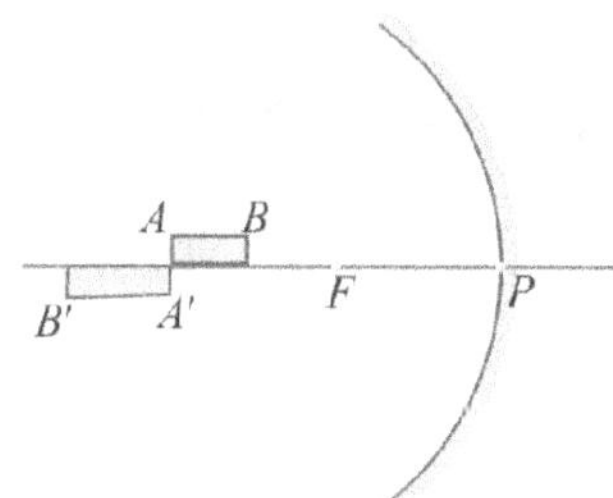

Fig. 1.52

$$u = -\left(2f - \frac{f}{3}\right)$$
$$= \frac{-5f}{3}$$

For concave mirror, $\qquad f = -f.$

By mirror formula, $\quad \dfrac{1}{u} + \dfrac{1}{v} = \dfrac{1}{f},$ we have

$$\frac{1}{\dfrac{-5f}{3}} + \frac{1}{v} = \frac{1}{-f}$$

On solving, we get $\qquad v = \dfrac{-5f}{2}.$

Thus the length of the image $\quad = A'B' = \dfrac{5f}{2} - 2f = \dfrac{f}{2}$

Magnification $\qquad m_L = -\dfrac{\text{length of the image}}{\text{length of the object}}$

$$= -\dfrac{\dfrac{f}{2}}{\dfrac{f}{3}} = -\dfrac{3}{2}. \qquad \textbf{\textit{Ans.}}$$

Here negative sign shows that the image is inverted with respect to the object.

Ex. 19
Prove that for spherical mirrors the product of the distances of the object and the image to the principal focus is always equal to the square of the principal focal length.

Sol.

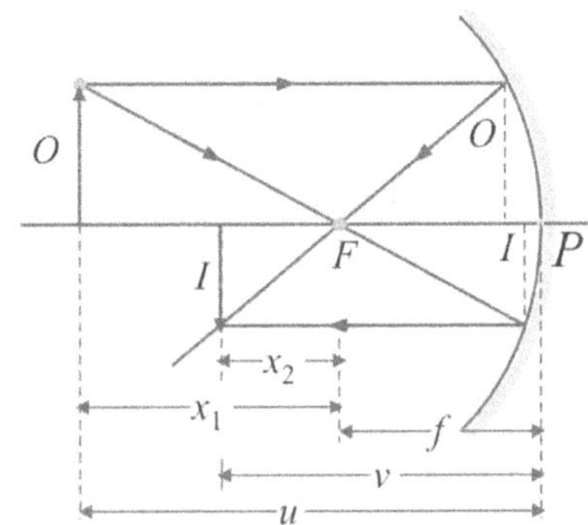

Fig. 1.53

See figure. For small aperture mirror; and in similar triangles

$$\frac{O}{I} = \frac{x_1}{f} \qquad \text{...(i)}$$

Also

$$\frac{O}{I} = \frac{f}{x_2} \qquad \text{...(ii)}$$

$$\therefore \qquad \frac{x_1}{f} = \frac{f}{x_2}$$

If we place the distances with the signs, then

$$\frac{-x_1}{-f} = \frac{-f}{-x_2}$$

or $\qquad x_1 x_2 = f^2 \qquad\qquad \textbf{\textit{Proved}}$

Ex. 20
A concave mirror forms the real image of a point source lying on the optic axis at a distance of 50 cm from the mirror. The focal length of the mirror is 25 cm. The mirror is cut in two and its halves are drawn at a distance of 1 cm apart in a direction perpendicular to the optical axis (see *fig.* 1.54). How will the images formed by the halves of the mirror be arranged ?

Sol.

For the upper half of the mirror the distance of the object O becomes 0.5 cm below its optic axis. As object is placed at coc, so its image will also form on coc and 0.5 cm above the optic axis. Similarly by the lower half. Thus the distance between the two images becomes 2 cm, see ray diagram.

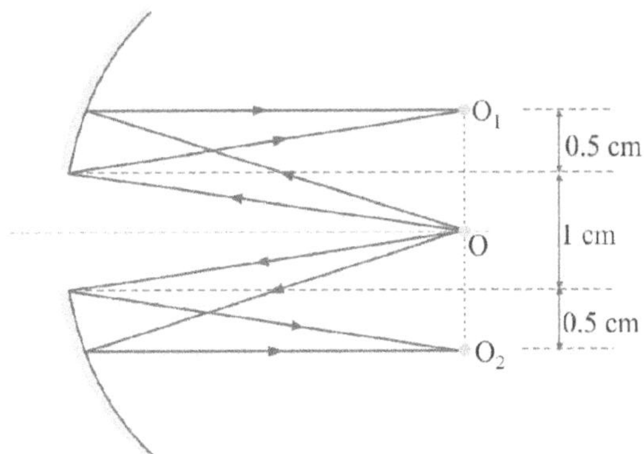

Fig. 1.54

Ex. 21
An object is placed in front of a convex mirror at a distance of 50 cm. A plane mirror is introduced covering lower half of the mirror. If the distance between the object and the plane mirror is 30 cm, it is found that there is no parallax between the images formed by two mirrors. What is the radius of curvature of the convex mirror ?

Sol.

The distance of the object from the plane mirror is 30 cm and so the distance of its image is also 30 cm from the mirror. As images formed by both the mirrors concide, so distance of image for convex mirror is = 10 cm.

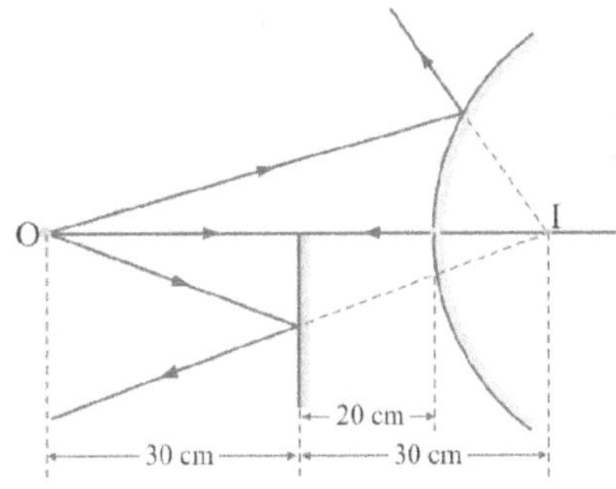

Fig. 1.55

By mirror formula $\dfrac{1}{u} + \dfrac{1}{v} = \dfrac{1}{f}$, we have

$$\frac{1}{10} + \frac{1}{-50} = \frac{1}{f}$$

which on solving gives $f = 12.5$ cm.

$\therefore$ Radius of curvature $R = 2f = 25$ cm. $\qquad \textbf{\textit{Ans.}}$

Ex. 22
A converging mirror M_1, a point source S and a diverging mirror M_2 are arranged as shown in *fig.* 1.56. The source is placed at a distance of 30 cm from M_1. The focal length of each of the mirrors is 20 cm. Consider only the images formed by a maximum of two reflections. It is found that one image is formed on the source itself.

(a)   Find the distance between the mirrors.

(b)   Find the location of the image formed by the single reflection from M_2.

Sol.

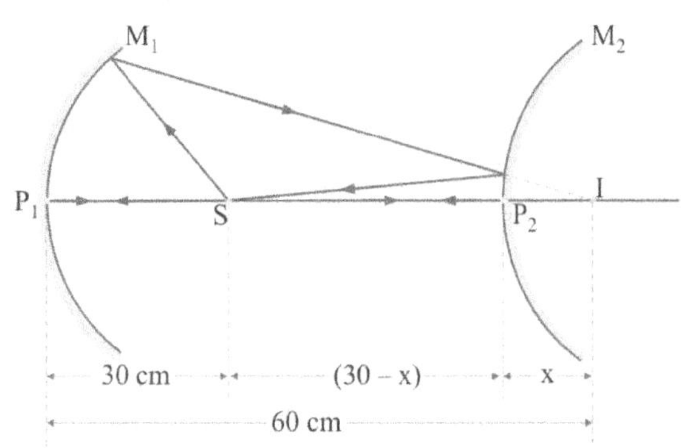

Fig. 1.56

For mirror M_1 :

$$u = -30 \text{ cm},$$
$$f = -20 \text{ cm}$$

By mirror formula, $\dfrac{1}{u}+\dfrac{1}{v} = \dfrac{1}{f}$, we have

$$\frac{1}{-30}+\frac{1}{v} = \frac{1}{-30}$$

which on solving gives, $v = -60$ cm.

For mirror M_2 : The image formed by mirror M_1 behaves like virtual object for mirror M_2. Let it is at a distance x from the pole of mirror M_2. Thus

$$u_2 = +x$$
$$v_2 = -(30-x)$$

Again by mirror formula, we have

$$\frac{1}{x}+\frac{1}{-(30-x)} = \frac{1}{20}$$

which on solving gives $x = 10$ cm or 60 cm,

$x = 60$ cm is not possible, $\therefore$ $x = 10$ cm.

(a)   Thus the separation between the mirrors $= 60 - 10 = 50$ cm.

(b)   The image formed by mirror M_2 is at a distance 10 cm.   ***Ans.***

Ex. 23

A gun of mass M fires a bullet of mass m with a horizontal speed v. The gun is fitted with a concave mirror of focal length f facing towards the receding bullet. Find the speed of separation of the bullet and image just after the gun was fired.

Sol.

If v' is the recoil velocity of the gun, then by conservation of linear momentum,

$$O = mv + Mv'$$

$$\therefore \qquad v' = -\frac{mv}{M}.$$

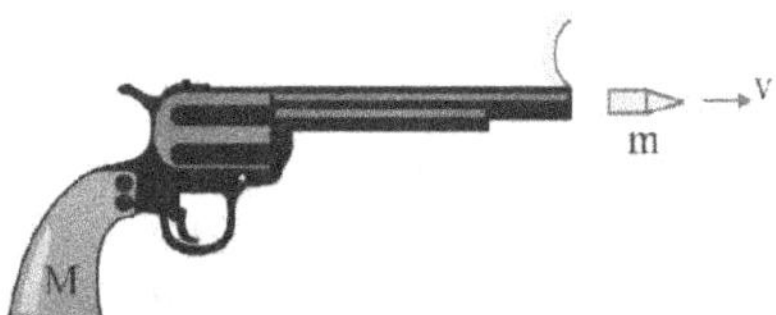

Fig. 1.57

The velocity of the bullet with respect to the mirror

$$[\vec{v}_{bullet}]_{mirror} = [\vec{v}_{bullet}]_g - [\vec{v}_{mirror}]_g$$
$$= v - v'$$

$$= v-\left(-\frac{mv}{M}\right)$$

$$= \left(1+\frac{m}{M}\right)v$$

or $\qquad \dfrac{du}{dt} = \left(1+\dfrac{m}{M}\right)v.$

By the defination, the image velocity,

$$\frac{dv}{dt} = -\frac{v^2}{u^2}\left(\frac{du}{dt}\right).$$

At the instant of firing, bullet and its image are at the pole of the mirror,

so $\dfrac{v}{u}=1.$ Thus

$$\frac{dv}{dt} = -\left(\frac{du}{dt}\right).$$

or the velocity of image w.r.t. mirror = velocity of bullet w.r.t. mirror
The speed of separation between bullet and its image

$$= 2\left(\frac{du}{dt}\right)$$

$$= 2\left(1+\frac{m}{M}\right)v .\qquad ***Ans.***$$

Ex. 24

A point object is moving towards and parallel to principal axis of a concave mirror of focal length 30 cm at a distance of 2 cm from principal axis of the mirror. Find velocity of its image when object is at a distance of 20 cm from the mirror.

Sol.

The distance of image for $u = -20$ cm,

$$\frac{1}{v}+\frac{1}{-20} = \frac{1}{-30}$$

$$\therefore \qquad v = +60 \text{ cm}$$

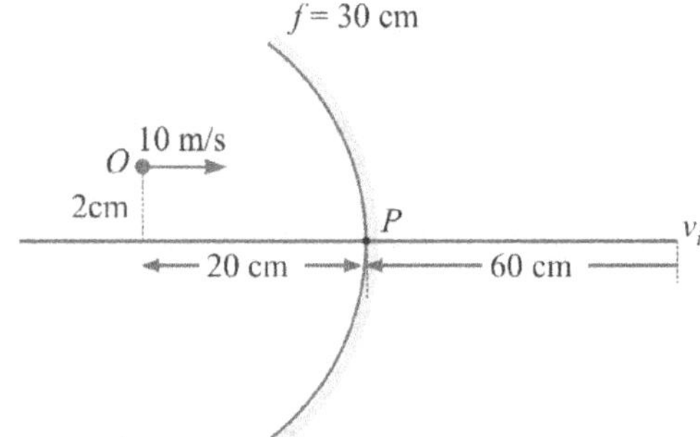

Fig. 1.58

The velocity of image is shown in figure. It has two components;

For x -component of velocity , v_{ix} :

$$v_{ix} = -\frac{v^2}{u^2}v_0$$

$$= -\frac{(+60)^2}{(-20)^2}\times 10 = -90 \text{ m/s}.$$

For y-component of velocity, v_{iy} :

Lateral magnification, $\qquad m = \dfrac{h_i}{h_o} = -\dfrac{v}{u}$

or $\qquad h_i = -h_o\dfrac{v}{u}$

Now $\qquad v_{iy} = -h_o\dfrac{\left[u\dfrac{dv}{dt} - v\dfrac{du}{dt}\right]}{u^2}$

$\qquad\qquad = -2\dfrac{[-20(-90) - (+60)\times 10]}{(-20)^2}$

$\qquad\qquad = -6 \text{ m/s}.$

Thus velocity of image;

$$\vec{v_i} = \vec{v_{ix}} + \vec{v_{iy}}$$

$$= (-90\hat{i} - 6\hat{j})\,\text{m/s} \qquad \textbf{\textit{Ans.}}$$

Ex. 25 Two concave mirrors of equal radii of curvature R are fixed on a stand facing opposite directions. The whole system has a mass *m* and is kept on a frictionless horizontal table (*fig. 1.59*).

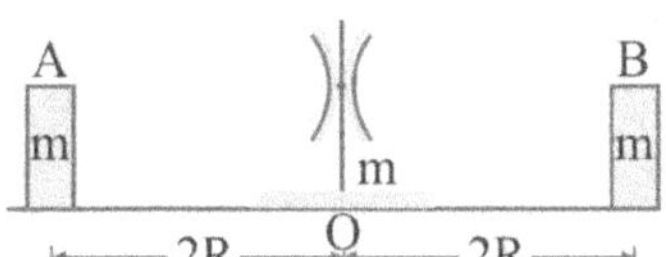

Fig. 1.59

Two block *A* and *B*, each of mass *m*, are placed on the two sides of the stand. At *t* = 0, the separation between *A* and the mirror is 2*R* and also the separation between *B* and the mirror is 2*R*. The block *B* moves towards the mirror at a speed v. All collisions which take place are elastic. Taking the original position of the mirrors standard system to be *x* = 0 and x-axis along *AB*, find the position of

the images of *A* and *B* at ; (a) $t = \dfrac{R}{v}$ (b) $t = \dfrac{3R}{v}$ (c) $t = \dfrac{5R}{v}$.

Sol.

(a) At $t = \dfrac{R}{v}$.

For block A, $\qquad u = -2R$

$\therefore \qquad \dfrac{1}{v} + \dfrac{1}{-2R} = \dfrac{2}{-R}$

or $\qquad v = \dfrac{-2R}{3}$.

For block B : The distance travels by block B in time $\dfrac{R}{v}$

$$x = v\times\dfrac{R}{v} = R.$$

Thus $\qquad u = -R$

$\therefore \qquad \dfrac{1}{v} + \dfrac{1}{-R} = \dfrac{2}{-R}$

or $\qquad v = -R$

The x-coordinate of the image of the block with respect to the mirror will be +R.

(b) At $t = \dfrac{3R}{v}$.

The block *B* will collide with the stand after time $\dfrac{2R}{v}$.

After collision block *B* becomes at rest and mirror starts moving with the same velocity *v*. In the remaining time *R/v*, the distance moved by the mirror

$$x = v\times\dfrac{R}{v} = R.$$

The position of blocks and mirror are shown in figure.

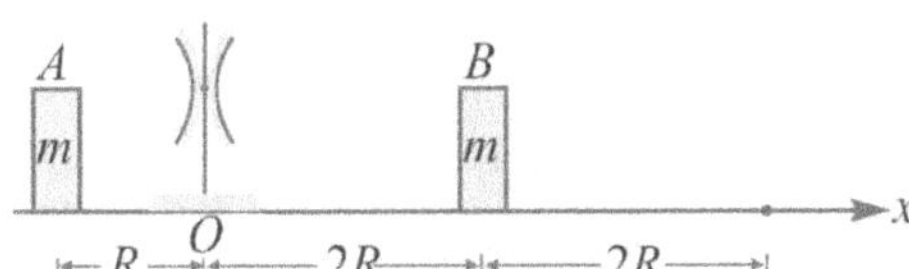

Fig. 1.60

At this time the blocks lie at the centre of curvature of the respective mirrors. Their images will form at the centres of curvature. So their co-ordinates are :

For block A, $\qquad x = -R$

For block B, $\qquad x = +R$

(c) At $t = \dfrac{5R}{v}$.

Fig. 1.61

The block *B* will collide to the mirror after a time $\dfrac{2R}{v}$. Thereafter mirror starts moving towards block A with velocity *v*. At $t = \dfrac{4R}{v}$, the mirror will collide with block A and stops after collision. The positions of blocks and mirror are shown in *fig. 1.61*.

For block *A*; Its image will form on the same place. Therefore the positions of the blocks are

$$x_A = -3R.$$

For block *B* ; $\qquad u = -2R$

$$\dfrac{1}{v} + \dfrac{1}{-2R} = \dfrac{2}{-R}$$

$$v = -\dfrac{2R}{3}$$

The coordinates of B are $-\left(2R - \dfrac{2R}{3}\right)$

$$= \dfrac{-4R}{3}. \qquad \textbf{\textit{Ans.}}$$

Ex. 26 A concave and a convex mirror are placed on two parallel optic axis as shown. Find the co-ordinates of image of point object P formed after two successive reflections; first reflection at concave mirror and then at convex mirror.

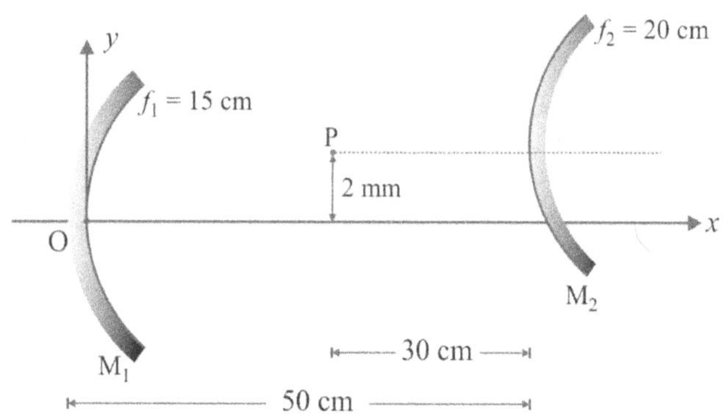

Fig. 1.62

Sol.

For concave mirror M_1 :
$$u = -20 \text{ cm}, \quad f_1 = -15 \text{ cm}$$

Now
$$\frac{1}{v_1} + \frac{1}{-20} = \frac{1}{-15}$$

or
$$v_1 = -60 \text{ cm}$$

Also
$$\frac{I_1}{O} = -\frac{v_1}{u}$$

or
$$\frac{I_1}{2} = -\frac{(-60)}{(-20)}$$

$$\therefore \quad I_1 = -6 \text{ mm}$$

For convex mirror M_2 :
$$\frac{1}{v_2} + \frac{1}{10} = \frac{1}{+20}$$

$$\therefore \quad v_2 = -20 \text{ cm}$$

For optic axis of convex mirror, $O_2 = (6 + 2) = 8$ mm

Now
$$\frac{I_2}{-8} = \frac{-(-20)}{+10}$$

$$\therefore \quad I_2 = -16 \text{ mm}$$

Thus co-ordinates of image point from O, are (30 cm, −14 mm). (see figure.)

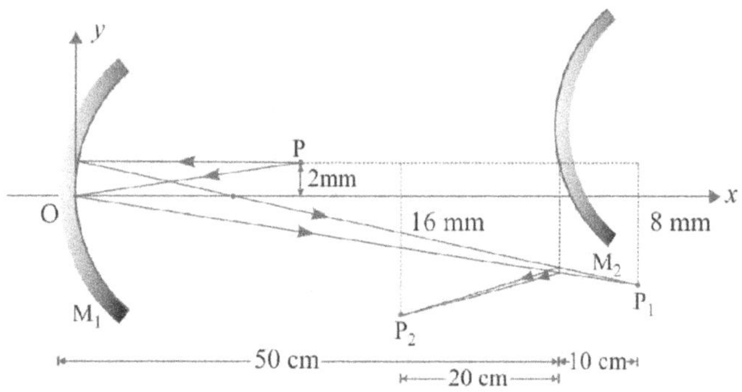

Fig. 1.63

Ex. 27 A parallel beam of light ray parallel to the x-axis is incident on a parabolic reflecting surface $x = 2by^2$ as shown in the fig. After reflecting it passes through focal point F. What is the focal length of the reflecting surface?

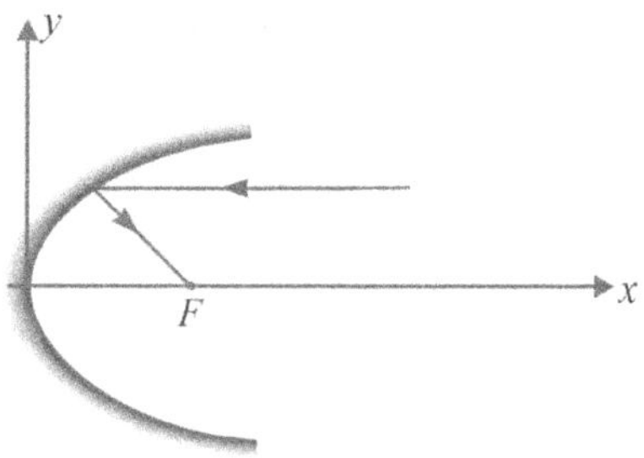

Fig. 1.64

Sol.

We can write,
$$x = 2by^2$$

or
$$y^2 = \frac{x}{2b}$$

On comparing with standard parabola $y^2 = 4ax$,

we get,
$$4a = \frac{1}{2b}$$

or
$$a = \frac{1}{8b}$$

Thus focal length, $f = a$

$$= \frac{1}{8b}.$$

Review of formulae & Important Points

1. **Laws of reflection**
   Law 1 : The incident ray, the reflected ray and the normal at the point of incident lie in the same plane,
   Law 2 : Angle of incidence is always equal to the angle of reflection. Thus $\angle i = \angle r$

2. **Real and virtual image**
   Real image is always inverted and virtual image is always erect. Real image can be taken on the screen but virtual image can not be taken on the screen.

3. **Formation of image by plane mirror**
   It is virtual and erect of the same size as the object, laterally inverted and as far behind the mirror as the object in front.

4. The minimum size of mirror required to see the image of the observer himself is half of his height and its lower end must be placed half of the eye level.

5. **Deviation produced by a mirror**
   (i) By single mirror; at an angle of incidence i, it is
   $$\delta = 180° - 2i.$$

   (ii) By two mirrors at an angle θ, the deviation
   $$\delta = 360° - 2\theta.$$

6. **Number of images**
   Suppose θ is the angle between the mirrors, then
   (i) if $\dfrac{360°}{\theta}$ is even integer, then number of images
   $$n = \dfrac{360°}{\theta} - 1 \text{ for all positions of the object.}$$

   (ii) if $\dfrac{360°}{\theta}$ is odd integer, then
   $$n = \dfrac{360°}{\theta} \text{ if the object is placed off the bisector of the}$$
   mirrors, and $\left(\dfrac{360°}{\theta} - 1\right)$, when object is placed on the axis.
   $n = 3$ for $\theta = 90°$ and 5 for $60°$ and $72°$.

7. **Spherical mirror**
   For radius of curvature R, the focal length of spherical mirror will be $f = R/2$. For convex mirror it is $+ f$ and for concave mirror it is $- f$.

8. **Mirror Formula**
   $$\frac{1}{v} + \frac{1}{u} = \frac{1}{f} = \frac{2}{R}$$

9. **Magnification**
   $$m = \frac{\text{size of image}}{\text{size of object}}.$$

   Lateral magnification, $m = \dfrac{I}{O} = -\dfrac{v}{u}$

   Longitudinal magnification for short object
   $$m_L = -\frac{v^2}{u^2} = -m^2.$$

   Magnification of area $m_{\text{area}} = \dfrac{A_i}{A_0} = \dfrac{-v^2}{u^2}.$

10. Velocity of image
    $$v_i = \left[-\frac{v^2}{u^2}\right] v_0$$

★ ★ ★

LEVEL - 1

Only one option correct

1. A plane mirror is approaching you at a speed of 10 cm/s you can see your image in it. At what speed will your image approach you

(a) 10 cm/s   (b) 5 cm/s

(c) 20 cm/s   (d) 15 cm/s

2. Figure shows the multiple reflections of a light ray along a glass corridor where the walls are either parallel or perpendicular to one another. If the angle of incidence at point a is 30°, then the angles of reflections of light ray at points d, e and f respectively are ;

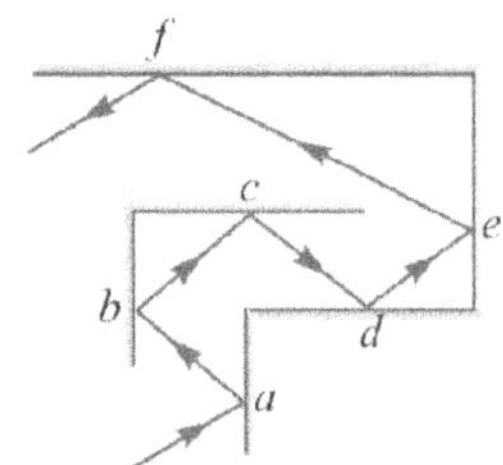

(a) 30°, 30°, 30°   (b) 30°, 60°, 60°

(c) 60°, 30°, 60°   (d) none of these.

3. Images formed of an object placed between two plane mirrors at angle 90° lie on a

(a) circle   (b) ellipse

(c) straight line   (d) none of these

4. What should be the angle between two plane mirrors so that whatever be the angle of incidence, the incident ray and the reflected ray from the two mirrors be parallel to each other

(a) 60°   (b) 90°

(c) 120°   (d) 175°

5. Figure shows an overhead view of a corridor with a plane mirror M mounted at one end. A burglar B sneaks along the corridor directly towards the centre of the mirror. If d = 2.0 m, then the distance of B from the mirror at which the security guard S first see her in the mirror is

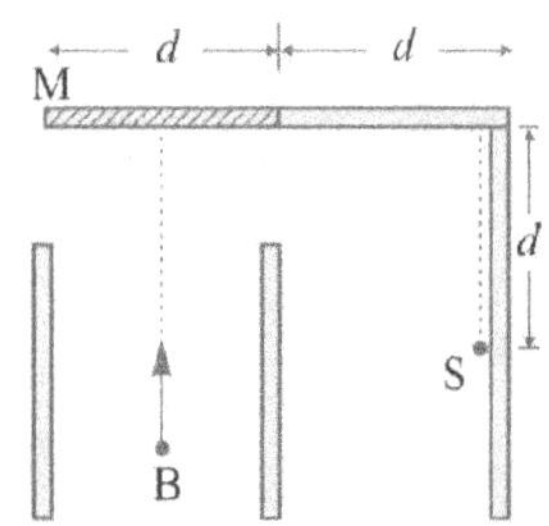

6. It is desired to photograph the image of an object placed at a distance of 3m from the plane mirror. The camera which is at a distance of 4.5 m from the mirror should be focused for a distance of

(a) 1 m   (b) 2 m

(c) 3 m   (d) none of these

(a) 3 m   (b) 4.5 m

(c) 6 m   (d) 7.5 m

7. When a plane mirror is placed horizontally on a level ground at a distance of 60 m from the foot of a tower, the top of the tower and its image in the mirror subtend an angle of 90° at the eye. The height of the tower will be

(a) 30 m   (b) 60 m

(c) 90 m   (d) 120 m

8. Two plane mirrors are at right angles to each other. A man stands between them and combs his hair with his right hand. In how many of the images will he be seen using his right hand

(a) 3   (b) 1

(c) 2   (d) none

9. A watch shows time as 3 : 25 when seen through a mirror, time appeared will be

(a) 8 : 35   (b) 9 : 35

(c) 7 : 35   (d) 8 : 25

10. A small object is placed 10 cm in front of a plane mirror. If you stand behind the object 30 cm from the mirror and look at its image, the distance focused for your eye will be

(a) 60 cm   (b) 20 cm

(c) 40 cm   (d) 80 cm

11. Two plane mirrors are inclined at an angle of 72°. The number of images of a point object placed between them will be

(a) 2   (b) 3

(c) 4   (d) 5

12. A convex mirror of focal length f forms an image which is $\dfrac{1}{n}$ times the object. The distance of the object from the mirror is

(a) $(n-1)f$ (b) $\left(\dfrac{n-1}{n}\right)f$

(c) $\left(\dfrac{n+1}{n}\right)f$ (d) $(n+1)f$

Answer Key	1	(c)	2	(c)	3	(a)	4	(b)	5	(a)	6	(d)
Sol. from page 36	7	(b)	8	(b)	9	(a)	10	(c)	11	(c)	12	(a)

13. An object 1 cm tall is placed 4 cm in front of a mirror. In order to produce an upright image of 3 cm height one needs a

(a) convex mirror of radius of curvature 12 cm

(b) concave mirror of radius of curvature 12 cm

(c) concave mirror of radius of curvature 4 cm

(d) plane mirror of height 12 cm

14. Under which of the following conditions will a convex mirror of focal length f produce an image that is erect, diminished and virtual

(a) only when $2f > u > f$ (b) only when $u = f$

(c) only when $u < f$ (d) always

15. In an experiment to find the focal length of a concave mirror a graph is drawn between the magnitudes of u and v. The graph looks like

(a) 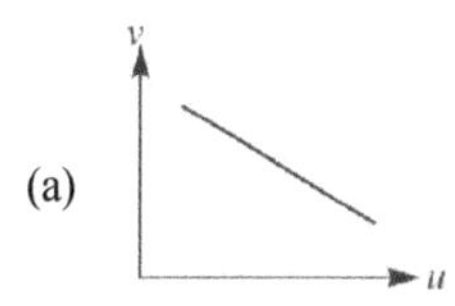   (b) 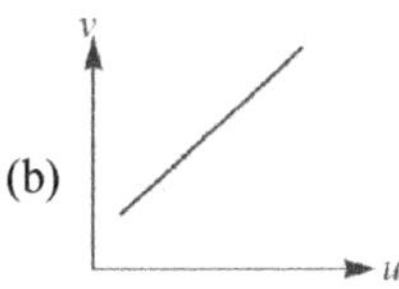

(c) 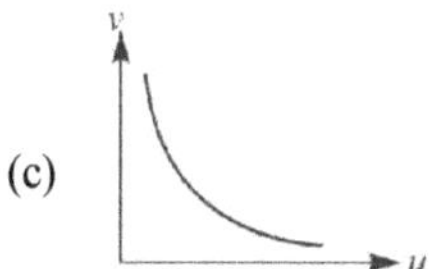   (d) 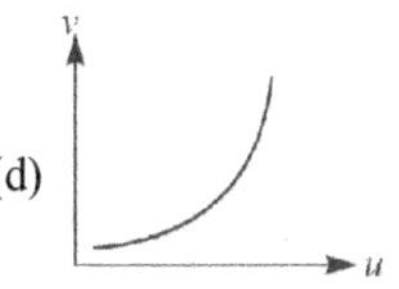

16. The graph shows variation of v with change in u for a mirror. Points plotted above the point P on the curve are for values of v

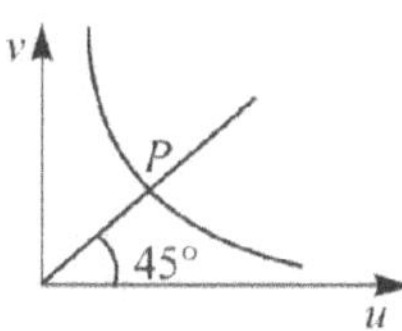

(a) smaller than f (b) smaller than $2f$

(c) larger than $2f$ (d) larger than f

17. For a concave mirror, if real image is formed the graph between $\dfrac{1}{u}$ and $\dfrac{1}{v}$ is of the form

(a) 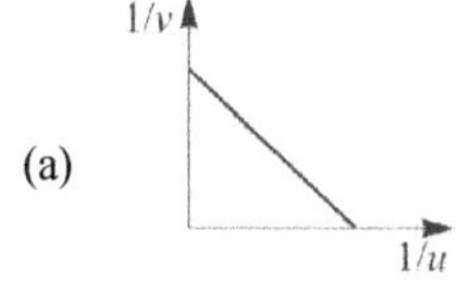   (b) 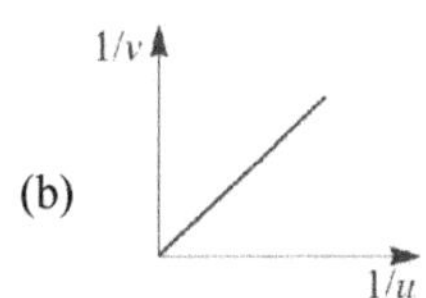

(c) 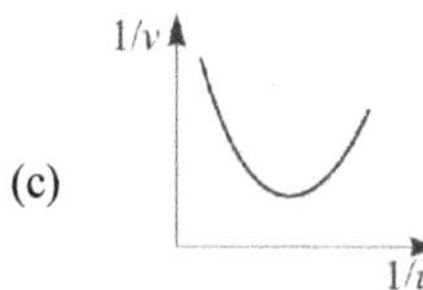   (d) 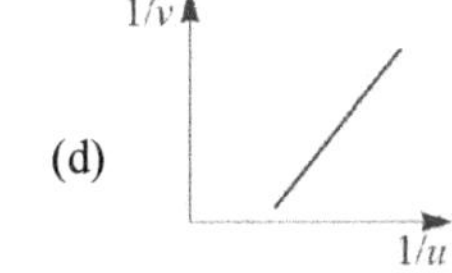

18. The graph between u and v for a convex mirror is

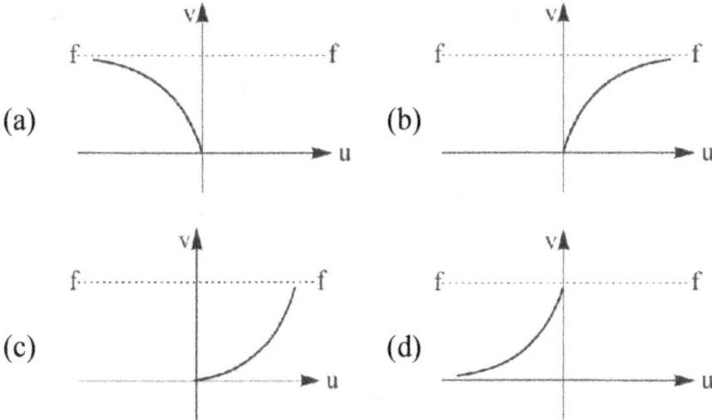

19. A plane mirror is placed at origin parallel of y-axis, facing the positive x-axis. An object starts from (2m, 0, 0) with a velocity of $(2i + 2j)$ m/s. The relative velocity of image with respect to object is along :

(a) positive x-axis   (b) negative x-axis

(c) positive y - axis   (d) negative y - axis

20. In an experiment to determine the focal length f of a concave mirror by the u–v method, a student places the object pin A on the principal axis at a distance x from the pole P. The student looks at the pin and its inverted image from a distance keeping his/her eye in line with PA. When the student shifts his/her eye towards left, the image appears to the right of the object pin. Then,

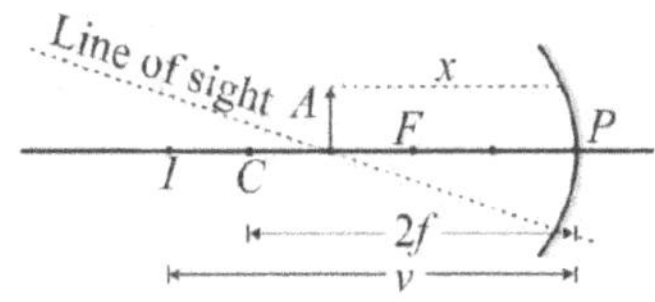

(a) $x < f$ (b) $f < x < 2f$

(c) $x = 2f$ (d) $x > 2f$

21. In the headlights of automobiles, the reflectors employed are parabolic because :

(a) it helps in providing a wide beam of light

(b) it increases the intensity of light

(c) it minimizes spherical aberration and provides a sharp image of the source

(d) it eliminates all colour effects in the beam of light

22. What is the relative velocity of the image in mirror (1) with respect to the image in the mirror (2) in situation as shown in figure ?

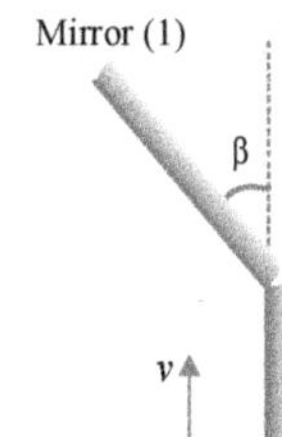

(a) $\dfrac{2v}{\sin\beta}$

(b) $2v\sin\beta$

(c) $\dfrac{2v}{\sin 2\beta}$

(d) none

Answer Key	13	(b)	14	(d)	15	(c)	16	(c)	17	(a)	18	(a)
Sol. from page 36	19	(b)	20	(b)	21	(c)	22	(b)				

23. Figure shows a square enclosure. The inner surfaces are plane mirrors. A ray of light enters a small hole in the centre of mirror. At what angle θ must the ray enter in order to exit through the hole after being reflected one by each mirrors ?

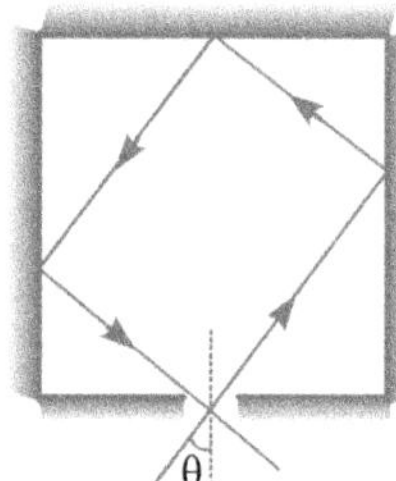

(a)   15°   (b) 30°
(c)   45°   (d) none

24. An object is placed 40 cm from a concave mirror of focal length 20 cm. The image formed is
(a)   real, inverted and same in size
(b)   real, inverted and smaller
(c)   virtual, erect and larger
(d)   virtual, erect and smaller

25.

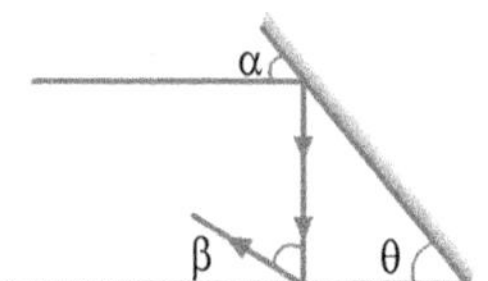

The figure given above shows two successive reflections from two mirrors inclined to each other at an angle θ. The net deviation after two successive deviations depends on :
(a) α and θ (b) β and θ
(c) α and β (d) θ only

26. The figure shows paths of three light rays emerging at the same time from the focus of a parabolic mirror and reaching the screen which is perpendicular to the axis of parabola. Which ray has the least optical path?

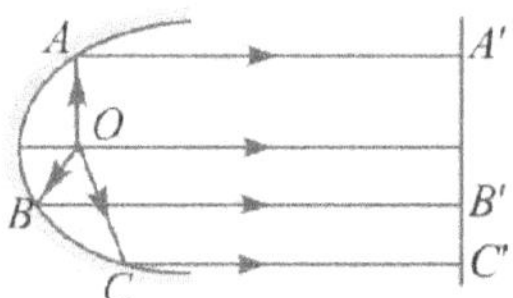

(a)   OAA'   (b) OBB'
(c)   OCC '
(d)   All have the same optical path.

Answer Key	23	(c)	24	(a)	25	(d)	26	(d)
Sol. from page 36								

Only one option correct

1. In the figure you look into a system of two horizontal parallel mirrors A and B separated by a distance d. A point object is placed at point O, a distance 0.2 d from mirror A (see figure). The distance of first and , second images in mirror A are ;

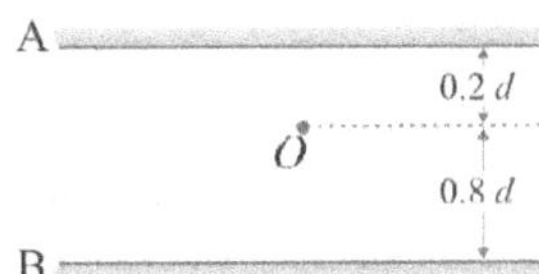

(a) $0.8\,d,\, 1.8\,d$
(b) $0.2d,\, 1.8\,d$
(c) $1.8\,d,\, 2.2\,d$
(d) none of these

2. A point source of light S is placed at a distance d from a screen; the intensity at the centre of the screen is I. When a perfectly reflecting mirror M is placed a distance d behind the source, then intensity at the centre of the screen becomes :

(a) I
(b) $2I$
(c) $\dfrac{10}{9}I$
(d) $4I$

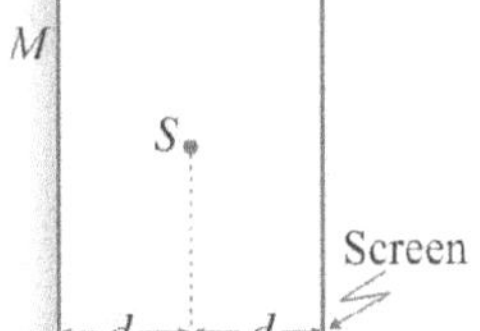

3. A person is in a room whose ceiling and two adjacent walls are mirrors. How many images are formed?

(a) 5
(b) 6
(c) 7
(d) 8

4. A ray of light is incident at $50°$ on the middle of one of the two mirrors arranged at an angle of $60°$ between them. The ray then touches the second mirror, get reflected back to the first mirror, making an angle of incidence of

(a) $50°$
(b) $60°$
(c) $70°$
(d) $80°$

5. The focal length of a concave mirror is f and the distance from the object to the principle focus is x. The ratio of the size of the image to the size of the object is

(a) $\dfrac{f+x}{f}$
(b) $\dfrac{f}{x}$
(c) $\sqrt{\dfrac{f}{x}}$
(d) $\dfrac{f^2}{x^2}$

6. A short linear object of length ℓ lies along the axis of a concave mirror of focal length f at a distance u from the pole of the mirror. The size of the image is approximately equal to

(a) $\ell\left(\dfrac{u-f}{f}\right)^{1/2}$
(b) $\ell\left(\dfrac{u-f}{f}\right)^{2}$
(c) $\ell\left(\dfrac{f}{u-f}\right)^{1/2}$
(d) $\ell\left(\dfrac{f}{u-f}\right)^{2}$

7. A cube of side 2 m is placed in front of a concave mirror of focal length 1m with its face P at a distance of 3 m and face Q at a distance of 5 m from the mirror. The distance between the image of face P and Q is

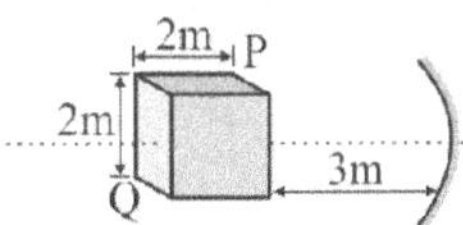

(a) 1 m
(b) 0.5 m
(c) 0.5 m
(d) 0.25 m

8. In a lamp and scale arrangement to measure small deflection, the arrangement is shown in the figure SS′ is the glass scale placed at a distance of 1 m from the plane mirror MM and I is the position of the light spot formed after reflection from the undeflected mirror MM. The mirror is deflected by $10°$ and comes to the deflected position M′M′. The distance moved by the spot on the scale (IR) is :

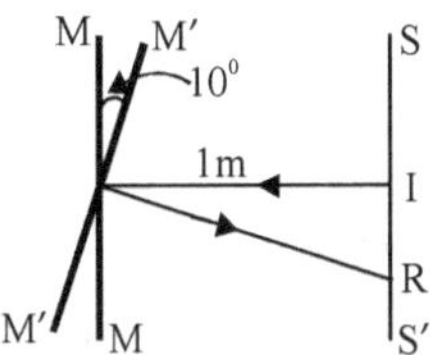

(a) 24.6 cm
(b) 36.4 cm
(c) 46.4 cm
(d) 34.6 cm

9. When an object is placed at a distance of 25 cm from a mirror, the magnification is m_1. The object is moved 15cm further away with respect to the earlier position, and the magnification becomes m_2. If $m_1/m_2 = 4$, the focal length of the mirror is :

(a) 10 cm
(b) 30 cm
(c) 15 cm
(d) 20 cm

10. Two plane mirrors are inclined to each other at a certain angle. A ray of light first incident on one of them at an inclination of $10°$ with the mirror retraces its path after five reflections. The angle between the mirrors is :

(a) $12°$
(b) $22°$
(c) $30°$
(d) $20°$

11. Two mirrors, one concave and the other convex, are placed 60 cm apart with their reflecting surfaces facing each other. An object is placed 30 cm from the pole of either of them on their axis. If the focal lengths of both the mirrors are 15 cm, the position of the image formed by reflection, first at the convex and then at the concave mirror, is :

(a) 19.09 cm from the pole of the concave mirror
(b) 19.09 cm from the pole of the convex mirror
(c) 11.09 cm from the pole of the concave mirror
(d) 11.09 cm from the pole of the convex mirror

Answer Key	1	(b)	2	(c)	3	(c)	4	(c)	5	(b)	6	(d)
Sol. from page 37	7	(d)	8	(b)	9	(d)	10	(d)	11	(a)		

12. A point source has been placed as shown in the figure. What is the length on the screen that will receive reflected light from the mirror?

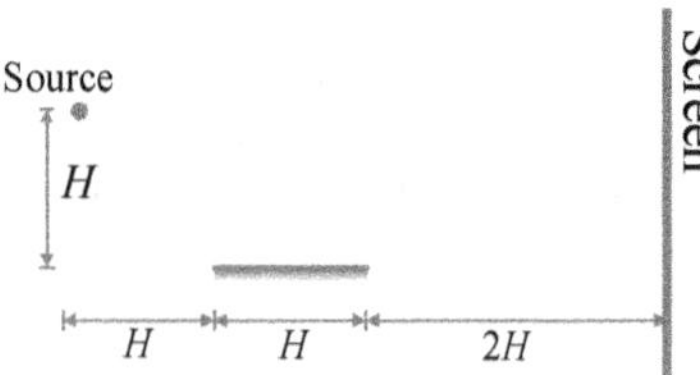

(a) $2H$
(b) $3H$
(c) H
(d) none

13. A boy is walking under an inclined mirror at a constant velocity v m/s along the x- axis as shown in figure. If the mirror is inclined at an angle θ with the horizontal then what is the velocity of the image?

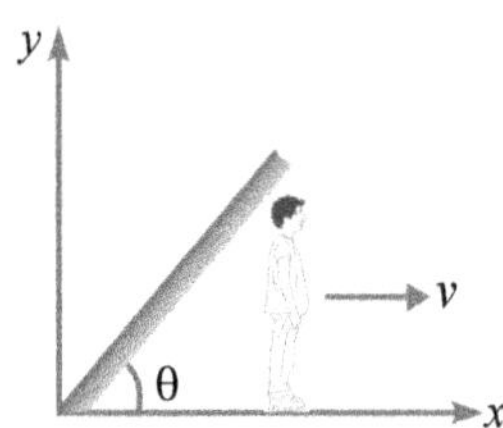

(a) $v \sin \theta i + v \cos \theta j$
(b) $v \cos \theta i + v \sin \theta j$
(c) $v \sin 2\theta i + v \cos 2\theta j$
(d) $v \cos 2\theta i + v \sin 2\theta j$

14. A child is standing in front of a straight plane mirror. His father is standing behind him, as shown in the figure. The height of the father is double the height of the child. What is the minimum length of the mirror required so that the child can completely see his own image and his father's image in the mirror? Given the height of father is $2H$.

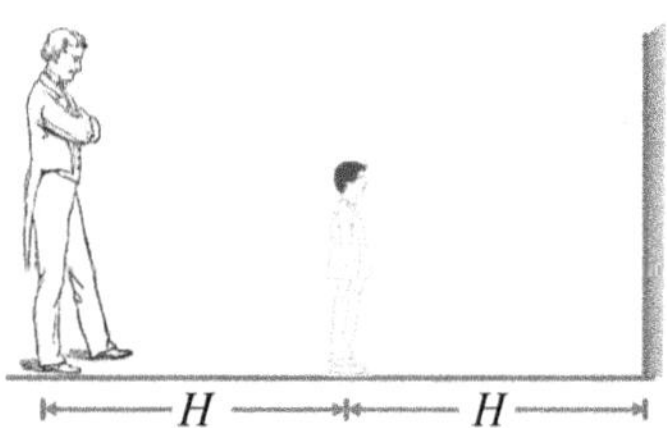

(a) $H/2$
(b) $5H/6$
(c) $3H/2$
(d) none

15. An infinitely long rod lies along the axis of a concave mirror of focal length f. The near end of the rod is at a distance $u > f$ from the mirror. Its image will have a length.

(a) $\dfrac{f^2}{u-f}$
(b) $\dfrac{uf}{u-f}$

(c) $\dfrac{f^2}{u+f}$
(d) $\dfrac{uf}{u+f}$

16. The reflecting surface is represented by the equation $2x = y^2$ as shown in the figure. A ray travelling horizontal becomes vertical after reflection. The co-ordinates of the point of incidence are :

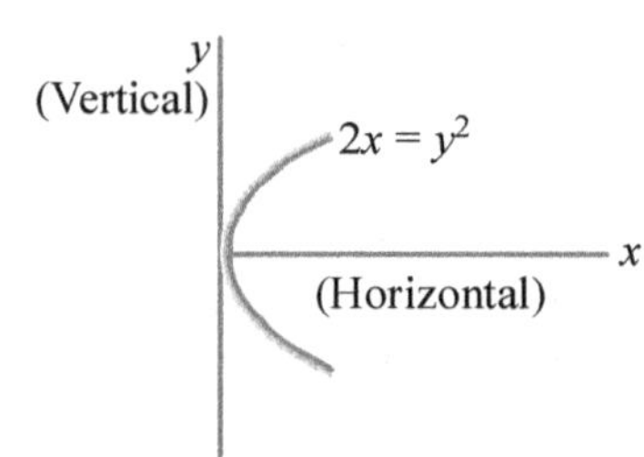

(a) $(1/2, 1)$
(b) $(1, 1/2)$
(c) $(1/2, 1/2)$
(d) none

17. A boy of height h is walking away from a street lamp with a constant speed v. The height of the street lamp is $3h$. The rate at which the length of the boy's shadow is increasing when he is at a distance of $10h$ from the base of the street lamp is :
(a) $2v$
(b) v
(c) $v/2$
(d) $v/3$

18. A particle is projected on a horizontal xy-plane, at an angle $45°$ with horizontal, as shown. The particle is projected from focus F of a concave mirror of curvature R, with speed $v = \sqrt{gR}$. Velocity of image of the particle as it is just about to strike the horizontal plane is

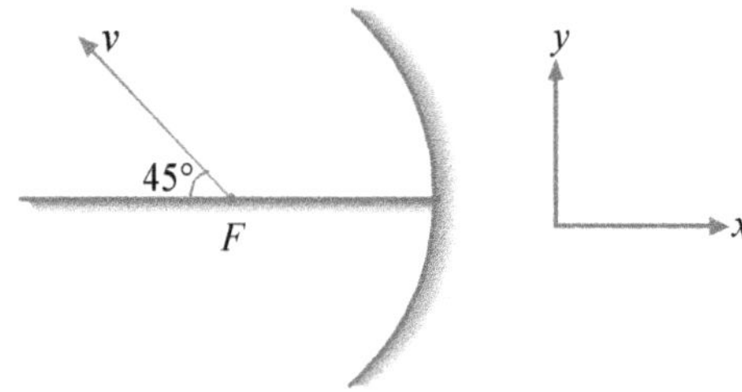

(a) $\dfrac{v}{4\sqrt{2}}\hat{i} - \dfrac{v}{4\sqrt{2}}\hat{j}$
(b) $\dfrac{v}{2\sqrt{2}}\hat{i} + \dfrac{v}{2\sqrt{2}}\hat{j}$

(c) $\dfrac{v}{4\sqrt{2}}\hat{i} - \dfrac{v}{2\sqrt{2}}\hat{j}$
(d) $\dfrac{-v}{2\sqrt{2}}\hat{i} + \dfrac{v}{4\sqrt{2}}\hat{j}$

19. A ray parallel to principal axis is incident at $30°$ from normal on concave mirror having radius of curvature R. The point on principal axis where rays are focussed is Q such that PQ is

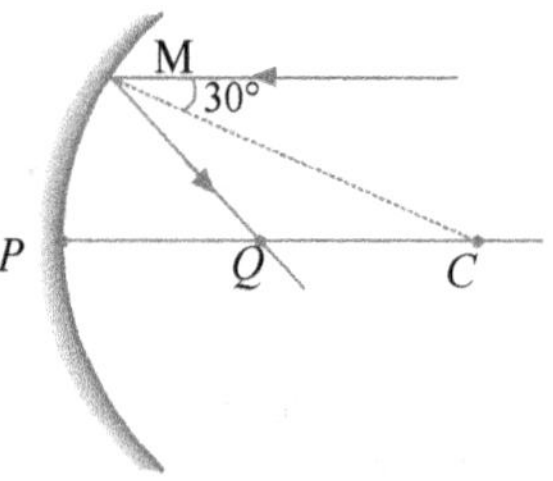

(a) $\dfrac{R}{2}$
(b) $\dfrac{R}{\sqrt{3}}$

(c) $\dfrac{2\sqrt{R} - R}{\sqrt{2}}$
(d) $R\left(1 - \dfrac{1}{\sqrt{3}}\right)$

Answer Key	12	(a)	13	(d)	14	(b)	15	(a)
Sol. from page 38	16	(a)	17	(c)	18	(c)	19	(d)

20. A mirror of parabolic shape is shown. The equation of mirror surface is $y^2 = 8x$. Rays parallel to principal axis are focussed at

(a)　$(2, 0)$

(b)　$(0, 2)$

(c)　$(4, 0)$

(d)　$(6, 0)$

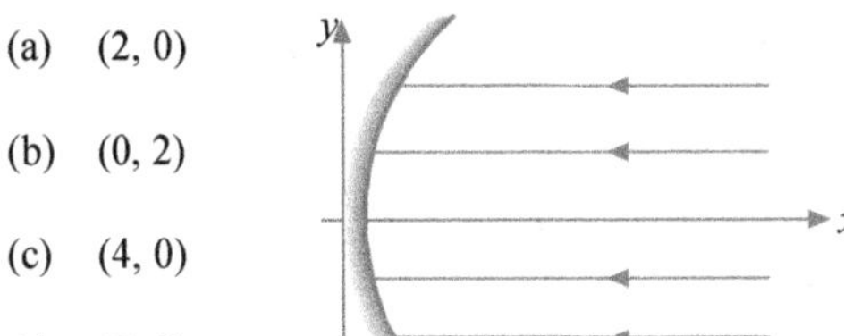

21. A plane mirror is moving with $-2\hat{i} + 4\hat{j} + \hat{k}$ m/s in x-z plane. Velocity of image of a point object moving with velocity $\hat{i} + 2\hat{j} - 5\hat{k}$ m/s is (assume that object is located on front side of the mirror)

(a)　$-2\hat{i} + 4\hat{j} - \hat{k}$ m/s

(b)　$\hat{i} + 4\hat{j} - 5\hat{k}$ m/s

(c)　$2\hat{i} - 3\hat{j} + \hat{k}$ m/s

(d)　$-\hat{i} + 5\hat{j} - 4\hat{k}$ m/s .

Answer Key Sol. from page 38	20	(a)	21	(b)				

Optics	**MCQ Type 2**	*Exercise 1.2*

Multiple correct options

1. The magnification produced by a spherical mirror is –4. The image is

(a)　real, inverted

(b)　virtual, inverted

(c)　virtual, erect

(d)　on the side of the object

2. A plane mirror reflecting a ray of incident light is rotated through an angle θ about an axis through the point of incidence in the plane of the mirror perpendicular to the plane of incidence, then

(a)　the reflected ray does not rotate

(b)　the reflected ray rotates through an angle θ

(c)　the reflected ray rotates through an angle 2θ

(d)　the incident ray is fixed

3. Which of the following form(s) a virtual and erect image for all positions of the object

(a)　convex lens

(b)　concave lens

(c)　convex mirror

(d)　concave mirror

4. Which of the following (referred to a spherical mirror) do (does) not depend on whether the rays are paraxial or not ?

(a)　pole

(b)　focus

(c)　radius of curvature

(d)　principal axis

5. The image of an extended object, placed perpendicular to the principal axis of a mirror, will be erect if :

(a)　the object and the image are both real

(b)　the object and the image are both virtual

(c)　the object is real but the image is virtual

(d)　the object virtual but the image is a real.

6. A plane mirror M is arranged parallel to a wall W at a distance l from it. The light produced by a point source S kept on the wall is reflected by the mirror and produces a light spot on the wall. The mirror moves with velocity v towards the wall. Then

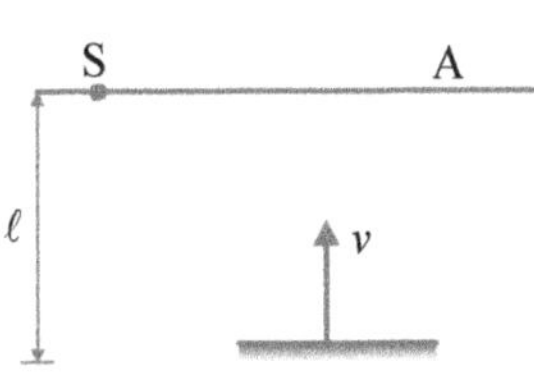

(a)　the spot of light will move with the speed v on the wall.

(b)　the spot of light will not move on the wall.

(c)　as the mirror comes closer, the spot of the light will becomes larger and shift away from the wall with speed larger then v.

(d)　the size of the light spot on the wall remains the same.

7. A ball is projected with initial speed v at distance 20 cm from pole of a concave mirror. Speed of image cannot be

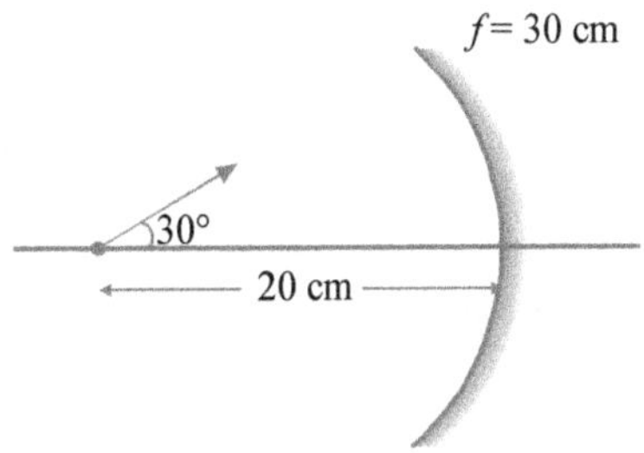

(a)　greater than v

(b)　less than v

(c)　equal to v

(d)　zero

8. For a real object, magnification produced by a mirror is +2.5. Choose the correct statements regarding the mirror.

(a)　Mirror must be a convex mirror

(b)　Mirror can be a concave or a convex mirror

(c)　Mirror cannot be a plane mirror

(d)　Mirror must be concave mirror, with object between pole and focus

Answer Key Sol. from page 40	1	(a, d)	2	(c, d)	3	(b, c)	4	(a, c, d)
	5	(c, d)	6	(b, d)	7	(b, c, d)	8	(c, d)

Optics — # Statement Questions — *Exercise 1.3*

Read the two statements carefully to mark the correct option out of the options given below. Select the right choice.

(a) If both the statements are true and the *Statement - 2* is the correct explanation of *Statement - 1*.

(b) If both the statements are true but *Statement - 2* is not the correct explanation of the *Statement - 1*.

(c) If *Statement - 1* true but *Statement - 2* is false.

(d) If *Statement - 1* is false but *Statement - 2* is true.

1. *Statement - 1* : Plane mirror may form real image.

 Statement - 2 : Plane mirror forms virtual image, if object is real.

2. *Statement - 1* : Virtual image can not be photographed.

 Statement - 2 : Real image can be photographed after taking on the screen.

3. *Statement - 1* : Figure shows two rays being reflected by a mirror; the mirror is plane.

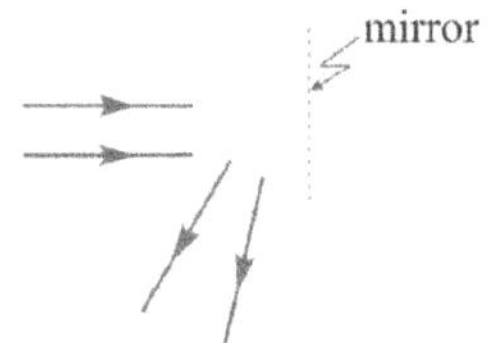

 Statement - 2 : The mirror must be spherical

4. *Statement - 1* : The focal length of the convex mirror will increase, if the mirror is placed in water.

 Statement 2 : The focal length of a convex mirror of radius R is equal to , $f = R/2$.

5. *Statement - 1* : Chromatic aberration in spherical mirror can be minimised by using stops.

 Statement - 2 : Spherical mirrors do not produce any chromatic aberration.

6. *Statement - 1* : The image formed by a concave mirror is certainly real if the object is virtual.

 Statement - 2 : The image formed by a concave mirror is certainly virtual if the object is real.

7. *Statement - 1* : The image of an extended object placed perpendicular to the principal axis of a mirror, will be erect if the object is real but the image is virtual.

 Statement - 2 : The image of an extended object, placed perpendicular to the principal axis of a mirror, will be erect if the object is virtual but the image is real.

8. *Statement - 1* : The height of plane mirror needed to form full image of an object is half the height of the object.

 Statement - 2 : The height of plane mirror needed to form full image of an object may by less than half of the height of the object.

9. *Statement - 1* : An object is placed at a distance of f from a convex mirror of focal length f its image will form at infinity.

 Statement - 2 : The distance of image in convex mirror can never be infinity.

10. *Statement - 1* : In motor vehicles, a convex mirror is attached near the driver's seat to get larger image of the traffic behind.

 Statement - 2 : The field of view of convex mirror is largest in all the mirrors.

11. *Statement - 1* : The focal length of concave mirror for red colour is greater than the focal length for blue colour.

 Statement - 2 : The focal length of concave mirror is same for both the colours.

12. *Statement - 1* : In the head light of automobiles, the reflectors used are parabolic.

 Statement - 2 : Parabolic reflector minimise spherical aberration and provide a sharp image of the source.

Answer Key	1	(b)	2	(d)	3	(d)	4	(d)	5	(d)	6	(c)	7	(b)
Sol. from page 40	8	(d)	9	(d)	10	(d)	11	(d)	12	(a)				

Optics | # Passage & Matrix | *Exercise 1.4*

PASSAGES

Passage for (Q. 1 & 2) :

An object of height h sits cautiously before a spherical mirror whose focal length has absolute value $|f| = 40$ cm. The image of the object produced by the mirror has the same orientation as the object and has height $h' = 0.20\, h$.

1. The magnification is
   (a) 0.10   (b) 0.30
   (c) 0.40   (d) 0.20

2. The position of the object is
   (a) −40 cm   (b) −120 cm
   (c) −160 cm   (d) −100 cm

Passage for (Q. 3 - 5)

A wire frame in the form of a small cube 3 cm on a side is placed with its centre on the axis of a concave mirror of radius of curvature 30 cm. The sides of the cube are parallel or perpendicular to the axis. The face toward the mirror is 60 cm to the left of the vertex (pole).

3. The position of the image of the cube is
   (a) −10 cm   (b) −15 cm
   (c) −15 cm   (d) − 20

4. The lateral magnification is
   (a) $-\dfrac{1}{2}$ (b) $-\dfrac{1}{4}$
   (c) $-\dfrac{1}{3}$ (d) −1

5. The longitudinal magnification is
   (a) $-\dfrac{1}{9}$ (b) $-\dfrac{1}{3}$
   (c) $-\dfrac{2}{3}$ (d) −1

MATRIX MATCHING

6. Match **Column-I** with **Column-II** and select the correct answer using the codes given below the lists:

Column – I	Column – II
(Position of the object)	**(Magnification)**
A. An object is placed at focus before a convex mirror	(p) Magnification is $-\infty$
B. An object is placed at centre of curvature before a concave mirror	(q) Magnification is 0.5
C. An object is placed at focus before a concave mirror	(r) Magnification is +1
D. An object is placed at centre of curvature before a convex mirror	(s) Magnification is −1
	(t) Magnification is 0.33

7. For an object placed in front of a mirror, magnification (m) is given in **Column I**, **Column II** gives the possible nature of the mirror or that of image. Match appropriately.

Column – I	Column – II
A. $m = \dfrac{1}{4}$	(p) Concave mirror
B. $m = -1$	(q) Convex mirror
C. $m = 2$	(r) Plane mirror
D. $m = 1$	(s) Real
	(t) Virtual

Answer Key	1	(d)	2	(c)	3	(d)	4	(c)
Sol. from page 40	5	(a)	6	A-(q); B-(s); C-(p); D-(t)	7	A-(q, t); B-(p, s); C-(p,t); D-(r,t)		

 # Subjective Integer Type   *Exercise 1.5*

Solution from page 41

1. A mirror 1 m high hangs on a wall. A man stands a distance of 2 m away from the mirror what is the height of the position of the opposite wall in the room that can be seen by the man in the mirror without changing the position of his head ? The wall is 4 m from the mirror.

Ans. 3 m.

2. Two plane mirrors A and B are aligned parallel to each other as shown in figure.

A light ray is incident at an angle of 30° at a point just inside one end of A. The plane of incidence with the plane of the figure. Find the maximum number of reflections (including the first one) the light ray suffers before it emerges out.

Ans. 30

3. The image produced by a concave mirror is one quarter the size of the object. If the object is moved b = 5 cm closer to the mirror the image will only be half the size of the object. Find the focal length of the mirror.

Ans. 25 mm.

 # Subjective   *Exercise 1.6*

Solution from page 41

1. Rays of light strike a horizontal plane mirror at an angle of 45°. At what angle should a second plane mirror be placed in order that the reflected ray finally be reflected horizontally from the second mirror ?

Ans. 22.5.

2. A point object is moving with a speed of v before an arrangement of two mirrors as shown in figure. Find the velocity of the image in mirror M, with respect to the image in mirror M_2.

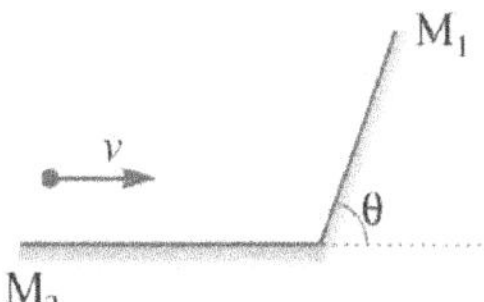

Ans. 2v sin θ

3. Determine graphically the positions of the eye when an observer can simultaneously use in a flat mirror of finite dimensions the image of a point and a section of a straight line placed with respect to the mirror as shown in figure.

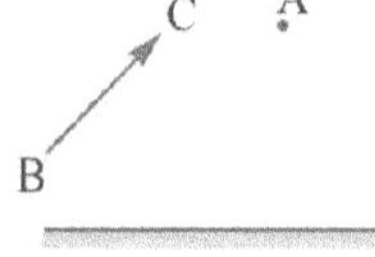

4. A small concave mirror L is suspended from a thread in a mirror galvanometer to read the angles of turn. A scale A A_1 is placed at a distance $\ell = 1$ m from the mirror and a lamp S is adjusted underneath the scale. What should the focal length of the mirror be to obtained on the scale the real image of the aperture in the lamp? To what distance d will the image be shifted on the scale in the mirror is turned through a small angle θ ?

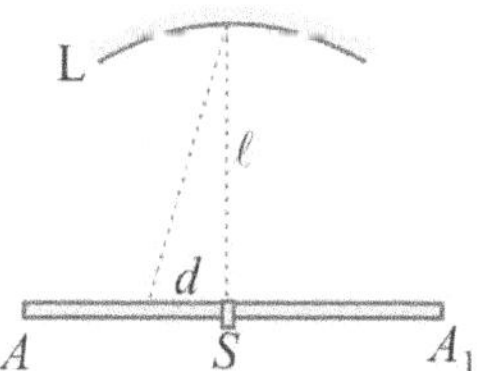

Ans. f = $\ell/2$ = 50 cm ; d = 2ℓθ.

5. An object is placed exactly midway between a concave mirror of radius of curvature 40 cm and a convex mirror of radius of curvature 30 cm. The mirrors face each other and are 50 cm apart. Determine the nature and position of the image formed by the successive reflections, first at the concave mirror and then at the convex mirror.

Ans. The virtual image is formed behind the convex mirror at a distance of 21.43 cm.

6. Find the diameter of the image of the moon formed by a spherical concave mirror of focal length 7.6 m. The diameter of the moon is 3450 km and the distance between the earth and the moon is 3.8×10^5 km.

Ans. 6.9 cm

7. A metal block of mass m and a concave mirror radius R fitted with a stand lie on a smooth horizontal table with a distance d between them. The mirror together with its stand has a mass m. The block is pushed at $t = 0$ towards the mirror so that it starts moving towards the mirror at a constant speed v_0 and collides with it. The collision is perfectly elastic. Find the velocity of the image (a) at time $t < \dfrac{d}{v_0}$ (b) at a time $t > \dfrac{d}{v_0}$.

Ans. (a) $-\dfrac{R^2 v_0}{[2(d - v_0 t) - R]^2}$ (b) $v_0\left[1 + \dfrac{R^2}{\{2(v_0 t - d) - R\}^2}\right].$

8. A mass $m = 50$ g is dropped on a vertical spring of spring constant 500 N/m from a height $h = 10$ cm as shown in figure. The mass stick to the spring and executes simple harmonic oscillations after that. A concave mirror of focal length 12 cm facing the mass is fixed with its principal axis coinciding with the line of motion of the mass, its pole being at a distance of 30 cm from the free end of the spring. Find the length in which the image of the mass oscillates.

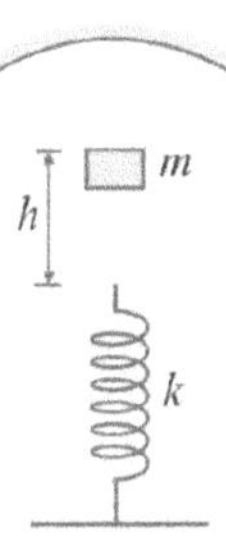

Ans. 1.26 cm.

9. Two spherical mirrors, one convex and the other concave, each of same radius of curvature R are arranged coaxially at a distance $2R$ from each other . A small circle of radius a is drawn on the convex mirror near the pole as shown in the figure. Find the radii of the first three images of the circle.

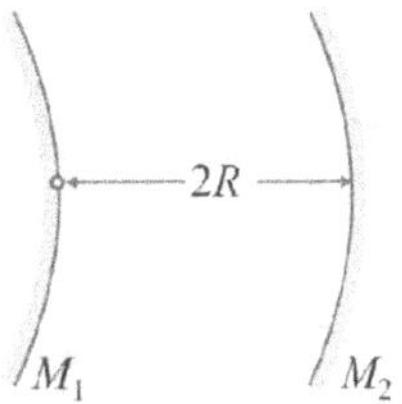

Ans. $a/3, a/11, a/41.$

★ ★ ★

Hints & Solutions

1. (c) Velocity of object w.r.t mirror = 10 cm/s
So velocity of image w.r.t you = 2 × 10 = 20 cm/s.

2. (c) Using law of reflection the angles are shown in figure

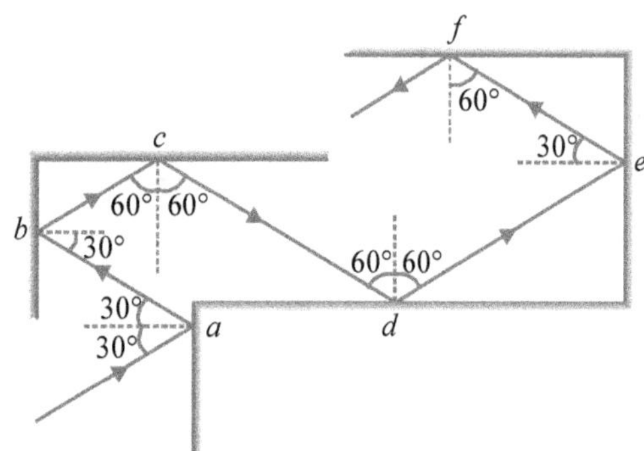

3. (a)

4. (b) For reflected ray becomes parallel to incident ray, angle of deviation, $\delta = 180°$. We have
$$\delta = 360° - 2\theta$$
or $$180° = 360° - 2\theta$$
or $$\theta = 90°.$$

5. (a) If y is the required distance, then
$$\frac{d/2}{y} = \frac{d}{d}$$
or $$y = \frac{d}{2} = \frac{2}{2} = 1 \text{ m}.$$

6. (d) The distance of the image from mirror = 3 m.
The distance of image from camera
$$= 3 + 4.5 = 7.5 \text{ m}$$

7. (b)

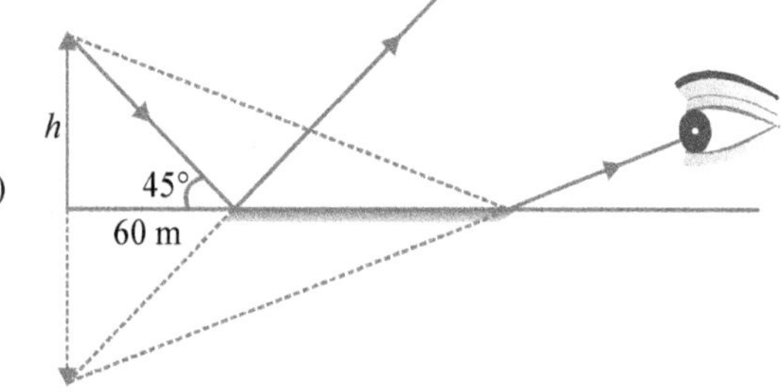

The angle subtended by tower will be 45°.
$$\therefore \quad \frac{h}{60} = \tan 45°$$
$$= 1$$
or $$h = 60 \text{ m}$$

8. (b) One of the images by mirror is formed after two reflections, and so it looks like as the object.

9. (a)

10. (c) The distance of image from the mirror will be 10 cm. The distance of image from observer = 10 + 30 = 40 cm.

11. (c) $n = \dfrac{360°}{\theta} - 1 = \dfrac{360°}{72} - 1 = 4$.

12. (a) $$m = \frac{1}{n} = \frac{-v}{u} \text{ or } v = \frac{-u}{n}$$

Now, $$\frac{1}{v} + \frac{1}{u} = \frac{1}{f}$$

or $$\frac{1}{\dfrac{-u}{n}} + \frac{1}{u} = \frac{1}{f}$$

$$\therefore \quad u = -(n-1)f.$$

13. (b) $$m = -\frac{v}{u}$$

or $$\frac{3}{1} = \frac{-v}{-4}$$

or $$v = 12 \text{ cm}$$

Now $$\frac{1}{12} + \frac{1}{-4} = \frac{1}{f}$$

or $$f = -6 \text{ cm}$$

14. (d) Convex mirror gives erect image for all possible positions of the object.

15. (c)

16. (c) At point P, $u = v$ and this happens when $u = 2f$. For point above P, $u > 2f$.

17. (a) $\dfrac{1}{v} + \dfrac{1}{u} = \dfrac{1}{f}$ or $x + y = c$, so it represent a straight line

between $\dfrac{1}{v}$ and $\dfrac{1}{u}$.

18. (a) For convex mirror for negative value of u, v will be positive and cannot be greater than f.

19. (b) The velocity of image w.r.t. mirror

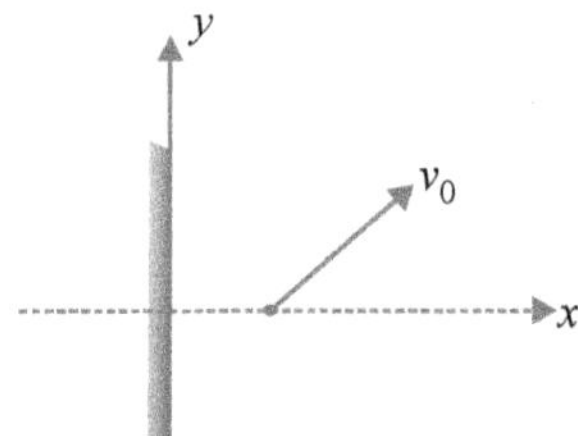

$$\vec{v}_i = (-2\hat{i} + 2\hat{j}) \text{ m/s}$$
So velocity of image w.r.t. object
$$= (-2\hat{i} + 2\hat{j}) - (2\hat{i} + 2\hat{j})$$
$$= -4\hat{i} \text{ m/s}.$$

20. (b)
21. (c) Parabolic mirror minimise spherical aberration.
22. (b) The required velocity is the velocity of image w.r.t. object.

Thus, $v_{i0} = 2(v_0)_1 = 2v\sin\beta$

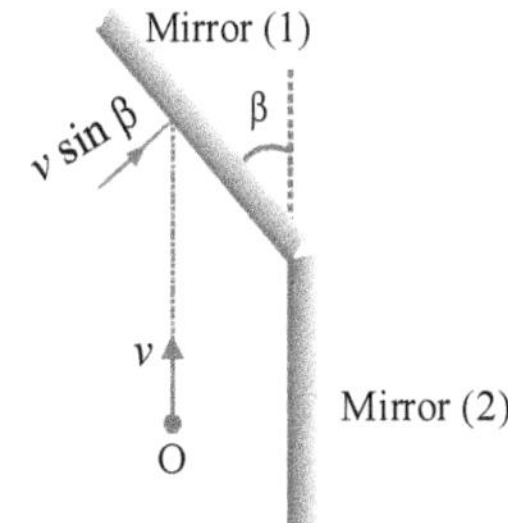

23. (c) For the ray back to the hole
$$90° - \theta = \theta$$
$$\therefore \qquad \theta = 45°$$

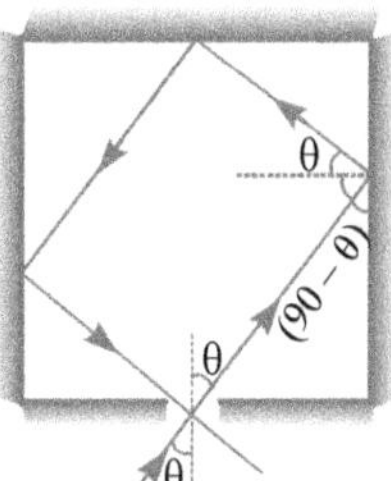

24. (a) For $u = -40$ cm and $f = -20$ cm,
$v = -40$ cm, so image will be real, inverted and equal in size of object.

25. (d) The angle of deviation produced by two mirrors in contact is given by $\delta = 360° - 2\theta$,

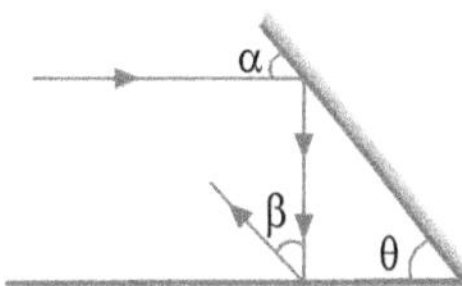

which depends only on angle between the mirrors.

26. (d)

1. (b) The distance of object and first image from B are 0.2d and 1.8 d from mirror A. So image distances are 0.2d and 1.8d.

2. (c) Intensity, $I = \dfrac{k}{r^2}$

Intensity at the screen without mirror

$$I_1 = \dfrac{k}{d^2}$$

Intensity at the screen with mirror

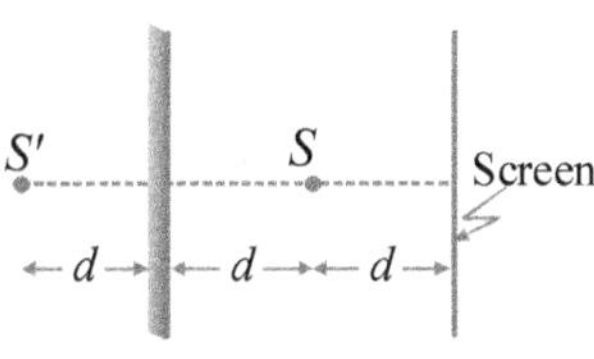

$$I_2 = \dfrac{k}{d^2} + \dfrac{k}{(3d)^2}$$

$$= \dfrac{10k}{9d^2} .$$

3. (c) Number of images formed by two mirror placed mutually perpendicular are three. These three images together with object becomes four objects for ceiling mirror. So total no of images are $= 3 + 4 = 7$.

4. (c) See geometry of the figure.

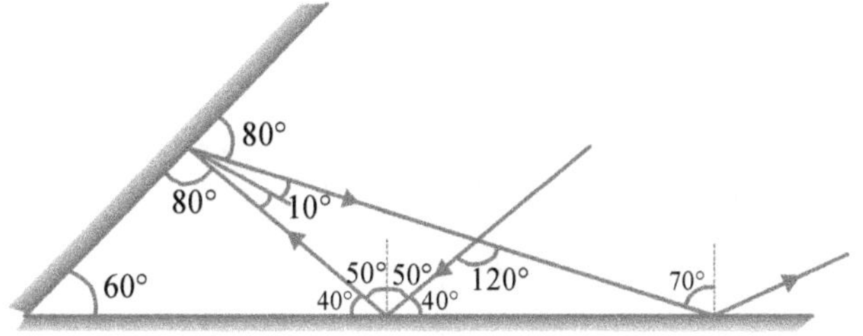

5. (b) From similar triangles, we have

$$\dfrac{I}{O} = \dfrac{f}{x} .$$

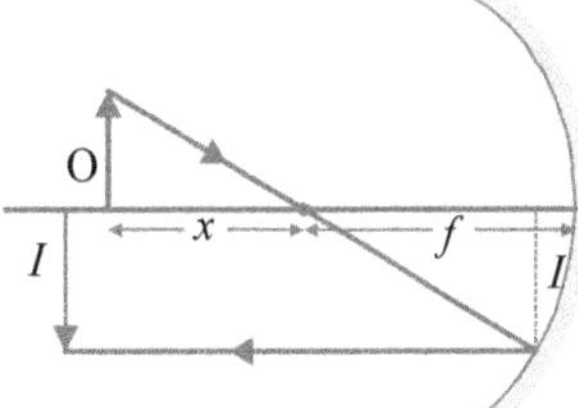

6. (d) The axial magnification

$$\delta v = -\dfrac{v^2}{u^2}(\delta u)$$

$$= \left(\dfrac{f}{u-f}\right)^2 \ell .$$

7. (d) For P : $\qquad \dfrac{1}{v} + \dfrac{1}{u} = \dfrac{1}{f}$

or $\qquad \dfrac{1}{v_P} + \dfrac{1}{-3} = \dfrac{1}{-1}$

or $\qquad v_P = -\dfrac{3}{2} m$

For Q : $\qquad \dfrac{1}{v_Q} + \dfrac{1}{-5} = \dfrac{1}{-1}$

or $\qquad v_Q = \dfrac{-5}{4} m$

So horizontal distance between image of P and Q is 0.25 m

8. (b)
$$IR = x\theta$$
$$= 1 \times 20°$$
$$= 1 \times \frac{20° \times \pi}{180°} \times 100$$
$$= 36.4 \text{ cm}$$

9. (d)
$$m = -\frac{v}{u} = -\left(\frac{f}{u-f}\right)$$

Now
$$m_1 = -\left(\frac{f}{25-f}\right) \qquad \ldots (i)$$

and
$$m_2 = -\left(\frac{f}{40-f}\right) \qquad \ldots (ii)$$

$\therefore$
$$\frac{m_1}{m_2} = \frac{40-f}{25-f}$$

or
$$4 = \frac{40-f}{25-f}$$

or
$$f = 20 \text{ cm}.$$

10. (d)

11. (a) For convex mirror :

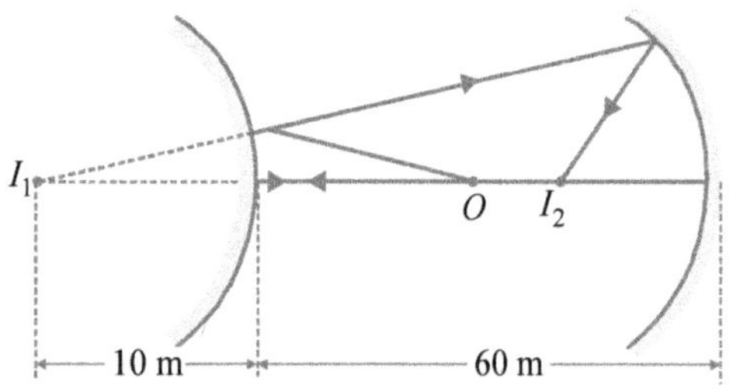

$$\frac{1}{v} + \frac{1}{-30} = \frac{1}{+15}$$
or
$$v = 10 \text{ m}$$

For concave mirror :
$$\frac{1}{v} + \frac{1}{-70} = \frac{1}{-15}$$
or
$$v = -19.09 \text{ m}$$

12. (a) In ΔABD,
$$\frac{BD}{3H} = \tan 45°$$

or
$$BD = 3H$$

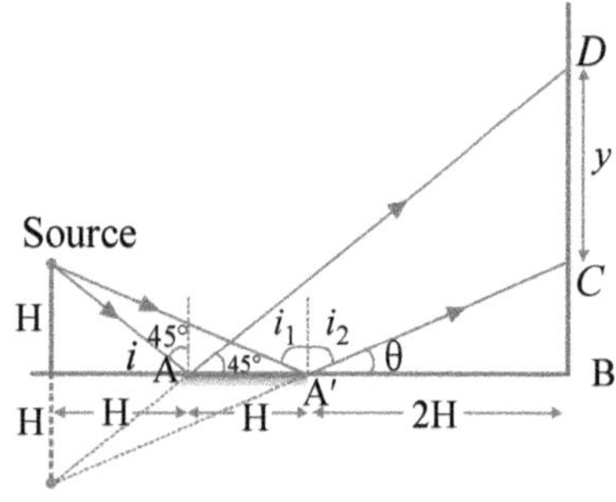

And in $\Delta A'BC$,
$$\frac{BC}{2H} = \tan \theta$$

$$= \frac{1}{2}$$

or
$$BC = H$$
Now, $y = BD - BC = 3H - H = 2H.$

13. (d)

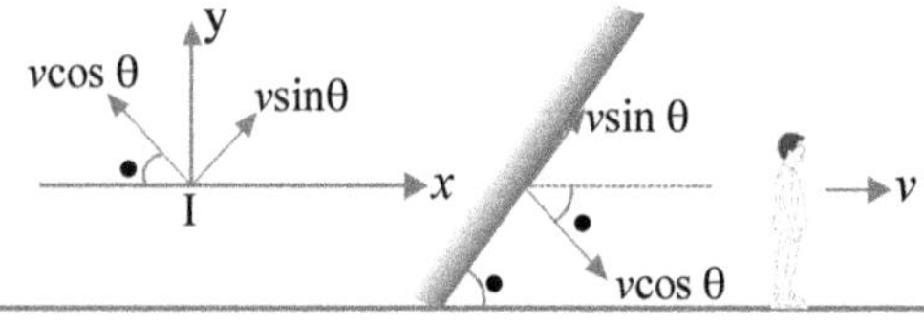

Velocity of image of boy is shown in figure. Thus
$$\vec{v}_i = [(v\sin\theta)\sin\theta - (v\cos\theta\cos\theta)]\hat{i}$$
$$+ [v\sin\theta\cos\theta + v\cos\theta\sin\theta]\hat{j}$$
$$= v[\cos 2\theta\,\hat{i} + \sin 2\theta\,\hat{j}].$$

14. (b)

15. (a) The image of end B will be at focus F.
For image of A,
$$\frac{1}{v_A} + \frac{1}{-u} = \frac{1}{-f}$$

or
$$v_A = \left(\frac{uf}{u-f}\right)$$

Thus length of the image
$$= v_A - f = \left(\frac{uf}{u-f}\right) - f$$
$$= \left(\frac{f^2}{u-f}\right).$$

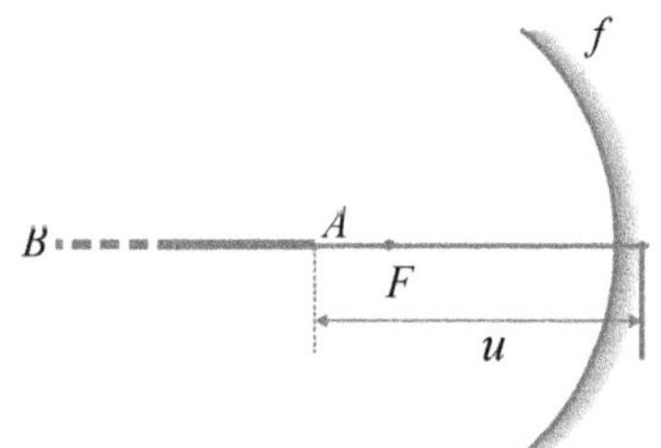

16. (a)

$i + r = 90°$, and $\angle i = \angle r$
$\therefore$
$$i = 45°$$
Also
$$i + \theta = 90°$$
$\therefore$
$$\theta = 90° - i = 90° - 45° = 45°$$
Given
$$y^2 = 2x$$

or
$$2y\frac{dy}{dx} = 2$$

$$\therefore \qquad \frac{dy}{dx} = \frac{1}{y}$$

$$\text{or} \qquad \tan 45° = \frac{1}{y}$$

$$\therefore \qquad y = 1$$

$$\text{Now} \qquad x = \frac{y^2}{2} = \frac{1^2}{2} = \frac{1}{2}$$

17. (c) Let x be the length of the shadow of the boy, when he is at a distance y from the lamp. From similar triangles, we have

$$\frac{h}{x} = \frac{3h}{x+y}$$

$$\text{or} \qquad x = y/2.$$

$$\text{Thus} \qquad \frac{dx}{dt} = \frac{dy/dt}{2}$$

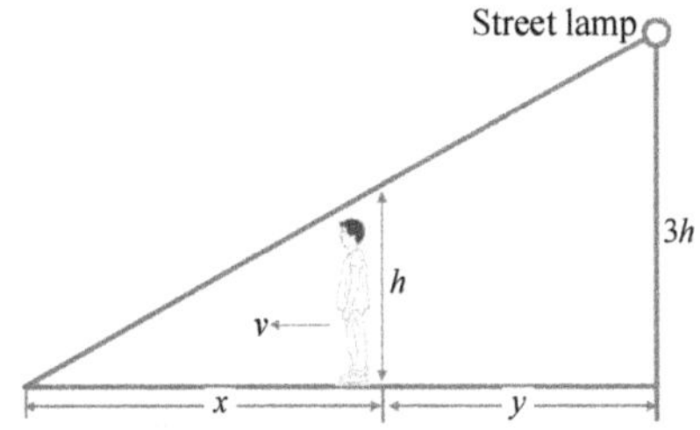

18. (c) The situation of the particle is shown in figure.

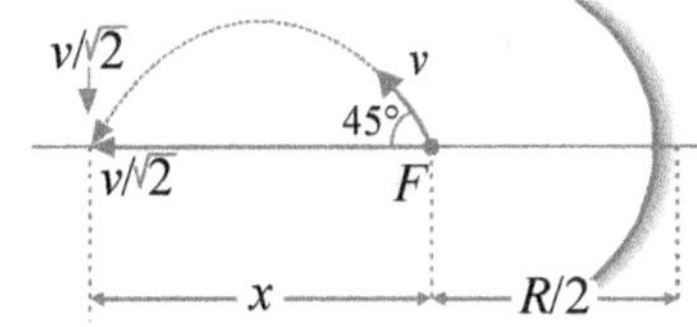

The distance of the particle at which it will hit the ground,

$$x = \frac{v^2}{g} = \frac{gR}{g} = R$$

$$\text{Thus,} \qquad u = -\left(\frac{R}{2}+R\right) = \frac{-3R}{2}$$

Velocity of image along the optic axis,

$$v_i = -\frac{v^2}{u^2} \times v_0$$

$$= -\frac{\left(-\dfrac{3R}{4}\right)^2}{\left(-\dfrac{3R}{2}\right)^2} \times \frac{v}{\sqrt{2}}$$

$$= -\frac{v}{4\sqrt{2}} \text{ (Opposite of particle velocity)}$$

Velocity perpendicular to optic axis

$$v_i = +\frac{v}{u} \times v_0$$

$$= \frac{-3R/4}{-3R/2} \times \frac{v}{\sqrt{2}} = \frac{v}{2\sqrt{2}}$$

$$\text{Thus} \qquad \vec{v}_i = \frac{v}{4\sqrt{2}}\hat{i} - \frac{v}{2\sqrt{2}}\hat{j}.$$

19. (d) From similar triangles,

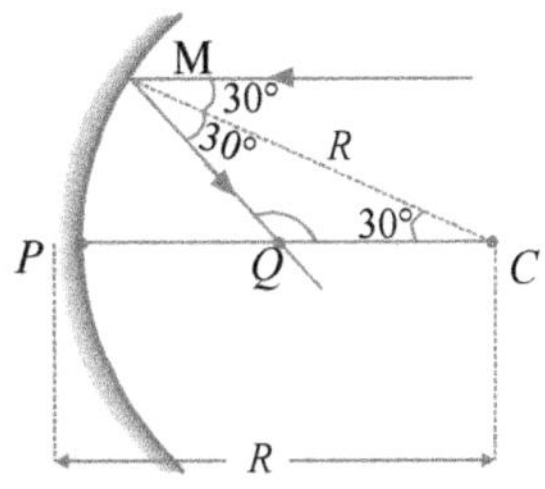

$$\frac{QC}{\sin 30°} = \frac{R}{\sin 120°}$$

$$\text{or} \qquad QC = R \times \frac{\sin 30°}{\sin 120°}$$

$$= \frac{R}{\sqrt{3}}$$

$$\text{Thus} \qquad PQ = PC - QC$$

$$= R - \frac{R}{\sqrt{3}}$$

$$= R\left(1 - \frac{1}{\sqrt{3}}\right)$$

20. (a) Given, $y^2 = 8x$

Compare with standard equation of parabola, $y^2 = 4ax$, we get

$$x = 2$$

Thus co-ordinates of focus are : (2, 0)

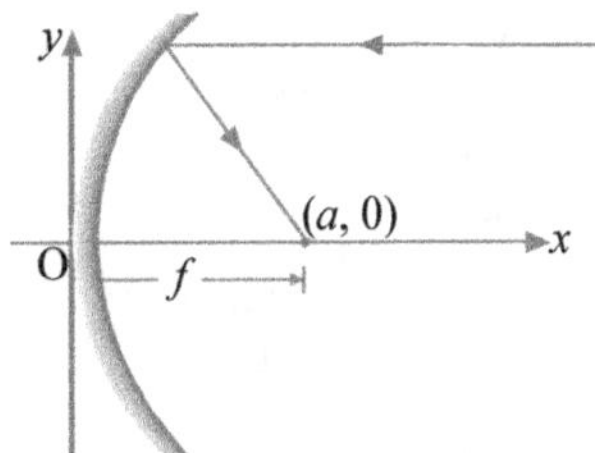

21. (b) Velocity of object w.r.t. mirror

$$\vec{v}_{0m} = \vec{v}_0 - \vec{v}_m$$

$$= (\hat{i} + 2\hat{j} - 5\hat{k}) - (-2\hat{i} + 3k + \hat{k})$$

$$= (3\hat{i} - \hat{j} - 6\hat{k}) \text{ m/s.}$$

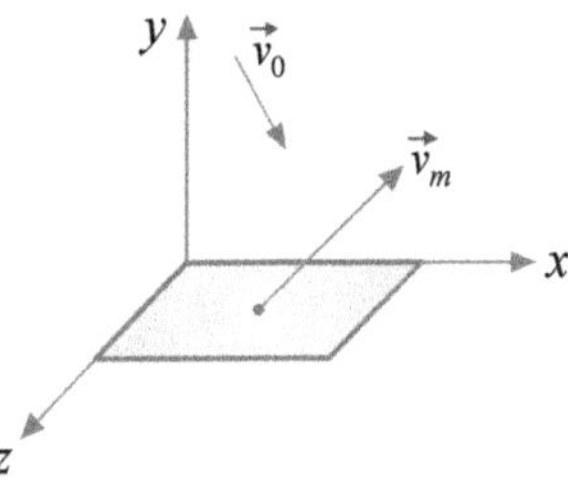

Velocity of image w.r.t. mirror (only y component of velocity of objects will reverse), and so

$$\vec{v}_{im} = (3\hat{i} + \hat{j} - 6\hat{k}) \text{ m/s}$$

Now velocity of image w.r.t. ground

$$\vec{v}_i = \vec{v}_{im} + \vec{v}_m$$

$$= (3\hat{i} + \hat{j} - 6\hat{k}) + (-2\hat{i} + 3\hat{j} + \hat{k}) \text{ m/s}$$

$$= (\hat{i} + 4\hat{j} - 5\hat{k}) \text{ m/s}$$

Solutions EXERCISE 1.2

1. (a, d) The magnification negative is for real and inverted image. The image will be on the side of the object.
2. (c, d)
3. (b, c)
4. (a, c, d)
5. (c, d)
6. (b, d) The situation is shown for two positions of the mirror.

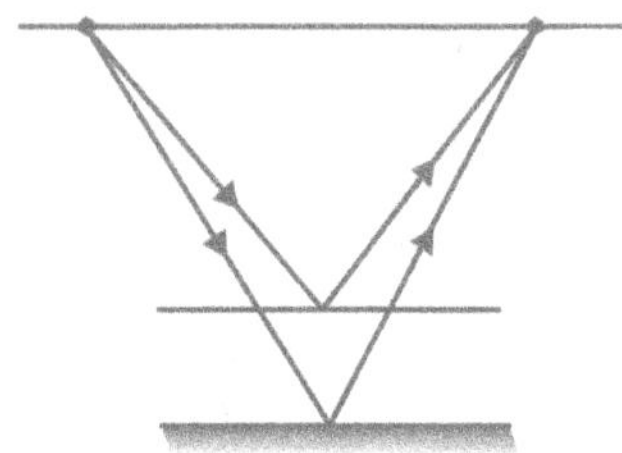

7. (b, c, d)
   The speed of the image,

   $$v_i = -v_0 \left(\frac{v^2}{u^2} \right)$$

   For $u = -20$ cm,

   $$\frac{1}{v} + \frac{1}{-20} = \frac{1}{-30}, \quad \therefore v = 60 \text{ cm}$$

   Thus $\quad v_i = -v \left(\frac{60}{-20} \right)^2 = 2v$

8. (c, d)

Solutions EXERCISE 1.3

1. (b) Plane mirror may form real image, if object is virtual.

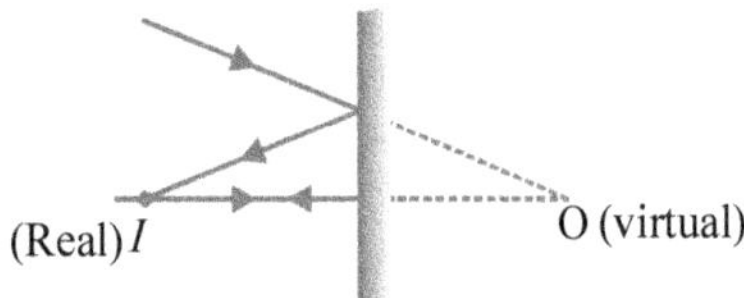

2. (d) Virtual image can be photographed. Anyone can take photograph of his image standing in front of plane mirror.
3. (d) The spacing between the reflected ray increases and so mirror must be spherical.
4. (d) Focal length of the spherical mirror does not depend on the medium in which it placed.
5. (d) There is no chromatic abberration in mirror.
6. (c) The image of real object may be real in case of concave mirror.
7. (b)
8. (d) The size of plane mirror to form full image of the object may be of any size.
9. (d) The distance of image in convex mirror is always $v \leq f$.
10. (d) In motor vehicles, the convex mirror is employed because it has largest field of view.
11. (d) Focal length of spherical mirror does not depend on colour of light used.
12. (a)

Solutions EXERCISE 1.4

Passage for (Qs. 1 & 2) :

1. (d) The image has the same orientation as that of the object and

   $$m = \frac{0.20h}{h} = 0.20 .$$

   These imformations give us an idea that the image is virtual and smaller in size and so mirror must be convex.

2. (c) Magnification, $0.20 = -\dfrac{v}{u}$

   $$\therefore \quad v = -0.20 \, u.$$

   Using mirror formula, $\dfrac{1}{v} + \dfrac{1}{u} = \dfrac{1}{f}$, we have

   $$\frac{1}{-0.20u} + \frac{1}{u} = \frac{1}{+40}$$

   After solving, we get $u = -160$ cm. **Ans.**

Passage for (Qs. 3 - 5) :

3. (d) Let us calculate the position of the image of a point centre of the right face of the cube.

   $$u = -60 \text{ cm}, R = -30 \text{ cm}$$

   $$\therefore \quad f = -15 \text{ cm}$$

   Using mirror formula

   $$\frac{1}{u} + \frac{1}{v} = \frac{1}{f}, \text{ we have}$$

   $$\frac{1}{-60} + \frac{1}{v} = \frac{1}{-15}$$

   $$\therefore \quad v = -20 \text{ cm}$$

   The image of this point is 20 cm to the left of the pole and is real.
   Ans.

4. (c) Lateral magnification,

   $$m = -\frac{v}{u}$$

   $$= -\frac{-20}{-60} = -\frac{1}{3} \quad \textbf{\textit{Ans.}}$$

5. (a) As the size of the object (3cm) is small in comparison to the object distance (60 cm), so we can get longitudinal magnification by

   $$m_L = -m^2 = -\left(\frac{1}{3}\right)^2 = -\frac{1}{9} . \textbf{\textit{Ans.}}$$

6. A-q : For $u = -f$,

$$\frac{1}{v} + \frac{1}{-f} = \frac{1}{f}$$

$$\therefore \quad v = \frac{f}{2}$$

and $\quad M = -\frac{v}{u} = -\frac{f/2}{(-f)} = 0.5$.

B-s : $u = -2f$, so $\quad v = -2f$

$$M = -\frac{v}{u} = -\left(\frac{-2f}{-2f}\right) = -1$$

C-p : In concave mirror, $u = -2f$, $v = -\infty$

$$\therefore \quad M = -\frac{v}{u} = -\infty.$$

D-t : In convex mirror $\quad u = -2f$

so $\quad \dfrac{1}{v} + \dfrac{1}{-2f} = \dfrac{1}{f} \Rightarrow v = \dfrac{2f}{3}$.

Now $\quad M = -\dfrac{v}{u} = \dfrac{1}{3}$.

7. A-(q, t) : $M = \dfrac{1}{4}$ is for erect or virtrual image and so it is possible for convex mirror.

B-(p, s): $m = -1$, negative magnification is possible in concave mirror.

C-(p, t) : $m = 2$, is possible for concave mirror when object is put between focal point and pole of the mirror.

D- (r, t) : $m = 1$ is possible for plane mirror.

Solutions EXERCISE 1.5

1. The position of the man and image of the visible portion of the wall in the mirror are shown in figure.

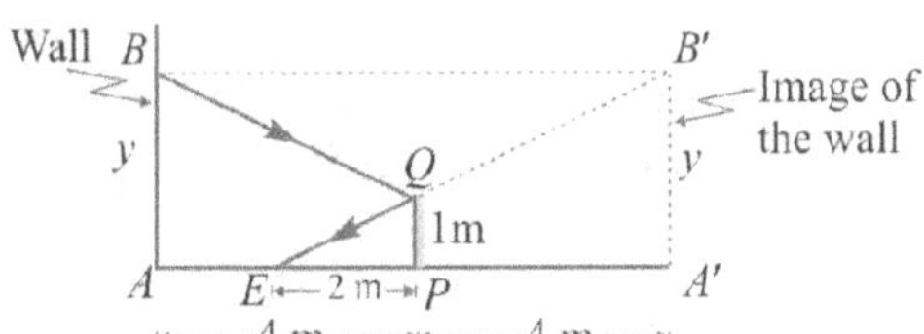

Suppose y height of the wall can be seen by the man. The distance of the image of the wall is 4 m from the mirror. E is the eye of the man. In similar triangles EPQ and EA'B', we have

$$\frac{1}{2} = \frac{y}{6}$$

$\therefore \quad y = 3$ m. ***Ans.***

2. Suppose x is the distance occupied by the ray in one reflection. Then $x = 0.2 \tan 30° = 0.2 / \sqrt{3}$ m.

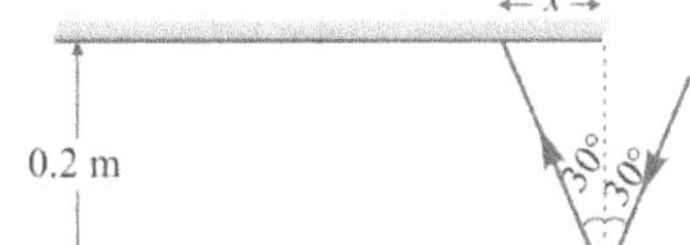

The number of reflections

$$= \frac{\text{length of mirror}}{x}$$

$$= \frac{2\sqrt{3}}{0.2/\sqrt{3}} = 30. \quad \textit{Ans.}$$

3. If u_1 and v_1 are the initial distance of the object and the image from the mirror, then

$$\frac{v_1}{u_1} = -\frac{1}{4} \qquad \text{... (i)}$$

and $\quad \dfrac{1}{v_1} + \dfrac{1}{u_1} = \dfrac{1}{f} \qquad$ ... (ii)

When object moves towards the mirror a distance b then

$$\frac{v_2}{(u_1 - b)} = -\frac{1}{2} \qquad \text{... (iii)}$$

and $\quad \dfrac{1}{v_2} + \dfrac{1}{(u_1 - b)} = \dfrac{1}{f}$. ... (iv)

On substituting the values and solving above equations, we get

$$f = 2.5 \text{ cm}. \quad \textit{Ans.}$$

Solutions EXERCISE 1.6

1. The situation is shown in figure.

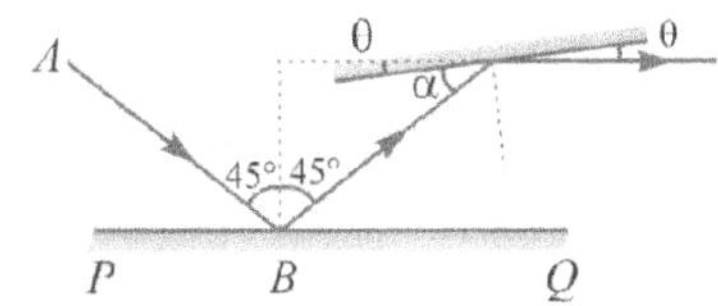

If θ is the inclination of second mirror from horizontal, then angle $\alpha = 45° - \theta$.

By law of reflection,

$$45° - \theta = \theta$$

$\therefore \quad \theta = 22.5°. \quad$ ***Ans.***

2.

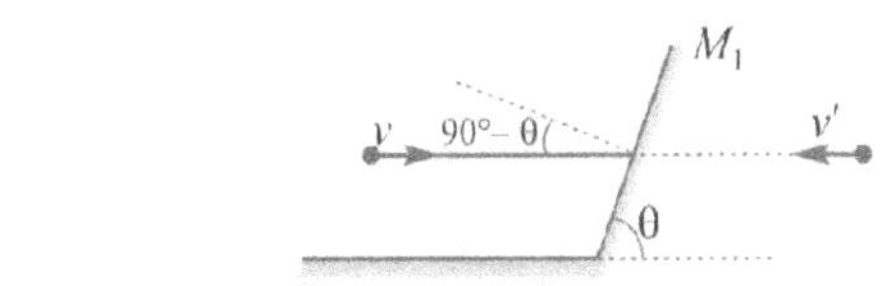

The component of velocity of the object perpendicular to the mirror M_1 is $v\sin\theta$. The velocity of its image is also $v\sin\theta$ with respect to the mirror M_1 along perpendicular. The velocity of the image in M_1 with respect to the image in M_2 (or object) will be $2v\sin\theta$.

3. The ray diagram is shown in figure. The observer can be the image of point and straight line when the eye is placed inside the triangles *DEH* limited by the rays *DG* and *EF*.

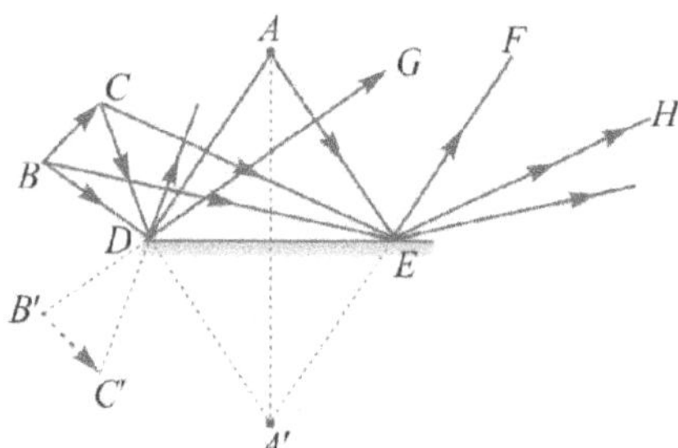

4. To get the image at the distance of object, $\ell = R$.

$$\therefore \qquad f = \frac{R}{2} = \frac{\ell}{2} = \frac{1}{2}m \,.$$

When mirror turns through an angle θ, the reflected ray and so image will shift an angle 2θ. Thus $d = 2\ell\,\theta$

5. For concave mirror; $u = -25$ cm, $f = -20$ cm

From mirror formula, $\dfrac{1}{u} + \dfrac{1}{v} = \dfrac{1}{f}$, we have

$$\frac{1}{-25} + \frac{1}{v} = \frac{1}{-20}$$

$$\therefore \qquad v = -100 \text{ cm}$$

In the absence of convex mirror, concave mirror forms the real image at a distance of 100 cm from it. This image now becomes the virtual object for the convex mirror, thus

$$u = +(100 - 50) = 50 \text{ cm}$$
$$f = +15 \text{ cm.}$$

Again by mirror formula, we have

$$\frac{1}{50} + \frac{1}{v} = \frac{1}{15}$$

$$\therefore \qquad v = 21.42 \text{ cm}$$

It shows that a virtual image is formed at a distance of 21.42 cm from convex mirror (see figure).

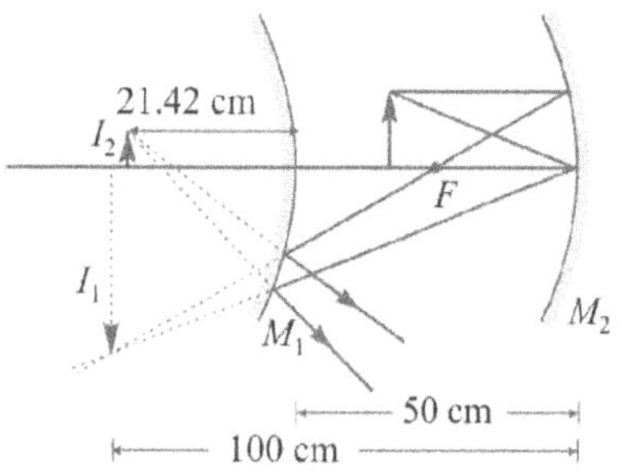

6. The angle subtended by moon at the pole of the mirror

$$\theta = \frac{D}{s}$$

$$= \frac{3450}{3.8 \times 10^5} = 9.1 \times 10^{-3} \text{ rad} \,.$$

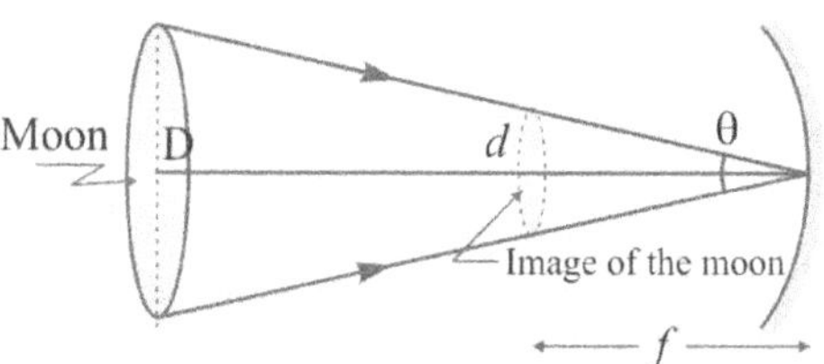

The image of the moon is formed at the focal plane of the mirror (see figure). If d is the diameter of the image of the moon, then

$$\theta = \frac{d}{f}$$

$$\therefore \qquad d = \theta f$$
$$= 9.1 \times 10^{-3} \times 7.6$$
$$= 6.9 \times 10^{-2} \text{ m.} \qquad \textbf{\textit{Ans.}}$$

7. (a) In time t ($t < d/v$) block has moved a distance $= v_0 t$. Its distance from the pole of the mirror becomes equal to $(d - v_0 t)$. Thus

$$u = -(d - v_0 t)$$

By mirror formula, $\dfrac{1}{u} + \dfrac{1}{v} = \dfrac{1}{f}$, we have

$$\frac{1}{-(d - v_0 t)} + \frac{1}{v} = \frac{1}{-R/2}$$

$$\therefore \qquad v = -\frac{R}{2}\left[\frac{(d - v_0 t)}{(d - v_0 t) - R}\right]$$

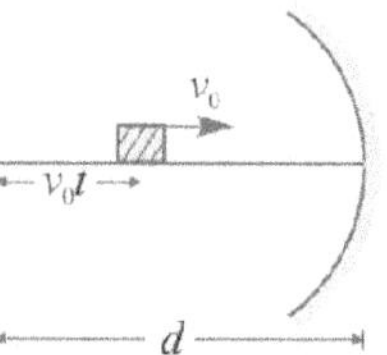

The velocity of the image (w.r.t. mirror ; here mirror is at rest) is given by

$$v_{image} = -\frac{v^2}{u^2} v_{object}$$

$$= -\frac{\left[-\dfrac{R}{2}\dfrac{(d - v_0 t)}{(d - v_0 t) - R}\right]^2}{(d - v_0 t)^2}$$

$$= -\frac{R^2 v_0}{[2(d - v_0 t) - R]^2} \,.$$

(b) For $t > \dfrac{d}{v_0}$, the block after making elastic collision with the

mirror will stop and the mirror starts moving with constant velocity v_0. The situation is shown in figure.

The distance of the block from the mirror

$$u = -(v_0 t - d)$$

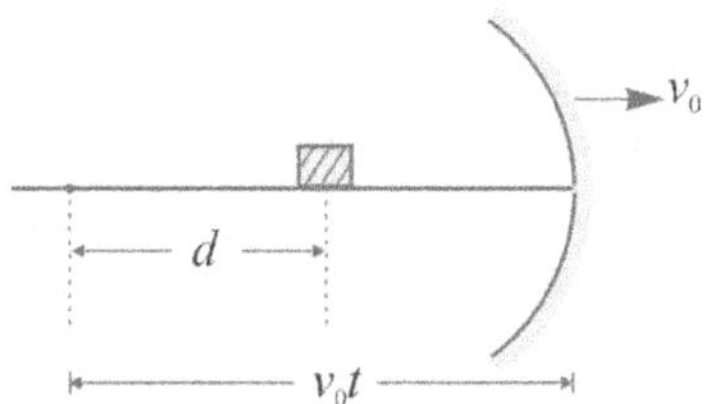

By mirror formula $\dfrac{1}{u} + \dfrac{1}{v} = \dfrac{1}{f}$, we have

$$\frac{1}{-(v_0 t - d)} + \frac{1}{v} = -\frac{2}{R}$$

$$\therefore \qquad v = \left[\frac{R(v_0 t - d)}{-2(v_0 t - d) + R} \right]$$

The velocity of the block with respect to mirror

$$v_{\text{object}} = 0 - v_0 = -v_0$$

The velocity of image of the block (w.r.t. mirror) is given by

$$\left[v_{\text{image}} \right]_{\text{mirror}} = -\frac{v^2}{u^2} v_{\text{object}}$$

$$= \frac{-\left[\dfrac{R(v_0 t - d)}{-2(v_0 t - d) + R} \right]^2}{[v_0 t - R]^2} \times (-v_0)$$

$$= \frac{R^2 v_0}{[2(v_0 t - d) - R]^2}.$$

The velocity of image of the block with respect to mirror is given by

$$\left[\vec{v}_{\text{image}} \right]_{\text{mirror}} = \left[\vec{v}_{\text{image}} \right]_{\text{ground}} - \left[\vec{v}_{\text{mirror}} \right]_{\text{ground}}$$

$$\therefore \quad \left[\vec{v}_{\text{image}} \right]_{\text{ground}} = \left[\vec{v}_{\text{image}} \right]_{\text{mirror}} + \left[\vec{v}_{\text{mirror}} \right]_{\text{ground}}$$

$$= \frac{R^2 v_0}{[2(v_0 t - d) - R]^2} + v_0$$

$$= v_0 \left[1 + \frac{R^2}{[2(v_0 t - d) - R]^2} \right]. \; \textbf{\textit{Ans.}}$$

8.   Suppose y is the compression of the spring. By conservation of mechanical energy, we have

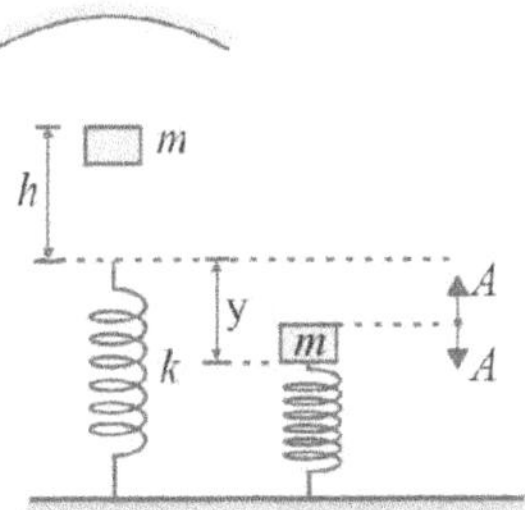

$$mg(h + y) = \frac{1}{2} k y^2$$

$$\text{or} \; \frac{1}{2} k y^2 - mgy - mgh = 0$$

$$\therefore \qquad y = \frac{mg \pm \sqrt{(mg)^2 + 4(mgh)\dfrac{k}{2}}}{2\dfrac{k}{2}}$$

$$\text{or} \qquad y = \frac{mg}{k} \pm \frac{\sqrt{(mg)^2 + 2mghk}}{k}$$

The amplitude of motion will be

$$A = \frac{\sqrt{(mg)^2 + 2mghk}}{k}$$

Given $m = 0.050$ kg, $h = 0.1$ m, $k = 500$ N/m

$$\therefore \qquad A = 1.42 \times 10^{-2} \text{ m} = 1.42 \text{ cm}$$

On being small amplitude, we can write

$$\delta u = 1.42 \text{ cm}$$

For concave mirror, $u = -30$ cm, $f = -12$ cm

By mirror formula, $\dfrac{1}{v} + \dfrac{1}{u} = \dfrac{1}{f}$, we have

$$\frac{1}{v} + \frac{1}{-30} = \frac{1}{-12}$$

$$\therefore \qquad v = -20 \text{ cm}.$$

If δv is the length of the image and object of length δu, then

$$\delta v = -\frac{v^2}{u^2} \delta u$$

$$= -\frac{(-20)^2}{(-30)^2} \times (1.42)$$

$$= 0.63 \text{ cm}.$$

Then the length in which image of the mass oscillates $= 2(\delta v) = 1.26$ cm.   **\textit{Ans.}**

9. **First image :** The first image is formed by reflection from the concave mirror M_2. Thus

$$\frac{1}{v_1} + \frac{1}{-2R} = -\frac{2}{R}$$

$$\therefore \quad v_1 = -\frac{2}{3}R$$

If I_1 is the radius of first image, then

$$\frac{I_1}{O} = -\frac{v}{u}$$

or $\quad |I_1| = \left(\frac{2R/3}{2R}\right) a = \frac{a}{3}.$

Second image : The image I_1 then becomes the object for mirror M_1. Thus

$$u_2 = -\left(2R - 2\frac{R}{3}\right) = -\frac{4R}{3}$$

$$\frac{1}{v_2} + \frac{1}{-4R/3} = +\frac{2}{R}$$

$$\therefore \quad v_2 = \frac{4R}{11}$$

It I_2 is the radius of the second image, then

$$|I_2| = \left[\frac{4R/11}{4R/3}\right] \times \frac{a}{3} = \frac{a}{11}.$$

Third image : The image I_2 acts as an object for M_1. Thus

$$u_3 = -\left(2R + \frac{4R}{11}\right) = \frac{-26R}{11}$$

$$\therefore \quad \frac{1}{v_3} + \frac{1}{\dfrac{-26R}{11}} = -\frac{2}{R}$$

$$\therefore \quad v_3 = -\frac{26R}{41}.$$

If I_3 is the radius of the third image, then

$$|I_3| = \left[\left(\frac{26R}{41}\right) \Big/ \left(\frac{26R}{11}\right)\right]\left(\frac{a}{11}\right)$$

$$= \frac{a}{41}$$

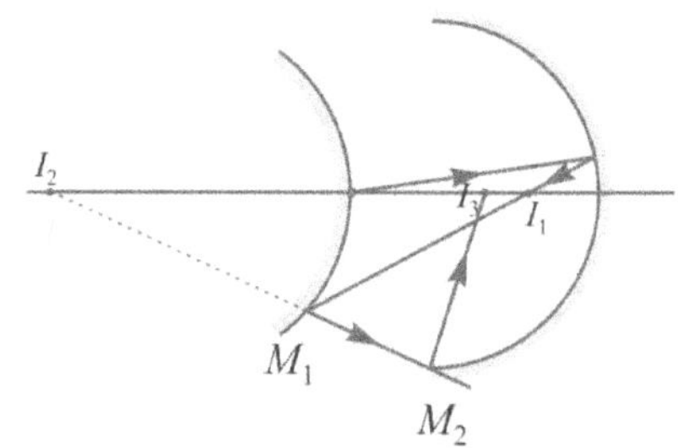

★ ★ ★

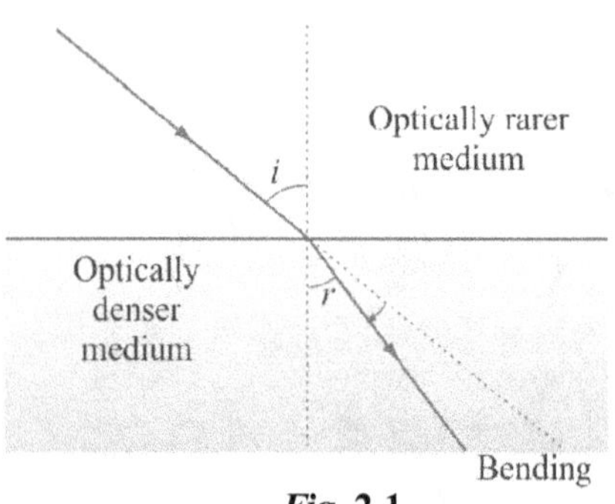

Fig. 2.1

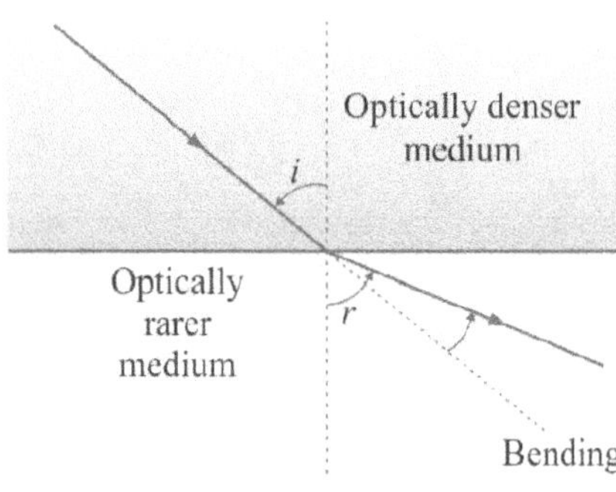

Fig. 2.2

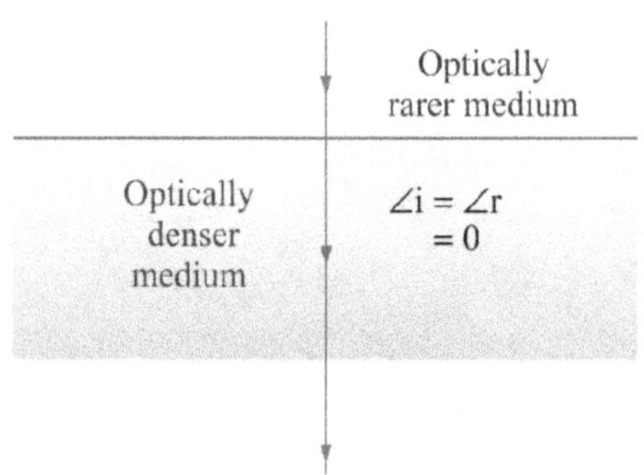

Fig. 2.3

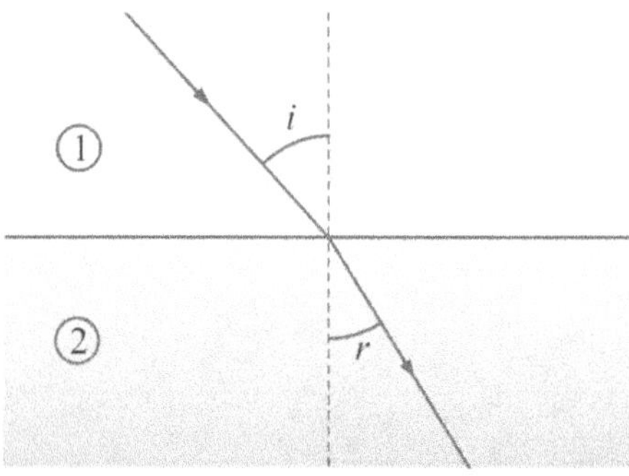

Fig. 2.4

2.1 INTRODUCTION : REFRACTION

Light will not change its path until it strikes with any obstruction or it travels into other medium. Experiments show that when light incident obliquely on the interface of different mediums, it bends from original path. The phenomenon due to which light deviates from its initial path, while travelling from one optical medium to another optical medium is called **refraction.**

The direction in which the light bends depends on :

(i)   The medium through which light is initially travelling.

(ii)   The optical density of two media which gives rise to the phenomenon of refraction.

The following are the cases of refraction of light :

(a)   If a ray of light passes from optically rarer medium (say air) to optically denser medium (say glass), then it always bends towards normal, drawn at the point of incidence. Thus in this case angle of refraction r, will be smaller than angle of incidence i.

(b)   If a ray of light passes from optically denser medium (say glass) to optically rarer medium (say air), then it bends away from the normal, drawn at the point of incidence. Thus angle of refraction r will be greater than angle of incidence i.

(c)   If a ray of light is incident normally at a surface separating two media i.e., with zero angle of incident, then it does not deviate from its original path. The angle of refraction is also zero.

Note :

1.   Optical denser medium is one in which speed of light is lesser. The medium of greater density is usually an optically denser medium.

2.   Optically denser medium is rarer medium for sound waves, because speed of sound is smaller in medium of greater density.

Laws of refraction

The laws of refraction are :

1.   The incident ray, the refracted ray and the normal at the point of incidence lie in the same plane.

2.   The ratio of sine of the angle of incidence to the sine of angle of refraction for two media is a constant. This is called **Snell's law**. It was first stated by Willibrod Snell in 1621. The constant is called refractive index and represented by a letter μ or n. Thus for light ray passing from medium 1 with angle of incidence i to the second medium 2 with angle of refraction r, this can be written as :

$$_1\mu_2 = \frac{\sin i}{\sin r} \qquad \ldots(1)$$

and

$$_2\mu_1 = \frac{\sin r}{\sin i}.$$

Here $_1\mu_2$ is called refractive index of medium 2 with respect to medium 1. If μ_1 and μ_2 are the refractive indices for the mediums 1 and 2 respectively, then we can write

$$_1\mu_2 = \frac{\mu_2}{\mu_1}. \qquad \ldots(2)$$

Thus equation (1) can be written as :

$$\mu_1 \sin i = \mu_2 \sin r.$$

Note :

The laws of reflection and refraction can tell about the directions of the corresponding rays but say nothing about the intensities of the reflected and refracted rays. These depend on the angle of incidence; for the present we simply state that the fraction is smallest for normal incidence, and it is 100% for the grazing incidence.

Defining refractive index

The speed of light is same for all colours (or wavelengths) in vacuum. However, if the light (of any colour) travels through any other optical medium, it slows down. The extend of slowing down depends on the optical density of the second medium and the colour of the light. Experiments show that :

$$_1\mu_2 = \frac{\text{speed of light in medium 1}}{\text{speed of light in medium 2}}.$$

Absolute refractive index

The refractive index of any optical medium with respect to vacuum (or air), is called absolute refractive index. Thus

$$_{\text{vacuum}}\mu_{\text{medium}} = \frac{\text{speed of light in vacuum}}{\text{speed light in medium}}$$

or

$$_{\text{vac}}\mu_{\text{med}} = {_{\text{air}}}\mu_{\text{med}} = \frac{c}{v_m} \qquad ...(3)$$

We can write

$$v_m = \frac{c}{_a\mu_m}. \qquad ...(4)$$

A note on Refractive Index

The absolute refractive index of a medium is defiend as:

$$\mu = \frac{\text{Speed of light in free space (c)}}{\text{Speed of light in medium (v)}}$$

If ϵ_0 and ϵ are the permittivity of the free space and medium and μ_0 and μ are the corresponding permeability then

$$\mu = \frac{\sqrt{\dfrac{1}{\mu_0\,\epsilon_0}}}{\sqrt{\dfrac{1}{\mu\,\epsilon}}} = \sqrt{\left(\frac{\mu}{\mu_0}\right)\left(\frac{\epsilon}{\epsilon_0}\right)} = \sqrt{\mu_r\,\epsilon_r}$$

Here ϵ_r is the relative permittivity of the medium and μ_r is the relative permeability of the medium.

Metamaterial: The refractive index of the metamaterial medium is negative. So refraction in such medium is as follows :

$$-\mu = \frac{\text{Sin } i}{\text{Sin } r}$$

or,

$$\text{Sin } r = \frac{\sin i}{(-\mu)}$$

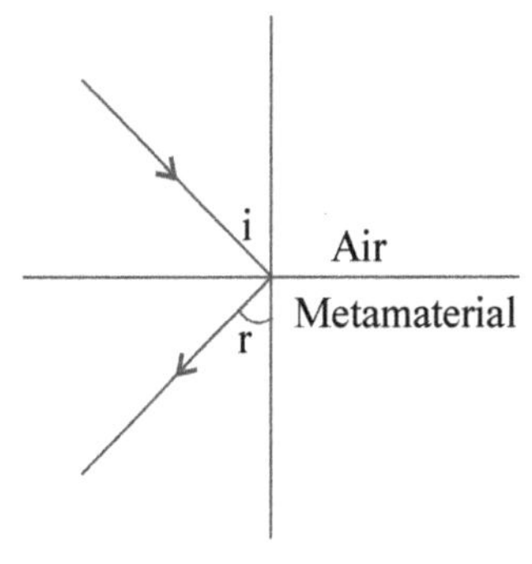

Medium	Index
Vacuum	1
Air (STP)	1.0003
Water (20°C)	1.33
Glass	1.50
Crown glass	1.52
Flint glass	1.65
Diamond	2.42

Some indexes of refraction (for yellow light)

When light moves from medium 1 to medium 2, its wavelength changes but its frequency remains the same. Wavelength of light wave decreases when it travels from a rarer medium (air) to a denser medium (glass). Thus

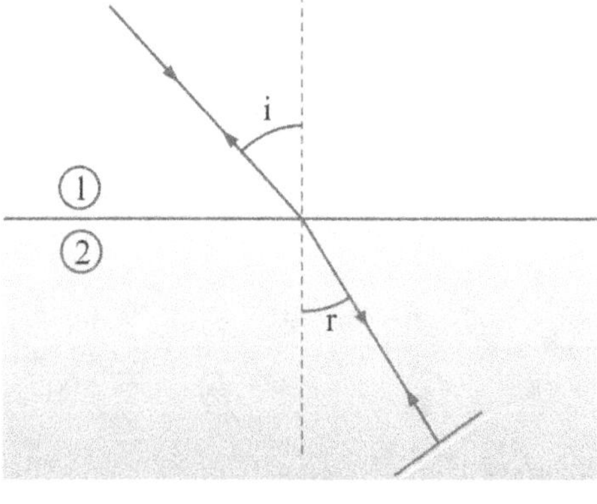

Air   Glass

Fig. 2.5

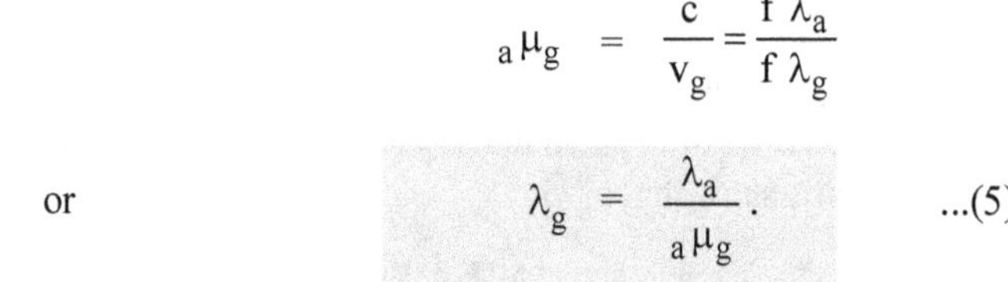

$$_a\mu_g = \frac{c}{v_g} = \frac{f\,\lambda_a}{f\,\lambda_g}$$

or
$$\lambda_g = \frac{\lambda_a}{_a\mu_g}. \qquad ...(5)$$

Principle of reversibility of path of light

If a ray of light is incident in first medium at an angle i, it will refract into second medium at an angle r. According to the principle of reversibility of light, if the ray of light in second medium is incident at an angle r, then it will refract into first medium at an angle i.

Thus for two media 1 and 2, we have

$$_1\mu_2 = \frac{\sin i}{\sin r} \qquad ...(i)$$

Also
$$_2\mu_1 = \frac{\sin r}{\sin i}. \qquad ...(ii)$$

Thus,
$$_1\mu_2 \times {_2\mu_1} = \frac{\sin i}{\sin r} \times \frac{\sin r}{\sin i} = 1,$$

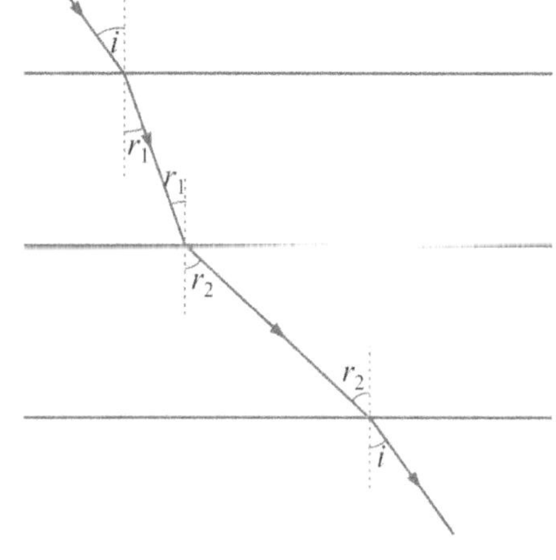

Fig. 2.6

or
$$_1\mu_2 = \frac{1}{_2\mu_1}. \qquad ...(6)$$

Refraction through many mediums

Consider a number of mediums placed parallel to one another (see figure). If first and the last medium is same, then angle of emergence will be equal to angle of incidence in the first medium. Thus we can have

$$_1\mu_2 = \frac{\sin i}{\sin r_1},$$

$$_2\mu_3 = \frac{\sin r_1}{\sin r_2}$$

$$_3\mu_1 = \frac{\sin r_2}{\sin i}$$

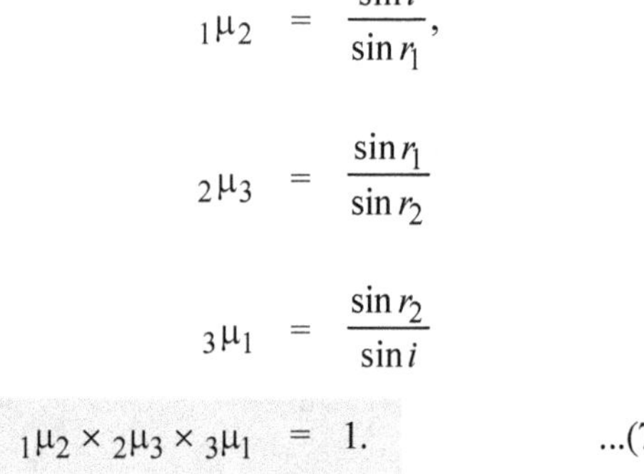

Thus
$$_1\mu_2 \times {_2\mu_3} \times {_3\mu_1} = 1. \qquad ...(7)$$

Fig. 2.7

Ex. 1 The velocity of light in glass is found 2×10^8 m/s. Find its refractive index.

Sol. By the definition

$$_a\mu_g = \frac{c}{v_g} = \frac{3\times10^8}{2\times10^8}$$

$$= 1.5. \qquad \textit{Ans.}$$

Ex. 2 Given $_a\mu_w = \dfrac{4}{3}$ and $_a\mu_g = \dfrac{3}{2}$, **find** $_w\mu_g$.

Sol. By the definition

$$_w\mu_g = \frac{_a\mu_g}{_a\mu_w}$$

$$= \frac{3/2}{4/3} = \frac{9}{8}. \qquad \textit{Ans.}$$

2.2 OPTICAL PATH

We know that the speed of light in any medium is given by $v_m = \dfrac{c}{\mu}$. Thus the distance

travelled by light in time Δt in the medium, $x_{med} = v_m t = \dfrac{c\Delta t}{\mu}$. The distance travelled

by light in air in the same time, $x_{air} = c\Delta t$. Thus we can write

$$x_{med} = \frac{x_{air}}{\mu}. \qquad ...(1)$$

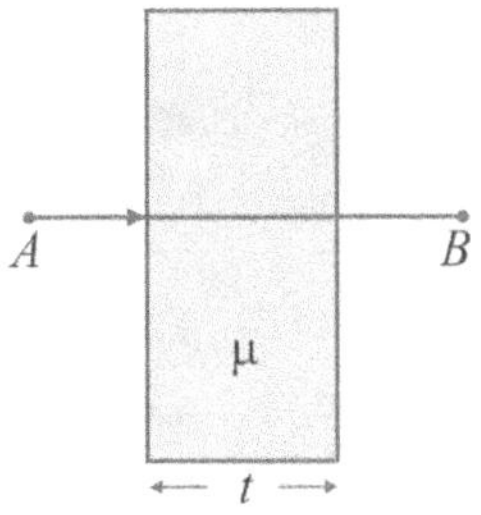

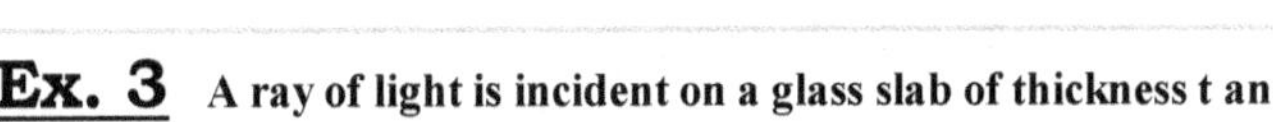

Now consider a ray of light going across the optical medium of thickness t and refractive index μ. Take its geometric path A to B. If light travels entirely into air for the same time, then optical path of AB

$$= \left(AB - t\right) \text{ in air} + t \text{ in medium}$$

$$= [\left(AB - t\right) + \mu t] \text{ in air}$$

$$= AB + (\mu - 1)t.$$

As geometric path is AB, so path length is increased by

$$\Delta = (\mu - 1)t. \qquad ...(2)$$

Fig. 2.8

Ex. 3 A ray of light is incident on a glass slab of thickness t and refractive index μ, at a small angle of incidence i. Show that lateral displacement

$$\delta = t\left(1 - \frac{1}{\mu}\right)i.$$

Sol.

Consider a ray of light incident on upper face of the slab at an angle i. After refraction in the slab, it rendered parallel to the incident ray (see figure). Let r be the angle of refraction, then in triangle ABC,

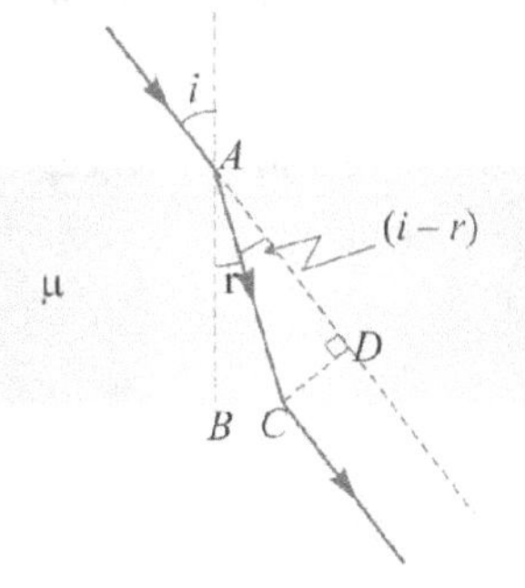

Fig. 2.9

$$AC = \frac{AB}{\cos r}.$$

Now in triangle ACD, deviation

$$\delta = CD = AC \sin (i - r)$$

$$= \frac{AB}{\cos r} \sin(i - r) \qquad ...(1)$$

For small angle of incidence i, r is also small.

$$\therefore \qquad \frac{\sin i}{\sin r} \simeq \frac{i}{r} = \mu$$

$$\text{or} \qquad r = \frac{i}{\mu}, \text{ and } \cos r = 1.$$

Also $\sin (i - r) \simeq (i - r)$ and $AB = t$.

$$\text{Thus} \qquad \delta = t\,(i - r) = t\left(i - \frac{i}{\mu}\right)$$

$$\text{or} \qquad \delta = t\left(1 - \frac{1}{\mu}\right)i.$$

2.3 IMAGE FORMATION BY REFRACTION

(a) Object in denser medium and observer in rarer medium

Consider an object O placed in an optically denser medium (say water), such that rays emerge from it in all directions. A ray of light which travels along OA, on striking the interface of separation at right angles will pass undeviated along AE. Another ray which travels along OB, making an angle i with the normal of interface gets refracted at an angle r and goes along BC. The refracted rays AE and BC on reaching eye, appear to originate from I. Thus I becomes the virtual image of O.

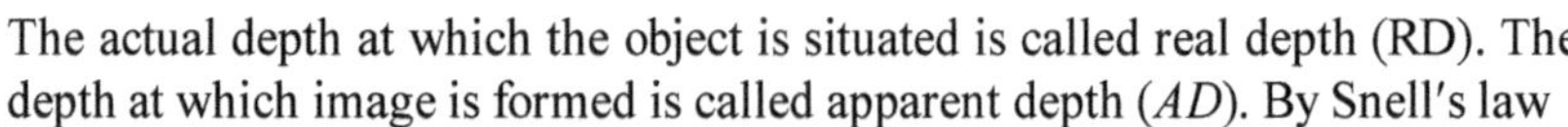

Fig. 2.10

The actual depth at which the object is situated is called real depth (RD). The depth at which image is formed is called apparent depth (AD). By Snell's law

$$_{denser}\mu_{rarer} = \frac{\sin i}{\sin r} \qquad ...(i)$$

In triangle AOB, $\sin i = \dfrac{AB}{OB}$ and in triangle AIB, $\sin r = \dfrac{AB}{IB}$. On substituting these values in equation (i), we have

$$_{denser}\mu_{rarer} = \frac{AB/OB}{AB/IB} = \frac{IB}{OB} \qquad ...(ii)$$

For small value of i, point B will be close to A and so

$$OB \simeq OA = \text{real depth and } IB \simeq IA = \text{apparent depth}$$

Thus equation (ii) becomes

$$_{denser}\mu_{rarer} = \frac{\text{apparent depth}}{\text{real depth}}$$

or

$$_{rarer}\mu_{denser} = \frac{\text{real depth (RD)}}{\text{apparent depth (AD)}} \qquad ...(1)$$

The shift in position of object

$$S = \text{Real depth} - \text{apparent depth}$$

$$= RD - \frac{RD}{\mu}$$

$$S = RD\left(1 - \frac{1}{\mu}\right). \qquad ...(2)$$

(b)   **Size of object situated in water**

(i)   **When extended object is situated perpendicular to the refracting surface :**

Consider an object of height h is in water of refractive index $_a\mu_w$. Its image is shown in figure. For the observer overhead the object

$$_a\mu_w = \frac{\text{real size of object}}{\text{apparent size of object}}$$

$$= \frac{h}{h'}$$

$$\therefore \qquad h' = \frac{h}{_a\mu_w}.$$

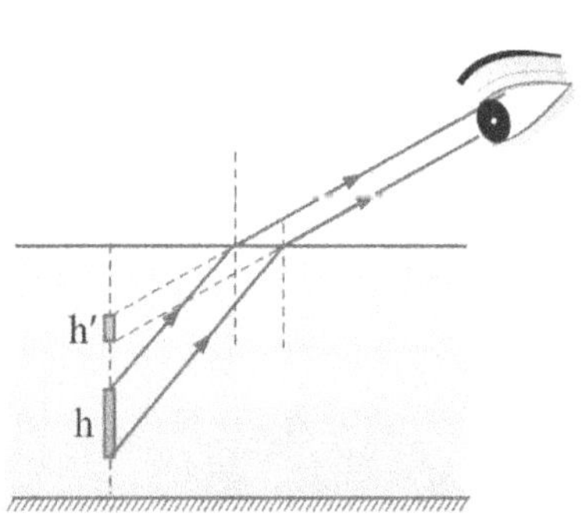

Fig. 2.11

(ii)   **When extended object is situated parallel to the refracting surface :**

Consider an object of width b is in water of refractive index $_a\mu_w$. Its image is shown in figure. Here the size of image is found equal to the size of the object. Thus width of image

$$b' = b.$$

Thus for an object of size $b \times h$ situated vertically in water, its area of image will be :

$$A_i = b'h' = b \times \frac{h}{_a\mu_w} = \frac{bh}{_a\mu_w}$$

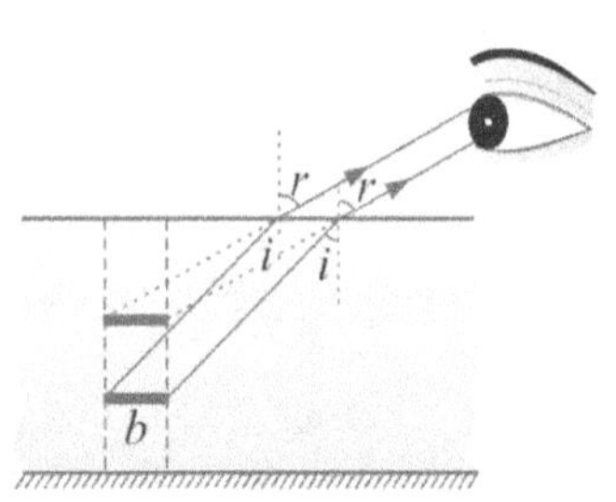

Fig. 2.12

If $bh = A_o$, area of the object, then

$$A_i = \frac{A_o}{a\mu_w}.$$

(c) Object in rarer medium (air) and observer in denser medium (water)

Consider an object O situated at a height h from the free surface of water. Take two rays OA and OB; after refraction, they form the virtual image I. If i and r are the angle of incidence and angle of refraction, then by Snell's law

$$_{rarer}\mu_{denser} = \frac{\sin i}{\sin r}$$

For small angles (observer below the line of object)

$$\frac{\sin i}{\sin r} \simeq \frac{\tan i}{\tan r} = \frac{AB/AO}{AB/AI} = \frac{AI}{AO}$$

Thus we have

$$_{rarer}\mu_{denser} = \frac{AI}{AO}$$

or

$$_{rarer}\mu_{denser} = \frac{\text{apparent height}}{\text{real height}} \quad ...(3)$$

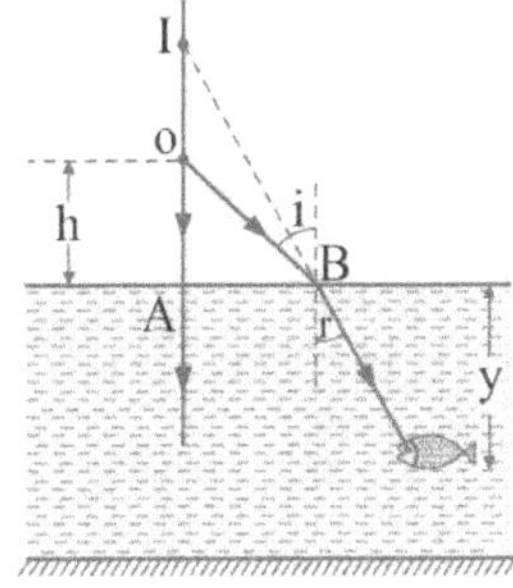

Fig. 2.13

If the observer (fish) at a depth y below the free surface of water, then apparent distance of the image from the observer,

$$x = AI + y$$
$$= \mu h + y. \quad ...(4)$$

It should be remembered that y is the distance of observer's medium, so it appears the same. In case when observer or object or both move perpendicular to the refracting surface, then velocity of the image with respect to the observer can be obtained by differentiating equation (4) with respect to the time.

Thus we have

$$\frac{dx}{dt} = \mu\frac{dh}{dt} + \frac{dy}{dt}.$$

or

$$\left[v_{image}\right]_{observer} = \mu v_{object} + v_{observer} \quad ...(5)$$

Here $\dfrac{dh}{dt}$ is taken positive when object moves up (away from the abserver). $\dfrac{dy}{dt}$ is taken positive when observer moves down.

(d) Shift produced by a slab

Consider an object O placed at a distance x from the left face of a glass slab of thickness t and refractive index μ. The left face of the slab forms the image at I', which acts as an object for the right face, the final image is formed at I (see figure).

For the left face

$$AI' = \mu(AO) = \mu x$$

For the right face of the slab

$$\frac{BI'}{BI} = \mu$$

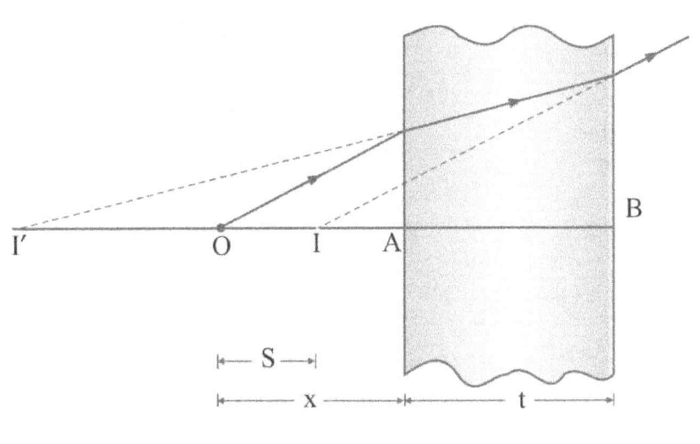

Fig. 2.14

$$\text{or} \qquad \frac{BA + AI'}{BI} = \mu$$

$$\text{or} \qquad \frac{t + \mu x}{BI} = \mu$$

$$\therefore \qquad BI = \frac{t + \mu x}{\mu}$$

$$AI = BI - AI$$

$$= \frac{t + \mu x}{\mu} - t$$

$$= \frac{t + \mu(x - t)}{\mu}$$

$$S = AO - AI$$

$$= x - \frac{t + \mu(x - t)}{\mu}$$

$$S = t\left(1 - \frac{1}{\mu}\right).$$

Ex. 4   A small air bubble is inside a glass cube of side 12 cm. When looking the top face, the bubble appears at a distance of 3 cm and when seen from the opposite face, it appears at a distance of 5 cm. Find refractive index of the glass.

Sol.

Suppose the bubble is at a distance x from the top face of the cube. We know that

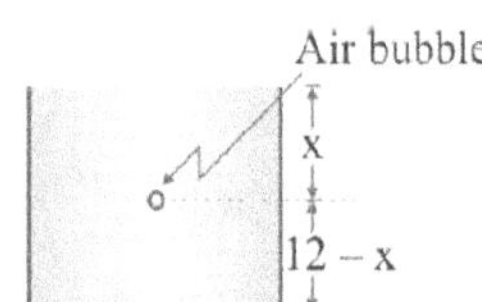

Fig. 2.15

$$\mu = \frac{\text{real depth}}{\text{apparent depth}}$$

$$\text{or} \qquad \mu = \frac{x}{3} \qquad ...(i)$$

$$\text{and} \qquad \mu = \frac{12 - x}{5} \qquad ...(ii)$$

On solving equations (i) and (ii), we get

$$x = \frac{9}{2}\text{cm}$$

$$\text{and} \qquad \mu = 1.5. \qquad \textit{Ans.}$$

Ex. 5   A fish rising vertically to the surface of water in a lake uniformly at the rate of 3 m/s observes a king-fisher diving vertically towards the fish at a rate of 9 m/s vertically above it. If the refractive index of water is 4/3, find the actual velocity of the dive of the bird.

Sol.

We know that apparent distance of the king fisher from the fish
$x = \mu h + y$

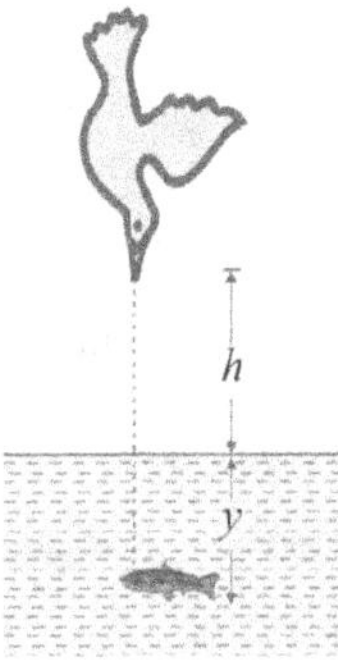

Fig. 2.16

On differentiating with respect to the time, we get

$$\left[v_{\text{image}}\right]_{\text{fish}} = \mu v_{\text{king fisher}} + v_{\text{fish}}$$

$$\text{or} \qquad -9 = \frac{4}{3} v_{\text{king fisher}} - 3$$

On solving, we get

$$v_{\text{king fisher}} = -4.5 \text{ m/s}. \qquad \textit{Ans.}$$

Apparent depth when observer is not overhead the object

Consider an object O situated at a depth h from the free surface of the water. The line of sight makes an angle θ with the normal, then I will be the virtual image of the object. Let its depth is h' from free surface of water.

From the triangle ABO, $AB = h \tan \alpha$ and from the triangle $AB'I$, $AB' = h' \tan\theta$

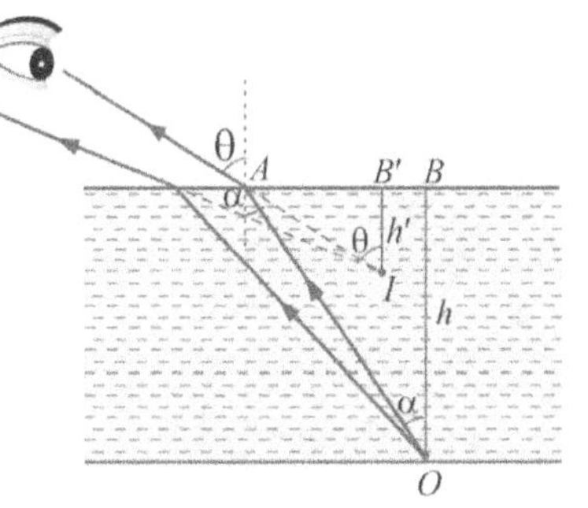

$$\therefore \quad BB' = AB - AB'$$
$$= h \tan \alpha - h' \tan\theta \qquad ...(i)$$

As BB' is parallel to the refracting surface, and so it remains constant with small variation in θ. Thus $\dfrac{d(BB')}{d\theta} = 0$.

Differentiating equation (i) with respect to θ, we have

$$\frac{d(BB')}{d\theta} = \frac{d}{d\theta}\left[h\tan\alpha - h'\tan\theta\right]$$

or
$$0 = h\sec^2\alpha\,\frac{d\alpha}{d\theta} - h'\sec^2\theta$$

$\therefore$
$$h' = h\frac{\sec^2\alpha}{\sec^2\theta}\left(\frac{d\alpha}{d\theta}\right) \qquad ...(ii)$$

By Snell's law
$$\mu = \frac{\sin\theta}{\sin\alpha}$$

or
$$\sin\alpha = \frac{\sin\theta}{\mu} \qquad ...(iii)$$

Differentiating with respect to θ, we get

$$\cos\alpha\,\frac{d\alpha}{d\theta} = \frac{\cos\theta}{\mu}$$

or
$$\frac{d\alpha}{d\theta} = \frac{1}{\mu}\left(\frac{\cos\theta}{\cos\alpha}\right) \qquad ...(iv)$$

Also from equation (iii), $\cos\alpha = \sqrt{1-\sin^2\alpha} = \sqrt{1-\dfrac{\sin^2\theta}{\mu^2}}$.

From equations (i) and (iv), we have
$$h' = \frac{h\cos^2\theta}{\cos^2\alpha}\left(\frac{1}{\mu}\frac{\cos\theta}{\cos\alpha}\right)$$

$$= \frac{h}{\mu}\frac{\cos^3\theta}{\cos^3\alpha}$$

$$= \frac{h}{\mu}\frac{\cos^3\theta}{\left(1-\sin^2\alpha\right)^{3/2}}$$

$$= \frac{h}{\mu}\frac{\cos^3\theta}{\left(1-\dfrac{\sin^2\theta}{\mu^2}\right)^{3/2}}$$

or
$$h' = \frac{h\mu^2\cos^3\theta}{\left(\mu^2-\sin^2\theta\right)^{3/2}} .$$

Fig. 2.17

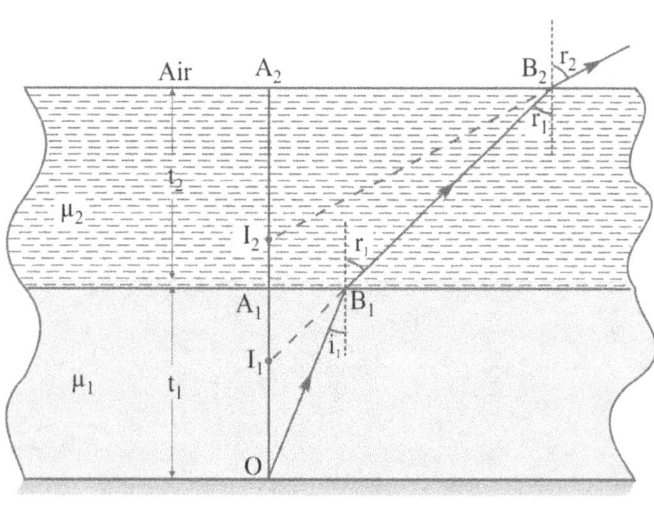

Fig. 2.18

Object is situated inside two or more optical mediums

Consider two immiscible liquids of refractive indexes μ_1 and μ_2 and of thicknesses t_1 and t_2 lie one over the other. An object O is situated as shown in *fig.* 2.18. The first liquid forms the image at I_1, which becomes object for the second liquid. Finally second liquid will form the image I_2.

For the refraction between the interface of two mediums 1 and 2, by Snell's law

$$\frac{\mu_2}{\mu_1} = \frac{\sin i}{\sin r_1}$$

For small angle of incidence i, (overhead observer), we can write

$$\frac{\mu_2}{\mu_1} = \frac{\sin i}{\sin r_1} \simeq \frac{\tan i}{\tan r_1}$$

$$= \frac{A_1 B_1 / A_1 O}{A_1 B_1 / A_1 I_1} = \frac{A_1 I_1}{A_1 O}.$$

or $\qquad A_1 I_1 = \dfrac{\mu_2}{\mu_1} A_1 O = \dfrac{\mu_2}{\mu_1} t_1.$ $\qquad$ ...(i)

Now refraction from medium 2 to air :

$$_2\mu_{air} = \frac{\mu_{air}}{\mu_2} = \frac{\sin r_1}{\sin r_2}$$

or $\qquad \dfrac{1}{\mu_2} \simeq \dfrac{\tan r_1}{\tan r_2}$ $\qquad$ (As $\mu_{air} = 1$)

$$= \frac{A_2 I_2}{A_2 I_1}$$

or $\qquad A_2 I_2 = \dfrac{A_2 I_1}{\mu_2}$

or $\qquad A_2 I_2 = \dfrac{A_2 A_1 + A_1 I_1}{\mu_2}$ $\qquad$ ...(iii)

From equations (i) and (ii), we have

$$A_2 I_2 = \frac{\left(t_2 + \dfrac{\mu_2}{\mu_1} t_1 \right)}{\mu_2}$$

$$= \frac{t_1}{\mu_1} + \frac{t_2}{\mu_2}$$

Thus apparent depth $\qquad = \dfrac{t_1}{\mu_1} + \dfrac{t_2}{\mu_2},$

and total shift $\qquad S = t_1\left(1 - \dfrac{1}{\mu_1} \right) + t_2\left(1 - \dfrac{1}{\mu_2} \right).$

For n-mediums of thicknesses; $t_1, t_2, ..., t_n$ of refractive indexes; $\mu_1, \mu_2, ..., \mu_n$,

the real depth $= t_1 + t_2 + ..., t_n$. Apparent depth $= \dfrac{t_1}{\mu_1} + \dfrac{t_2}{\mu_2} + ... + \dfrac{t_n}{\mu_n}$.

If μ is the effective value of refractive indexes, then

$$\mu = \frac{\text{real depth}}{\text{apparent depth}}$$

$$= \frac{t_1 + t_2 + ... + t_n}{\left(\dfrac{t_1}{\mu_1} + \dfrac{t_2}{\mu_2} + ... + \dfrac{t_n}{\mu_n}\right)}.$$

Ex. 6   A plane mirror of thickness 3 cm of material of refractive index $\dfrac{3}{2}$ is silvered on the back surface. A point object is placed at a distance of 9 cm from the unsilvered face of the mirror. Find the position of the brightest image.

Sol.

Because of multiple reflections and refractions, there will form infinite images; second of them will be brightest, which is formed by the reflection from the silvered face. Suppose M' is the apparent position of the mirror at a distance x from the unsilvered face of the mirror. Then

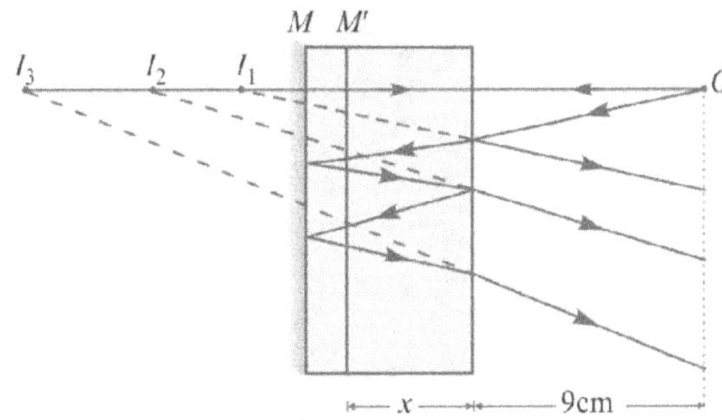

Fig. **2.19**

$$x = \frac{\text{real depth}}{\mu}$$

$$= \frac{3}{3/2} = 2 \text{ cm}$$

The position of the object from $M' = 9 + 2 = 11$ cm.
By the definition, the position of the image
$$= 11 \text{ cm from } M'$$
The position of the image from unsilvered face
$$= 11 + 2 = 13 \text{ cm} \qquad \textit{Ans.}$$

Ex. 7   An object is placed 21 cm in front of a concave mirror of radius of curvature 20 cm. A glass slab of thickness 3 cm and refractive index 1.5 is placed close to the mirror in the space between object and the mirror. Find the position of the final image formed. The distance of the nearer surface of the slab from the mirror is 10 cm.

Sol.

The shift produced by slab towards mirror

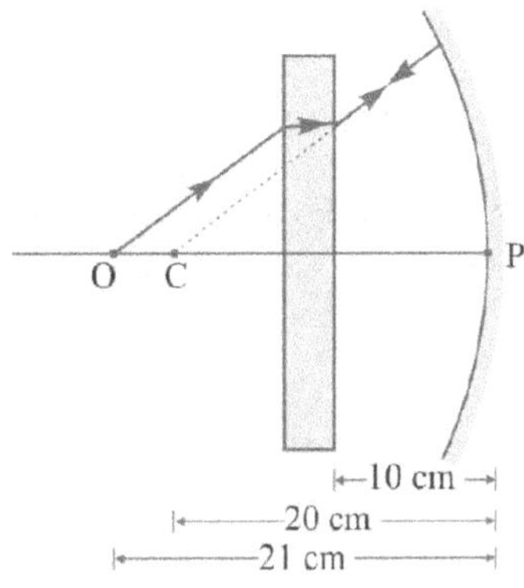

Fig. **2.20**

$$S = t\left(1 - \frac{1}{\mu}\right)$$

$$= 3\left(1 - \frac{1}{1.5}\right)$$

$$= 1 \text{ cm.}$$

The apparent position of the object from the mirror
$$= 21 - 1 = 20 \text{ cm.}$$

By mirror formula, $\dfrac{1}{u} + \dfrac{1}{v} = \dfrac{1}{f}$, we have

$$\frac{1}{-20} + \frac{1}{v} = \frac{1}{-20}$$

or $\qquad v = -20$ cm

Thus mirror will form real image at a distance of 20 cm in the absence of the slab. The slab now obtructed the reflected rays, which after refraction displaces the image by 1 cm. So the final position of the image = 20 + 1 = 21 cm from the mirror. i.e., image and object will coincide.

Ex. 8 A concave mirror of radius R is kept on a horizontal table. Water is poured in upto a height h. Where should an object be placed so that its image is formed on itself ?

Sol.

Suppose the object is placed at O, at a height y from the surface of the water. For the observer at the position of the mirror inside water, the apparent distance of the object becomes

$$= \mu y + h.$$

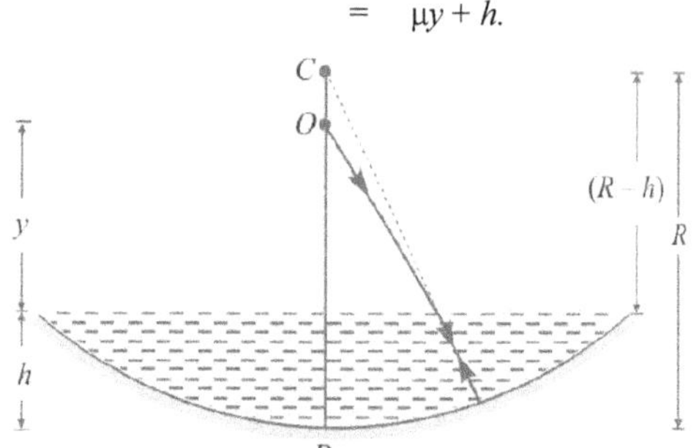

Fig. 2.21

The image will form on the object itself when mirror forms virtual image at C. i.e., at a distance R from P. Thus

$$\mu y + h = R$$

or $$y = \frac{R-h}{\mu}.$$ **Ans.**

Ex. 9 A concave mirror is placed inside water with its shinny surface upwards and principal axis vertical as shown. Rays are incident parallel to the principal axis of the concave mirror. Find position of the image.

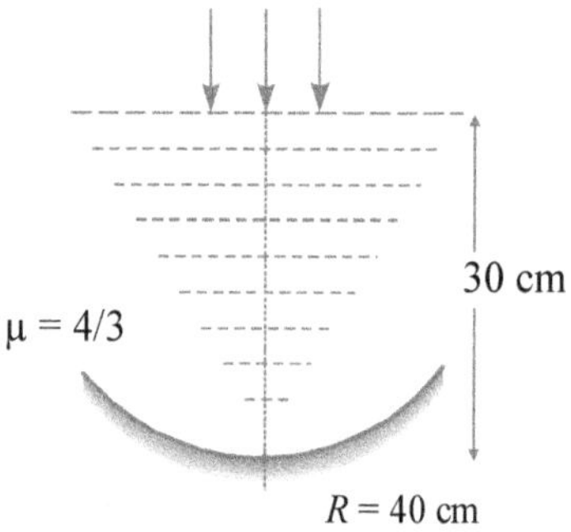

Fig. 2.22

Sol. Focal length of the mirror, $f = \dfrac{40}{2} = 20$ cm.

Thus the image of the far object will form at the focal point of the mirror. This image is at a distance of 10 cm from the free surface of the water, which finally appears at a distance $\dfrac{10}{\mu} = \dfrac{10}{4/3} = 7.5$ cm from the free surface of water.

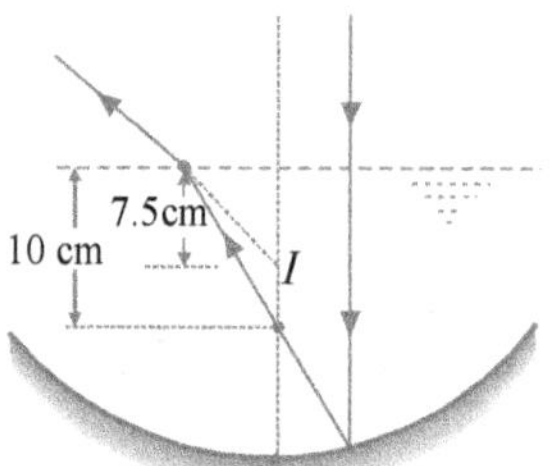

Fig. 2.23

Ex. 10 A cylindrical vessel, whose diameter and height both are equal to 30 cm, is placed on a horizontal surface and a small particle P is placed in it at a distance of 5.0 cm from the centre. An eye is placed at a position such that the edge of the bottom is just visible. The particle P is in the plane of the drawing. Upto what minimum height should water be poured in the vessel to make the particle P visible ?

Sol.

In emply vessel, the line of sight makes an angle

$$\tan r = \frac{30}{30} = 1$$

$$\therefore \qquad r = 45°.$$

Let h is the required height of the water in the vessel. The rays after refraction from the particle P must reach at the eye again.

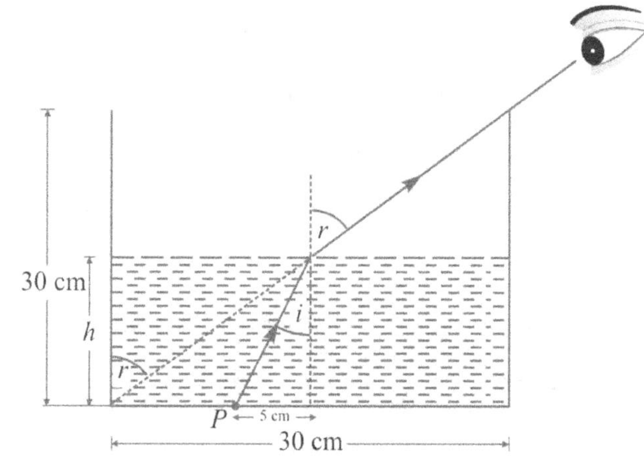

Fig. 2.24

By Snell's law

$$\frac{\sin 45°}{\sin i} = {}_a\mu_w$$

$$= \frac{4}{3}$$

$$\sin i = \frac{3}{4\sqrt{2}} \qquad ...(i)$$

From geometry $$\sin i = \frac{h-10}{\sqrt{h^2 + (h-10)^2}} \qquad ...(ii)$$

From equations (i), (ii)

$$\frac{(h-10)}{\sqrt{h^2 + (h-10)^2}} = \frac{3}{4\sqrt{2}}$$

After solving $$h = 26.7 \text{ cm} \qquad \textit{Ans.}$$

Ex. 11 Consider the situation shown in *fig.* 2.25. The bottom of the pot is a reflecting plane mirror, S is a small fish and T is a human eye. Refractive index of water is μ.

(a) At what distance(s) from itself will the fish see the images of the eye ?

(b) At what distance(s) from itself will the eye see the image(s) of the fish?

Sol.

(a) For fish to be an observer, the apparent distance of eye from water surface = μh. The apparent distance of eye from the fish = $\left(\mu h + \dfrac{h}{2}\right)$ above itself. The other image will be seen through the mirror.

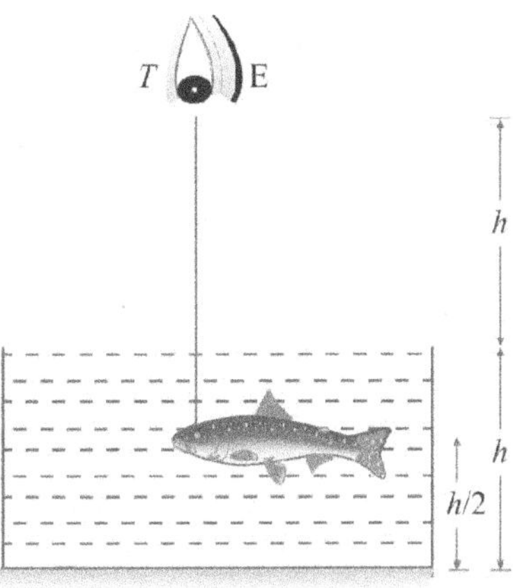

Fig. 2.25

The apparent position of eye from the mirror = $\mu h + h$.
Thus the image of the eye will be $(\mu h + h)$ from the mirror.
The distance of the second image of the eye

$$= (\mu h + h) + \frac{h}{2}$$

$$= \left(\mu h + \frac{3h}{2}\right) \text{ below itself.}$$

(b) For T as the observer, the apparent distance of the fish from the water surface

$$= \frac{h/2}{\mu} = \frac{h}{2\mu}$$

The apparent distance of fish from eye T

$$= \left(\frac{h}{2\mu} + h\right).$$

The other image of fish is formed by mirror, the distance of fish from mirror (both have same medium) is $\dfrac{h}{2}$. Its image is also at $\dfrac{h}{2}$ from the mirror. The distance of fish from the surface of water

$$= h + \frac{h}{2} = \frac{3h}{2}.$$

Its apparent distance from the surface of water

$$= \frac{3h}{2\mu}.$$

Thus the apparent distance of image of fish from the eye T

$$= \left(\frac{3h}{2\mu} + h\right). \qquad \textbf{\textit{Ans.}}$$

Ex. 12 In a river 2 m deep, a water level measuring post embedded into the river stands vertically with 1 m of it above the water surface. If the angle of inclination of the sun above the horizon is 30°, calculate the length of the post on the bottom of the river (μ of water = 4/3).

Sol.

The ray starting from S will cast the shadow at the bottom of the river, which is equal to BE. From the geometry

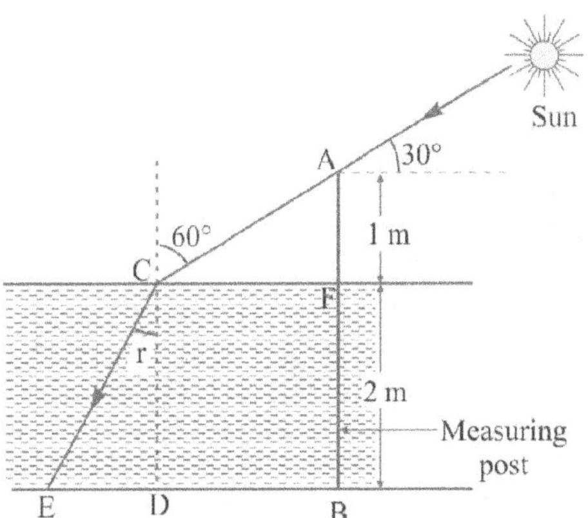

Fig. 2.26

$$BE = BD + DE$$
$$= CF + DE \,...(i)$$

In triangle ACF,
$$CF = AF \tan 60°$$
$$= 1 \times \sqrt{3} = \sqrt{3}\ m$$

By Snell's law
$$\frac{\sin 60°}{\sin r} = {}_a\mu_w$$

$$= \frac{4}{3}$$

$$\therefore \quad \sin r = \frac{3}{4}\sin i$$

$$= \frac{3}{4} \times \sin 60°$$

$$= \frac{3}{4} \times \frac{\sqrt{3}}{2} = \frac{3\sqrt{3}}{8}$$

$$\cos r = \sqrt{1 - \sin^2 r} = \sqrt{1 - \left(\frac{3\sqrt{3}}{8}\right)^2}$$

$$= \frac{\sqrt{37}}{8}$$

$$\therefore \quad \tan r = \frac{\sin r}{\cos r} = \frac{3\sqrt{3}/8}{\sqrt{37}/8} = \frac{3\sqrt{3}}{\sqrt{37}}$$

Now in triangle CDE,
$$DE = CD \tan r$$

$$= 2 \times \frac{3\sqrt{3}}{\sqrt{37}} = \frac{6\sqrt{3}}{\sqrt{37}}$$

Substituting these values in equation (i), we get

$$= \sqrt{3} + \frac{6\sqrt{3}}{\sqrt{37}}$$

$$= 3.44\ m \qquad \textbf{\textit{Ans.}}$$

Ex. 13 A concave mirror of radius 40 cm lies on a horizontal table and water is filled in it upto a height of 5.0 cm as shown in *fig.* 2.27. A small dust particle floats on the water surface at a point P vertically above the point of contact of the mirror with the table. Locate the image of the dust particle as seen from a point directly above it. The refractive index of water is 1.33.

Sol.

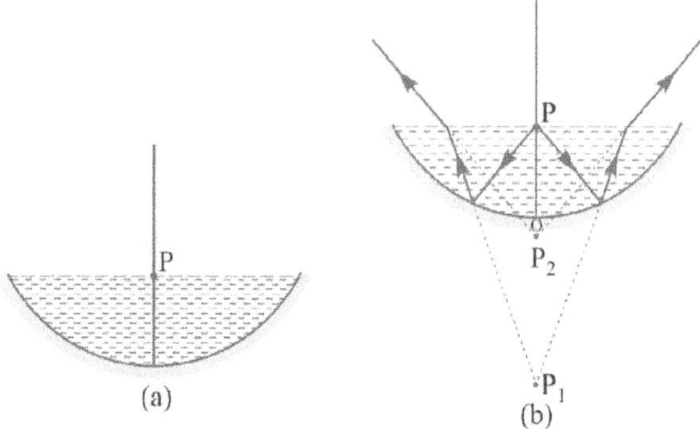

Fig. 2.27

First image P_1, is formed by the mirror, which acts as an object for water-air interface. Final image will form at P_2. For concave mirror

$$f = -20 \text{ cm}, u = -5 \text{ cm (measured from O)}$$

By mirror formula, $\dfrac{1}{u} + \dfrac{1}{v} = \dfrac{1}{f}$, we have

$$\frac{1}{-5} + \frac{1}{v} = \frac{1}{-20}$$

$$\therefore \qquad v = \frac{+20}{3} = +6.67 \, cm$$

As v is positive, so the image formed will be below the mirror. The distance of point P_1 from free surface of water

$$= 6.67 + 5.0 = 11.67 \text{ cm}.$$

Now using

$$_a\mu_w = \frac{\text{real depth}}{\text{apparent depth } (PP_2)}$$

or

$$1.33 = \frac{11.67}{\text{apparent depth } (PP_2)}$$

$$\therefore \quad \text{apparent depth } (PP_2) = \frac{11.67}{1.33}$$

$$= 8.77 \text{ cm} \qquad \textit{Ans.}$$

Ex. 14 A ray of light travelling in air is incident at grazing angle (incident angle = 90°) on a large rectangular slab of a transparent medium of thickness t = 1.0 m (see *fig.* 2.28). The point of incident is the origin A (0, 0).

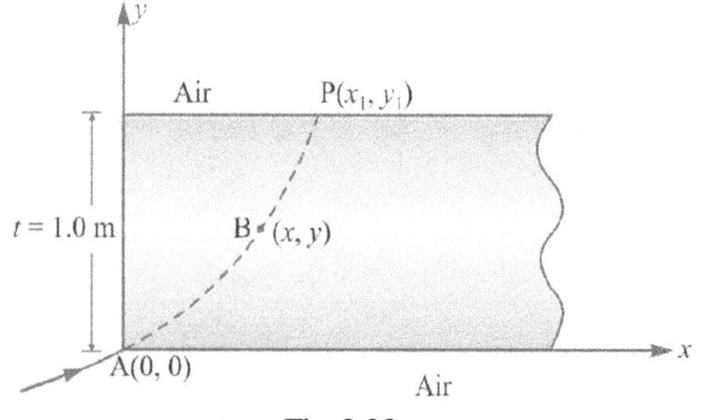

Fig. 2.28

The medium has a variable index of refraction μ(y) given by

$$\mu(y) = \left(ky^{3/2} + 1\right)^{1/2}$$

where $k = 1.0 \text{ m}^{-3/2}$.
The refractive index of air is 1.0.

(a) Obtain a relation between the slope of the trajectory of the ray at point B(x, y) in the medium and the incident angle at that point.

(b) Obtain an equation for the trajectory y(x) of the ray in the medium.

(c) Determine the coordinates (x_1, y_1) of the point P, where the ray intersects the upper surface of the slab-air boundary.

(d) Indicate the path of the ray subsequently.

Sol.

Suppose θ is the angle of incident at any point (x, y) in the medium. The slope of the trajectory,

$$\frac{dy}{dx} = \tan\left(90° - \theta\right)$$

$$= \cot\theta$$

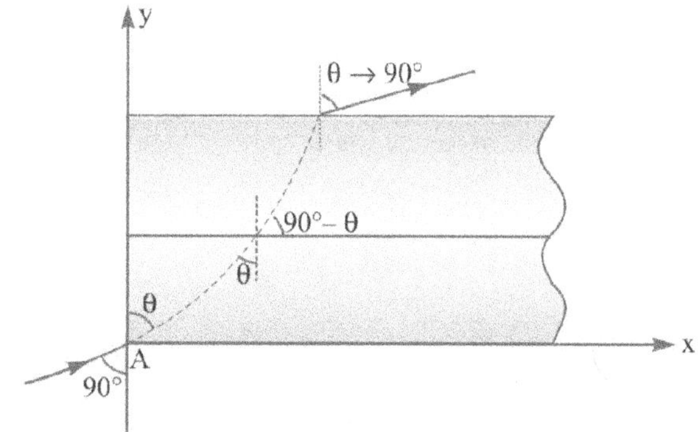

Fig. 2.29

(a) By Snell's law

$$\mu \sin\theta = 1 \sin 90° \qquad ...(i)$$

$$\therefore \qquad \sin\theta = \frac{1}{\mu}$$

and

$$\cos\theta = \sqrt{1 - \sin^2\theta}$$

$$= \sqrt{1 - \frac{1}{\mu^2}} = \frac{\sqrt{\mu^2 - 1}}{\mu}$$

Slope

$$\cot\theta = \frac{\cos\theta}{\sin\theta}$$

$$= \frac{\dfrac{\sqrt{\mu^2 - 1}}{\mu}}{\dfrac{1}{\mu}}$$

$$= \sqrt{\mu^2 - 1} \, . \textit{Ans.}$$

(b) From equation (i),

$$\mu \sin\theta = 1$$

or

$$\mu^2 \sin^2\theta = 1$$

or

$$\mu^2 = \frac{1}{\sin^2\theta} = \csc^2\theta$$

$$= 1 + \cot^2\theta$$

$$\therefore \quad \left(ky^{3/2} + 1\right) = 1 + \left(\frac{dy}{dx}\right)^2$$

or $$ky^{3/2} = \left(\frac{dy}{dx}\right)^2$$

or $$\frac{dy}{dx} = k^{1/2} y^{3/4}$$

or $$\frac{dy}{y^{3/4}} = k^{1/2} dx$$

On integrating, we get

$$4y^{1/4} = k^{1/2} x + c$$

At $x = 0$, $y = 0$ and so $c = 0$,

$$\therefore \quad k^{1/2} x = 4y^{1/4}$$

(c) At $y = 1$, $$x = \frac{4(1)^{1/4}}{1^{1/2}} = 4.$$

Thus coordinates of the upper surface, where ray intersect are (4, 1) *Ans.*

(d) At upper interface

$$\mu \sin e = 1$$

or $$\sin e = \frac{1}{\mu} = \frac{1}{1} = 1$$

$$\therefore \quad e = 90°$$

Thus the path of the emerging ray will be grazing one.

Ans.

Ex. 15 Due to a vertical temperature gradient in the atmosphere, the refractive index varies; $\mu = \mu_0 (1 + ay)^{1/2}$, where μ_0 is the refractive index at the surface and $a = 2.0 \times 10^{-6}$/m. A person of height 2.0 m stands on a level surface. Beyond what distance will he not see the runway?

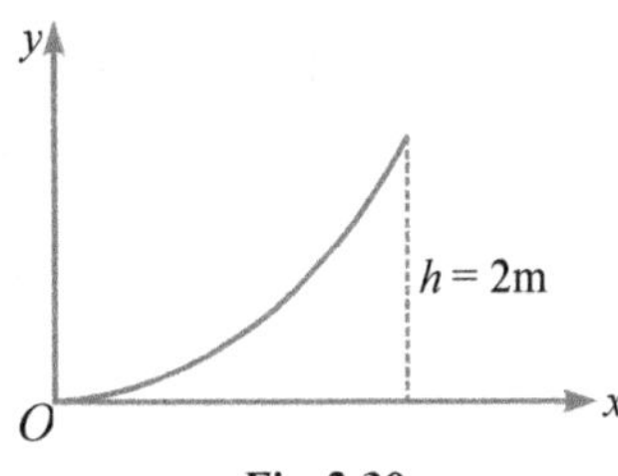

Fig. 2.30

Sol. If x is the required distance, then situation is shown in figure. If θ is the angle of refraction for the horizontal rays, then

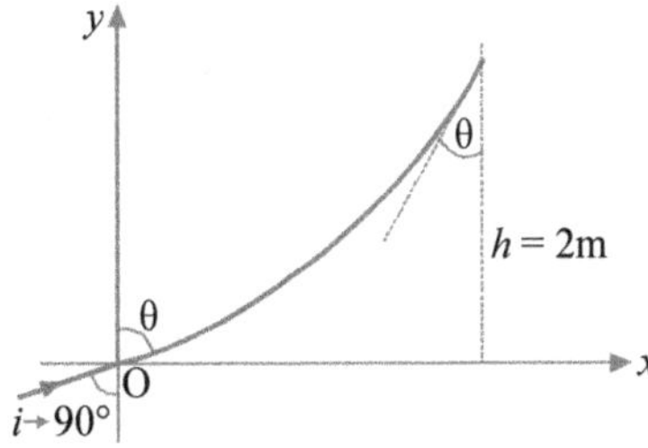

Fig. 2.31

$$\frac{\mu}{\mu_0} = \frac{\sin 90°}{\sin\theta}$$

or $$(1 + ay)^{1/2} = \frac{1}{\sin\theta}$$

or $$\sin\theta = \frac{1}{(1+ay)^{1/2}}$$

$$\therefore \quad \tan\theta = \frac{1}{(ay)^{1/2}}$$

or $$\frac{dx}{dy} = \frac{1}{(ay)^{1/2}}$$

or $$\int_0^x dx = a^{-1/2} \int_0^2 y^{-1/2} dy$$

$$\therefore \quad x = 2a^{-1/2} y^{1/2}$$

$$= 2 \times (2 \times 10^{-6})^{1/2} \times 2^{1/2} = 2000 \text{ m}$$

Ex. 16 The *xy*-plane is the boundary between two transparent media. Medium –1 with $z \geq 0$ has a refractive index $\sqrt{2}$ and medium 2 with $z \leq 0$ has a refractive index $\sqrt{3}$. A ray of light in medium –1 given by the vector $\vec{A} = 6\sqrt{3}\,\hat{i} + 8\sqrt{3}\,\hat{j} - 10\hat{k}$ is incident on the plane of separation. Find the unit vector in the direction of the refractive ray in medium –2.

Sol.

The vector of incident ray is given by

$$\vec{AB} = 6\sqrt{3}\,\hat{i} + 8\sqrt{3}\,\hat{j} - 10\hat{k}$$

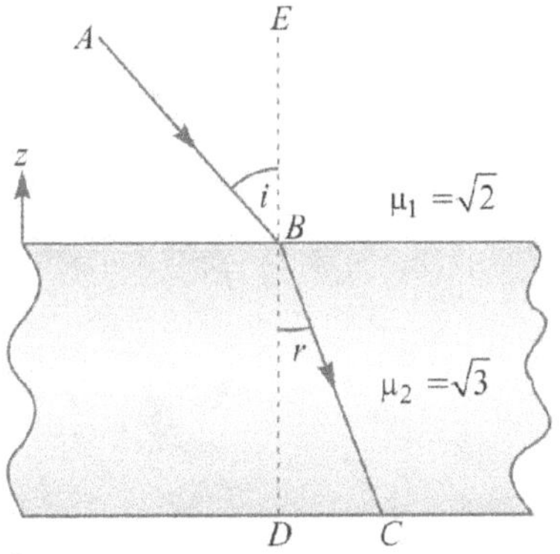

Fig. 2.32

In triangle *ABE*,

$$\vec{AB} = \vec{EB} + \vec{AE}$$

$$\therefore \quad \vec{AE} = 6\sqrt{3}\,\hat{i} + 8\sqrt{3}\,\hat{j} \text{ and } \vec{EB} = -10\hat{k}.$$

The angle of incidence i between AB and EB can be obtained as:

$$\cos i = \frac{\overrightarrow{AB}\cdot\overrightarrow{EB}}{(AB)(EB)}$$

$$= \frac{\left(6\sqrt{3}\,\hat{i}+8\sqrt{3}\,\hat{j}-10\hat{k}\right)\cdot\left(-10\hat{k}\right)}{\sqrt{\left(6\sqrt{3}\right)^2+\left(8\sqrt{3}\right)^2+(-10)^2}\ \sqrt{(-10)^2}}$$

$$= \frac{100}{\left(\sqrt{36\times3+64\times3+100}\right)(10)} = \frac{1}{2}$$

and $\qquad \sin i = \sqrt{1-\cos^2 i} = \sqrt{1-\left(\frac{1}{2}\right)^2} = \frac{\sqrt{3}}{2}.$

By Snell's law $\qquad \mu_1 \sin i = \mu_2 \sin r$

or $\qquad \sqrt{2}\times\frac{\sqrt{3}}{2} = \sqrt{3}\sin r$

$\therefore \qquad \sin r = \frac{1}{\sqrt{2}}$

Also $\qquad \cos r = \frac{1}{\sqrt{2}}$

The vector of refracted ray can be written as

$$\overrightarrow{BC} = \overrightarrow{BD}+\overrightarrow{DC}$$

$$= BC\cos r\left(-\hat{k}\right)+BC\sin r\,\hat{e}$$

Unit vector along $\overrightarrow{DC}$, $\quad \hat{e} = \dfrac{6\sqrt{3}\,\hat{i}+8\sqrt{3}\,\hat{j}}{\sqrt{\left(6\sqrt{3}\right)^2+\left(8\sqrt{3}\right)^2}}$

$$= \frac{6\hat{i}+8\hat{j}}{10}$$

Thus $\qquad \dfrac{\overrightarrow{BC}}{BC} = -\cos r\,\hat{k}+\sin r\,\hat{e}$

$$= -\frac{\hat{k}}{\sqrt{2}}+\frac{1}{\sqrt{2}}\frac{6\hat{i}+8\hat{j}}{10}$$

$$= \frac{1}{10\sqrt{2}}\left(6\hat{i}+8\hat{j}-10\hat{k}\right)\ \textit{Ans.}$$

Ex. 17 Derive Snell's law from Fermat's principle.

Sol.

According to Fermate principle, the path taken by a ray of light in passing from one point to the other is the path of minimum time. Consider a ray of light going from medium of refractive index μ_1 to the medium of refractive index μ_2 (see figure). If c is the speed of light in vacuum, then speed of light in first and second medium will be $v_1 = \dfrac{c}{\mu_1}$ and $v_2 = \dfrac{c}{\mu_2}$ respectively. Suppose ray incident at O, at a distance x from C. The point of incident must be between C and D and so CD is constant.

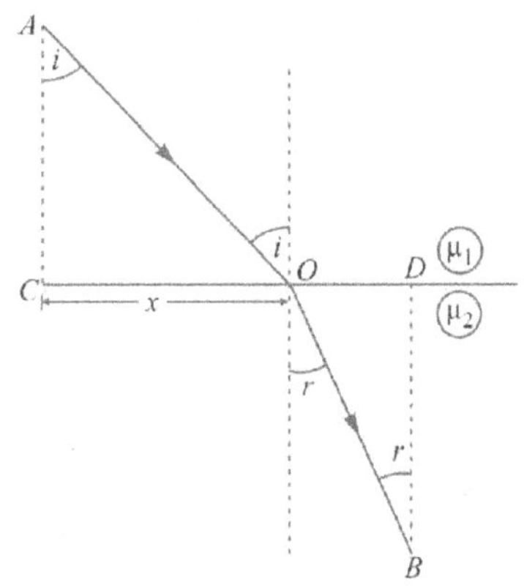

Fig. 2.33

The time taken by light ray from A to B

$$t = \frac{AO}{v_1}+\frac{OB}{v_2}$$

$$t = \frac{\sqrt{x^2+AC^2}}{\dfrac{c}{\mu_1}}+\frac{\sqrt{(CD-x)^2+BD^2}}{\dfrac{c}{\mu_2}} \qquad ...(i)$$

Differentiating equation (i) w.r.t. x, we have

$$\frac{dt}{dx} = \frac{\mu_1}{2c}\left(x^2+AC^2\right)^{-1/2}\times2x\frac{dx}{dt}$$

$$+\frac{\mu_2}{2c}\left[(CD-x)^2+BD^2\right]^{-1/2}\times2(CD-x)\left(-\frac{dx}{dt}\right)$$

For t to be minimum, $\qquad \dfrac{dt}{dx} = 0$

$$\therefore \quad 0 = \mu_1\frac{x}{\sqrt{x^2+AC^2}}-\mu_2\frac{(CD-x)}{\sqrt{(CD-x)^2+BD^2}}$$

or $\qquad 0 = \mu_1 \sin i-\mu_2 \sin r$

or $\qquad \dfrac{\sin i}{\sin r} = \dfrac{\mu_2}{\mu_1}.$

This proves the Snell's law.

2.4 PRACTICAL PHENOMENA BASED ON REFRACTION

1. **Twinkling of stars :** Earth's atmosphere consists of number of layers of varying densities, such that the most dense layer is near the earth's surface. These layers of air are not stationary, but contantly inter-mingle, and so rapidly changing in density. In figure S is the true position of the star. Due to the refraction by the atmosphere, its image is formed at S'. Thus S' is the apparent position of the star. When different layers in atmosphere change in density and so in refractive index, will change the apparent position of the star. Thus when star is within the line of sight, it is visible. However when it falls out of line of sight, it is no longer visible. The collective effect of the above changes in apparent position of a star is known as twinkling. Planets do not twinkle, because they are very close to us as compared to stars. Their refraction and hence apparent shift in position of planets are quite small, and so they appear at their original position.

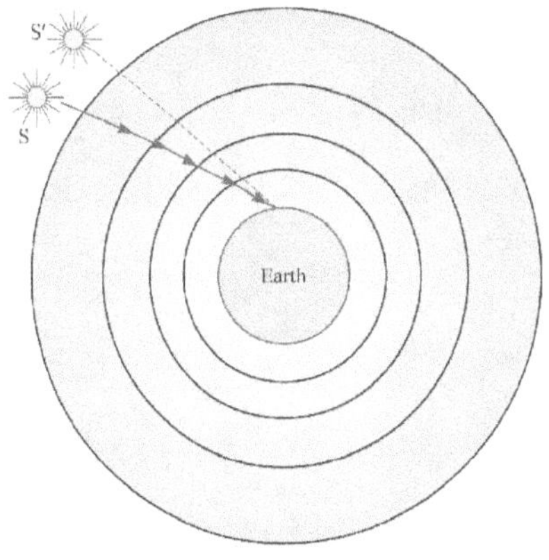

Fig. 2.34

2. **Why sun appears bigger during sun-set or sun-rise ?**
Sun is our near star and so looks larger in size. Due to refraction its image appears more closer to eye than its actual size. Since during sun-set and sun-rise, the rays of light travel through maximum length of atmosphere, and therefore refraction is also maximum. Hence apparent image of sun is very much closer to eye. Thus it appears bigger in size.

2.5 TOTAL INTERNAL REFLECTION

We know that when light ray is incident in optical denser medium, it bends away from the normal in rarer medium. With the increase in angle of incidence in denser medium, angle of refraction also increases. For particular value of angle of incidence, the angle of refraction in rarer medium becomes 90°. The angle of incidence for which the refracted ray emerges tangent to the interface between the mediums, is called the **critical angle** and is designated by C. If the angle of incidence in denser medium is greater than the **critical angle**, the ray does not pass into the rarer medium but is totally internally reflected at the boundary surface and return back into the same medium. This is known as **total internal reflection (TIR).**

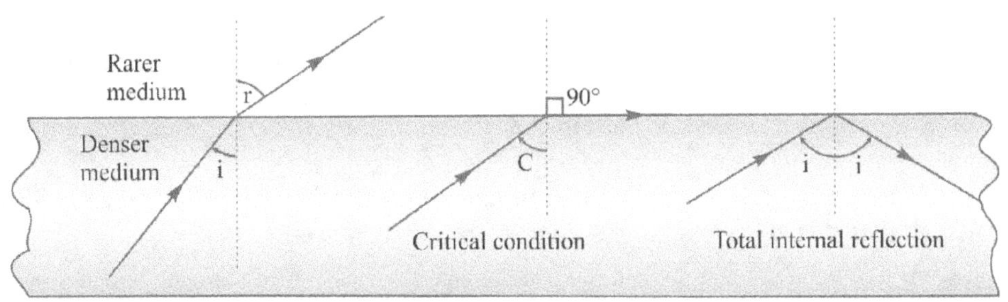

Fig. 2.35

Critical angle : The critical angle for two given material mediums may be obtained by setting r = 90° in Snell's law. We then have

$$_{denser}\mu_{rarer} = \frac{\sin C}{\sin 90°}$$

$$= \sin C$$

or

$$\sin C = \frac{1}{_{rarer}\mu_{denser}} = \frac{1}{\mu}.$$

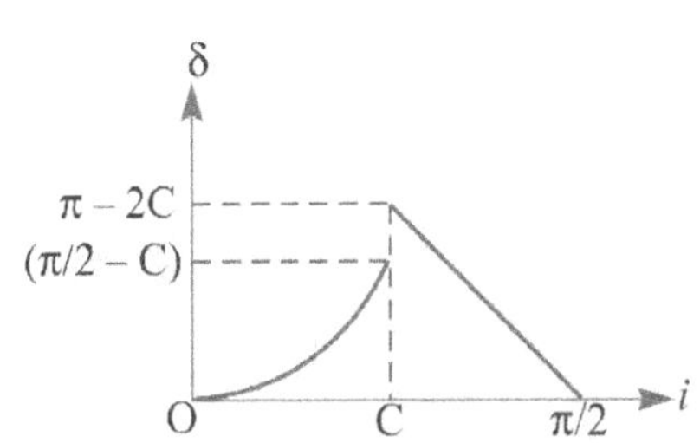

Fig.2.36. Variation of δ with i.

Light passes from	Refractive index μ	Critical angle, C
Glass to air	3/2	42°
Water to air	4/3	49°
Diamond to air	2.4	24°

Variation of angle of deviation with angle of incidence

When angle of incidence in denser medium is less than critical angle, the angle of deviation is given

$$\delta = r - i$$

By Snell's law

$$\frac{\sin r}{\sin i} = \mu$$

or

$$r = \sin^{-1}(\mu \sin i)$$

$$\therefore \qquad \delta = \sin^{-1}(\mu \sin i) - i$$

The maximum value of δ will occur when $i = C$, and is given by

$$\delta_{max} = \frac{\pi}{2} - C$$

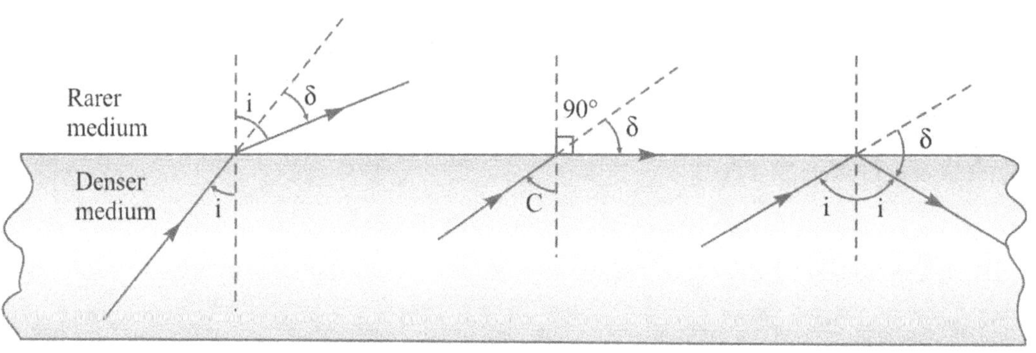

Fig. **2.37**

When angle of incidence in denser medium is greater than critical angle, the angle of deviation is given by

$$\delta = \pi - 2i$$

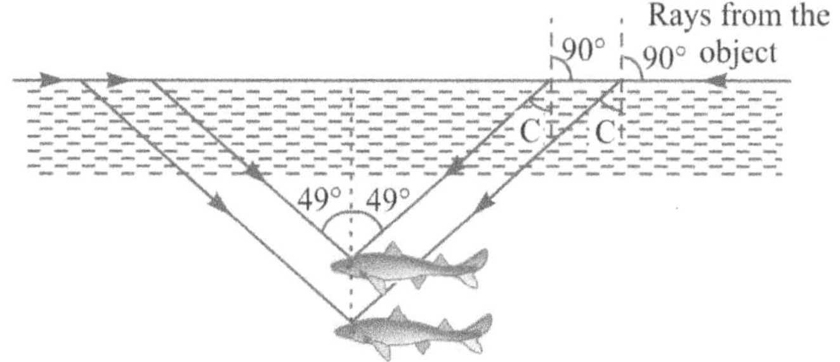

Fig. **2.38**

Field of view of a fish

For the objects situated at the banks of the pond, the rays incident at 90° will reach the fish inside water at an angle C = 49° (see *fig.* 2.38). The maximum angular width of field of vision of fish lies within a cone of semi vertex angle of 49°, which does not depend on the depth of the fish.

Ex. 18 Find critical angle for the light ray when incident on glass-water interface.

Sol.

We have
$$\sin C = \frac{1}{_{rarer}\mu_{denser}}$$

$$= \frac{1}{_{w}\mu_{g}}$$

$$= \frac{\mu_w}{\mu_g}$$

$$= \frac{4/3}{3/2} = \frac{8}{9}$$

Thus
$$C = \sin^{-1}\left(\frac{8}{9}\right). \qquad \textbf{Ans.}$$

Ex. 19 A point source of light S is placed at the bottom of a vessel containing a liquid of refractive index 5/3. A person is viewing the source from above the surface. There is an opaque disc of radius 1 cm floating on the surface. The centre of the disc lies vertically above the source. The liquid from the vessel is gradually drained out through a tap. What is the maximum height of the liquid for which the source can not at all be seen from above.

Sol. The source will not be seen from above, if rays after refraction become parallel to surface of liquid or totally reflected into it. For maximum height h, the angle of refraction $r = 90°$.

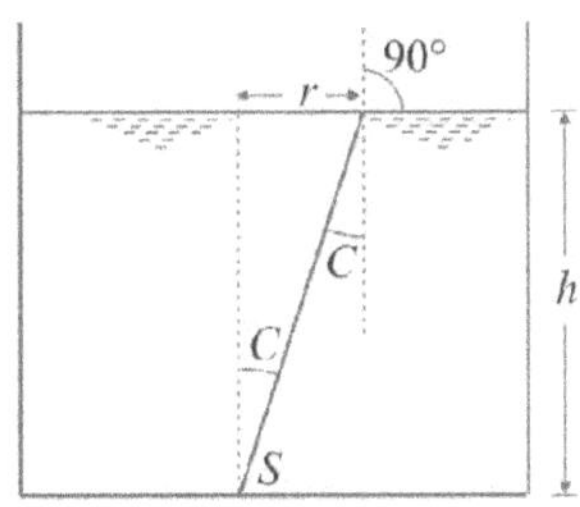

Fig. 2.39

Thus by Snell's law
$$\frac{\sin 90°}{\sin C} = \mu$$

or
$$\sin C = \frac{1}{\mu} = \frac{1}{5/3}$$

$$= \frac{3}{5}$$

$$\therefore \qquad \tan C = \frac{3}{4}.$$

From the geometry
$$\tan C = \frac{r}{h}$$

$$\therefore \qquad h = \frac{r}{\tan C}$$

$$= \frac{1}{3/4} = \frac{4}{3} \text{ cm} \qquad \textbf{Ans.}$$

Ex. 20 A rectangular block of glass is placed on a printed page lying on a horizontal surface. Find the minimum value of the refractive index of glass for which the letters on page are not visible from any of the vertical faces of the block.

Sol. Let a rectangular block $ABCD$ is placed on the printed page. A thin air film is enclosed between page and the block. The rays from the letter O incident almost normally on the lower face of the block, and so angle of refraction inside block becomes critical angle C. These rays now incident on vertical face of the block at an angle $(90°-C)$. If they totally reflected inside the block, then the letter will not be seen from the vertical face of the block. Thus at vertical face BC

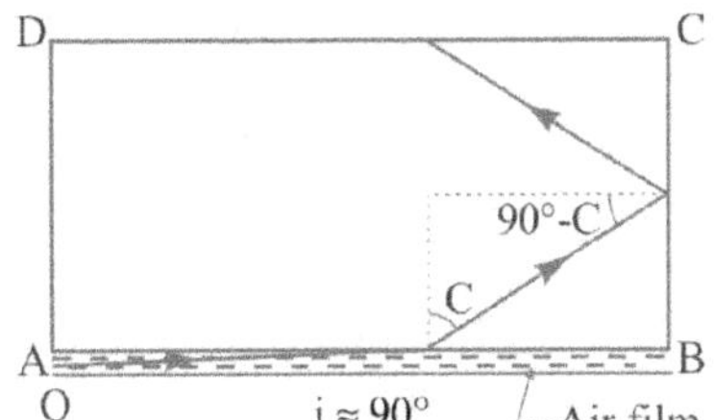

Fig. 2.40

$$\text{angle of incidence } (90°-C) > \text{critical angle } C$$
$$\text{or} \qquad 90°-C > C$$
$$\text{or} \qquad 2C < 90°$$
$$\text{or} \qquad C < 45°$$

For minimum value of refractive index,
$$C_{max} = 45°, \text{ and so}$$

$$\mu_{min} = \frac{1}{\sin C_{max}}$$

$$= \frac{1}{\sin 45°} = \sqrt{2} \qquad \textbf{Ans.}$$

Ex. 21 A point source of light is placed at a distance h below the surface of a large and deep lake. Show that the fraction f of light energy that escapes directly from the water surface is independent of h and is given by

$$f = \frac{1}{2}\left[1 - \sqrt{\left(1 - \frac{1}{\mu^2}\right)}\right].$$

Sol.

Only those rays can escape from surface of water for which angle of incidence $i \leq C$. So required fraction

$$f = \left[\frac{\text{Surface area of sphere outside water}}{\text{total area of sphere}}\right]$$

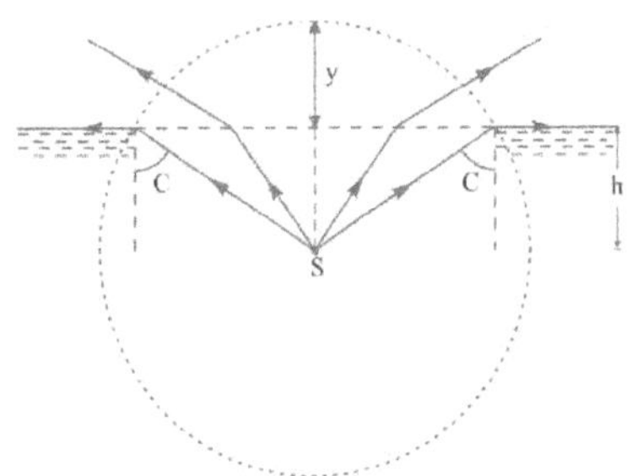

Fig. 2.41

If R is the radius of sphere and y is the part of it which is above the water surface, then

$$f = \frac{2\pi Ry}{4\pi R^2} = \frac{y}{2R}$$

As h is the depth of the source from the free surface of water, so

$$y = R - h$$

$$\therefore \quad f = \frac{R-h}{2R}$$

$$= \frac{1}{2}\left[1 - \frac{h}{R}\right]$$

From the geometry of the figure,

$$\cos C = \frac{h}{R}$$

$$\therefore \quad f = \frac{1}{2}[1 - \cos C]$$

or $$f = \frac{1}{2}\left[1 - \sqrt{1 - \sin^2 C}\right]$$

But $$\sin C = \frac{1}{\mu}$$

$$\therefore \quad f = \frac{1}{2}\left[1 - \sqrt{\left(1 - \frac{1}{\mu^2}\right)}\right]. \quad \textbf{\textit{Proved}}$$

Ex. 22 A rod made of glass ($\mu = 1.5$) and of square cross-section is bent into the shape shown in *fig.* 2.42. A parallel beam of light falls perpendicular on the plane flat surface A. Referring to diagram, d is the width of a side and R is the radius of inner semicircle. Find the maximum value of ratio $\dfrac{d}{R}$ so that all light entering the glass through surface A emerge from the glass through surface B.

Sol.

The path of two rays 1 and 2 are shown in figure. The angle of incidence of ray 1 is greater than that of angle of incidence of ray 2 $(i_2 > i_1)$. If ray 1 get totally reflected, then ray 2 also be reflected. Therefore for ray 1:

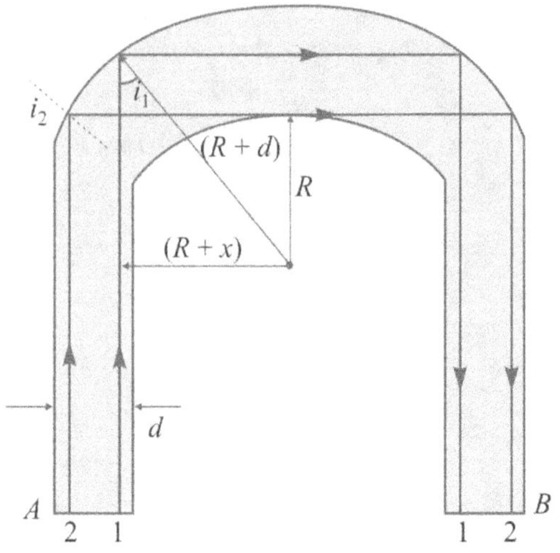

Fig. 2.42

$$\sin i_1 = \frac{R+x}{R+d}$$

For minimum value of i_1, $x = 0$. Thus

$$\sin i_1 = \frac{R}{R+d}$$

For TIR, $i_1 > C$, and $\sin C = \dfrac{1}{\mu} = \dfrac{1}{3/2} = \dfrac{2}{3}$.

$$\therefore \quad \frac{R}{R+d} > \frac{2}{3}$$

or $$d < \frac{R}{2}$$

or $$\frac{d}{R} < \frac{1}{2}$$

Thus maximum value of $\dfrac{d}{R} = \dfrac{1}{2}$ *Ans.*

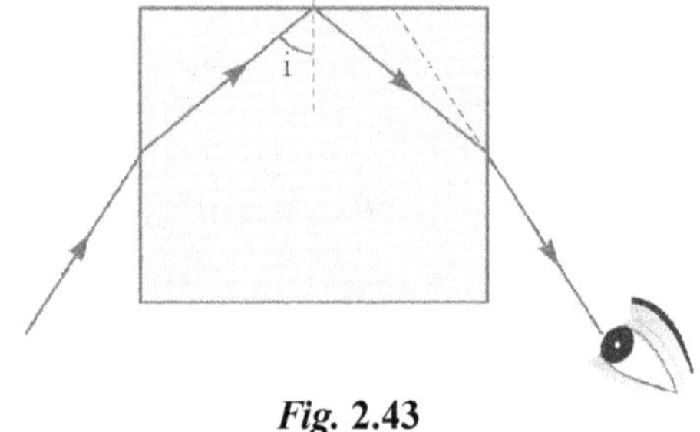

Fig. 2.43

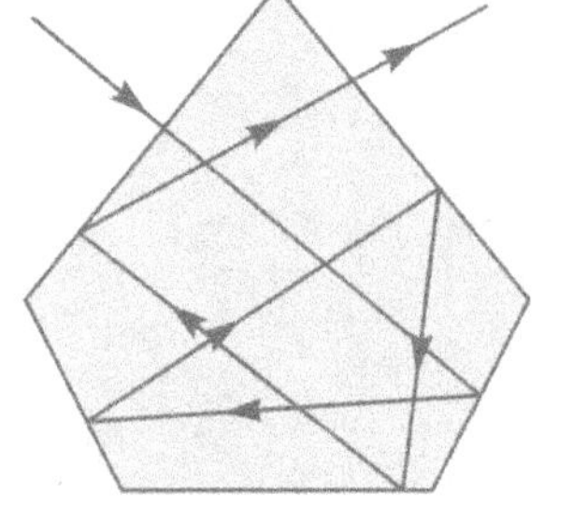

Fig. 2.44

2.6 PHENOMENA BASED ON TIR

(i) **Surface of water contained in a beaker held above eye level appears silvery :** Critical angle for water-air is 49°. The rays of light entering in water from below, suffer refraction from the vertical face of the beaker. Thereafter they strike the water surface. If angle of incidence i at the interface is greater than critical angle 49°, then they get totally reflected. These rays on emerging out of water appear to come from the upper surface of water which in turn appear silvery.

(ii) **Sparkling of diamond :** The critical angle for diamond is only 24°. Moreover, diamonds are cut at very sharp angles, making number of refracting surfaces of angle of incidence slightly greater than C. When a ray of light enters into a diamond, it suffers a series of total internal reflections because of very small critical angle. Thus the ray gets trapped within the diamond for some time. It is the trapped light energy, which makes it sparkle. It is for the same reason that cut glass articles sparkle.

(iii) **Mirage :** In summer season, the ground surface becomes very hot and then the layers of air above it. Thus the layers of air closest to ground surface are hottest and optically least dense whereas the layers high up are colder and optically more dense. In this situation, the rays coming from the tall object like tree, pass from denser to rarer medium and so angle of refraction increases. This continues till a stage comes when angle of incidence in optically denser layer becomes greater than the critical angle. Thus total reflection takes place. When these reflected rays reach to the observer's eyes, they appear to come from the image of the tree. Thus an image of tree will appear without the presence of water. This is called mirage.

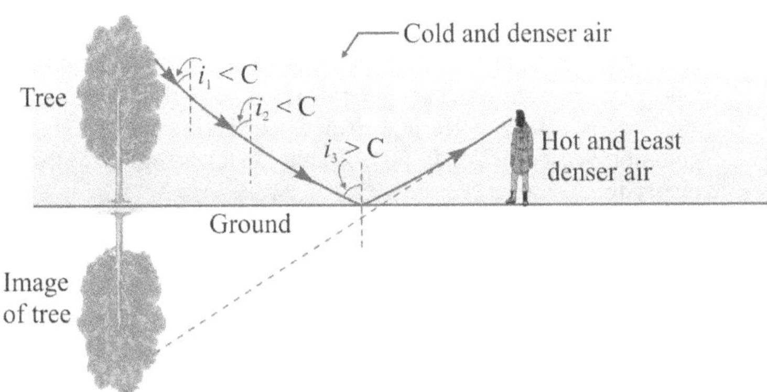

Fig. **2.45 Formation of mirage**

Note :

The size of image of tree will appear smaller than the actual size of the tree.

(iv) **Optical fibre :** An optical fibre is a thin and flexible fibre. It has a thin core made of transparent medium like glass or plastic. The core is surrounded by a cladding, whose refractive index is lower than the core. Because of cladding (like air), the light rays inside the core get totally reflected at different points along the length of the fibre and emerge from the other end. Optical fibre can be used to send telephone signals. Doctors use optical fibre tube, to examine stomach, which is called **endoscopy.**

The maximum value of angle of θ, so that a ray can be propagated through the fibre.

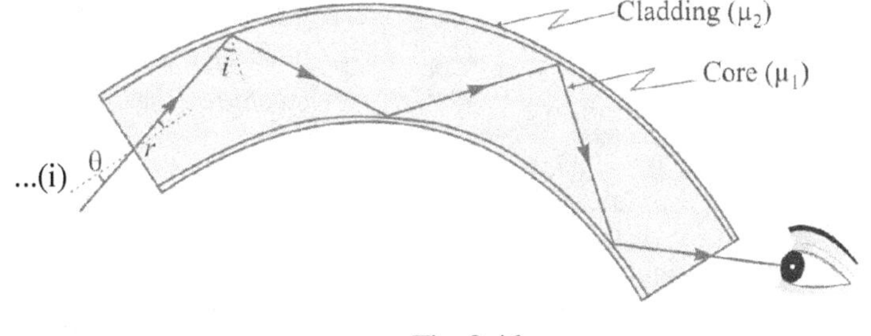

Fig. **2.46**

By Snell's law

$$\frac{\sin\theta}{\sin r} = \mu_1$$

or $\qquad \sin\theta = \mu_1 \sin r \qquad \ldots(i)$

From the geometry of the figure, angle of incidence

$$i = 90° - r.$$

For TIR, $\qquad 90° - r > C$

or $\qquad \sin(90° - r) > \sin C$

$$> \frac{\mu_2}{\mu_1}$$

or $\qquad \cos r > \dfrac{\mu_2}{\mu_1} \qquad \ldots(ii)$

From equations (i) and (ii), we get

$$\sin\theta_{max} = \mu_1\sqrt{1-\cos^2 r}$$

$$= \mu_1\sqrt{1-\left(\frac{\mu_2}{\mu_1}\right)^2}$$

or

$$\sin\theta_{max} = \sqrt{\mu_1^2 - \mu_2^2}\,.$$

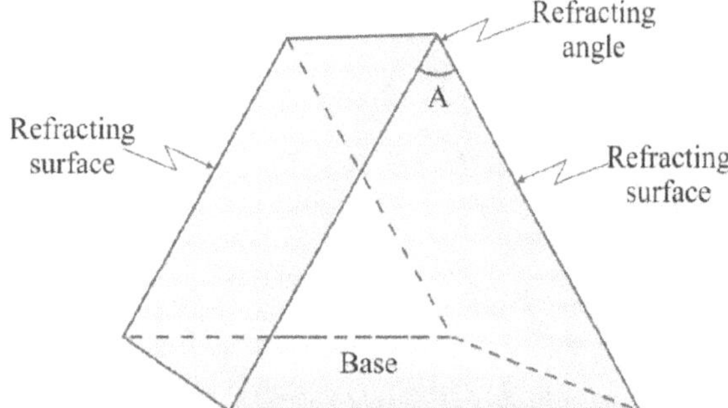

Fig. 2.47 . A triangular prism

2.7 THE PRISM

When two refracting surfaces are inclined at some angle, they constitute a prism. Figure shows a triangular prism. The angle between the inclined surfaces is called angle of prism or refracting angle. The angle of commonly used prism is 60°. Prism can cause deviation as well as dispersion.

Note:

1. When two non parallel faces of the slab is used for refraction, the angle of refraction will be 90°.

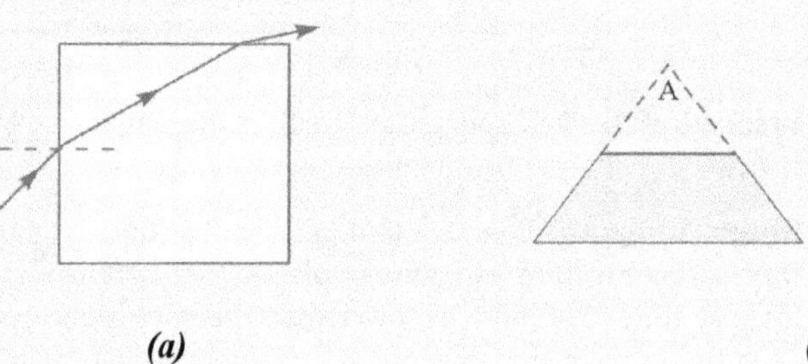

Fig. 2.48

2. In the figure, the angle between two refracting surfaces is A.

Refraction through a prism

Consider a monochromatic ray of light incident at an angle i on the face *AB* of the prism. It gets refraced at an angle r_1 into the prism, after this the ray incident on the other face *AC* of the prism at an angle r_2, and then finally emerges from this face with an angle *e* (see figure). By Snell's law

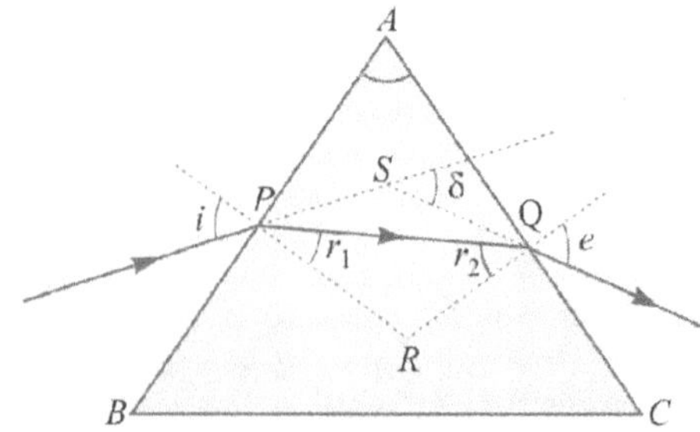

Fig. 2.49. Principal section of prism

$$\mu = \frac{\sin i}{\sin r_1} = \frac{\sin e}{\sin r_2}. \qquad ...(1)$$

2.8 DEVIATION PRODUCED BY PRISM

Because of the inclination between the refracting surfaces, the incident ray and emerging ray are not parallel. The angle between the incident ray and emerging ray is called angle of deviation and designated by δ. In figure

$$\angle A + \angle R = 180°$$

$$\therefore \qquad \angle R = 180° - A$$

In ΔPQR,

$$\angle R + \angle r_1 + \angle r_2 = 180°$$

or $\quad \left(180° - A\right) + r_1 + r_2 = 180°$

$$\therefore \quad r_1 + r_2 = A \qquad \qquad ...(2)$$

Angle of deviation,

$$\delta = \angle SPQ + \angle SQP$$

$$= \left(i - r_1\right) + \left(e - r_2\right)$$

$$= \left(i + e\right) - \left(r_1 + r_2\right)$$

$$= \left(i + e\right) - A$$

$$\therefore \quad i + e = A + \delta \qquad \qquad ...(3)$$

Deviation produced by small angled prism

From equation (1), for small angle, we have

$$\mu = \frac{i}{r_1} = \frac{e}{r_2}$$

$$\therefore \quad i = \mu\, r_1 \text{ and } e = \mu\, r_2$$

Now from equation (3), we have

$$\mu\, r_1 + \mu\, r_2 = A + \delta$$
$$\text{or} \quad \mu(r_1 + r_2) = A + \delta$$
$$\text{or} \quad \mu A = A + \delta$$
$$\therefore \quad \delta = (\mu - 1)A \qquad \qquad ...(4)$$

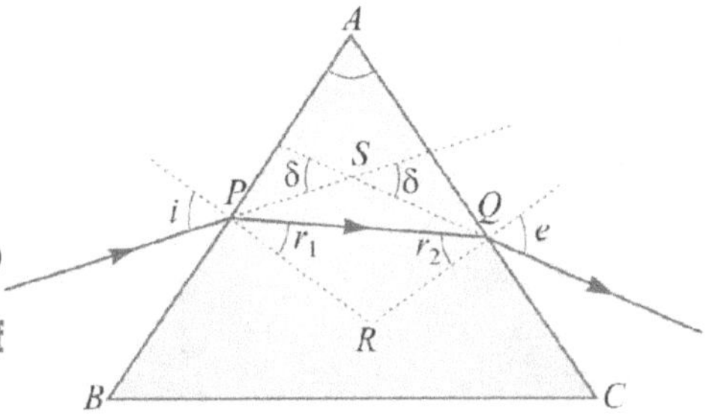

There are two values for angle of incidence for same angle of deviation :

When a ray is incident at an angle i, it emerges at an angle e, with a deviation angle δ. If the ray is incident at an angle e, then it will emerge at an angle i having same angle of deviation (see *fig.* 2.50). Thus there are two angles of incidence for same angle of deviation. These are $i_1 = i$ and $i_2 = e$.

Minimum deviation

We know that

$$i + e = A + \delta$$
$$\therefore \quad \delta = (i + e) - A$$

From the above equation, we can say that angle of deviation depends on angle of incidence. Experiments show that with the increase in angle of incidence, the angle of deviation first decreases, passes through minimum and then increases. Thus for a certain value of the angle of incidence ($i_1 = i_2$), the light passing through prism suffers minimum deviation. The angle of deviation at this position is called the minimum angle of deviation (δ_m). Figure shows the minimum deviation and graph shows the variation of angle of deviation with angle of incidence.

In minimum deviation position, $\quad \delta = \delta_m$

$$i = e$$

and so $\quad r_1 = r_2 = r \text{ (say)}$

From equations (2) and (3), we get

$$r = \frac{A}{2} \text{ and } i = \frac{A + \delta_m}{2}.$$

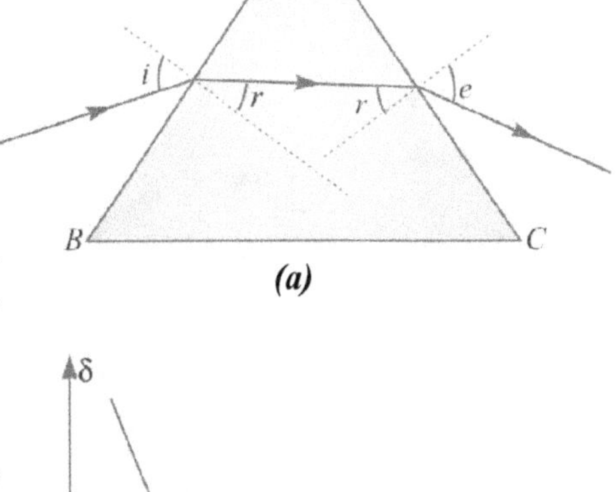

Fig. 2.50

(a)

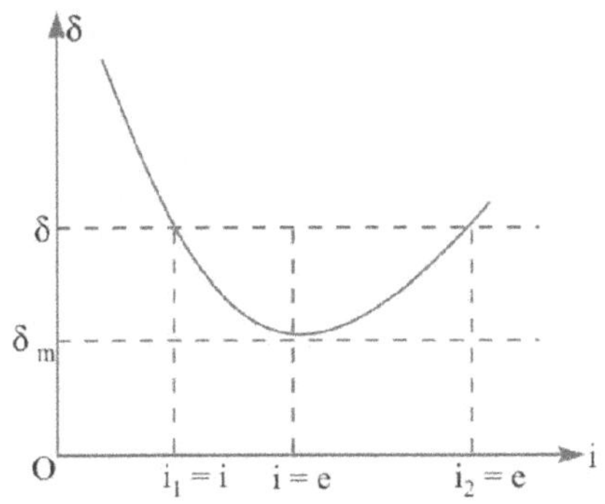

(b)

Fig. 2.51

If μ is the refractive index of material of the prism, then by Snell's law

$$\mu = \frac{\sin i}{\sin r}$$

or

$$\mu = \frac{\sin\left(\dfrac{A+\delta_m}{2}\right)}{\sin\dfrac{A}{2}}. \qquad \ldots(5)$$

This is called prism formula.

Maximum deviation

We know that, angle of deviation

$$\delta = (i+e)-A.$$

The deviation angle will be maximum, when either of i or e is maximum. Thus for

$$i = 90^\circ,$$
$$\delta_{max} = (90^\circ + e)-A. \qquad \ldots(i)$$

At face AB of the prism,

$$\mu = \frac{\sin 90^\circ}{\sin r_1}$$

$$\therefore \qquad \sin r_1 = \frac{1}{\mu}$$

or

$$r_1 = \sin^{-1}\left(\frac{1}{\mu}\right) = C$$

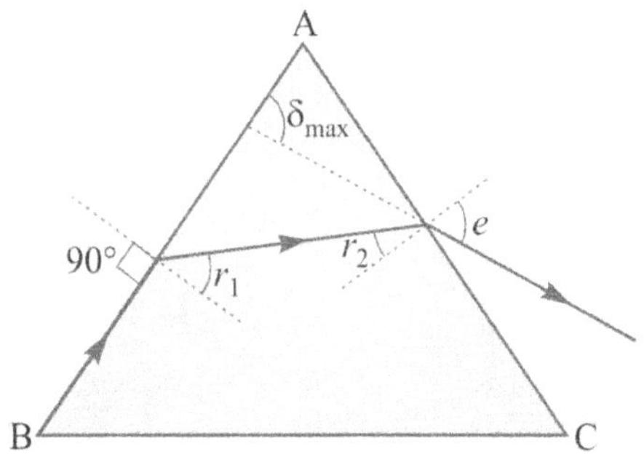

Fig. 2.52

We have

$$r_1 + r_2 = A$$
$$\therefore \qquad r_2 = A - r_1 = A - C$$

Now for face AC,

$$\mu = \frac{\sin e}{\sin(A-C)}$$

or

$$\sin e = \mu \sin(A-C)$$

or

$$e = \sin^{-1}\left[\mu \sin(A-C)\right] \qquad \ldots(ii)$$

Thus

$$\delta_{max} = 90^\circ + \sin^{-1}\left[\mu \sin(A-C)\right] - A. \qquad \ldots(6)$$

Condition of no emergence

A ray of light will not emerge out from the prism, if it gets totally reflected from the other face of the prism, even for angle of incidence on first face is 90°. Thus angle of incidence on second face should be greater than critical angle. i.e.,

$$r_2 > C.$$

For $i \to 90^\circ, r_1 \to C$. Thus for no emergence from any face of the prism, angles

$$r_1 + r_2 = A,$$
$$\therefore \qquad A > 2C \qquad \ldots(7)$$

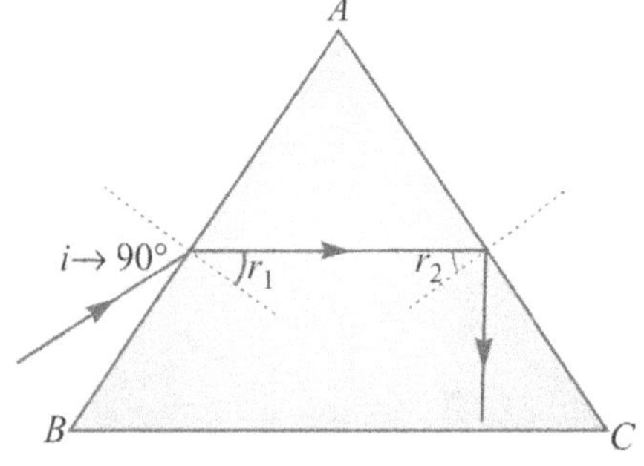

Fig. 2.53

So, a ray of light will not emerge out from the prism, if $A > 2C$.

Totally reflecting prism

The critical angle for glass-air interface is 42°. Thus if we make a prism in such a way, that light ray incident into it at an angle greater than critical, then it becomes totally reflecting prism. Such a prism may be right angled isosceles (45° – 90° – 45°). They can be used to deviate rays through 90° or 180°.

Erecting prism

This is also the right-angled isosceles prism. In this case rays of light should be parallel to the hypotenuse. By doing so the rays invert themselves and an inverted object appears as erect.

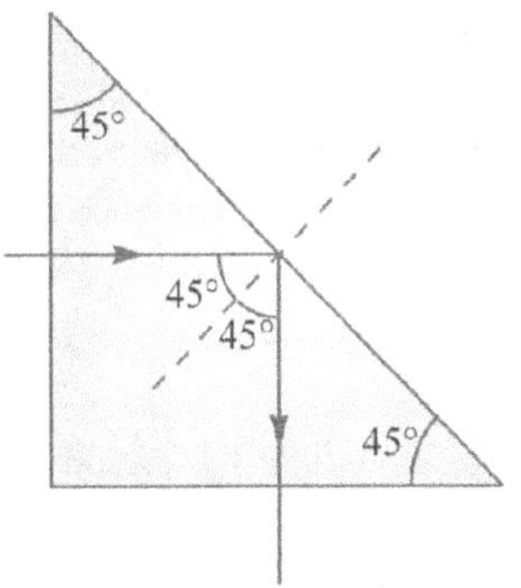
(a) Deviation of ray through 90°

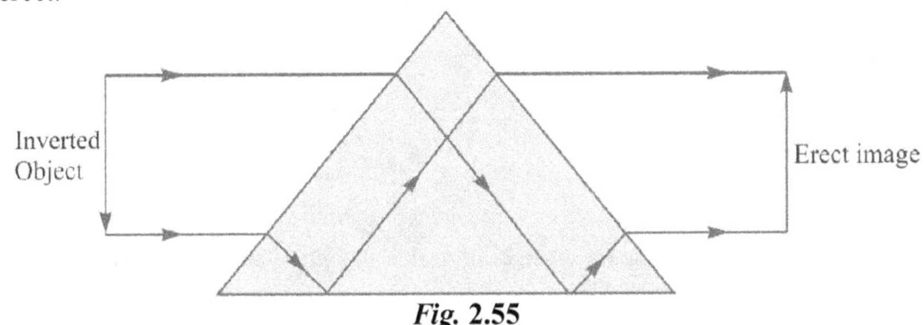

Fig. **2.55**

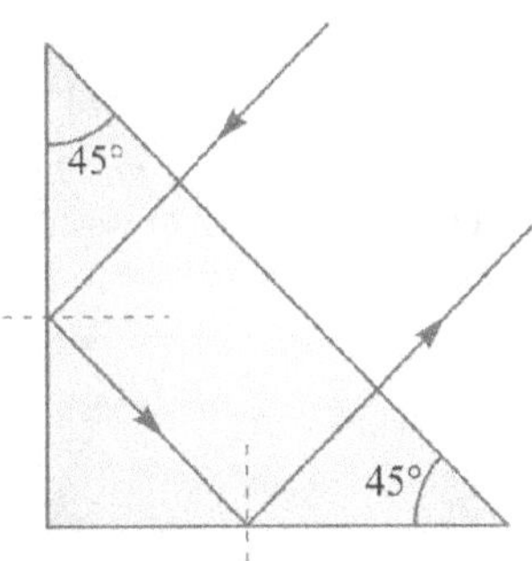
(b) Deviation of ray through 180°.
Fig. **2.54**

Ex. 23 Two identical thin isosceles prisms angle A and refractive index μ are placed with their bases touching each other. This system can act as a crude converging lens. Draw a neat diagram showing the path of parallel incident rays. Obtain the focal length of the system. The height of incident is h.

Sol. The deviation produced by thin prism

$$\delta = (\mu - 1)A.$$

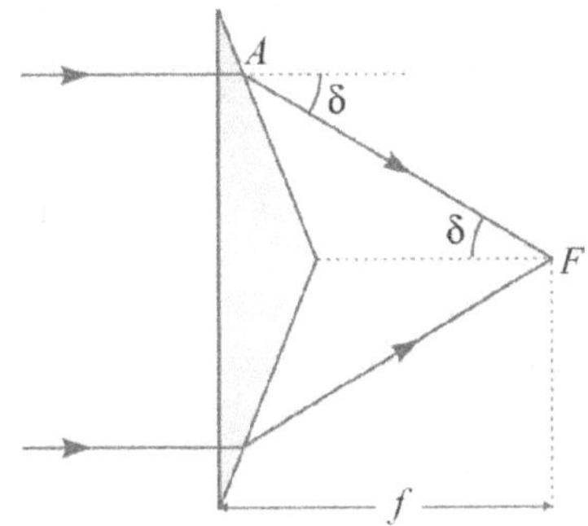

Fig. **2.56**

For small angled prism

$$\delta \simeq \tan\delta = \frac{h}{f}$$

$$\therefore \quad \frac{h}{f} = (\mu - 1)A$$

$$\text{or} \quad f = \frac{h}{(\mu - 1)A} \quad \textit{Ans.}$$

Ex. 24 An isosceles prism of angle 120° has a refractive index $\sqrt{2}$. Two parallel monochromatic rays enter the prism parallel to each other in air as shown in *fig.* 2.57. Find the angle between the emerging rays.

Sol.

The angle of incidence on the inclined face of the prism is 30°. If r is the angle of refraction, then by Snell's law

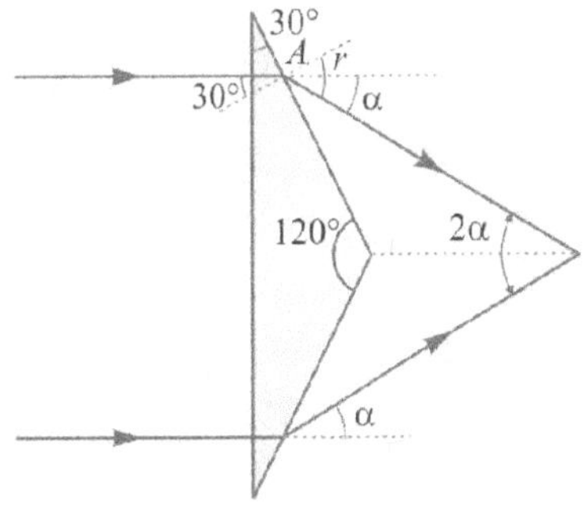

Fig. **2.57**

$$\frac{\sin r}{\sin 30°} = \sqrt{2}$$

$$\text{or} \quad \sin r = \frac{1}{\sqrt{2}}$$

$$\therefore \quad r = 45°$$

$$\text{Angle} \quad \alpha = 45° - 30° - 15°$$

$$\text{The required angle} = 2\alpha$$

$$= 2 \times 15° = 30° \quad \textit{Ans.}$$

Ex. 25 A glass prism of refractive index 1.5 is immersed in water (refractive index 4/3). A light beam incident normally on the face AB as shown in *fig.* 2.58 is totally reflected to reach the face BC. Find θ.

Sol.

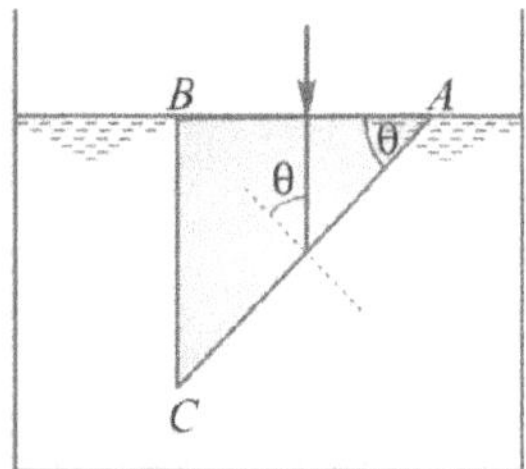

Fig. **2.58**

The critical angle from glass to water is

$$\sin C = \frac{1}{_w\mu_g} = \frac{_a\mu_w}{_a\mu_g}$$

$$= \frac{4/3}{3/2} = \frac{8}{9}$$

The angle of incidence at the face AC is θ. For the ray to be totally reflected, the angle θ must be greater than critical angle. Thus

$$\theta > C$$

or $$\sin\theta > \sin C$$

$$> \frac{8}{9} \qquad \textit{Ans.}$$

Ex. 26 A glass prism of angle 72° and index of refraction 1.66 is immersed in a liquid of refractive index 1.33. Find the angle of minimum deviation for a parallel beam in light passing through the prism.

Sol.   Given $_a\mu_g$ =1.66 and $_a\mu_w$ = 1.33

$$\therefore \qquad _w\mu_g = \frac{_a\mu_g}{_a\mu_w} = \frac{1.66}{1.33}$$

If δ_m is the required angle, then

$$\frac{\sin\left(\dfrac{A+\delta_m}{2}\right)}{\sin\dfrac{A}{2}} = \frac{1.66}{1.33}$$

or $$\frac{\sin\left(\dfrac{72°+\delta m}{2}\right)}{\sin 36°} = \frac{1.66}{1.33}$$

After simplifying, $$\delta_m = 22°22' \qquad \textit{Ans.}$$

Ex. 27 A ray of light is incident at an angle of 60° on one face of a prism which has an angle of 30°. The ray emerging out of the prism makes an angle 30° with the incident ray. Show that the emergent ray is perpendicular to the face through which it emerges and calculate the refractive index of the material of the prism.

Sol.

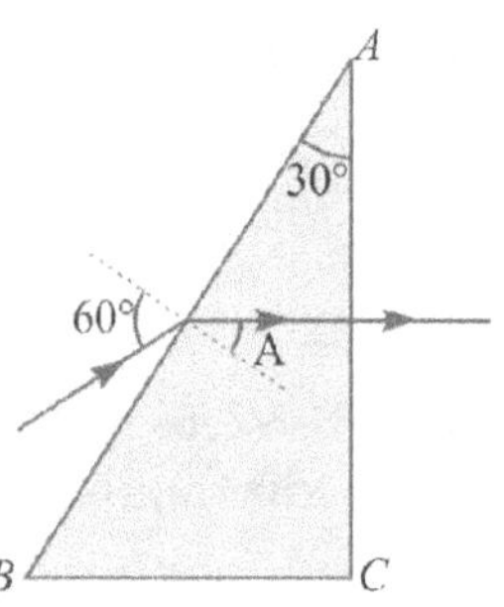

Fig. **2.59**

Given, $$i = 60°, \delta = 30°, A = 30°$$
We have, $$i + e = A + \delta$$
or $$60° + e = 30° + 30°$$
$$\therefore \qquad e = 0$$

Thus the ray emerges normal to the other face of the prism.
By Snell's law

$$\mu = \frac{\sin i}{\sin r_1}$$

Here $r_1 = 30°$ and $i = 60°$

$$\therefore \qquad \mu = \frac{\sin 60°}{\sin 30°}$$

$$= \frac{\dfrac{\sqrt{3}}{2}}{\dfrac{1}{2}} = \sqrt{3}. \qquad \textit{Ans.}$$

Ex. 28 A ray of light undergoes deviation of 30° when incident on an equilateral prism of refractive index $\sqrt{2}$. What is the angle subtended by the ray inside the prism with base of prism ?

Sol.

Suppose the prism had been in the position of minimum deviation. Then

$$\mu = \frac{\sin\left(\dfrac{A+\delta_m}{2}\right)}{\sin\dfrac{A}{2}}$$

$$= \frac{\sin\left(\dfrac{60°+30°}{2}\right)}{\sin\left(\dfrac{60°}{2}\right)}$$

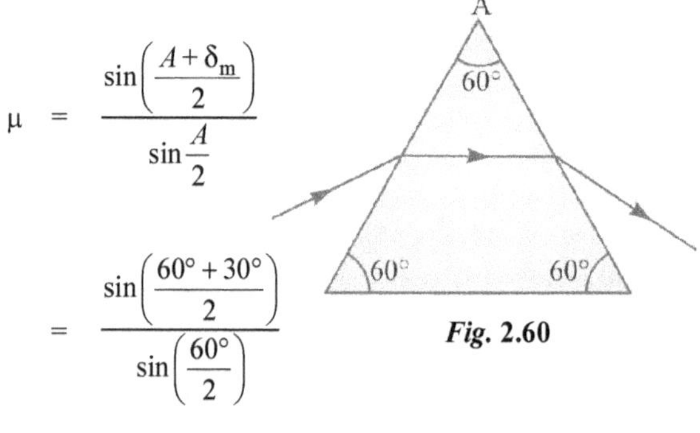

Fig. **2.60**

$$= \frac{\sin 45°}{\sin 30°} = \frac{1/\sqrt{2}}{1/2} = \sqrt{2}.$$

Given value of refractive index is also $\sqrt{2}$, and so the prism is the position of minimum deviation. The ray inside prism thus becomes parallel to base. i.e., it makes zero angle with the base of the prism.

Ex. 29 If one face of a prism of prism angle 30° and $\mu = \sqrt{2}$ is silvered, the incident ray retraces its initial path. What is the angle of incidence ?

Sol.

Suppose angle of incidence is i. The angle of refraction on first face of the prism will be 30° (see figure). Now by Snell's law

$$\mu = \frac{\sin i}{\sin r}$$

$$\sqrt{2} = \frac{\sin i}{\sin 30°}$$

$$\therefore \quad \sin i = \sqrt{2}\sin 30° = \sqrt{2}\times\frac{1}{2}$$

$$= \frac{1}{\sqrt{2}}$$

or $i = 45°$.   **Ans.**

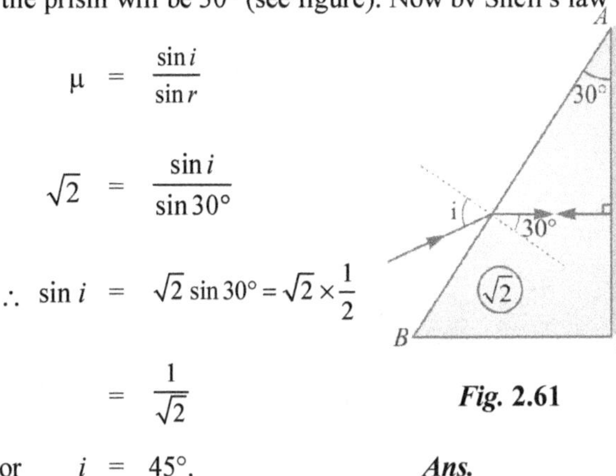

Fig. 2.61

Ex. 30 A prism of refracting angle 30° is coated with a thin film of transparent material of refractive index 2.2 on face AC of the prism as shown in *fig. 2.62*. A light of wavelength 6600Å is incident on face such that angle of incidence is 60°. Find

a)   the angle of emergence, (given refractive index of the material of the prism is $\sqrt{3}$) and

(b)   the minimum value of thickness of the coated film on the face, AC for which the light emerging from the face has maximum intensity.

Sol.

(a)   By Snell's law on face *AB*

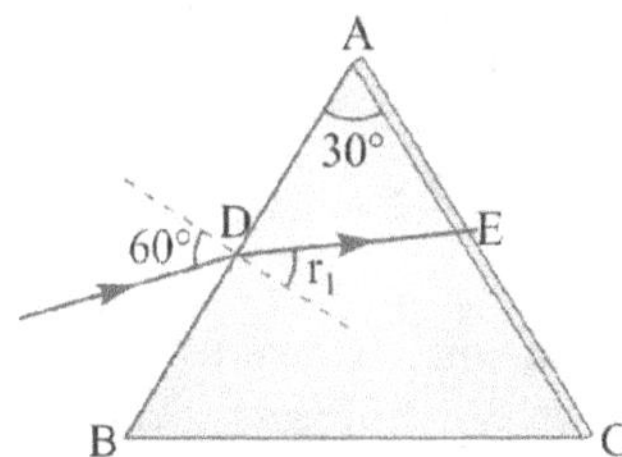

Fig. 2.62

$$\mu = \sqrt{3} = \frac{\sin 60°}{\sin r_1}$$

$$\therefore \quad \sin r_1 = \frac{\sin 60°}{\sqrt{3}}$$

$$= \frac{\sqrt{3}/2}{\sqrt{3}} = \frac{1}{2}$$

or $r_1 = 30°$

In figure $\angle ADE = 90° - r_1 = 90° - 30°$
$$= 60°$$

The $\angle AED = 90°$.

(b)   Thus angle of emergence on the second face will be zero.

For maximum intensity, there should be constructive interference. Thus

$$2\mu t \cos 0° = n\lambda$$

or $t = \dfrac{n\lambda}{2\mu}$

For minimum t, $n = 1$.

$$\therefore \quad t = \frac{\lambda}{2\mu} = \frac{6600}{2\times 2.2}$$

$$= 1500 \text{ Å}. \qquad \textbf{Ans.}$$

Ex. 31 Light passes symmetrically through a 60° prism. After emergence, it is incident on a plane mirror fixed to the base of the prism extending beyond it. Find the deviation produced. (The μ of the prism material is 1.54).

Sol.

As light in the prism passes symmetrically, so $r_1 = r_2 = r$.

Thus $r = \dfrac{A}{2} = \dfrac{60°}{2} = 30°$

By Snell's law $\dfrac{\sin i}{\sin 30°} = 1.54$

or $\sin i = 0.77$

$\therefore$ $i = 50°$

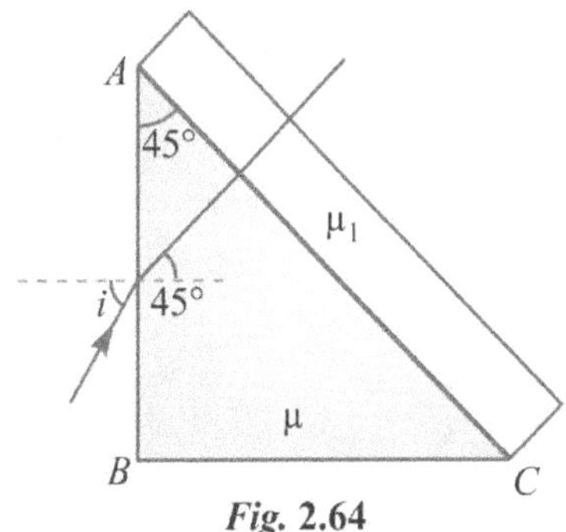

Fig. 2.63

The angle of deviation produced by the prism.

$$\delta = (i+e) - A$$

$$= (50° + 50°) - 60° = 40°.$$

The light ray after emerging from the prism, incident on the mirror at an 70°. The reflected ray then makes 20° with the horizontal axis, and so it is parallel to the incident ray. Thus deviation produced by the system is zero.

Ex. 32 A right angle prism (45° – 90° – 45°) of refractive index μ has a plate of refractive index $\mu_1 (\mu_1 < \mu)$ cemented to its diagonal face. The assembly is in air. A ray is incident on *AB*.

Fig. 2.64

(i) Calculate the angle of incidence at AB for which the ray strikes the diagonal face at the critical angle.

(ii) Assuming $\mu = 1.352$, calculate the angle of incidence at AB for which the refracted ray passes through the diagonal face undeviated.

Sol.

(i) If C is the critical angle at the face AC, then

$$\sin C = \frac{\mu_1}{\mu} \qquad \ldots(i)$$

Let the required angle of incidence be i and angle of refraction on face AB is r_1. Then

$$r_1 + C = 45°$$
$$\therefore \qquad r_1 = 45° - C$$

For the face AB $\quad \mu = \dfrac{\sin i}{\sin r_1} = \dfrac{\sin i}{\sin(45° - C)}$

or $\quad \sin i = \mu \sin(45° - C)$

$$\therefore \qquad i = \sin^{-1}\left[\mu\sin\left(45° - \sin^{-1}\frac{\mu_1}{\mu}\right)\right] \cdot \textbf{\textit{Ans.}}$$

(ii) For the ray passes undeviated through the face AC, $r = 45°$.

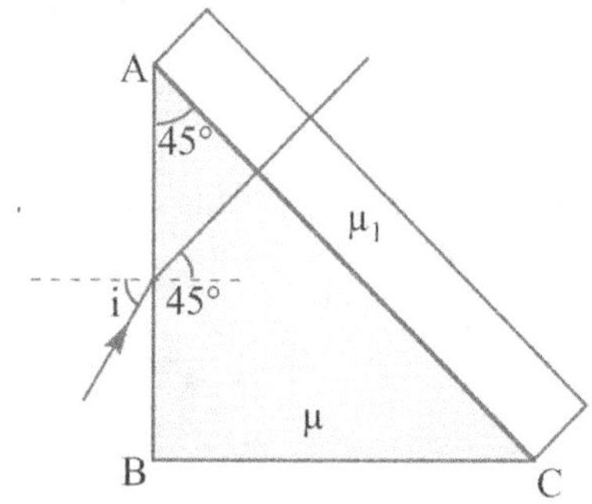

Fig. 2.65

Thus $\quad \dfrac{\sin i}{\sin 45°} = 1.352$

or $\qquad \sin i = 1.352 \times \sin 45°$

or $\qquad i \simeq 73°.$ **_Ans._**

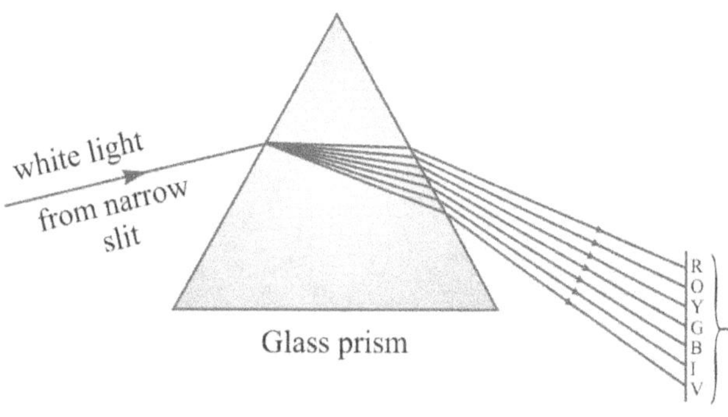

Fig. 2.66

2.9 DISPERSION OF LIGHT

In **Riga Veda**, it is mentioned that light is made of many colours. In 1665, **Sir Isaac Newton** showed that natural light actually consists of seven colours. All the colours of light mixed together appears white.

When white light is incident on one face of the prism, a band of seven colours is seen on the other side of the prism. These colours are : Violet, Indigo, Blue, Green, Yellow, Orange and Red. The order of the colours can be remembered by forming a word **VIBGYOR**.

The splitting of white light into its constituent colours is called dispersion of light. The band of colours formed on a screen due to dispersion is called, **spectrum**.

> *Note:*
>
> Theoretically each wavelength is associated with its own colour, therefore there are infinite colours in the natural light. Our eyes can differentiate only six colours, indigo and violet can not be differentiable. So in further study we consider only six colours in the spectrum of white light in wavelength range (4000Å to 7000Å).

Causes of dispersion

The refractive index of a any medium depends on wavelength of light. It approximately is given by Cauchy's equation as :

$$\mu = A + \frac{B}{\lambda^2}. \qquad \ldots(1)$$

Here A and B are constants. As the wavelength of red light is longer than violet light and so $\mu_V > \mu_R$. The deviation angle in specific case is given by $\delta = (\mu - 1)A$. Hence deviation of violet colour in maximum and so violet colour is at the lower end and red coloured is at the upper end of the spectrum.

Angular dispersion

Figure shows the deviation for two extreme colours. i.e., red violet. If δ_R and δ_V are the angles of deviations for red and violet colours, then

angular dispersion $\qquad = \delta_V - \delta_R.$

Thus angular dispersion is defined as the difference in the angles of deviation of two extreme colours. The mean deviation of all the colours is noticed for yellow colour. If A is the angle of prism, then

$$\delta_R = (\mu_R - 1) A$$

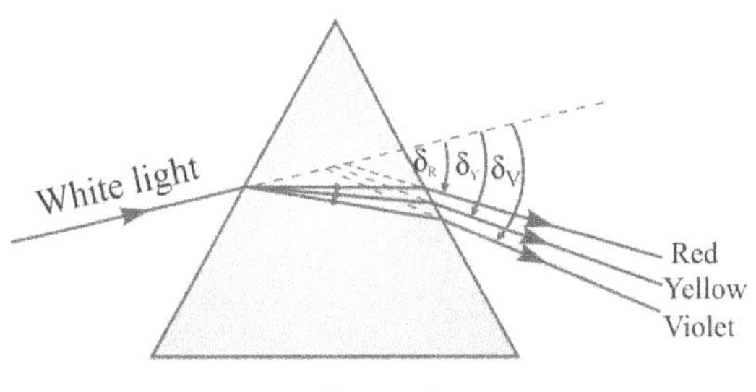

Fig. 2.67

and $$\delta_V = (\mu_V - 1) A.$$

Thus angular dispersion

$$\delta_V - \delta_R = (\mu_V - \mu_R) A. \qquad \ldots(2)$$

2.10 DISPERSIVE POWER

Dispersive power tells about the light bending capability of the prism or lens. Mathematically dispersive power of material of the prism

$$\omega = \frac{\text{angular dispersion}}{\text{mean deviation}}$$

or $$\omega = \frac{\delta_V - \delta_R}{\delta_Y} \qquad \ldots(1)$$

For thin prism, $$\delta_V = (\mu_V - 1) A, \delta_R = (\mu_R - 1) A \text{ and}$$

$$\delta_Y = (\mu_Y - 1) A.$$

$$\therefore \qquad \omega = \frac{(\mu_V - 1) A - (\mu_R - 1) A}{(\mu_Y - 1) A}$$

or $$\omega = \frac{\mu_V - \mu_R}{\mu_Y - 1}. \qquad \ldots(2)$$

In terms of differentiation

$$\omega = \frac{d\mu}{\mu - 1}. \qquad \ldots(3)$$

According to Cauchy's formula

$$\mu = A + \frac{B}{\lambda^2}$$

Differentiating above equation,

$$\frac{d\mu}{d\lambda} = -\frac{2B}{\lambda^3}.$$

Here $\dfrac{d\mu}{d\lambda}$ is known as dispersive power of the medium. Therefore dispersive power of violet colour ($\lambda = 4000\text{Å}$) is nearly eight times the dispersive power of red colour ($\lambda = 7000\text{Å}$). It means the spectral lines are more dispensed near the violet end of the spectrum than at the red end.

Note:

1. Dispersive power is the material property and always positive. The formula of ω is derived for thin prism. But the same can be used for lens etc.
2. When white light is incident on glass slab, it disperses into the slab. But emerging light appears white because all the colours of light emerge with same angle.
3. A beam of white light passing through a hollow prism gives no spectrum. The faces of the prism behaves like plates.

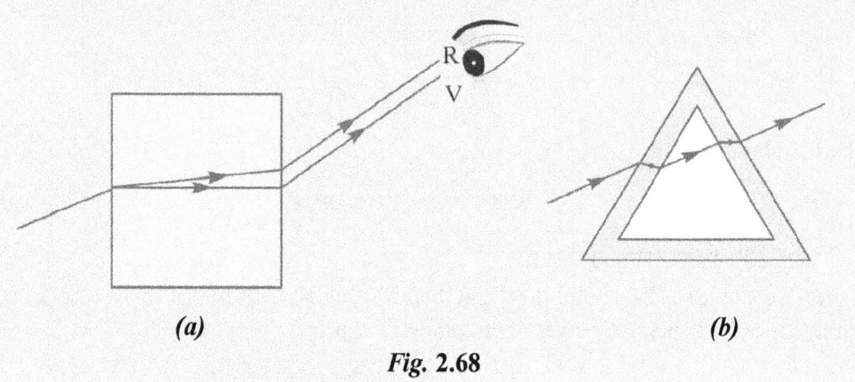

(a) *(b)*

Fig. 2.68

2.11 COMBINATION OF PRISMS

A prism produces both deviation and dispersion. It can not give deviation without dispersion and vice-versa when white light is incident on it. However a suitable combination of two prisms can do so.

(i) **Dispersion without deviation :**

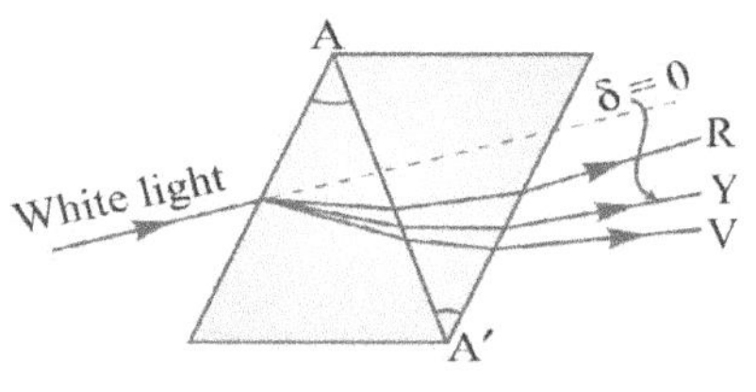

Fig. 2.69

Consider two prisms of refracting angles A and A′ and refractive indexes μ and μ' respectively. The deviation produced by first prism for mean colour (yellow colour) $\delta_Y = (\mu_Y - 1)A$ and by second prism $\delta_Y' = (\mu_Y' - 1)A'$. The total deviation produced by two prisms to be zero

$$\delta_Y + \delta_Y' = 0$$

or

$$(\mu_Y - 1)A + (\mu_Y' - 1)A' = 0$$

or

$$A' = -\frac{(\mu_Y - 1)}{(\mu_Y' - 1)}A \qquad ...(1)$$

The negative sign shows that two prisms must be placed with their angles oppositely. The situation is shown in figure. This combination will produce some dispersion. The dispersion produced by first prism is $(\delta_V - \delta_R)$ and by second prism is $(\delta'_V - \delta'_R)$. The total dispersion

$$D = (\delta_V - \delta_R) + (\delta'_V - \delta'_R)$$

or

$$D = (\mu_V - \mu_R)A + (\mu'_V - \mu'_R)A' \qquad ...(2)$$

On substituting the value of A', we get

$$D = (\mu_V - \mu_R)A + (\mu'_V - \mu'_R)\left\{\frac{-(\mu_Y - 1)A}{(\mu'_Y - 1)}\right\}$$

$$= (\mu_V - \mu_R)A - \left(\frac{\mu'_V - \mu'_R}{\mu_Y - 1}\right)(\mu_Y - 1)A$$

or

$$D = (\mu_Y - 1)A(\omega - \omega') \qquad ...(3)$$

(ii) Deviation without dispersion :

Total dispersion produced by two prisms is zero, if $D = 0$.

or $(\mu_V - \mu_R)A + (\mu'_V - \mu'_R)A' = 0$

$$\therefore \quad A' = \frac{-(\mu_V - \mu_R)A}{(\mu'_V - \mu'_R)} \qquad \dots(4)$$

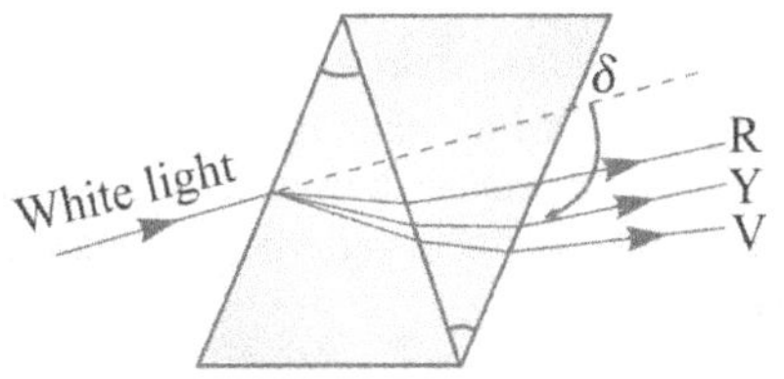

The negative sign shows that two prisms must be placed with their angles oppositely. The situation is shown in figure. The deviation produced by the combination for mean colour is

$$\delta = \delta_Y + \delta'_Y$$

or $$\delta = (\mu_Y - 1)A + (\mu_Y' - 1)A' \qquad \dots(5)$$

On substituting the value of $A,'$ we get

$$\delta = (\mu_Y - 1)A + (\mu'_Y - 1)\left\{-\left(\frac{\mu_V - \mu_R}{\mu'_V - \mu'_R}\right)A\right\}$$

$$= \left[(\mu_Y - 1) - \left(\frac{\mu'_Y - 1}{\mu'_V - \mu'_R}\right)(\mu_V - \mu_R)\right]A$$

$$= (\mu_Y - 1)A\left[1 - \left(\frac{\mu'_Y - 1}{\mu'_V - \mu'_R}\right)\left(\frac{\mu_V - \mu_R}{\mu_Y - 1}\right)\right]$$

or $$\delta = (\mu_Y - 1)A\left[1 - \frac{\omega}{\omega'}\right] \qquad \dots(6)$$

Fig. 2.70. Deviation without dispersion

Note :

Two identical prisms of same material placed in contact will give light without deviation and dispersion.

Ex. 33 A thin prism P_1 with angle 4° and made from glass of refractive index 1.54 is combined with another prism P_2 made from glass of refractive index 1.72 to produce dispersion without deviation. What is the angle of prism P_2?

Sol. Given $A_1 = 4°$, $\mu_1 = 1.54$, $\mu_2 = 1.72$

The angle of second prism for no total deviation

$$A_2 = -\frac{(\mu_1 - 1)A_1}{(\mu_2 - 1)} = -\frac{(1.54 - 1)}{(1.72 - 1)} \times 4°$$

$$= -3°.$$

Hence, the angle of the second prism should be 3° and it should be placed opposite to the first.

Ex. 34 The refractive indexes of the crown glass for blue and red lights are 1.51 and 1.49 respectively and those of the flint glass are 1.77 and 1.73 respectively. An isosceles prism of angle 6° is made of crown glass. A beam of white light is incident at a small angle on this prism. The other flint glass isosceles prism is combined with the crown glass prism such that there is no deviation of the incident

light. Determine the angle of the flint glass prism. Calculate the net dispersion of the combined system.

Sol.

The refractive index for crown glass for mean colour (yellow) is given by

$$\mu_Y = \frac{1.51 + 1.49}{2} = 1.50.$$

Similarly, the refractive index for flint glass for mean colour is given by

$$\mu_Y' = \frac{1.77 + 1.73}{2} = 1.75$$

For no deviation by the system of two prisms

$$A' = -\frac{(\mu_Y - 1)A}{(\mu_Y' - 1)}$$

$$= -\frac{(1.50 - 1)}{(1.75 - 1)} \times 6°$$

$$= -4°$$

Net dispersion

$$D = (\mu_V - \mu_R)A + (\mu'_V - \mu'_R)A'$$
$$= (1.51 - 1.49)\times 6 - (1.77 - 1.73)\times 4$$
$$= -0.04° \qquad \text{Ans.}$$

Ex. 35 Three right-angled prisms of refractive indices μ_1, μ_2 and μ_3 are fitted together as shown in the *fig.* 2.71. If a ray passes through the prisms without suffering any deviation, then find the relation between the three refractive indices of the prism.

Sol.

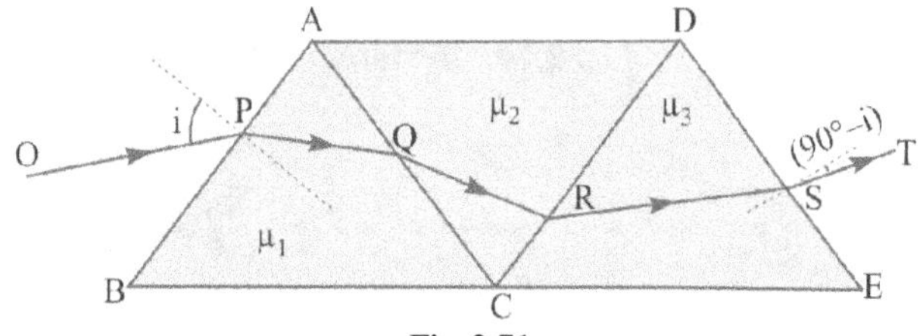

Fig. 2.71

Suppose $OPQRST$ be the ray through the prisms. According to the given condition the incident ray OP should be parallel to emerging ray ST. Let the angles of incidence and of refraction at P be i and r_1. The angle of incidence at Q is $(90°-r_1)$. Let the angle of refraction at Q is r_2. The angle of incidence at R becomes $(90-r_2)$. Let angle of refraction at R be r_3. The angle of incidence at S is $(90°-r_3)$. Since the ray ST is parallel to OP, so the angle of emergence at S will be $(90°-i)$. Thus :

For refraction at P :
$$\sin i = \mu_1 \sin r_1$$
or
$$\sin^2 i = \mu_1^2 \sin^2 r_1 \qquad ...(i)$$

For refraction at Q :
$$\mu_2 \sin r_2 = \mu_1 \sin(90° - r_1)$$
$$\therefore \qquad \mu_2^2 \sin^2 r_2 = \mu_1^2 \cos^2 r_1 \qquad ...(ii)$$

For refraction at R :
$$\mu_2 \sin(90° - r_2) = \mu_3 \sin r_3$$
or
$$\mu_2^2 \cos^2 r_2 = \mu_3^2 \sin^2 r_3 \qquad ...(iii)$$

For refraction at S:
$$\sin(90° - i) = \mu_3 \sin(90° - r_3)$$
or
$$\cos^2 i = \mu_3^2 \cos^2 r_3. \qquad ...(iv)$$

On adding equations (i), (ii), (iii) and (iv), we get
$$1 + \mu_2^2 = \mu_1^2 + \mu_3^2. \qquad \text{Ans.}$$

Ex. 36 A prism of refractive index μ_1 and another prism of refractive index μ_2 are stuck together without a gap as shown in *fig.* 2.72.

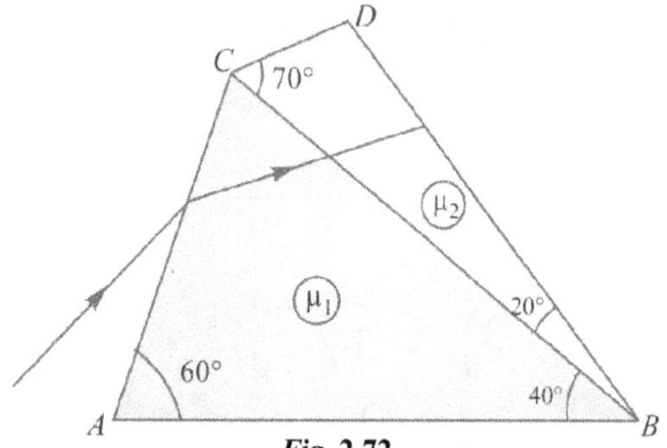

Fig. 2.72

The angles of the prisms are as shown, μ_1 and μ_2 depend on λ, the wavelength of light according to $\mu_1 = 1.20 + \dfrac{10.8 \times 10^4}{\lambda^2}$ and

$\mu_2 = 1.45 + \dfrac{1.80 \times 10^4}{\lambda^2}$, where λ is in nm.

(a)   Calculate the wavelength λ_0, for which rays incident at any angle on the interface BC pass through without bending at that interface.

(b)   For light of wavelength λ_0, find the angle of incidence i on the face AC such that the deviation produced by the combination of prisms is minimum.

Sol.

(a)   For the ray passes undeviated through CB, $\mu_1 = \mu_2$. Thus for $\lambda = \lambda_0$,

$$1.20 + \frac{10.8 \times 10^4}{\lambda_0^2} = 1.45 + \frac{1.80 \times 10^4}{\lambda_0^2}$$

or
$$\frac{9 \times 10^4}{\lambda_0^2} = 0.25$$

or
$$\lambda_0 = 600 \text{ nm.} \qquad \text{Ans.}$$

(b)   As both the prisms are of same refractive indices, so they behave like a single prism of prism angle 60° (on extending the refracting surfaces). Thus for λ_0

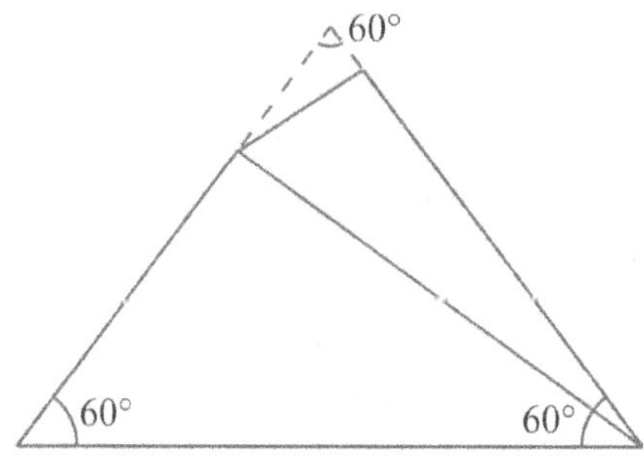

Fig. 2.73

$$\mu = 1.20 + \frac{10.8 \times 10^4}{(600)^2} = 1.50$$

We have
$$\mu = \frac{\sin i}{\sin A/2}$$

$$1.50 = \frac{\sin i}{\sin\left(\dfrac{60°}{2}\right)}$$

or
$$\sin i = 1.50 \times \frac{1}{2} = \frac{3}{4}a$$

$$\therefore \qquad i = 48.6°. \qquad \text{Ans.}$$

2.12 LINE, BAND AND CONTINUOUS SPECTRUM

The line spectrum are known to arise from the single free atoms in a heated gas. Molecules of two or more atoms give rise to spectrum lines grouped together into what are called bands. Continuous spectra are usually produced by the matter in liquid or solid state.

The sun's spectrum

The solar spectrum, consisting of a bright coloured continuous spectrum interspersed by thousands of dark lines discovered by Fraunhofer in 1817.

2.13 RAINBOW

Rainbow is produced due to the dispersion of light by small raindrops floating in the air after rain. The rainbow is seen when the sun is behind the observer.

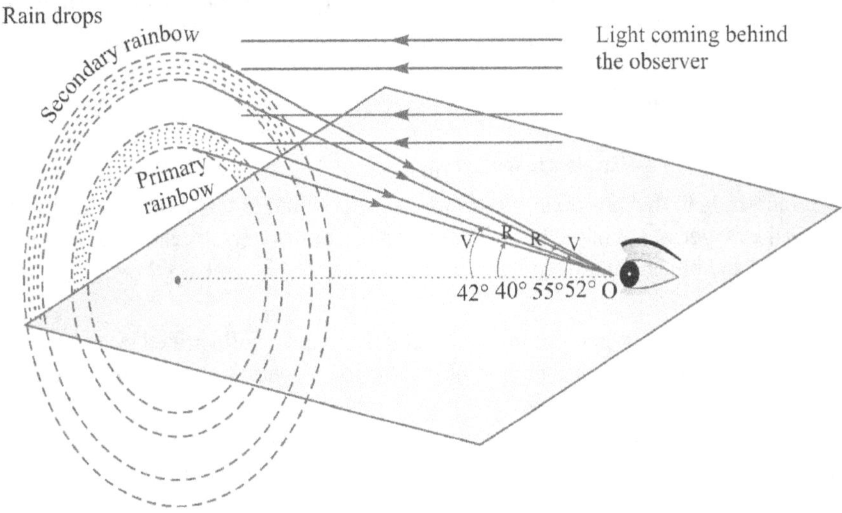

Fig. **2.74** Primary and secondary rainbow as seen by the observer at O.

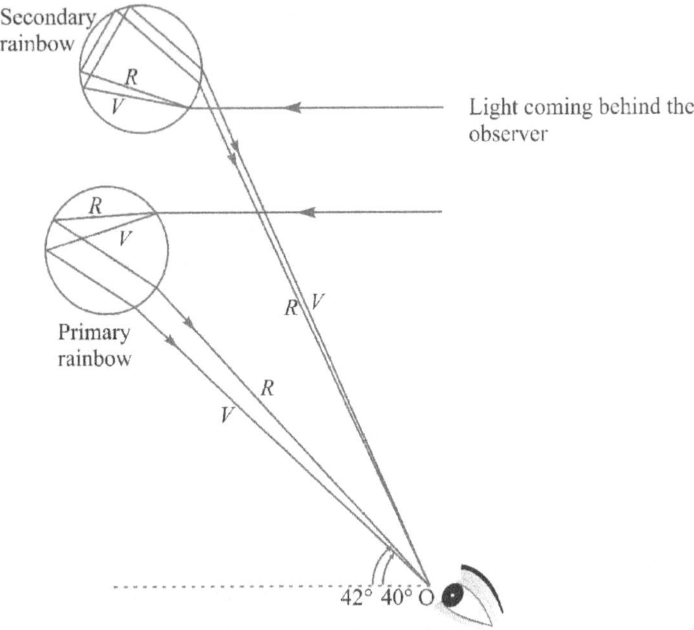

Fig. **2.75** Dispersion of light through each drop.

(i)   **Primary rainbow :** The primary rainbow is formed when sun light suffers one reflection and two refractions before emerging from water droplets. In this case the violet colour is on the lower side and red colour is on upper side of the rainbow. It has been observed that violet colour makes an angle 40° and red makes an angle 42° at eye with the axis of rainbow (see figure).

(ii) **Secondary rainbow :** Sometimes secondary rainbow which is fainter than primary rainbow is also observed. This is formed by the sunrays which suffer two internal reflections and two refractions from the water droples and giving rise violet colour on upperside and red on lower side of the rainbow (see figure).

2.14 SCATTERING AND BLUE SKY

When light is incident on small particles, it is absorbed by them. This absorbed light is then sends into all directions. This phenomenon is called **scattering**. The blue of the sky and the red of the sunset are due to scattering.

Experiments show that the scattering is inversely proportional to the fourth power of the wavelength. Thus

$$\text{scattering} \propto \frac{1}{\lambda^4}$$

This is known as **Rayleigh scattering formula.**

According to this law the light of short waves (violet) is scattered about ten times as the longer waves of red light. Thus when sun light enters the earth's atmosphere, violet and blue light are scattered the most, followed by green, yellow, orange and red.

At noon on a clear day when the sun is directly overhead, as illustrated by an observer in *fig.* 2.76, the whole sky appears light **blue**. This is the composite colour of the mixture of colours scattered most effectively by the air molecules.

It can be demonstrated that light blue can be obtained by mixing of violet, blue, green and yellow.

The red sunset

At sunrise or sunset, the sun's rays have to pass through a larger distance in the atmosphere (fig.). Most of the blue and other shorter wavelengths are removed by scattering. The least scattered light reaching our eye, therefore the sun looks reddish. This explains the reddish appearance of the sun near the horizion.

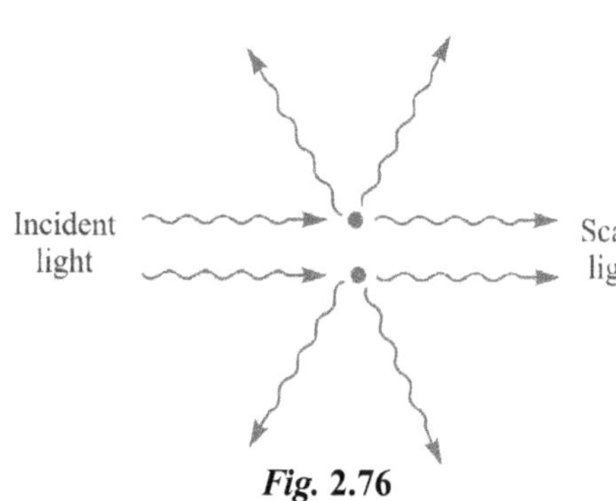

Fig. **2.76**

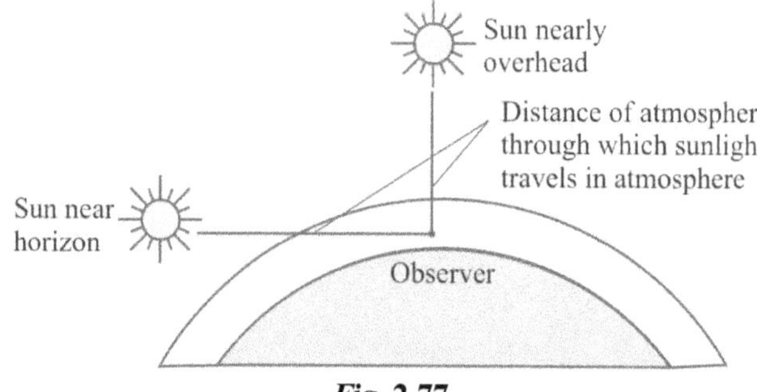

Fig. **2.77**

Any colour can be made from red, green and blue light

Any colour may be made by adding together red, green and blue light in the correct amount. If a mixture of red and green light hits eye, your red-sensitive and green-sensitive cones send impulses to your brain. Your brain interprets this as yellow light.

A colour television works in this way. The picture on the screen is made up of dots of light. The colours are made up of red, green and blue dots, in different combinations and of different intensities. If you look closely at a television screen, you can see these dots.

Fig. 2.78. Mixed red, green and blue light produces white light. which coloured lights produce cyan (turquoise), magenta and yellow ?

Red, green and blue are called the primary colours of light. You can make any colour from red, green and blue light. But you cannot make red, green or blue light from any other coloured light.

Colours which can be made by adding any two of the primary colours of light are called secondary colours of light. Figure shows how the three secondary colours-yellow, magenta and cyan- are made.

Objects look different in different colours of light

If you shine white light onto a red book, the book looks red because it reflects only the red light into your eyes. If you look at the book in red light, it still looks red, because it reflects the red light. But if you look at the book in green light it looks black. There is no red light for it to reflect, so it does not reflect any light at all, and it looks black.

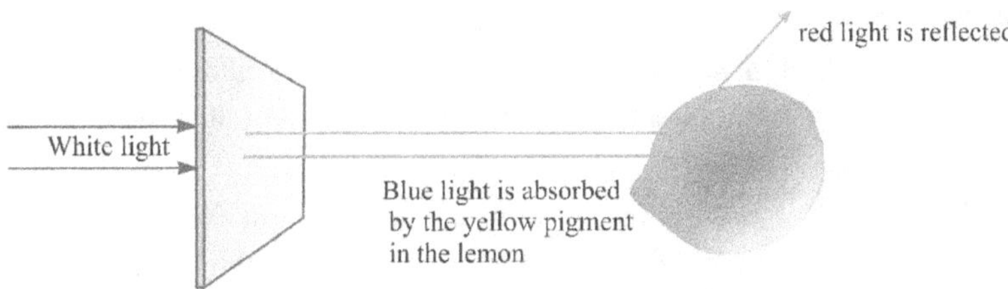

Fig. 2.79

What happens if you shine yellow light onto the red book? Yellow light is a mixture of red and green light. The book will absorb the green part of the yellow light, and reflect the red part. So it still reflects red light into your eye, and still looks red.

Complementary colours

A pair of colour on mixing give white colour are called complementary colours. Ex.

Green + magenta = White.

So, green and magenta colours are complementary to each other.

Blue + Yellow = White

So, blue and yellow colours are complementary to each other.

Red + Cyan (greenish-blue) = White

So, red and cyan colours are complementary to each other.

<u>Ex. 37</u> **The beams of light, one of red colour and other green fall on the same spot on a white screen. The colour on the screen will appear to be**

(a) magenta (b) blue (c) cyan (d) yellow.

Sol. Red and green colour combine to give yellow colour.

So, the correct answer is (d).

2.15 COLOUR OF AN OBJECT

We see objects of many different colours around us. The science of colours is a very interesting. We discuss some basic facts about the colours in this section.

Colour of opaque objects

The colour of a non-luminous, opaque object depends upon the colour of the light reflected by it. The colour of the reflected light depends upon the colour of the light falling on the object.

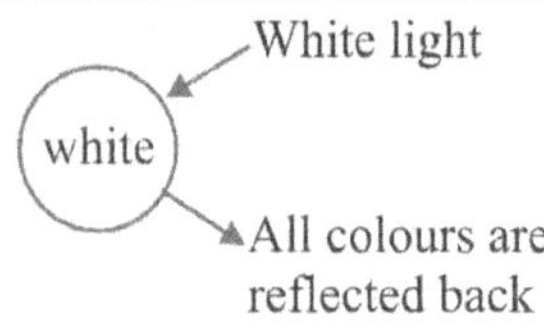

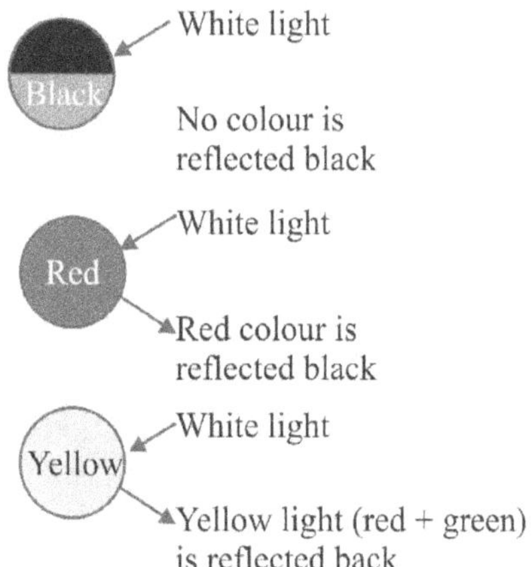

Fig.2.80. Colour of opaque objects

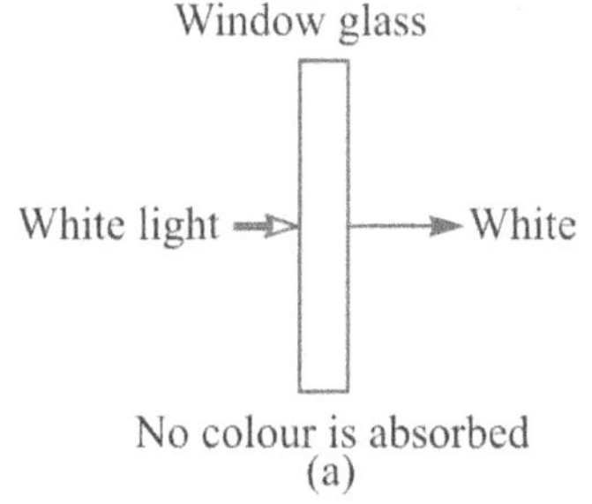

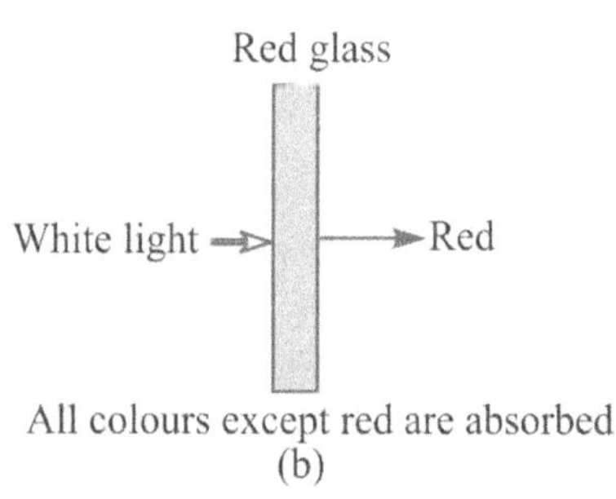

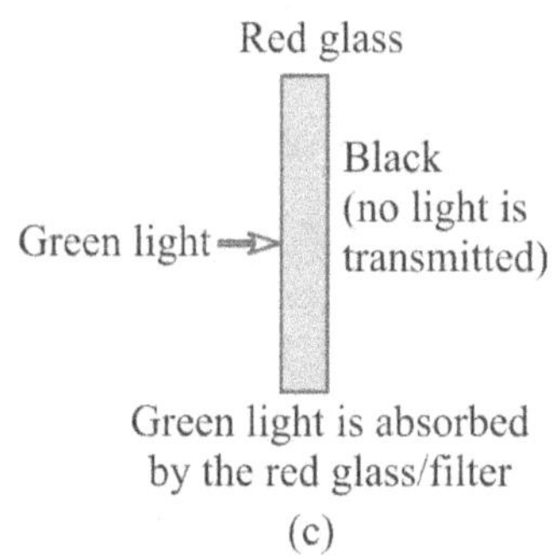

Fig. 2.81

Two cases are discussed below:

When white light falls on the object. When white light falls on a non-luminous opaque object, the following situations become possible:

(i) **When all the colours of white light are reflected back by the object.** In such a situation, the opaque object appears white because all the colours recompose to give white light.

(ii) **When all the colours of the white light are absorbed by the object.** In such a situation, the opaque object appears black because no colour of the white light is reflected back by the object.

(iii) **When all the colours except one are absorbed by the object.** In such a situation, the object appears to have the colour of reflected light. For example, a red rose during day light appears red because it reflects red light, and absorbs all other colours present in the white light.

When coloured light falls on the object. The colour of a non-luminous opaque object also depends upon the colour of the light falling on it. Following situations may become possible:

(i) **When white coloured object is seen in coloured light.** When coloured light falls on a white object it does not absorb any light and the light falling on it is reflected back. Therefore, the white object seen in a coloured light appears to have the colour of the coloured light. For example, a white flower appears red in red light, and blue in blue light because it reflects the light falling on it.

(ii) **When a coloured object is seen in a coloured light.** When coloured light falls on a coloured object it is absorbed by it and the object appears black because no light is reflected from the body. For example, a red rose when seen in blue (or green) light appears black because blue (or green) light is absorbed by the rose, and there is no other colour to reflect back.

A magenta-coloured object when seen in yellow light appears red. This is because yellow light consists of red and green lights. The magenta-coloured object absorbs green colour to give white colour, and reflects the red colour.

Colour of transparent objects

The objects which allow light to pass through them are called transparent objects. The colour of any transparent object is the colour of the light transmitted by it. **For example.**

(i) Ordinary window glass appears white because it allow all the colours in the white light to pass through it (Figure).

(ii) A red filter (or red glass) appears red in white light. This is because it absorbs all colours except red, and transmits only red light.

(iii) A red filter (or red glass) when seen in green light appears black because it absorbs green light (Figure).

(iv) A red flower when seen through a green filter light appears black because the red light from the rose is absorbed by the green filter (Figure)

Ex. 38 A red rose appears black when seen in dark at night.

Sol.   At night and in dark there is no light to fall on the rose. As a result, no light is reflected by the rose. So, a red rose appears black in dark at night.

Review of Formulae & Important Points

1. Snell's law

$$_1\mu_2 = \mu = \frac{\sin i}{\sin r}$$

Also

$$_1\mu_2 = \frac{v_1}{v_2},$$

and

$$_1\mu_2 = \frac{1}{_1\mu_2}$$

2.

$$\chi_{med} = \frac{\chi_{air}}{\mu}.$$

3. Image formation by refraction

(i) When object is in denser medium and observer in rarer medium, then

$$\mu = \frac{RD}{AD}.$$

Apparent shift $S = RD\left(1 - \frac{1}{\mu}\right).$

(ii) When object is in rarer medium and observer in denser medium, then

$$\mu = \frac{AH}{RH}.$$

4. Total internal reflection (TIR)

(i) TIR occurs when light ray passes from denser to rarer medium.

(ii) Angle of incidence in denser medium must be greater than critical angle. Critical angle is given by

$$\sin C = \frac{1}{\mu}.$$

Critical angle for water to air is 49° and for glass to air is 42°.

(iii) A fish inside water at a depth h can see outside world in horizontal circle of radius r, where

$$r = \frac{h}{\sqrt{\mu^2 - 1}}.$$

5. Deviation produced by prism

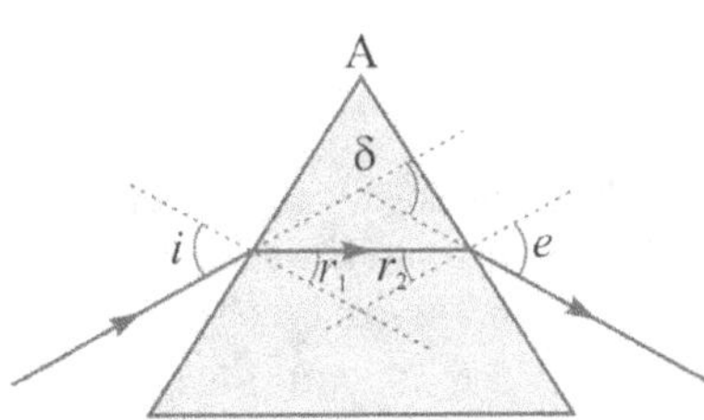

For the prism, angle of refraction A, we have

$$r_1 + r_2 = A$$

and

$$i + e = A + \delta$$

At minimum deviation,

$$\delta = \delta_m, \; r_1 = r_2, \; i = e.$$

We have

$$\mu = \frac{\sin\left(\dfrac{A + \delta_m}{2}\right)}{\sin \dfrac{A}{2}}.$$

For small angled prism

$$\delta = (\mu - 1)A$$

(i) Condition of minimum deviation $i = e$ and $r_1 = r_2$.

(ii) Condition of maximum deviation; either of i or e should be 90°.

(ii) Condition of no emergence, $A > 2C$

6. Dispersion produced by prism

The refractive index of material of a prism depends on wavelength of light. It approximately is given by Cauchy's equation as :

$$\mu = A + \frac{B}{\lambda^2}.$$

Here A and B are constants.

Dispersive power, $\omega = \dfrac{\text{angular dispersion}}{\text{mean deviation}} = \dfrac{\delta_v - \delta_R}{\delta_y}$

or

$$\omega = \frac{\mu_v - \mu_R}{\mu_y - 1}$$

7. Combination of prisms

(i) **Dispersion without deviation :**

For two small angled prisms, we have

$$A' = -\frac{(\mu_y - 1)}{(\mu'_y - 1)}A$$

The total dispersion

$$D = (\mu_v - \mu_R)A + (\mu'_v - \mu'_R)A'$$

(ii) **Deviation with dispersion :**

For two small angled prisms, we have

$$A' = -\frac{(\mu_v - \mu_R)}{(\mu'_v - \mu'_R)}A$$

The total deviation

$$\delta = (\mu_y - 1)A + (\mu'_y - 1)A'.$$

Rainbow

Rainbow is produced due to the dispersion of light by small raindrops floating in air after rain. In primary rainbow there are one reflection and two refractions before emerging from water droplets. In secondary rainbow, there are two reflections and two refractions from the water droplets.

Blue of the sky

It is due to the scattering of light by the small particles present in the atmosphere. The scattering of the blue colour will be the greatest.

★★★

Optics **MCQ Type 1** *Exercise 2.1*

LEVEL - 1

Only one option correct

1. Figure shows rays of monochromatic light passing through three materials I, II, III. The materials according to their indexes of refraction, greatest first;

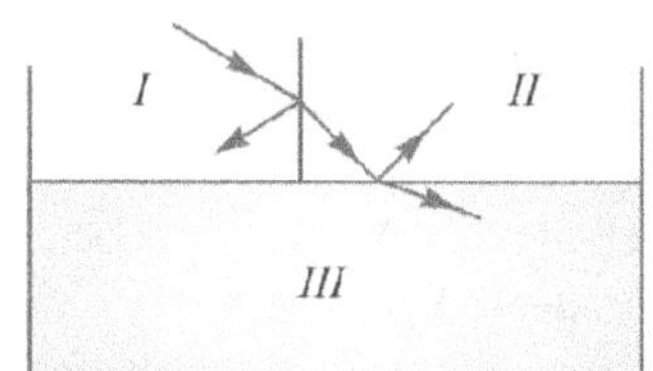

  (a) I, II, III   (b) II, I, III
  (c) III, II, I   (d) none of these

2. A glass plate of thickness 1 cm and of refractive index 1.50 is held horizontal and its lower face is 4 cm above a printed page. The distance of the page from top face of the plate as seen from above is
  (a) 5 cm   (d) 3.33 cm
  (c) 4.67 cm   (d) 2.50 cm

3. Each part of figure shows light that refracts through an interface between two materials. The incident ray consists of red and blue light. The approximate index of refraction for visible light is indicated for each material. Which of the three parts show physically possible refraction?

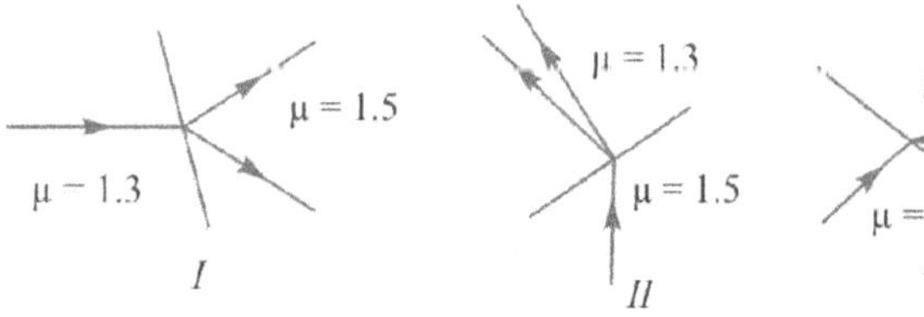

  (a) I   (b) II
  (c) III   (d) none

4. When light travels from one medium to the other of which the refractive index is different, then which of the following will change
  (a) frequency, wavelength and velocity
  (b) frequency and wavelength
  (c) frequency and velocity
  (d) wavelength and velocity

5. How much water should be filled in a container 21 cm in height, so that it appears half filled when viewed from the top of the container (given that $_a\mu_\omega = 4/3$)

  (a) 8.0 cm   (b) 10.5 cm
  (c) 12.0 cm   (d) None of the above

6. A vessel of depth 2d cm is half filled with a liquid of refractive index μ_1 and the upper half with a liquid of refractive index μ_2. The apparent depth of the vessel seen perpendicularly is

  (a) $d\left(\dfrac{\mu_1\mu_2}{\mu_1+\mu_2}\right)$ (b) $d\left(\dfrac{1}{\mu_1}+\dfrac{1}{\mu_2}\right)$

  (c) $2d\left(\dfrac{1}{\mu_1}+\dfrac{1}{\mu_2}\right)$ (d) $2d\left(\dfrac{1}{\mu_1\mu_2}\right)$

7. A beam of light is converging towards a point I on a screen. A plane glass plate whose thickness in the direction of the beam $= t$, refractive index $= \mu$, is introduced in the path of the beam, The convergence point is shifted by

  (a) $t\left(1-\dfrac{1}{\mu}\right)$ away   (b) $t\left(1+\dfrac{1}{\mu}\right)$ away

  (c) $t\left(1-\dfrac{1}{\mu}\right)$ nearer   (d) $t\left(1+\dfrac{1}{\mu}\right)$ nearer

8. Light takes 8 min 20 sec to reach from sun on the earth. If the whole atmosphere is filled with water, the light will take the time $\left(_a\mu_w = 4/3\right)$
  (a) 8 min 20 sec.   (b) 8 min
  (c) 6 min 11 sec   (d) 11 min 6 sec

9. If $_i\mu_j$ represents refractive index when a light ray goes from medium i to medium j, then the product $_2\mu_1 \times {}_3\mu_2 \times {}_4\mu_3$ is equal to
  (a) $_3\mu_1$ (b) $_3\mu_2$

  (c) $\dfrac{1}{_1\mu_4}$ (d) $_4\mu_2$

10. The wavelength of light diminishes μ times ($\mu = 1.33$ for water) in a medium. A diver from inside water looks at an object whose natural colour is green. He sees the object as
  (a) green   (b) blue
  (c) yellow   (d) red

Answer Key	1	(a)	2	(c)	3	(d)	4	(d)	5	(c)
Sol. from page 96	6	(b)	7	(a)	8	(d)	9	(c)	10	(a)

11. If ε_0 and μ_0 are respectively the electric permittivity and the magnetic permeability of free space, ε and μ the corresponding quantities in a medium, the refractive index of the medium is

(a) $\sqrt{\dfrac{\mu\varepsilon}{\mu_0\varepsilon_0}}$

(b) $\dfrac{\mu\varepsilon}{\mu_0\varepsilon_0}$

(c) $\sqrt{\dfrac{\mu_0\varepsilon_0}{\mu\varepsilon}}$

(d) $\sqrt{\dfrac{\mu\mu_0}{\varepsilon\,\varepsilon_0}}$

12. In the adjoining diagram, a wavefront AB, moving in air is incident on a plane glass surface XY. Its position CD after refraction through a glass slab is shown also along with the normals drawn at A and D. The refractive index of glass with respect to air ($\mu = 1$) will be equal to

(a) $\dfrac{\sin\theta}{\sin\theta'}$

(b) $\dfrac{\sin\theta}{\sin\phi'}$

(c) $\dfrac{\sin\phi'}{\sin\theta}$

(d) $\dfrac{AB}{CD}$

13. On a glass plate a light wave is incident at an angle of 60°. If the reflected and the refracted waves are mutually perpendicular, the refractive index of material is

(a) $\dfrac{\sqrt{3}}{2}$

(b) $\sqrt{3}$

(c) $\dfrac{3}{2}$

(d) $\dfrac{1}{\sqrt{3}}$

14. Electromagnetic radiation of frequency f, wavelength λ, travelling with velocity v in air, enters a glass slab of refractive index μ. The frequency, wavelength and velocity of light in the glass slab will be respectively.

(a) $\dfrac{f}{\mu},\dfrac{\lambda}{\mu},\dfrac{v}{\mu}$

(b) $f,\dfrac{\lambda}{\mu},\dfrac{v}{\mu}$

(c) $n,\lambda,\dfrac{v}{\mu}$

(d) $\dfrac{n}{\mu},\dfrac{\lambda}{\mu},v$

15. A ray of light passes through four transparent media with refractive indices μ_1, μ_2, μ_3, and μ_4 as shown in the figure. The surfaces of all media are parallel. If the emergent ray CD is parallel to the incident ray AB, we must have

(a) $\mu_1 = \mu_2$

(b) $\mu_2 = \mu_3$

(c) $\mu_3 = \mu_4$

(d) $\mu_4 = \mu_1$

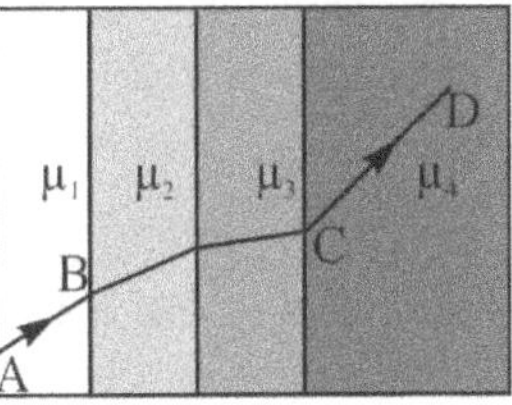

16. An object is immersed in a fluid. In order that the object becomes invisible, it should

(a) behave as a perfect reflector

(b) absorb all light falling on it

(c) have refractive index one

(d) have refractive index exactly matching with that of the surrounding fluid

17. A diver in a swimming pool wants to signal his distress to a person lying on the edge of the pool by flashing his water proof flash light

(a) he must direct the beam vertically upwards

(b) he has to direct the beam horizontally

(c) he has to direct the beam at an angle to the vertical which is slightly less than the critical angle of incidence for total internal reflection

(d) he has to direct the beam at an angle to the vertical which is slightly more than the critical angle of incidence for the total internal reflection

18. The reason for shining of air bubble in water is

(a) diffraction of light

(b) dispersion of light

(c) scattering of light

(d) total internal reflection of light

19. Air has refractive index 1.0003. The thickness of air column, which will have one more wavelength of yellow light (6000Å) than in the same thickness of vacuum is

(a) 2 mm

(b) 2 cm

(c) 2 m

(d) 2 km

20. Consider telecommunication through optical fibres. Which of the following statements is not true

(a) optical fibres may have homogeneous core with a suitable cladding

(b) optical fibres can be of graded refractive index

(c) optical fibres are subject to electromagnetic interference from outside

(d) optical fibres have extremely low transmission loss

21. White light is incident on the interface of glass and air as shown in the figure. If green light is just totally internally reflected then the emerging ray in air contains

(a) yellow, orange, red

(b) violet, indigo, blue

(c) all colours

(d) all colours except green

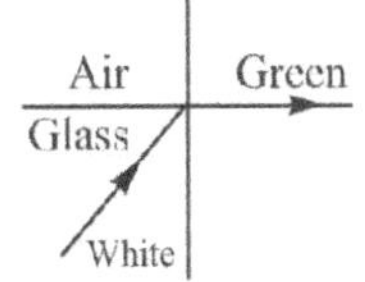

Answer Key	11	(a)	12	(b)	13	(b)	14	(b)	15	(d)	16	(d)
Sol. from page 96	17	(c)	18	(b)	19	(a)	20	(c)	21	(a)		

22. A spectrum is formed by a prism of dispersive power ω. If the angle of deviation is 'δ', then the angular dispersion is
(a) ω/δ
(b) δ/ω
(c) $1/\omega\,\delta$
(d) $\omega\,\delta$

23. A diverging beam of light from a point source S having divergence angle α, falls symmetrically on a glass slab as shown. The angles of incidence of the two extreme rays are equal. If the thickness of the glass slab is t and the refractive index μ, then the divergence angle of the emergent beam is

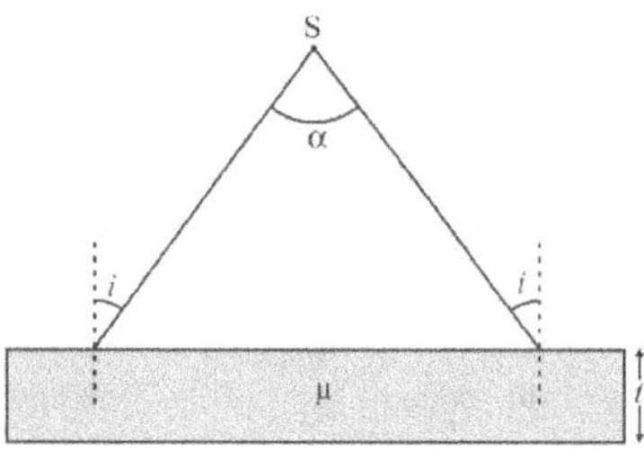

(a) zero
(b) α
(c) $\sin^{-1}(1/\mu)$
(d) $2\sin^{-1}(1/\mu)$

24. In the figure shown, the value of $\dfrac{\sin i}{\sin r}$ is :

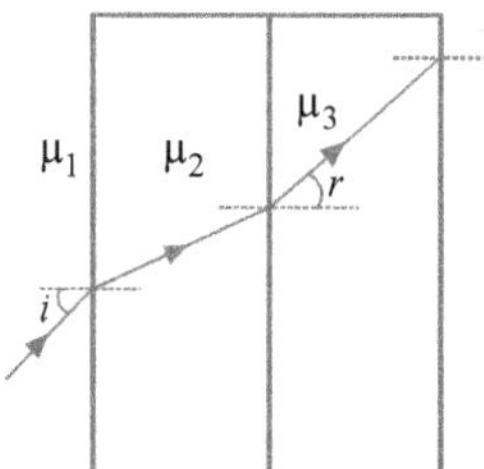

(a) $\dfrac{\mu_1}{\mu_2}$
(b) $\dfrac{\mu_2}{\mu_3}$
(c) $\dfrac{\mu_3}{\mu_1}$
(d) $\dfrac{\mu_1\mu_3}{\mu_2^{\,2}}$

25. Which of the following graphs shows appropriate variation of refractive index μ with wavelength λ

(a) 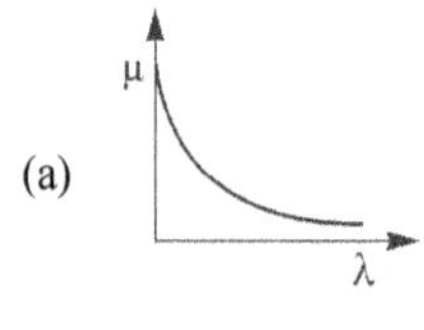
(b) 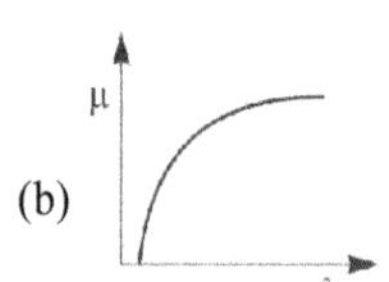
(c) 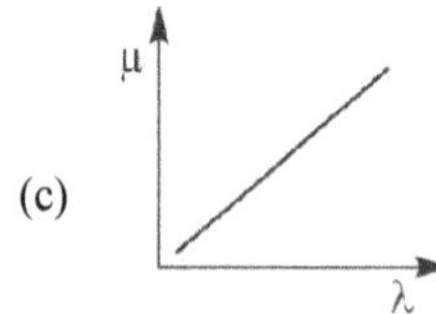
(d) 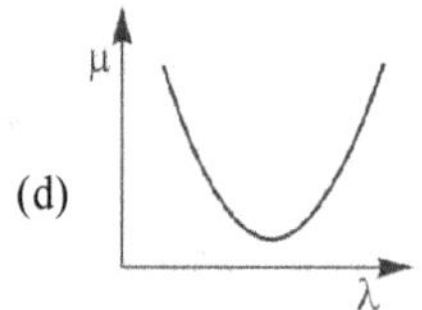

26. A thin prism P_1 with angle $4°$ and made from glass of refractive index 1.54 is combined with another thin prism P_2 made from glass of refractive index 1.72 to produce dispersion without deviation. The angle of prism P_2 is
(a) $2.6°$
(b) $3°$
(c) $4°$
(d) $5.33°$

27. The figures represent three cases of a ray passing through a prism of angle A. The case corresponding to minimum deviation is

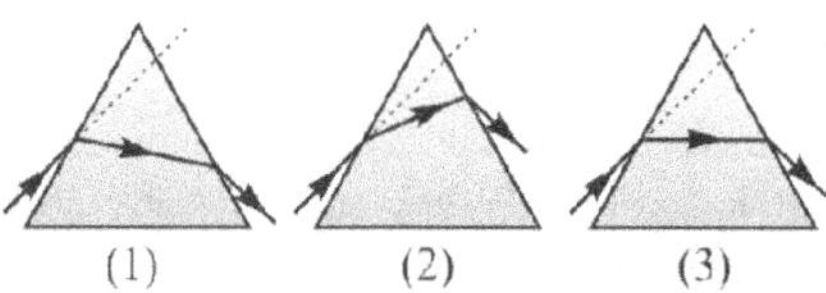

(a) 1
(b) 2
(c) 3
(d) none of these

28. Three glass prisms A, B and C of same refractive index are placed in contact with each other as shown in figure, with no air gap between the prisms. Monochromatic ray of light OP passes through the prism assembly and emerges as QR. The conditions of minimum deviation is satisfied in the prisms

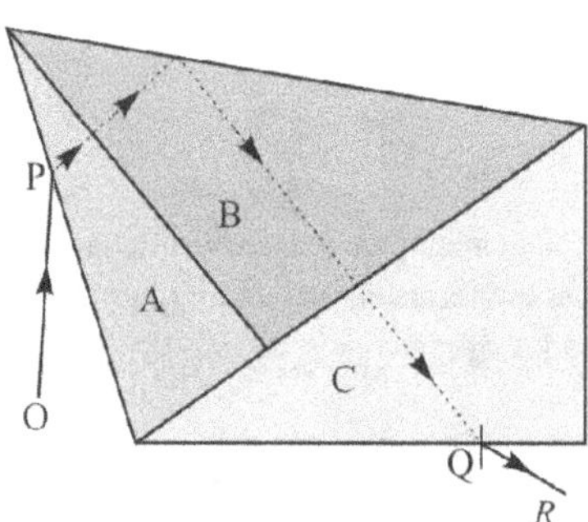

(a) A and C
(b) B and C
(c) A and B
(d) in all prisms A, B and C

29. Which of the following diagrams, shows correctly the dispersion of white light by a prism

(a) 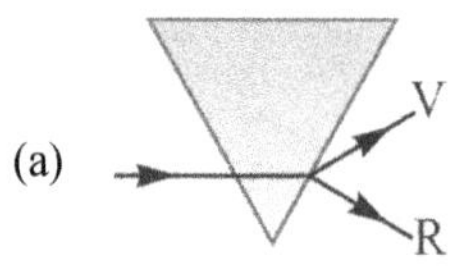
(b) 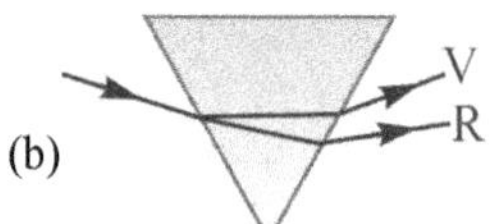
(c) 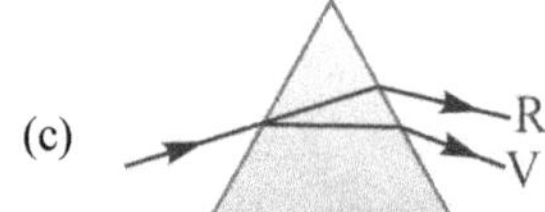
(d) 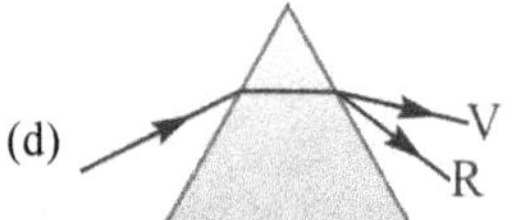

Answer Key	22	(d)	23	(b)	24	(c)	25	(a)
Sol. from page 96	26	(b)	27	(c)	28	(c)	29	(b)

30. A triangular prism of glass is shown in the figure. A ray incident normally to one face is totally reflected, if $\theta = 45°$, the index of refraction of glass is

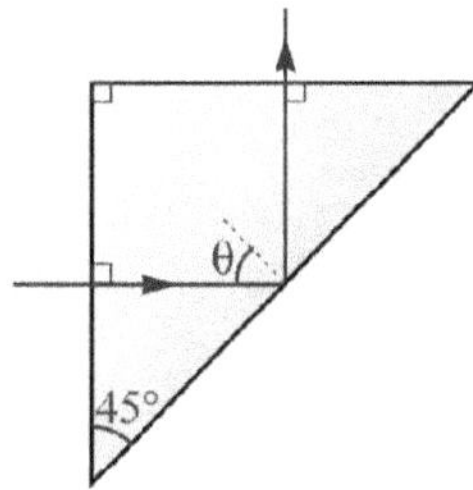

   (a) less than 1.41
   (b) equal to 1.41
   (c) greater than 1.41
   (d) none of the above

31. A given ray of light suffers minimum deviation in an equilateral prism P. Additional prisms Q and R of identical shape and material are now added to P as shown in the figure. The ray will suffer

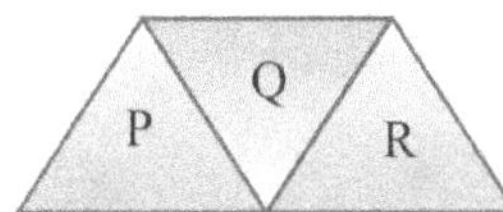

   (a) greater deviation
   (b) same deviation
   (c) no deviation
   (d) total internal reflection

32. A horizontal ray of light passes through a prism P of index 1.50 whose apex angle is $4°$ and then strikes a vertical mirror M as shown. For the ray after reflection to become horizontal, the mirror must be rotated through an angle of :

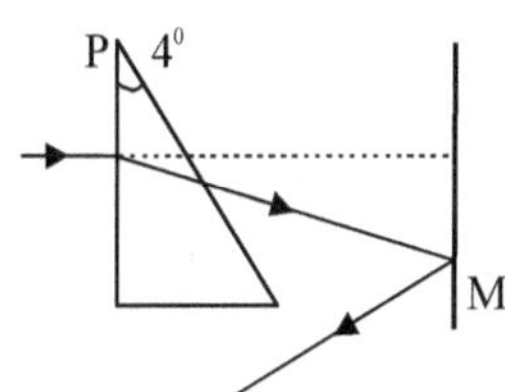

   (a) $6°$
   (b) $4°$
   (c) $1°$
   (d) $18°$

33. The refractive index of a certain glass is 1.5 for light whose wavelength in vacuum is 6000Å. The wavelength of this light when it passes through glass is

   (a) 4000 Å
   (b) 6000 Å
   (c) 9000 Å
   (d) 15000 Å

34. The optical path of a monochromatic light is same if it goes through 4.0 cm of glass or 4.5 cm of water. If the refractive index of glass is 1.53, the refractive index of the water is

   (a) 1.30
   (b) 1.36
   (c) 1.42
   (d) 1.46

35. If the critical angle for total internal reflection from a medium to vacuum is $30°$, the velocity of light in the medium is

   (a) 3×10^8 m/s
   (b) 1.5×10^8 m/s
   (c) 6×10^8 m/s
   (d) $\sqrt{3} \times 10^8$ m/s

36. The ratio of angle of minimum deviation of a prism in air and when dipped in water will be $\left(_a\mu_g = 3/2 \text{ and } _a\mu_w = 4/3\right)$

   (a) 8
   (b) 2
   (c) 3/4
   (d) 4

37. The angle of minimum deviation measured with a prism is $30°$ and the angle of prism is $60°$. The refractive index of prism material is

   (a) $\sqrt{2}$
   (b) 2
   (c) 3/2
   (d) 4/3

38. If the refractive indices of a prism for red, yellow and violet colours be 1.61, 1.63 and 1.65 respectively, then the dispersive power of the prism will be

   (a) $\dfrac{1.65 - 1.62}{1.61 - 1}$
   (b) $\dfrac{1.62 - 1.61}{1.65 - 1}$
   (c) $\dfrac{1.65 - 1.61}{1.63 - 1}$
   (d) $\dfrac{1.65 - 1.63}{1.61 - 1}$

39. Minimum deviation is observed with a prism having angle of prism A, angle of deviation δ, angle of incidence i and angle of emergence e. We then have generally

   (a) $i > e$
   (b) $i < e$
   (c) $i = e$
   (d) $i = e = \delta$

40. A prism of refractive index μ and angle A is placed in the minimum deviation position. If the angle of minimum deviation is A, then the value of A in terms of μ is

   (a) $\sin^{-1}\left(\dfrac{\mu}{2}\right)$
   (b) $\sin^{-1}\sqrt{\dfrac{\mu - 1}{2}}$
   (c) $2\cos^{-1}\left(\dfrac{\mu}{2}\right)$
   (d) $\cos^{-1}\left(\dfrac{\mu}{2}\right)$

41. Which source is associated with a line emission spectrum

   (a) electric fire
   (b) neon street sign
   (c) red traffic light
   (d) sun

42. Band spectrum is obtained when the source emitting light is in the form of

   (a) atoms
   (b) molecules
   (c) plasma
   (d) none of the above

43. Fraunhofer spectrum is a

   (a) line absorption spectrum
   (b) band absorption spectrum
   (c) line emission spectrum
   (d) bane emission spectrum

Answer Key	**30**	(c)	**31**	(b)	**32**	(c)	**33**	(a)	**34**	(b)	**35**	(b)	**36**	(d)
Sol. from page 96	**37**	(a)	**38**	(c)	**39**	(c)	**40**	(c)	**41**	(b)	**42**	(b)	**43**	(a)

44. Colour of the sky is blue due to
   (a) scattering of light   (b) total internal reflection
   (c) total emission   (d) none of the above

45. In the formation of a rainbow light from the sun on water droplets undergoes
   (a) dispersion only
   (b) only total internal reflection
   (c) dispersion and total internal reflection
   (d) none of these

46. If the refractive index of the material of a prism is cot $(A/2)$ and vertex angle of the prism is A, what is the angle of minimum deviation?
   (a) $\pi - 2A$ (b) $\pi - A$
   (c) $(\pi/2) - 2A$ (d) $(\pi/2) - A$

Answer Key	44	(a)	45	(c)	46	(a)		
Sol. from page 96								

LEVEL -2

1. A ray of light travelling in water in incident on its surface open to air. The angle of incidence is θ, which is less than the critical angle. Then there will be
   (a) only a reflected ray and no refracted ray
   (b) only a refracted ray and no reflected ray
   (c) a reflected ray and a refracted ray and the angle between them would be less than $180° - 2\theta$
   (d) a reflected ray and a refracted ray and the angle between them would be greater than $180° - 2\theta$.

2. Material A has critical angle i_A, and material B has critical angle i_B $(i_B > i_A)$, then which of the following is true
   (i) light can be totally internally reflected when it passes from B to A
   (ii) light can be totally internally reflected when it passes from A to B
   (iii) critical angle for total internal reflection is $i_B - i_A$
   (iv) critical angle between A and B is $\sin^{-1}\left(\dfrac{\sin i_A}{\sin i_B}\right)$

   (a) (i) and (iii)   (b) (i) and (iv)
   (c) (ii) and (iii)   (d) (ii) and (iv)

3. If light travels a distance x in t_1 sec in air and $10x$ distance in t_2 sec in a medium, the critical angle of the medium will be
   (a) $\tan^{-1}\left(\dfrac{t_1}{t_2}\right)$ (b) $\sin^{-1}\left(\dfrac{t_1}{t_2}\right)$
   (c) $\sin^{-1}\left(\dfrac{10t_1}{t_2}\right)$ (d) $\tan^{-1}\left(\dfrac{10t_1}{t_2}\right)$

4. A prism ABC of angle $30°$ has its face AC silvered. A ray of light incident at an angle of $45°$ at the face AB retraces its path after refraction at face AB and reflection at face AC. The refractive index of the material of the prism is
   (a) 1.5
   (b) $\dfrac{3}{\sqrt{2}}$
   (c) $\sqrt{2}$
   (d) $\dfrac{4}{3}$

5. The apparent depth of water in cylindrical water tank of diameter $2R$ cm is reducing at the rate of x cm/minute when water is being drained out at a constant rate. The amount of water drained in c.c. per minute is (μ_1 = refractive index of air, μ_2 = refractive index of water
   (a) $x\,\pi R^2\,\mu_1/\mu_2$ (b) $x\,\pi R^2\,\mu_2/\mu_1$
   (c) $2\,\pi R\,\mu_1/\mu_2$ (d) $\pi R^2\,x$

6. A black spot is present just inside one of the face of an equilateral prism. A man places his eye directly at the opposite corner. He sees two images of the spot at an angular separation of $60°$. Then the minimum value of refractive index of the prism is :
   (a) $\mu = \dfrac{\sqrt{3}}{2}$
   (b) $\mu = 2$
   (c) $\mu = \dfrac{3}{2}$
   (d) $\mu = \dfrac{2}{\sqrt{3}}$

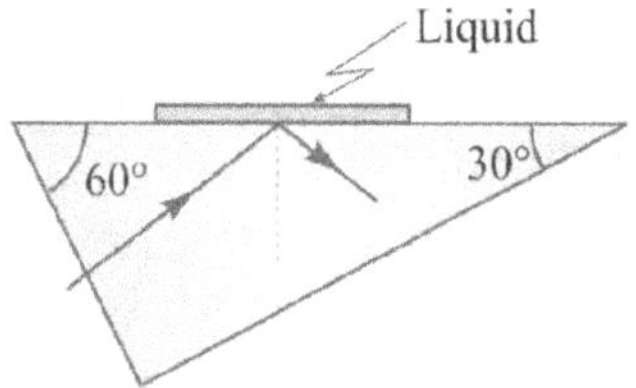

7. On a hypotenuse of a right prism $(30° - 60° - 90°)$ of refractive index 1.50, a drop of liquid is placed as shown in figure. Light is allowed to fall normally on the short face of the prism. In order that the ray of light may get totally reflected, the maximum value of refractive index is :
   (a) 1.30   (b) 1.47
   (c) 1.20   (d) 1.25

8. Light takes 4.5×10^{-10}s to travel 10 cm in a transparent medium. The optical path length covered by it :
   (a) 11.5 cm   (b) 13.5 cm
   (c) 15.5 cm   (d) 17.5 cm

Answer Key	1	(c)	2	(d)	3	(c)	4	(c)
Sol. from page 97	5	(b)	6	(d)	7	(a)	8	(b)

9. If $\hat{i}$ denotes a unit vector along incident light ray, $\hat{r}$ a unit vector along refracted ray into a medium of refractive index μ and $\hat{n}$ unit vector normal to boundary of medium directed towards incident medium, then law of refraction is

   (a) $\hat{i}.\hat{n} = \mu(\hat{r}.\hat{n})$ (b) $\hat{i} \times \hat{n} = \mu(\hat{n} \times \hat{r})$

   (c) $\hat{i} \times \hat{n} = \mu(\hat{r} \times \hat{n})$ (d) $\mu(\hat{i} \times \hat{n}) = \hat{r} \times \hat{n}$

10. A ray of light is incident at an angle i from denser to rare medium. The reflected and the refracted rays are mutually perpendicular. The angle of reflection and the angle of refraction are respectively r and r′, then the critical angle will be

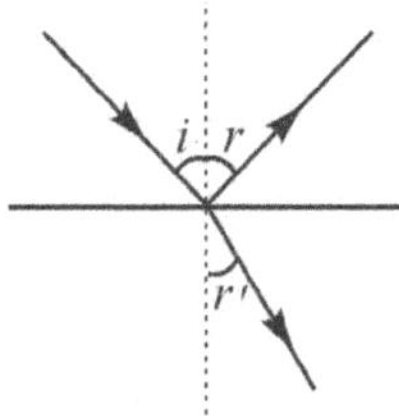

   (a) $\sin^{-1}(\sin r)$ (b) $\sin^{-1}(\tan r')$

   (c) $\sin^{-1}(\tan i)$ (d) $\tan^{-1}(\sin i)$

11. In the figure shown, for an angle of incidence 45°, at the top surface, what is the minimum refractive index needed for total internal reflection at vertical face?

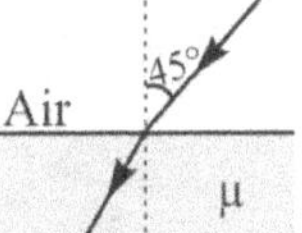

   (a) $\dfrac{\sqrt{2}+1}{2}$ (b) $\sqrt{\dfrac{3}{2}}$

   (c) $\sqrt{\dfrac{1}{2}}$ (d) $\sqrt{2}+1$

12. A fish looking up through the water sees the outside world contained in a circular horizon. If the refractive index of water is $\dfrac{4}{3}$ and the fish is 12 cm below the surface, the radius of this circle in cm is

   (a) $36\sqrt{5}$ (b) $4\sqrt{5}$

   (c) $36\sqrt{7}$ (d) $36/\sqrt{7}$

13. A rectangular glass slab ABCD, of refractive index μ_1, is immersed in water of refractive index μ_2 $(\mu_1 > \mu_2)$. A ray of light is incident at the surface AB of the slab as shown. The maximum value of the angle of incidence $\alpha_{max,}$ such that the ray comes out only from the other surface CD is given by

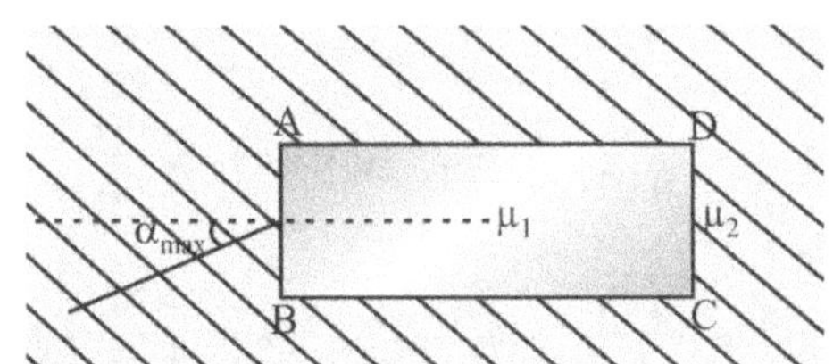

   (a) $\sin^{-1}\left[\dfrac{\mu_1}{\mu_2}\cos\left(\sin^{-1}\dfrac{\mu_2}{\mu_1}\right)\right]$ (b) $\sin^{-1}\left[\mu_1\cos\left(\sin^{-1}\dfrac{1}{\mu_2}\right)\right]$

   (c) $\sin^{-1}\left(\dfrac{\mu_1}{\mu_2}\right)$ (d) $\sin^{-1}\left(\dfrac{\mu_2}{\mu_1}\right)$

14. An observer can see through a pinhole the top end of a thin rod of height h, placed as shown in the figure. The beaker height is 3h and its radius h. When the beaker is filled with a liquid upto a height 2h, he can see the lower end of the rod. Then the refractive index of the liquid is

   (a) 5/2

   (b) $\sqrt{(5/2)}$

   (c) $\sqrt{(3/2)}$

   (d) 3/2

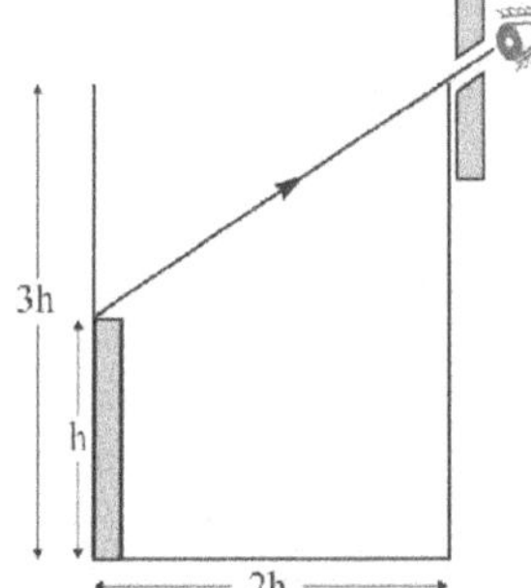

15. A ray of light is incident at the glass-water interface at an angle i, it emerges finally parallel to the surface of water, then the value of μ_g would be

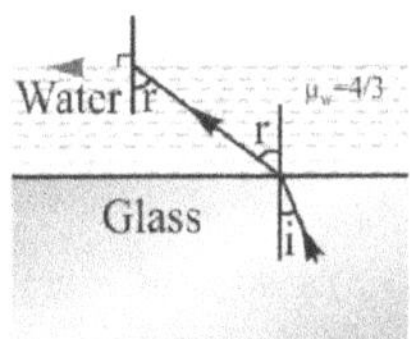

   (a) (4/3) sin i   (b) 1/sin i

   (c) 4/3   (d) 1

16. A container is filled with water (μ = 1.33) upto a height of 33.25 cm. A concave mirror is placed 15 cm above the water level and the image of an object placed at the bottom is formed 25 cm below the water level. The focal length of the mirror is

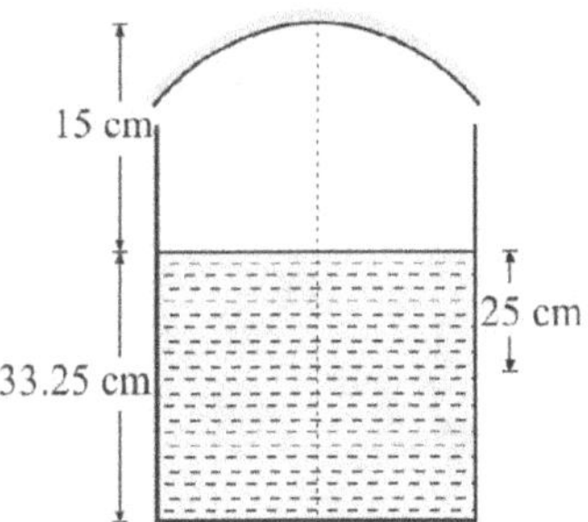

   (a) 10 cm   (b) 15 cm

   (c) 18.30 cm   (d) 25 cm

Answer Key	9	(c)	10	(c)	11	(b)	12	(d)
Sol. from page 97	13	(a)	14	(b)	15	(b)	16	(c)

17. A plane mirror is placed at the bottom of the tank containing a liquid of refractive index μ. P is a small object at a height h above the mirror. An observer O-vertically above P outside the liquid see P and its image in the mirror. The apparent distance between these two will be

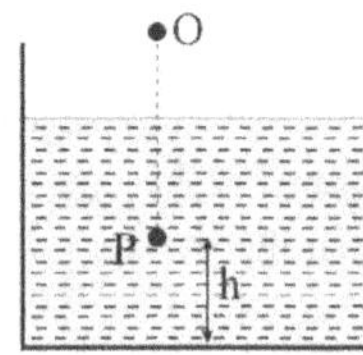

(a) $2\mu h$

(b) $\dfrac{2h}{\mu}$

(c) $\dfrac{2h}{\mu - 1}$

(d) $h\left(1 + \dfrac{1}{\mu}\right)$

18. An optical fibre consists of core of μ_1 surrounded by a cladding of $\mu_2 < \mu_1$. A beam of light enters from air at an angle α with axis of fibre. The highest α for which ray can be travelled through fibre is

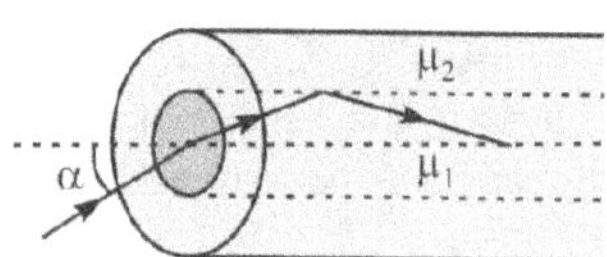

(a) $\cos^{-1}\sqrt{\mu_2^2 - \mu_1^2}$

(b) $\sin^{-1}\sqrt{\mu_1^2 - \mu_2^2}$

(c) $\tan^{-1}\sqrt{\mu_1^2 - \mu_2^2}$

(d) $\sec^{-1}\sqrt{\mu_1^2 - \mu_2^2}$

19. A rod of glass ($\mu = 1.5$) and of square cross section is bent into the shape shown in the figure. A parallel beam of light falls on the plane flat surface A as shown in the figure. If d is the width of a side and R is the radius of circular arc then for what maximum value of $\dfrac{d}{R}$ light entering the glass slab through surface A emerges from the glass through B

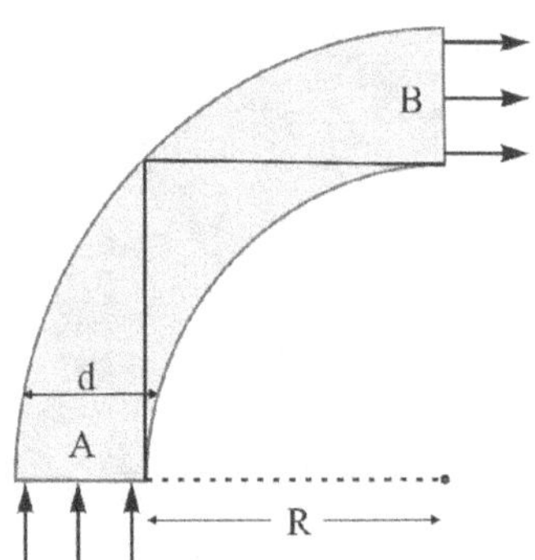

(a) 1.5

(b) 0.5

(c) 1.3

(d) none of these

20. While an aquarium is being filled with water, a motionless fish looks up vertically through the surface of the water at a monochromatic plane wave source of frequency f. If the index of refraction of water is μ and water level rises at a rate of dh/dt, the shift in the frequency df/f, that the fish observes is (velocity of light is c) :

(a) $\dfrac{(\mu - 1)dh/dt}{c}$

(b) $\dfrac{\mu}{c}\dfrac{dh}{dt}$

(c) $\dfrac{c\, dh/dt}{(\mu - 1)}$

(d) $\dfrac{c}{\mu}\dfrac{dh}{dt}$

21. The xy - plane separates two media A and B of refractive indices $\mu_1 = 1.5$ and $\mu_2 = 2$. A ray of light travels from A to B. Its directions in the two media are given by unit vectors $\hat{u}_1 = ai + bj$ and $\hat{u}_2 = ci + dj$. Then :

(a) $(a/c) = (4/3)$

(b) $(a/c) = (3/4)$

(c) $(b/d) = (4/3)$

(d) $(b/d) = (3/4)$

22. A light beam is travelling from Region I to Region IV (refer figure). The refractive index in Region I, II, III and IV are $\mu_0, \dfrac{\mu_0}{2}, \dfrac{\mu_0}{6}$ and $\dfrac{\mu_0}{8}$, respectively. The angle of incidence θ for which the beam just misses entering Region IV is

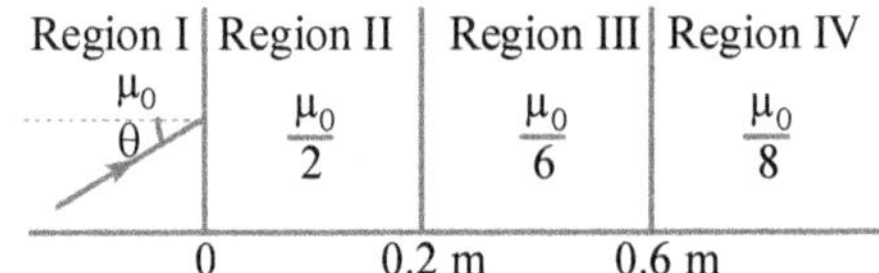

(a) $\sin^{-1}\left(\dfrac{3}{4}\right)$

(b) $\sin^{-1}\left(\dfrac{1}{8}\right)$

(c) $\sin^{-1}\left(\dfrac{1}{4}\right)$

(d) $\sin^{-1}\left(\dfrac{1}{3}\right)$.

23. A plane mirror is held at a height h above the bottom of an empty beaker. The beaker is now filled with water up to depth d. The general expression for the distance from a scratch at the bottom of the beaker to its image in terms of h and the depth d of water in the beaker is :

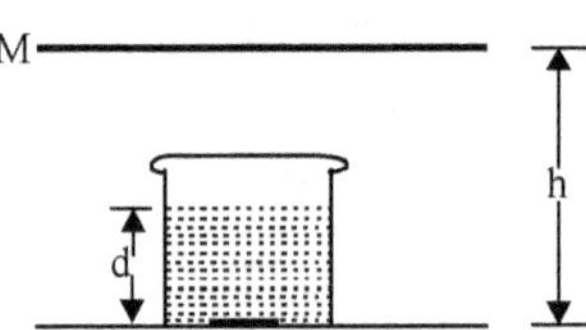

(a) $2h - d\left(\dfrac{\mu}{\mu - 1}\right)$

(b) $2h - \dfrac{d}{2}\left(\dfrac{\mu - 1}{\mu}\right)$

(c) $2h - d\left(\dfrac{\mu - 1}{\mu}\right)$

(d) $2h - d\left(\dfrac{2\mu - 1}{\mu}\right)$

Answer Key	**17**	(b)	**18**	(b)	**19**	(b)	**20**	(a)
Sol. from page 97	**21**	(a)	**22**	(b)	**23**	(c)		

24. An object O is located in a medium of refractive index μ_1 and observer is in medium of refractive index μ_3. The apparent distance of the object from the observer from the data shown in the figure is

(a) $\left(\dfrac{t_1}{\mu_1}+\dfrac{t_2}{\mu_2}\right)$

(b) $\left(\dfrac{t_1}{\mu_1}+\dfrac{t_2}{\mu_3}\right)$

(c) $\left(\mu_1\dfrac{t_1}{\mu_3}+\dfrac{t_2\mu_2}{\mu_3}\right)$

(d) $\mu_3\left(\dfrac{t_1}{\mu_1}+\dfrac{t_2}{\mu_3}\right)$

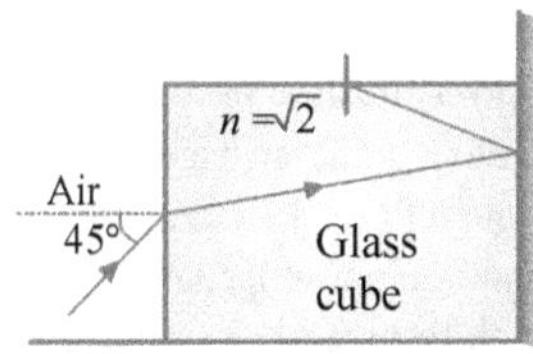
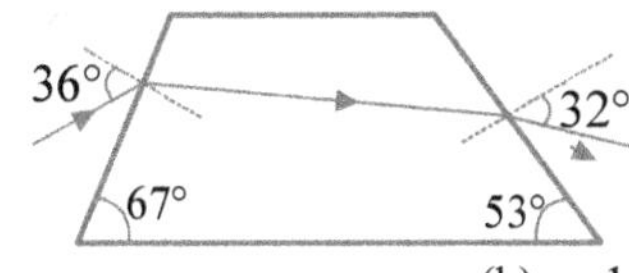

25. A ray of light strikes a plane mirror M at an angle of $45°$ as shown in the figure. After reflection, the ray passes through a prism of index 1.50 whose apex angle is $4°$. In order to have the total deviation of the ray equal to $90°$, the angle though which the mirror should be rotated is :

(a) $1°$

(b) $4°$

(c) $30°$

(d) $3°$

26. A slab of glass, Q of thickness 6 cm and refractive index 1.5, is placed in front of a concave mirror, the faces of the slab being perpendicular to the principal axis of the mirror. If the radius of curvature of the mirror is 40 cm and the reflected image coincides with the object, then the distance of the object from the mirror is
(a) 30 cm   (b) 22 cm
(c) 42 cm   (d) 28 cm

27. Right face of a glass cube is silvered as shown. A ray of light is incident on left face of the cube as shown. The deviation of the ray when it comes out of the glass cube is

(a) $0°$ (b) $90°$
(c) $180°$ (d) $270°$

28. Upper part of a prism is cut. The ray diagram of a ray incident at first refracting surface is as shown in figure. The minimum deviation that can be produced by the prism is

(a) $12°$ (b) $16°$
(c) $8°$ (d) less than $8°$

29. A long rectangular slab of transparent medium of thickness d is placed on a table with length parallel to x-axis and width parallel to y-axis. A ray of light is traveling along y-axis at origin. The refractive index μ of the medium varies as, $\mu=\sqrt{1+e^{x/d}}$. The refractive index of air is 1. The value of x, where the ray intersects the upper surface of the slab-air boundary is :

(a) $d\ln 2$

(b) $d\ln 4$

(c) $3d\ln 2$

(d) none of these

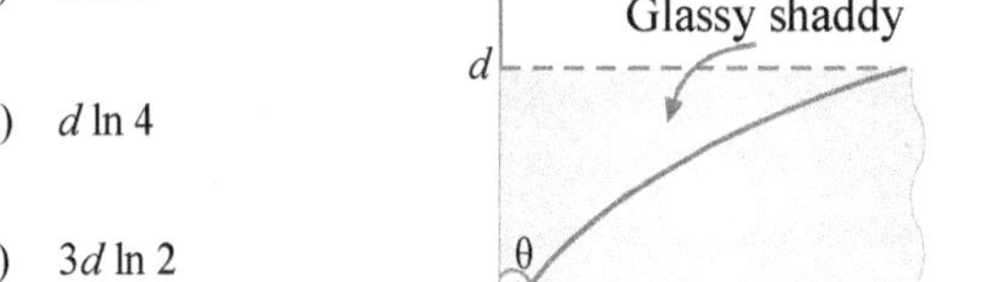
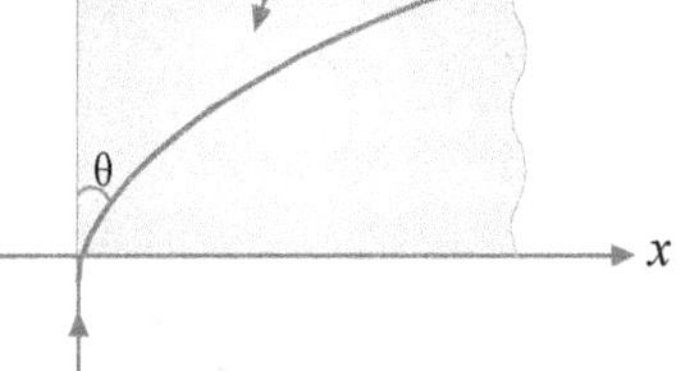

30. The refractive index of a medium varies, when $0\le x\le 1$, as $\eta(x)=1.5(2-x)$ where 1.5 is a number having dimension $[L^{-1}]$. What is the optical path of a ray moving from $x=0$ to $x=1$?
(a) 1.5   (b) 2.25
(c) 3.0   (d) 0.75

31. A ray of light is incident on a surface of glass slab at an angle $45°$. If the lateral shift produced per unit thickness is $\dfrac{1}{\sqrt{3}}$ m, the angle of refraction produced is

(a) $\tan^{-1}\left(\dfrac{\sqrt{3}}{2}\right)$

(b) $\tan^{-1}\left(1-\sqrt{\dfrac{2}{3}}\right)$

(c) $\sin^{-1}\left(1-\sqrt{\dfrac{2}{3}}\right)$

(d) $\tan^{-1}\left(\sqrt{\dfrac{2}{\sqrt{3}-1}}\right)$

32. Angle of prism is A and its one surface is silvered. Light rays falling at an angle of incidence $2A$ on first surface return back through the same path after suffering reflection at second silvered surface. Refractive index of the material of prism is
(a) $2\sin A$ (b) $2\cos A$
(c) $\dfrac{1}{2}\cos A$ (d) $\tan A$

33. For light incident from air on a meta-material, the oppropriate ray diagram is :

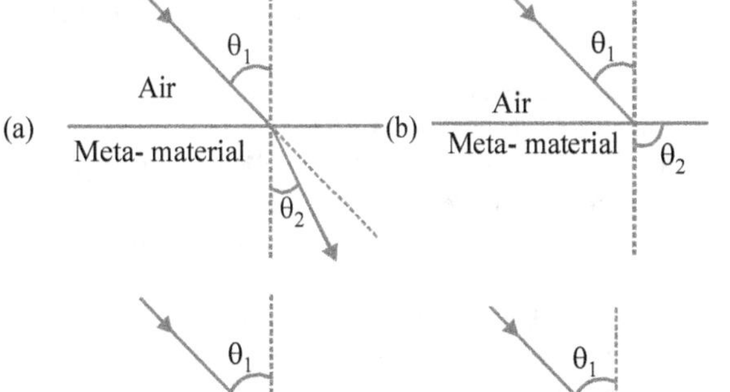

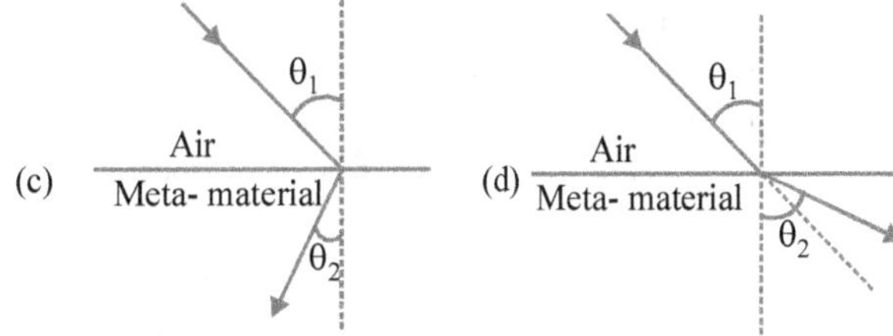

Answer Key	24	(d)	25	(a)	26	(c)	27	(c)	28	(d)
Sol. from page 97	29	(b)	30	(b)	31	(b)	32	(b)	33	(c)

1. Figure shows a fish and a fish stalker in water

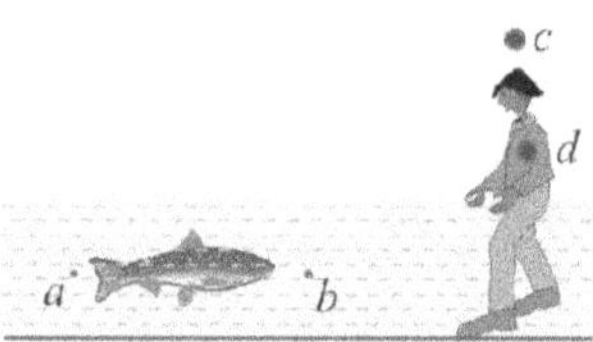

(a) the stalker sees the fish in the region a.
(b) the stalker sees the fish in the region b.
(c) the fish sees the eyes of the stalker at c.
(d) the fish sees the eyes of the stalker at d.

2. When light is incident on a medium at angle i and refracted into a second medium at an angle r, the graph of $\sin i$ vs $\sin r$ is as shown in the graph. From this, one can conclude that

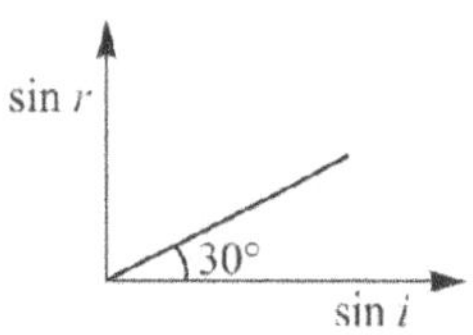

(a) velocity of light in the second medium is 1.73 times the velocity of light in the I medium
(b) velocity of light in the I medium is 1.73 times the velocity in the II medium
(c) the critical angle for the two media is given by $\sin i_c = \dfrac{1}{\sqrt{3}}$
(d) $\sin i_c = \dfrac{1}{2}$

3. If the light moving in a straight line bends by a small but fixed angle, it may be a case of
(a) reflection   (b) refraction
(c) diffraction   (d) dispersion

4. A narrow beam of white light goes through a slab having parallel faces :
(a) the light never splits in different colours.
(b) the emergent beam is white.
(c) the light inside the slab is split into different colours
(d) the light inside the slab is white.

5. By properly combining two prisms made of different materials, it is possible to
(a) have dispersion without average deviation
(b) have deviation without dispersion
(c) have both dispersion and average deviation
(d) have neither disperson nor average deviation

6. A ray of light is incident grazingly of face AB to a right angled prism as shown. It emerges out of face AC, as shown, $e =$ angle of emergence. Refractive indices of different media have been shown in the diagram. Choose the correct alternatives

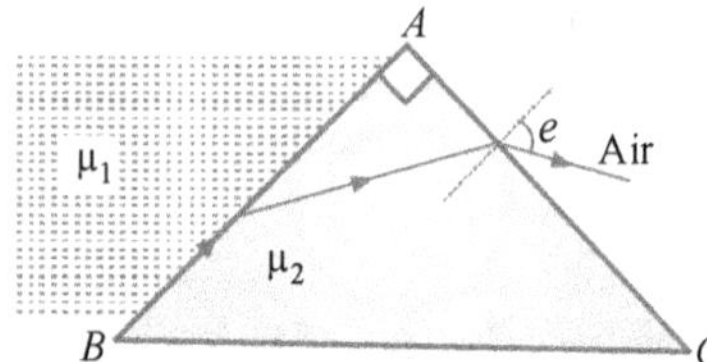

(a) $\mu_1^2 + \sin^2 e = \mu_2^2$ (b) $\mu_2^2 + \sin^2 e = \mu_1^2$

(c) $\mu_1^2 + \cos^2 e = \mu_2^2$

(d) If the ray just fails to emerge out of the face AC of the prism, for $\mu_2 = \sqrt{3}$, angle of refraction of face AB is $\sin^{-1}\sqrt{\dfrac{2}{3}}$

7. Rays of different colours are passing through a slab as shown. Which of the following is/are incorrect ?

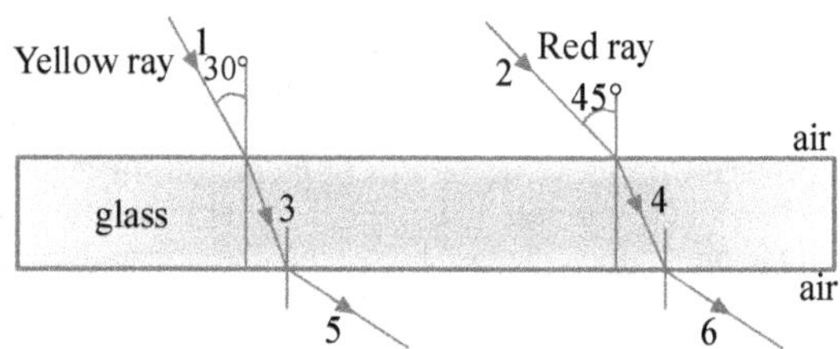

(a) Ray 1 and ray 2 are parallel
(b) Ray 5 and ray 6 are parallel
(c) Ray 1 and ray 5 are parallel
(d) Ray 3 and ray 1 must be parallel

8. A ray of light travelling in a transparent medium falls on a surface separating the medium from air at an angle of incidence of 45°. The ray undergoes total internal reflection. If μ is the refractive index of the medium with respect to air, select the possible value (s) of μ from the following
(a) 1.3   (b) 1.4
(c) 1.5   (d) 1.6

Answer Key	1	(a, c)	2	(b, c)	3	(a,b)	4	(b, c)	5	(a,b, c)
Sol. from page 101	6	(a, d)	7	(b, d)	8	(c, d)				

 # Statement Questions *Exercise 2.3*

Read the two statements carefully to mark the correct option out of the options given below. Select the right choice.

(a) If both the statements are true and the *Statement - 2* is the correct explanation of *Statement - 1*.

(b) If both the statements are true but *Statement - 2* is not the correct explanation of the *Statement - 1*.

(c) If *Statement - 1* true but *Statement - 2* is false.

(d) If *Statement - 1* is false but *Statement - 2* is true.

1. *Statement -1* : A man with a metre scale goes inside water ($_a\mu_w = 4/3$). The length of the scale as observed by the man will be 3/4 metre.

    Statement - 2 : To the man inside water, the length of the metre scale will be one metre.

2. *Statement -1* : Different colours of light travel with different speed in vacuum.

    Statement - 2 : Wavelength of any colour of refractive index μ is given by $\lambda = \dfrac{\lambda_{air}}{\mu}$.

3. *Statement -1* : The setting sun appears red.

    Statement - 2 : Scattering of light is directly proportional to the wavelength.

4. *Statement - 1* : The stars twinkle while the planets do not.

    Statement - 2 : The stars are much bigger in size than the planet.

5. *Statement - 1* : The frequencies of incident, reflected and refracted beam of monochromatic light incident from one medium to another are same.

    Statement - 2 : The reflected and refracted rays are mutually perpendicular.

6. *Statement - 1* : Diamond glitters brilliantly.

    Statement - 2 : Diamond does not absorb sunlight.

7. *Statement - 1* : Refractive index of a prism depends only of the kind of the glass of which it is made of and colour of light used.

Statement - 2 : The refractive index of a prism depends upon the refractive angle of the prism and the angle of minimum deviation..

8. *Statement - 1* : The refractive index of diamond is $\sqrt{6}$ and that of liquid is $\sqrt{3}$. If the light travels from diamond to the liquid, it will totally reflected when the angle of incidence is 30°.

    Statement - 2 : The critical angle C is given by $\sin C = \dfrac{1}{\mu}$, where μ is the refractive index of diamond with respect to the liquid.

9. *Statement - 1* : The equation for dispersive power

    $\omega = \dfrac{\mu_v - \mu_r}{\mu_y - 1}$ is derived for small angled prism. The value of dispersive power ω can be used for lens of same material.

    Statement - 2 : The dispersive power for lens will be less than ω.

10. *Statement - 1* : In optical fibre, the diameter of the core is kept small.

     Statement - 2 : The smaller diameter of the core ensures that the fibre should have incident angle more than the critical angle required for total internal reflection.

11. *Statement - 1* : There is no dispersion of light refracted through a rectangular glass slab.

     Statement - 2 : The parallel faces of the slab cancel the mutual dispersion effect.

Answer Key	1	(d)	2	(d)	3	(c)	4	(b)	5	(c)	6	(b)	7	(c)
Sol. from page 101	8	(d)	9	(c)	10	(a)	11	(a)					

| Optics | **Passage & Matrix** | *Exercise 2.4* |

PASSAGES

Passage for (Qs. 1 - 3) :

The figure shows a surface XY separating two transparent media, medium-1 and medium-2. The lines ab and cd represent wavefronts of a light wave travelling in medium-1 and incident of XY. The lines ef and gh represent wavelengths of the light wave in medium-2 after refraction.

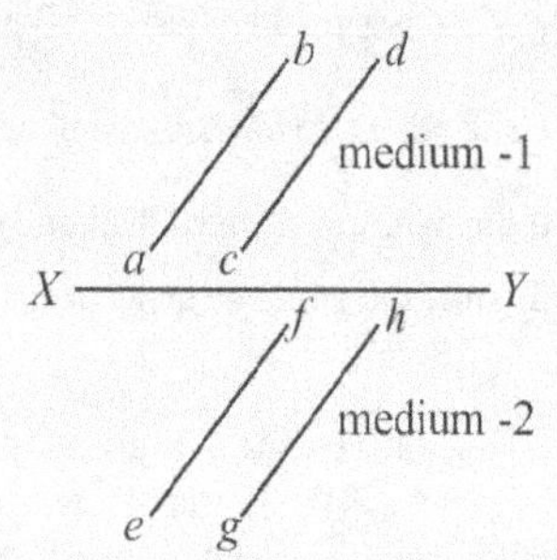

1. Light travels as a
   (a) parallel beam in each medium
   (b) convergent beam in each medium
   (c) divergent beam in each medium
   (d) divergent beam in one medium and convergent beam in the other medium.

2. The phases of the light wave at c, d, e and f are ϕ_c, ϕ_d, ϕ_e and ϕ_f respectively. It is given that $\phi_c \neq \phi_{f'}$

   (a) ϕ_c cannot be equal to ϕ_d
   (b) ϕ_d can be equal to ϕ_e
   (c) $(\phi_d - \phi_f)$ is equal to $(\phi_c - \phi_e)$
   (d) $(\phi_d - \phi_c)$ is not equal to $(\phi_f - \phi_e)$.

3. Speed of light is
   (a) the same in medium-1 and medium-2
   (b) larger in medium-1 than in medium-2
   (c) larger in medium-2 than in medium-1
   (d) different at b and d.

Passage for (Qs. 4 & 5) :

A right prism is made by selecting a proper material and the angle A and B ($B << A$) as shown in figure. It is desired that a ray of light incident on the face AB emerges parallel to the incident direction after two internal reflections.

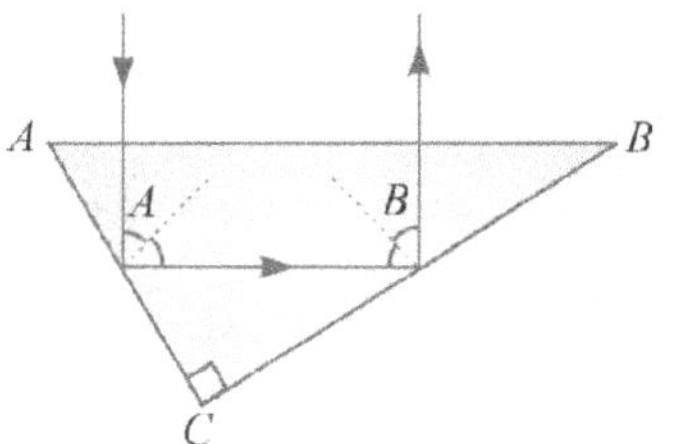

4. What should be the minimum refractive index μ for this to be possible ?
   (a) $\sqrt{3}$
   (b) 1.5
   (c) $\sqrt{2}$
   (d) 1.8

5. For $\mu = \dfrac{5}{3}$ the critical angle is
   (a) 30°
   (b) 35°
   (c) 45°
   (d) 37°

Answer Key	**1**	(a)	**2**	(c)	**3**	(b)	**4**	(c)
Sol. from page 102	**5**	(d)						

6. Angle of deviation is given in **Column -I** and ray diagram for angle of deviation in **Column -II**

Column – I		Column – II	

A. $60°$　　　　　　　　　　　　(p) 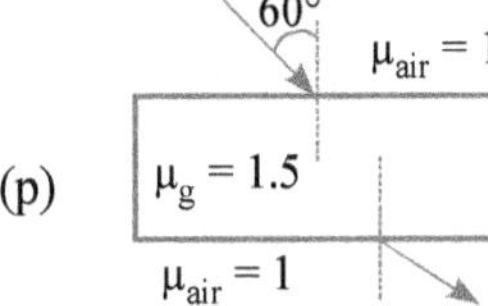

B. $0°$　　　　　　　　　　　　(q) 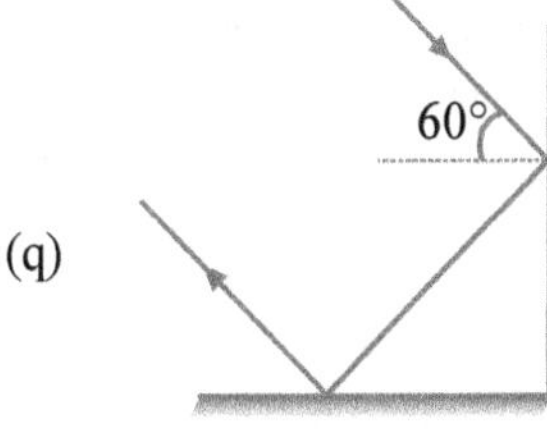

C. $180°$　　　　　　　　　　　(r) 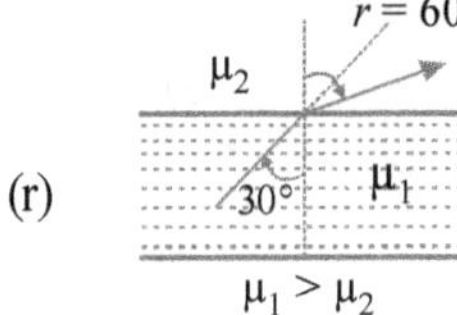

D. $30°$　　　　　　　　　　　(s) 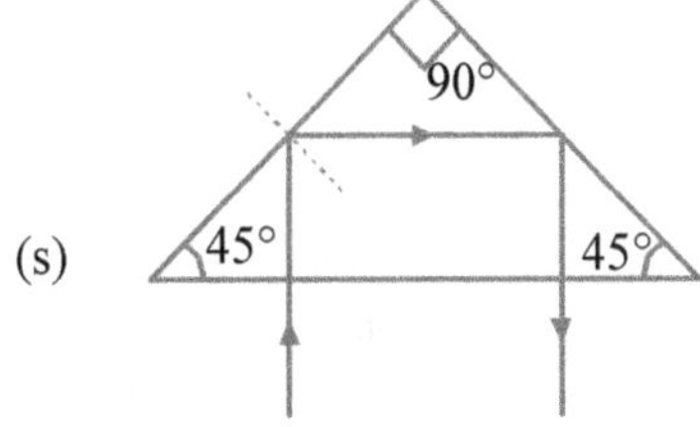

(t) 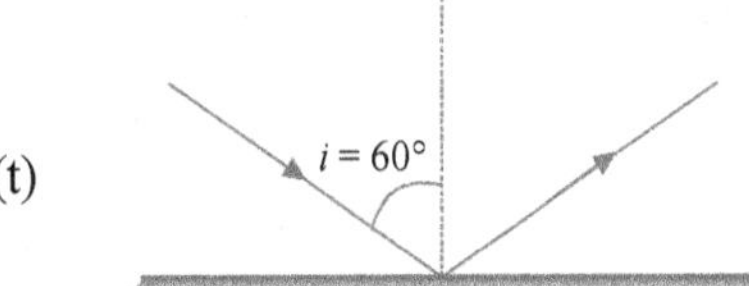

Answer Key	6	A-(t) ; B-(p) ; C-(q, s) ; D-(r)				
Sol. from page 102						

Solution from page 102

1. A ray of light falls on a glass plate of refractive index $\mu = 1.5$. What is the angle of incidence of the ray if the angle between the reflected and refracted rays is $90°$?

   Ans. $\simeq 57°$.

2. A coin lies on the bottom of a vessel filled with water to a depth of 40 cm. At what height should a small electric lamp be placed above the water surface so that its image produced by the rays reflected from the water surface coincides with the image of the coin formed by the refracted rays?

   Ans. 30 cm.

3. AB and CD are surfaces of two slabs as shown in figure. The medium between the slabs has refractive index 2, refractive index of slab above AB is $\sqrt{2}$ and below CD is $\sqrt{3}$. Find the minimum angle of incidence at θ, so that the ray is totally reflected by both the slabs.

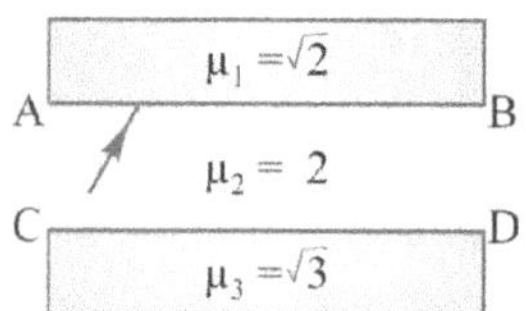

Ans. $\theta_{\min} = 60°$.

4. A $60°$ glass prism has refractive index of 1.5.
   (i) Calculate the angle of incidence for minimum deviation,
   (ii) the minimum deviation
   (iii) the angle of emergence of the light at maximum deviation.

   Ans. (i) $48°$ (ii) $37°$ (iii) $28°$

Solution from page 103

1. A light ray is incident at an angle $45°$ with the normal to a $\sqrt{2}$ cm thick plate ($\mu = 2$). Find the shift in the path of the light as it emerges out from the plate.

   Ans. 0.62 cm.

2. (a) A point source of light is arranged at a height h above the surface of water. Where will the image of this source in the flat mirror like bottom of a vessel be if the depth of the vessel full of water is d?
   (b) What is the apparent distance from the surface of water to the image formed by a mirror if the observer is standing in air and views the image vertically downwards?

   Ans. (a) $\left(d \pm \dfrac{4h}{3}\right)$ (b) $\left(\dfrac{3d}{2} + h\right)$.

3. A fixed cylindrical tank of height $H = 4$ m and area A , is filled up with a liquid. An observer through a telescope fitted at the top of the wall of the tank and inclined at $\theta = 45°$ with the vertical. When the tank is completely filled with liquid, he notices an insect, which is at the centre of the bottom of the tank. At $t = 0$, he opens a cork of area a at the bottom of the tank. The insect moves in such a way that it is visible for a certain time. Determine

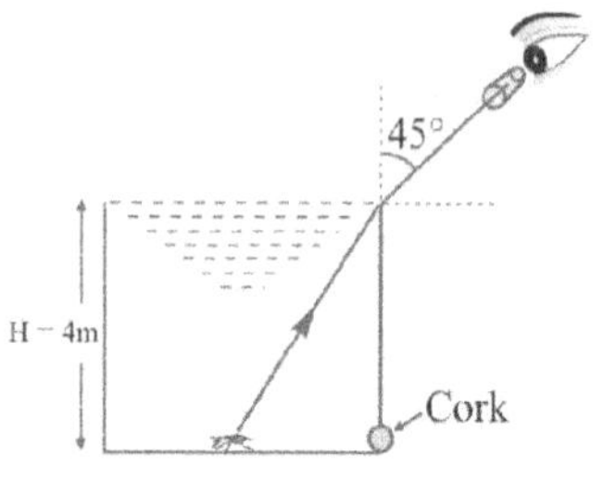

   (a) the refractive index of the liquid
   (b) the velocity at any time.

   Ans. $v = \dfrac{a\sqrt{8g}}{4A}\left[1 - \dfrac{a}{8A}\sqrt{8gt}\right]$.

4. A point source is placed at a depth h below the surface of water (refractive index μ). Find the area through which light escapes from the water surface.

   Ans. $\left[\dfrac{\pi h^2}{\mu^2 - 1}\right]$.

5. One face of a prism with a refractive angle of $30°$ is coated with silver. A ray incident and reflected from the silver -coated face and retraces its path. What is the refractive index of the prism?

   Ans. $\sqrt{2}$.

6. Light is incident at an angle α on one planar end of a transparent cylindrical rod of refractive index μ. Determine the least value of μ, so that the light entering the rod does not emerge from the curve surface of the rod irrespective of the value of α.

   Ans. $\mu_{\min} = \sqrt{2}$.

7. Monochromatic light is incident on a plane interface AB between two media of refractive indices μ_1 and μ_2 ($\mu_2 > \mu_1$) at an angle of incidence θ as shown in figure. The angle θ is infinite similarly greater than the critical angle for the two media so that total internal reflection takes place. Now if a transparent slab DEFG of uniform thickness and refractive index μ_2 is introduced on the interface,

show that for any value of μ_3 all light will ultimately be reflected back again into medium II. Consider separately cases (i) $\mu_3 < \mu_1$ and (ii) $\mu_2 > \mu_1$.

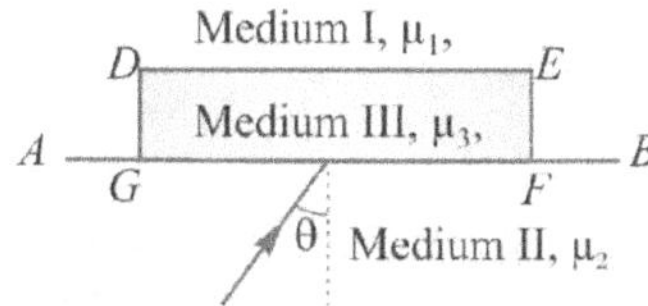

8. The cross-section of a glass prism has the form of an isosceles triangle. One of the refracting faces is silvered. A ray of light falling normally on the other refracting face, being reflected twice emerges through the base of the prism perpendicular to it. Find the angles of the prism.

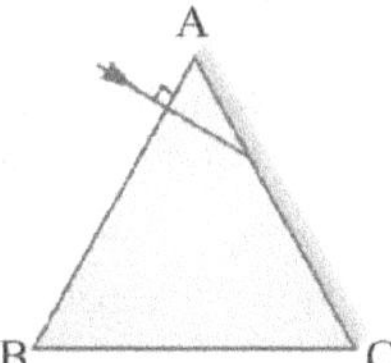

Ans. 36°, 72°, 72°.

9. The refractive indices of the crown glass for blue and red lights are 1.51 and 1.49 respectively and those of the flint glass are 1.77 and 1.73 respectively. An isosceles prism of angle 6° is made of crown glass. A beam of white light is incident at a small angle on this prism. The other flint glass isosceles prism is combined with the crown glass prism such that there is no deviation of the incident light. Determine the angle of the flint glass prism. Calculate the net dispersion of the combined system.

Ans. $\Delta\delta = 0.04°$.

10. A concave mirror of radius 40 cm lies on a horizontal table and water is filled in it upto a height of 5.0 cm. A small dust particle P floats on the surface of water. Particle P lies vertically above the point of contact of the mirror with the table. Locate the image of the dust particle as seen from a point directly above it. The refractive index of water is 4/3.

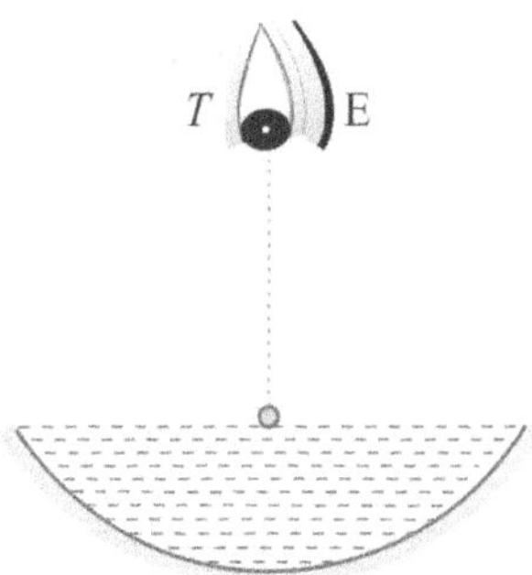

Ans. 8.75 cm below water surface.

11. A thin prism of angle 6.0°, $\omega = 0.07$ and $\mu_y = 1.50$ is combined with another thin prism having $\omega = 0.08$ and $\mu_y = 1.60$. The combination produces no deviation in the mean ray. (a) Find angle of the second prism (b) Find the angular dispersion produced by the combination when a beam of white light passes through it. (c) If the prisms are similarly directed, what will be the deviation in the mean ray?

Ans. (a) 5° (b) 0.03° (c) 6°.

12. A ray of light is incident on a prism ABC of refractive index $\sqrt{3}$ as shown in figure.

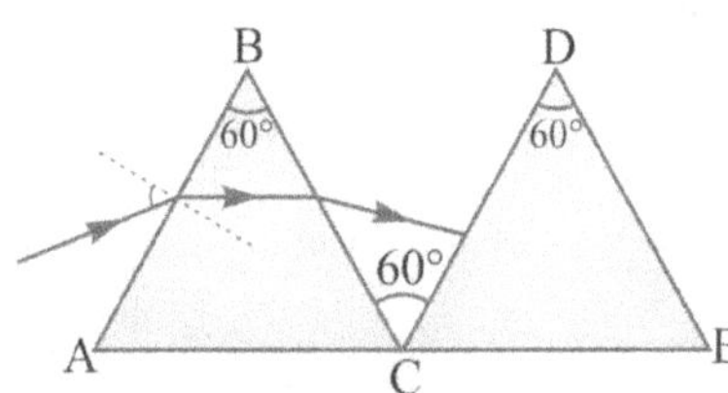

(a) Find the angle of incidence for which the deviation of light ray by prism ABC is minimum.

(b) By what angle the second prism must be rotated, so that the final ray suffers net minimum deviation.

Ans. (a) 60° (b) $\delta_{net} = 0$

13. A concave mirror of radius of curvature 1 m is placed at the bottom of a tank filled with water. The mirror forms an image of the sun when it is directed overhead. Calculate, the distance of the image from the mirror for different depths, 80 cm and 40 cm of the water in the tank.

Ans. 50 cm, 47.5 cm.

★★★

Hints & Solutions

1. (a) The angle of refraction is second medium is greater than angle of incidence in first medium, so $\mu_2 < \mu_1$. Also angle of refraction in third medium is greater than angle of incidence in second medium and so $\mu_2 > \mu_3$.

2. (c) $$x = 4 + \frac{1}{1.5} = 4.67 \text{ cm.}$$

3. (d)

4. (d) Frequency of wave is a fundamental quantity which will not change, but wavelength and velocity will change.

5. (c) If x is the height of water in the container, then apparent depth $21 - x$. So

$$\frac{x}{21-x} = \frac{4}{3}$$

$$\therefore \qquad x = 12 \text{ cm.}$$

6. (b) Apparent depth, $x = \dfrac{d}{\mu_1} + \dfrac{d}{\mu_2}$

7. (a) The shift produced,

$$s = t\left(1 - \frac{1}{\mu}\right).$$

8. (d) Time taken by light to travel in water

$$= \mu \times t_{air} = \frac{4}{3} \times 8 \text{ min } 20 \sec$$

$$= 11 \text{ min } 6 \text{ sec.}$$

9. (c) $$_2\mu_1 \times {_3}\mu_2 \times {_4}\mu_3 = \frac{\mu_1}{\mu_2} \times \frac{\mu_2}{\mu_3} \times \frac{\mu_3}{\mu_4} = \frac{\mu_1}{\mu_4} = \frac{1}{_1\mu_4},$$

10. (a)

11. (a) $$\mu = \frac{c}{v} = \frac{1/\sqrt{\mu_0 \in_0}}{1/\sqrt{\mu \in}} = \sqrt{\frac{\mu \in}{\mu_0 \in_0}}$$

12. (b) $$\mu = \frac{\text{distance BD}}{\text{distance AC}}$$

$$= \frac{\text{BD/AD}}{\text{AC/AB}}$$

$$= \frac{\sin\theta}{\sin\phi}$$

13. (b) $$\mu = \tan\phi$$

$$= \tan 60°$$

$$= \sqrt{3}.$$

14. (b)

15. (d) $$\frac{\mu_2}{\mu_1} \times \frac{\mu_3}{\mu_2} \times \frac{\mu_4}{\mu_3} = \frac{\sin r_1}{\sin i} \times \frac{\sin r_2}{\sin r_4} \times \frac{\sin r_3}{\sin r_2}$$

$$\text{or} \qquad \mu_4 = \mu_1.$$

16. (d)

17. (c) The signal will transmitted to the edge of the pool only if angle of incidence in water is less than critical angle.

18. (b)

19. (a) If t is the required thickness, then

$$\frac{t}{\lambda_{air}} + 1 = \frac{t}{\lambda_{vac}}$$

$$\text{or} \quad \frac{t}{(600/1.0003)} + 1 = \frac{t}{6000}$$

$$\therefore \qquad t = 2 \times 10^{-3} \text{ m}$$

20. (c)

21. (a) Critical angle for wavelength greater than green will be greater and so they will be refracted into air.

22. (d) $$\omega = \frac{\text{angular dispersion}}{\text{mean deviation } (\delta)}$$

$$\therefore \text{ angular dispersion } = \omega\delta.$$

23. (b) Glass slab will not produce any deviation and so it remains α.

24. (c) $$\frac{\sin i}{\sin r} = \frac{\sin i}{\sin r_1} \times \frac{\sin r_1}{\sin r}$$

$$= \frac{\mu_2}{\mu_1} \times \frac{\mu_3}{\mu_2} = \frac{\mu_3}{\mu_1}$$

25. (a) As $\mu = A + \dfrac{B}{\lambda^2}$; so with increase in λ, μ will decrease.

26. (b) For no deviation,

$$(\mu_1 - 1)A_1 + (\mu_2 - 1)A_2 = 0$$

$$\therefore \quad A_2 = -\frac{(\mu_1 - 1)A_1}{(\mu_2 - 1)} = -\frac{(1.54 - 1) \times 4}{(1.72 - 1)} = -3°$$

27. (c) In case of minimum deviation, the light ray inside prism becomes parallel to base of the prism.

28. (c)

29. (b)

30. (c) $$C_{max} = \theta = 45°$$

$$\mu_{min} = \frac{1}{\sin C_{max}}$$

$$= \frac{1}{\sin 45°}$$

$$= \sqrt{2}.$$

31. (b) If δ is the deviation produced by each prism, then total deviation,

$$\delta' = \delta - \delta + \delta = \delta.$$

32. (c) The deviation produced by prism

$$\delta = (\mu - 1)A = (1.50 - 1) \times 4 = 2°.$$

To counter balance this deviation, the minor should be rotated by 1°.

33. (a) $$\lambda = \frac{\lambda_{air}}{\mu} = \frac{6000}{1.5} = 4000 \text{ Å}$$

34. (b)
$$\mu_g x_1 = \mu_w x_2$$
or $\quad 1.53 \times 4 = \mu_w \times 4.5$
$$\therefore \quad \mu_w = 1.36$$

35. (b)
$$\mu = \frac{1}{\sin C} = \frac{1}{\sin 30°}$$
or $\quad \dfrac{c}{v} = \dfrac{1}{(1/2)}$
$$\therefore \quad v = \frac{c}{2}$$
$$= \frac{3 \times 10^8}{2} = 1.5 \times 10^8 \text{ m/s}.$$

36. (d)
$$\delta = (\mu - 1)A.$$
$$\therefore \quad \frac{\delta_{air}}{\delta_w} = \frac{(_a\mu_g - 1)}{(_w\mu_g - 1)}$$
$$= \frac{(_a\mu_g - 1)}{\left(\dfrac{_a\mu_g}{_a\mu_w} - 1\right)}$$
$$= \frac{(3/2 - 1)}{\left(\dfrac{3/2}{4/3} - 1\right)} = 4$$

37. (a) We have
$$\mu = \frac{\sin\left(\dfrac{A + \delta m}{2}\right)}{\sin(A/2)}$$
$$= \frac{\sin\left(\dfrac{30° + 60°}{2}\right)}{\sin\left(\dfrac{60°}{2}\right)}$$
$$= \frac{\sin 45°}{\sin 30°} = \sqrt{2}$$

38. (c)
$$\omega = \frac{\mu_v - \mu_R}{\mu_y - 1}$$
$$= \left(\frac{1.65 - 1.61}{1.63 - 1}\right).$$

39. (c) For minimum deviation, $i = e$.

40. We have,
$$\mu = \frac{\sin\left(\dfrac{A + \delta_m}{2}\right)}{\sin\dfrac{A}{2}}$$
$$= \frac{\sin\left(\dfrac{A + A}{2}\right)}{\sin\dfrac{A}{2}}$$
$$= \frac{\sin A}{\sin A/2}$$
$$= \frac{2\sin A/2 \cos A/2}{\sin A/2}$$
$$\therefore \quad A = 2\cos^{-1}(\mu/2)$$

41. (b) Source with atomic state is associated with line spectrum. So neon street sign produces line spectrum.

42. (b) Band spectrum is obtained in molecular state of substance.

43. (a)

44. (a)

45. (c)

46. (a) We know that
$$\mu = \frac{\sin\left(\dfrac{A + \delta m}{2}\right)}{\sin\dfrac{A}{2}}$$
or $\quad \cot\dfrac{A}{2} = \dfrac{\sin\left(\dfrac{A + \delta m}{2}\right)}{\sin\dfrac{A}{2}}$
$$\therefore \quad \delta_m = \pi - 2A.$$

1. (c) The angle between reflected and refracted rays,
$$= 180° - (\theta + r)$$

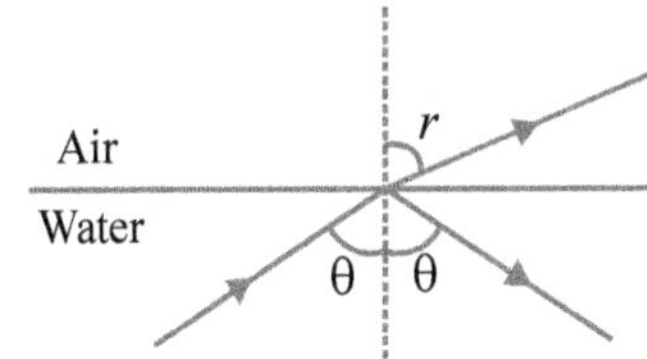

As $r > \theta$, $\therefore 180° - (\theta + r) < (180° - 2\theta)$

2. (d) We know that $C = \sin^{-1}\left(\dfrac{1}{\mu}\right)$. Given $i_B > i_A$, $\therefore \mu_B < \mu_A$.

So B is rarer and A is denser. Light will be totally reflected, when it passes from A to B. Now critical angle for A to B

$$C_{AB} = \sin^{-1}\left(\frac{1}{_B\mu_A}\right) = \sin^{-1}(_A\mu_B)$$

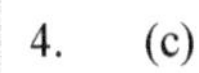

$$= \sin^{-1}\left(\frac{\mu_B}{\mu_A}\right) = \sin^{-1}\left(\frac{i_B}{i_A}\right).$$

3. (c) $v_1 = x/t_1$ and $v_2 = 10x/t_2$.
$$\therefore \; _1\mu_2 = \frac{v_1}{v_2} = \frac{x/t_1}{10x/t_2} = \frac{t_2}{10t_1}$$

Now critical angle, $\sin C = \dfrac{1}{_1\mu_2} = \left(\dfrac{10t_1}{t_2}\right)$

4. (c)
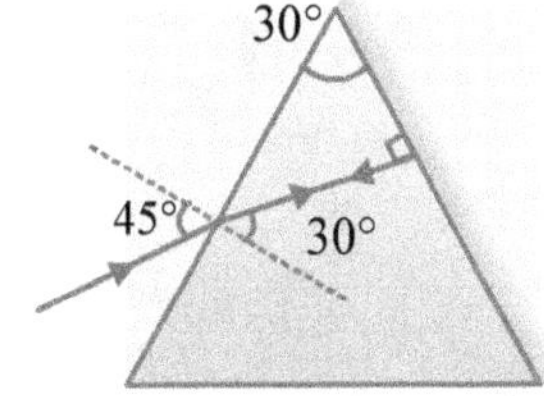

$$\mu = \frac{\sin 45°}{\sin 30°}$$

$$= \frac{1/\sqrt{2}}{1/2} = \sqrt{2} .$$

5. (b)

$$\frac{RD}{AD} = \frac{\mu_2}{\mu_1}$$

$$\therefore \quad RD = AD\,\frac{\mu_2}{\mu_1} = x\pi R^2\,\frac{\mu_2}{\mu_1} .$$

6. (d)

$$\frac{\sin 60°}{\sin 90°} = \frac{1}{\mu} \Rightarrow \mu = \frac{2}{\sqrt{3}}$$

7. (a)

$$C_{max} = 60°$$

$$\therefore \quad _r\mu_d = \frac{1}{\sin 60°}$$

$$\text{or} \quad \frac{\mu_g}{\mu_\ell} = \frac{2}{\sqrt{3}}$$

$$\therefore \quad \mu_\ell = \frac{\sqrt{3}}{2}\mu_g = \frac{\sqrt{3}}{2} \times 1.5$$

$$= 1.3$$

8. (b) Speed,

$$v = \frac{10 \times 10^{-2}}{4.5 \times 10^{-10}} = 2.22 \times 10^8 \text{ m/s}$$

$$\mu = \frac{c}{v} = \frac{3 \times 10^8}{2.22 \times 10^8} = 1.35$$

Optical path $= \mu t = 1.35 \times 10 = 13.5$ cm

9. (c)

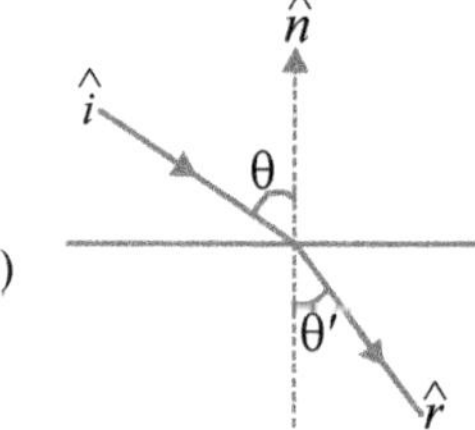

$$1 \times 1 \times \sin \theta = \mu \times 1 \times \sin \theta'$$

$$\therefore \quad \frac{\sin \theta}{\sin \theta'} = \mu.$$

10. (c) We have, $r + r' = 90°$

or $\qquad r' = 90° - r = 90° - i$

Now $\qquad _d\mu_r = \dfrac{\sin i}{\sin r'} = \dfrac{\sin i}{\sin(90° - i)}$

$$= \tan i$$

Critical angle, $\sin C = \dfrac{1}{_r\mu_d} = {_d\mu_r}$

$$= \tan i$$

$$\therefore \quad C = \sin^{-1}(\tan i)$$

11. (b) If θ is the angle of refraction, then

$$\frac{\sin 45°}{\sin \theta} = \mu \text{ or } \mu = \frac{1}{\sqrt{2}\sin \theta}$$

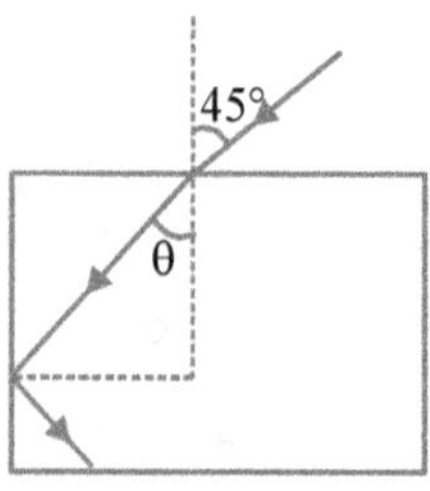

At vertical face, angle of incidence is $(90° - \theta)$. For TIR at vertical face

$$(90° - \theta) > C$$

or $\qquad \sin(90° - \theta) > \sin C$

or $\qquad \cos \theta > \dfrac{1}{\mu}$

$$> \sqrt{2}\sin \theta$$

or $\qquad \tan \theta < \dfrac{1}{\sqrt{2}}$

or $\qquad \sin \theta < \dfrac{1}{\sqrt{3}}$

$$\therefore \quad \mu_{min} = \frac{1}{\sqrt{2} \times \dfrac{1}{\sqrt{3}}}$$

$$= \sqrt{\frac{3}{2}} .$$

12. (d)

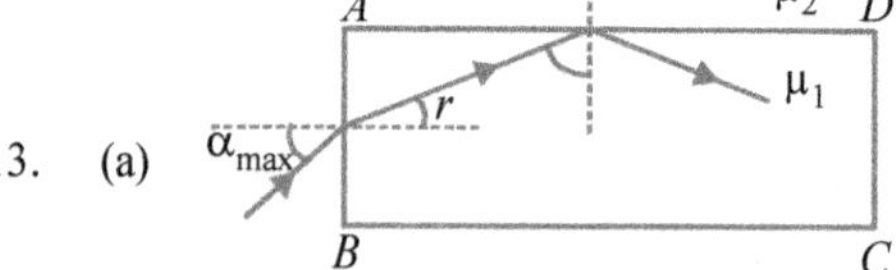

$$\sin C = \frac{1}{\mu} = \frac{1}{4/3} = \frac{3}{4} .$$

Now $\qquad r = h\tan C$

$$= 12 \times \frac{3}{\sqrt{7}}$$

$$= \frac{36}{\sqrt{7}} \text{ cm}$$

13. (a)

Ray comes out from CD, when it get reflected from AD.

$$\frac{n_1}{n_2} = \frac{\sin \alpha_{max}}{\sin r_1}$$

$$\Rightarrow \quad \alpha_{max} = \sin^{-1}\left[\frac{\mu_1}{\mu_2}\sin r_1\right]$$

Also $\qquad r_1 = 90° - \theta = 90° - C$

or $\qquad r_1 = 90° - \sin^{-1}\left(\dfrac{1}{2\mu_1}\right)$

or $\qquad r_1 = 90° - \sin^{-1}\left(\dfrac{\mu_2}{\mu_1}\right)$

$\therefore \quad \alpha_{max} = \sin^{-1}\left[\dfrac{\mu_1}{\mu_2}\sin\left\{90° - \sin^{-1}\dfrac{\mu_2}{\mu_1}\right\}\right]$

$\qquad\qquad = \sin^{-1}\left[\dfrac{\mu_1}{\mu_2}\cos\left\{\sin^{-1}\left(\dfrac{\mu_2}{\mu_1}\right)\right\}\right]$

14. (b)

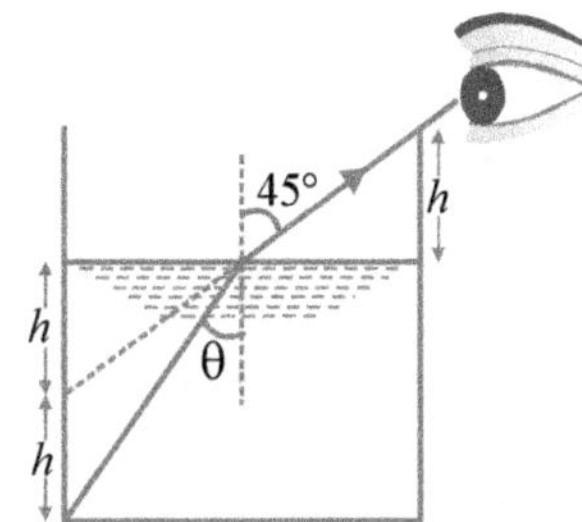

$$\sin\theta = \dfrac{h}{\sqrt{h^2 + (2h)^2}} = \dfrac{1}{\sqrt{5}}$$

$\therefore \qquad \mu = \dfrac{\sin 45°}{\sin\theta}$

$$= \dfrac{1/\sqrt{2}}{1/\sqrt{5}} = \sqrt{\dfrac{5}{2}}.$$

15. (b) For glass-water interface,

$$_g\mu_w = \dfrac{\sin i}{\sin r}$$

For water-air interface

$$_w\mu_a = \dfrac{\sin i}{\sin 90°}$$

Now $\quad _g\mu_w \times {_w\mu_a} = \dfrac{\sin i}{\sin r} \times \dfrac{\sin r}{\sin 90°} = \sin i$

$\Rightarrow \quad \dfrac{\mu_w}{\mu_g} \times \dfrac{\mu_a}{\mu_w} = \sin i, \quad \therefore \ \mu_g = \dfrac{1}{\sin i}.$

16. (c) The distance of object from mirror

$$= 15 + \dfrac{33.25}{4} \times 3 = 39.93 \text{ cm}$$

Distance of image from mirror

$$= 15 + \dfrac{25 \times 3}{4} = 33.75 \text{ cm}$$

Using mirror formula,

$$\dfrac{1}{v} + \dfrac{1}{u} = \dfrac{1}{f}$$

or $\dfrac{1}{-33.93} + \dfrac{1}{-33.75} = \dfrac{1}{f}$

$\therefore \qquad\qquad f = -18.3 \text{ cm}$

17. (b) The apparent height of object from mirror is $= \dfrac{h}{\mu}$.

So distance between object and its image $= \dfrac{2h}{\mu}$.

18. (b) See example.

19. (b)

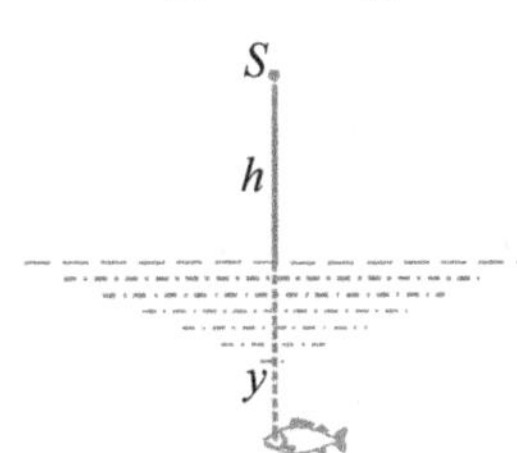

For TIR, $\qquad i > C$

or $\qquad\qquad \sin i > \sin C$

or $\qquad\qquad \dfrac{R}{R+d} > \dfrac{1}{1.5}$

or $\qquad\qquad d < 0.5\,R$

or $\qquad\qquad \dfrac{d}{R} < 0.5$

$\therefore \qquad \left(\dfrac{d}{R}\right)_{max} = 0.5$

20. (a) Given, $\qquad \dfrac{dy}{dt} = \dfrac{-dh}{dt}$

The apparent distance of source from fish,

$$x = \mu h + y$$

or $\qquad \dfrac{dx}{dt} = \mu\dfrac{dh}{dt} + \dfrac{dy}{dt}$

or $\qquad v = \mu\dfrac{dh}{dt} - \dfrac{dh}{dt}$

$$= (\mu - 1)\dfrac{dh}{dt} \quad \dots \text{(i)}$$

We know that

$$\dfrac{df}{f} = \dfrac{v}{c}$$

or $\qquad v = c\dfrac{df}{f} \qquad \dots \text{(ii)}$

Now from equations (i) and (ii), we have

$$\dfrac{df}{f} = \dfrac{(\mu - 1)}{c}\dfrac{dh}{dt}.$$

21. (a)

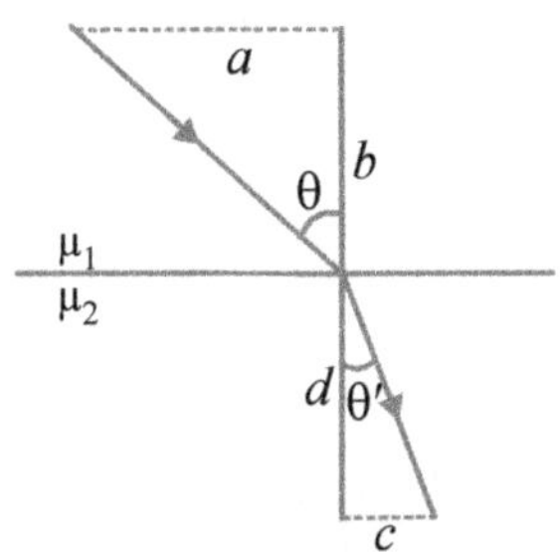

As $\hat{u}_1$ and $\hat{u}_2$ and the unit vectors and so

$$\sqrt{a^2 + b^2} = \sqrt{c^2 + d^2}$$

Now using Snell's law, we have

$$\frac{\mu_2}{\mu_1} = \frac{\sin\theta}{\sin\theta'}$$

or

$$\frac{2}{1.5} = \frac{a/\sqrt{a^2+b^2}}{c/\sqrt{c^2+d^2}}$$

or

$$\frac{4}{3} = \frac{a}{c}.$$

22. (b)

$$\sin\theta = \frac{1}{_r\mu_d} = \frac{\mu_r}{\mu_d}$$

$$= \frac{\mu_0/8}{\mu_0} = \frac{1}{8}$$

or

$$\theta = \sin^{-1}\left(\frac{1}{8}\right)$$

23. (c) The distance of bottom of the beaker from mirror

$$= h - d\left(1 - \frac{1}{\mu}\right)$$

So it will be at a distance $= h - d\left(1 - \frac{1}{\mu}\right)$ from mirror. Now

distance between bottom of beaker and image

$$= h + h - d\left(1 - \frac{1}{\mu}\right) = 2h - d\left(\frac{\mu-1}{\mu}\right).$$

24. (d) The apparent distance of O $= \dfrac{t_1}{3\mu_1} + \dfrac{t_2}{3\mu_2}$

$$= \frac{t_1}{\mu_1/\mu_3} + \frac{t_2}{\mu_2/\mu_3}$$

$$= \mu_3\left(\frac{t_1}{\mu_1} + \frac{t_2}{\mu_2}\right).$$

25. (a) The deviation produced by prism

$$\delta = (\mu - 1)A$$
$$= (1.5 - 1) \times 4 = 2°$$

Thus the angle through which mirror should be rotated is 1°.

26. (c) The shift produced by the slab towards mirror

$$= t\left(1 - \frac{1}{\mu}\right)$$

$$= 6\left(1 - \frac{1}{1.5}\right) = 2\,\text{cm}$$

If the object is placed at $40 + 2 = 42$ cm, its apparent distance from mirror will be 40 cm and so its image will coincide with the object.

27. (c)

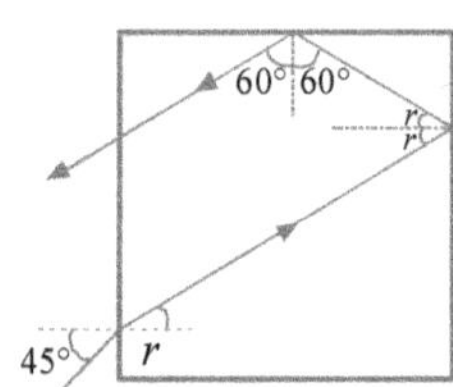

From Snell's law,

$$\frac{\sin 45°}{\sin r} = \sqrt{2}$$

or

$$\sin r = \frac{1}{2}$$

$$\therefore \qquad r = 30°$$

Critical angle, $\sin C = \dfrac{1}{\mu} = \dfrac{1}{\sqrt{2}}$

$$\therefore \qquad C = 45°$$

So ray comes out antiparallel to the incident ray.

28. (d) The angle of prism, $A = 180° - (67° + 53°)$
$$= 60°$$

The deviation ,

$$A + \delta = i + e$$

or $\qquad 60° + \delta = 36° + 32°$

$$\therefore \qquad \delta = 8°$$

For minimum deviation $i = e$, and so angle of deviation should be less than 8°.

29. (b) Using Snell's law (at origin),

$$\mu = \frac{\sin 90°}{\sin\theta} \quad \text{or } \sin\theta = \frac{1}{\mu}$$

$$\therefore \tan\theta = \frac{1}{\sqrt{\mu^2 - 1}} = \frac{1}{\sqrt{1 + e^{x/d}} - 1} = e^{-\frac{x}{2d}}$$

or

$$\frac{dy}{dx} = e^{-x/2d}$$

or

$$\int_0^d dy = \int_0^x e^{-x/2d}\,dx$$

$$\therefore \qquad x = d\ln 4.$$

30. (b) Optical path $= \displaystyle\int_0^1 \mu\,dx$

$$= \int_0^1 1.5(2 - x)\,dx$$

$$= \left|3x - \frac{1.5x^2}{2}\right|_0^1 = 2.25$$

31. (b) Lateral shift is given by

$$\delta = t(\sin\theta - \cos\theta\tan r)$$

or $\qquad \dfrac{1}{\sqrt{3}} = 1(\sin 45° - \cos 45°\tan r)$

$$\therefore \qquad r = \tan^{-1}(1 - \sqrt{2/3})$$

32. (b)

$$\mu = \frac{\sin 2A}{\sin A}$$

$$= \frac{2\sin A\cos A}{\sin A}$$

$$= 2\cos A$$

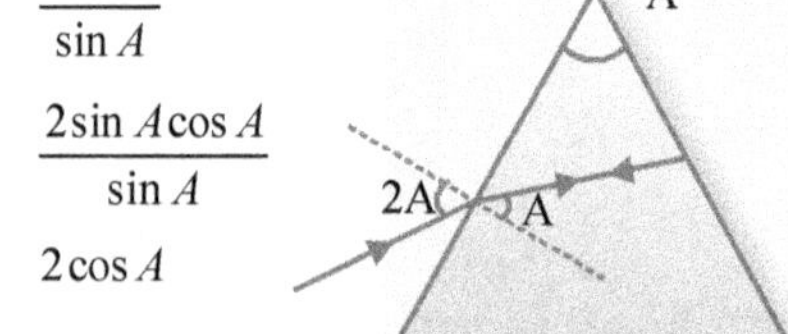

33. (c) Meta material has a negative refractive index

$$\therefore \text{(c) } \sin\theta_2 = \frac{\mu_1}{\mu_2}\sin\theta_1 \Rightarrow \mu_2 \text{ is negative}$$

$$\therefore \theta_2 \text{ negative.}$$

Solutions EXERCISE 2.2

1. (a, c)

2. (b, c)

We can write,

$$\frac{v_1}{v_2} = \frac{\sin i}{\sin r} = \cot 30°$$

$$= \sqrt{3} = 1.732.$$

Critical angle, $\sin C = \frac{1}{\mu} = \frac{1}{\sqrt{3}}$

3. (a, b)

4. (b, c)

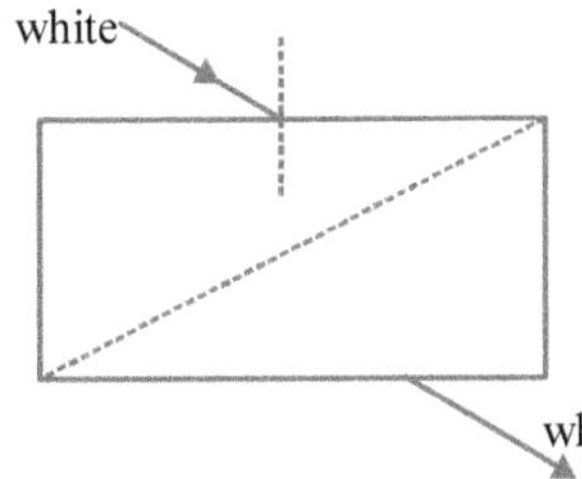

A slab can be assumed to made of two identical prisms placed oppositely. So they cancel dispersion to each other and produces white light.

5. (a, b, c)

6. (a, d)

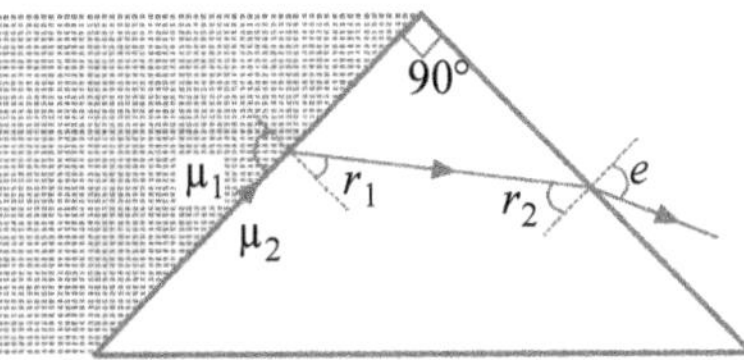

By Snell's law,

$$\frac{\mu_2}{\mu_1} = \frac{\sin 90°}{\sin r_1}$$

or $\sin r_1 = \left(\frac{\mu_1}{\mu_2}\right)$

Similarly,

$$\frac{\sin e}{\sin r_2} = \mu_2$$

or $\sin r_2 = \dfrac{\sin e}{\mu_2}$

or $\sin(90° - r_1) = \dfrac{\sin e}{\mu_2}$

or $\cos r_1 = \dfrac{\sin e}{\mu_2}$

or $\sqrt{1 - \sin^2 r_1} = \dfrac{\sin e}{\mu_2}$

or $\sqrt{1 - \left(\dfrac{\mu_1}{\mu_2}\right)^2} = \dfrac{\sin e}{\mu_2}$

$\therefore \quad \mu_1^2 + \sin^2 e = \mu_2^2$

Also $\sin e = \dfrac{1}{\mu_2} = \dfrac{1}{\sqrt{3}}$

Now $r_1 = 90° - r_2 = 90° - e$

or $\sin r_1 = \sin(90° - e)$

$= \cos e$

$= \sqrt{1 - \sin^2 e}$

$= \sqrt{\dfrac{2}{3}}$

7. (b, d) Ray 1 and Ray 2 may have any angle between them. Similarly ray 5 and ray 6 may have any angle between them. This depends on angle of incidence on first face.

8. (c, d) $C_{max} = 45°$

$\therefore \quad \mu_{min} = \dfrac{1}{\sin C_{max}}$

$= \dfrac{1}{\sin 45°}$

$= \sqrt{2} = 1.414$

Solutions EXERCISE 2.3

1. (d) The medium of object and observer are same so length of scale remains same.

2. (d) Different colours of light travel with same speed in vacuum.

3. (c) Setting sun appears red. Scattering of light in proportional

$$\propto \frac{1}{\lambda^4}.$$

4. (b) Stars are large distance from earth.

5. (c) Reflected and refracted ray are mutually perpendicular in a specific case.

6. (b) Glittering of diamond is due to total interval reflection.

7. (c)

8. (d) The critical angle, $\sin C = \dfrac{1}{_r\mu_d} = \dfrac{\sqrt{3}}{\sqrt{6}} = \dfrac{1}{\sqrt{2}}$, or $C = 45°$.

9. (c) Dispersive power depends on material only.

10. (a) Statement -2 explains statement -1

11. (a)

Solutions EXERCISE 2.4

1. (a) For plane wave fronts the beam of light is parallel.

2. (c) Since points c and d are on the same wavefront, therefore $\phi_d = \phi_c$

Similarly, $\phi_e = \phi_f$

$\therefore \quad \phi_d - \phi_f = \phi_c - \phi_f$

3. (b) The gap between consecutive wavefronts in medium 2 is less than that is medium 1. Therefore, wavelength of light in medium 2 is less than that in medium 1. Therefore, speed of light is more in medium 1 and less in medium 2.

4. (c) The ray is incident on face AC at an angle A, after reflection, it incident of face BC at an angle B. Thus

$$\angle A + \angle B = 90°.$$

As $B < A$, so the ray if totally reflected from face BC, it must be reflected from AC also. For this angle B should be greater than critical angle C. For minimum value of μ, B can be infinitesimally than C, so $B = C$ (critical angle).We know that

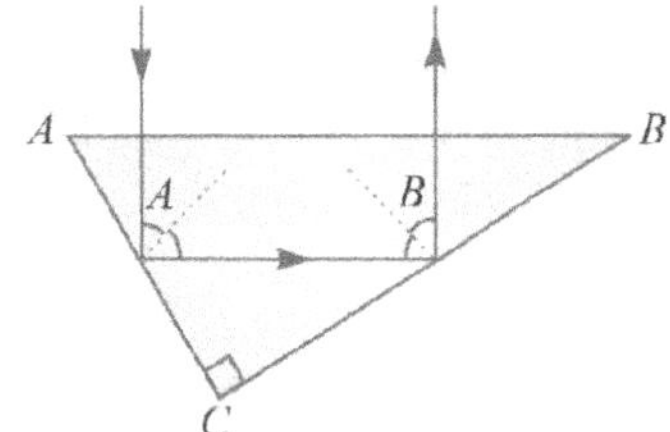

$$\mu = \frac{1}{\sin C}$$

$$= \frac{1}{\sin B}$$

For $A = B$, $\quad B = 45°$

$$\therefore \quad \mu_{min} = \frac{1}{\sin 45°} = \sqrt{2}$$

5. (d) When $\mu = 5/3$, then

$$\sin C = \frac{1}{5/3} = \frac{3}{5}$$

or $\quad C = 37°$.

In this case, the angle of incidence $B = 30°$, which is less than the critical angle, so the condition can not be achieved.

6. A-t : The angle of deviation, $\delta = 180° - 2i = 180° - 2 \times 60° = 60°$

B-p : Glass slab produces no deviation and so $\delta = 0$.

C-q, s : Deviation in both the cases are $180°$.

D-r : $\delta = 60° - 30° = 30°$

Solutions EXERCISE 2.5

1. If i and r are the angle of incident and angle of refraction respectively, then

$$i + r = 90°$$
$$\therefore \quad r = 90° - i$$

By Snell's law, $\quad \dfrac{\sin i}{\sin r} = \mu$

or $\quad \dfrac{\sin i}{\sin(90° - i)} = \mu$

or $\quad \dfrac{\sin i}{\cos i} = \mu$

or $\quad \tan i = \mu$

$\therefore \quad i = \tan^{-1}(\mu) = \tan^{-1}(1.5)$

$$\simeq 57° \qquad \textit{Ans.}$$

2. If y is the apparent distance of the coin, then

$$y = \frac{40}{\mu}$$

$$= \frac{40}{4/3} = 30 \, cm$$

If h is the height of the lamp from the water surface, then its image will be at a distance h below the water surface. Both the images to be coincide, $h = 30$ cm

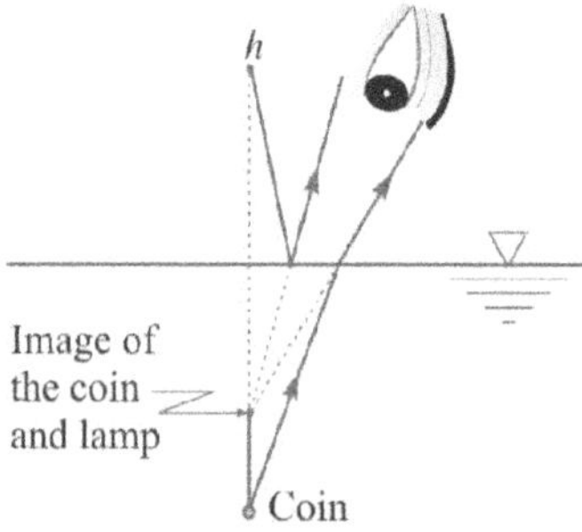

3. Let θ is the angle of incidence and C_1 is the critical angle, then

$$\sin \theta > \sin C,$$

$$> \frac{\mu_1}{\mu_2}$$

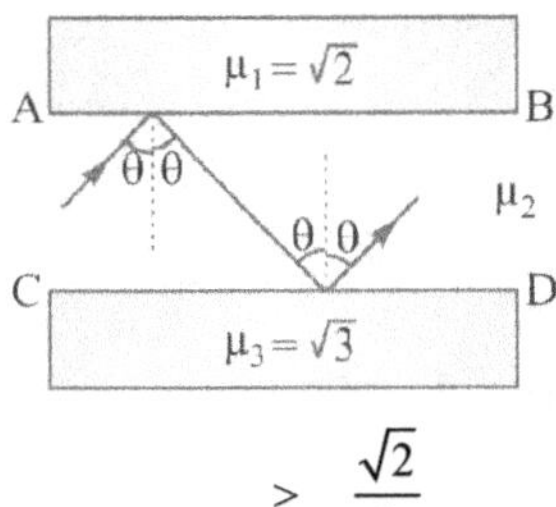

$$> \frac{\sqrt{2}}{2}$$

$$\therefore \qquad \theta > 45°.$$

For total internal reflection at the face CD

$$\sin\theta > \sin C_2$$

$$> \frac{\mu_3}{\mu_2}$$

$$> \frac{\sqrt{3}}{2}$$

$$\therefore \qquad \theta > 60°$$

For total internal reflection at both the surfaces

$$\theta_{\min} = 60°. \qquad\qquad Ans.$$

4. (i) & (ii) Given, $A = 60°$ and $\mu = 1.5$.
We know that

$$\mu = \frac{\sin\left(\dfrac{A + \delta_m}{2}\right)}{\sin(A/2)}$$

or

$$1.5 = \frac{\sin\left(\dfrac{60° + \delta_m}{2}\right)}{\sin(60°/2)}$$

or

$$\sin\left(\frac{60° + \delta_m}{2}\right) = 1.5\sin 30°$$

After solving, $\qquad \delta_m = 37°$.

Angle of incidence $\qquad i = \dfrac{A + \delta_m}{2}$

$$= \frac{60° + 37°}{2} = 48°$$

(iii) For maximum deviation, $\quad i = 90°$

$$\therefore \quad r_1 = C = \sin^{-1}\left(\frac{1}{1.5}\right) = 42°.$$

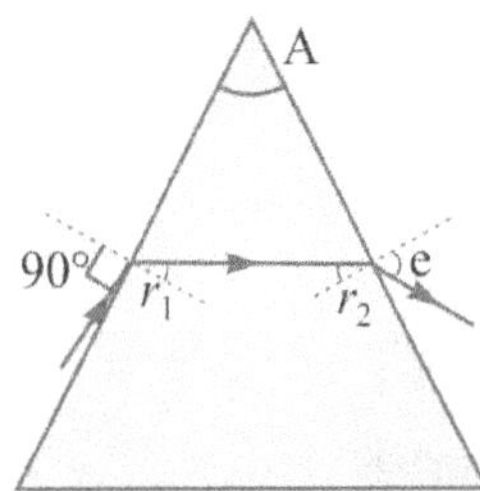

We know that, $\quad r_1 + r_2 = A = 60°$

$$\therefore \qquad r_2 = 60° - r_1 = 60° - 42°$$
$$= 18°.$$

Now by Snell's law

$$\frac{\sin e}{\sin 18°} = 1.5$$

$$\therefore \qquad e = 28°$$

1. By Snell's law

$$\frac{\sin i}{\sin r} = \mu$$

$$\therefore \qquad \sin r = \frac{\sin i}{\mu} \qquad\qquad \dots (i)$$

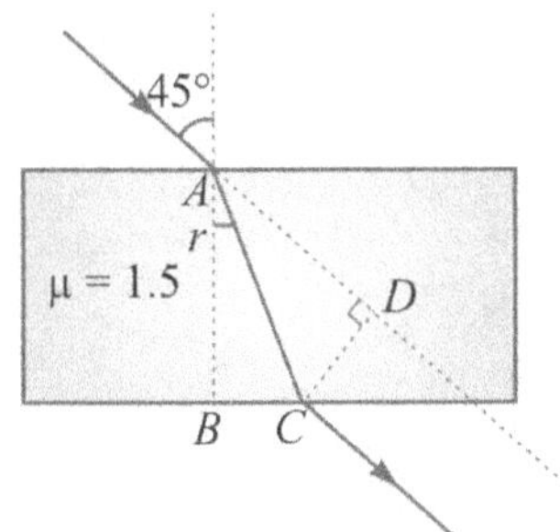

In $\triangle ABC$, $\qquad AC = \dfrac{AB}{\cos r}$

In $\triangle ACD$, $\qquad CD = AC\sin(i - r)$

$$= \frac{AB}{\cos r}\sin(i - r) \qquad \dots (ii)$$

On substituting $\quad AB = \sqrt{2}$ cm, $i = 45°$
and solving $\qquad CD = 0.62$ cm. $\qquad$ ***Ans.***

2. (a) The image S' of the point S is shown in figure. The apparent height of the image S is given by $h' = \mu h$.
Thus apparent distance of S' from the bottom of the vessel will be

$$= d + \mu h$$

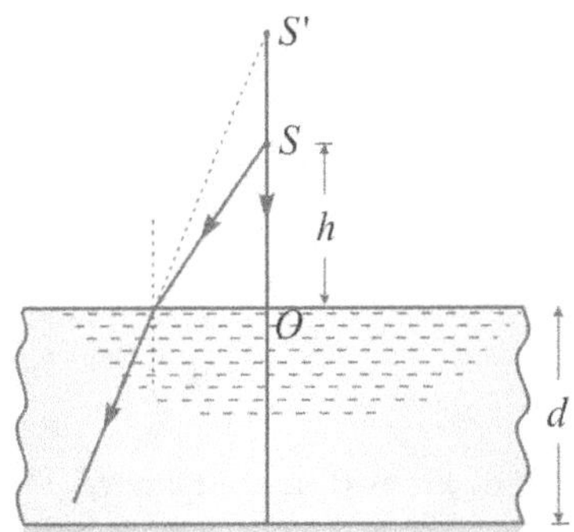

The image of S' thus will be at a distance of $(d + \mu h)$ below the bottom of the vessel.

(b) The distance of the image S_1 of S' from the surface of the water,

$$OS_1 = d + (d + \mu h)$$
$$= (2d + \mu h).$$

Now by using the formula

$$\frac{\text{real depth}}{\text{apparent depth}} = \mu$$

We have

$$\frac{OS_1}{OS_2} = \mu$$

$$OS_2 = \frac{OS_1}{\mu}$$

$$= \frac{(2d + \mu h)}{\mu}$$

$$= \frac{2d}{\mu} + h = \frac{2d}{4/3} + h$$

$$= \frac{3d}{2} + h \qquad \textbf{Ans.}$$

3. The angle of incidence i is equal to, $\sin i = \dfrac{3}{5}$.

By Snell's law $\qquad \dfrac{\sin 45°}{\sin i} = \mu$

or $\qquad \dfrac{\sin 45°}{3/5} = \mu$

$\therefore \qquad \mu = \dfrac{5}{3\sqrt{2}}.$

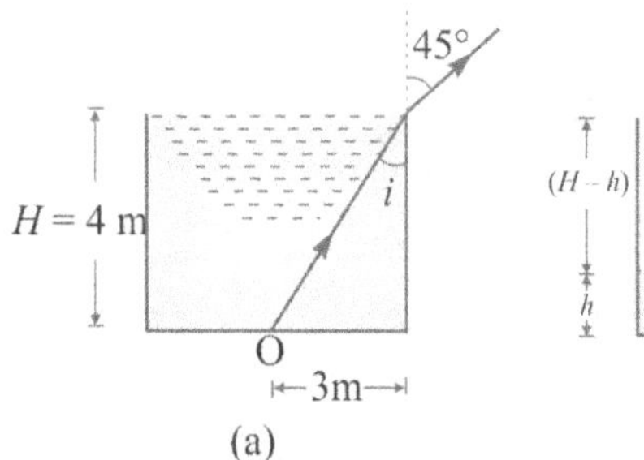

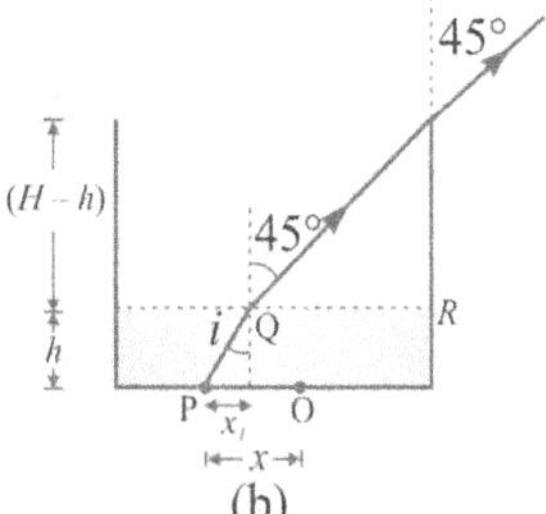

When the cork is opened, the level of liquid in the tank decreases. Let h be the height and P is the position of the insect after time t. As the insect is still visible, so ray after refraction at the surface of liquid will reach the observer at an angle $45°$. Therefore

$$\tan i = \frac{h}{x_1}$$

Also $\qquad \tan i = \dfrac{3}{4}$

$\therefore \qquad \dfrac{h}{x_1} = \dfrac{3}{4}$

or $\qquad x_1 = \dfrac{3h}{4}.$

The distance of the insect from the centre,

$$x = (QR - 3) + x_1$$

$$= (H - h) - 3 + \frac{3h}{4}$$

$$= 4 - h - 3 + \frac{3h}{4}$$

$$= 1 - \frac{h}{4}$$

or $\qquad h = 4(1 - x).$

On differentiating, we have

$$\frac{dx}{dt} = -\frac{1}{4}\left(\frac{dh}{dt}\right)$$

or $\qquad \dfrac{dh}{dt} = -4\left(\dfrac{dx}{dt}\right). \qquad \ldots (i)$

From the equation of continuity

$$A\left(\frac{-dh}{dt}\right) = a\sqrt{2gh} \qquad \ldots (ii)$$

Here A is the area of the tank and a is the area of hole (cork). From equations (i) and (ii), we have

$$(4A)\frac{dx}{dt} = a\sqrt{2g \times 4(1-x)}$$

$$= a\sqrt{8g}(1-x)^{1/2}$$

or $\qquad 4A\displaystyle\int_0^x (1-x)^{-1/2}\,dx = a\sqrt{8g}\int_0^t dt$

or $\qquad -\Big|2(1-x)^{1/x}\Big|_0^x = \dfrac{a}{4A}\sqrt{8g}\,t$

or $\qquad -(1-x)^{1/2} + 1 = \dfrac{a\sqrt{8g}}{8A}t$

or $\qquad (1-x)^{1/2} = 1 - \dfrac{a\sqrt{8g}}{8A}t \qquad \ldots (iii)$

From equations (ii) and (iii), we have

$$4A\frac{dx}{dt} = a\sqrt{8g}\left[1 - \frac{a}{8A}\sqrt{8g}\,t\right]$$

As $\dfrac{dx}{dt} = v$, so the speed of the insect

$\therefore \qquad v = \dfrac{a\sqrt{8g}}{4A}\left[1 - \dfrac{a}{8A}\sqrt{8g}t\right] Ans.$

4. The situation is shown in figure. If C is the critical angle, then

$$\sin C = \frac{1}{\mu}$$

$\therefore \qquad \tan C = \dfrac{1}{\sqrt{\mu^2 - 1}}.$

From the geometry,

$$\frac{r}{h} = \tan C = \frac{1}{\sqrt{\mu^2 - 1}}$$

$\therefore \qquad r = \dfrac{h}{\sqrt{\mu^2 - 1}}.$

The area $\quad A = \pi r^2 = \pi\left[\dfrac{h}{\sqrt{\mu^2 - 1}}\right]^2 = \dfrac{\pi h^2}{\mu^2 - 1}. \quad \textbf{Ans.}$

5. The path of the ray to be retraced, the angle of refraction at the first face must be $30°$. Thus by Snell's law

$$\mu = \frac{\sin 45°}{\sin 30°} = \sqrt{2}.$$

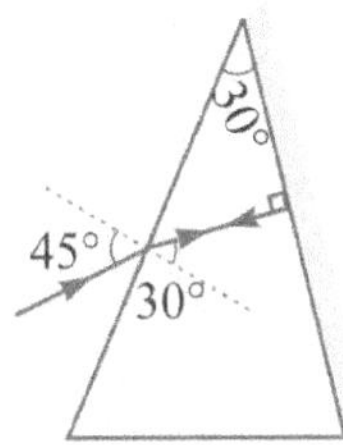

6. If r is the angle of refraction on a plane face of the rod, then

$$\mu = \frac{\sin \alpha}{\sin r}$$

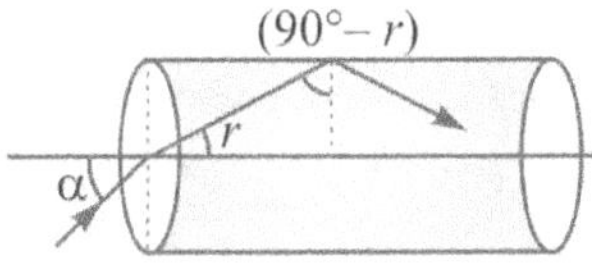

$$\therefore \quad \sin r = \frac{\sin \alpha}{\mu}.$$

The angle of incidence on curved surface of the rod $= 90° - r$. For ray to be totally reflected, $90° - r \geq C$, where C is the critical angle or we can write

$$\sin(90° - r) \geq \sin C$$

or $$\cos r \geq \sin C$$

or $$\sqrt{1 - \sin^2 r} \geq \sin C$$

or $$1 - \left(\frac{\sin \alpha}{\mu}\right)^2 \geq \sin^2 C$$

As $\sin C = \dfrac{1}{\mu}$

$$\therefore \quad 1 - \frac{\sin^2 \alpha}{\mu^2} \geq \frac{1}{\mu^2}$$

or $$\frac{1 + \sin^2 \alpha}{\mu^2} \leq 1$$

or $$1 + \sin^2 \alpha \leq \mu^2$$

The maximum value of $\sin^2 \alpha = +1$

$$\therefore \quad \mu^2 \geq 2$$

or $$\mu \geq \sqrt{2}$$

or $$\mu_{min} = \sqrt{2}. \qquad \textbf{\textit{Ans.}}$$

7. (i) Let us consider the case when $\mu_3 < \mu_1$

Since $\mu_1 < \mu_2$, $\therefore \mu_3 << \mu_2$

If C_1 is the critical angle for medium II to III, then

$$\sin C_1 = \frac{\mu_3}{\mu_2}$$

Similarly critical angle from II to I,

$$\sin C_2 = \frac{\mu_1}{\mu_2}$$

Clearly $C_1 < C_2$.

Thus if $\sin \theta > \sin C_2$, then $\sin \theta$ will be greater than $\sin C_1$.

Hence the ray incident on AB at an angle θ will reflected back into II medium.

(ii) Now consider the case when $\mu_3 > \mu_1$:

$$\sin C_1 = \frac{\mu_3}{\mu_2} \text{ and } \sin C_2 = \frac{\mu_1}{\mu_2}$$

Here $C_2 < C_1$, $\therefore$ for $\theta > C_2$, the angle θ may be less than C and so refraction will takesplace on face AB. The angle of refraction θ' is given by

$$\frac{\sin \theta'}{\sin \theta} = \frac{\mu_2}{\mu_3}$$

$$\therefore \quad \sin \theta' = \frac{\mu_2}{\mu_3} \sin \theta$$

or $$\sin \theta' > \frac{\mu_2}{\mu_3} \sin C_2$$

$$> \frac{\mu_2}{\mu_3} \times \frac{\mu_1}{\mu_2}$$

Thus $$\sin \theta' > \frac{\mu_1}{\mu_3}.$$

This shows that total internal reflection will take place at face DE. The situation is shown in figure.

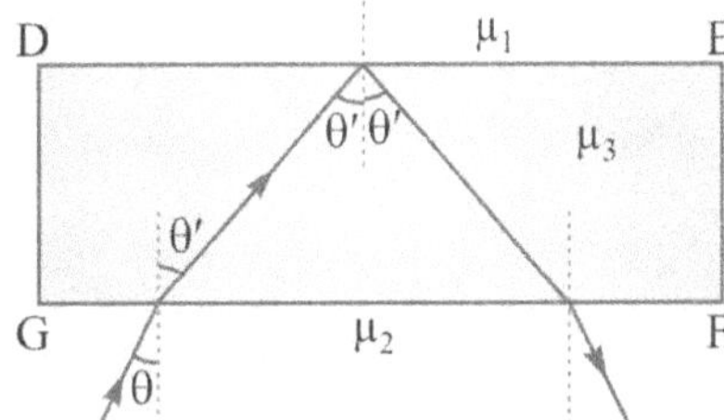

8. Suppose the angle of refraction of prism is α. The angle of incidence of ray on second face becomes α, which on reflection incident on first face at an angle 2α (see figure). Thus $\beta = 2\alpha$. Also $\alpha + 2\beta = 180°$

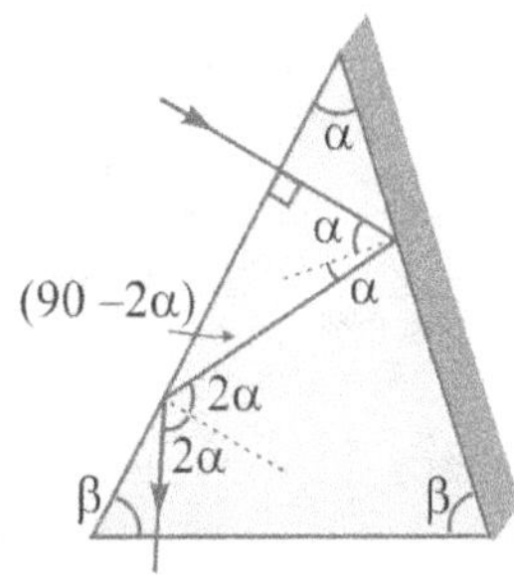

or $$\alpha + 2(2\alpha) = 180°$$

$\therefore \alpha = 36°$ and $\beta = 72°$ **Ans**

9. For crown glass, $$\mu_y = \frac{\mu_v + \mu_R}{2} = \frac{1.51 + 1.49}{2}$$
$$= 1.50$$

For flint glass, $$\mu'_y = \frac{1.77 + 1.73}{2} = 1.75$$

If δ_y and δ'_y are the deviations produced by crown and flint glass respectively, then for no deviation

$$\delta_y + \delta'_y = 0$$

or $(\mu_y - 1)A + (\mu'_y - 1)A' = 0$

$\therefore \qquad A' = -\dfrac{(\mu_y - 1)A}{(\mu'_y - 1)}$

$$= -\dfrac{(1.50 - 1) \times 6°}{(1.75 - 1)} = -4°$$

The total dispersion is given by

$$\Delta\theta = (\mu_v - \mu_R)A + (\mu'_v - \mu'_R)A'$$
$$= (1.51 - 1.49) \times 6° + (1.77 - 1.73) \times (-4°)$$
$$= -0.04$$
$$= 0.04 \text{ (numerically)}$$

10. For concave mirror, $u = -5$ cm, $f = -20$ m

By mirror formula, $\dfrac{1}{v} + \dfrac{1}{u} = \dfrac{1}{f}$, we have

$$\dfrac{1}{v} + \dfrac{1}{-5} = \dfrac{1}{-20}$$

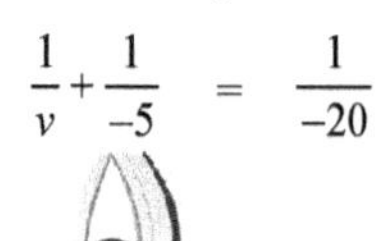

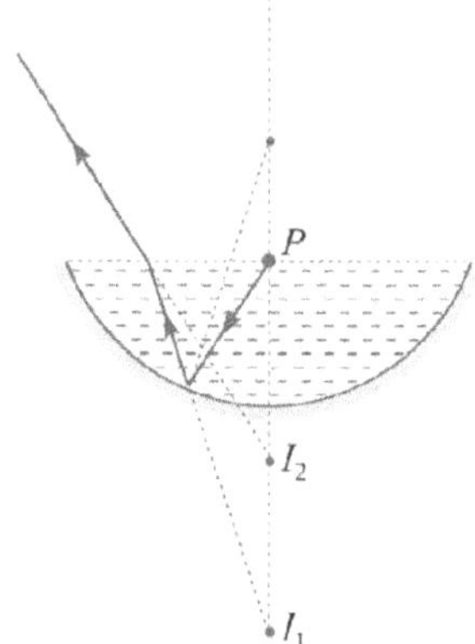

$\therefore \qquad v = +\dfrac{20}{3}$ cm

Thus $OI' = \dfrac{20}{3}$ cm

$$= 11.67 \text{ cm}$$

The distance $PI' = \dfrac{20}{3} + 5$

$$= 11.67 \text{ cm.}$$

Now for the refraction through water surface, we have

$$\mu = \dfrac{RD}{AD}$$

$\therefore \qquad AD = \dfrac{RD}{\mu} = \dfrac{11.67}{4/3}$

or $PI_2 = 8.75$ cm.   Ans.

11. (a) For no deviation, the angle of second prism is given by

$$A' = -\dfrac{(\mu_y - 1)}{(\mu'_y - 1)}A$$

$$= -\dfrac{(1.50 - 1)}{(1.60 - 1)} \times 6.0°$$

$$= -5°$$

(b) We know that , $\omega = \dfrac{\delta_v - \delta_R}{\delta_y} = \dfrac{(\mu_v - \mu_R)}{(\mu_y - 1)}$

$\therefore \qquad (\mu_v - \mu_R) = \omega(\mu_y - 1)$
$$= 0.07 (1.50 - 1)$$
$$= 0.035 \qquad Ans.$$

For second prism
$$(\mu'_v - \mu'_R) = \omega'(\mu'_y - 1)$$
$$= 0.08 (1.60 - 1)$$
$$= 0.048$$

The net angular dispersion is given by

$$\Delta\theta = (\mu_v - \mu_R)A + (\mu'_v - \mu'_R)A'$$
$$= 0.035 \times 6.0° + 0.048 (-5°)$$
$$= 0.03° \text{ (numerically)}$$

(c) When prisms are similarly directed, the total deviation

$$\delta = \delta + \delta'$$
$$= (\mu_y - 1)A + (\mu'_y - 1)A'$$
$$= (1.50 - 1) \times 6° + (1.60 - 1) \times 5°$$
$$= 6° \qquad Ans.$$

12. (a) For the minimum deviation by the prism ABC
$$r_1 = r_2 = A/2$$
$$= \dfrac{60°}{2} = 30°$$

By Snell's law, we have

$$\dfrac{\sin i}{\sin 30°} = \sqrt{3}$$

or $\sin i = \sqrt{3} \times \sin 30°$

On solving $i = 60°$

(b) Net minimum deviation will occur when prism CDE is rotated anticlockwise by 60°.

In this situation, deviation produced by prism ABC will cancel out by deviation produced by CDE. Thus

$$\delta_{net} = 0 \text{ (see figure).}$$

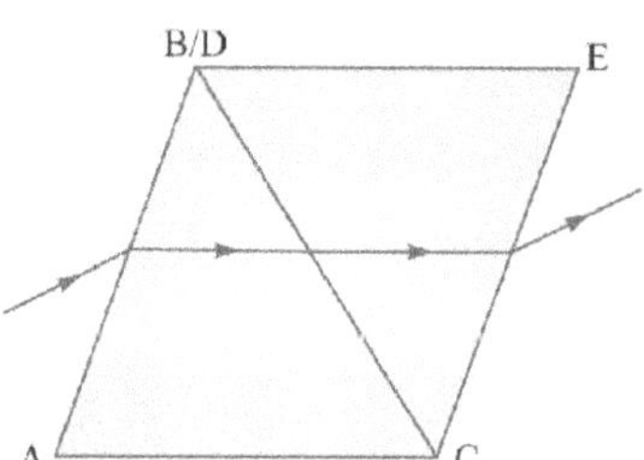

13. The focal length of the mirror $f = -50$ cm.

For the sun, practically at infinite distance, its real image will form at the focus of the mirror. Since water level is 80 cm from the mirror, so the image will form inside water. Therefore image distance will be 50 cm from the mirror.

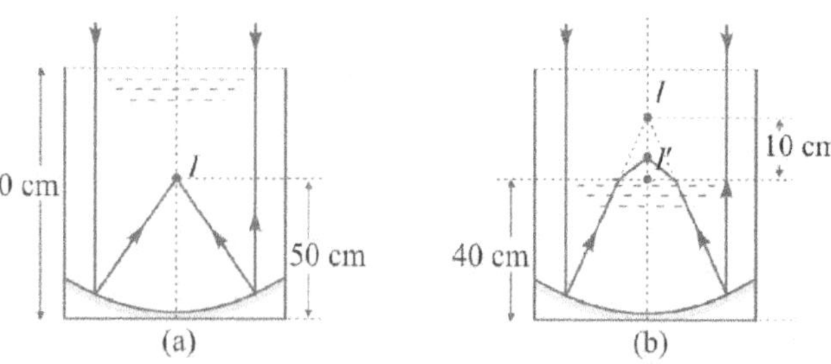

In case when water in the tank is 40 cm, the rays after reflection from mirror, get refracted from free surface of water and form final image at I'. For free surface of water virtual object distance is 10 cm, its image I' will be $40 + 7.5 = 47.5$ cm from the mirror.

Chapter 3

Refraction at Spherical Surface Lenses and Photometry

(107- 182)

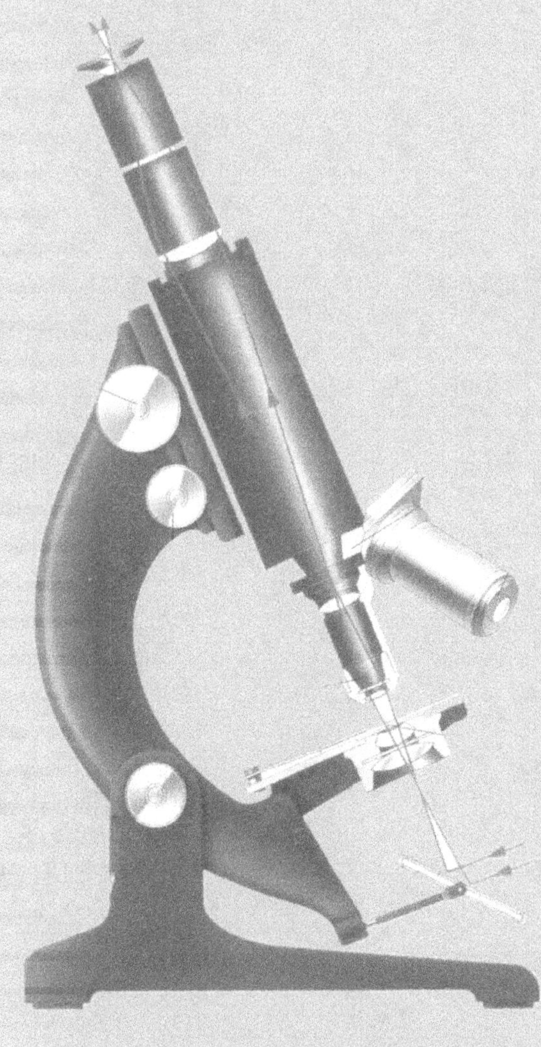

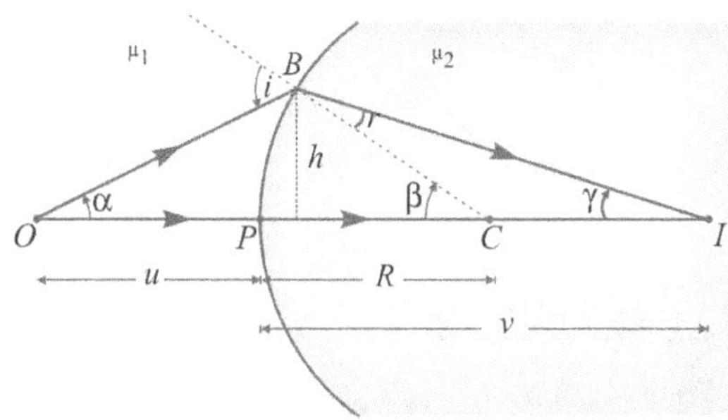

Fig. 3.1

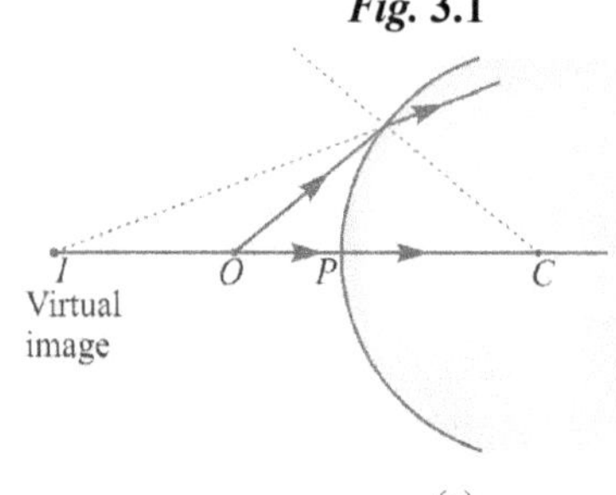

(a)

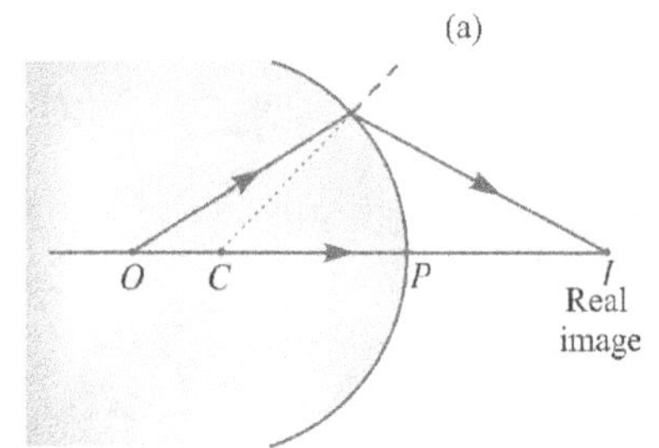

(b)

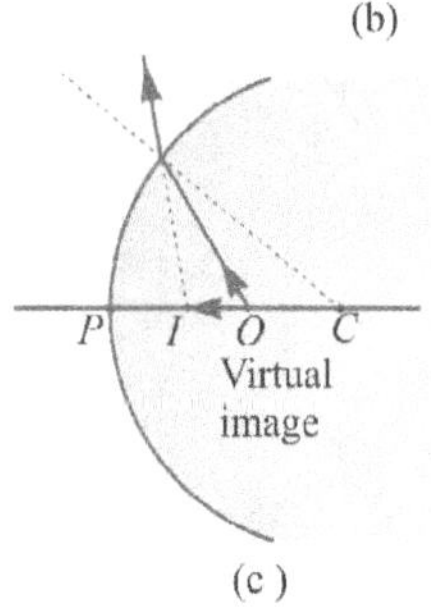

(c)

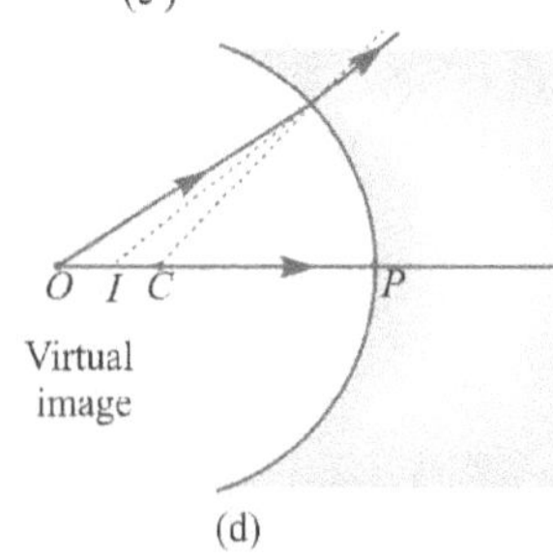

(d)

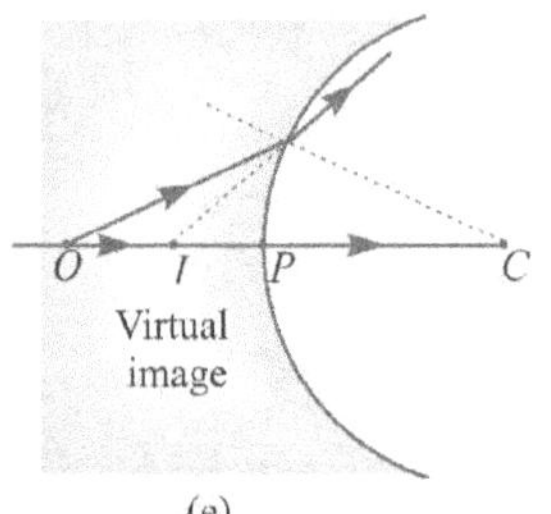

(e)

Fig. 3.2

3.1 REFRACTION AT A SPHERICAL SURFACE

Consider a spherical surface of radius R. The refractive indexes at left and right of the surface are μ_1 and μ_2 respectively. Let an object O be placed at a distance u from pole P of the surface in a medium of refractive index μ_1. Ray OP, incident normally, passes into the second medium without deviation. Ray OB, making an angle α with the principal axis, is incident at an angle i with the normal and is refracted at an angle r. These rays intersect at I at a distance v to the right of pole P. Thus I is the real image of the object O.

From the triangles OBC and IBC, we have

$$i = \alpha + \beta$$

and
$$\beta = r + \gamma \text{ or } r = \beta - \gamma$$

From Snell's law

$$\frac{\mu_2}{\mu_1} = \frac{\sin i}{\sin r}$$

or
$$\mu_1 \sin i = \mu_2 \sin r$$

For small angle of incidence i, we can write

$$\sin i \simeq i \text{ and } \sin r \simeq r$$

Thus
$$\mu_1 i = \mu_2 r$$

or
$$\mu_1 (\alpha + \beta) = \mu_2 (\beta - r) \qquad \text{...(i)}$$

As i is small, and so α, β and γ are also small. Thus

$$(\alpha + \beta) = \tan\alpha + \tan\beta$$

$$= \frac{h}{-u} + \frac{h}{+R}$$

and
$$(\beta - \gamma) = \frac{h}{R} - \frac{h}{v}$$

On substituting these values in equation (i), we have

$$\mu_1 \left[\frac{h}{-u} + \frac{h}{+R} \right] = \mu_2 \left[\frac{h}{R} - \frac{h}{v} \right]$$

After simplifying, we get

$$\frac{\mu_2}{v} - \frac{\mu_1}{u} = \frac{\mu_2 - \mu_1}{R} \qquad \text{...(1)}$$

Also
$$\frac{\frac{\mu_2}{\mu_1}}{v} - \frac{1}{u} = \frac{\frac{\mu_2}{\mu_1} - 1}{R}$$

or
$$\frac{_1\mu_2}{v} - \frac{1}{u} = \frac{_1\mu_2 - 1}{R}. \qquad \text{...(2)}$$

The above formula is derived for convex surface and for real image. But the same can be used for concave surface and virtual image. The following are the five more cases of spherical surfaces:

---

1. When angle of incidence is not small, the correct relation will be

$$\frac{\mu_2}{v} - \frac{\mu_1}{u} = \frac{\mu_2 \cos r - \mu_1 \cos i}{R}$$

2. For plane refracting surface, $R = \infty$,

$$\therefore \quad \frac{v}{u} = \frac{\mu_2}{\mu_1}.$$

3.2 PRINCIPAL FOCI

Each refracting surface has two focal points. These are called principal focal points and their distances from pole are called focal lengths. These are :

(i)   First principal focus : This is the point on principal axis on object side; the rays starting from this point become parallel to the principal axis after refraction. Thus if f_1 is the first focal length, then from

$$\frac{\mu_2}{v} - \frac{\mu_1}{u} = \frac{\mu_2 - \mu_1}{R}, \text{ we have}$$

$$u = f_1, v = \infty$$

$$\therefore \qquad \frac{\mu_2}{\infty} - \frac{\mu_1}{f_1} = \frac{\mu_2 - \mu_1}{R}$$

or
$$f_1 = \frac{-\mu_1 R}{\mu_2 - \mu_1}. \qquad \qquad ...(3)$$

(ii)   Second principal focus : This is the point on the principal axis on image side at which parallel incident rays converge or appear to converge. Thus if f_2 is the second principal focal length, then we have

$$u = \infty, v = f_2$$

$$\therefore \qquad \frac{\mu_2}{f_2} - \frac{\mu_1}{\infty} = \frac{\mu_2 - \mu_1}{R}$$

or
$$f_2 = \frac{\mu_2 R}{\left(\mu_2 - \mu_1\right)}. \qquad \qquad ...(4)$$

From equations (3) and (4), we have

$$\frac{f_1}{f_2} = -\frac{\mu_1}{\mu_2}. \qquad \qquad ...(5)$$

3.3 MAGNIFICATION

It is the ratio of size of image to that of size of the object. This ratio depends on the position of the object. Here we will discuss two types of magnifications. These are :

(i)   Lateral magnification : When object is placed perpendicular to the principal axis, its image will also be perpendicular to the principal axis. Thus lateral magnification,

$$m = \frac{\text{height of image} \left(I\right)}{\text{height of object} \left(O\right)}$$

To find lateral magnification, let us see the image I of the object O formed by convex spherical surface as shown in figure.

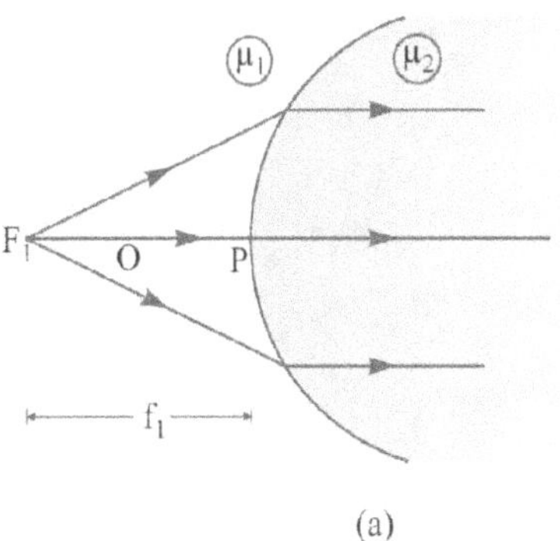

(a)

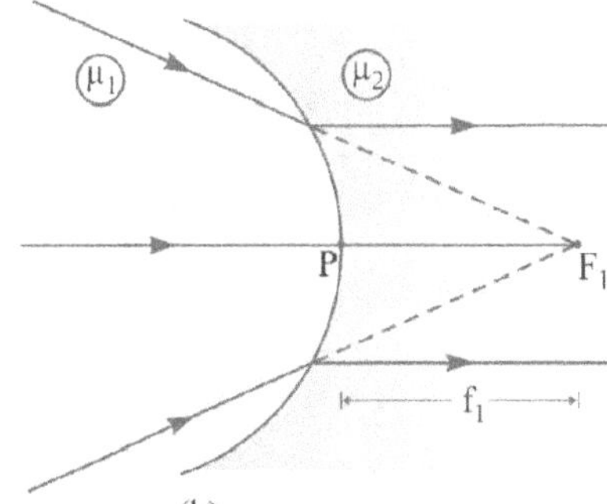

(b)

Fig. 3.3(a) First principal focal point of convex surface.

(b)   First principal focal point of concave surface.

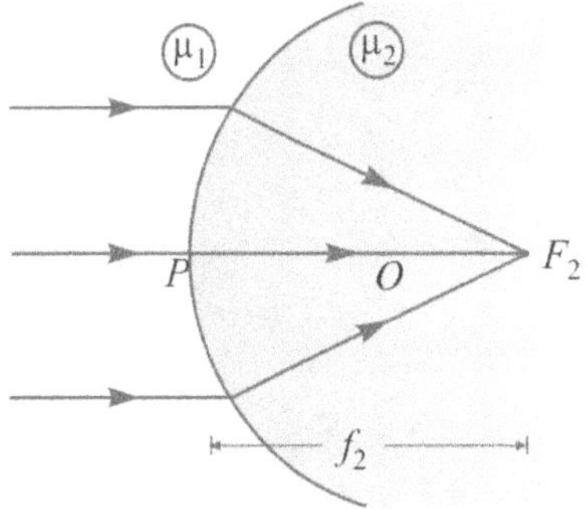

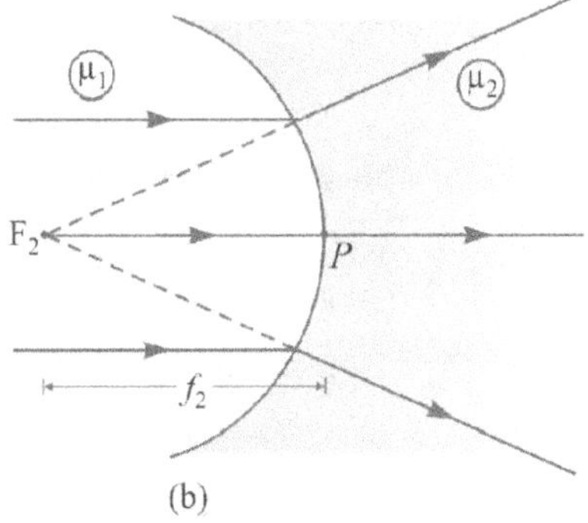

(b)

Fig. 3.4. (a) Second principal focal point of convex surface.

(b)   Second principal focal point of concave surface.

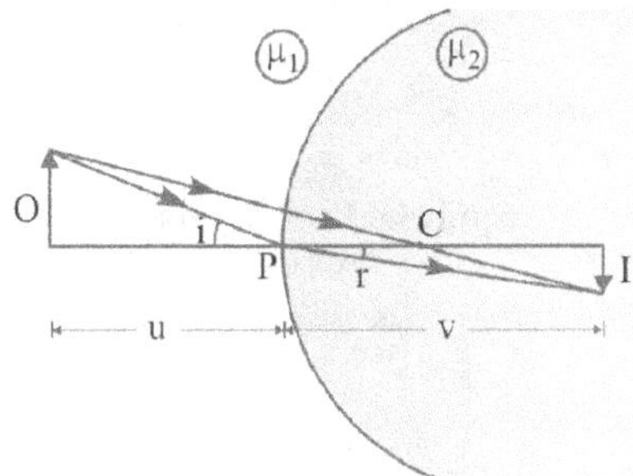

Fig. 3.5

From Snell's law

$$\frac{\mu_2}{\mu_1} = \frac{\sin i}{\sin r}$$

For small angle of incidence, we can write

$$\frac{\sin i}{\sin r} \simeq \frac{\tan i}{\tan r} = \frac{O/(-u)}{-I/(+v)}$$

Thus

$$\frac{\mu_2}{\mu_1} = \frac{O}{I}\left(\frac{v}{u}\right)$$

or

$$\frac{I}{O} = \frac{\mu_1}{\mu_2}\frac{v}{u}.$$

By the definition of lateral magnification, we have

$$m = \frac{I}{O} = \frac{\mu_1}{\mu_2}\frac{v}{u} \qquad \ldots (6)$$

(ii) **Longitudinal magnification :** When object is placed along the principal axis, its image will form along the principal axis. Thus longitudinal magnification

$$m_L = \frac{\text{length of the image}}{\text{length of the object}}.$$

For small object, we can write length of the object and length of the image as δu and δv respectively, then

$$m_L = \frac{\delta v}{\delta u}$$

We know that;

$$\frac{\mu_2}{v} - \frac{\mu_1}{u} = \frac{\mu_2 - \mu_1}{R}$$

Differentiating above equation, we have

$$-\frac{\mu_2}{v^2}\frac{\delta v}{\delta u} + \frac{\mu_1}{u^2} = 0$$

or

$$\frac{\delta v}{\delta u} = \frac{\mu_1}{\mu_2}\frac{v^2}{u^2}.$$

Thus by the definition of longitudinal magnification, we have

$$m_L = \frac{\delta v}{\delta u} = \frac{\mu_1}{\mu_2}\frac{v^2}{u^2}. \qquad \ldots (7)$$

Also

$$m_L = \frac{\mu_2}{\mu_1}\left[\frac{\mu_1 v}{\mu_2 u}\right]^2$$

or

$$m_L = \frac{\mu_2}{\mu_1}m^2. \qquad \ldots (8)$$

Summary of spherical reflecting and refracting surfaces :

	Spherical mirror	Spherical refracting surfaces
Object, image distance relation	$\dfrac{1}{u} + \dfrac{1}{v} = \dfrac{1}{f} = \dfrac{2}{R}$	$\dfrac{\mu_2}{v} - \dfrac{\mu_1}{u} = \dfrac{\mu_2 - \mu_1}{R}$
Lateral magnification	$m = \dfrac{v}{u}$	$m = \dfrac{\mu_1}{\mu_2}\dfrac{v}{u}$
Longitudinal magnification	$m_L = \dfrac{v^2}{u^2}$	$m_L = \dfrac{\mu_1}{\mu_2}\dfrac{v^2}{u^2}$

Ex. 1 The slab of material of refractive index 2 shown in *fig.* 3.6 has a curved surface *APB* of radius of curvature 10 cm and a plane surface *CD*. On the left of *APB* is air and on the right of *CD* is water of refractive index 4/3. An object *O* is placed at a distance of 15 cm from the pole *P*. Find the distance of the final image of *O* from *P* as viewed from left.

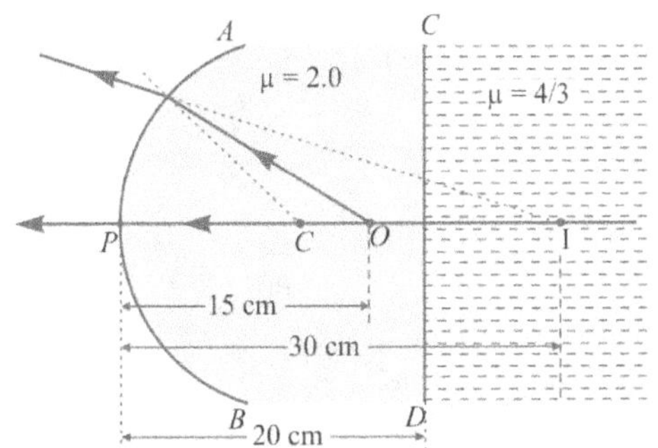

Fig. 3.6

Sol. We know that;

$$\frac{\mu_2}{v} - \frac{\mu_1}{u} = \frac{\mu_2 - \mu_1}{R}$$

Here $\mu_1 = 2$, for object medium and so

$$\frac{1}{v} - \frac{2}{-15} = \frac{1-2}{-10}$$

or $\qquad v = -30$ cm

The virtual image I will form inside the water, and so no more refraction will take place. Thus image distance from P remains 30 cm.

Ex. 2 A glass dumbbell of length 30 cm and refractive index 1.5 has ends of 3 cm radius of curvature. Find the position of the image formed due to refraction at one end only, when the object is situated in air at a distance of 12 cm from the end of the dumbbell along the axis.

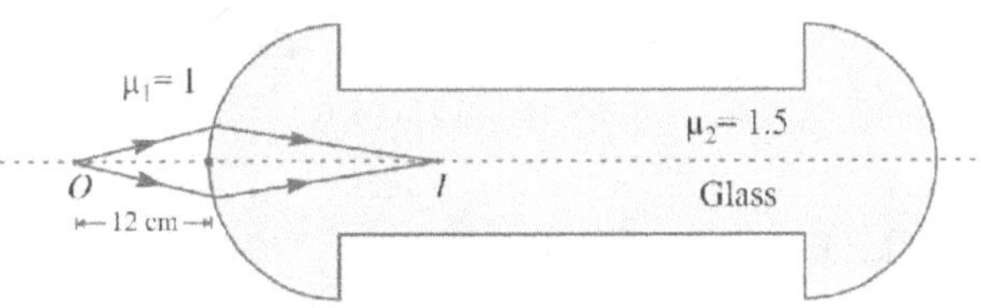

Fig. 3.7

Sol. From refraction formula

$$\frac{\mu_2}{v} - \frac{\mu_1}{u} = \frac{\mu_2 - \mu_1}{R}, \text{ we have}$$

$$\frac{1.5}{v} - \frac{1}{-12} = \frac{1.5-1}{+3}$$

$\therefore \qquad v = 18$ cm $\qquad$ *Ans.*

Thus real image is formed at a distance of 18 cm inside glass.

Ex. 3 A glass rod has ends as shown in *fig.* 3.8. The refractive index of glass is μ. The object *O* is at a distance $2R$ from the surface of larger radius of curvature. The distance between apexes of ends is $3R$. Find the distance of image formed of the point object from right hand vertex. What is the condition to be satisfied if the image is to be real ?

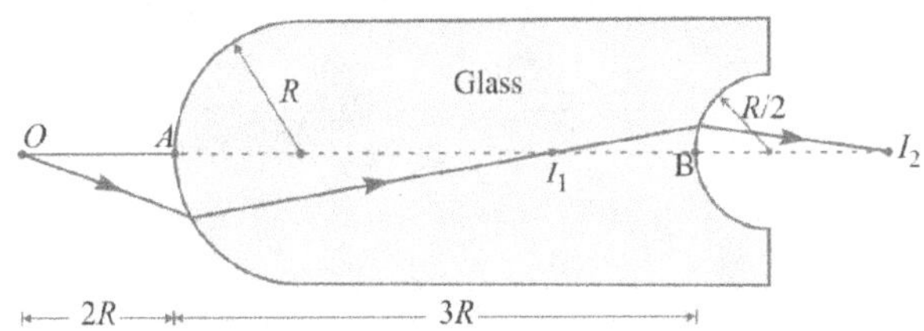

Fig. 3.8

Sol. If v_1 is the distance of the image formed by the surface A, then by

$$\frac{\mu_2}{v_1} - \frac{\mu_1}{u} = \frac{\mu_2 - \mu_1}{R_1}$$

or $\qquad \dfrac{\mu}{v_1} - \dfrac{1}{-2R} = \dfrac{\mu-1}{R}$

$\therefore \qquad v_1 = \dfrac{2\mu R}{(2\mu - 3)}$

Now for surface B; $\quad \mu_1 = \mu,\ \mu_2 = 1,$

$$u_2 = -\left(3R - \frac{2\mu R}{2\mu - 3}\right)$$

$\therefore \quad \dfrac{1}{v_2} - \dfrac{\mu}{-\left(3R - \dfrac{2\mu R}{2\mu - 3}\right)} = \dfrac{1-\mu}{R/2}$

or $\qquad \dfrac{1}{v_2} = \dfrac{2-2\mu}{R} - \dfrac{\mu(2\mu - 3)}{(6\mu R - 9R - 2\mu R)}$

$\qquad\qquad = \dfrac{2-2\mu}{R} - \dfrac{\mu(2\mu - 3)}{R(4\mu - 9)}$

$\qquad\qquad = \dfrac{(9-4\mu)R}{10\mu^2 - 29\mu + 18}$

$\therefore \qquad v_2 = \dfrac{(9-4\mu)R}{(10\mu - 9)(\mu - 2)}$ $\qquad$ *Ans.*

For real image μ of the glass should be between 2 and 9/4.

Ex. 4 A plano-convex lens has thickness 4 cm. When placed on a horizontal table with the curved surface in contact with it the apparent depth of the bottommost point of the lens is found to be 3 cm. If the lens is inverted such that the plane face is in contact with the table, the apparent depth of the centre of plane face of the lens is found to be $\dfrac{25}{8}$ cm. Find the focal length of the lens.

Sol. When the curved surface of the lens is in contact with the table, the refraction occurs due to plane face, and if μ is the refractive index of the material of the lens, then by refraction formula;

$$\frac{\mu_2}{v} - \frac{\mu_1}{u} = \frac{\mu_2 - \mu_1}{R}.$$

Here $\qquad \mu_1 = \mu,\ \mu_2 = 1$ and $R_1 = \infty$

$\qquad\qquad u = -4$ cm, $v = -3$ cm

(distances are measured from top of the lens)

$$\therefore \qquad \frac{1}{-3} - \frac{\mu}{-4} = \frac{1-\mu}{\infty}$$

or $\qquad \mu = 4/3.$

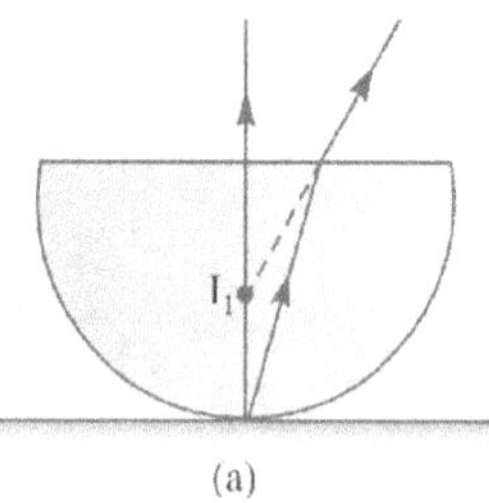

(a)

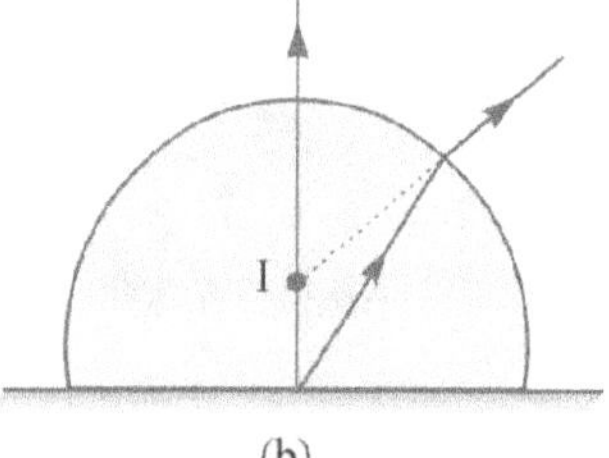

(b)

Fig. 3.9

In the second case : $\qquad \mu_1 = \mu, \mu_2 = 1, R_2 = -R$

$$m = -4 \text{ cm}, v = \frac{-25}{8} \text{ cm}$$

$$\therefore \qquad \frac{\mu_1}{-25/8} - \frac{\mu}{-4} = \frac{1-\mu}{-R}$$

On substituting value of $\mu = 4/3$, we get

$$R = 25 \text{ cm}.$$

The focal length of the lens can be obtained by lens maker's formula;

$$\frac{1}{f} = (\mu - 1)\left(\frac{1}{R_1} - \frac{1}{R_2}\right)$$

$$\therefore \qquad \frac{1}{f} = \left(\frac{4}{3} - 1\right)\left(\frac{1}{\infty} - \frac{1}{-25}\right)$$

or $\qquad f = 75 \text{ cm} \qquad\qquad$ ***Ans.***

Ex. 5 In *fig.* 3.10 light is incident on a thin lens as shown in figure. The radius of curvature of both surfaces is R. Determine the focal length of this system.

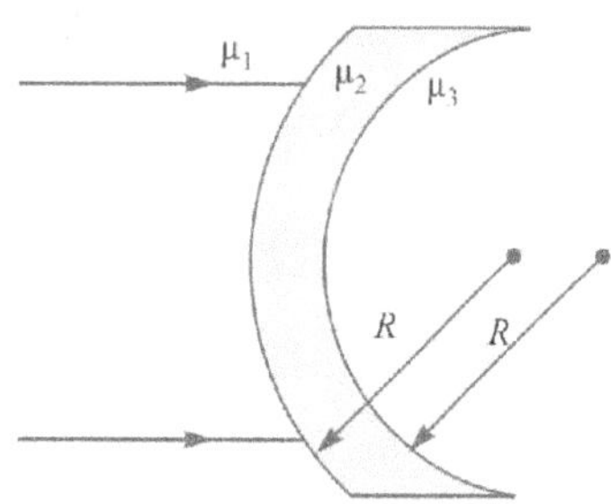

Fig. 3.10

Sol. For the refraction at first surface :

$$u_1 = \infty$$

$$\therefore \qquad \frac{\mu_2}{v_1} - \frac{\mu_1}{\infty} = \frac{\mu_2 - \mu_1}{+R} \qquad ...(i)$$

For the second surface : $\qquad u_2 = v_1$ and $v_2 = f$

Thus $\qquad \dfrac{\mu_3}{f} - \dfrac{\mu_2}{v_1} = \dfrac{\mu_3 - \mu_2}{+R} \qquad ...(ii)$

On adding equations (i) and (ii), we get

$$\frac{\mu_3}{f} = \frac{\mu_3 - \mu_1}{R}$$

$$\therefore \qquad f = \frac{\mu_3 R}{\mu_3 - \mu_1} \qquad\qquad ***Ans.***$$

Ex. 6 *Fig.* 3.11 shows an irregular block of material of refractive index $\sqrt{2}$. A ray of light strikes the face *AB* as shown in figure. After refraction it is incident on a spherical surface *CD* of radius of curvature 0.4 m and enter a medium of refractive index 1.514 to meet *PQ* at *E*. Find the distance *OE* upto two places of decimal.

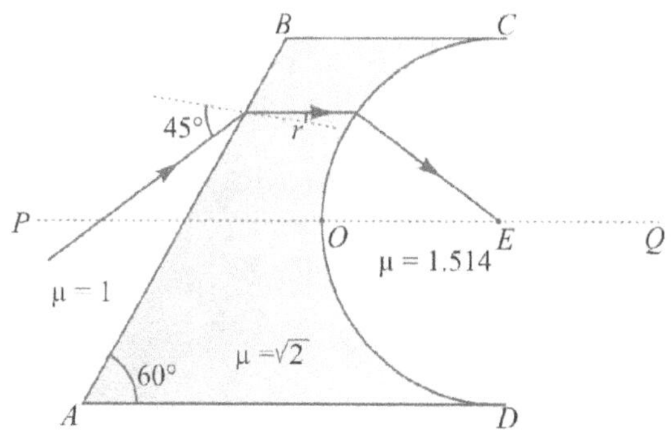

Fig. 3.11

Sol. By Snell's law

$$\frac{\mu_2}{\mu_1} = \frac{\sin i}{\sin r}$$

or $\qquad \dfrac{\sqrt{2}}{1} = \dfrac{\sin 45°}{\sin r}$

or $\qquad \sin r = \dfrac{1}{\sqrt{2}\,\sqrt{2}} = \dfrac{1}{2}$

$$\therefore \qquad r = 30°.$$

It shows that the refractive ray thus becomes parallel to *AD* inside the block. So parallel ray is incident on spherical surface *CD*.

$$\therefore \quad u = \infty, R = 0.4 \text{ m}, \mu_1 = \sqrt{2}, \mu_2 = 1.514$$

From $\qquad \dfrac{\mu_2}{v} - \dfrac{\mu_1}{u} = \dfrac{\mu_2 - \mu_1}{R}$, we have

$$\frac{1.514}{v} - \frac{\sqrt{2}}{\infty} = \frac{1.514 - \sqrt{2}}{0.4}$$

After simplification, we get $v = 6.06$ m $\qquad$ ***Ans.***

Thus required distance $OE = 6.06$ m.

Ex. 7 A small filament is at the centre of a hollow glass sphere of inner and outer radii 8 cm and 9 cm respectively. The refractive index of glass is 1.50. Calculate the position of the image of the filament when viewed from outside the sphere.

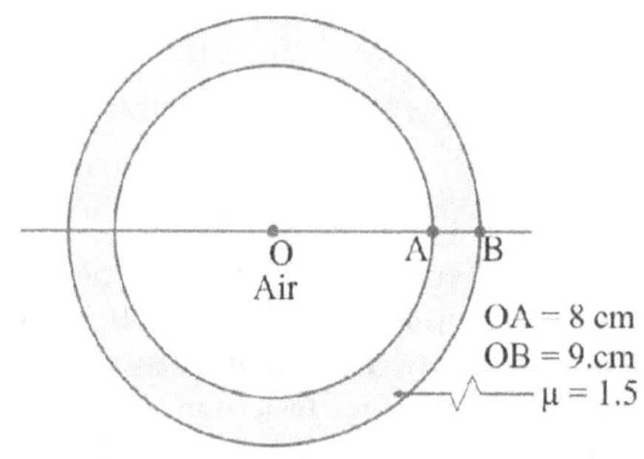

Fig. 3.12

Sol. For the refraction at first surface;

$u_1 = -8$ cm, $R_1 = -8$ cm

$\mu_1 = 1$, $\mu_2 = 1.5$. (distances are measured from A)

From $\dfrac{\mu_2}{v} - \dfrac{\mu_1}{u} = \dfrac{\mu_2 - \mu_1}{R}$, we have

$$\frac{1.5}{v_1} - \frac{1}{-8} = \frac{1.5 - 1}{-8}$$

or $v_1 = -8$ cm

It shows that the image is formed at the position of object. For the second surface;

$u_2 = -9$ cm, $R_2 = -9$ cm

$\mu_1 = 1.5$, $\mu_2 = 1$

(distances are measured from B)

$\therefore \quad \dfrac{\mu_2}{v_2} - \dfrac{\mu_1}{u_2} = \dfrac{\mu_2 - \mu_1}{R_2}$

or $\dfrac{1}{v_2} - \dfrac{1.5}{-9} = \dfrac{1 - 1.5}{-9}$

On solving, we get $v_2 = -9$ cm *Ans.*

Thus the final image is formed at the centre of the sphere.

Ex. 8 *Fig.* 3.13 *shows a transparent hemisphere of radius 3.0 cm made of a material of refractive index 2.0 :*

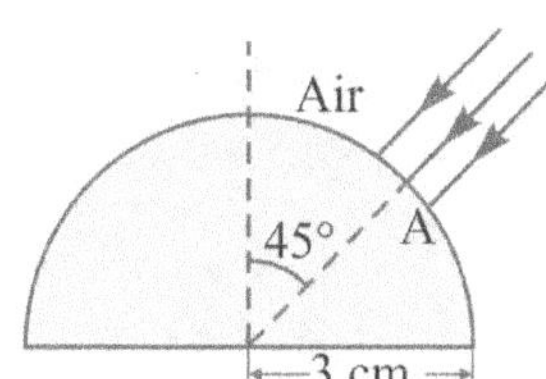

Fig. 3.13

(a) **A narrow beam of parallel rays is incident on the hemisphere as shown in figure. Are the rays totally reflected at plane surface ?**

(b) **Find the image formed by refraction at the first surface.**

(c) **Find the image formed by the reflection or by refraction at the plane surface.**

Sol. (a) The critical angle for material-air interface

$$\sin C = \frac{1}{\mu}$$

$$= \frac{1}{2}$$

$\therefore \quad C = 30°$

The rays are incident normally on the spherical surface, so they pass undeviated and then incident on plane face at an angle 45°. As the angle of incidence is greater than critical angle (30°), so rays get totally reflected.

(b) For spherical surface :

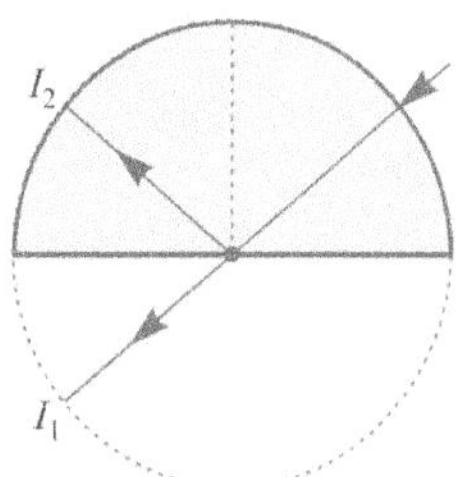

Fig. 3.14

$u = \infty$

We have $\dfrac{\mu_2}{v} - \dfrac{\mu_1}{u} = \dfrac{\mu_2 - \mu_1}{R}$

or $\dfrac{2}{v} - \dfrac{1}{\infty} = \dfrac{2 - 1}{R}$

$\therefore \quad v = 2R.$

Thus the image will form on diametrically opposite point.

(c) Some of the rays get totally reflected and so they will form the image at I_2.

Ex. 9 **A quarter cylinder of radius R and refractive index 1.5 is placed on a table. A point object P is kept at a distance of mR from it. Find the value of m for which a ray from P will emerge parallel to the table as shown in the** *fig.* **3.15.**

Sol. Refraction at plane surface :

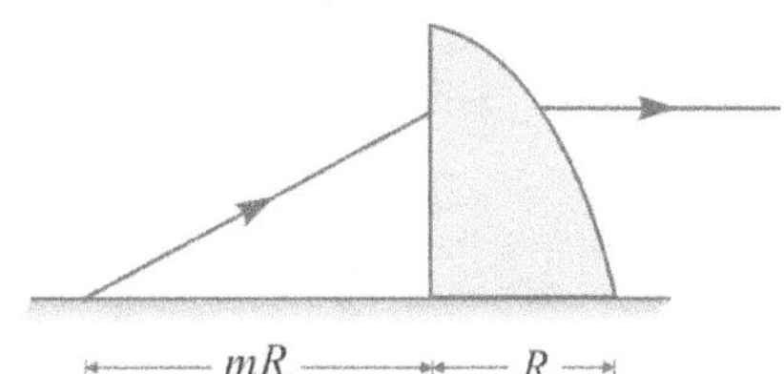

Fig. 3.15

$u = -mR$, $R_1 = \infty$

$\mu_1 = 1$, $\mu_2 = 1.5$.

By refraction formula

$$\frac{\mu_2}{v} - \frac{\mu_1}{u} = \frac{\mu_2 - \mu_1}{R}$$

We have

$$\frac{1.5}{v_1} - \frac{1}{-mR} = \frac{1.5 - 1}{\infty}$$

$\therefore \quad v_1 = -1.5\, mR$

For refraction at curved surface;

$u_2 = -(1.5\, mR + R) = -(1.5\, m + 1)\, R$

$R_2 = -R$, $v_2 = \infty$

$\mu_1 = 1.5$, $\mu_2 = 1$

$\therefore \quad \dfrac{\mu_2}{v_2} - \dfrac{\mu_1}{u_2} = \dfrac{\mu_2 - \mu_1}{R_2}$

or $\dfrac{1}{\infty} - \dfrac{1.5}{-(1.5\, m + 1)R} = \dfrac{1 - 1.5}{-R}$

or $1.5\, m + 1 = 3$

$\therefore \quad m = 4/3.$ *Ans.*

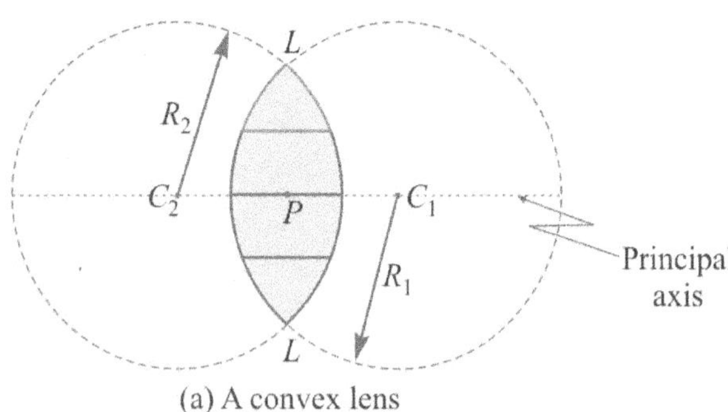

(a) A convex lens

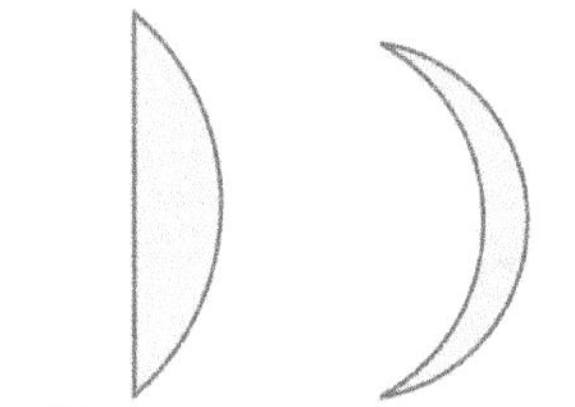

(b) Plano-convex and concavo-convex

Fig. 3.16

3.4 LENSES

Lenses play very important role in our life. They are used in microscopes, telescopes and movie cameras etc. We have natural lenses in our eyes. A lens consists of two refracting surfaces (at least one spherical) inclined at some angle. In thin lens the spacing between the refracting surfaces is negligibly small. In thick lens the spacing between the refracting surfaces at the centre of the lens is large enough. Basically a lens is the combination of many prisms. Thus lens can also produce deviation and dispersion (aberration). Lenses are of two types. We shall study the special case of thin lens in which the thickest part is thin compared to the object distance or focal length of the lens.

Convex lens

A lens which is thicker at the middle and thinner at the edges is known as convex or converging lens.

Concave lens

A lens which is thinner at the middle and thicker at the edges is known as concave or diverging lens.

Note:

For convex lens $R_1 = +$ ve, $R_2 = -$ ve.
For concave lens $R_1 = -$ ve, $R_2 = +$ ve.

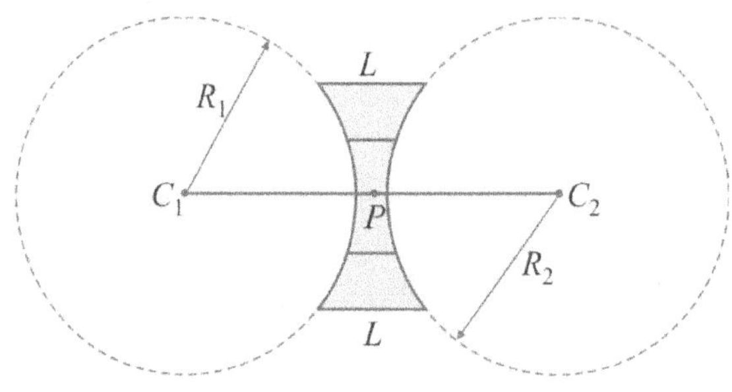

(a) A concave lens

(b) Plano-concave and convexo-concave lenses

Fig. 3.17

The following are the terms used with the lenses:

(i)   **Aperture :** The effective width of a lens from which refraction takes place is called aperture. In figure LL is the aperture of the lens.

(ii)   **Optical centre :** The centre of a lens is called its optical centre. It is denoted by letter P. A ray of light passing through optical centre does not suffer any deviation.

(iii)   **Principal or optic axis :** The line joining the centres of curvatures of the lens is known as principal axis (PA).

(iv)   **Principal focus and focal length :** A point on the principal axis at which parallel rays of light after refraction from the lens converge or appear to diverge from it is known as focus. It is denoted by a letter F. The distance of focal point from optical centre is known as focal length of the lens. It is denoted by f.

Guidelines for image formation

On the basis of laws of refractions, the following rays coming from the object are usually used for constructing ray diagram for image:

(i)   A ray of light coming parallel to the principal axis; after refraction from the lens will pass or appears to pass through focus and vice-versa.

(ii)   A ray of light passing through the optical centre of the lens goes straight without deviation. This is however, is true for a thin lens because the two sides of a lens at its centre are almost parallel only when the lens is thin.

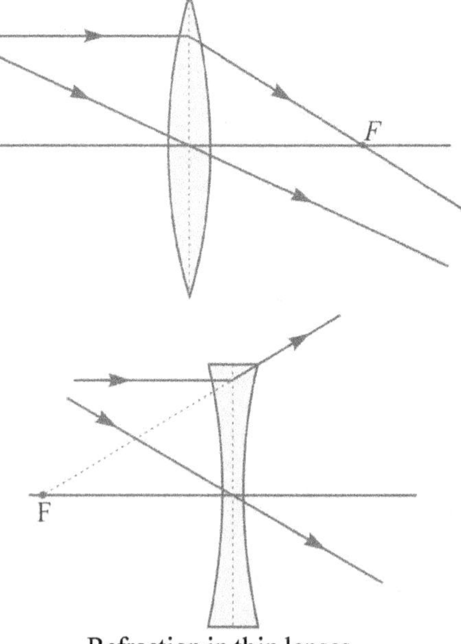

Refraction in thin lenses.

Fig. 3.18

Image formation by convex lens

Object position	Ray diagram	Position and nature of image
At ∞	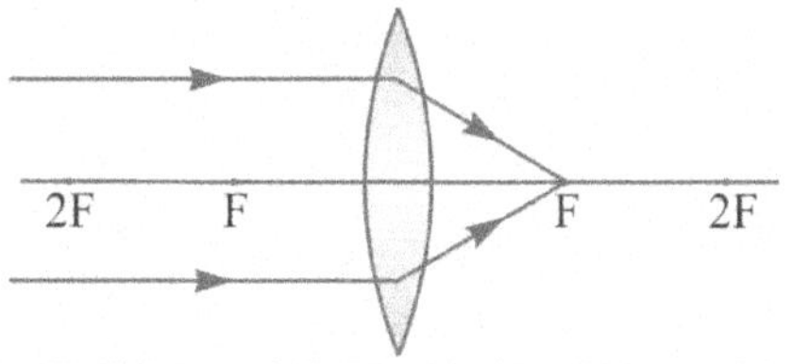	Image at focus. Real, inverted and diminished image.
Between 2F and ∞	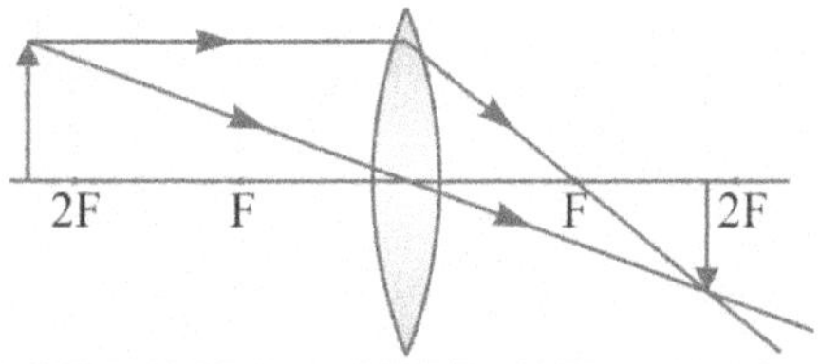	Between F and 2F. Real, inverted and diminished.
At 2F	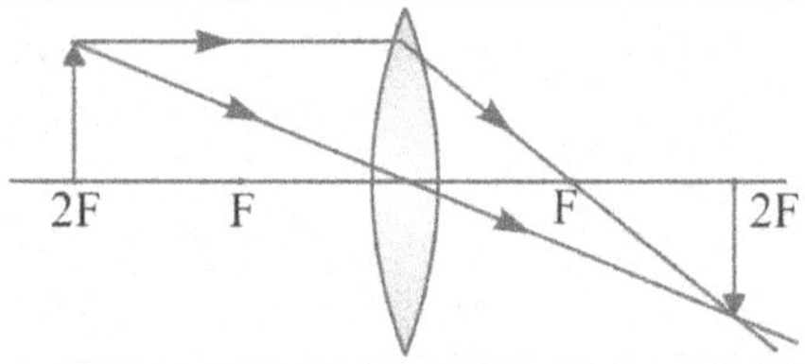	At 2F. Real, inverted and same size of the object.

Object position	Ray diagram	Position and nature of image
Between 2F and F	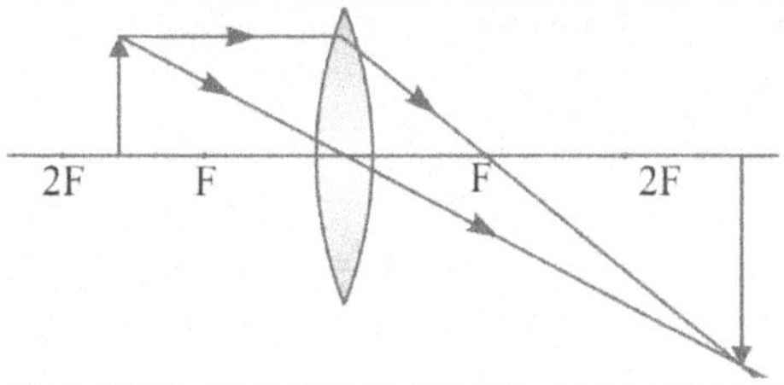	Beyond 2F. Real inverted and larger than object.
At F	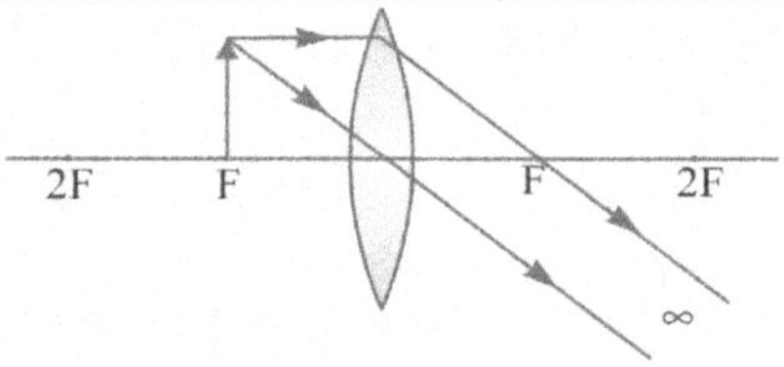	At ∞. Real, inverted and very larger than object.
Between F and P	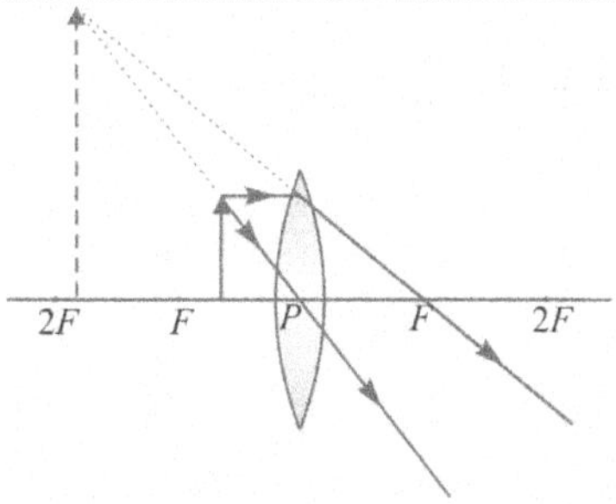	On the side of the object. Virtual, erect and larger than object.

Image formation by concave lens

Object position	Ray diagram	Position and nature of image
At ∞		At focus. Virtual erect and diminished.
Anywhere between ∞ and P		Between P and F. Virtual, erect and smaller than object.

3.5. THE THIN LENS FORMULAS

Consider a thin lens made of a material of refractive index μ_2 and situated in a medium of refractive index μ_1 on its both sides. Let R_1 and R_2 be the radii of curvature of the two co-axial spherical surfaces. Suppose an object O is placed at a distance u from the optical centre of the lens.

An image I' is formed by refraction at the first surface of the lens, at a distance v' from the pole of the surface.

Then by refraction formula, we have

$$\frac{\mu_2}{v'} - \frac{\mu_1}{u} = \frac{\mu_2 - \mu_1}{R_1}. \qquad \text{...(i)}$$

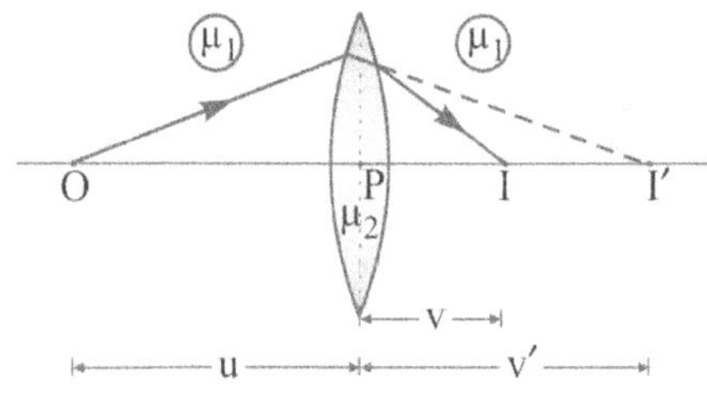
Fig. 3.19

The image I' becomes the virtual object for the second surface of the lens, and which forms the image I at a distance v from this surface. Then

$$\frac{\mu_1}{v} - \frac{\mu_2}{v'} = \frac{\mu_1 - \mu_2}{R_2}. \qquad \text{...(ii)}$$

In this case rays are going from medium of refractive index μ_2 to the medium of refractive index μ_1. Moreover do not place the sign with R_1 and R_2, because they have already signed.

Adding equations (i) and (ii), we have

$$\frac{\mu_1}{v} - \frac{\mu_1}{u} = (\mu_2 - \mu_1)\left(\frac{1}{R_1} - \frac{1}{R_2}\right)$$

or

$$\frac{1}{v} - \frac{1}{u} = \left(\frac{\mu_2}{\mu_1} - 1\right)\left(\frac{1}{R_1} - \frac{1}{R_2}\right)$$

If the lens is placed in air, then $\mu_1 = 1$, and putting $\mu_2 = \mu$, we have

$$\frac{1}{v} - \frac{1}{u} = (\mu - 1)\left(\frac{1}{R_1} - \frac{1}{R_2}\right) \quad \text{...(1)}$$

Note :

1. The equation derived will hold only for paraxial rays and for a thin lens.
2. While solving numerical problems, proper signs are to be placed for all the given values, and no sign for unknowns.

Equation (1) is known as the thin lens formula and is usually written in the form

$$\frac{1}{v} - \frac{1}{u} = \frac{1}{f}. \qquad ...(2)$$

where f is known as focal length of the lens, and is given by

$$\frac{1}{f} = (\mu - 1)\left(\frac{1}{R_1} - \frac{1}{R_2}\right) \qquad ....(3)$$

The above formula is known as lens maker's formula.

$$\frac{1}{v} - \frac{1}{u} = \frac{1}{f}$$

Graph of u vs. v for a lens : According to lens formula it is a hyperbola, as shown in figure.

(a)   **Convex lens**

$u =$	$-\infty$	$-2f$	$-f$	$-\dfrac{f}{2}$	$-\dfrac{f}{4}$	0	$+f$	$+2f$	$+\infty$
$v =$	$+f$	$+2f$	$+\infty$	$-f$	$-\dfrac{f}{3}$	0	$+\dfrac{f}{2}$	$+\dfrac{2f}{3}$	$+f$

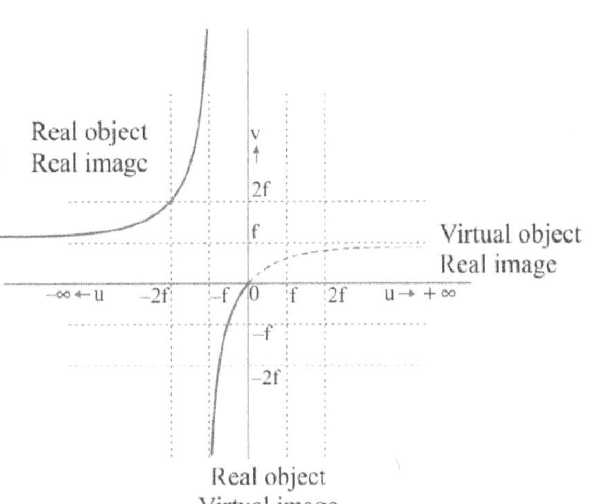

Fig. 3.20

(b)   **Concave lens**

$u =$	$-\infty$	$-2f$	$-f$	$-\dfrac{f}{2}$	0	$+\dfrac{f}{2}$	$+f$	$+f$	$+2f$	$+\infty$
$v =$	$-f$	$\dfrac{-2f}{3}$	$-\dfrac{f}{2}$	$-\dfrac{f}{3}$	0	$+f$	$+\infty$	$+\infty$	$-2f$	$-f$

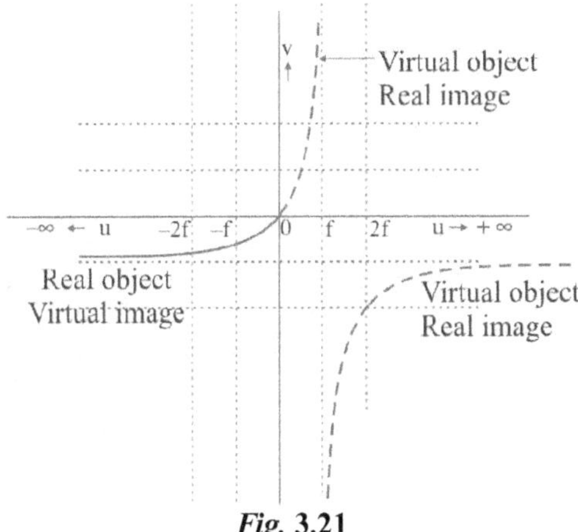

Fig. 3.21

Lens with different mediums on its sides

In case when there are different mediums on both sides of the lens say μ_1 and μ_3, then we can write

for first surface;
$$\frac{\mu_2}{v'} - \frac{\mu_1}{u} = \frac{\mu_2 - \mu_1}{R_1} \qquad ...(iii)$$

and for second surface;
$$\frac{\mu_3}{v} - \frac{\mu_2}{v'} = \frac{\mu_3 - \mu_2}{R_2}. \qquad ..(iv)$$

Adding equations (iii) and (iv), we have

$$\frac{\mu_3}{v} - \frac{\mu_1}{u} = \frac{\mu_2 - \mu_1}{R_1} + \frac{\mu_3 - \mu_2}{R_2} \qquad ....(4)$$

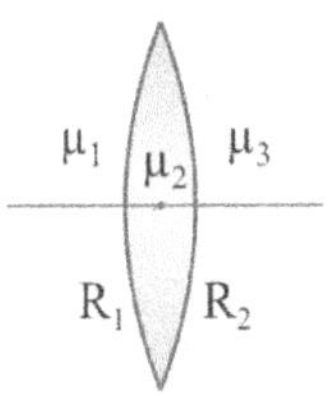

Fig. 3.22

3.6 PRINCIPAL FOCI

There are two principal foci of any lens. These are :

(i)   **First principal focus** : For the first focus F_1, $v = \infty$, $u = f_1$. Thus by equation (4)

$$\frac{1}{f_1} = -\frac{1}{\mu_1}\left(\frac{\mu_2-\mu_1}{R_1}+\frac{\mu_3-\mu_2}{R_2}\right) \quad ...(5)$$

Here f_1 is called first focal length.

For the convex lens it will be on object side and for concave lens it will on image side.

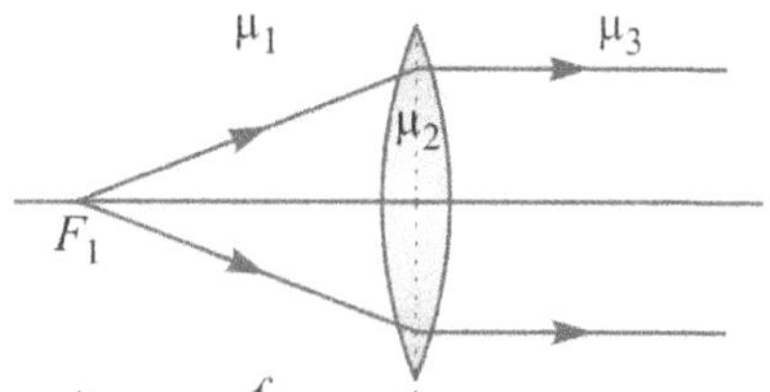

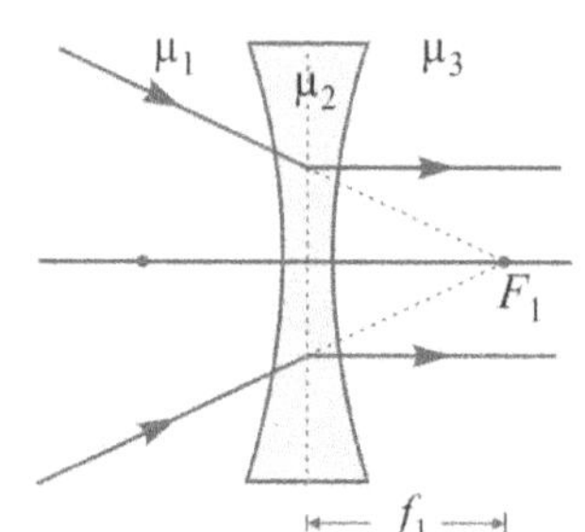

Fig. 3.23

(ii)   **Second principal focus** : For the second focus F_2, $u = -\infty$, $v = f_2$. Thus

$$\frac{1}{f_2} = \frac{1}{\mu_3}\left[\frac{\mu_2-\mu_1}{R_1}+\frac{\mu_3-\mu_2}{R_2}\right] \quad ...(6)$$

Now from equations (5) and (6), we get

$$\frac{f_1}{f_2} = -\frac{\mu_1}{\mu_3} \quad ...(7)$$

In case when $\mu_1 = \mu_3$, $f_1 = -f_2$. In this case we will simply use f as the focal length.

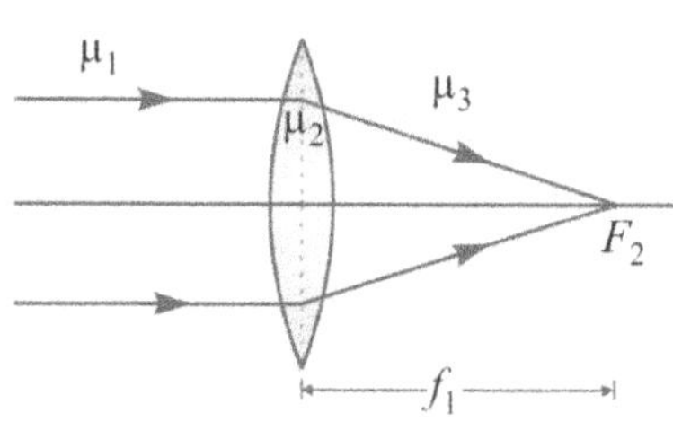

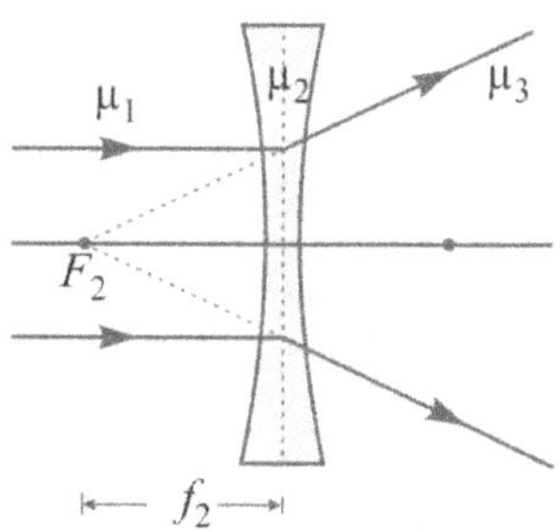

Fig. 3.24

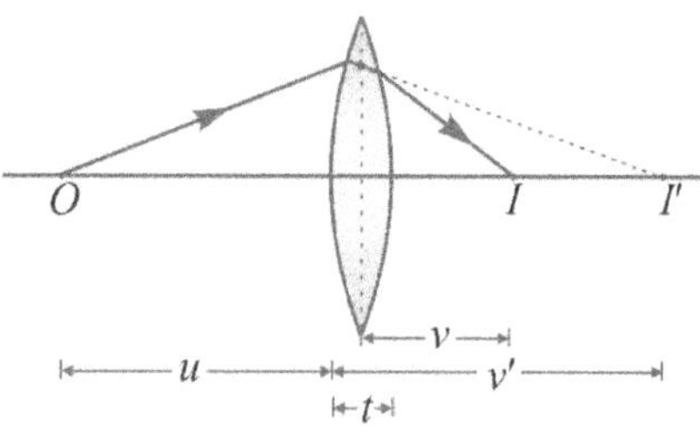

Fig. 3.25

Note:

1. In case, if t is the thickness of the lens at the centre, then we can solve the problem in two steps :

$$\frac{\mu_2}{v'}-\frac{\mu_1}{-u} = \frac{\mu_2-\mu_1}{+R_1} \quad ...(i)$$

and

$$\frac{\mu_1}{v}-\frac{\mu_2}{(v'-t)} = \frac{\mu_1-\mu_2}{-R_2} \quad ...(ii)$$

On solving (i) and (ii), we can get v.

2. If distances of the object and the image are measured from first and second focus respectively, then $x_1\, x_2 = f_1 f_2$.

This known as Newton's formula.

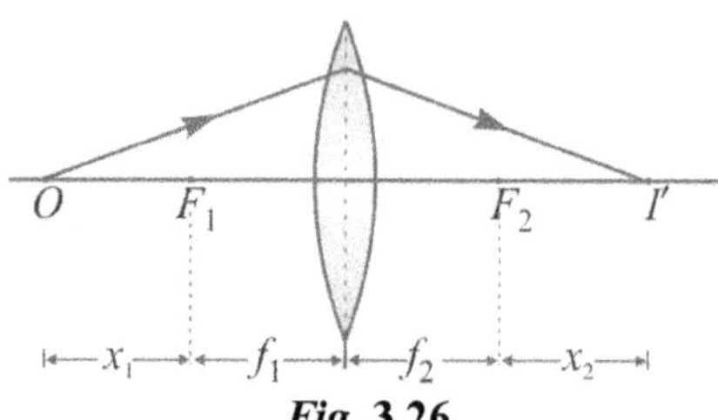

Fig. 3.26

More about focal length

According to our sign conventions;

For convex lens,

$$R_1 = +R, \quad R_2 = -R;$$

$$\therefore \quad \frac{1}{f} = (\mu-1)\left(\frac{1}{R} - \frac{1}{-R}\right)$$

or

$$f = \frac{R}{2(\mu-1)}.$$

For concave lens,

$$R_1 = -R, \quad R_2 = +R.$$

$$\therefore \quad \frac{1}{f} = (\mu-1)\left(\frac{1}{-R} - \frac{1}{+R}\right)$$

or

$$f = -\frac{R}{2(\mu-1)}.$$

Thus the focal length of convex lens is positive and that of concave is negative.

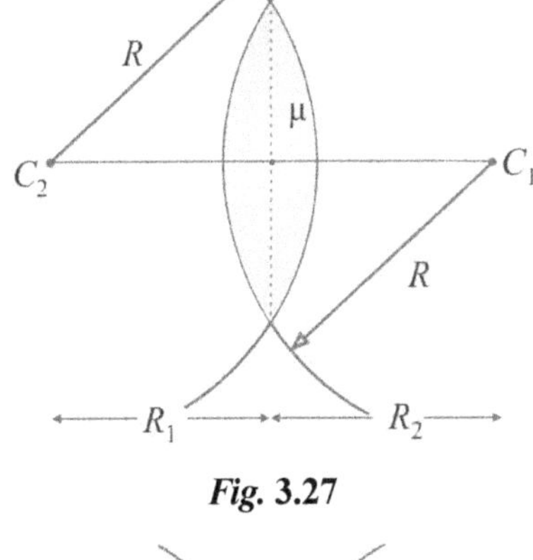

Fig. 3.27

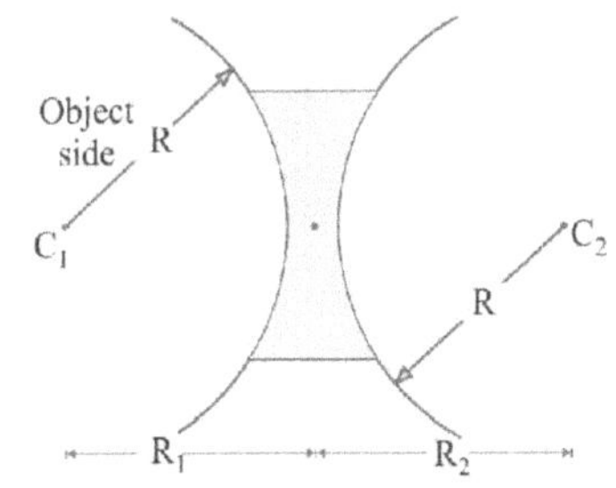

Fig. 3.28

Note:

In case when parallel ray are not parallel to principal axis, they intersect at a point which is not on the axis. Plane through this point is called focal plane.

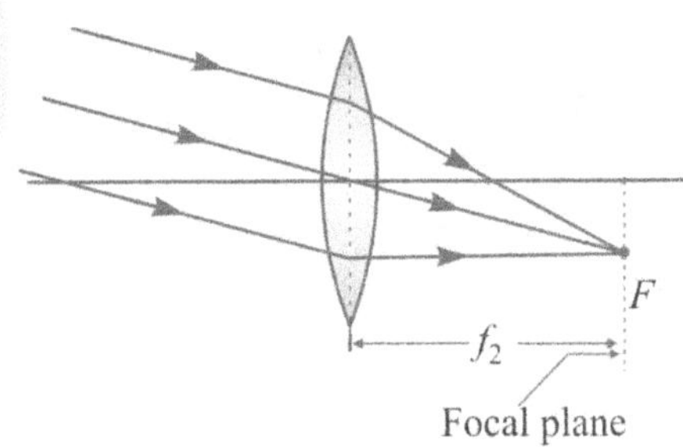

Fig. 3.29

Ex. 10 An equi-convex lens of refractive index (3/2) and focal length 10 cm is held with its axis vertical and its lower surface immersed in water ($\mu = 4/3$), the upper surface being in air. At what distance will a vertical beam of parallel light incident on the lens be focused ?

Sol.

According to lens maker's formula for glass lens in air, we have

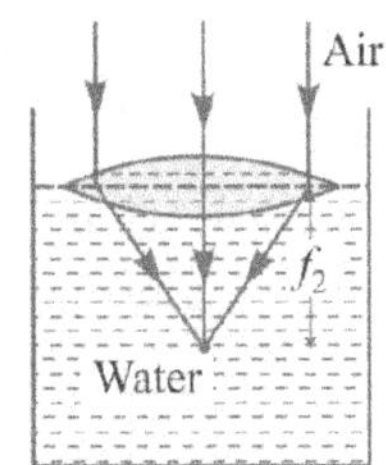

Fig. 3.30

$$\frac{1}{f} = \left(_a\mu_g - 1\right)\left(\frac{1}{R_1} - \frac{1}{R_2}\right)$$

or

$$\frac{1}{10} = \left(\frac{3}{2} - 1\right)\left(\frac{1}{R} - \frac{1}{-R}\right)$$

or

$$R = 10 \text{ cm}$$

Now for two different mediums on both sides of the lens, we have

$$\frac{1}{f_2} = \frac{1}{\mu_3}\left[\frac{\mu_2 - \mu_1}{R_1} + \frac{\mu_3 - \mu_2}{R_2}\right]$$

$$= \frac{1}{4/3}\left[\frac{3/2 - 1}{10} + \frac{4/3 - 3/2}{-10}\right]$$

$$\Rightarrow \quad f_2 = 20 \text{ cm.} \qquad \textit{Ans.}$$

3.7 MAGNIFICATION

It is the ratio of size of image to the size of the object. Its value depends on the position of the object.

(i) Lateral magnification

When an object is placed perpendicular to the principal axis, its image will be perpendicular to the principal axis. Thus

lateral magnification, $\qquad m = \dfrac{\text{height of image }(I)}{\text{height of object }(O)}$

Consider an object AB of height O is situated in front of a convex lens at a distance u from it. Its image A′B′ is formed at a distance v from the lens. The height of image is I. From the similar triangles PAB and PA′B′,

$$\frac{-I}{O} = \frac{v}{-u}$$

or $\qquad \dfrac{I}{O} = \dfrac{v}{u}$

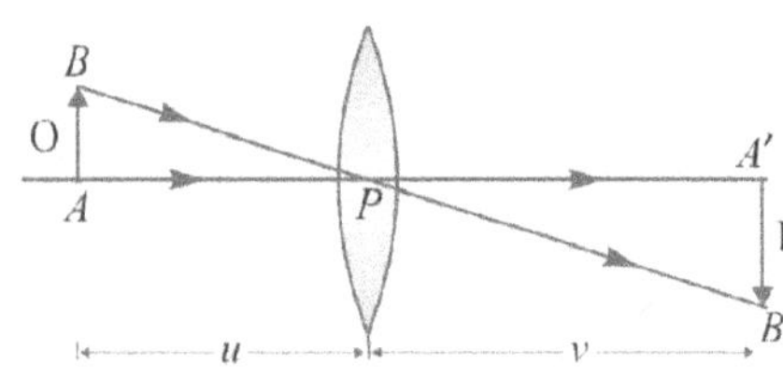

Fig. 3.31

Thus $\qquad m = \dfrac{I}{O} = \dfrac{v}{u}. \qquad \ldots(8)$

For the lens of focal length f, we have

$$\frac{1}{v} - \frac{1}{-u} = \frac{1}{f}$$

or $\qquad \dfrac{u}{v} + 1 = \dfrac{u}{f}$

or $\qquad \dfrac{v}{u} = \dfrac{f}{u-f}$

Thus $\qquad \dfrac{I}{O} = \dfrac{f}{u-f}. \qquad \ldots(9)$

According to sign conventions, m is put positive for erect image and negative for inverted image.

(ii) Longitudinal magnification

When an object is placed parallel the principal axis, its longitudinal magnification is defined as :

$$m_L = \frac{\text{length of the image}}{\text{length of the object}}$$

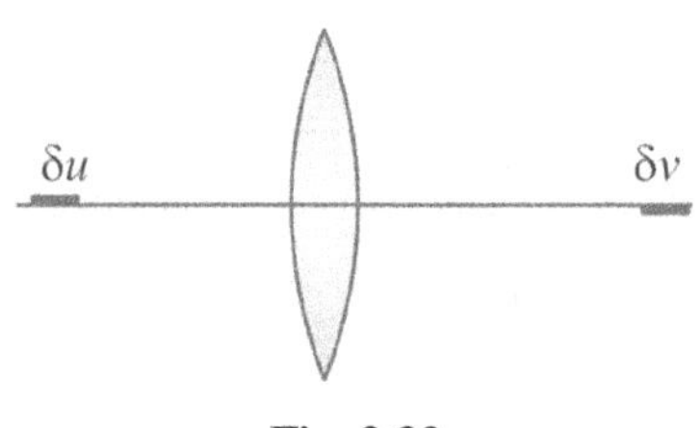

Fig. 3.32

For short linear object, we can write δu for length of the object and δv, for length of the image. So

$$m_L = \frac{\delta v}{\delta u}.$$

We have, $\qquad \dfrac{1}{v} - \dfrac{1}{u} = \dfrac{1}{f}.$

On differentiating, we get

$$-\frac{\delta v}{v^2}+\frac{\delta u}{u^2} = 0$$

or

$$\frac{\delta v}{\delta u} = \frac{v^2}{u^2}$$

Thus

$$m_L = \frac{\delta v}{\delta u} = \frac{v^2}{u^2} = m^2 \quad ...(10)$$

Here positive value of m_L indicates that object and its image are along the same direction.

Velocity of image

Consider an object moving along the principal axis of a lens with a constant velocity v_o. Its image velocity v_i can be obtained as :

We have,

$$\frac{1}{v}-\frac{1}{u} = \frac{1}{f}$$

Differentiating above equation with respect to time, we get

$$-\frac{1}{v^2}\frac{dv}{dt}+\frac{1}{u^2}\frac{du}{dt} = 0$$

or

$$\frac{dv}{dt} = \frac{v^2}{u^2}\left(\frac{du}{dt}\right).$$

Here

$$\frac{du}{dt} = v_o \quad \text{and} \quad \frac{dv}{dt}=v_i$$

Thus

$$v_i = \frac{v^2}{u^2}v_0. \quad ...(11)$$

Here $\dfrac{v^2}{u^2}$ is a positive term and so v_i and v_o have same direction.

3.8 LEAST POSSIBLE DISTANCE BETWEEN AN OBJECT AND ITS REAL IMAGE FOR A CONVEX LENS

Consider a convex lens of focal length f. Let the distance between object and its real image be D. Suppose x is the distance of the object from the lens, then image distance will be $(D-x)$. Thus

$$u = -x, \quad v = +(D-x).$$

By lens formula,

$$\frac{1}{v}-\frac{1}{u} = \frac{1}{f}$$

$$\frac{1}{(D-x)}-\frac{1}{-x} = \frac{1}{f}$$

or

$$x^2 - Dx + fD = 0$$

$$\therefore \quad x = \frac{D\pm\sqrt{D^2-4fD}}{2}$$

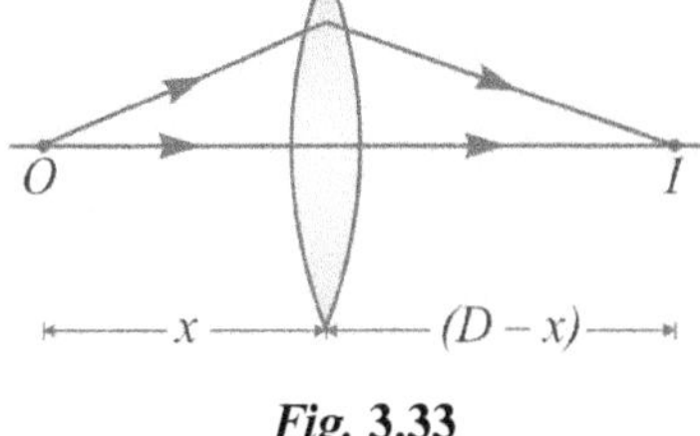

Fig. 3.33

For real image, x to be real and so

$$D^2 - 4fD \geq 0$$

or $$D \geq 4f.$$

Thus minimum and maximum distance between object and its real image will be $4f$ and ∞ respectively.

Focal length of convex lens by displacement method

Consider a convex lens, whose focal length is to be determined. Let D is the separation between object and its real image (screen). Suppose u and v are the object and image distances from the lens, then $D = u + v$. If we make the object distance v by displacing the lens, then image distance will be u (according to reversibility of path of light). Let the displacement of the lens be x. If I_1 and I_2 are the heights of images for the two positions of the lens, then

$$\frac{I_1}{O} = \frac{v}{u} \text{ and } \frac{I_2}{O} = \frac{u}{v}$$

$$\therefore \quad \frac{I_1}{O} \times \frac{I_2}{O} = 1 \text{ or } O = \sqrt{I_1 I_2} \qquad ....(12)$$

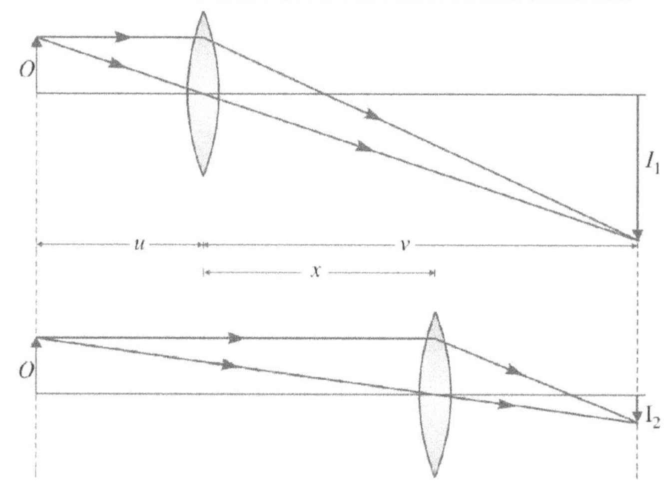

Fig. 3.34

We have $$u + v = D \qquad ...(i)$$
and $$v - u = x \qquad ...(ii)$$

On adding equations (i) and (ii), we get

$$u = \frac{D - x}{2}$$

and $$v = \frac{D + x}{2}$$

Now by lens formula, $\dfrac{1}{v} - \dfrac{1}{u} = \dfrac{1}{f}$, we have

$$\frac{1}{+\left(\dfrac{D+x}{2}\right)} - \frac{1}{-\left(\dfrac{D-x}{2}\right)} = \frac{1}{+f}$$

After solving, we get

$$f = \frac{D^2 - x^2}{4D} \qquad ...(13)$$

Ex. 11 The distance between object and its real image in convex lens is D and magnification in m. Find focal length of the lens.

Sol.

If x is the object distance, then image distance $v = D - x$. Thus

$$m = \frac{v}{u} = \frac{D - x}{x}$$

or
$$D - x = m x$$

$$\therefore \quad x = \frac{D}{(1 + m)}$$

and
$$D - x = \frac{mD}{1 + m}$$

Now using lens formula, $\dfrac{1}{v} - \dfrac{1}{u} = \dfrac{1}{f}$, we have

$$\frac{1}{+\left(\dfrac{mD}{1+m}\right)} - \frac{1}{-\left(\dfrac{D}{1+m}\right)} = \frac{1}{f}$$

After solving, we get

$$f = \frac{mD}{(1+m)^2}. \qquad \textit{Ans.}$$

Ex. 12 The graph shows the variation of magnification $|m|$ produced by a convex lens with the real image distance $|v|$. Find the focal length of the lens.

Sol.

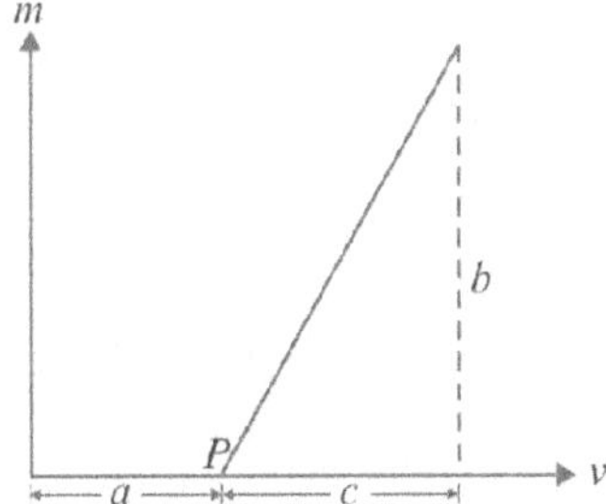

Fig. 3.35

We know that
$$m = \frac{v}{u}$$

Also
$$\frac{1}{f} = \frac{1}{v} - \frac{1}{u}.$$

For convex lens,
$$u = -u \text{ and}$$
$$v = +v.$$

$$\therefore \quad \frac{1}{f} = \frac{1}{v} - \frac{1}{-u} = \frac{1}{v} + \frac{1}{u}$$

or
$$\frac{v}{u} = \frac{v}{f} - 1$$

$$\therefore \quad m = \frac{v}{f} - 1 \qquad \text{...(i)}$$

Differentiating equation (i) with respect to v, we get

$$\frac{dm}{dv} = \frac{1}{f}$$

or
$$f = \frac{1}{\left(\dfrac{dm}{dv}\right)}.$$

From the graph, $\quad \dfrac{dm}{dv} = \dfrac{b}{c}$

$$\therefore \quad f = \frac{1}{b/c} = \frac{c}{b} \qquad \textit{Ans.}$$

Also, $\quad u = \infty, v = f$

and $\quad m = \dfrac{v}{u} = \dfrac{f}{\infty} = 0.$

Therefore at P, $\quad f = a. \qquad \textit{Ans.}$

Thus there are two possible values of f ; c/b and a. These two must be equal.

Ex. 13 A point object O is placed on the principal axis of a convex lens of focal length $f = 20$ cm at a distance of 40 cm to the left of it. The diameter of the lens is 10 cm. An eye is placed 60 cm to the right of the lens and a distance h below the principal axis. What is the maximum value of h ?

Sol.

For the maximum value of h, the rays should be coming from edges of the lens after refraction.

For convex lens, $u = -40, f = +20$ cm

$$\therefore \quad \frac{1}{v} - \frac{1}{-40} = \frac{1}{+20}$$

or
$$v = 40 \text{ cm}$$

The situation is shown in **fig. 3.36**.

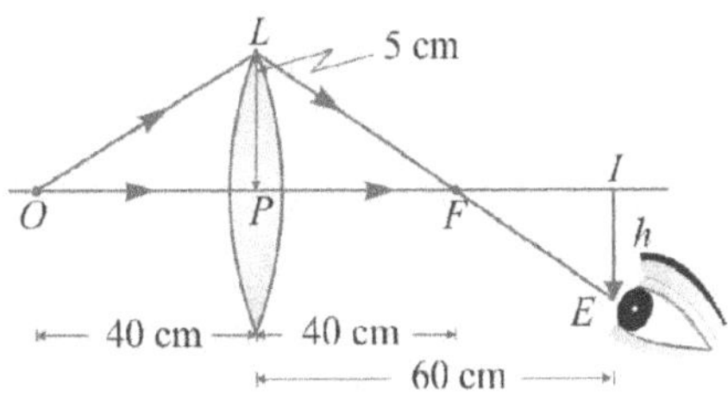

Fig. 3.36

In similar triangles PLF and IEF, we have

$$\frac{5}{h} = \frac{40}{20}$$

$$\therefore \quad h = 2.5 \text{ cm.} \qquad \textit{Ans.}$$

Ex. 14 A converging lens of focal length 15 cm and a converging mirror of focal length 20 cm are placed with their principal axis coinciding. A point source S is placed on the principal axis at a distance of 12 cm from the lens as shown in *fig. 3.37*. It is found that the final beam comes out parallel to the principal axis. Find the separation between the mirror and the lens.

Sol. For convex lens; $u = -12$ cm, $f = +15$ cm

$$\frac{1}{v} - \frac{1}{u} = \frac{1}{f}$$

or $$\frac{1}{v} - \frac{1}{-12} = \frac{1}{+15}$$

$$\therefore \quad v = -60 \text{ cm}$$

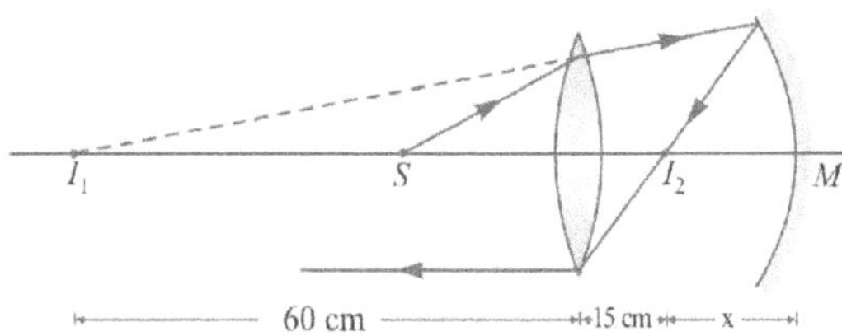

Fig. 3.37

The negative sign shows that the image is formed on the side of the object. For the final beam becomes parallel to the principal axis, the mirror should form the image at the focus of the lens. Thus for the mirror, I_1 becomes object and I_2 the image.

$$\therefore \quad u = -(60 + 15 + x) = -(75 + x)$$
$$v = -x \text{ and } f = -20 \text{ cm}.$$

Now by mirror formula, $\dfrac{1}{v} + \dfrac{1}{u} = \dfrac{1}{f}$, we have

$$\frac{1}{-x} + \frac{1}{-(75 + x)} = \frac{1}{-20}$$

On solving, we get, $x = 25$ cm, -60 cm.

Only $x = 25$ cm can be accepted. Thus the separation between lens and the mirror

$$= 15 + 25 = 40 \text{ cm}. \qquad \textit{Ans.}$$

Ex. 15 The diameter of aperture of a plano-convex lens is 6 cm and its maximum thickness is 3 mm. If the velocity of light in the material of lens is 2×10^8 m/s, calculate the focal length of the lens.

Sol. Given thickness of the lens at the centre $t = 0.3$ cm. If R be the radius of the spherical surface of the lens, then

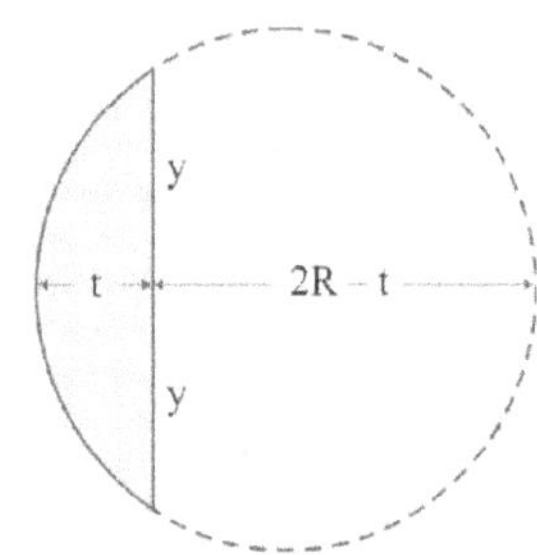

Fig. 3.38

$$(2R - t)\,t = y^2$$
or $$2Rt - t^2 = y^2$$
As $t << R$, $\therefore$ $$2Rt \simeq y^2$$

and $$R = \frac{y^2}{2t} = \frac{(3)^2}{2 \times 0.3} = 15 \text{ cm}$$

If μ is the refractive index of material of the lens, then

$$\mu = \frac{3 \times 10^8}{2 \times 10^8} = 1.5.$$

Now by lens maker's formula, we have

$$\frac{1}{f} = (\mu - 1)\left(\frac{1}{R_1} - \frac{1}{R_2}\right)$$

$$= (1.5 - 1)\left(\frac{1}{15} - \frac{1}{\infty}\right)$$

$$\therefore \quad f = 30 \text{ cm}. \qquad \textit{Ans.}$$

3.9 DEVIATION PRODUCED BY A LENS

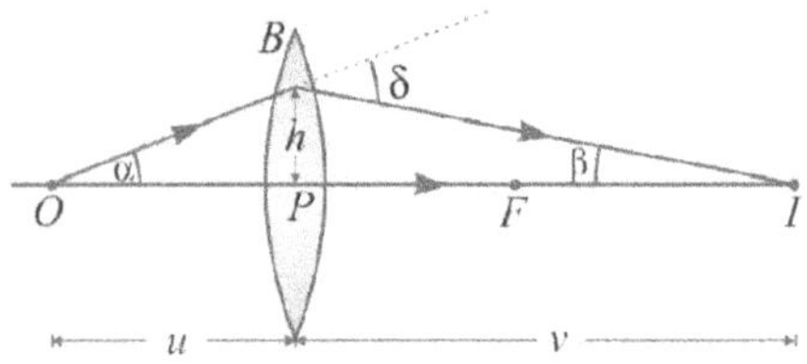

Consider a ray OB coming from the object and incident at a height h on the lens of focal length f. The ray intersect the principal axis at I. So the deviation δ produced by the lens

$$\delta = \angle BOP + \angle BIP$$
$$= \alpha + \beta$$

For small angles

$$\alpha \simeq \tan \alpha = \frac{h}{-u}$$

and

$$\beta \simeq \tan \beta = \frac{h}{v}$$

Fig. 3.39

$$\therefore \qquad \delta \;=\; \frac{h}{-u} + \frac{h}{v}$$

or
$$\delta \;=\; h\left[\frac{1}{v} - \frac{1}{u}\right]$$

or
$$\delta \;=\; \frac{h}{f}.$$

The above formula holds for the rays, for which h is small.

3.10 Power of a Lens

When light ray is incident on a lens, it bends either towards the principal axis (in convex lens) or away from the principal axis (in concave lens). The ability of a lens to bend the ray towards the principal axis is called power of the lens. As convex lens bends the rays towards the principal axis, so its power is taken a positive while concave lens bends the rays away from the principal axis, so its power is negative. Mathematically, power of a lens is defined as :

$$\text{power} \;=\; \frac{1}{\text{focal length of the lens}}$$

or
$$P \;=\; \frac{1}{f}.$$

The unit of power is diopter, if unit of f is metre.

3.11 Combined Focal Length

(i) Two lenses are placed in contact

Consider two thin lenses of focal lengths f_1 and f_2 are placed in contact on the same optic axis. An object O is placed at a distance u from the lenses. The image I_1 formed by first lens becomes the object for second lens; second lens forms the image I at a distance v from it. If v_1 is the distance of I_1, then for first lens;

$$\frac{1}{v_1} - \frac{1}{u} \;=\; \frac{1}{f_1} \qquad \text{...(i)}$$

For the second lens;

$$\frac{1}{v} - \frac{1}{v_1} \;=\; \frac{1}{f_2} \qquad \text{...(ii)}$$

Adding equations (i) and (ii), we get

$$\frac{1}{v} - \frac{1}{u} \;=\; \frac{1}{f_1} + \frac{1}{f_2} \qquad \text{... (iii)}$$

If f_e is the focal length of the equivalent lens, then

$$\frac{1}{v} - \frac{1}{u} \;=\; \frac{1}{f_e} \qquad \text{...(iv)}$$

On comparing equations (iii) and (iv), we get

$$\frac{1}{f_e} \;=\; \frac{1}{f_1} + \frac{1}{f_2} \qquad \text{...(14)}$$

Also equivalent power;

$$P \;=\; P_1 + P_2 \qquad \text{...(15)}$$

The above formulas are applicable to any type and any number of thin lenses in contact.

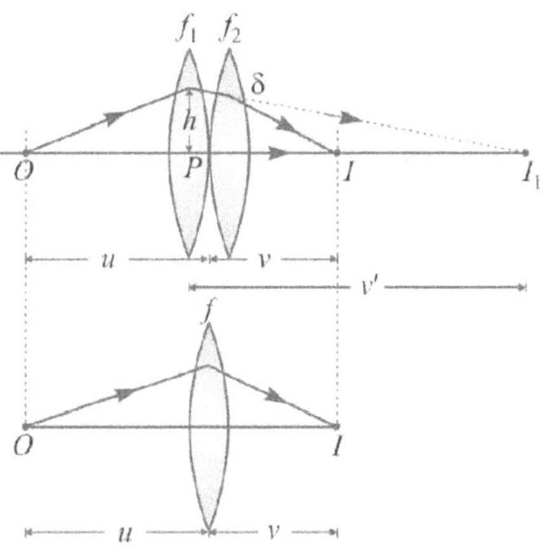

Fig. **3.40**

(ii)   **Total magnification**

Suppose m_1 and m_2 are the magnifications produced by lenses separately. For the first lens

$$\frac{I_1}{O} = m_1$$

$$\therefore \qquad I_1 = m_1 O.$$

The image formed by first lens becomes the object for second lens, and so $O_2 = I_1 = m_1 O$, and

$$\frac{I_2}{O_2} = m_2$$

or

$$\frac{I_2}{m_1 O} = m_2$$

or

$$\frac{I_2}{O} = m_1 m_2. \qquad \text{...(i)}$$

If M is the total magnification produced by the system, then

$$\frac{I_2}{O} = M \qquad \text{...(ii)}$$

On comparing equations (i) and (ii), we get

$$M = m_1 m_2.$$

For n-thin lenses, we can write

$$M = m_1 \times m_2 \times \text{.......} \times m_n. \quad \text{... (16)}$$

(iii)   **Two lenses separated by a finite distance**

Let two lenses of focal lengths f_1 and f_2 are placed on the same optic axis at a separation d.

Suppose a ray AB is incident on first lens at a height h_1. The refracted ray BC is then incident on the second lens at a height h_2, F_1 and F are the focal points of first and equivalent lens. If δ_1 and δ_2 are the deviations produced by the lenses separately, then total deviation produced

$$\delta = \delta_1 + \delta_2$$

$$\frac{h_1}{f_e} = \frac{h_1}{f_1} + \frac{h_2}{f_2} \qquad \text{...(i)}$$

where f_e is the focal length of equivalent lens. From similar triangles $P_1 B F_1$ and $P_2 C F_1$, we have

$$\frac{h_1}{f_1} = \frac{h_2}{(f_1 - d)}$$

$$\therefore \qquad h_2 = \frac{h_1 (f_1 - d)}{f_1}.$$

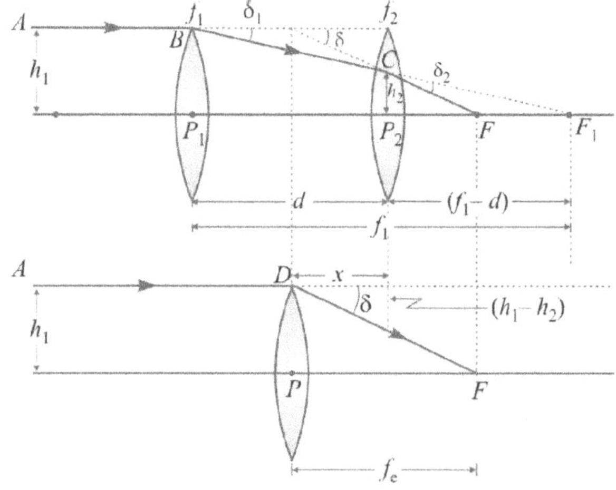

Fig. **3.41**

Substituting the value of h_2 in equation (i), we have

$$\frac{h_1}{f_e} = \frac{h_1}{f_1} + \frac{h_1}{f_1 f_2}(f_1 - d)$$

or
$$\frac{1}{f_e} = \frac{1}{f_1} + \frac{1}{f_2} - \frac{d}{f_1 f_2} \quad ...(17)$$

Equivalent power;
$$P = P_1 + P_2 - d\, P_1 P_2 \quad ...(18)$$

The distance of the equivalent lens from the second lens

Let x be the required distance. In figure

$$\delta \simeq \tan\delta = \frac{h_1 - h_2}{x}$$

or
$$\frac{h_1}{f_e} = \frac{h_1 - h_2}{x}$$

$$\therefore \quad x = \frac{f_e}{h_1}(h_1 - h_2)$$

$$= f_e\left[h_1 - h_1\left(\frac{f_1 - d}{f_1}\right)\right]$$

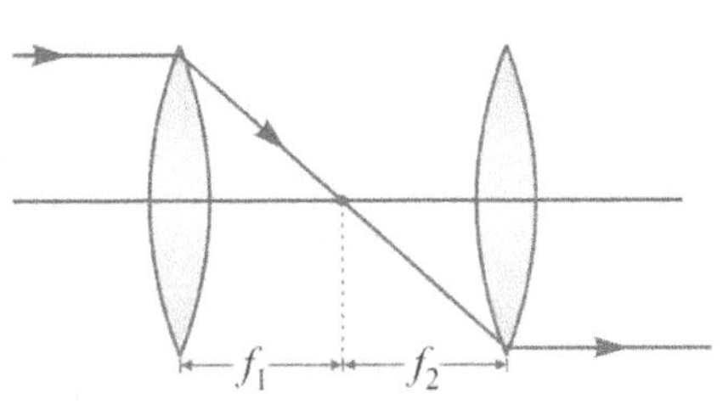

Fig. 3.42

or
$$x = \frac{f_e d}{f_1}$$

Special case : If parallel incident ray on first lens emerges parallel from the second lens, then $f_e = \infty$.

$$\therefore \quad \frac{1}{\infty} = \frac{1}{f_1} + \frac{1}{f_2} - \frac{d}{f_1 f_2}$$

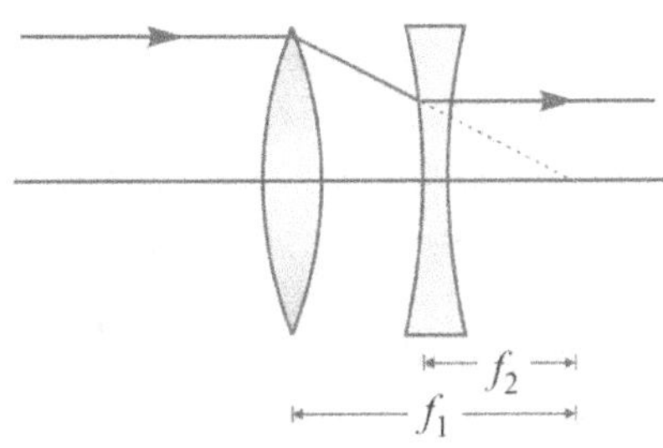

or
$$d = f_1 + f_2$$

Fig. 3.43

(i) If both the lenses are convex, then $\quad d = f_1 + f_2$.

(ii) If second lens is concave, then $\quad d = f_1 + (-f_2) = f_1 - f_2$.

More about lenses

1. If a lens of focal length f is cut into two identical lenses as shown in figure, then focal length of each lens will be $2f$.

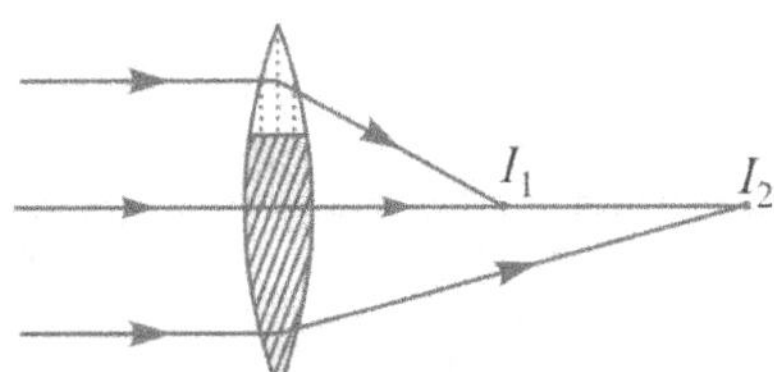

Fig. 3.45

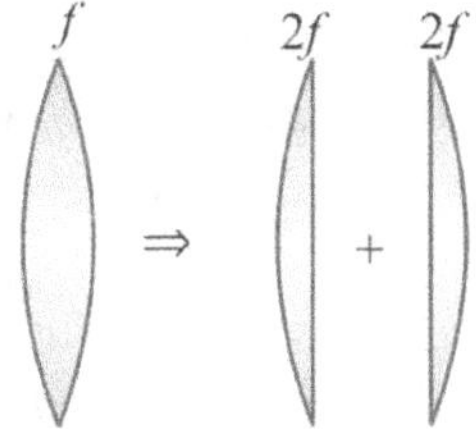

Fig. 3.44

2. If a lens is made of two or more materials (placed one over other), then it will have two or more focal lengths and hence separate images.

3. If a lens is made of two or more material and are placed side by side, then there will be one focal length and hence one image.

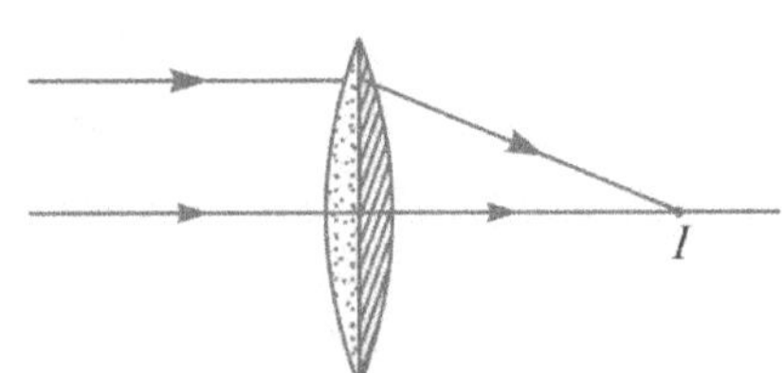

Fig. 3.46

4. Intensity of image is proportional to the area of the lens exposed to incident rays. A quarter of a lens can form full image but its intensity will be one forth that of full lens.

Ex. 16 A lens of focal length f (in air) is made of material of refractive index $_a\mu_g = 1.5$, is immersed in a liquid. Find its focal length, if the refractive index of liquid is

(a) $_a\mu_\ell = 1.2$ (b) $_a\mu_\ell = 1.8$ (c) $_a\mu_\ell = 1.5$.

Sol.

The focal length of the lens is given by

$$\frac{1}{f_{air}} = \left(_a\mu_g - 1\right)\left(\frac{1}{R_1} - \frac{1}{R_2}\right) \quad ...(i)$$

When lens is immersed in liquid, its focal length is given by

$$\frac{1}{f_{liq}} = \left(_\ell\mu_g - 1\right)\left(\frac{1}{R_1} - \frac{1}{R_2}\right) \quad ...(ii)$$

Dividing equation (i) by (ii), we have

$$f_{liq} = f_{air}\left[\frac{_a\mu_g - 1}{_\ell\mu_g - 1}\right]$$

$$= f_{air}\left[\frac{_a\mu_g - 1}{\dfrac{_a\mu_g}{_a\mu_\ell} - 1}\right]$$

(a)   For $_a\mu_g = 1.5$, $_a\mu_\ell = 1.2$

$$f_{liq} = f_{air}\left[\frac{1.5 - 1}{\dfrac{1.5}{1.2} - 1}\right] = 2f_{air} = 2f \quad \textbf{Ans.}$$

(b)   For $_a\mu_g = 1.5$, $_a\mu_\ell = 1.8$

$$f_{liq} = f_{air}\left[\frac{1.5 - 1}{\dfrac{1.5}{1.8} - 1}\right] = -3f_{air} = -3f \,\textbf{Ans.}$$

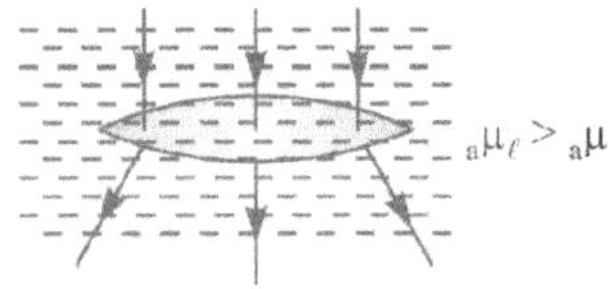

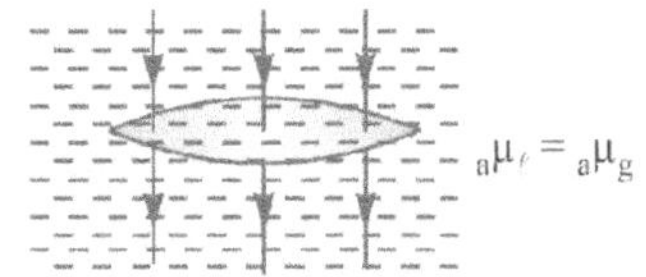

Fig. 3.47

(c) $_a\mu_g = 1.5$, $_a\mu_\ell = 1.5$

$$f_{liq} = f_{air}\left[\frac{1.5 - 1}{\dfrac{1.5}{1.5} - 1}\right] = \infty$$

The lens behaves like a plate and becomes invisible.

From the above calculations, it can be concluded that focal length of the lens in each case will increase when lens is immersed in a liquid.

Ex. 17 Two thin convex lenses of focal lengths f_1 and f_2 are separated by a horizontal distance d ($d < f_1$ and $d < f_2$) and their centres are displaced by a vertical separation Δ as shown in *fig. 3.48*. Taking the origin of coordinates O as the centre of first lens, what would be the x and y co-ordinates of the focal point of this lens system for a parallel beam of rays coming from left ?

Sol.

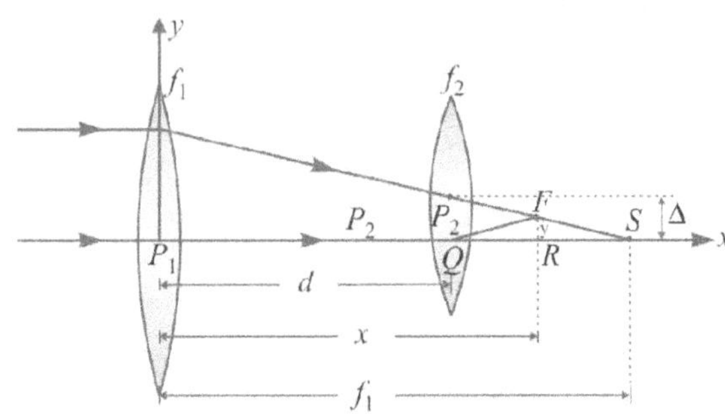

Fig. 3.48

In the absence of second lens, the parallel incident rays will focus at S, at a distance f_1 from the first lens. These rays now intercepted by second lens, and finally focus at point F. Thus for second lens;

$$u_2 = +(f_1 - d)$$
$$f = +f_2$$

By lens formula, $\dfrac{1}{v} - \dfrac{1}{u} = \dfrac{1}{f}$, we have

$$\frac{1}{v} - \frac{1}{(f_1 - d)} = \frac{1}{f_2}$$

After simplifying, we get $v = \dfrac{f_2(f_1 - d)}{(f_1 + f_2 - d)}$

The x coordinate of the focus

$$x = d + v$$

$$= d + \frac{f_2(f_1 - d)}{(f_1 + f_2 - d)}$$

$$= \frac{f_1 f_2 + d(f_1 - d)}{(f_1 + f_2 - d)}. \quad \textit{Ans.}$$

The y co-ordinate of the focus F can be obtained as :

In similar triangles $P_2\,QS$ and FRS, we have

$$\frac{\Delta}{y} = \frac{(f_1 - d)}{(f_1 - x)}$$

or $\qquad y = \dfrac{\Delta(f_1 - x)}{(f_1 - d)}$

$$= \frac{\Delta\left[f_1 - \left\{\dfrac{f_1 f_2 + d(f_1 - d)}{(f_1 + f_2 - d)}\right\}\right]}{(f_1 - d)}$$

$$= \frac{\Delta(f_1 - d)}{(f_1 + f_2 - d)}. \quad \textit{Ans.}$$

3.12 SILVERING OF LENSES

When one face of the lens is silvered, what it behaves like ? To understand this let us suppose an object is placed in front of a silvered plano-convex lens. The ray from the object first gets refracted from the curved surface, thereafter reflected by the silvered face. Again refracted from the curved surface and finally emerges out from the lens. The I becomes the image of the object O. Its action is like a concave mirror. The focal length of the system is equivalent to two lenses and a mirror in contact (two refraction and a reflection). Thus is f_{lens} and f_{mirror} be the focal lengths of lens and mirror respectively, then equivalent focal length f_e of the system can be obtained as :

$$\frac{1}{f_e} = \frac{1}{f_{\text{lens}}} + \frac{1}{f_{\text{lens}}} + \frac{1}{f_{\text{mirror}}}$$

or

$$\frac{1}{f_e} = \frac{2}{f_{\text{lens}}} + \frac{1}{f_{\text{mirror}}}$$

Focal length of mirror

Thus in solving the problems of silvered lens, first find the focal length by using the above formula and then use mirror formula; $\dfrac{1}{u} + \dfrac{1}{v} = \dfrac{1}{f}$. In this formula put the value of f_e with negative sign (assuming concave mirror).

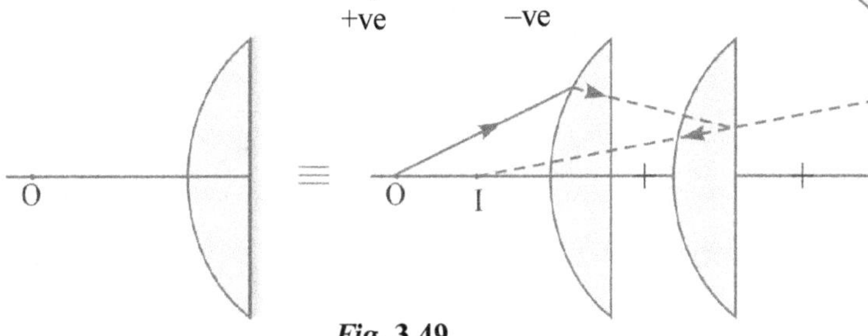

Fig. 3.49

Ex. 18 Find the focal length of the lens in the following cases : The radius of curvature of curved surface is R and refractive index of material of lens is μ.

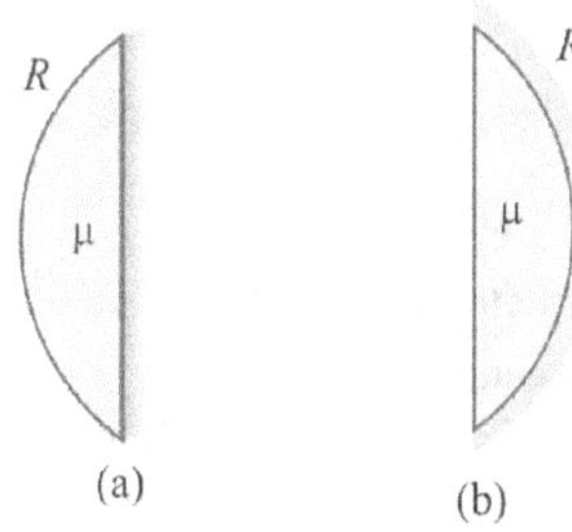

Fig. 3.50

Sol.

(a) Here the plane face is silvered and so $f_{\text{mirror}} = \infty$. The focal length of the lens;

$$\frac{1}{f_{lens}} = (\mu-1)\left(\frac{1}{R} - \frac{1}{\infty}\right)$$

$$= \frac{(\mu-1)}{R}.$$

The equivalent focal length of the silvered lens

$$\frac{1}{f_e} = \frac{2}{f_{lens}} + \frac{1}{f_{mirror}}$$

$$= \frac{2(\mu-1)}{R} + \frac{1}{\infty}$$

or

$$f_e = \frac{R}{2(\mu-1)}.$$ **Ans.**

(b) In this case curved face is silvered and so $f_{\text{mirror}} = R/2$ (put no sign). Thus

$$\frac{1}{f_e} = \frac{2(\mu-1)}{R} + \frac{1}{R/2}$$

or

$$f_e = \frac{R}{2\mu}.$$ **Ans.**

Ex. 19 The convex surface of a thin concavo-convex lens (refractive index 1.5) has a radius of curvature 20 cm. The concave surface has a radius of 60 cm. The convex side is silvered and is placed on a horizontal surface. At what distance from the lens should a pin be placed on the optic axis such that its image is formed at the same place ?

Sol. For the lens, $R_1 = -60$ cm

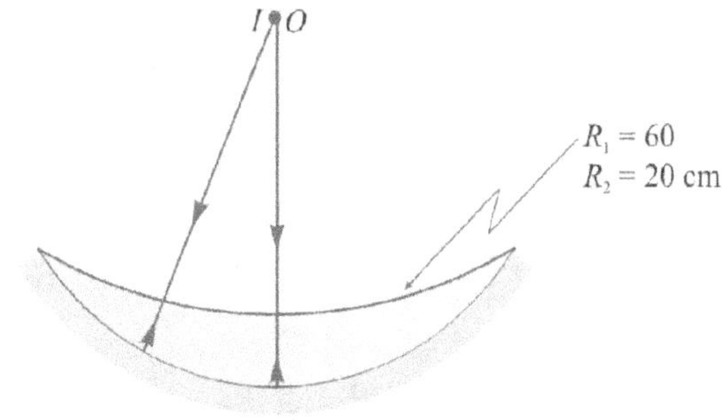

Fig. 3.51

and
$$R_2 = -20 \text{ cm.}$$

Thus
$$\frac{1}{f_{lens}} = (\mu - 1)\left(\frac{1}{R_1} - \frac{1}{R_2}\right)$$

$$= (1.5 - 1)\left(\frac{1}{-60} - \frac{1}{-20}\right)$$

On solving, we get
$$f_{lens} = 60 \text{ cm}$$

The focal length of the equivalent lens;

$$\frac{1}{f_e} = \frac{2}{f_{lens}} + \frac{1}{f_{mirror}}$$

$$= \frac{2}{60} + \frac{1}{10}$$

or
$$f_e = 7.5 \text{ cm.}$$

The system behaves like a concave mirror. Thus
$$f = -7.5 \text{ cm}$$

By mirror formula, $\dfrac{1}{u} + \dfrac{1}{v} = \dfrac{1}{f}$ and for $v = u$,

$$\frac{1}{u} + \frac{1}{u} = \frac{1}{-7.5}.$$

$$\therefore \qquad u = -15 \text{ cm.}$$

Thus image and object will coincide if object is placed at a distance of 15 cm from the lens.

Ex. 20

Two thin similar convex glass pieces are joined together, front to front, with its rear-portion silvered such that a sharp image of a distinct object is formed at 0.2 m. When the air between the glass pieces is replaced by water ($\mu = 4/3$), find the position of the image.

Sol.

The system is equivalent to two air lenses each of focal length $f_{air} = \infty$ and a mirror of focal length $f_m = R/2$. Also for distinct object, $u = -\infty$,

$$\therefore v = f_e.$$

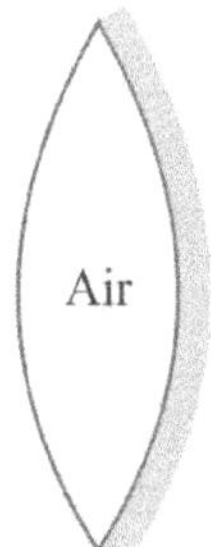

Fig. 3.52

Thus
$$\frac{1}{f_e} = \frac{2}{f_{air}} + \frac{1}{f_m}$$

or
$$\frac{1}{-0.2} = \frac{2}{\infty} + \frac{1}{R/2}$$

or
$$R = -0.4 \text{ m.} \ |R| = 0.4 \text{ m.}$$

When air is replaced by water, then

$$\frac{1}{f_{water}} = \left(_a\mu_w - 1\right)\left(\frac{1}{R_1} - \frac{1}{R_2}\right)$$

$$= \left(\frac{4}{3} - 1\right)\left(\frac{1}{0.4} - \frac{1}{-0.4}\right)$$

or
$$f_{water} = 0.6 \text{ m.}$$

The focal length of the equivalent lens now

$$\frac{1}{f_e'} = \frac{2}{f_{water}} + \frac{1}{f_{mirror}}$$

$$= \frac{2}{0.6} + \frac{1}{0.4/2}$$

or
$$f'_e = 0.12 \text{ m}$$

Thus new position of image for distinct object will be 0.12 m.

Ex. 21

An equi-convex lens of focal length 10 cm and refractive index ($_a\mu_g = 1.5$) is placed in a liquid whose refractive index varies with time as $_a\mu_l = 1 + \dfrac{t}{10}$. If the lens was placed in the liquid at $t = 0$, after what time will the lens act as concave lens of focal length 20 cm?

Sol. We know that, focal length of the lens in liquid is given by

$$f_e = f_a\left[\frac{_a\mu_g - 1}{\dfrac{_a\mu_g}{_a\mu_l} - 1}\right] \quad \text{or} \quad -20 = 10\left[\frac{1.5 - 1}{\dfrac{1.5}{\left(1 + \dfrac{t}{10}\right)} - 1}\right]$$

After simplifying, we get $t = 10$ s.

Ex. 22

A plane glass plate is constructed by combining a plano-convex lens and a plano-concave lens of different materials as shown in *fig. 3.53*. Will it act as a lens ? If so, find its focal length.

Sol.

On being different refractive indexes of two parts, it will bend the parallel incident rays and so behaves like a lens. If f_1 and f_2 are the focal lengths of two parts, then effective focal length of the system

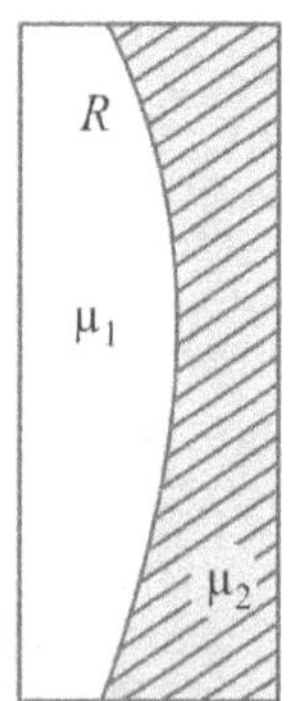

Fig. 3.53

$$\frac{1}{f} = \frac{1}{f_1} + \frac{1}{f_2}.$$

where

$$\frac{1}{f_1} = (\mu_1 - 1)\left(\frac{1}{\infty} - \frac{1}{-R}\right)$$

$$= \frac{(\mu_1 - 1)}{R}$$

and

$$\frac{1}{f_2} = (\mu_2 - 1)\left(\frac{1}{-R} - \frac{1}{\infty}\right)$$

$$= \frac{-(\mu_2 - 1)}{R}$$

Thus

$$\frac{1}{f} = \left[\frac{\mu_1 - 1}{R}\right] + \left[\frac{-(\mu_2 - 1)}{R}\right]$$

$$= \frac{\mu_1 - \mu_2}{R}$$

or

$$f = \frac{R}{\mu_1 - \mu_2}. \qquad Ans.$$

Ex. 23 A hemispherical portion of the surface of a solid glass sphere ($\mu = 1.5$) of radius r is silvered to make the inner side reflecting. An object is placed on the axis of the hemisphere at a distance $3r$ from the centre of the sphere. The light from the object is refracted at the unsilvered part, then reflected from the silvered part and again refracted at the unsilvered part. Locate the final image formed.

Sol. For the refraction through unsilvered face

$$u = -2r, \ R = +r$$

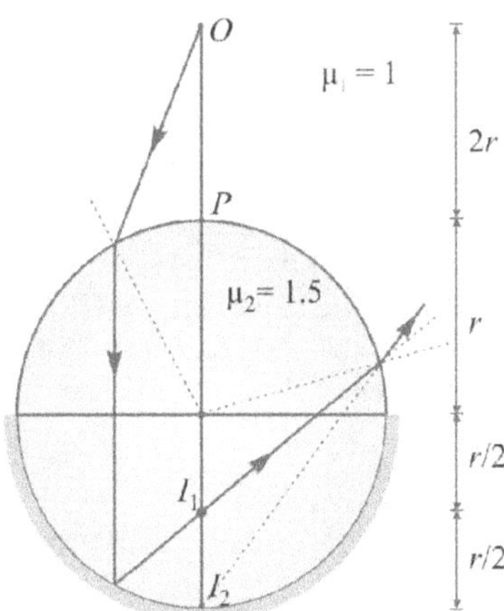

Fig. 3.54

We have

$$\frac{\mu_2}{v} - \frac{\mu_1}{u} = \frac{\mu_2 - \mu_1}{R}$$

or

$$\frac{1.5}{v} - \frac{1}{-2r} = \frac{1.5 - 1}{r}$$

which gives

$$v = \infty$$

The image formed by unsilvered face becomes object for silvered face. For which

$$u = \infty,$$

$$\therefore \qquad \frac{1}{v} + \frac{1}{\infty} = \frac{1}{-r/2} \Rightarrow v = \frac{-r}{2}.$$

This image again becomes object for unsilvered face, and so

$$u = +\frac{3r}{2}, \mu_1 = 1.5, \mu_2 = 1$$

$$\therefore \qquad \frac{1}{v} - \frac{1.5}{\left(\dfrac{3r}{2}\right)} = \frac{1 - 1.5}{r}$$

After solving, we get

$$v = +2r$$

Thus the final image is formed on the silvered face.

Ex. 24 A diverging lens of focal length 20 cm and a converging mirror of focal length 10 cm are placed coaxially at a separation of 5 cm. Where should an object be placed so that a real image is formed at the object itself ?

Sol.

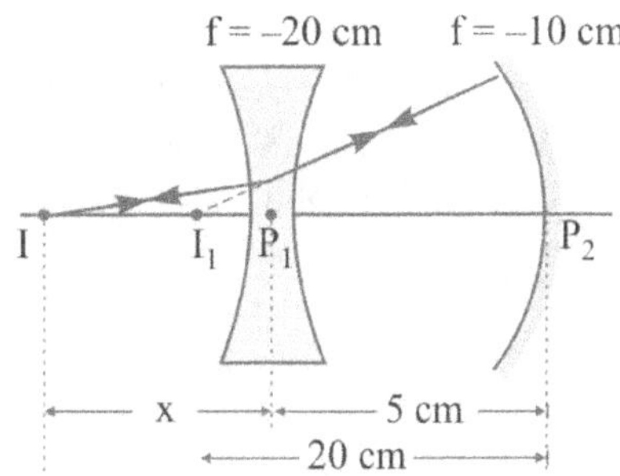

Fig. 3.55

The image will form on the object itself when rays after reflection from mirror retrace the path. It is possible when rays after refraction from lens incident normally on the mirror. In the absence of lens the mirror will form the image at I_1. But lens displaces it to I. Therefore for lens

$$u = +15 \text{ cm}$$
$$v = +x \text{ cm}$$
$$f = -20 \text{ cm}$$

By lens formula

$$\frac{1}{+x} - \frac{1}{+15} = \frac{1}{-20}$$

or $\qquad\qquad x = 60 \text{ cm} \qquad\qquad Ans.$

The object is to be placed at 60 cm from the lens further away from mirror.

Ex. 25 A converging lens and a diverging mirror are placed at a separation of 15 cm. The focal length of the lens is 25 cm and that of mirror is 40 cm. Where should a point source be placed between the lens and the mirror so that the light, after getting reflected by the mirror and then getting transmitted by the lens, comes out parallel to principal axis ?

Sol.

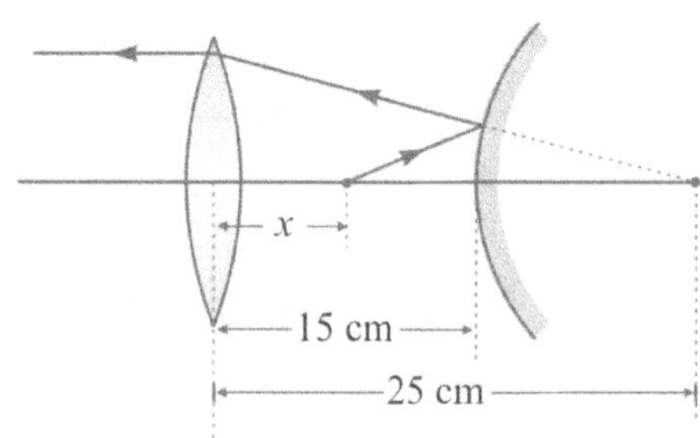

Fig. 3.56

The light is reflected by the mirror in such a way that it appears to come from its focus.

For mirror
$$u = -(15-x)$$
$$v = +10 \text{ cm}$$

By mirror formula $\dfrac{1}{v}+\dfrac{1}{u} = \dfrac{1}{f}$, we have

$$\frac{1}{+10}+\frac{1}{-(15-x)} = \frac{1}{+25}$$

After solving $\qquad x = 1.67 \text{ cm}$. *Ans.*

Ex. 26 A diverging lens of focal length 20 cm and a converging lens of focal length 30 cm are placed 15 cm apart with their principal axes coinciding. Where should an object the placed on the principal axis so that the image is formed at infinity ?

Sol.

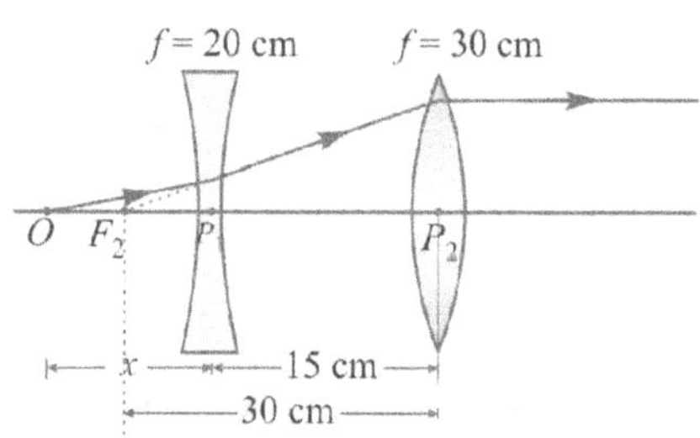

Fig. 3.57

(a) The final image will form at infinity when rays after refraction from concave lens appears to come from focal point of the convex lens. Let object be placed at a distance of x from the concave lens.

For concave lens,
$$u = -x$$
$$v = -15x$$

We have
$$\frac{1}{-15}-\frac{1}{-x} = \frac{1}{-20}$$

or $\qquad \dfrac{1}{x} = \dfrac{1}{-20}+\dfrac{1}{15}$

$\therefore \qquad x = 60 \text{ cm}$. *Ans.*

(b)

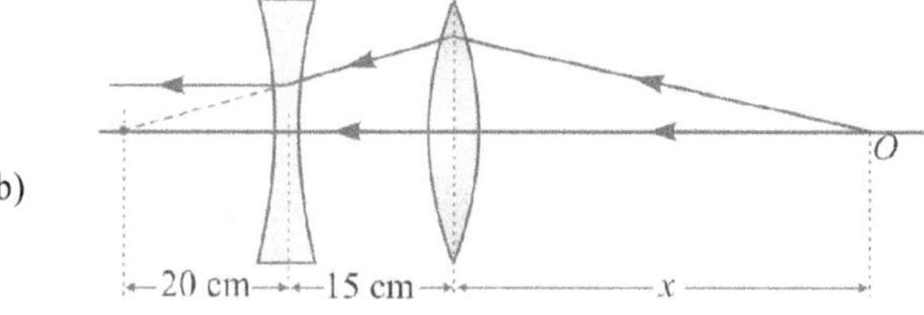

Fig. 3.58

Object can also be placed on the right of convex lens. Let it be placed at a distance x from lens. The final image will form at infinity; if rays after refraction from converging lens, incident along focus of diverging lens.

$$u = -x$$
$$v = +35$$

By lens formula $\dfrac{1}{v}-\dfrac{1}{u} = \dfrac{1}{f}$, we have

$$\frac{1}{+35}-\frac{1}{-x} = \frac{1}{+30}$$

or $\qquad \dfrac{1}{x} = \dfrac{1}{30}-\dfrac{1}{35}$

or $\qquad x = 210 \text{ cm}$. *Ans.*

Ex. 27 A small angled prism (refractive index μ and angle α) and a convex lens are arranged as shown in *fig. 3.59*. A point object O is placed as shown.

(a) Calculate the angle of deviation of the rays hitting the prism at nearly normal incidence

(b) If the distance between object, prism and the lens are shown in the figure, locate the position of the image both along and transverse to the axis.

Sol.

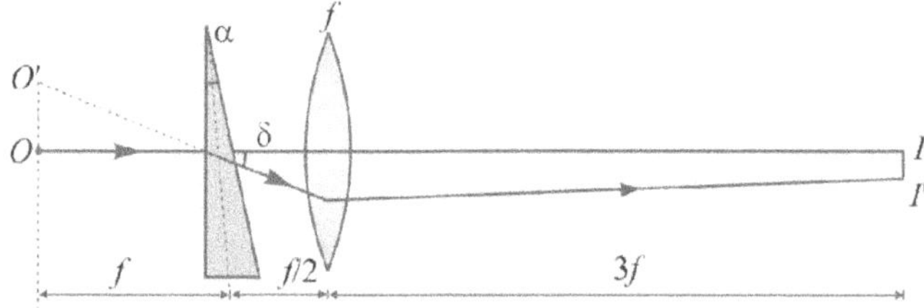

Fig. 3.59

(a) The deviation produced by the prism
$$\delta = (\mu-1)\alpha$$

(b) The prism forms image of the object at O'.
$$\therefore \qquad OO' = \delta f = (\mu-1)\,\alpha f$$
The image O' becomes object for lens.

Now using lens formula $\dfrac{1}{v}-\dfrac{1}{u} = \dfrac{1}{f}$

where $\qquad u = -\dfrac{3f}{2}$

$\therefore \qquad \dfrac{1}{v}-\dfrac{1}{\dfrac{3f}{2}} = \dfrac{1}{f}$

or $\qquad \dfrac{1}{v} = \dfrac{1}{3f}$

or $\qquad v = 3f$

Also
$$\frac{II'}{OO'} = \frac{v}{u}$$

$$= \frac{3f}{\left(\frac{3f}{2}\right)} = 2$$

which gives
$$II' = 2(OO')$$
$$= 2(\mu - 1)\alpha f$$

Thus image position is $3f$ on the right side of the lens along the axis, and $2(\mu-1)\alpha f$ transverse to axis.

Ex. 28 A thin plano convex lens of focal length f is split into two halves, one of the halves is shifted along the optical axis (*fig.* 3.60). The separation between object and image planes is 1.8 m. The magnification of the image formed by one of the half lenses is 2. Find the focal length of the lens and separation between two halves. Draw the ray diagram for image formation.

Sol.

Given :
$$u + v = 1.8$$

and
$$\frac{v}{u} = 2$$

After solving we get $u = 0.6$ and $v = 1.2$ m

Since position of object and screen are fixed and therefore distances u and v for one half of lens; become v and u for second half.

By lens formula $\dfrac{1}{v} - \dfrac{1}{u} = \dfrac{1}{f}$, we have

$$\frac{1}{1.2} - \frac{1}{-0.6} = \frac{1}{f}$$

or
$$f = 0.4 \, \text{m}$$

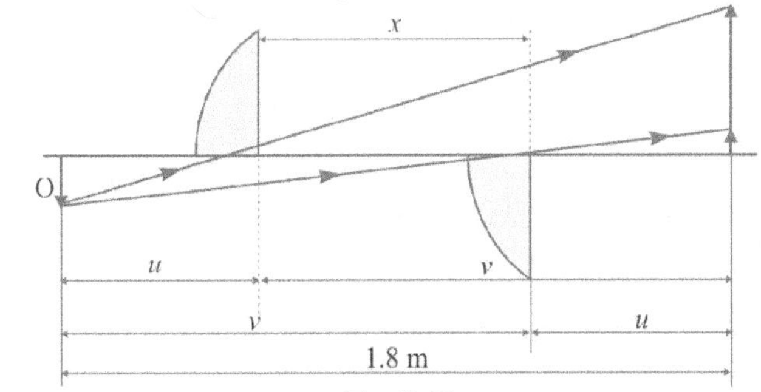

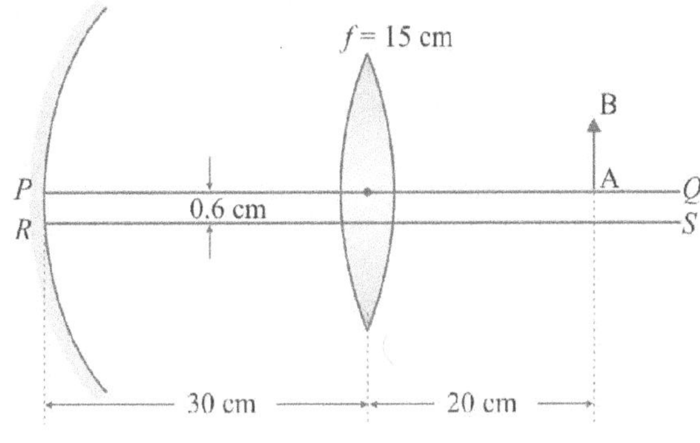

Fig. 3.60

From the figure $x = 0.6$ m.

Ex. 29 A point object is placed at a distance of 0.3 m from a convex lens (focal length 0.2 m) cut into two halves each of which is displaced by 0.0005 m as shown in the *fig.* 3.61. Find the position of the image. If more than one image is formed find their number and the distance between them.

Sol. Both halves of lens behave separately and form two images.

From lens formula, $\dfrac{1}{v} - \dfrac{1}{u} = \dfrac{1}{f}$

where
$$u = -0.3 \, \text{m}$$
$$f = +0.2 \, \text{m}$$

$$\therefore \quad \frac{1}{v} - \frac{1}{-0.3} = \frac{1}{0.2}$$

or
$$\frac{1}{v} = \frac{1}{0.6}$$

or
$$v = 0.6 \, \text{m}.$$

Each half lens forms the image at a distance 0.6 m from the lens. If I_1 and I_2 are the images form by two halves, then from similar triangles OP_1P_2 and OI_1I_2, we have

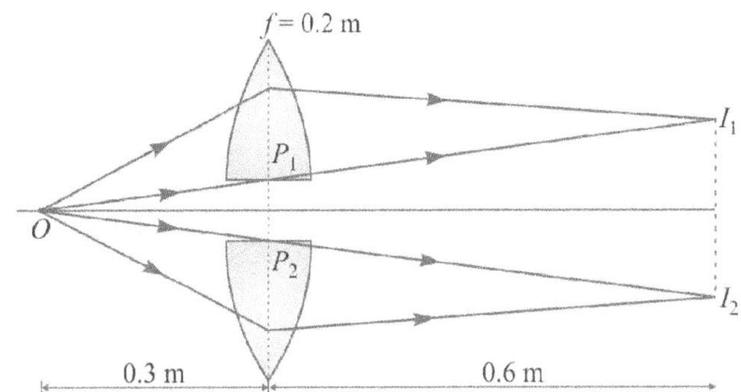

Fig. 3.61

$$\frac{I_1I_2}{P_1P_2} = \frac{(0.6 + 0.3)}{0.3}$$

or
$$I_1I_2 = 0.3 \, P_1P_2$$
$$= 3 \times 0.001$$
$$= 0.003 \, \text{m}. \qquad \textit{Ans.}$$

Ex. 30 A convex lens of focal length 15 cm and a concave mirror of focal length 30 cm are kept with their optic axis *PQ* and *RS* parallel but separated in vertical direction by 0.6 m as shown. The distance between lens and mirror is 30 cm. An upright object *AB* of height 1.2 m is placed on the optic axis *PQ* of the lens at a distance of 20 cm from the lens. If *A'B'* is the image after refraction from the lens and reflection from the mirror, find the distance of *A'B'* from the pole of the mirror and obtain magnification. Also locate position of *A'* and *B'* with respect to the optic axis *RS*.

Fig. 3.62

Sol. Given $u = -20$ cm, $f = +15$ cm

From lens formula $\dfrac{1}{v} - \dfrac{1}{u} = \dfrac{1}{f}$, we have

$$\therefore \quad \frac{1}{v} - \frac{1}{-20} = \frac{1}{+15}$$

$$\text{or} \quad v = 60 \text{ cm}$$

$$\text{and} \quad \frac{I}{O} = \frac{v}{u}$$

$$\text{or} \quad I = \frac{v}{u}O = \frac{60}{-20} \times 1.2$$

$$= -3.6 \text{ cm}$$

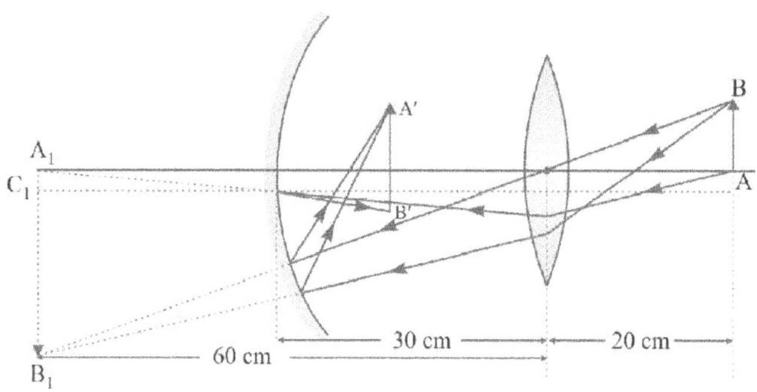

Fig. 3.63

The image formed by lens acts as an object. Its $(3.6 - 0.6)$ cm lies below the principal axis of the mirror and 0.6 cm lies above principal axis. Let image of C_1B_1 is $C'B'$, and that of C_1A_1 is $C'A'$

Now by mirror formula, $\dfrac{1}{v} + \dfrac{1}{u} = \dfrac{1}{f}$, we have

$$\frac{1}{v} + \frac{1}{+30} = \frac{1}{-30}$$

$$\therefore \quad v = -15 \text{ cm}$$

Now

$$\frac{C'B'}{3.0} = \frac{-v}{+u}$$

$$= -\frac{15}{30} = -\frac{1}{2}$$

or

$$C'B' = -1.5 \text{ cm}$$

Also

$$\frac{C'A'}{0.6} = \frac{-v}{u}$$

$$= \frac{15}{30}$$

which gives

$$C'A' = -0.3 \text{ cm}$$

$$A'B' = C'B' + C'A'$$

$$= 1.5 + 0.3 = 1.8 \text{ cm}$$

The 1.5 cm of image lies above principal axis and 0.3 cm lies below principal axis.

Ex. 31 A thin biconvex lens of refractive index 3/2 is placed on a horizontal plane mirror as shown in the *fig.* 3.67. The space between the lens and the mirror is then filled with water of refractive index 4/3. It is found that when a point object is placed 15 cm above the lens on its principal axis, the object coincides with its own image. On repeating with another liquid, the object and the image again coincide at a distance 25 cm from the lens. Calculate the refractive index of the liquid.

Sol.

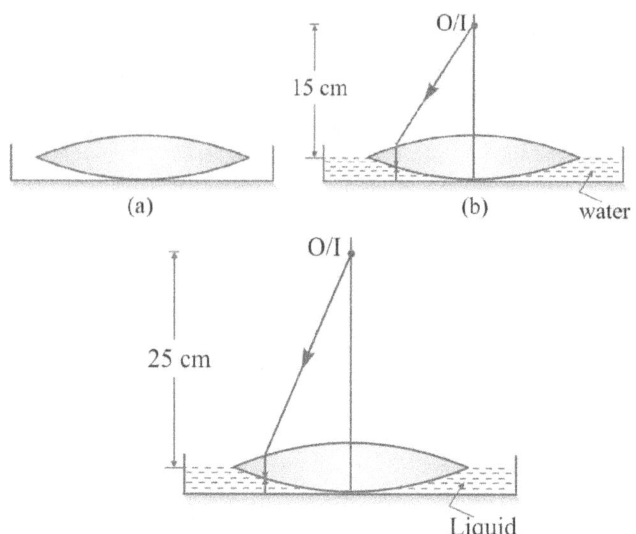

Fig. 3.64

Focal length of the convex lens

$$\frac{1}{f} = (\mu - 1)\left(\frac{1}{R_1} - \frac{1}{R_2}\right)$$

where $R_1 = +R$, $R_2 = -R$ and $\mu = 3/2$

$$\therefore \quad \frac{1}{f} = (3/2 - 1)\left(\frac{1}{R} - \frac{1}{-R}\right)$$

or

$$f = R. \qquad \textit{Ans.}$$

Now focal length of concave lens which is formed by water between lens and mirror

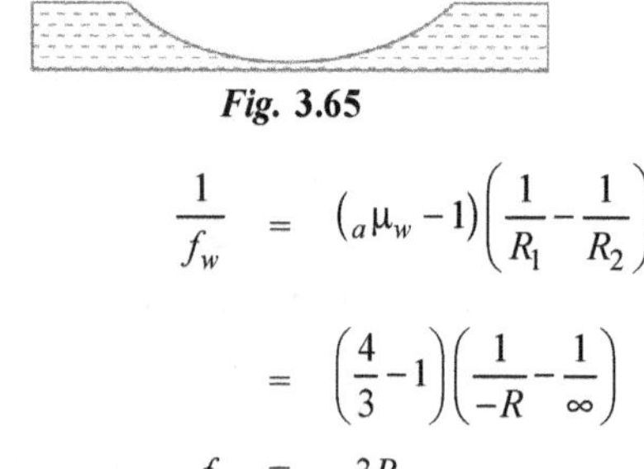

Fig. 3.65

$$\frac{1}{f_w} = \left({}_a\mu_w - 1\right)\left(\frac{1}{R_1} - \frac{1}{R_2}\right)$$

$$= \left(\frac{4}{3} - 1\right)\left(\frac{1}{-R} - \frac{1}{\infty}\right)$$

or

$$f_w = -3R$$

The effective system is equivalent of two glass lenses plus two water lenses. Therefore

$$\frac{1}{f_{e_1}} = \frac{2}{f} + \frac{2}{f_w}$$

We have

$$2f_{e_1} = 15 \text{ cm} \Rightarrow f_{e_1} = \frac{15}{2} \text{ cm}$$

$$\therefore \qquad \frac{1}{\left(\dfrac{15}{2}\right)} = \frac{2}{R} + \frac{2}{-3R}$$

or
$$\frac{1}{15} = \frac{1}{R} - \frac{1}{3R}$$

Which gives $\qquad R = 10 \qquad \therefore f = 10$ cm

When space between mirror and lens is filled with liquid, then

$$2f_{e_2} = 25 \text{ cm}$$

or
$$2f_{e_2} = \frac{25}{2} \text{ cm}$$

Also
$$\frac{1}{f_{e_2}} = \frac{2}{f} + \frac{2}{f_\ell}$$

or
$$\frac{1}{\left(\dfrac{25}{2}\right)} = \frac{2}{10} + \frac{2}{f_\ell}$$

or
$$f_\ell = -\frac{50}{3} \text{ cm}$$

For liquid lens

$$\frac{1}{f_\ell} = \left({}_a\mu_\ell - 1\right)\left(\frac{1}{R_1} - \frac{1}{R_2}\right)$$

or
$$\frac{1}{\left(-\dfrac{50}{3}\right)} = \left({}_a\mu_\ell - 1\right)\left(\frac{1}{-10} - \frac{1}{\infty}\right)$$

After solving $\qquad {}_a\mu_\ell = 1.6.$ ***Ans.***

Ex. 32
A thin equiconvex lens made of glass of refractive index
$\mu = \dfrac{3}{2}$ **and of focal length 0.3 m in air is sealed into an opening at one end of a tank filled with water ($\mu = 4/3$). On the opposite side of the lens a mirror is placed inside the tank on the tank wall perpendicular to the lens axis as shown in *fig. 3.66*. The separation between the lens and mirror is 0.8 m. A small object is placed outside the tank in front of the lens at a distance 0.9 m from the lens along its axis. Find the position (relative to lens) of the image of the object formed by the system.**

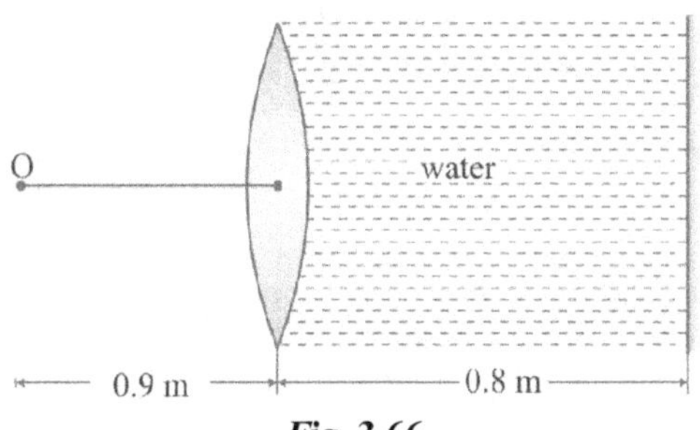

Fig. 3.66

Sol. We know that $\qquad \dfrac{1}{f} = (\mu - 1)\left(\dfrac{1}{R_1} - \dfrac{1}{R_2}\right)$

or
$$\frac{1}{0.3} = \left(\frac{3}{2} - 1\right)\left(\frac{1}{+R} - \frac{1}{-R}\right)$$

or
$$R = 0.3 \text{ m.}$$

Consider refraction through left glass surface

$$\frac{\mu_2}{v} - \frac{\mu_1}{u} = \frac{\mu_2 - \mu_1}{R_1}$$

or
$$\frac{3/2}{v} - \frac{1}{-0.9} = \frac{3/2 - 1}{+0.3}$$

or
$$v = 2.7 \text{ m}$$

The image formed becomes object for second curvature of the lens

Now using
$$\frac{\mu_2}{v} - \frac{\mu_1}{u} = \frac{\mu_2 - \mu_1}{R_2}$$

or
$$\frac{4/3}{v} - \frac{3/2}{2.7} = \frac{4/3 - 3/2}{-0.3}$$

or
$$v = 1.2 \text{ m.}$$

The image formed by the lens is 1.2 m away from the lens or $(1.2 - 0.8)$ = 0.4 m behind the mirror. Mirror will form the final image 0.4 m in front of it. This image on being real; the rays now incident on lens again, and so it becomes object for lens.

$$\therefore \qquad \frac{\left(\dfrac{3}{2}\right)}{v} - \frac{\dfrac{4}{3}}{-0.4} = \frac{\dfrac{3}{2} - \dfrac{4}{3}}{+0.3}$$

which gives
$$v = -\frac{2.7}{5} \text{ m.}$$

Now refraction by glass air interface

$$\frac{1}{v} - \frac{\dfrac{3}{2}}{\left(\dfrac{-2.7}{5}\right)} = \frac{1 - \dfrac{3}{2}}{-0.3}$$

which gives $\qquad v = -0.9 \text{ m.}$

Thus the final image is formed on the object itself

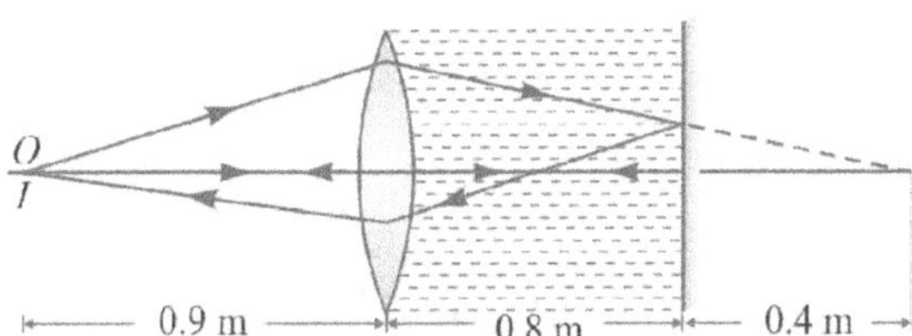

Fig. 3.67

Ex. 33
A strong source of light when used with a convex lens produces a number of images of the source owing to feeble internal reflections and refraction called flare spots as shown in *fig. 3.68*. These extra images are F_1, F_2, ------. If F_n is the position of nth flare spot, then show that

$$\frac{1}{f_n} = \frac{(n+1)\mu - 1}{f(\mu - 1)}.$$

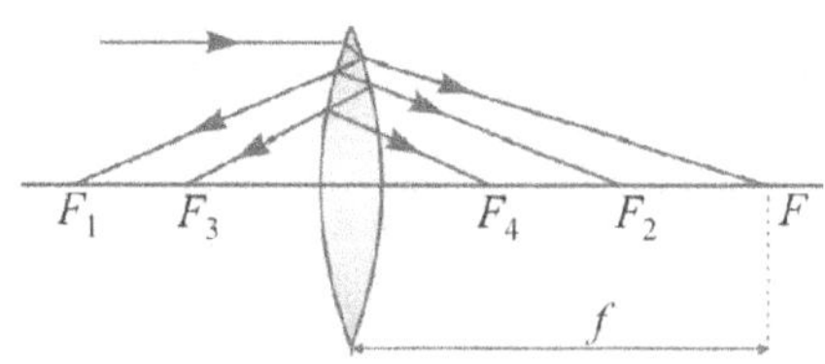

Fig. 3.68

Sol. Light converges at F_1 after two refractions and one reflection from the lens. Therefore

$$\frac{1}{F_1} = \frac{2}{f_e} + \frac{1}{f_m},$$

where

$$\frac{1}{f_e} = (\mu-1)\left(\frac{1}{R_1} - \frac{1}{R_2}\right)$$

or

$$\frac{1}{f} = (\mu-1)\left(\frac{1}{+R} - \frac{1}{-R}\right)$$

$$= (\mu-1)\frac{2}{R} \Rightarrow R = 2(\mu-1)f$$

$$\therefore \quad \frac{1}{F_1} = \frac{2}{f} + \frac{2}{2(\mu-1)f}$$

$$= \frac{2\mu-1}{(\mu-)f}.$$

For F_2, there are three refractions and two reflections

$$\therefore \quad \frac{1}{F_2} = \frac{3}{f_l} + \frac{2}{f_m}$$

$$= \frac{3}{f} + \frac{2}{R/2} = \frac{3}{f} + \frac{4}{R}$$

$$= \frac{3}{f} + \frac{4}{2(\mu-1)f}$$

$$= \frac{3}{f} + \frac{2}{(\mu-1)f}$$

$$= \frac{3(\mu-1)+2}{(\mu-1)f} = \frac{3\mu-1}{(\mu-1)f}$$

$$\therefore \quad \frac{1}{F_n} = \frac{(n+1)\mu-1}{(\mu-1)f}.$$

Ex. 34 A converging beam of rays passes through a round aperture in a screen as shown in *fig.* 3.69. The apex of the beam A is at a distance of 15 cm from the screen. How will the distance from the focus of the rays to the screen change if a convergent lens is inserted in the aperture with a focal length of 30 cm ? Plot the path of the rays after the lens is fitted.

Sol.

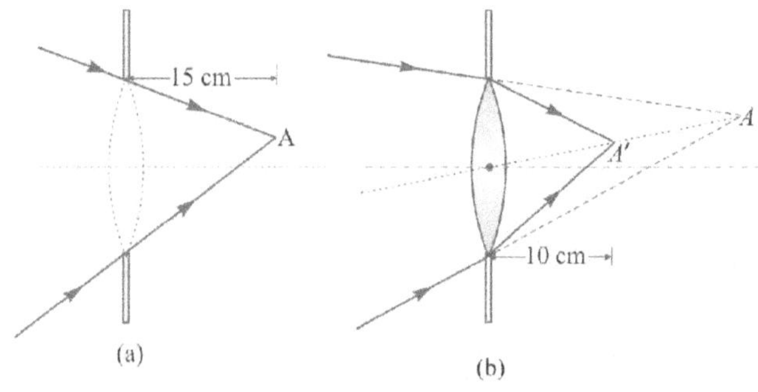

(a)   (b)

Fig. 3.69

By using lens formula $\dfrac{1}{v} - \dfrac{1}{u} = \dfrac{1}{f}$,

where $u = +15$ cm, $f = +30$ cm

we have

$$\frac{1}{v} - \frac{1}{+15} = \frac{1}{+30}$$

which gives $v = +10$ cm

The plot of rays is shown in *fig* **3.69.**

Ex. 35 A thin converging lens of focal length f = 1.5 m is placed along y-axis such that its optical centre coincides with the origin. A small light source S is placed at (–2.0 m, 0.1 m). Where should a plane mirror inclined at an angle θ, tan θ = 0.3 be placed such that y-coordinates of final image is 0.3 m. Also find x co-ordinate of final image.

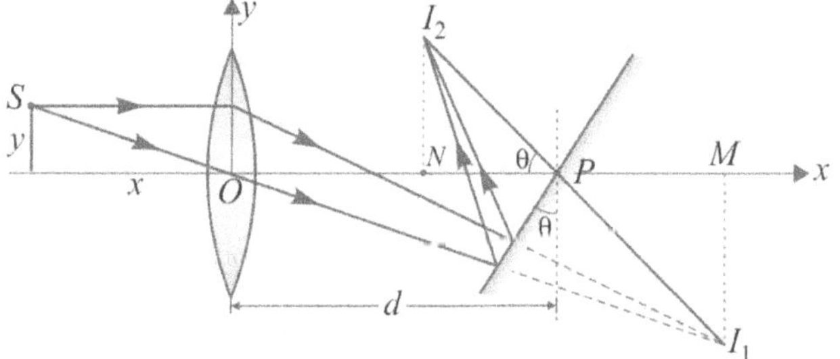

Fig. 3.70

Sol. For lens

$$u = -2.0 \text{ m}$$
$$f = +1.5 \text{ m}$$

By using lens formula, $\dfrac{1}{v} - \dfrac{1}{u} = \dfrac{1}{f}$, we have

$$\frac{1}{v} - \frac{1}{-2.0} = \frac{1}{+1.5}$$

or $v = 6.0$ m

Let (x_1, y_1) be the coordinates of image formed by lens, then

$$x_1 = +6.0 \text{ m, and}$$

$$\frac{y_1}{y} = \frac{v}{u}$$

or

$$y_1 = \frac{6.0}{-2.0} \times 0.1$$

$$= -0.3 \text{ m} = MI_1$$

This image I_1, becomes object for mirror, then mirror forms the image at I_2 at $y = +0.3$ m.

From figure $PI_1 = PI_2$ and I_1PI_2 will be perpendicular to mirror. Now in $\Delta I_2 PN$, we have

$$\frac{I_2N}{NP} = \tan\theta$$

$$\Rightarrow \qquad NP = \frac{I_2N}{\tan\theta} = \frac{0.3}{0.3} = 1\text{ m}$$

Also $\qquad PM = 1\text{ m}$

$\therefore \qquad d = 5\text{ m} \qquad\qquad Ans$

The co-ordinates of image are $(ON, NI_2) = (4\text{m}, 0.3\text{ m})$.

Ex. 36 An object of height 4 cm is kept to the left of and on the axis of a converging lens of focal length 10 cm as shown in *fig.* 3.71. A plane mirror is placed inclined at 45° to the lens axis 10 cm to the right of the lens. Find the position and size of the image formed by the lens and mirror combination. Trace the path of rays forming the image.

Sol.

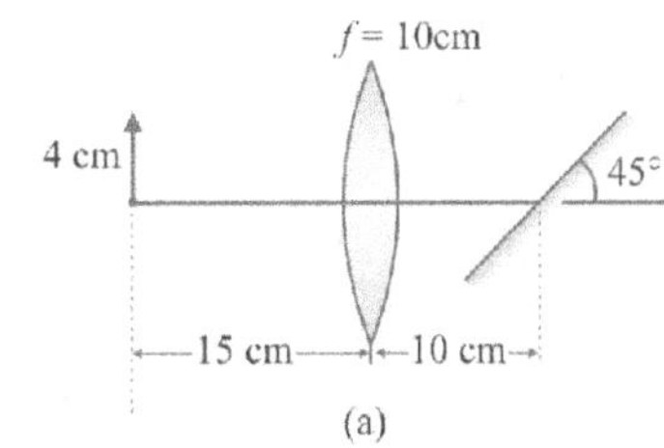

(a)

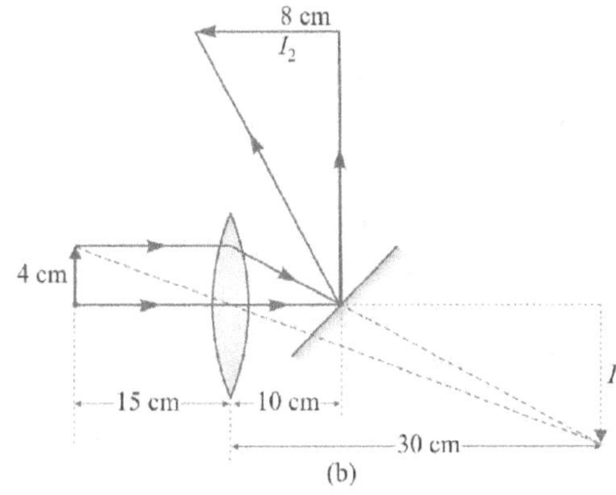

(b)

Fig. 3.71

For lens; $\qquad u = -15\text{ cm}, f = +10\text{ cm}$

Using lens formula, $\dfrac{1}{v} - \dfrac{1}{u} = \dfrac{1}{f}$

or $\qquad \dfrac{1}{v} - \dfrac{1}{-15} = \dfrac{1}{+10}$

which gives $\qquad v = +30\text{ cm}$

The magnification $\qquad \dfrac{I}{O} = \dfrac{v}{u}$

or $\qquad I = \dfrac{v}{u}O$

$\qquad\qquad = \dfrac{30}{-15} \times 4 = -8\text{ cm} = I_1$

This image becomes object for mirror. Mirror forms its image as I_2 as shown in figure. The image is at a distance of 20 cm from its pole.

Ex. 37 In the given *fig.* 3.72 there are two thin lenses of same focal length f arranged with their principal axes inclined at an

angle α. The separation between the optical centres of the lenses is $2f$. A point object lies on the principal axis of the convex lens at a large distance to the left of convex lens.

(a) Find the co-ordinates of the final image formed by the system of lenses taking O as the origin of co-ordinate axes, and

(b) draw the ray diagram.

Sol.

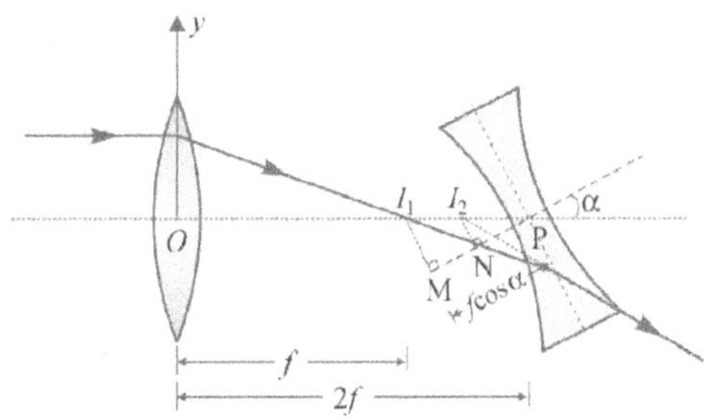

Fig. 3.72

For convex lens, $\qquad u = \infty,\ f = +f$

Using lens formula, $\qquad \dfrac{1}{v} - \dfrac{1}{u} = \dfrac{1}{f}$

$$\dfrac{1}{v} - \dfrac{1}{\infty} = \dfrac{1}{f}$$

$\Rightarrow \qquad v = f$

Now for concave lens, the distance of object which is equal to the image formed by convex lens from optical centre of concave lens

$$u = -f\cos\alpha$$
$$f = -f$$

Now by lens formula

$$\frac{1}{v} - \frac{1}{-f\cos\alpha} = \frac{1}{f}$$

$\therefore \qquad v = -\left(\dfrac{f\cos\alpha}{1+\cos\alpha}\right)$

Magnification $\qquad m = \dfrac{v}{u}$

$$= \frac{1}{(1+\cos\alpha)}$$

Length of $I_2N = \left(\dfrac{1}{1+\cos\alpha}\right) \times I_1M$

where $\qquad I_1M = f\sin\alpha$

$\therefore \qquad I_2N = \left(\dfrac{f\sin\alpha}{1+\cos\alpha}\right)$

x-coordinate $= 2f - (PN/\cos\alpha)$

$$= 2f - \left(\frac{f\cos\alpha}{1+\cos\alpha}\right)\Big/\cos\alpha$$

$$= 2f - \frac{f}{1+\cos\alpha}$$

$$= \frac{f(2+2\cos\alpha - 1)}{1+\cos\alpha}$$

$$= f\left(\frac{2\cos\alpha + 1}{1+\cos\alpha}\right)$$

Therefore co-ordinates of final image are

$$= \left[f\left(\frac{2\cos\alpha + 1}{1+\cos\alpha}\right), 0\right] \qquad Ans.$$

3.13 DEFECTS OF IMAGES : ABERRATION

The equations and relations derived in previous chapter hold for paraxial light rays or for the rays making small angles with the optic axis. In practice, however lenses are used to form images of points which are off the axis. Also, if light coming from an object is not monochromatic, a number of overlapped coloured images are formed by the lens. Thus in actual practice the image of a point and white object is not sharp and white. This defect of lens is called **aberration**. The coloured image formed by lens of a white object is called **chromatic aberration**. The other aberration in which lens is unable to form actual size of the image even using monochrotic light, is called **monochromatic aberration.**

Chromatic aberration

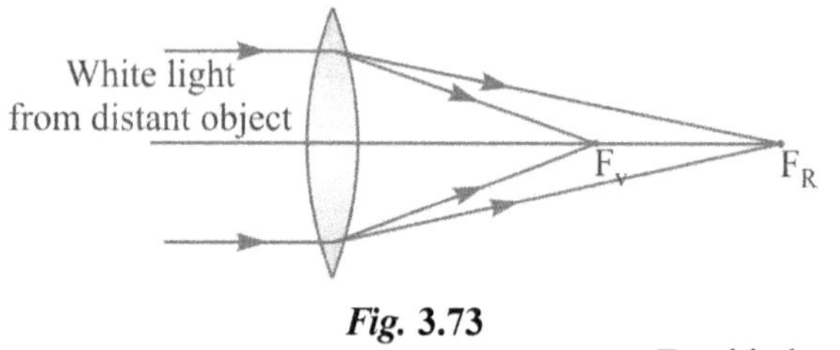

The refractive index of the material of a lens is different for different colours (wavelengths) of light. Hence the focal length of a lens is different for different colours. It is longest for red and shortest for violet colour. Thus light coming from the object will split when emerges from the lens. The distance between focal point of red colour and violet colour is called **axial or longitudinal chromatic aberration.** Thus if f_R and f_V are the focal lengths for extreme colours, then axial chromatic aberration is given by

$$\delta f = f_r - f_v.$$

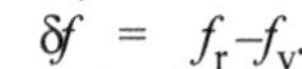

Fig. 3.73

For thin lens, the expression for chromatic aberration can easily be derived. The focal length of a thin lens is given by

$$\frac{1}{f} = (\mu - 1)\left(\frac{1}{R_1} - \frac{1}{R_2}\right). \qquad ...(i)$$

If a small change in μ say $\delta\mu$ results in a small change in f say δf then by differentiating equation (i), we have

$$\frac{-\delta f}{f^2} = \delta\mu\left(\frac{1}{R_1} - \frac{1}{R_2}\right). \qquad ...(ii)$$

Dividing equation (ii) by (i), we get

$$df = \left(\frac{-\delta\mu}{\mu - 1}\right)f, \qquad ...(1)$$

which represents the axial chromatic aberration of a lens. If μ_v and μ_r represent the refractive indexes for the violet and red colours respectively, then we can write

$$f_r - f_v = \left(\frac{\mu_v - \mu_r}{\mu_y - 1}\right)f_y.$$

As $\left(\dfrac{\mu_v - \mu_r}{\mu_y - 1}\right)$ is the dispersive power ω of the lens material, and so

$$f_r - f_v = \omega f_y. \qquad ...(2)$$

Achromatism : The achromatic doublet

The minimisation or removal of chromatic aberration is called achromatism. This can be possible by using two lenses of opposite nature. The system of two lenses which is free from chromatic aberration is called **achromatic doublet**.

Consider two lenses of focal lengths f_1 and f_2 and dispersive powers ω_1 and ω_2 are put in contact. If f is the focal length of the combination, then

$$\frac{1}{f_1} + \frac{1}{f_2} = \frac{1}{f} \qquad ...(i)$$

Differentiating equation (i) partially, we have

$$\frac{-\delta f_1}{f_1^2} - \frac{\delta f_2}{f_2^2} = \frac{-\delta f}{f^2}$$

For achromatism, $\delta f = 0$,

$$\therefore \qquad \frac{-\delta f_1}{f_1^2} - \frac{\delta f_2}{f_2^2} = 0$$

Also from (2), $\qquad \dfrac{\delta f_1}{f_1} = \omega_1 \quad$ and $\quad \dfrac{\delta f_2}{f_2} = \omega_2,$

$$\therefore \qquad \frac{\omega_1}{f_1} + \frac{\omega_2}{f_2} = 0 \qquad \qquad ...(3)$$

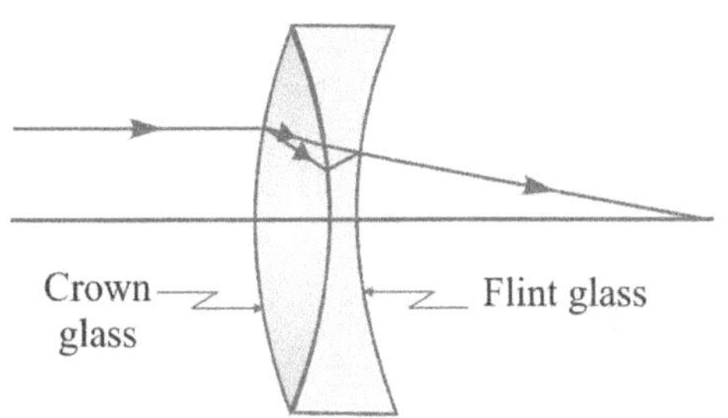

Fig. **3.74.** Achromatic doublet.

This is the required condition of achromatism.
The equation (3) can be written as :

$$\frac{f_1}{f_2} = -\frac{\omega_1}{\omega_2}. \qquad \qquad ...(4)$$

Here negative sign shows that either of f_1 or f_2 must be negative, because dispersive power is always a positive quantity. Thus if one of the lenses is converging, then other must be diverging. For converging doublet, the converging lens is made of crown glass and diverging lens is made of flint glass.

Achromatism by separated doublet

Consider two convex lenses of focal lengths f_1 and f_2, separated by a suitable distance d. The focal length of the combination is given by

$$\frac{1}{f_1} + \frac{1}{f_2} - \frac{d}{f_1 f_2} = \frac{1}{f}. \qquad \qquad ...(i)$$

Differentiating above equation, we get

$$\frac{-\delta f_1}{f_1^2} - \frac{\delta f_2}{f_2^2} - d\left[\left(\frac{-\delta f_1}{f_1^2}\right)\frac{1}{f_2} + \left(\frac{-\delta f_2}{f_2^2}\right)\frac{1}{f_1}\right] = \frac{-\delta f}{f^2}$$

For achromatism, $\delta f = 0$

$$\therefore \left(\frac{\delta f_1}{f_1}\right)\frac{1}{f_1} + \left(\frac{\delta f_2}{f_2}\right)\frac{1}{f_2} - d\left[\frac{1}{f_1 f_2}\left(\frac{\delta f_2}{f_2}\right) + \frac{1}{f_1 f_2}\left(\frac{\delta f_1}{f_1}\right)\right] = 0$$

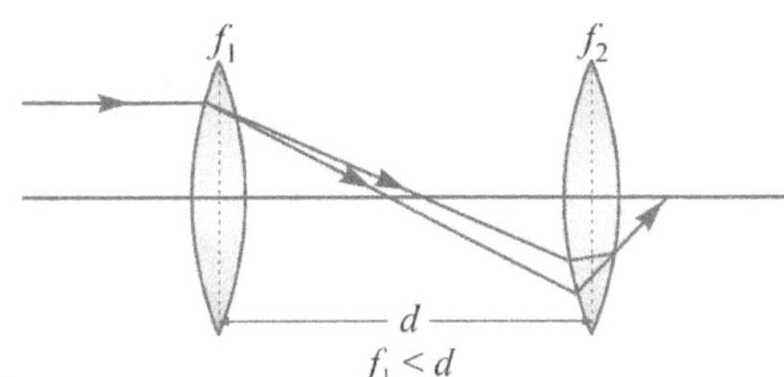

Fig. **3.75** Achromatic doublet with separated lenses.

Putting $\dfrac{\delta f_1}{f_1} = \omega_1$ and $\dfrac{\delta f_2}{f_2} = \omega_2$, and simplifying, we get

$$d = \frac{\omega_1 f_2 + \omega_2 f_1}{\omega_1 + \omega_2}. \qquad \qquad ...(5)$$

In case, when lenses are of same material

$$\omega_1 = \omega_2 = \omega$$

and so $\qquad\qquad d = \dfrac{f_1 + f_2}{2}. \qquad \qquad ...(6)$

Thus two lenses of same nature can be free from chromatic aberration if they are placed

at a separation $\dfrac{f_1 + f_2}{2}$. Such a combination is shown in figure.

Monochromatic aberration

The size of the image as formed by a lens is not according to theoretical calculation, even using monochromatic light. The image formed will spread both along and perpendicular to principal axis of the lens. Also the shape of the image is not according to the shape of the object. Monochromatic aberration can be divided into following heads.

(i) Spherical aberration

Fig. **3.76** shows the image formed by different parts of a lens of a point object. The paraxial rays of light form the image at a longer distance from the lens than the marginal rays. The image is not sharp at any point on the axis. The image will spread perpendicular to the principal axis. This effect is called **spherical aberration.** If the screen is placed perpendicular to the principal axis at AB, the image appears to be a circular patch of diameter AB. This patch AB is called **circle of least confusion**. Spherical aberration can be minimised by using **stops** or by using crossed lens.

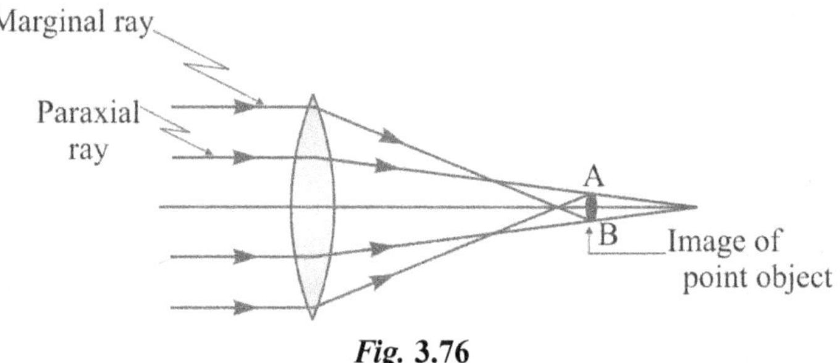

Fig. **3.76**

(ii) Coma

When object is situated off the axis, its image will spread obliquely perpendicular to the principal axis. It looks like a comet and so called **coma.**

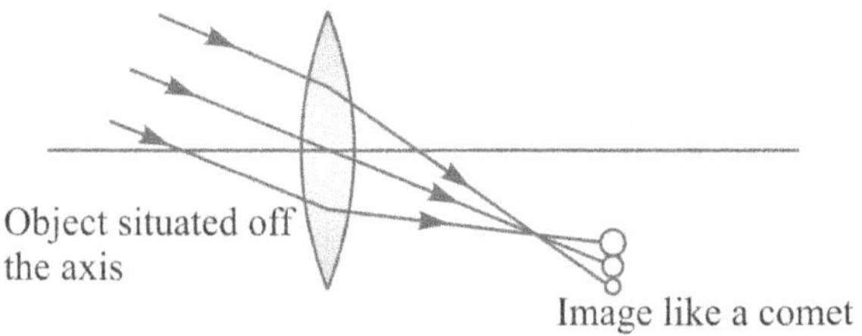

Fig. **3.77**

(iii) Astigmatism

The spread of image along the principal axis of the lens is known as **astigmatism.** The object situated off the axis, its image will spread along and perpendicular to the principal axis (see figure).

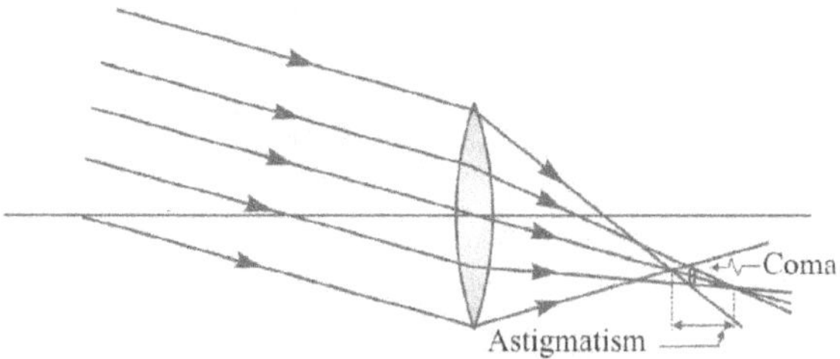

Fig. **3.78**

(iv) Curvature

The image of an extended plane object formed by lens is not a flat but curved. This defect is called the **curvature**. This defect is due to the fact that the paraxial focal length is greater than marginal focal length. This defect is present even if the aperture of the lens is reduced by a suitable stop.

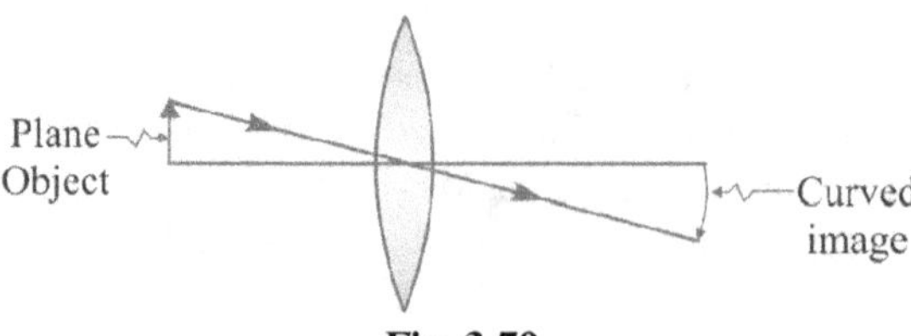

Fig. **3.79**

(v) Distortion

The variation in the magnification produced by a lens for different axial distances results in the aberration called **distortion.**

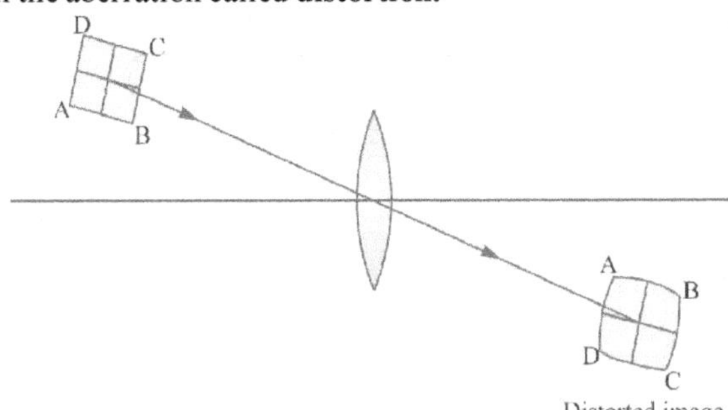

Fig. **3.80**

Ex. 38
A convex lens made of material 'A' is combined with a concave lens made of material 'B' so as to form an achromatic doublet. If an object of height 6 cm is placed 30 cm in front of the doublet, it forms an erect image of size 2 cm. Find the focal lengths of the component lenses, given that the ratio of dispersive powers of materials A and B is 2 : 1.

Sol. The erect and small size of the image shows that doublet should be of diverging nature. For erect image

$$\frac{v}{u} = \frac{I}{O} = \frac{2}{6}$$

or
$$v = u/3$$

Given
$$u = -30 \text{ cm}$$

$$\therefore \quad v = \frac{-30}{3} = -10 \text{ cm}$$

By lens formula, $\dfrac{1}{v} - \dfrac{1}{u} = \dfrac{1}{f}$, we have

$$\frac{1}{-10} - \frac{1}{-30} = \frac{1}{f}$$

or
$$f = -15 \text{ cm}$$

Here f is the focal length of the achromatic doublet. If f_A and f_B are the focal lengths of the lenses, then

$$\frac{1}{f_A} + \frac{1}{f_B} = \frac{1}{-15} \qquad \text{...(i)}$$

Also
$$\frac{f_A}{f_B} = -\frac{\omega_A}{\omega_B}$$

$$= -2 \qquad \text{...(ii)}$$

Solving equation (i) and (ii), we get
$$f_A = 15 \text{ cm}$$

and
$$f_B = -7.5 \text{ cm.} \qquad \textbf{Ans.}$$

3.14 The Human Eye

Eye is the most precious optical instrument given by the nature to human being. It mainly consist of a lens and a retina behind it, which acts as a screen where image is formed.

The retina contains light sensitive cells, rods and cones. These send messages along the optic nerve to the brain. The brain sorts out the messages, so that we see a picture of the image formed on our retina. The image on the retina is inverted. The brain automatically interprets the erect image.

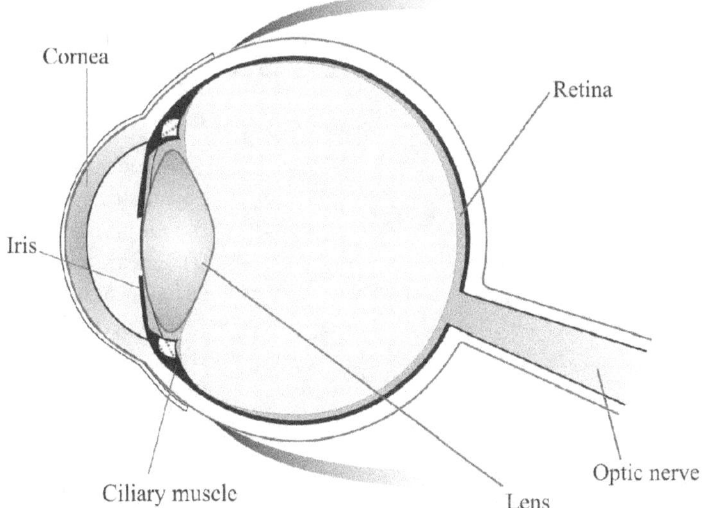

Fig. **3.81**

Accommodation of eye

The normal human eye can see the objects situated at any distance from infinity upto about 25 cm in front of the eye. This is made possible by changing the focal length of the eye lens. When relaxed, the normal eye is focused on objects at infinity. When it is desired to view an object nearer than infinity, the ciliary muscle tenses and the eye lens becomes nearly spherical and will get shorter focal length. The ability of eye to change focal length of its lens is called **power of accommodation**. The extremes of the range over which the clear vision is possible are known as the far point and the near point of the eye. The far point of a normal eye is at infinity. The position of near point changes with age; on average it is 25 cm.

Age	Near point (cm)
10	7
20	10
30	14
40	22
50	40
60	200

Note:

1. The retina is nearly 2.5 cm behind the eye lens, and so maximum focal length of the eye lens that can be 2.5 cm for relaxed eye.
2. The minimum focal length corresponds to, when object is at near point. Thus :
$$u = -25 \text{ cm}, v = +2.5 \text{ cm}$$
$$\therefore \quad \frac{1}{f} = \frac{1}{v} - \frac{1}{u} = \frac{1}{2.5} - \frac{1}{-25}; \text{ or } f \simeq 2.2 \text{ cm}$$

Why an optical instrument needed ?

The size of the object as viewed by the eye depends upon the angle subtended by the object at the eye. This angle is known as **visual angle**.

As the object is brought closer to eye, the image on retina becomes larger and larger on account of increase in visual angle. However, the object cannot be brought nearer to the eye beyond the certain minimum distance.

This minimum distance upto which eye can see the image of an object clearly is called **least distance of distinct** vision. It is 25 cm and represented by D. From the above discussion, it is clear that the visual angle can not be increased beyond a certain limit. It can be increased with the help of an optical instrument by making image of an object closer to eye.

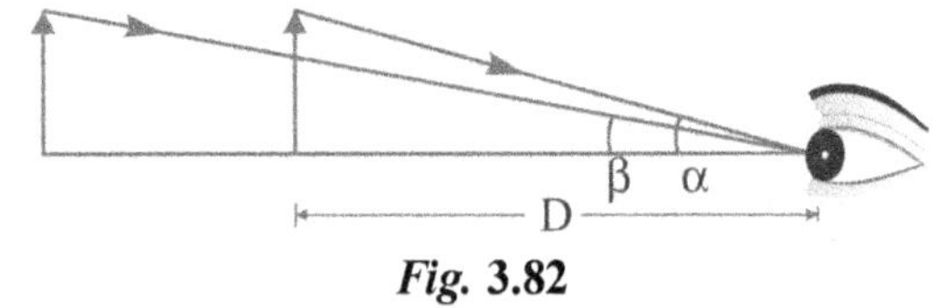

Fig. 3.82

3.15 DEFECTS OF VISION

1. Myopia or nearsightedness

A person suffering from this defect can see near object clearly but can not see far object clearly. The rays from the far object are focussed in front of retina. Thus the far point of myopic eye becomes less than infinity. For myopic eye :

(i) Near point distance is 25 cm.

(ii) Far point distance is less than infinity; may be few metres.

(iii) A diverging lens is required to make up this defect.

If x is the far point distance of myopic eye and f be the focal length of the lens required, then by lens formula,

$$\frac{1}{v} - \frac{1}{u} = \frac{1}{f}, \text{ we have}$$

$$\frac{1}{-x} - \frac{1}{-\infty} = \frac{1}{f}$$

or $$f = -x$$

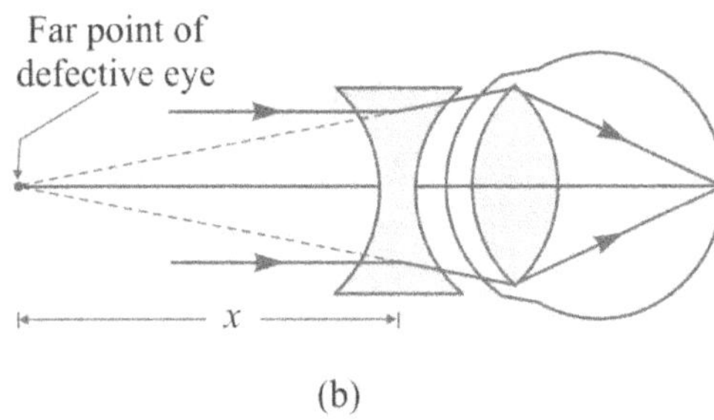

(a) Myopic eye.

(b)

Fig. 3.83

2. Hypermetropia or farsightedness

A person suffering from this defect can see far object clearly but can not see near object clearly. The image of near object will be formed behind

the retina. Thus the eye suffering from this defect :
(i)   The near point distance is greater than 25 cm.
(ii) The far point distance remains as such, i.e., infinite.
(iii) The lens required to make up this is of converging nature.
If y is the near point of defective eye and f be the focal length of the lens required, then by lens formula.

$$\frac{1}{v}-\frac{1}{u} = \frac{1}{f}, \text{ we have}$$

$$\frac{1}{-y}-\frac{1}{-25} = \frac{1}{f}$$

or $$f = \frac{25\,y}{y-25}.$$

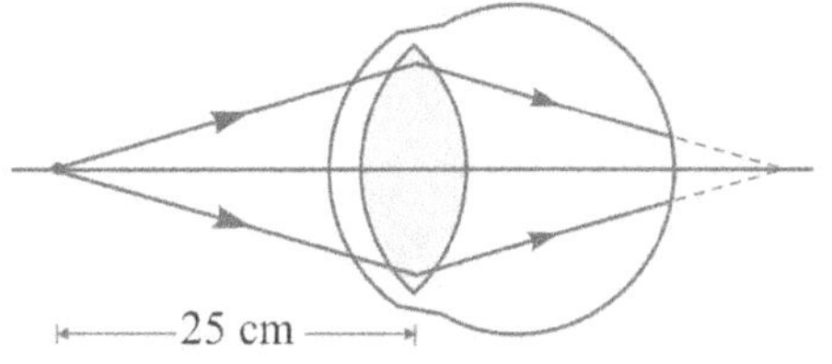
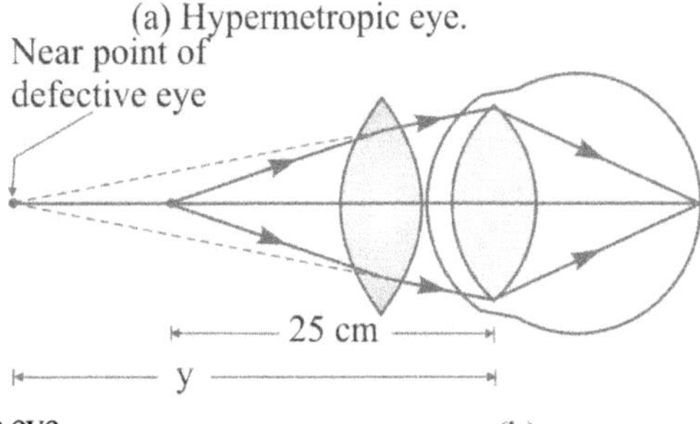

Fig. **3.84**

3.   Presbyopia

In old age the muscles become weak and so unable to change the focal length of the eye lens. The person therefore unable to see neither near object nor far object clearly. The remedy of this is either using two separate spectacles, one for myopia and other for hypermetropia or using single spectacle having bifocal lens. The upper part of bifocal lens should be concave while the lower part, a convex lens.

4.   Astigmatism

This kind of defect arises in the eye when the eye lens has different curvatures along different planes. Person suffering from this defect can not see all the directions equally well. This defect can be removed by using **cylindrical lens**.

3.16   SIMPLE MICROSCOPE OR MAGNIFIER

It consists of a converging lens of short focal length (2–5 cm). It can give a maximum magnification of 20 times. The object to be seen through a simple microscope is kept just inside the focal point of the lens. When viewed from the other side of the lens, a virtual, erect and enlarged image of the object is seen. Angular magnification M of a simple microscope is defined as :

$$M = \frac{\text{angle subtended by the image }(\beta)}{\left[\begin{array}{l}\text{angle subtended by the object when}\\ \text{placed at near point }(\alpha)\end{array}\right]}.$$

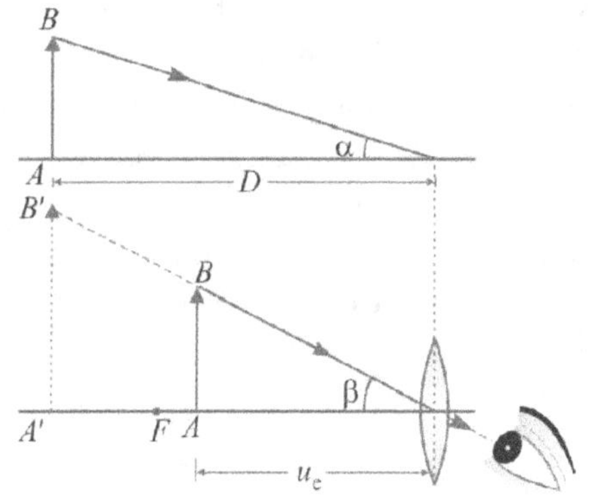

Fig. **3.85**

Consider an object AB placed at a distance u_e from the eyelens of focal length f_e ($u_e < f_e$). $A'B'$ is the virtual image of the object. If image is formed at the near point of the eye, then

$$M = \frac{\beta}{\alpha}$$

$$\simeq \frac{AB/u_e}{AB/D}$$

$$= \frac{D}{u_e}.$$

There are two possible cases :

(i)   When image is formed at infinity

For this, $v = \infty$, $u_e = f_e$. Thus

$$M = \frac{D}{f_e}.$$

In this situation, the eye is said to be normal, relaxed or unstrained.

(ii) When final image is formed at near point

For this,
$$v = -D, u = -u_e.$$

By lens formula, $\dfrac{1}{v} - \dfrac{1}{u} = \dfrac{1}{f}$, we have

$$\frac{1}{-D} - \frac{1}{-u_e} = \frac{1}{f_e}$$

or
$$\frac{1}{u_e} = \frac{1}{D}\left(1 + \frac{D}{f_e}\right)$$

$$\therefore \quad M = 1 + \frac{D}{f_e}.$$

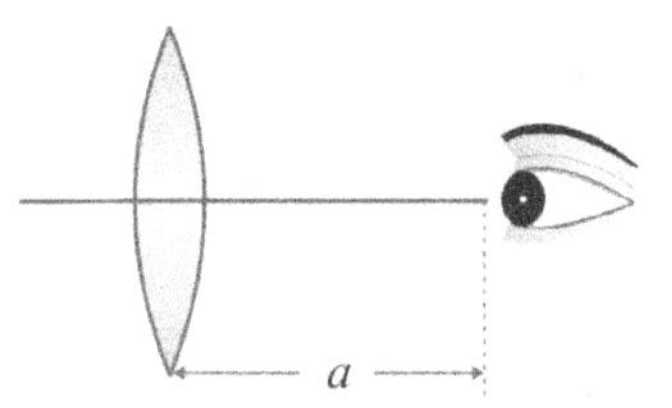

Fig. 3.86

Note :

1. In deriving these formulas, we have placed the lens very close to eye. If a is the separation between eye and the lens, then $v_e = -(D - a)$, then

$$M = 1 + \frac{D - a}{f_e}.$$

2. In the formula of M, put the value of $D = 25$ cm, without giving any sign.

Ex. 39 The angular magnification of a simple microscope is 10. Does the height of the image is ten times the height of the object ?

Sol. No. The angular size of the image is ten times the angular size of the object. For the image at its near point, the height will be nearly ten times the height of the object.

Ex. 40 A person wears glasses of power – 2.5D. Is the person farsighted or nearsighted ? What is the far point of the person without the glass?

Sol. Nearsighted. The focal length of the lens

$$f = -\frac{100}{2.5} \text{ cm} = -40 \text{ cm}.$$

Thus far point of the person is at 40 cm. **Ans.**

Ex. 41 A professor reads a greeting card received on his 50th birthday with + 2.5 D glasses keeping the card 25 cm away. Ten years later, he reads his farewell letter with the same glasses but he has to keep the letter 50 cm away. What power of lens should he now use?

Sol.

The image of the letters 25 cm away, now form at 50 cm away. Thus
$$u = -25 \text{ cm}, v = -50 \text{ cm}$$

By lens formula, $\dfrac{1}{v} - \dfrac{1}{u} = \dfrac{1}{f}$, we have

$$\frac{1}{-50} - \frac{1}{-25} = \frac{1}{f}$$

$$\therefore \quad f = 50 \text{ cm} = 0.5 \text{ m}$$

The additional power of the lens

$$P = \frac{1}{0.5} = 2D.$$

The total power of the lens required
$$= 2.5 + 2$$
$$= 4.5\, D \qquad \textit{Ans.}$$

Ex. 42 A man is looking at a small object placed at his near point. Without altering the position of his eye or the object, he put a simple microscope of magnifying power 8 X before his eye. Find the angular magnification achieved.

Sol.

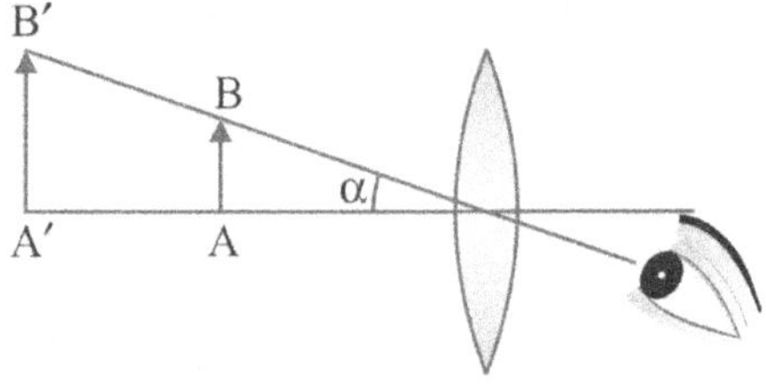

Fig. 3.87

Without changing the position of the object,
$$\beta = \alpha, \quad (\text{see } fig\ 3.87)$$
and so
$$M = 1. \qquad \textit{Ans.}$$

Ex. 43 A simple microscope is rated 5 X for a normal relaxed eye. What will be its magnifying power for a relaxed farsighted eye whose near point is 40 cm ?

Sol.

If f_e is the focal length of the lens of microscope, then

$$M = \frac{D}{f_e}$$

or

$$5 = \frac{25}{f_e}$$

$$\therefore \quad f_e = 5 \text{ cm}.$$

For farsighted person whose near point $D' = 40$ cm,

$$M' = \frac{D'}{f_e} = \frac{40}{5} = 8X \quad \textbf{Ans.}$$

Ex. 44 A person uses + 1.5 D glasses to have normal vision from 25 cm onwards. He uses a 20 D lens as a simple microscope to see an object. Find the maximum magnification power if he uses the microscope (a) together with his glass (b) without the glass.

Sol.

The focal length of the glasses (lens) used

$$f = \frac{100}{1.5} \text{ cm}$$

If y is the distance of near point, then

$$\frac{1}{y} - \frac{1}{-25} = \frac{1.5}{100}$$

or

$$y = -40 \text{ cm}$$

(a) The focal length of the lens of the microscope

$$f_e = \frac{1}{P} = \frac{100}{20} = 5 \text{ cm}$$

The magnifying power of the microscope together with the glass

$$M = 1 + \frac{D}{f_e} = 1 + \frac{25}{5}$$

$$= 6X \quad \textbf{Ans.}$$

(b) Without the glass, $D' = y = 40$ cm

$$\therefore \quad M' = 1 + \frac{D'}{f_e}$$

$$= 1 + \frac{40}{5} = 9X \quad \textbf{Ans.}$$

Ex. 45 The image of the moon is focused by a converging lens of focal-length 50 cm on a plane screen. The image is seen by an unaided eye from a distance of 25 cm. Find the angular magnification achieved due to the converging lens.

Sol.

The ray diagram of the image of moon formed by a lens is shown in **fig. 3.88**.

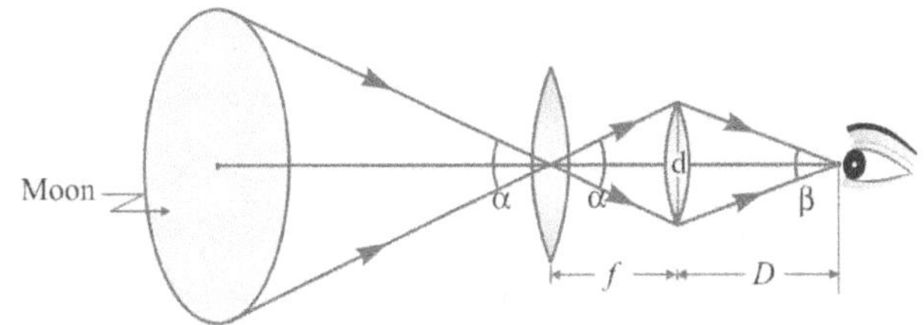

Fig. 3.88

Suppose d is the diameter of the image of the moon. If α and β are the angle made by moon and its image respectively, then

$$\alpha = \frac{d}{f}$$

and

$$\beta = \frac{d}{D}.$$

Angular magnification

$$M = -\frac{\beta}{\alpha}$$

$$= -\left|\frac{f}{D}\right| = -\left|\frac{50}{25}\right| = -2. \quad \textbf{Ans.}$$

3.17   COMPOUND MICROSCOPE

The magnifying power of a simple microscope is given by $M = 1 + \dfrac{D}{f_e}$. Its value can be increased by decreasing the value of focal length f_e of the lens. But due to constructional difficulties, the focal length of a lens can not be decreased beyond a certain limit. Therefore to increase the magnifying power, two lenses are used and so called **compound microscope**. The lens placed near to the object is called objective and the other which is nearer the eye is known as eye piece. Both the lenses are of converging nature. The objective is of small aperture (focal length) and eye piece is of larger aperture. These lenses are fitted in two cylindrical tubes, one can slide over the other.

Consider an object AB is placed at a distance slightly greater than the focal length f_o of the objective. An inverted image A_1B_1 is formed on the other side of the objective. This becomes the object for eye piece, which finally forms the enlarge image A_2B_2.

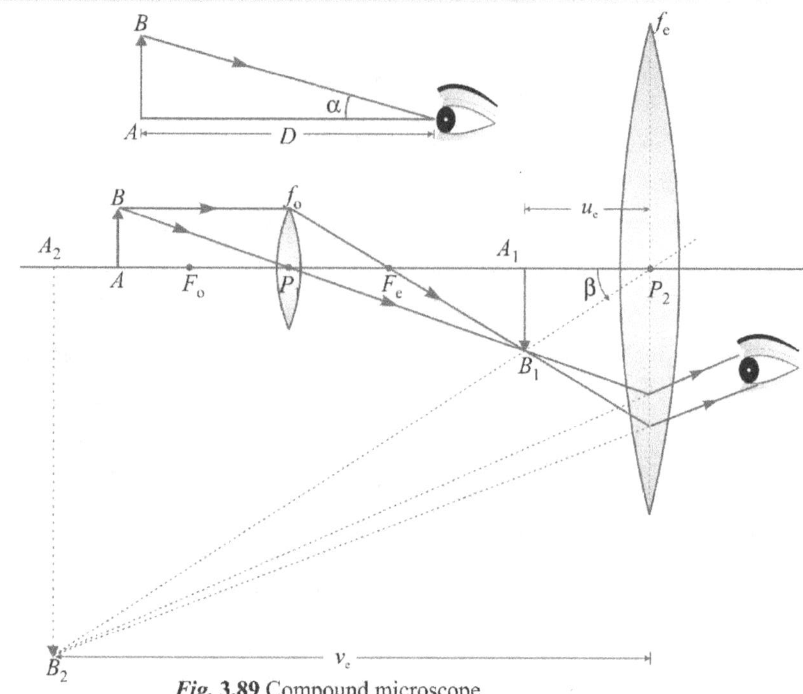

Fig. 3.89 Compound microscope

Angular magnification of the compound microscope is defined as :

$$M = \frac{\text{angle subtended by final image at eye } (\beta)}{\text{angle subtended by object when placed at near point } (\alpha)}$$

From the figure,

$$\frac{\beta}{\alpha} = \frac{-A_1 B_1 /(-u_e)}{(AB)/(-D)} = -\frac{A_1 B_1}{AB} \times \frac{D}{u_e} \quad …\text{(i)}$$

In similar triangles $P_1 AB$ and $P_1 A_1 B_1$, we have

$$\frac{A_1 B_1}{AB} = \frac{v_o}{u_o}$$

For eye lens;
$$u = -u_e$$
$$v = -v_e$$
$$f = +f_e$$

By lens formula, $\dfrac{1}{v} - \dfrac{1}{u} = \dfrac{1}{f},$ we have

$$\frac{1}{-v_e} - \frac{1}{-u_e} = \frac{1}{f_e}$$

$$\therefore \qquad \frac{1}{u_e} = \frac{1}{v_e}\left(1 + \frac{v_e}{f_e}\right) \qquad …\text{(iii)}$$

From equations (i), (ii) and (iii), we get

$$M = -\frac{v_o}{u_o}\frac{D}{v_e}\left(1 + \frac{v_e}{f_e}\right) \qquad …\text{(1)}$$

There are two possible adjustments of the compound microscope. These are :

(i) When final image is formed at near point i.e., $v_e = D$

$$\therefore \qquad M = -\frac{v_o}{u_o}\left(1+\frac{D}{f_e}\right)$$

The length of the microscope is the separation between the lenses.

$$\therefore \qquad L = v_o + |u_e|$$

Magnification of the compound microscope can also be written as:

$$M = M_o \times M_e$$

$$= -\frac{v_o}{u_o}\left(1+\frac{D}{f_e}\right).$$

(ii) When final image is formed at infinity

For this, $\qquad u_e = f_e$

$$\therefore \qquad M = -\frac{v_o}{u_o}\frac{D}{f_e}. \qquad\qquad ...(3)$$

The length of the microscope

$$L = v_o + f_e$$

Magnification in terms of length of the microscope

Usually focal length of the objective is very small, and so $\dfrac{v_o}{f_o} >> 1$. Also first image is close to eye piece and so $v_o \simeq L$.

By lens formula, $\qquad \dfrac{1}{v} - \dfrac{1}{u} = \dfrac{1}{f}$, we have

$$\frac{1}{v_o} - \frac{1}{-u_o} = \frac{1}{f_o}$$

or $\qquad\qquad 1 + \dfrac{v_o}{u_o} = \dfrac{v_o}{f_o}$

or $\qquad\qquad \dfrac{v_o}{u_o} = \dfrac{v_o}{f_o} - 1$

As, $\dfrac{v_o}{f_o} >> 1$ and $\qquad v_o \simeq L$

$$\therefore \qquad \frac{v_o}{u_o} \simeq \frac{L}{f_o}.$$

Thus for final image at near point,

$$M = -\frac{L}{f_o}\left(1+\frac{D}{f_e}\right) \text{ and }$$

For infinity, $\qquad M = -\dfrac{L}{f_o}\cdot\dfrac{D}{f_e}.$

Note:

In using formula of magnification, one should place the value of v_o, u_o, D, f_o and f_e without any sign, because sign has been used while deriving the formula.

3.18 TELESCOPE

Telescope is an optical instrument which is used to see distant objects like, planets, stars etc. There are basically two types of telescopes : refracting telescope and reflecting telescope. In refracting telescope lenses are used and in reflecting telescope a combination of lens and mirror is used. Here we are discussing about three basic refracting types of telescopes. These are :

Astronomical telescope

It consists of two converging lenses; objective lens and eyepiece or eye lens. Objective lens is of large aperture or focal length commonly 50 to 100 cm, while eye piece is of small aperture or focal length commonly 2 to 5 cm. These lenses are fitted in two cylindrical tubes; one can slide over the other according to the required adjustment. Consider a distant object AB. Its real inverted image A_1B_1 is formed at focal point of the objective. This image becomes object for eyepiece, which finally forms virtual image A_2B_2.

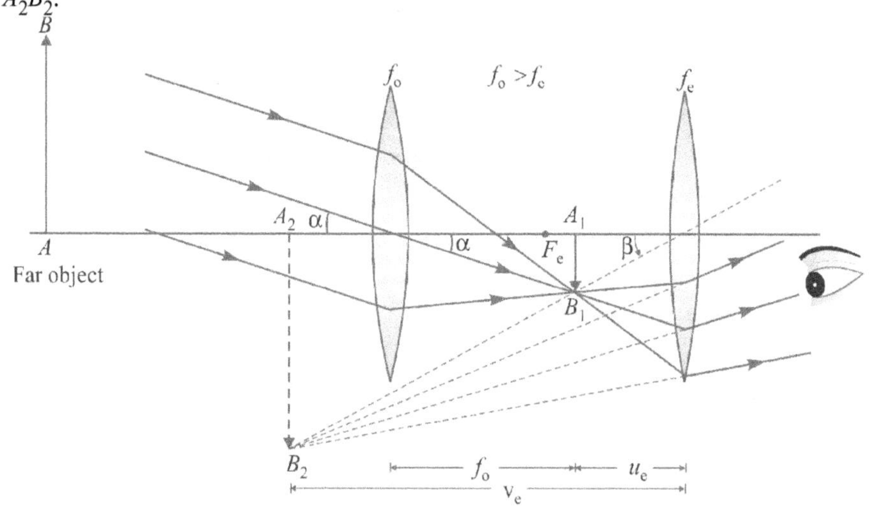

Fig. **3.90** Astronomical telescope.

Angular magnification of telescope is defined as :

$$M = \frac{\text{angle subtended by image } (\beta)}{\text{angle subtended by object at eye } (\alpha)}$$

For distant object, the angle forms by object at objective lens is nearly same as that at eye, and so

$$M = \frac{\beta}{\alpha}$$

From the figure,
$$\frac{\beta}{\alpha} = \frac{-A_1B_1/(-u_e)}{-A_1B_1/f_o} = -\frac{f_o}{u_e}$$

$\therefore$
$$M = -\frac{f_o}{u_e} \qquad \text{...(i)}$$

For eye piece;
$$u = -u_e, \; v = v_e, \; f = +f_e.$$

By lens formula,
$$\frac{1}{v} - \frac{1}{u} = \frac{1}{f}, \text{ we have}$$

$$\frac{1}{-v_e} - \frac{1}{-u_e} = \frac{1}{f_e}$$

or
$$\frac{1}{u_e} = \frac{1}{f_e} + \frac{1}{v_e}$$

$$= \frac{1}{f_e}\left(1+\frac{f_e}{v_e}\right)$$

From equation (i), we have

$$M = -\frac{f_o}{f_e}\left(1+\frac{f_e}{v_e}\right) \qquad ...(1)$$

There are two possible adjustments of the telescope. These are :

(i) When final image is formed at near point

$$v_e = D$$

$$\therefore \qquad M = -\frac{f_o}{f_e}\left(1+\frac{f_e}{D}\right). \qquad ...(2)$$

Length of the telescope is equal to the distance between the lenses and so

$$L = f_o + |u_e|$$

(ii) When final image is formed at infinity

For this, $$u_e = f_e$$

$$\therefore \qquad M = -\frac{f_o}{f_e} \qquad ...(3)$$

The length of the telescope, $L = f_o + f_e$.

Terrestrial telescope

The astronomical telescope forms inverted image and so it is not useful for viewing ground objects like cricket match. To get erect image terrestrial telescope is commonly used. In terrestrial telescope an erecting lens is fitted between objective and eyepiece. By doing so terrestrial telescope will produce erect image. The erecting lens is adjusted in such a way that it produces magnification of $+1$. So magnification formulae derived for astronomical telescope can be used for terrestrial telescope also.

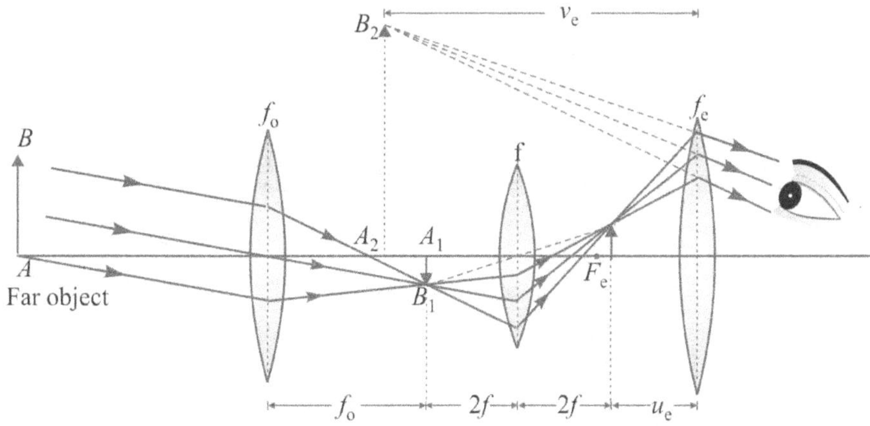

Fig. 3.91

For two adjustments, the angular magnification is given by

(i)   When final image is formed at near point

$$v_e = D, \qquad M = \frac{f_o}{f_e}\left(1+\frac{f_e}{D}\right)$$

and $\qquad L = f_o + 4f + u_e$

(ii) When final image is formed at infinity

$$v_e = \infty, \qquad M = \frac{f_o}{f_e}$$

and $\qquad L = f_o + 4f + f_e.$

Galileo's telescope

This telescope was first designed by Galileo in 1609, which provides an erect image. It consists of two lenses : one converging of large focal length, called objective and other diverging of short focal length, called eyepiece. The image of far object is formed at the focus of the objective, which becomes the virtual object for eyepiece. The eyepiece then forms the erect and enlarged image. Thus the angular magnification of the Galileo telescope is positive.

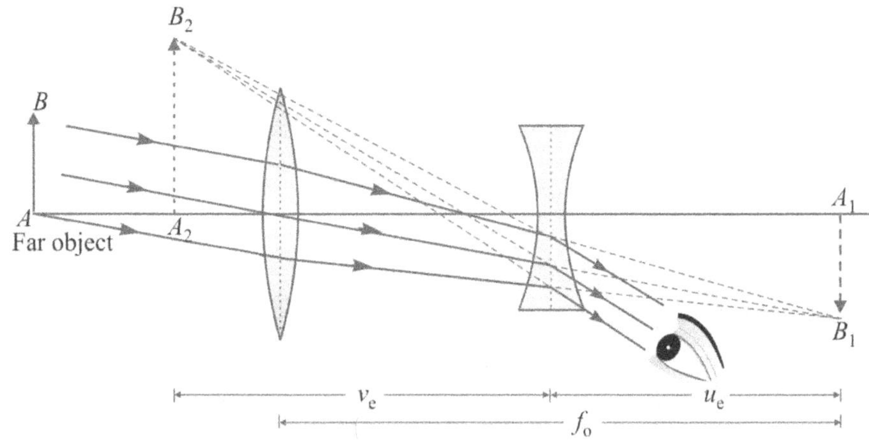

Fig. 3.92

There are two adjustments of the telescope. These are :

(i)   When final image is formed at near point

$$v_e = D.$$

$$M = \frac{f_o}{f_e}\left(1+\frac{f_e}{D}\right)$$

and $\qquad L = f_o - |u_e|.$

(ii) When final image is formed at infinity

$$v_e = \infty$$

$$M = \frac{f_o}{f_e}$$

and $\qquad L = f_o - f_e.$

Note:

In using formulas of magnification M and L one should put the value of f_o, f_e, D and u_e without any sign.

Ex. 46 The focal lengths of the objective and the eyepiece of a microscope are 2 cm and 5 cm respectively and the distance between them is 20 cm. Find the distance of the object from the objective when the final image seen by the eye is 25 cm from the eye-piece. Also find the magnifying power.

Sol. For eye piece; $f_e = 5$ cm, $v_e = -25$ cm.

By lens formula, $\dfrac{1}{v} - \dfrac{1}{u} = \dfrac{1}{f}$, we have

$$\frac{1}{-25} - \frac{1}{u_e} = \frac{1}{5}$$

$$\therefore \quad u_e = -\frac{25}{6} \text{ cm}.$$

Given the length of the microscope

$$v_o + |u_e| = 20$$

$$\therefore \quad v_o = 20 - |u_e|$$

$$= 20 - \frac{25}{6} = \frac{95}{6} \text{ cm},$$

Now for objective lens;

$$\frac{1}{v_o} - \frac{1}{u_o} = \frac{1}{f_o}$$

$$\frac{1}{95/6} - \frac{1}{u_o} = \frac{1}{2}$$

$$\therefore \quad u_o = -\frac{190}{83} \text{ cm}.$$

Magnifying power, $\quad M = \dfrac{-v_o}{u_o}\left(1 + \dfrac{D}{f_e}\right)$

$$= -\frac{(95/6)}{(190/86)}\left(1 + \frac{25}{5}\right)$$

$$= -41.5. \qquad \textit{Ans.}$$

Ex. 47 A compound microscope is used to enlarge an object kept at a distance of 0.03 m from its objective which consists of several convex lenses in contact and focal length 0.02 m. If the lens of focal length 0.1 m is removed from the objective, find out the distance by which the eye-piece of the microscope must be moved to refocus the image.

Sol.

Initially, $\quad u_o = -0.03$ m, $f_o = 0.02$ m.

By lens formula, $\dfrac{1}{v} - \dfrac{1}{u} = \dfrac{1}{f}$, we have

$$\frac{1}{v_o} - \frac{1}{-0.03} = \frac{1}{0.02}$$

$$\therefore \quad \frac{1}{v_o} = \frac{1}{0.02} - \frac{1}{0.03}$$

or $\quad v_o = 0.06$ m

When a lens of focal length 0.1 is removed, the focal length f_o' of the remaining is :

$$\frac{1}{0.02} = \frac{1}{0.1} + \frac{1}{f_o'}$$

$$\therefore \quad \frac{1}{f_o'} = \frac{1}{0.02} - \frac{1}{0.1}$$

or $\quad f_o' = \dfrac{0.02 \times 0.1}{0.1 - 0.02} = 0.025$ m

If v_o' now is the image position from the objective, then

$$\frac{1}{v_o'} - \frac{1}{-0.03} = \frac{1}{0.025}$$

$$\therefore \quad \frac{1}{v_o'} = \frac{1}{0.025} - \frac{1}{0.03}$$

or $\quad v_o' = 0.15$ m

Thus displacement of eye $= 0.15 - 0.06$

$$= 0.09 \text{ m}. \qquad \textit{Ans.}$$

Ex. 48 The eye-piece and objective of a microscope, having focal lengths of 0.3 m and 0.4 m, respectively are separated by a distance of 0.2 m. Now the eye-piece and the objective are to be interchanged such that the angular magnification of the instrument remains same. What is the new separation between the lenses ?

Sol.

Suppose the microscope is adjusted for relaxed eye. The magnification is given by

$$M = -\frac{v_o}{u_o}\frac{D}{f_e}.$$

In compound microscope, $u_o \simeq f_o$ and $v_o + f_e = L$ or

$$v_o = L - f_e,$$

$$\therefore \quad M = -\frac{(L - f_e)}{f_o}\frac{D}{f_e}. \qquad ...(i)$$

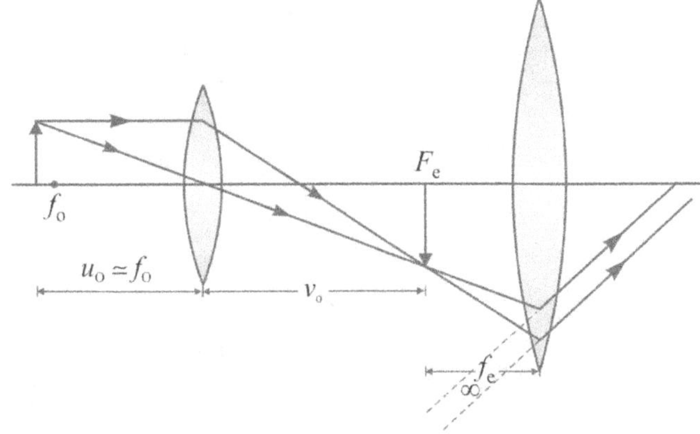

Fig. 3.93

When lenses are interchanged, let the new separation between the lenses be L', then

$$M' = -\frac{(L'-f_e)}{f_e} \cdot \frac{D}{f_o} \qquad ...(ii)$$

Given $\qquad M = M'$

$$\therefore \qquad \frac{L-f_e}{f_o} \frac{D}{f_e} = \frac{L'-f_o}{f_e} \frac{D}{f_o}$$

or $\qquad L - f_e = L' - f_o$

$$\therefore \qquad L' = (f_o - f_e) + L$$
$$= (0.4 - 0.3) + 0.2$$
$$= 0.3 \text{ m.} \qquad \textit{Ans.}$$

Ex. 49 A telescope has an objective of focal length 50 cm and an eye piece of focal length 5 cm. The least distance of distinct vision is 25 cm. The telescope is focussed for distinct vision on a scale 200 cm away from the objective. Calculate (a) the separation between objective and eyepiece and (b) the magnification produced

Sol.

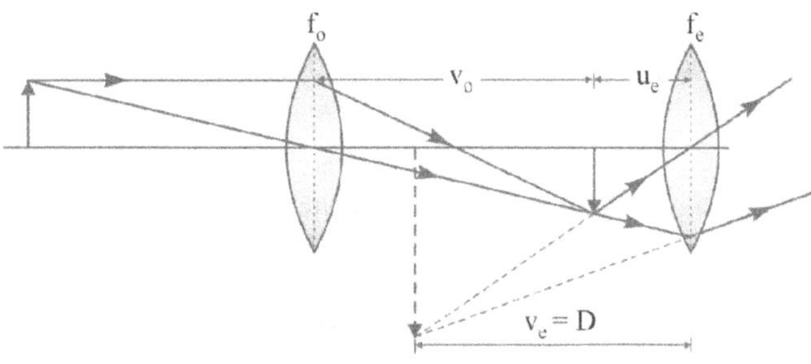

Fig. 3.94

(a) For objective lens $\quad u = -200$ cm, $f_o = +50$ cm

By lens formula, $\dfrac{1}{v} - \dfrac{1}{u} = \dfrac{1}{f}$, we have

$$\frac{1}{v_o} - \frac{1}{-200} = \frac{1}{50}$$

which gives $\qquad v_o = \dfrac{200}{3}$ cm

For eye piece, $\quad v_e = -25$ cm
$$f_e = +5 \text{ cm}$$

Now by lens formula,

$$\frac{1}{v} - \frac{1}{u} = \frac{1}{f}, \text{ we have}$$

$$\frac{1}{-25} - \frac{1}{u_e} = \frac{1}{+5}$$

which gives $\qquad u_e = -\dfrac{25}{6}$ cm

Length of the telescope

$$L = |v_o| + |u_e|$$
$$= \frac{200}{3} + \frac{25}{6} = 70.80 \text{ cm} \quad \textit{Ans.}$$

(b) Magnification $\quad M = -M_o \times M_e$

$$= -\frac{v_o}{u_o} \times \frac{v_e}{u_e}$$

$$= -\left(\frac{200/3}{200}\right) \times \frac{-25}{(-25/6)} = -2. \textit{Ans.}$$

3.19 PHOTOMETRY : AN INTRODUCTION

Photometry is the branch of optics which deals with the measurement of light; light is either emitted or reflected by the objects. So in this part we have to understand the emission and reflection characteristics of the objects.

Radiant flux

The total energy emitted by the source in unit time is called radiant flux. It includes visible and invisible radiations. Its SI unit is watt.

Luminous flux

The amount of light energy emitted by a source in one second is known as luminous flux. It is only that part of the radiant flux which is visible and can affect the eye. Its SI unit is lumen.

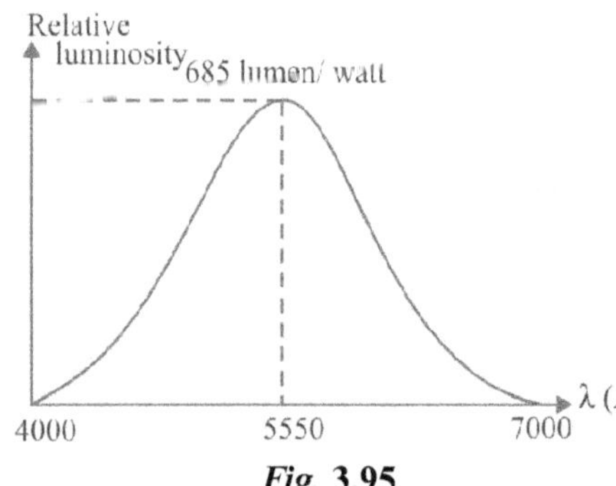

Fig. 3.95

Luminous efficiency

It is the ratio of luminous flux to the radiant flux. Thus

$$\text{luminous efficiency,} \qquad \eta = \frac{\text{luminous flux}}{\text{radiant flux}} \times 100.$$

Luminous efficiency of ordinary bulb is nearly 12% and that of tube light is 50%.

Relative luminosity

In the visible radiations, each colour has its own luminosity. It is greatest for yellow colour and least for red and violet. The graph shows the variation of relative luminosity with colour of light (wavelength). The relative luminosity for yellow-green region (5550Å) is 1. In this region each watt produces 685 lumen of luminous flux.

Ex. 50 The relative luminosity of a source is 0.60. Its power is 5W. Find the luminous flux produces by the source.

Sol.

The luminous flux produces by 5W for wavelength 5550Å = 685×5 = 3225 lumen

We know that
$$RL = \frac{\text{luminous flux of any wavelength}}{\text{luminous flux of wavelength } 5550\text{Å}}$$

or
$$0.6 = \frac{\Delta\phi}{3225}$$

$$\therefore \quad \Delta F = 3225 \times 0.6$$
$$= 1935 \text{ lumen.} \quad \textbf{\textit{Ans.}}$$

3.20 LUMINOUS INTENSITY

Luminous intensity of any source in any direction is the luminous flux per unit solid angle in that direction. Thus if $\Delta\phi$ is the luminous flux emitted in solid angle $\Delta\omega$, then luminous intensity,

$$L = \frac{\Delta\phi}{\Delta\omega}$$

Its SI unit is lumen/steradian. It is known as candela. For a point source, total solid angle is 4π steradian, and so total luminous flux becomes
$$\phi = L\omega = 4\pi L.$$

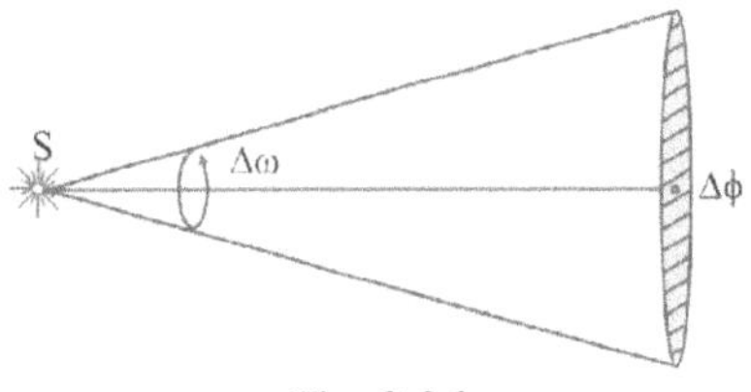

Fig. **3.96**

Note :

Intensity of the source is the power of the source per unit area perpendicular to the direction of propagation of light. Thus for a source of power P, its intensity
$$I = P/A. \quad \text{Its SI unit is W/m}^2.$$

3.21 ILLUMINANCE

The illuminance at any point of the surface is the luminous flux per unit surface area surrounding that point. If $\Delta\phi$ is the luminous flux striking a surface area ΔA, then illuminance E is given by

$$E = \frac{\Delta\phi}{\Delta A}.$$

It is the illuminance which is directly related to the brightness of an illuminated area. The SI unit of illuminance is lumen/m², which is called **lux**. Illuminance is also called illuminating power.

Luminance is related to the reflected power of the surface. If r is the coefficient of reflection, then

$$\text{luminance} = r \times \text{illuminance}$$

For perfectly reflecting surface, $r = 1$, and so luminance = illuminance.

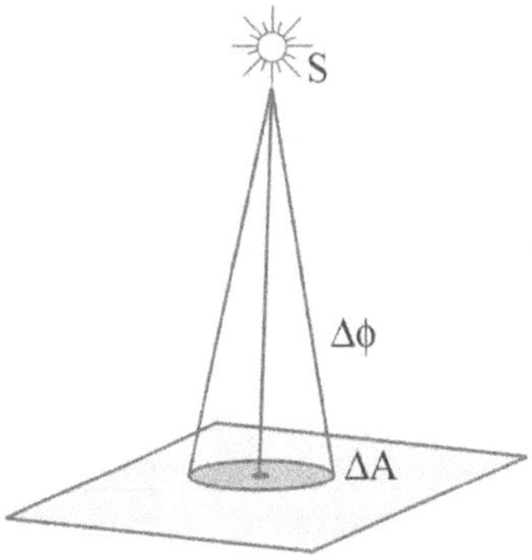

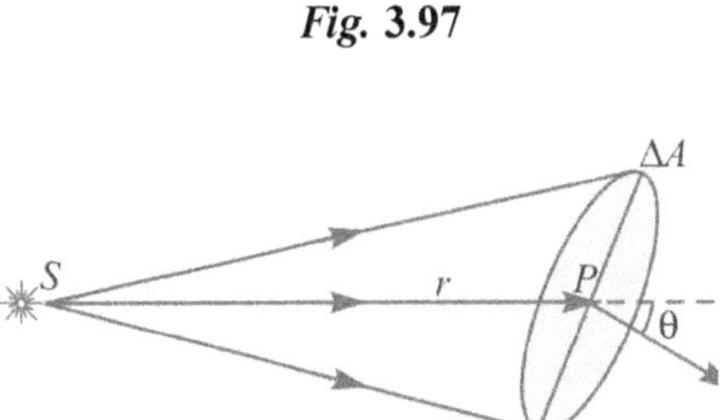

Fig. **3.97**

Inverse square law

Consider an isotropic source S and a small area ΔA. Choose a point P on the area at a distance r from the source S. Suppose the angle between SP and the normal of the area is θ. The solid angle subtended by the area ΔA at the source is

$$\Delta\omega = \frac{\Delta A \cos\theta}{r^2}.$$

Fig. **3.98**

If L is the luminous intensity of the source, then luminous flux incident on area ΔA is
$$\Delta\phi = L\Delta\omega$$

$$= \frac{L \Delta A \cos\theta}{r^2}.$$

The illuminance at any point P of the surface ΔA is

$$E = \frac{\Delta\phi}{\Delta A}$$

or
$$E = \frac{L\cos\theta}{r^2}.$$

As $E \propto \dfrac{1}{r^2}$, $\therefore$ illumination follows the inverse square law.

Lambert's cosine law

The relation $E = \dfrac{L\cos\theta}{r^2}$ is known as Lambert's cosine law i.e., the intensity of illumination is directly proportional to the cosine of the angle of incidence of light on the given surface. In a case when light incident normal to the surface, $\theta = 0$, and $\cos 0° = 1$,

$\therefore$
$$E = \frac{L}{r^2}.$$

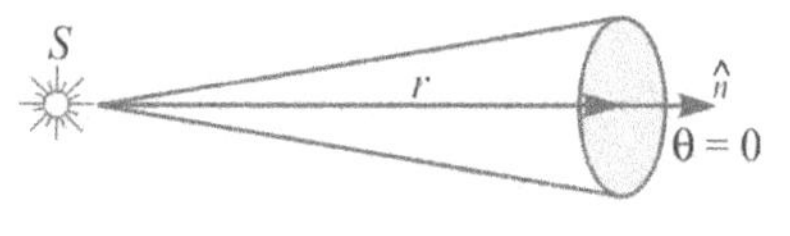

Fig. 3.99

3.22   PHOTOMETER

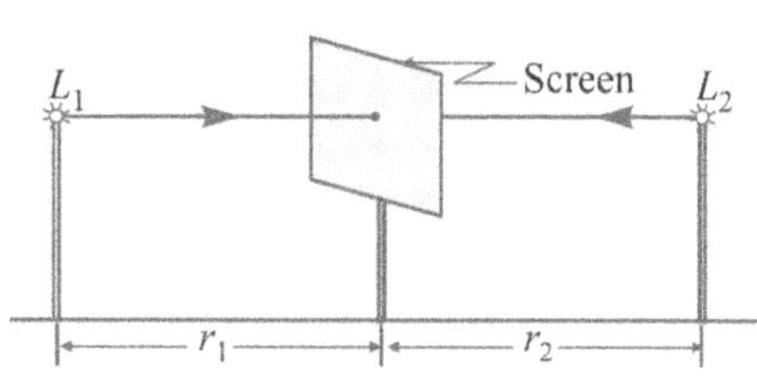

Fig.3.100 Photometer

Photometer is an instrument which is used to compare the luminous intensities of the different sources. The basic principle is that the illuminance produced by the sources on the screen are equal. Thus if L_1 and L_2 are the luminous intensities of the two sources at a distance r_1 and r_2 from the screen, then for equal illumination on the screen

$$\frac{L_1}{r_1^2} = \frac{L^2}{r_2^2}$$

or
$$\frac{L_1}{L_2} = \frac{r_1^2}{r_2^2}.$$

Ex. 51 A source is hanging over the centre of circular table of radius R. Calculate the height of source so that illuminance at the edge of the table is maximum.

Sol.   The illuminance at the edge of the table is equal to

$$E = \frac{I\cos\theta}{r^2}$$
$$= \frac{I(h/r)}{r^2} = \frac{Ih}{r^3}$$
$$= \frac{I\,h}{\left(R^2 + h^2\right)^{3/2}}$$

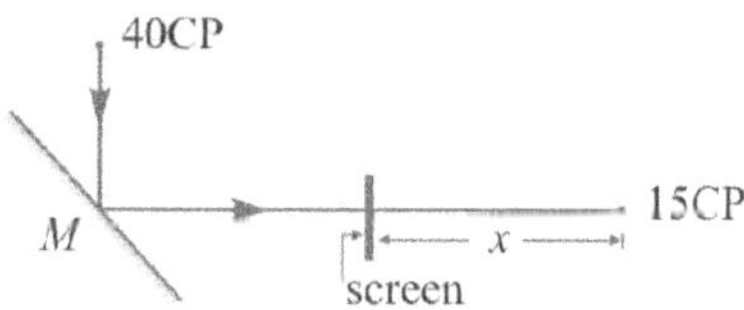

Fig. 3.101

E to be maximum, $dE/dh = 0$

or
$$\frac{d}{dh}\left[\frac{I\,h}{\left(R^2 + h^2\right)^{3/2}}\right] = 0$$

or $\left(R^2 + h^2\right)^{-3/2} \times 1 + h \times \left(-\dfrac{3}{2}\right)\left(R^2 + h^2\right)^{-5/2} \times 2h = 0$

After simplification, we get $h = \dfrac{R}{\sqrt{2}}$.   *Ans.*

Ex. 52 Light from a 40 candle power lamp falls on a silvered mirror M is reflected there to a grease spot photometer. The distance to the lamp to the screen via the mirror is 150 cm. The mirror reflects 80% of the light falling on it. A 15 candle power lamp is placed so that the grease spot vanishes. Calculate the approximate distance x of the lamp from the screen.

Fig. 3.102

Sol.

For photometric balance
$$E_1 = E_2$$

or
$$\frac{I_1}{r_1^2} = \frac{I_2}{r_2^2}$$

or
$$0.8 \times \frac{40}{\left(150\right)^2} = \frac{15}{x^2}$$

or $x = 103$ cm.   *Ans.*

Ex. 53 A plane mirror is placed 8 cm behind A, the plane of the mirror being normal to the line from A to the screen. It is found that, for a photometric balance, a source B must be moved 10 cm nearer the screen. In the beginning the two lamps A and B produce equal illuminance on the screen when A was 60 cm and B was 70 cm away from the screen. Find the reflecting power of the mirror.

Sol.

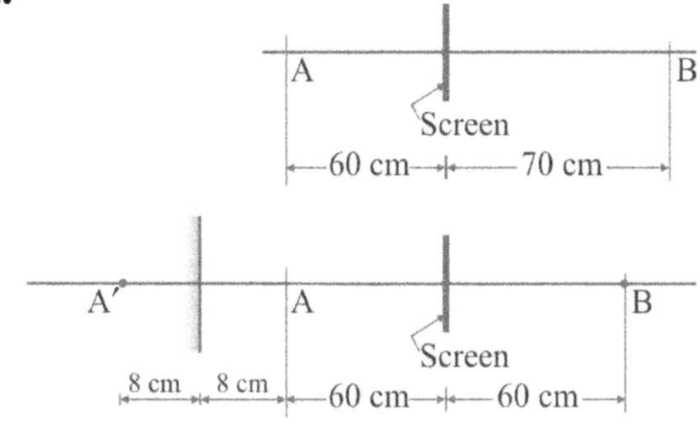

Fig. 3.103

Initially,
$$\frac{I_1}{60^2} = \frac{I_2}{70^2}$$

or
$$\frac{I_1}{I_2} = \frac{60^2}{70^2} \qquad (i)$$

when mirror is placed behind source A, its image is formed at A'. If k is the coefficient of reflection of the mirror. then

$$\frac{I_1}{60^2} + \frac{kI_1}{76^2} = \frac{I_2}{60^2}$$

or
$$\frac{(I_1/I_2)}{60^2} + \frac{k(I_1/I_2)}{76^2} = \frac{1}{60^2}$$

or
$$\frac{\left(60^2/70^2\right)}{60^2} + \frac{k\left(60^2/70^2\right)}{76^2} = \frac{1}{60^2}$$

or
$$k = 0.58. \qquad \textit{Ans.}$$

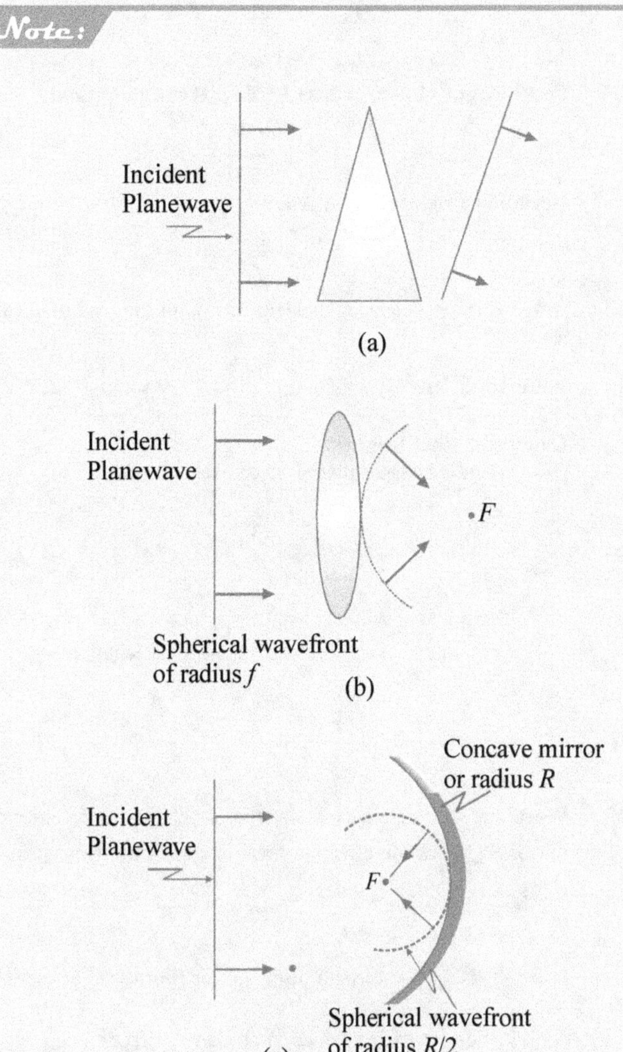

Refraction of a plane wave by (a) a thin prism, (b) a convex lens. (c) Reflection of a plane wave by a concave mirror

Review of Formulae & Important Points

1. Refraction formula through single spherical surface

$$\frac{_1\mu_2}{v} - \frac{1}{u} = \frac{_1\mu_2 - 1}{R}$$

or
$$\frac{\mu_2}{v} - \frac{\mu_1}{u} = \frac{\mu_2 - \mu_1}{R}.$$

2. (i) Lateral magnification

$$m = \frac{I}{O} = \frac{\mu_1 v}{\mu_2 u}.$$

(ii) Longitudinal magnification

$$m_L = \frac{\mu_1}{\mu_2} \frac{v^2}{u^2}$$

3. Lens formula

$$\frac{1}{v} - \frac{1}{u} = \frac{1}{f}.$$

Lens maker's formula

$$\frac{1}{f} = (\mu - 1)\left(\frac{1}{R_1} - \frac{1}{R_2}\right).$$

4. If μ_1 and μ_3 are the refractive indexes on both sides of the lens of material of refractive index μ_2, then

$$\frac{\mu_3}{v} - \frac{\mu_1}{u} = \frac{(\mu_2 - \mu_1)}{R_1} + \frac{(\mu_3 - \mu_2)}{R_2}$$

5. Lateral magnification,

$$m = \frac{I}{O} = \frac{v}{u} = \frac{f}{u - f}$$

6. Velocity of image

$$v_i = \frac{v^2}{u^2} v_o$$

7. Minimum distance between object and its real image

$$D_{\min} = 4f$$

and

$$D_{\max} = \infty .$$

8. Focal length of convex lens by displacement method

$$f = \frac{D^2 - x^2}{4D} .$$

9. Deviation produced by a lens

$$\delta = \frac{h}{f} .$$

where h is the height of incident of ray on the lens of focal length f.

10. Power of a lens $\qquad P = \dfrac{1}{f} .$

11. Combined focal length

(i) When lenses are placed in contact

$$\frac{1}{f} = \frac{1}{f_1} + \frac{1}{f_2} + ... ,$$

and $\qquad P = P_1 + P_2 + ...$

(ii) If two lenses of focal lengths f_1 and f_2 are placed at a separation of d, the equivalent focal length

$$\frac{1}{f} = \frac{1}{f_1} + \frac{1}{f_2} - \frac{d}{f_1 f_2} .$$

and $\qquad p = p_1 + p_2 - d p_1 p_2 .$

12. When one face of a lens is silvered, it behaves as a concave mirror. If f_e is the effective focal length of the lens, then

$$\frac{1}{f_e} = \frac{2}{f_\ell} + \frac{1}{f_m} .$$

Here f_m is the focal length of the mirror which is to be placed without sign.

(i) Plano-convex lens silvered at plane surface, then

$$f_e = \frac{R}{2(\mu - 1)} .$$

(ii) Plano-convex lens silvered at convex surface

$$f = \frac{R}{2\mu} .$$

13. Aberration

It is the defect in the image formed by the lens.
Axial or chromatic aberration

$$\delta f = f_R - f_v = \omega f_y .$$

14. Condition of achromatism

(i) For two lenses placed in contact

$$\frac{\omega_1}{f_1} + \frac{\omega_2}{f_2} = 0 .$$

(ii) For two lenses placed at a separation d,

$$d = \left[\frac{\omega_1 f_2 + \omega_2 f_1}{\omega_1 + \omega_2} \right] .$$

(iii) Two convex lens made of same material can be free from chromatic aberration, if

$$d = \frac{f_1 + f_2}{2} .$$

15. Simple microscope

Angular magnification, $M = 1 + \dfrac{D}{f_e}$

Here $D = 25$ cm.

16. Compound microscope

(i) When final image is formed at near point

$$M = -\frac{v_0}{u_0}\left(1 + \frac{D}{f_e}\right)$$

Length of the microscope

$$L = |v_0| + |u_e|$$

(ii) When final image is formed at infinity

$$M = -\frac{v_0}{u_0}\frac{D}{f_e}$$

Length of the microscope

$$L = |v_0| + f_e .$$

17. Astronomical telescope

(i) When final image is formed at near point

$$M = -\frac{f_0}{f_e}\left(1 + \frac{f_e}{D}\right) .$$

Length of the telescope,

$$L = f_0 + |u_e|$$

(ii) When final image is formed at infinity

$$M = -\frac{f_0}{f_e}$$

Length of the telescope,

$$L = f_0 + f_e .$$

18. Luminous efficiency

$$\eta = \frac{\text{luminous flux}}{\text{radiant flux}} \times 100$$

19. Relative luminosity

$$RL = \frac{\text{luminous flux of any wavelength}}{\text{luminous flux of wavelength 5550Å}}$$

20. Luminous intensity

$$L = \frac{\Delta\phi}{\Delta\omega}$$

The SI unit of luminous intensity is Candela.

The total luminous flux, $\phi = 4\pi L$

21. Illuminance, $\qquad E = \dfrac{L\cos\theta}{r^2}$

The unit of illuminance is lumen/m^2 which is called ℓux.

22. Principle of photometry

For two sources to be in photometric balance

$$E_1 = E_2$$

or $\qquad \dfrac{L_1}{r_1^2} = \dfrac{L_2}{r_2^2} .$

23. Total luminous energy falling on a plane surface of area A, in time t

$$Q = EAt$$

★ ★ ★

     # MCQ Type 1   *Exercise 3.1*

LEVEL - 1

Only one option correct

1. A diminished image of an object is to be obtained on a screen 1.0 m from it. This can be achieved by appropriately placing
   (a) a convex mirror of suitable focal length
   (b) a concave mirror of suitable focal length
   (c) a concave lens of suitable focal length
   (d) a convex lens of suitable focal length less than 0.25 m

2. A thin lens of focal length f_1 and its aperture has diameter d. It forms an image of intensity I. Now the central part of the aperture upto diameter $\dfrac{d}{2}$ is blocked by an opaque paper. The focal length and image intensity will change to
   (a) $\dfrac{f}{2}$ and $\dfrac{I}{2}$
   (b) f and $\dfrac{I}{4}$
   (c) $\dfrac{3f}{4}$ and $\dfrac{I}{2}$
   (d) f and $\dfrac{3I}{4}$

3. A convex lens of focal length 40 cm is in contact with a concave lens of focal length 25 cm. The power of combination is
   (a) -1.5 D
   (b) -6.5 D
   (c) $+6.5$ D
   (d) $+6.67$ D

4. A converging lens is used to form an image on a screen. When upper half of the lens is covered by an opaque screen
   (a) half the image will disappear
   (b) complete image will be formed of same intensity
   (c) half image will be formed of same intensity
   (d) complete image will be formed of decreased intensity

5. The ray diagram could be correct

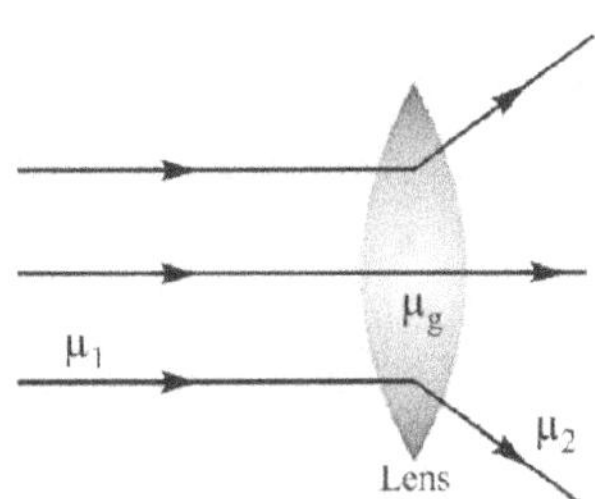

   (a) if $\mu_1 = \mu_2 = \mu_g$
   (b) if $\mu_1 = \mu_2$ and $\mu_1 < \mu_g$
   (c) if $\mu_1 = \mu_2$ and $\mu_1 > \mu_g$
   (d) under no circumstances

6. A lens behaves as a converging lens in air and a diverging lens in water. The refractive index of the material is
   (a) equal to unity
   (b) equal to 1.33
   (c) between unity and 1.33
   (d) greater than 1.33

7. A lens is placed between a source of light and a wall. It forms images of area A_1 and A_2 on the wall for its two different positions. The area of the source of light is
   (a) $\dfrac{A_1 + A_2}{2}$
   (b) $\left[\dfrac{1}{A_1} + \dfrac{1}{A_2}\right]^{-1}$
   (c) $\sqrt{A_1 A_2}$
   (d) $\left[\dfrac{\sqrt{A_1} + \sqrt{A_2}}{2}\right]^2$

8. A beam of parallel light rays from a laser is incident on a solid transparent sphere of index of refraction μ. If a point image is formed at the back of the sphere, then the value of μ is :

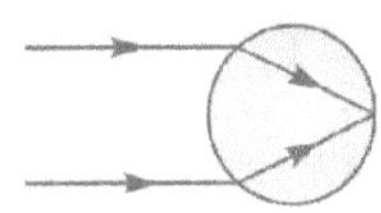

   (a) 1.2
   (b) 1.5
   (c) 1.8
   (d) 2.0

9. Figure given below shows a beam of light converging at point P. When a concave lens of focal length 16 cm is introduced in the path of the beam at a place O shown by dotted line such that OP becomes the axis of the lens, the beam converges at a distance x from the lens. The value x will be equal to

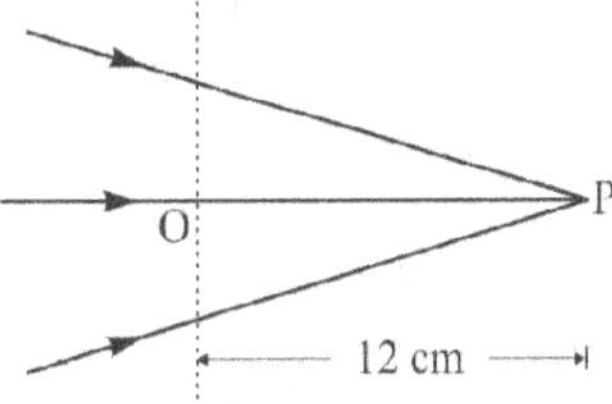

   (a) 12 cm
   (b) 24 cm
   (c) 36 cm
   (d) 48 cm

10. A point object is placed at the centre of a glass sphere of radius 6 cm and refractive index 1.5. The distance of the virtual image from the surface of the sphere is
   (a) 2 cm
   (b) 4 cm
   (c) 6 cm
   (d) 12 cm

Answer Key	1	(d)	2	(d)	3	(a)	4	(d)	5	(c)
Sol. from page 171	6	(c)	7	(c)	8	(d)	9	(d)	10	(c)

11. 1. 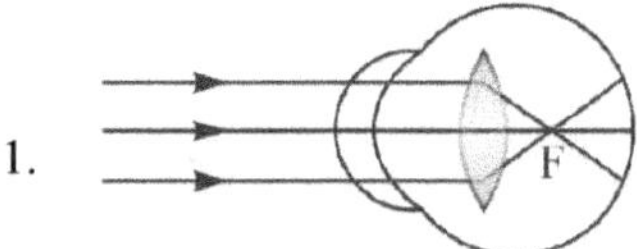

2. 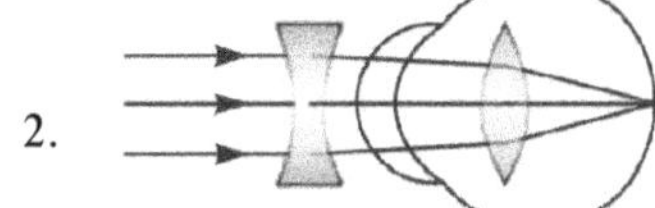

3. 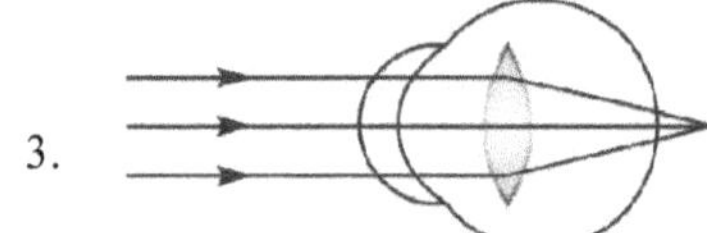

4. 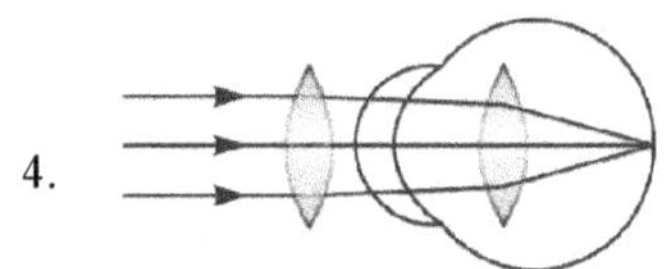

Identify the wrong description of the above figures

(a) 1 represents far-sightedness

(b) 2 correction for short sightedness

(c) 3 represents far sightedness

(d) 4 correction for far-sightedness

12. The focal length of the objective lens of a compound microscope is

(a) equal to the focal length of its eye piece

(b) less than the focal length of eye piece

(c) greater than the focal length of eye piece

(d) any of the above three

13. When the length of a microscope tube increases, its magnifying power

(a) decreases   (b) increases

(c) does not change   (d) may decrease or increase

14. The magnifying power of a microscope with an objective of 5 mm focal length is 40. The length of its tube is 20 cm. Then the focal length of the eye-piece is

(a) 200 cm   (b) 160 cm

(c) 2.5 cm   (d) 0.1 cm

15. In a compound microscope, the intermediate image is

(a) virtual, erect and magnified

(b) real, erect and magnified

(c) real, inverted and magnified

(d) virtual, erect and reduced

16. For a telescope to have large resolving power the

(a) focal length of its objective should be large

(b) focal length of its eye piece should be large

(c) focal length of its eye piece should be small

(d) aperture of its objective should be large

17. A drop of water is placed on a glass plate. A double convex lens having radius of curvature of each surface is 20 cm is placed on it. The focal length of water is ($\mu_w = 4/3$)

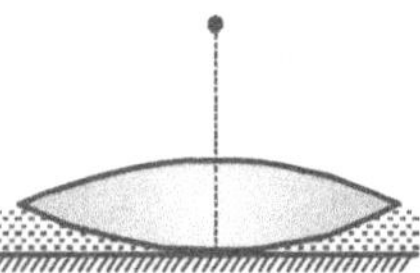

(a) -20 cm   (b) 60 cm

(c) 20 cm   (d) -60 cm

18. An observer looks at a tree of height 15 m with a telescope of magnifying power 10. To him, the tree appears

(a) 10 times taller   (b) 15 times taller

(c) 10 times nearer   (d) 15 times nearer

19. An astronomical telescope has an angular magnification of magnitude 5 for distant objects. The separation between the objective and the eye piece is 36 cm and the final image is formed at infinity. The focal length f_o of the objective and the focal length f_e of the eye piece are

(a) $f_o = 45$ cm and $f_e = -9$ cm

(b) $f_o = 7.2$ cm and $f_e = 5$ cm

(c) $f_o = 50$ cm and $f_e = 10$ cm

(d) $f_o = 30$ cm and $f_e = 6$ cm

20. The focal lengths of the objective and eye lenses of a telescope are respectively 200 cm and 5 cm. The maximum magnifying power of the telescope will be

(a) -40 (b) -48

(c) -60 (d) -100

21. Which one of the following spherical lenses does not exhibit dispersion? The radii of curvature of the surfaces of the lenses are as given in the diagrams

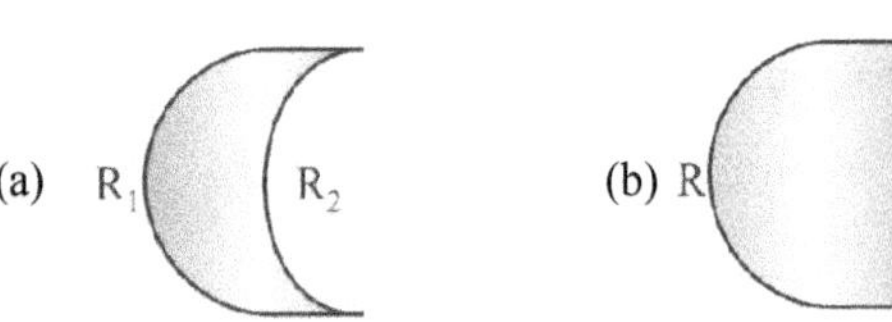

Answer Key														
	11	(a)	**12**	(b)	**13**	(b)	**14**	(c)	**15**	(c)	**16**	(d)	**17**	(d)
Sol. from page 171	**18**	(c)	**19**	(d)	**20**	(b)	**21**	(c)						

22. If in a plano-convex lens, the radius of curvature of the convex surface is 10 cm and the focal length of the lens is 30 cm, then the refractive index of the material of lens will be

(a) 1.5   (b) 1.66

(c) 1.33   (d) 3

23. A convex lens is made of 3 layers of glass of 3 different materials as in the figure. A point object is placed on its axis. The number of images of the object are

(a) 3

(b) 4

(c) 1

(d) 2

24. A beam of parallel rays is brought to a focus by a plano-convex lens. A thin concave lens of the same focal length is joined to the first lens. The effect of this is

(a) the focal point shifts away from the lens by a small distance

(b) the focus remains undisturbed

(c) the focus shifts to infinity

(d) the focal point shifts towards the lens by a small distance

25. In order to increase the magnifying power of a compound microscope.

(a) The focal lengths of the objective and the eye piece should be small

(b) Objective should have small focal length and the eye piece large

(c) Both should have large focal lengths

(d) The objective should have large focal length and eye piece should have small

26. Four lenses of focal length $+15$ cm, $+20$ cm, $+150$ cm and $+250$ cm are available for making an astronomical telescope. To produce the largest magnification, the focal length of the eye-piece should be

(a) $+15$ cm   (b) $+20$ cm

(c) $+150$ cm   (d) $+250$ cm

27. Spherical aberration is minimized by

1. use of stops.

2. use of plano-convex lens.

3. using two suitable lenses in contact.

4. using two plano-convex lenses separated by a distance.

Which of the above statements are correct?

(a) 3 and 4   (b) 1, 2 and 4

(c) 1, 2 and 3   (d) 1, 2, 3 and 4

28. A parallel beam of light is incident on the surface of a transparent hemisphere of radius R and refractive index 2.0 as shown in figure. The position of the image formed by refraction at the first surface is :

(a) $R/2$

(b) R

(c) $2R$

(d) $3R$

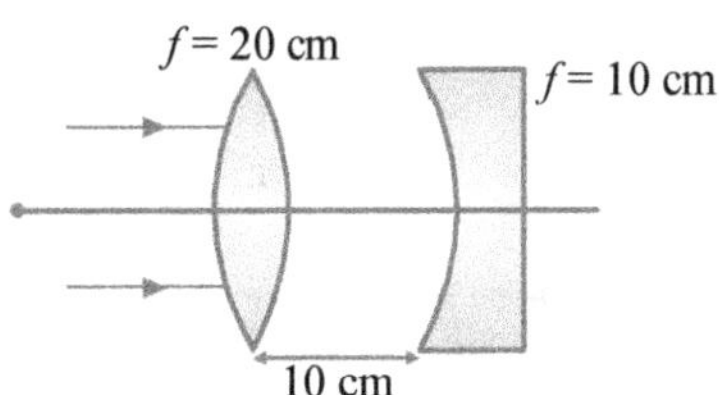

29. Parallel rays are focussed on a pair of lenses. Where will rays be focussed after refraction from both lenses ?

(a) At 40 cm from first lens   (b) At ∞ from first lens

(c) At 10 cm from first lens   (d) At 20 cm from first lens

30. An electric bulb illuminates a plane surface. The intensity of illumination on the surface at a point 2m away from the bulb is 5×10^{-4} phot (lumen/cm^2). The line joining the bulb to the point makes an angle of $60°$ with the normal to the surface. The intensity of the bulb in candela is

(a) $40\sqrt{3}$ (b) 40

(c) 20   (d) 40×10^{-4}

31. Total flux produced by a source of 1 cd is

(a) $\dfrac{1}{4\pi}$ (b) 8π

(c) 4π (d) $\dfrac{1}{8\pi}$

32. If the luminous intensity of 100 W unidirectional bulb is 100 candela, then total luminous flux emitted from the bulb is

(a) 861 lumen   (b) 986 lumen

(c) 1256 lumen   (d) 1561 lumen

33. A point source of light moves in a straight line parallel to a plane table. Consider a small portion of the table directly below the line of movement of the source. The illuminance at this portion varies with its distance r from the source as

(a) $E \propto \dfrac{1}{r}$ (b) $E \propto \dfrac{1}{r^2}$

(c) $E \propto \dfrac{1}{r^3}$ (d) $E \propto \dfrac{1}{r^4}$

Answer Key	22	(c)	23	(c)	24	(c)	25	(a)	26	(a)	27	(d)	28	(c)
Sol. from page 171	29	(b)	30	(b)	31	(c)	32	(c)	33	(c)				

LEVEL - 2

Only one option correct

1. A point object O is placed in front of a glass rod having spherical end of radius of curvature 30 cm. The image would be formed at

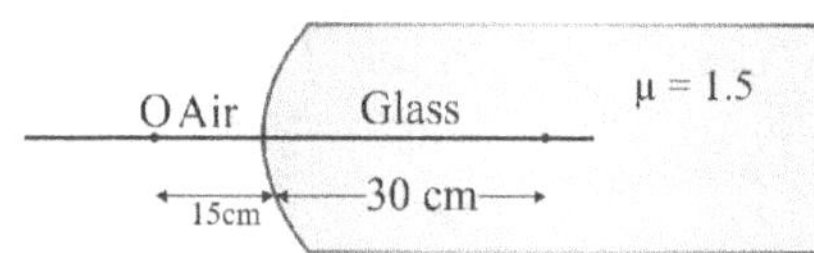

 (a) 30 cm left
 (b) infinity
 (c) 1 cm to the right
 (d) 18 cm to the left

2. The size of the image of an object, which is at infinity, as formed by a convex lens of focal length 30 cm is 2 cm. If a concave lens of focal length 20 cm is placed between the convex lens and the image at a distance of 26 cm from the convex lens, calculate the new size of the image
 (a) 1.25 cm
 (b) 2.5 cm
 (c) 1.05 cm
 (d) 2 cm

3. A spherical surface of radius of curvature R separates air (refractive index 1.0) from glass (refractive index 1.5). The centre of curvature is in the glass. A point object P placed in air is found to have a real image Q in the glass. The line PQ cuts the surface at a point O, and $PO = OQ$. The distance PO is equal to
 (a) $5R$
 (b) $3R$
 (c) $2R$
 (d) $1.5R$

4. A convex lens of focal length 40 cm is held co-axially 12 cm above a mirror of focal length 18 cm. An object held x cm above the lens gives rise to an image coincident with it. Then x is equal to :
 (a) 12 cm
 (b) 15 cm
 (c) 18 cm
 (d) 30 cm

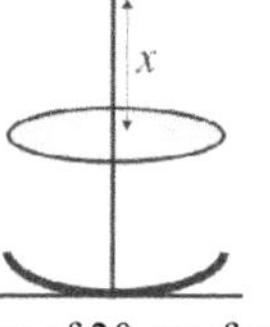

5. A point object is placed at a distance of 20 cm from a thin plano-convex lens of focal length 15 cm, if the plane surface is silvered. The image will form at :
 (a) 60 cm left of AB
 (b) 30 cm left of AB
 (c) 12 cm left of AB
 (d) 60 cm right of AB

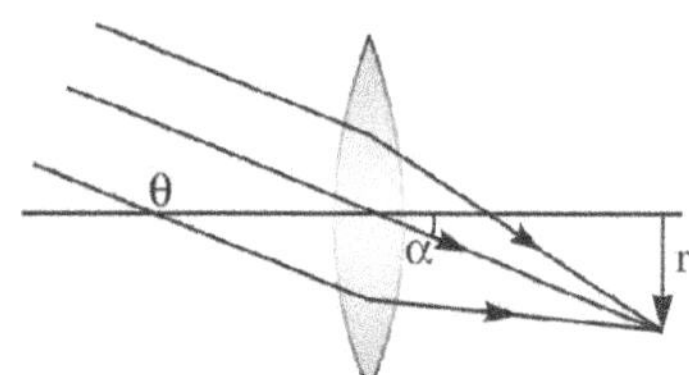

6. A biconvex lens of focal length f forms a circular image of sun of radius r in focal plane. Then :

 (a) $\pi r^2 \propto f$
 (b) $\pi r^2 \propto f^2$
 (c) If lower half part is covered by black sheet, then area of the image is equal to $\dfrac{\pi r^2}{2}$
 (d) If f is doubled, intensity will increase

7. A ray of light falls on a transparent sphere with centre at C as shown in figure. The ray emerges from the sphere parallel to line AB. The refractive index of the sphere is :

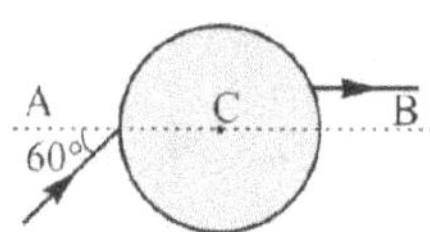

 (a) $\sqrt{2}$
 (b) $\sqrt{3}$
 (c) $3/2$
 (d) $1/2$

8. A parallel beam of light falls on a quarter cylinder of radius R, as shown in figure (A). Refractive index of the material of the cylinder is $\sqrt{3}$. Maximum value of OP, as shown in figure (B), so that rays don't suffer T.I.R at the curved surface is (consider refractive index of surrounding medium equal to 1)

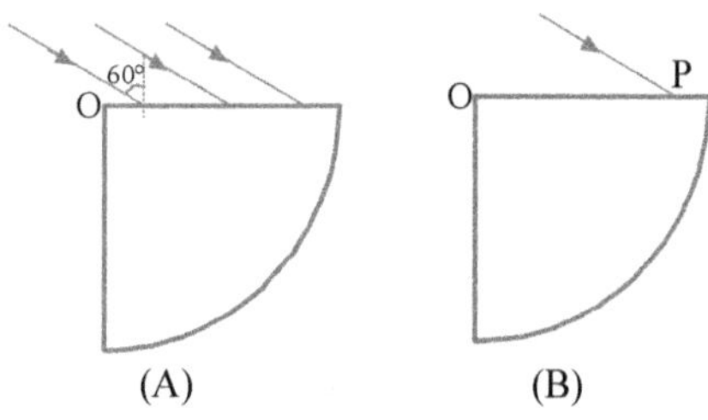

 (a) $\dfrac{R}{3}$
 (b) $\dfrac{2R}{3}$
 (c) $\dfrac{R}{2}$
 (d) $\dfrac{3R}{4}$

9. A hemisphere (made of material of refractive index $\sqrt{3}$) of radius r is placed on a horizontal surface with its base touching the surface. A vertical beam of cross sectional radius $\dfrac{\sqrt{3}}{2}r$ is incident symmetrically on its curved surface. Radius of the spot of light formed on the horizontal surface is
 (a) $\dfrac{r}{2}$
 (b) $\dfrac{r}{3}$
 (c) $\dfrac{r}{\sqrt{2}}$
 (d) $\dfrac{r}{\sqrt{3}}$

Answer Key	1	(a)	2	(b)	3	(a)	4	(b)	5	(c)	6	(b)
Sol. from page 172	7	(b)	8	(b)	9	(d)						

10. A ray is incident at an angle 60° on a sphere which is made of material having refractive index = $\sqrt{3}$, find angle by which the emergent ray is deviated

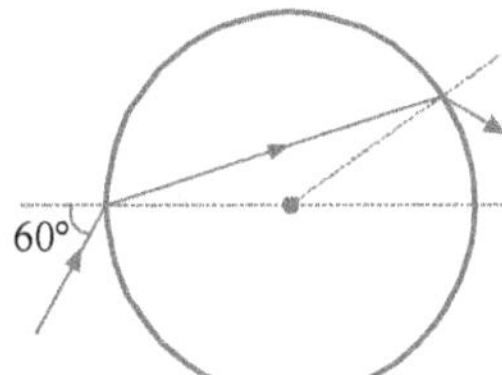

(a) 30° (b) 15°
(c) 45° (d) 60°

11. Consider the figure shown. Reflected ray AB and refracted ray AC are perpendicular. Refractive index of the material of the sphere is

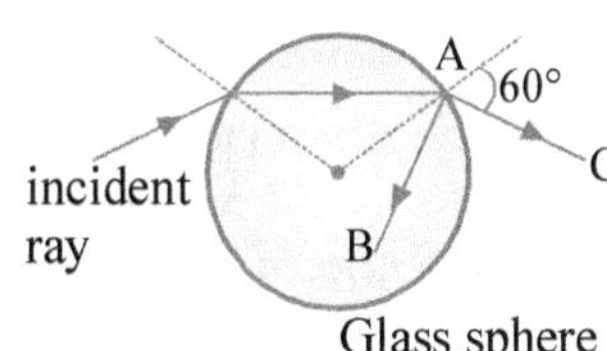

(a) $\sqrt{1.5}$ (b) $\sqrt{2}$
(c) $\sqrt{3}$ (d) $\sqrt{2.5}$

12. Parallel rays are focussed by the convex lens (lens is placed along y-axis) of focal length 20 cm at the point

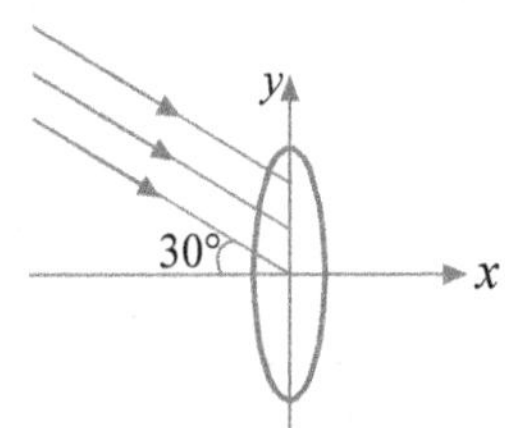

(a) (20, 0) (b) (20, –20)

(c) (20, –10) (d) $\left(20, -\dfrac{20}{\sqrt{3}}\right)$

13. A thin lens made of glass of refractive index 1.5 has a front surface + 11D power and back surface – 6D. If this lens is submerged in a liquid of refractive index 1.6, the resulting power of the lens is
(a) – 0.5 D (b) + 0.5D
(c) – 0.625 D (d) + 0.625 D

14. The distance between an object and the screen is 100 cm. A lens produces an image on the screen when placed at either of the positions 40 cm apart. The power of the lens is
(a) $\approx$ 3 diopters (b) $\approx$ 5 diopters
(c) $\approx$ 7 diopters (d) $\approx$ 9 diopters

15. Two plano-concave lenses (1 and 2) of glass of refractive index 1.5 have radii of curvature 25 cm and 20 cm. They are placed in contact with their curved surface towards each other and the space between them is filled with liquid of refractive index 4/3. Then the combination is

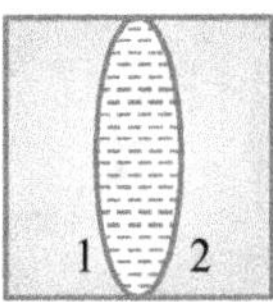

(a) convex of focal length 70 cm
(b) concave of focal length 70 cm
(c) concave of focal length 66.6 cm
(d) convex of focal length 66.6 cm

16. An object has image thrice of its original size when kept at 8 cm and 16 cm from a convex lens. Focal length of the lens is
(a) 8 cm (b) 16 cm
(c) between 8 cm and 16 cm (d) Less than 8 cm

17. A convex lens is in contact with concave lens. The magnitude of the ratio of their focal length is 2/3. Their equivalent focal length is 30 cm. What are their individual focal lengths?
(a) – 75, 50 (b) –10, 15
(c) 75, 50 (d) – 15, 10

18. The position of final image formed by the given lens combination from the third lens will be at a distance of f_1 = + 10cm, f_2 = – 10cm, f_3 = + 30 cm.

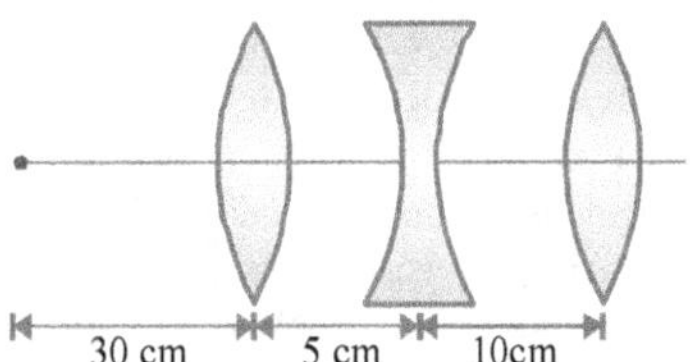

(a) 15 cm (b) infinity
(c) 45 cm (d) 30 cm

19. There is a concave lens of focal length f. A ray is incident on the lens at $y = b$. The equation of the refracted ray will be

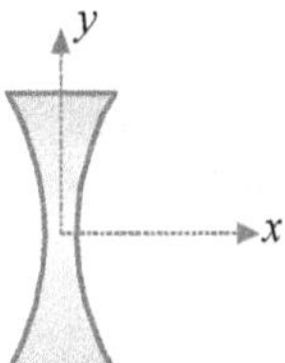

(a) $y = \dfrac{bx}{f} + b$ (b) $y = -\dfrac{bx}{f} + b$

(c) $y = \dfrac{bx}{f} - b$ (d) $y = \dfrac{fx}{b} + b$

Answer Key	**10**	(d)	**11**	(c)	**12**	(d)	**13**	(c)	**14**	(b)
Sol. from page 172	**15**	(c)	**16**	(c)	**17**	(d)	**18**	(d)	**19**	(b)

20. A converging lens of focal length 20 cm and diameter 5 cm is cut along the line AB. The part of the lens shown shaded in the figure is now used to form an image of a point P placed 30 cm away from it on the line xy, which is perpendicular to the plane of the lens. The image of P will be formed;

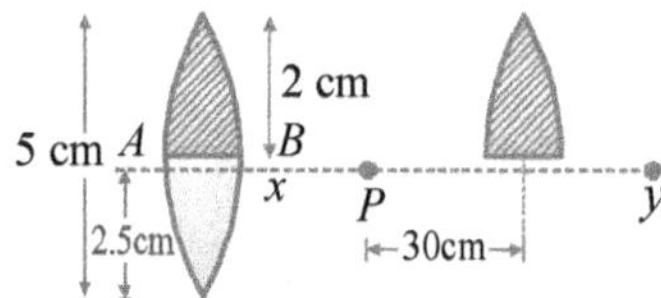

(a) 0.5 cm above xy.
(b) 1 cm below xy
(c) on xy
(d) 1.5 cm below xy

21. A convex lens of focal length 30 cm is kept coaxially at a distance of 20 cm from a concave lens of focal length 20 cm. What is the focal length of the combination?
(a) 20 cm
(b) 30 cm
(c) 60 cm
(d) 90 cm

22. A concave lens of glass, refractive index 1.5, has both surfaces of same radius of curvature R. On immersion in a medium of refractive index 1.75, it will behave as a
(a) convergent lens of focal length 3.5 R
(b) convergent lens of focal
(c) civergent lens of focal length 3.5 R
(d) divergent lens of focal length 3.0 R

23. A concave lens of focal length 20 cm placed in contact with a plane mirror acts as a
(a) convex mirror of focal length 10 cm
(b) concave mirror of focal length 40 cm
(c) concave mirror of focal length 60 cm
(d) concave mirror of focal length 10 cm

24. A plano-convex lens of refractive index 1.5 and radius of curvature 30 cm is silvered at the curved surface. Now this lens has been used to form the image of an object. At what distance from this lens an object be placed in order to have a real image of the size of the object
(a) 20 cm
(b) 30 cm
(c) 60 cm
(d) 80 cm

25. A bi-convex lens is formed with two thin plano-convex lenses as shown in the figure. Refractive index of the first lens is 1.5 and that of the second lens is 1.2. Both the curved surfaces are of the same radius of curvature R= 14 cm. for this bi-convex lens, for an object distance of 40 cm, the image distance will be

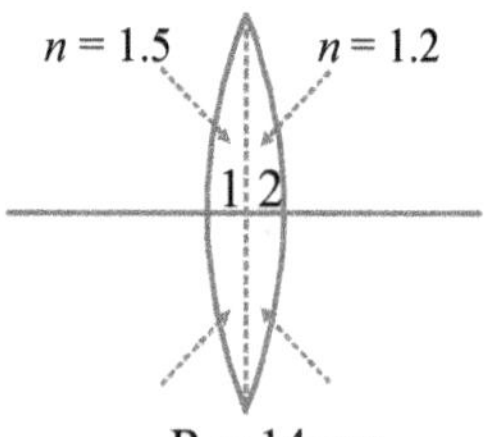

(a) −280.0 cm
(b) 40.0 cm
(c) 21.5 cm
(d) 13.3 cm

26. The focal lengths of the objective and the eye-piece of a compound microscope are 2.0 cm and 3.0 cm respectively. The distance between the objective and the eye-piece is 15.0 cm. The final image formed by the eye-piece is at infinity. The two lenses are thin. The distances in cm of the object and the image produced by the objective measured from the objective lens are respectively
(a) 2.4 and 12.0
(b) 2.4 and 15.0
(c) 2.3 and 12.0
(d) 2.3 and 3.0

27. A simple telescope, consisting of an objective of focal length 60 cm and a single eye lens of focal length 5 cm is focussed on a distant object is such a way that parallel rays comes out from the eye lens. If the object subtends an angle 2° at the objective, the angular width of the image
(a) 10°
(b) 24°
(c) 50°
(d) 1/6°

28. A telescope has an objective lens of focal length 200 cm and an eye piece with focal length 2 cm. If this telescope is used to see a 50 meter tall building at a distance of 2 km, what is the height of the image of the building formed by the objective lens
(a) 5 cm
(b) 10 cm
(c) 1 cm
(d) 2 cm

29. A plano-convex lens when silvered on the plane side behaves like a concave mirror of focal length 30 cm. However when silvered on the convex side, it behaves like a concave mirror of focal length 10 cm. Then refractive index of its material is :
(a) 1.5
(b) 2.0
(c) 2.5
(d) 3.0

30. A combination of two thin lenses with focal lengths f_1 and f_2 respectively forms an image of a distance object at distance 60 cm when lenses are in contact. The position of the image shift by 30 cm towards the combination when lenses are separated by 10 cm. The values of f_1 and f_2 will be :
(a) 30 cm, − 60 cm
(b) 20 cm, − 30 cm
(c) 15 cm, − 12 cm
(d) 12 cm, − 15 cm

31. A convex lens of focal length 12 cm is placed in contact with a plane mirror. If the object is placed at 20 cm from the lens, the position of final image is

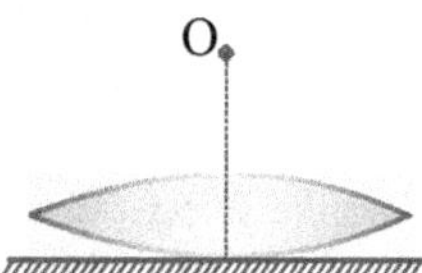

(a) 30 cm above lens
(b) 30 cm below lens
(c) 20 cm above lens
(d) 8.6 cm below lens

Answer Key	**20**	(d)	**21**	(c)	**22**	(a)	**23**	(a)	**24**	(a)	**25**	(b)
Sol. from page 172	**26**	(a)	**27**	(b)	**28**	(a)	**29**	(a)	**30**	(b)	**31**	(d)

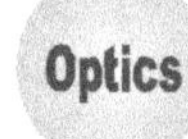 **Optics**

MCQ Type 2

Exercise 3.2

Multiple correct options

1. Which of the following quantities related to a lens depend on the wavelength or wavelengths of the incident light?
   - (a) Power
   - (b) Focal length
   - (c) Chromatic aberration
   - (d) Radii of curvature.

2. Which of the following quantities increase when wavelength is increased? Consider only the magnitude :
   - (a) The power of a converging lens
   - (b) The focal length of a converging lens
   - (c) The power of a diverging lens
   - (d) The focal length of a diverging lens.

3. The speed of light is 3×10^8 m/s :
   - (a) with respect to the earth
   - (b) with respect to the sun
   - (c) with respect to a train moving on the earth
   - (d) with respect to a spaceship going in outer space.

4. The object distance u, the image distance v and the magnification m in a lens follow certain linear relations. These are
   - (a) $\dfrac{1}{u}$ versus $\dfrac{1}{v}$
   - (b) m versus u
   - (c) u versus v
   - (d) m versus v

5. Consider the following statements :

   A compound microscope is better than single lens microscope because
   - (a) it can produce larger magnification
   - (b) it has better resolution
   - (c) it produces images free of all defects of these statements
   - (d) all the above

6. A planet is observed by an astronomical refracting telescope having an objective of focal length 16 m and an eye-piece of focal length 2 cm
   - (a) the distance between the objective and the eye-piece is 16.02 m
   - (b) the angular magnification of the planet is 800
   - (c) the image of the planet is inverted
   - (d) the objective is larger than the eye-piece

Answer Key	1	(a, b, c)	2	(b, d)	3	(a,b, c, d)	4	(a, d)
Sol. from page 176	5	(a, c)	6	(a, b, c, d)				

Optics | # Statement Questions | *Exercise 3.3*

Read the two statements carefully to mark the correct option out of the options given below. Select the right choice.
(a) **If both the statements are true and the** *Statement* **- 2** is the correct explanation of *Statement* **- 1**.
(b) If both the statements are true but *Statement* **- 2** is not the correct explanation of the *Statement* **- 1**.
(c) If *Statement* **- 1** true but *Statement* **- 2** is false.
(d) If *Statement* **- 1** is false but *Statement* **- 2** is true.

1. *Statement* -1 : The diameter of convex lens required to form full image of an object is half the height of the object.

   Statement **- 2** : The smaller diameter lens will give full image of lower intensity.

2. *Statement* -1 : For real image in convex lens; the minimum distance between object and its image must not be less than $2f$.

   Statement **- 2** : For a convex lens of focal length f, the distance between object and its real image can be $14f/3$.

3. *Statement* **- 1** : The image of a point object situated at the centre of hemispherical lens is also at the centre.

   Statement **- 2** : For hemisphere Snell's law is not valid.

4. *Statement* **- 1** : A convex lens forms a real image of an object placed on its optic axis. If the upper half of the lens is painted black; the size of he image becomes half.

   Statement **- 2** : The intensity of the image by the half painted lens will be half that due to unpainted lens.

5. *Statement* **- 1** : When a convex lens ($\mu_g = 3/2$) of focal length f is dipped in water, its focal length becomes $\dfrac{4}{3}f$.

   Statement **- 2** : The focal length of convex lens in water becomes $4f$.

6. *Statement* **- 1** : The object O is located as shown figure the apparent position of the object will be at 8/3 cm from the eye.

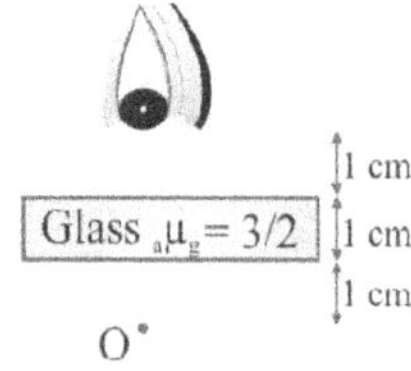

   Statement **- 2** : The apparent position of the object O will be 2 cm from the eye.

7. *Statement* **- 1** : The optical instruments are used to increase the size of the image of the object.

   Statement **- 2** : The optical instruments are used increase the visual angle.

8. *Statement* **- 1** : The resolving power of a telescope is more if the diameter of the objective lens is more.

   Statement **- 2** : Objective lens of large diameter collects more light.

9. *Statement* **- 1** : The image of an object placed at the focus of the concave lens will form at infinity.

   Statement **- 2** : The image of an object placed at the focus of the concave lens will form midway between the lens and the focus.

10. *Statement* **- 1** : A lens, whose radii of curvature are different, is forming the image of an object placed on its axis. If the lens is reversed, the position of the image will not change.

    Statement **- 2** : The focal length of a lens is given by

    $$\frac{1}{f} = (\mu - 1)\left(\frac{1}{R_1} - \frac{1}{R_2}\right),$$ and so focal length in both the cases is same.

11. *Statement* **- 1** : The focal length of an equiconvex lens of radius of curvature R made of material of refractive index $\mu = 1.5$, is R.

    Statement **- 2** : The focal length of the lens will be R/2.

12. *Statement* **- 1** : If the rays are diverging after emerging from a lens; the lens must be concave.

    Statement **- 2** : The convex lens can give diverging rays.

13. *Statement* **- 1** : The luminous flux of a source emitting microwaves is zero.

    Statement **- 2** : The wavelengths of microwaves are longer than 7000 Å.

14. *Statement* **- 1** : The illuminating power of a monochromatic source of wavelength 5550Å is always greater than that of a white light source of same power.

    Statement **- 2** : The illuminating power of a monochromatic source is always greater than that of a white light source of same power.

Answer Key	1	(d)	2	(d)	3	(c)	4	(d)	5	(d)	6	(c)	7	(d)
Sol. from page 177	8	(a)	9	(d)	10	(a)	11	(c)	12	(d)	13	(a)	14	(c)

15 *Statement - 1* : Luminous flux and radiant flux have same dimensions.

Statement - 2 : Luminous flux and radiant flux have same unit.

16. *Statement - 1* : The normal eye is not able to see objects closer than 25 cm.

Statement - 2 : The eye is not able to decrease the focal length beyond a certain limit.

17. *Statement - 1* : The near point of a farsighted eye is 50 cm. The magnifying power of a convex lens of focal length 5 cm is 10 X.

Statement - 2 : The magnifying power of a magnifying glass is given by $M = \dfrac{D}{f_e}$.

18. *Statement - 1* : The equation derived from spherical surface, $\dfrac{\mu_2}{v} - \dfrac{\mu_1}{u} = \dfrac{\mu_2 - \mu_1}{R}$ can be used for plane surfaces also.

Statement - 2 : For plane surface $\dfrac{v}{u} = \dfrac{\mu_2}{\mu_1}$.

Answer Key	**15**	(c)	**16**	(a)	**17**	(a)	**18**	(a)
Sol. from page 177								

Optics — Passage & Matrix — *Exercise 3.4*

PASSAGES

Passage for (Qs. 1 - 3) :
Two lenses of focal length 10 cm; one convex and other concave are placed on the same optic axis at a separation x. A plane mirror is also placed on the same optic axis at a distance of 10 cm from the concave lens. An object O is placed at a distance 30 cm from the convex lens.

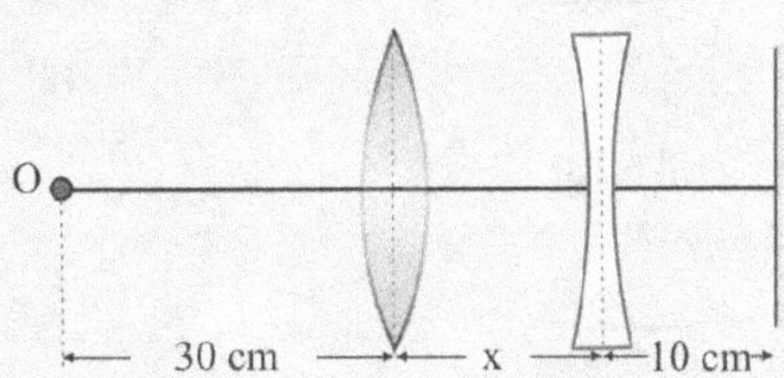

1. What should be the value of x show that image will coincide with the object?
(a) 5 cm
(b) 10 cm
(c) 20 cm
(d) none of these

2. If the mirror is replaced by a convex lens of focal length 30 cm, then the position of the final image formed (from second convex lens) by the system with the distance x between the lenses is :
(a) 30 cm
(b) 40 cm
(c) 50 cm
(d) none of these

3. The magnification of the system of three lenses is
(a) 0
(b) –3/2
(c) ∞
(d) none of these

Passage for (Qs. 4 - 6):
In a method of determining focal length of a convex lens, a luminous object and a screen are fixed distance D apart. A converging lens of focal length f is placed between object and the screen.

4. The image will be formed on the screen if
(a) $D = 2f$
(b) $D = 3f$
(c) $D = 4f$
(d) $D \geq 4f$

5. If a real image is formed on the screen for the two positions of lenses, then the separation x between these positions is
(a) $\sqrt{D(D - 4f)}$
(b) $D/2$
(c) $\sqrt{D(D - f)}$
(d) none of these

6. The ratio of the two image sizes for these two positions of the lens
(a) 1
(b) $\dfrac{D}{x}$
(c) $\left[\dfrac{D - x}{D + x}\right]^2$
(d) $\left[\dfrac{D + x}{D - x}\right]^2$

Passage for (Qs. 7 & 8) :
A concavo–convex lens made of glass ($\mu = 1.5$) has surfaces of radii 20 cm and 60 cm.

7. The distance of image of an object placed 80 cm to the left of the lens along the principal axis is
(a) 230 cm
(b) 240 cm
(c) 24 cm
(d) 2.4 cm

8. A similar lens is placed coaxially at a distance of 160 cm right to it. The position of the image is

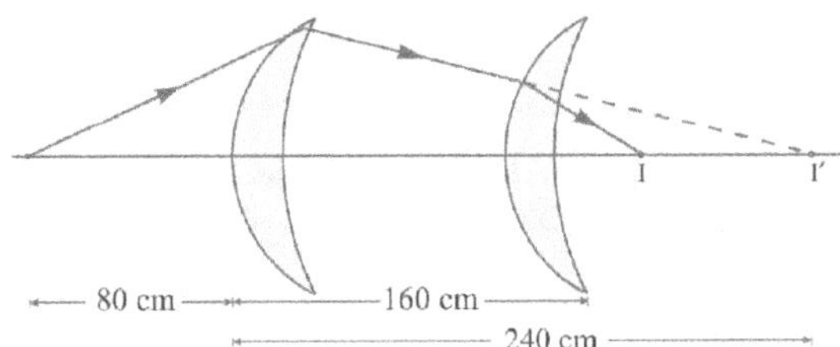

(a) 34.3 cm
(b) 35.5
(c) 31.5 cm
(d) 30 cm

Answer Key	**1**	(a)	**2**	(a)	**3**	(b)	**4**	(d)
Sol. from page 177	**5**	(a)	**6**	(c)	**7**	(b)	**8**	(a)

9. Two transparent media of refractive indices μ_1 and μ_3 have a solid lens shaped transparent material of refractive index μ_2 between them as shown in figures in **Column II**. A ray traversing these media is also shown in the figures. In **Column I** different relationships between μ_1, μ_2, and μ_3 are given. Match them to the ray diagrams shown in **Column II**.

Column I	Column II

A.　$\mu_1 < \mu_2$　　　　　　　　(p) 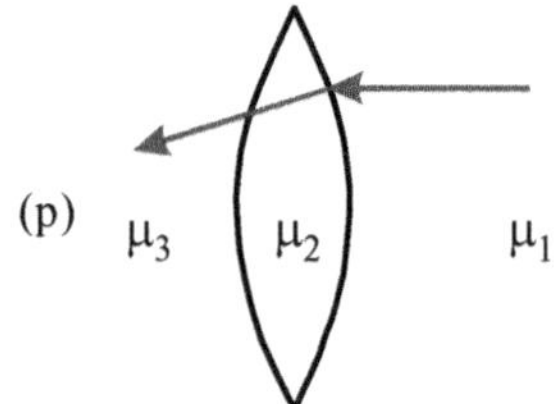

B.　$\mu_1 > \mu_2$　　　　　　　　(q) 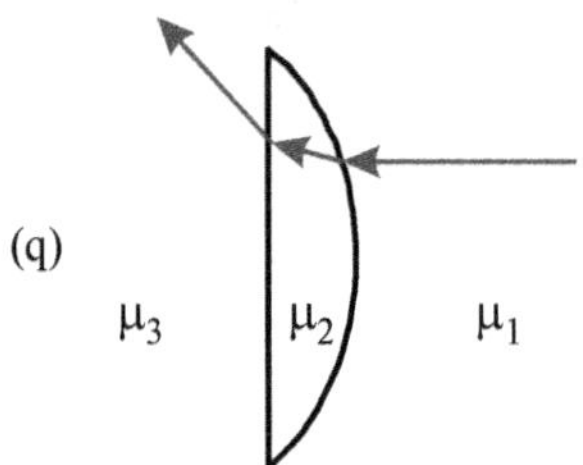

C.　$\mu_2 = \mu_3$　　　　　　　　(r) 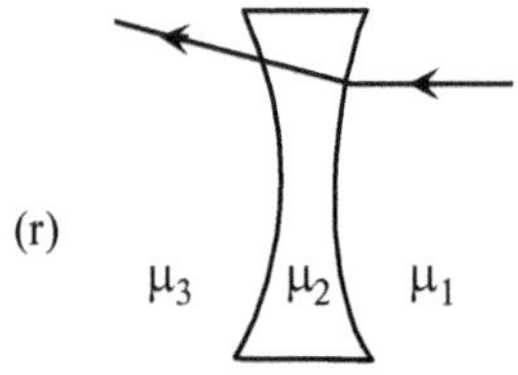

D.　$\mu_2 > \mu_3$　　　　　　　　(s) 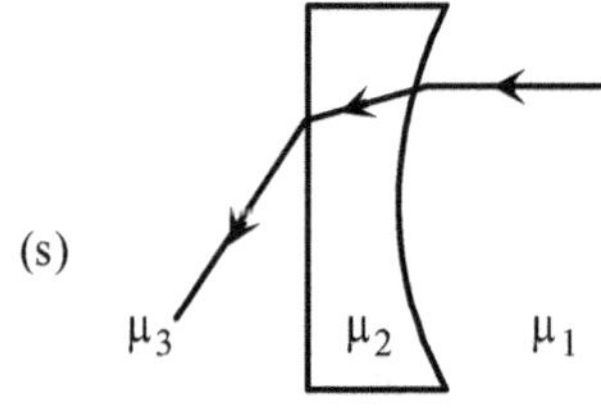

　　　　　　　　　　　　　　　　(t) 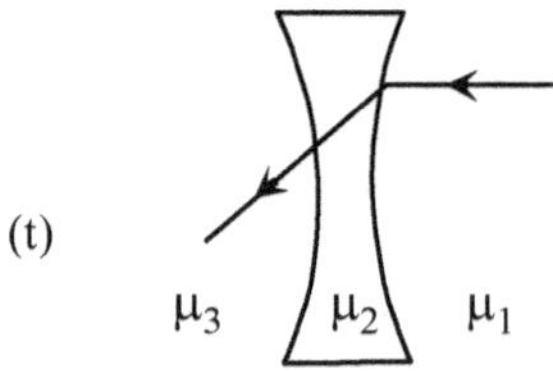

10. Match **Column I** with **Column II** and select the correct answer using the codes given below :

Column I		Column II
A.	Spherical aberration	(p) Heterochromatic on and off axis.
B.	Coma	(q) Monochromatic on and off axis
C.	Distortions	(r) Monochromatic off axis only
D.	Chromatic aberration	

Answer Key	**9**	A-(p, r); B-q, s, t ; C-(p, r, t) ; D-(q, s)	**10**	A-(q) ; B- (r) ; C- (r) ; D- (p)
Sol. from page 177				

11 An optical component and an object S placed along its optic axis are given in **Column I**. The distance between the object and the component can be visaed. The properties of images are given in **Column II**. Match all the properties of images from **Column II** with the appropriate components given in **Column I**.

Column I	Column II
(A) 	(p) Real image
(B)	(q) Virtual image
(C)	(r) Magnified image
(D)	(s) Image at infinity

12. Match the **Column-I** with the **Column-II** from the combinations shown

Column – I	Column – II
A. Presbyopia	(p) Sphero-cylindrical lens
B. Hypermetropia	(q) Convex lens of proper power may be used close to the eye
C. Astigmatism	(r) Concave lens of suitable focal length
D. Myopia	(s) Bifocal lens of suitable focal length

13. Match the following **Column II** gives nature of image formed in various cases given in **Column I**

Column – I	Column – II
A. 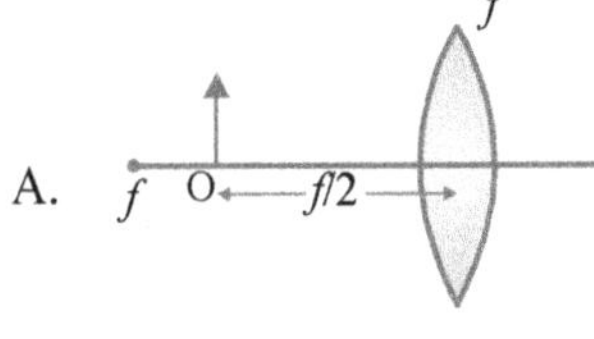	(p) Real
B. 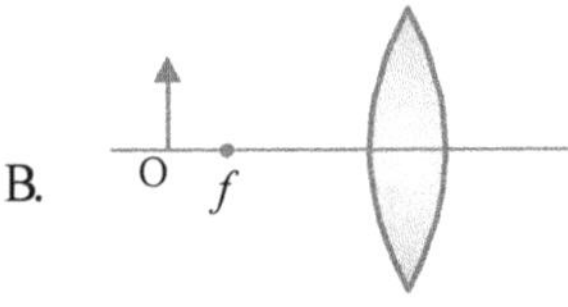	(q) Inverted
C. 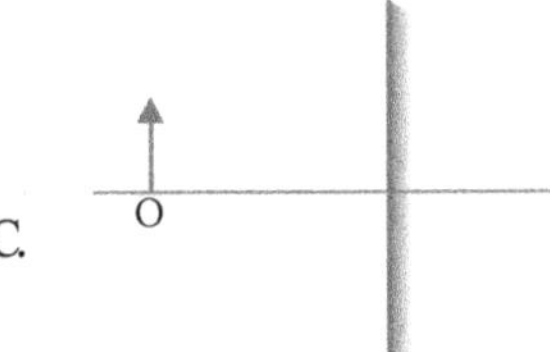	(r) Virtual
D. 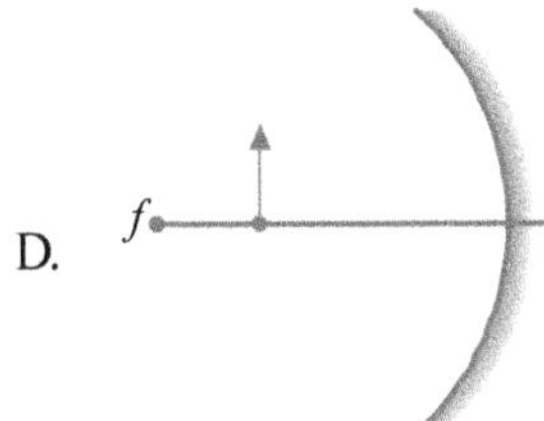	(s) Upright
	(t) Magnified

Answer Key	**11**	A-(p, q, r,s) ; B-(q) ; C-(p, q, r, s) ; D-(p, q, r, s)	
Sol. from page 177	**12**	A- (s) ; B-(q) ; C-(p) ; D-(r)	**13** A-((r, s, t) ; B-(p, q, t) ; C- (r, s) ; D - (r, s, t)

14. Match the following **Column -I** gives number of image formed, **Column-II** shows an arrangement and an objects

Column – I		Column – II

A. Number of images = 3   (p)

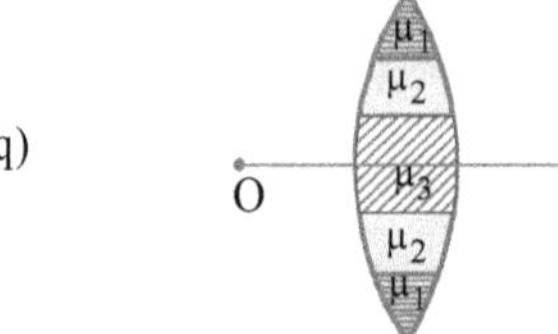

B. Number of images = 5   (q)

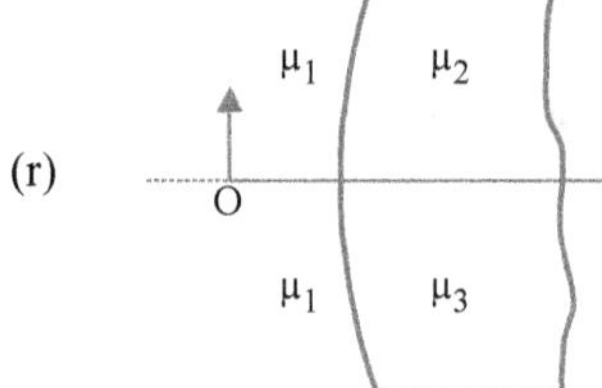

C. Number of images = 2   (r)

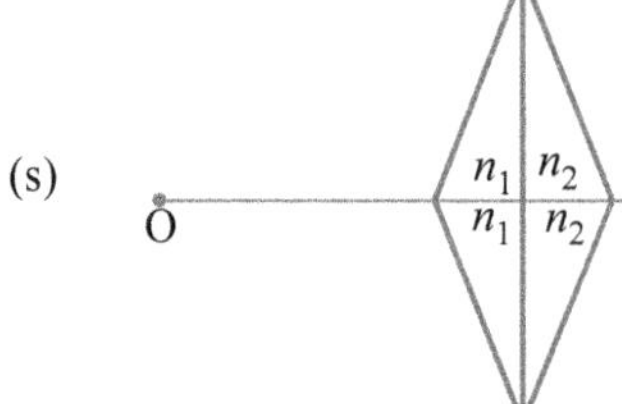

D. Number of image = 1   (s)

(t)

Answer Key	**14**	A-(q) ; B-(p) ; C-(r,) ; D-(s, t)
Sol. from page 177		

Optics

Subjective Integer Type — *Exercise 3.5*

Solution from page 278

1. A glass sphere of radius 5 cm has a small bubble 2 cm from its centre. The bubble is viewed along a diameter of the sphere from the side on which it lies. How far from the surface will it appear. Refractive index of glass is 1.5.

Ans. 25 cm

2. A converging beam of rays is incident on a diverging lens. Having passed through the lens the rays intersect at a point 15 cm from the lens. If the lens is removed the point where the rays meet will move 5 cm closer to the mounting that holds the lens. Find focal length of the lens.

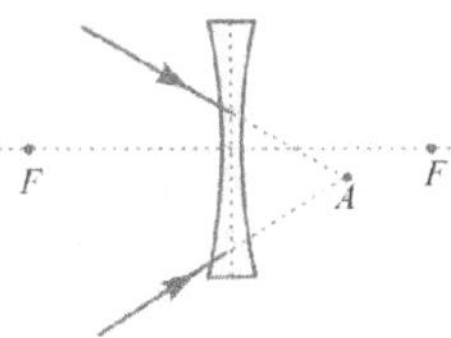

Ans. 30 cm.

3. A convergent lens forms on a screen an image of lamp magnified to twice its normal size. After the lens has been moved 36 cm closer to the screen it gives an image diminished by a factor of two. Find the focal length of the lens.

Ans. 24 cm.

4. An optical system consists of a convergent lens with a focal length of 30 cm and a flat mirror placed at a distance 15 cm from the lens. Determine the position of the image formed by this system is an object is at a distance 15 cm in front of the lens. Plot the path of the rays in this case.

Ans. 60 cm

5. Determine the position of the image produced by an optical system consisting of a concave mirror with a focal length of 10 cm and a convergent lens with a focal length of 20 cm. The distance from the mirror to the lens is 30 cm and from the lens to the object 40 cm. Plot the image.

Ans. 100 cm.

6. Photograph of the ground are taken from an aircraft at an altitude of 10 km by a camera fitted with a convex lens of focal length 1 m. The size of the film in the camera is 10 cm × 10 cm. What area of the ground can be photographed by this camera at any time?

Ans. 1km^2

Optics

Subjective — *Exercise 3.6*

Solution from page 179

1. A small fish, 0.4 m below the surface of a lake, is viewed through a simple converging lens of focal length 3m. The lens is kept at 0.2 m above the water surface such that the fish lies on the optical axis of the lens. Find the image of the fish seen by the observer. The refractive index of water is 4/3.

Ans. 0.4 m below the water surface.

2. A point source S is placed at a distance of 15 cm from a converging lens of focal length 10 cm on its principal axis. Where should a diverging mirror of focal length 12 cm be placed so that a real image is formed on the source itself ?

Ans. 6 cm from the right of lens.

3. A ball is kept at a height y_0 above the surface of a transparent sphere of radius R, made of material of refractive index μ. At t = 0, the ball is dropped to fall normally on the sphere. Find the speed of the image formed as a function of time for $t < \sqrt{\dfrac{2y_0}{g}}$.

Consider the image by a single refraction.

$$Ans. \quad \frac{\mu R^2 g t}{[(\mu-1)(y_0 - \frac{1}{2}gt^2) - R]^2}.$$

4. An object is approaching a thin convex lens of focal length 0.3 m with a speed of 0.01 m/s. Find the magnitude of the rate of change of position and lateral magnification of image when object is at a distance of 0.4 m from the lens.

Ans. 0.09 m/s, –0.3 per second

5. When observed from the earth the angular diameter of the solar disc is θ = 32' (minute). Determine the diameter of the image of the sun formed by a convergent lens with a focal length f = 0.50 m.

Ans. d = fθ = 4.70 mm

6. (a) A paperweight in the form of a hemisphere of radius 3.0 cm is used to hold a printed page. An observer looks at the page vertically through the paperweight. At what height above the page will the printed letters near the centre appear to the observer? (b) If the paperweight is inverted at its place so that the spherical surface touches the paper. What is the answer of part (a) ? [The refractive index of material of paperweight μ = 3/2]

Ans. (a) 3 cm (b) 2 cm

7. A convex lens of focal length 20 cm and a concave lens of focal length 10 cm are placed 10 cm apart on the same optic axis. A beam of light travelling parallel to the optic axis and having a beam diameter 5.0 mm, is incident on the convex lens. Show that the emergent beam is parallel to the incident one. Find the beam diameter of the emergent beam.

Ans. 2.5 mm.

8. In what position of the eye and for what distance between a point source and a convergent lens can an observer simultaneously see the source lying on the optical axis of the lens and its image produced by the lens ? The focal length of the lens of f and its diameter is *d*.

Ans. The source should be more than twice the focal length away from the lens.

9. Plot the image of an object in an optical system consisting of a convergent lens and a flat mirror arranged in the focal plane of the lens. The object is in front of the lens and between the focus and the double focal length of the lens. What will be size of the image be if the object is positioned arbitrarily.

Ans. Real image between focus and lens.

10. An image Y is formed by a point object X by a lens whose optic axis is AB as shown in figure. Draw a ray diagram to locate the lens and its focus. If the image Y of the object X is formed by a concave mirror (having the same optic axis AB) instead of lens, draw another ray diagram to locate the mirror and its focus. Write down the steps of construction of the ray diagrams.

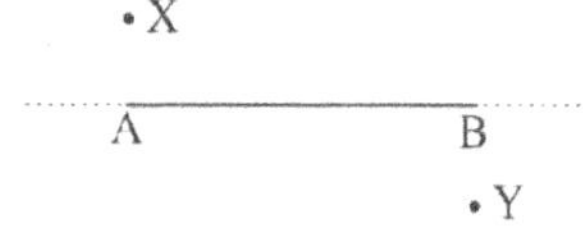

11. A convex lens of focal length 10 cm is placed on a plane mirror with its optic axis vertical. An object is placed at a distance 15 cm from the lens. Find the position of the final image.

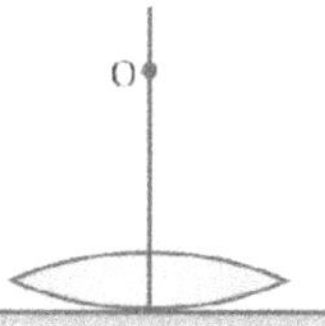

Ans. 7.5 cm from the lens on the sided of the object.

12. In a compound microscope the object and eyepiece have focal length of 0.95 cm and 5 cm respectively, and are kept at a distance of 20 cm. The last image is formed at a distance of 25 cm from eyepiece. Calculate the position of the object and total magnification

Ans. $u_0 = -\dfrac{95}{94}$ cm , M = –94.

13. A lady cannot see objects closer than 40 cm from the left eye and closer than 100 cm from the right eye. While on a mountaineering trip, she is lost from her team. She tries to make an astronomical electroscope from her reading glasses to look for her teammates.

(a) Which glass should she use as the eyepiece?

(b) What magnification can she get with relaxed eye?

Ans. right lens, 2.

14. A telescope has an objective of focal length 50 cm and eyepiece of focal length 5 cm. The distance of distinct vision is 25 cm. The telescope is focussed for distinct vision on a scale 200 cm away from the objective. Calculate;

(i) the separation between the objective and eyepiece,

(ii) the magnification produced.

Ans. 70.80 cm, 2.

★ ★ ★

Hints & Solutions

1. (d) For diminished real image

$$D \geq 4f$$

or

$$f \leq \frac{D}{4}$$

$$\leq \frac{1}{4}$$

$$\leq 0.25 \text{ m}$$

2. (d)

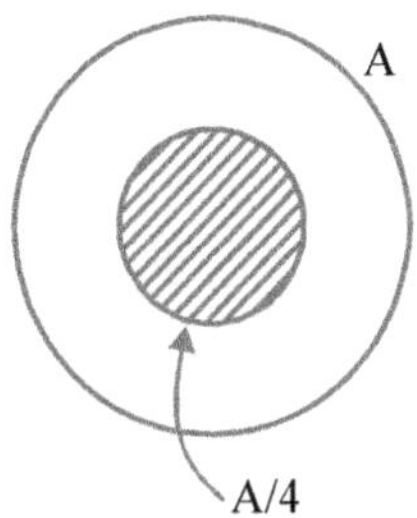

The exposed area of the lens becomes $= A - \dfrac{A}{4} = \dfrac{3A}{4}$.

So intensity of image will be $\dfrac{3I}{4}$.

Focal length remains as such

3. (a) Equivalent focal length,

$$\frac{1}{f} = \frac{1}{40} + \frac{1}{-25}$$

$$f = \frac{200}{3} \text{ cm}$$

$$= \frac{2}{3} \text{ m}$$

$$\therefore \quad \text{Power} = \frac{1}{f} = \frac{1}{2/3}$$

$$= \frac{3}{2} = 1.5 \text{ D}$$

4. (d) The size of image remains same but intensity of image becomes half the previous.

5. (c)

6. (c) When lens behaves like diverging in water, its material refractive index should be less than water so it will be less than 1.33.

7. (c) As $\quad I = \sqrt{I_1 I_2}$,

So $\quad A = \sqrt{A_1 A_2}$.

8. (d) Using $\quad \dfrac{\mu}{v} - \dfrac{1}{u} = \dfrac{\mu-1}{R}$

or $\quad \dfrac{\mu}{2R} - \dfrac{1}{\infty} = \dfrac{\mu-1}{R}$

$\therefore \quad \mu = 2$

9. (d) Given, $u = 12, f = -16$ cm

Now $\quad \dfrac{1}{v} - \dfrac{1}{12} = \dfrac{1}{-16}$

or $\quad v = 48$ cm.

10. (c)

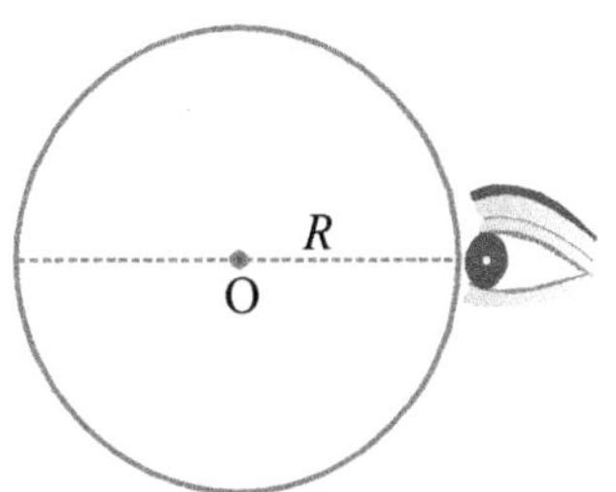

$$\frac{\mu_2}{v} - \frac{\mu_1}{u} = \frac{\mu_2 - \mu_1}{R}$$

or $\quad \dfrac{1}{v} - \dfrac{1.5}{-R} = \dfrac{1-1.5}{-R}$

$\therefore \quad v = -R$

$$= -6 \text{ cm}$$

11. (a)

12. (b)

13. (b) Magnifying power of compound microscope is proportional to length of the microscope.

14. (c)

$$M = -\frac{L}{f_0}\left(1 + \frac{D}{f_e}\right)$$

or $\quad -40 = -\dfrac{20}{5}\left(1 + \dfrac{25}{f_e}\right)$

or $\quad f_e = 2.5$ cm

15. (c)

16. (d) R. P. $\propto$ aperture of objective lens.

17. (d)

$$\frac{1}{f} = (\mu_w - 1)\left(\frac{1}{R_1} - \frac{1}{R_2}\right)$$

$$= \left(\frac{4}{3} - 1\right)\left(\frac{1}{-20} - \frac{1}{\infty}\right)$$

$\therefore \quad f = -60$ cm.

18. (c)

19. (d)

$$f_o + f_e = 36$$

and $\quad \dfrac{f_o}{f_e} = 5$

$\therefore \quad f_o = 6$ cm and $f_e = 30$ cm

20. (b)

$$M = -\frac{f_o}{f_e}\left(1 + \frac{f_e}{D}\right)$$

$$= \frac{-200}{5}\left(1 + \frac{5}{25}\right)$$

$$= -48$$

21. (c)

22. (c) Using
$$\frac{1}{f} = (\mu-1)\left(\frac{1}{R_1} - \frac{1}{R_2}\right),$$

we have
$$\frac{1}{30} = (\mu-1)\left(\frac{1}{10} - \frac{1}{\infty}\right)$$

$$\therefore \quad \mu = 1.33$$

23. (c)

24. (c)
$$\frac{1}{f_e} = \frac{1}{f} + \frac{1}{-f}$$

$$\Rightarrow \quad f_e = \infty$$

25. (a) Magnifying power,
$$M = -\frac{L}{f_o}\left(1 + \frac{D}{f_e}\right),$$

So magnifying power will increase with decrease in both f_o and f_e.

26. (a)
$$M = -\frac{f_o}{f_e}\left(1 + \frac{f_e}{D}\right), \text{ so for largest}$$

magnification, f_e should be least, which is 15 cm.

27. (d) The defect of convergence of light ray at different points on the principal axis due to different zones of the lens is called spherical aberration.

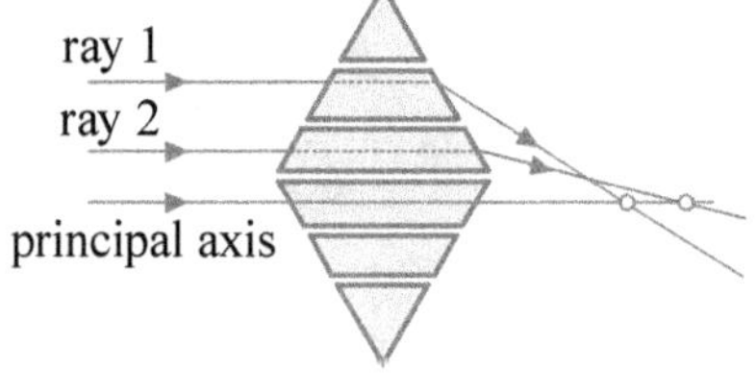

This aberration can be minimized by

(i) use of stops

(ii) use of plano-convex lenses

(iii) using two suitable lenses in contact

(iv) using two plano-convex lenses separated by distance equal to difference between their foci $d = f_1 - f_2$.

28. (c) Using,
$$\frac{\mu}{v} - \frac{1}{u} = \frac{\mu-1}{R}$$

or
$$\frac{2}{v} - \frac{1}{\infty} = \frac{2-1}{R}$$

$$\therefore \quad v = 2R$$

29. (b) The parallel rays will focus at focal point of concave lens, and so after refraction from it, they become parallel.

30. (b)
$$E = \frac{I\cos\theta}{r^2}$$

or
$$5 = \frac{I\cos 60°}{2^2}$$

$$\therefore \quad I = 40 \text{ Candela}$$

31. (c)
$$\phi = 4\pi I = 4\pi \times 1 = 4\pi$$

32. (c)
$$\phi = 4\pi L$$

$$= 4\pi \times 100 = 1256 \text{ Lumen}$$

33. (c)
$$E = \frac{L\cos\theta}{r^2}$$

$$= \frac{L \times h/r}{r^2} = \frac{Lh}{r^3}$$

1. (a) Using,
$$\frac{\mu}{v} - \frac{1}{u} = \frac{\mu-1}{R}$$

or
$$\frac{1.5}{v} - \frac{1}{-15} = \frac{1.5-1}{+30}$$

$$\therefore \quad v = -30 \text{ cm}$$

2. (b)

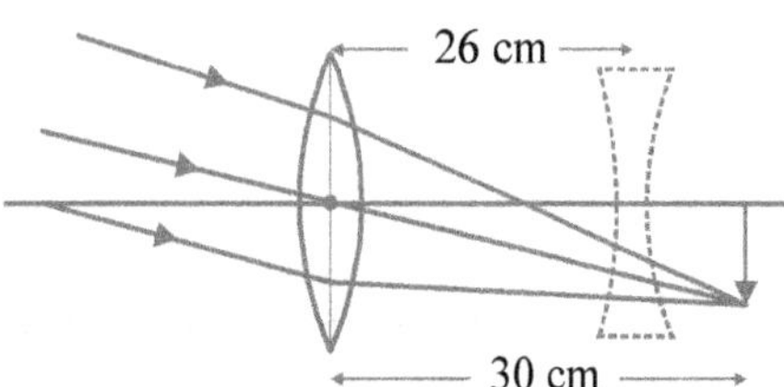

For concave lens,
$$u = +4 \text{ cm}$$
$$f = -20 \text{ cm}$$

$$\therefore \quad \frac{1}{v} - \frac{1}{4} = \frac{1}{-20}$$

or
$$v = 5 \text{ cm}$$

Now
$$\frac{I}{O} = \frac{v}{u}$$

or
$$\frac{I}{2} = \frac{5}{4}$$

or
$$I = 2.5 \text{ cm}$$

3. (a)

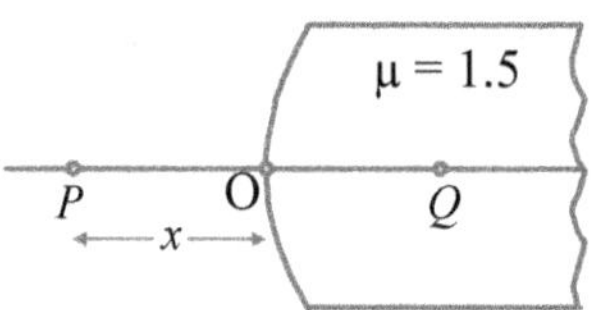

Using,
$$\frac{\mu}{v} - \frac{1}{u} = \frac{\mu-1}{R}$$

or
$$\frac{1.5}{x} - \frac{1}{-x} = \frac{(1.5-1)}{R}$$

$$\therefore \quad x = 5R$$

4.. **(b)**

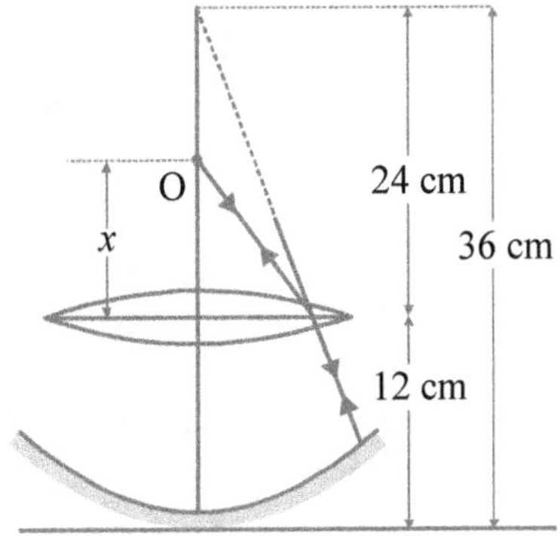

$u = 24$ cm, $v = x$

Using
$$\frac{1}{v} - \frac{1}{u} = \frac{1}{f}$$

or
$$\frac{1}{x} - \frac{1}{24} = \frac{1}{40}$$

$\therefore \qquad x = 15$ cm

5. **(c)** If f_e be the focal length of the lens, then

$$\frac{1}{f_e} = \frac{2}{15} + \frac{1}{\infty}$$

or $\qquad f_e = 7.5$ cm

Now using mirror formula, we have

$$\frac{1}{v} + \frac{1}{-20} = \frac{1}{-7.5}$$

$\therefore \qquad v = -12$ cm

6. **(b)** Form geometry

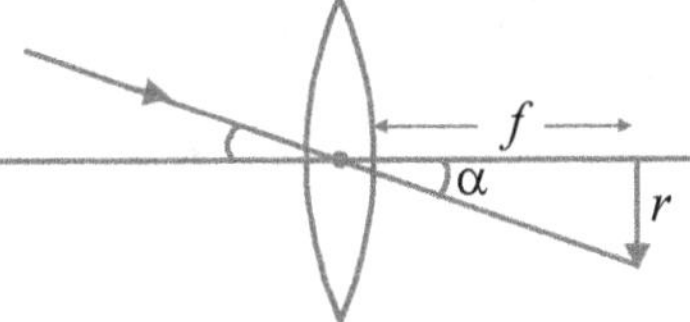

$$r = f \tan \alpha$$

$\therefore \qquad \pi r^2 = \pi f^2 \tan^2 \alpha$

or $\qquad \pi r^2 \propto f^2.$

7. **(b)**

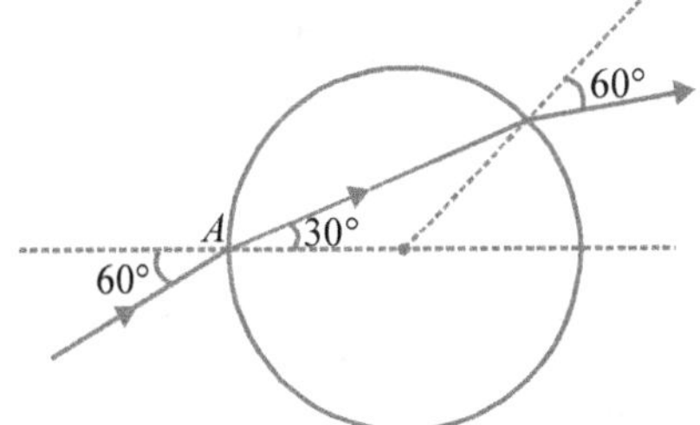

$$\mu = \frac{\sin 60°}{\sin 30°}$$

$$= \frac{\sqrt{3}/2}{1/2}$$

$$= \sqrt{3}.$$

8. **(b)**

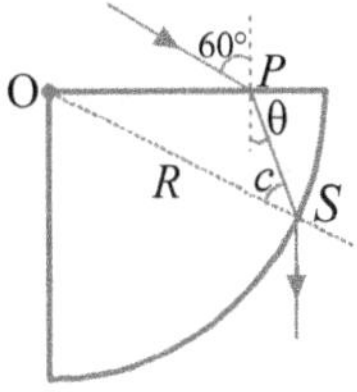

At P, $\qquad \dfrac{\sin 60°}{\sin \theta} = \sqrt{3}$

or $\qquad \sin \theta = \dfrac{1}{2}$

$\therefore \qquad \theta = 30°$

Also $\qquad \sin c = \dfrac{1}{\mu} = \dfrac{1}{\sqrt{3}}$

In ΔOPS, $\qquad \dfrac{OP}{\sin c} = \dfrac{R}{\sin(90° + \theta)}$

or $\qquad OP = \dfrac{\sin c}{\sin 120°} \times R$

$$= \frac{1}{\sqrt{3} \times \dfrac{\sqrt{3}}{2}} R$$

$$= \frac{2R}{3}$$

9. **(d)** Angle of incidence,

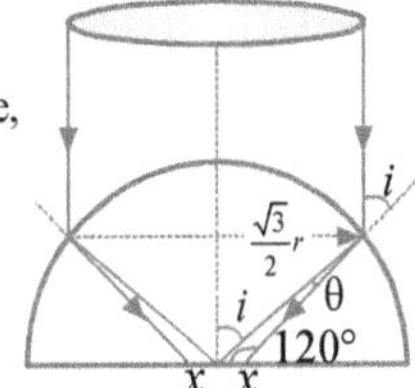

$$\sin i = \frac{\sqrt{3}r/2}{r}$$

$$= \sqrt{3}/2, \qquad i = 60°$$

By Snell's law $\qquad \mu = \dfrac{\sin i}{\sin \theta}$

or $\qquad \sqrt{3} = \dfrac{\sqrt{3}/2}{\sin \theta}$

or $\qquad \sin \theta = \dfrac{1}{2}$ or $\theta = 30°$

Now, $\qquad \dfrac{r}{\sin 120°} = \dfrac{x}{\sin \theta}$

$\therefore \qquad x = r \dfrac{\sin \theta}{\sin 120°} = \dfrac{r}{2} \times \dfrac{2}{\sqrt{3}} = \dfrac{r}{\sqrt{3}}.$

10. (d) From Snell's law,

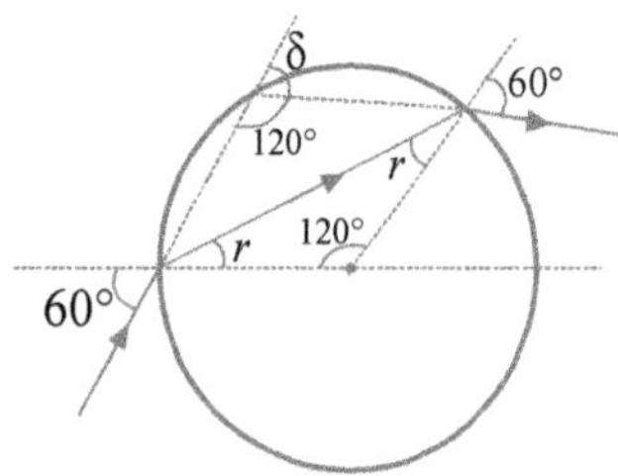

$$\frac{\sin 60°}{\sin r} = \sqrt{3}$$

or $\qquad \sin r = \dfrac{\sqrt{3}}{2 \times \sqrt{3}} = \dfrac{1}{2}$

$\therefore \qquad r = 30°$

Thus, $\qquad \delta = 60°$

11. (c) From Snell's law,

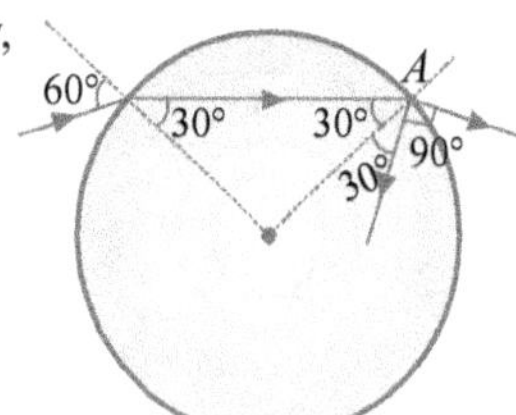

$$\mu = \frac{\sin 60°}{\sin 30°}$$

$$= \sqrt{3}$$

12. (d) From the geometry, we have

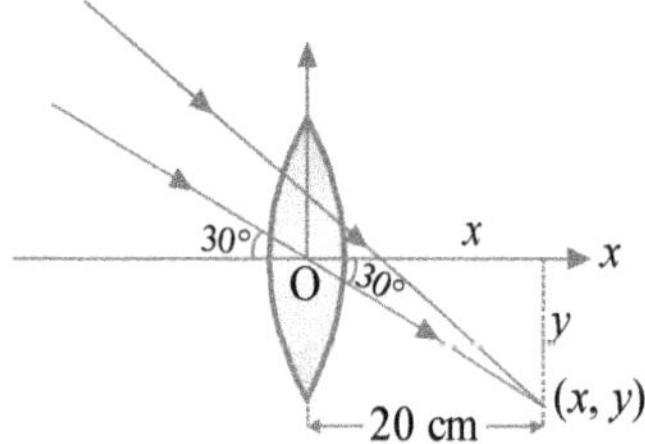

$$\frac{y}{x} = \tan 30°$$

or $\qquad y = x \tan 30°$

$$= \frac{20}{\sqrt{3}}$$

Thus co-ordinates of focus are : $\left(20, -\dfrac{20}{\sqrt{3}}\right)$.

13. (c) $\qquad P_a = P_1 + P_2 = 11 - 6 = 5D$

$$\frac{f_\ell}{f_a} = \frac{P_a}{P_\ell} = \frac{({}_a\mu_g - 1)}{({}_\ell\mu_g - 1)}$$

or $\qquad \dfrac{5}{P_\ell} = \left(\dfrac{1.5 - 1}{\dfrac{1.5}{1.6} - 1}\right)$

$\therefore \qquad P_\ell = -0.625 \, D$

14. (b) $\qquad f = \dfrac{D^2 - x^2}{4D}$

$$= \frac{100^2 - 40^2}{4 \times 100} = 21 \text{ cm}$$

$\therefore \qquad P = \dfrac{1}{f} = \dfrac{1}{21/100} \approx 5D$

15. (c) $\qquad \dfrac{1}{f_1} = \left(\dfrac{3}{2} - 1\right)\left(\dfrac{1}{\infty} - \dfrac{1}{25}\right) = -\dfrac{1}{50}$,

$$\frac{1}{f_2} = \left(\frac{4}{3} - 1\right)\left(\frac{1}{25} + \frac{1}{20}\right) = \frac{3}{100}$$

and $\qquad \dfrac{1}{f_3} = \left(\dfrac{3}{2} - 1\right)\left(\dfrac{1}{-20} - \dfrac{1}{\infty}\right) = -\dfrac{1}{40}$

Now $\qquad \dfrac{1}{f} = \dfrac{1}{f_1} + \dfrac{1}{f_2} + \dfrac{1}{f_3}$

$$= -\frac{1}{50} + \frac{3}{100} - \frac{1}{40}$$

$\therefore \qquad f = -66.6 \text{ cm}$

16. (c) $m = \pm 3$, using $\quad m = \dfrac{f}{f + u}$

For virtual image, $\quad 3 = \dfrac{f}{f - 8} \qquad \ldots \text{(i)}$

and for real image, $\quad -3 = \dfrac{f}{f - 16} \qquad \ldots \text{(ii)}$

After solving above equations, we get

$$f = 12 \text{ cm.}$$

17. (d) $\qquad \dfrac{f_1}{f_2} = \dfrac{2}{3} \qquad \ldots \text{(i)}$

and $\qquad \dfrac{1}{f_1} - \dfrac{1}{f_2} = \dfrac{1}{30} \qquad \ldots \text{(ii)}$

After solving above equations, we get

$f_1 = -15 \text{ cm}$ and $f_2 = 10 \text{ cm}$.

18. (d) For first lens :

$$\frac{1}{v_1} - \frac{1}{-30} = \frac{1}{10}$$

or $\qquad v_1 = 15 \text{ cm at I}_1.$

For second lens :

$$u_2 = 15 - 5 = 10 \text{ cm.}$$

The focal length of second lens is also 10 cm, and so it forms this image at infinity. Finally third lens forms the image at its focal point. i.e., 30 cm from it.

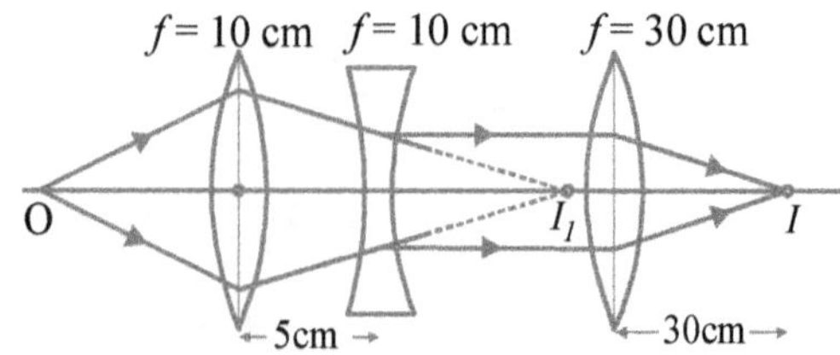

19. From the geometry of the figure

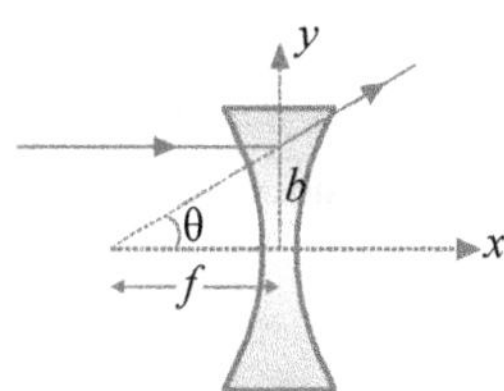

$$m = \tan\theta = \frac{b}{f}$$

Now the equation of the refracted ray

$$y = mx + c$$

or

$$y = \frac{bx}{f} + b$$

20. Using lens formula, $\dfrac{1}{v} - \dfrac{1}{u} = \dfrac{1}{f}$, we have

$$\frac{1}{v} - \frac{1}{-30} = \frac{1}{20}$$

or

$$v = +60 \text{ cm}$$

Magnification, $m = \dfrac{v}{u} = \dfrac{60}{30} = 2$.

As point P is 0.5 cm above the principal axis of the whole lens and so its image will be $2 \times 0.5 = 1$ cm, below this axis. It is $1 + 0.5 = 1.5$ cm below xy.

21. (c)

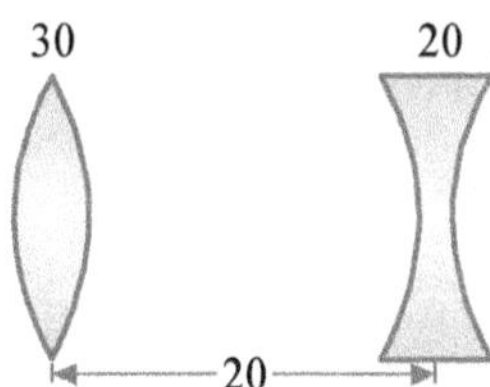

The equivalent focal length of the combination is given as

$$\frac{1}{F} = \frac{1}{f_1} + \frac{1}{f_2} - \frac{d}{f_1 f_2}$$

Here, $f_1 = 30 \text{ cm}$, $f_2 = -20 \text{ cm}$, $d = 20 \text{ cm}$

So,

$$\frac{1}{F} = \frac{1}{30} + \frac{1}{-20} - \frac{20}{30(-20)}$$

$$= \frac{1}{30} - \frac{1}{20} + \frac{20}{30 \times 20}$$

$$= \frac{1}{30} - \frac{1}{20} + \frac{1}{30}$$

$$= \frac{2 - 3 + 2}{60}$$

$$= \frac{1}{60}$$

$\Rightarrow \qquad F = 60 \text{ cm}$

22. (a)

$$\frac{1}{f_a} = (\mu - 1)\left(\frac{1}{R_1} - \frac{1}{R_2}\right)$$

$$= (1.5 - 1)\left(\frac{1}{-R} - \frac{1}{+R}\right)$$

or $\qquad f_a = -R$

Focal length in liquid

$$f_l = f_a\left(\frac{{}_a\mu_g - 1}{\dfrac{{}_a\mu_g}{{}_a\mu_l} - 1}\right)$$

$$= -R\left(\frac{1.5 - 1}{\dfrac{1.5}{1.75} - 1}\right)$$

$$= 3.5 R$$

23. (a)

Equivalent focal length

$$\frac{1}{f_e} = \frac{2}{f_l} + \frac{1}{f_m}$$

$$= \frac{2}{-20} + \frac{1}{\infty}$$

or $\qquad f_e = -10 \text{ cm}$

So $\qquad f = -(-10) = 10 \text{ cm}$.

This system behaves like a convex lens of focal length 10 cm.

24. (a)

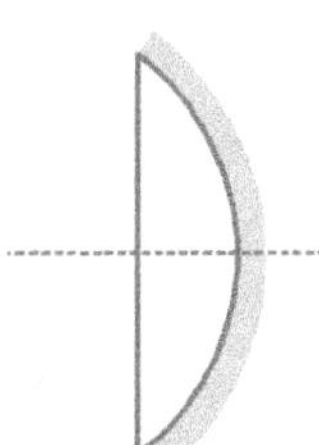

$$\frac{1}{f_e} = \frac{2}{f_l} + \frac{1}{f_m}$$

where

$$\frac{1}{f_l} = (\mu - 1)\left(\frac{1}{R} - \frac{1}{\infty}\right)$$

$$= (1.5 - 1)\left(\frac{1}{30}\right)$$

or $\qquad f_l = 60 \text{ cm}$

Now,

$$\frac{1}{f_e} = \frac{2}{60} + \frac{1}{15}$$

$\therefore \qquad f_e = 10 \text{ cm}$

If object is put on $2f_e = 20$ cm, then its image will coincide with the object.

25. (b)

$$\frac{1}{f_1} = (\mu - 1)\left[\frac{1}{R_1} - \frac{1}{R_2}\right]$$

$$\frac{1}{f_1} = (1.5 - 1)\left[\frac{1}{14} - \frac{1}{\infty}\right]$$

$$\frac{1}{f_1} = \frac{0.5}{14}$$

$$\frac{1}{f_1} = (1.2 - 1)\left[\frac{1}{\infty} - \frac{1}{-14}\right]$$

$$\frac{1}{f_2} = \frac{0.2}{14}$$

$$\frac{1}{f} = \frac{1}{f_1} + \frac{1}{f_2} = \frac{0.5}{14} + \frac{0.2}{14}$$

$$\frac{1}{f} = \frac{0.7}{14}$$

$$\frac{1}{v} = \frac{7}{140} - \frac{1}{40} = \frac{1}{20} - \frac{1}{40}$$

$$\frac{1}{v} = \frac{2-1}{40}$$

$$v = 40 \text{ cm}$$

26. (a) $f_0 = 2\text{cm}$, $f_e = 3$ cm, $L = 15$ m

we have $v_0 + f_e = 15$

or $v_0 + 3 = 15$

or $v_0 = 12$ cm

For objective lens,

$$\frac{1}{v_0} - \frac{1}{u_0} = \frac{1}{f_0}$$

or

$$\frac{1}{+12} - \frac{1}{u_0} = \frac{1}{2}$$

$\therefore$ $u_0 = -2.4$ cm

27. (b) $f_0 = 60$ cm and $f_e = 5$ cm

Magnification $M = \dfrac{f_0}{f_e} = \dfrac{\beta}{\alpha}$

or

$$\frac{60}{5} = \frac{\beta}{2°}$$

$\therefore$ $\beta = 24°$

28. (a)

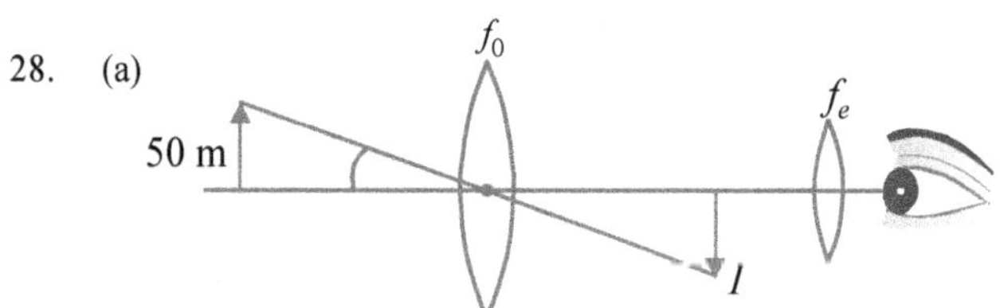

From similar triangle,

$$\frac{50\text{m}}{2\text{km}} = \frac{I}{200 \text{ cm}}$$

$\therefore$ $I = 5$ cm

29. (a)   Focal length of plano-convex lens

$$f_e = \frac{R}{\mu - 1}$$

When plane side is silvered

Now

$$\frac{1}{f} = \frac{2}{f_e} + \frac{1}{f_m}$$

or

$$\frac{1}{30} = 2\frac{(\mu - 1)}{R} + \frac{1}{\infty} \qquad \ldots \text{(i)}$$

when convex side is silvered

$$\frac{1}{f} = \frac{2}{f_e} + \frac{1}{f_m}$$

or

$$\frac{1}{10} = \frac{2(\mu - 1)}{R} + \frac{2}{R} \qquad \ldots \text{(ii)}$$

On solving above equations we get

$$\mu = 1.5$$

30. (b)   When lenses are in contact

$$\frac{1}{f_1} + \frac{1}{f_2} = \frac{1}{60} \qquad \ldots \text{(i)}$$

When lenses are at separation,

$$\frac{1}{f_1} + \frac{1}{f_2} - \frac{10}{f_1 f_2} = \frac{1}{30} \qquad \ldots \text{(ii)}$$

On solving above equations, we get

$$f_1 = 20\text{cm}, \ f_2 = -30\text{cm}.$$

31. (d)   If f_e is the effective focal length of the system, then

$$\frac{1}{f_e} = \frac{2}{f_e} + \frac{1}{f_m}$$

$$= \frac{2}{12} + \frac{1}{\infty}$$

$\therefore$ $f_e = 6$ cm

Now using mirror formula,

$$f = -6 \text{ cm}$$

$$\frac{1}{v} + \frac{1}{-20} = \frac{1}{-6}$$

$\therefore$ $v = -8.6$ cm   **Ans.**

Solutions EXERCISE 3.2

1. (a, b, c)

$$\mu = A + \frac{B}{\lambda^2}, \text{ also} \quad \frac{1}{f} = (\mu - 1)\left(\frac{1}{R_1} - \frac{1}{R_2}\right) \text{ and}$$

so focal length, power and chromatic aberration depend on wavelength.

2. (b, d)

3. (a, b, c, d)

The speed of light in air is same in all frames.

4. (a, d)

In lens formula $\dfrac{1}{v} - \dfrac{1}{u} = \dfrac{1}{f}$, $\dfrac{1}{u}$ and $\dfrac{1}{v}$ are linearly related.

Also $m = \dfrac{v}{u} = 1 - \dfrac{v}{f}$,

so m and v are linearly related.

5. (a, c)

6. (a, b, c, d)

Magnification, $M = -\dfrac{f_0}{f_e} = -\dfrac{1600}{2}$

$$= -800.$$

$$L = f_0 + f_e$$

$$= 16 + 0.02 = 16.02 \text{ m}$$

Solutions EXERCISE 3.3

1. (d) Any size of lens, can form full image, only intensity of image decreases with decrease in size.

2. (d) In convex lens the minimum distance between object and its real image will be $4f$.

3. (c) The rays from centre of hemisphere cut at the centre after refraction - Snell's law is valid in each case of refraction.

4. (d) Half painted lens forms full image with half intensity.

5. (d)
$$f_w = f\frac{_a\mu_g - 1}{\left(\dfrac{_a\mu_g}{_a\mu_w} - 1\right)} = f\frac{\left(\dfrac{3}{2} - 1\right)}{\left(\dfrac{3/2}{4/3} - 1\right)}$$
$$= 4f$$

6. (c) Apparent distance, $x = 1 + \dfrac{1}{\mu} + 1$
$$= 1 + \dfrac{1}{3/2} + 1 = \dfrac{8}{3} \text{ cm.}$$

7. (d)

8. (a) RP $\propto$ diameter of objective.

9. (d) $\dfrac{1}{v} - \dfrac{1}{-f} = \dfrac{1}{-f}$; $\therefore$ $v = \dfrac{f}{2}$.

10. (a)

11. (c)
$$\frac{1}{f} = (\mu - 1)\left(\frac{1}{R_1} - \frac{1}{R_2}\right)$$
$$= (1.5 - 1)\left(\frac{1}{R} - \frac{1}{-R}\right)$$
or $\quad f = R$.

12. (d) If the rays cross focal point of convex lens, they become diverging.

13. (a) Microwaves produce no luminous flux.

14. (c)

15. (c) Dimensions of lumnous flux and radiant flux are same but the unit of luminous flux is luimen while that of radiant flux is watt.

16. (a)

17. (a) $\quad M = \dfrac{D}{f_e} = \dfrac{50}{5} = 10.$

18. (a) $\dfrac{\mu_2}{v} - \dfrac{\mu_1}{u} = \dfrac{\mu_2 - \mu_1}{R}$, can be used for plane surfaces, if $R = \infty$.

Solutions EXERCISE 3.4

Passage for (Qs. 1 - 3) :

1. (a) For convex lens :
$$\frac{1}{v} - \frac{1}{-30} = \frac{1}{10}$$
or $\quad v = 15$ cm

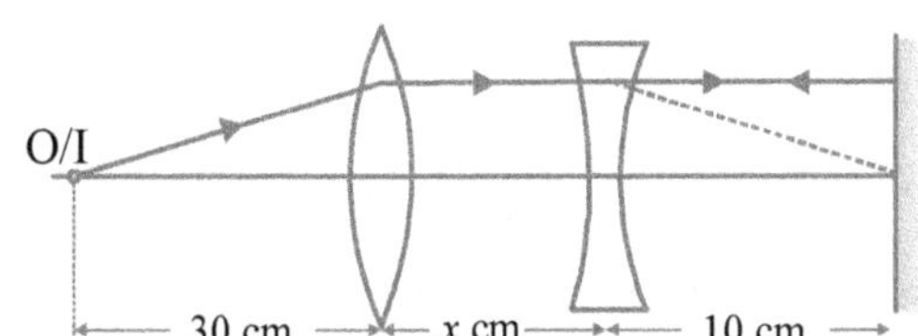

For $x = 5$ cm, the rays will retrace the path after reflection from mirror and the final image is formed on object itself.

2. (a) For second convex lens ;
$u = \infty$, and so $v = 30$ cm

3. (d)

Passage for (Qs. 4 - 6) :

4. (d) Also $\quad \dfrac{1}{v} - \dfrac{1}{u} = \dfrac{1}{f}$
or $\quad \dfrac{1}{(D-x)} - \dfrac{1}{-x} = \dfrac{1}{f}$
or $\quad x^2 - Dx + fD = 0$
$\therefore \quad x = \dfrac{D \pm \sqrt{D^2 - 4fD}}{2}$

For real image, $D^2 - 4fD \geq 0$, or $D \geq 4f$.

5. (a)
$$u + v = D$$
and $\quad v - u = x$
$\therefore \quad u = \dfrac{D-x}{2}$, and $v = \dfrac{D+x}{2}$

Using lens formula, we have
$$\frac{1}{\left(\dfrac{D+x}{2}\right)} - \frac{1}{-\left(\dfrac{D-x}{2}\right)} = \frac{1}{f}$$
or $\quad f = \left(\dfrac{D^2 - x^2}{4D}\right)$
or $\quad x = \sqrt{D(D - 4f)}$.

6. (c) $I_1 = \dfrac{v}{u}o$ and $I_2 = \dfrac{u}{v}o$
$$\therefore \quad \frac{I_2}{I_1} = \frac{u^2}{v^2}$$
$$= \left[\frac{(D-x)/2}{(D+x)/2}\right]^2$$
$$= \left[\frac{D-x}{D+x}\right]^2.$$

Passage for (Qs. 7 & 8) :

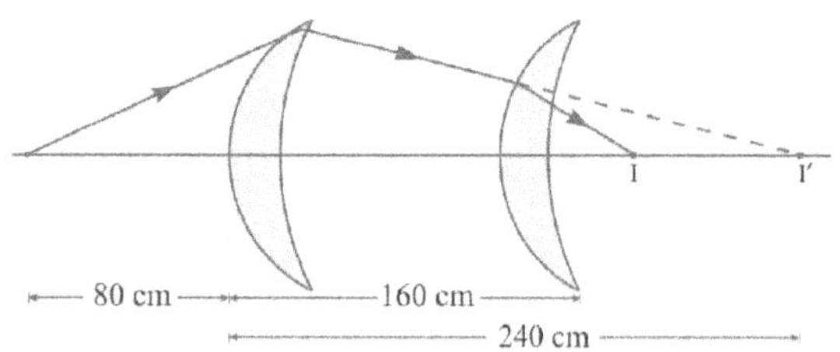

For the given lens, $R_1 = +20$ cm, $R_2 = 60$ cm.

Focal length of the lens is given by

$$\frac{1}{f} = (\mu - 1)\left(\frac{1}{R_1} - \frac{1}{R_2}\right)$$

or

$$\frac{1}{f} = (1.5 - 1)\left(\frac{1}{20} - \frac{1}{60}\right)$$

or $\qquad f = 60$ cm

7   (b)   For $\quad u = -20$ cm,

$$\frac{1}{v} - \frac{1}{-80} = \frac{1}{60}$$

or

$$\frac{1}{v} = \frac{1}{60} - \frac{1}{80}$$

$\therefore \qquad v = 240$ cm.

Thus the real image will form on the right of the lens. If we reverse the face of the lens, then the position of image will not change.

8.   (a)   When second lens is placed, the image of first lens becomes object for it and so for the second lens;

$$u = +(240 - 160) = 80 \text{ cm}$$

$\therefore \qquad \dfrac{1}{v} - \dfrac{1}{80} = \dfrac{1}{60}$

or $\qquad \dfrac{1}{v} = \dfrac{7}{240}$

$\therefore \qquad v = 34.3$ cm.

The final image is thus formed to the right of second lens at a distance of 34.3 cm.

9.   **A-p, r; B-q,s,t; C-p,r,t, D-q,s**

(a)   When $\mu_1 < \mu_2$, the ray of light while entering the lens will bend towards the normal. Therefore p, r are the correct options

(B)   When $\mu_1 > \mu_2$, the ray of light while entering the lens will bend away from the normal. Therefore q,s,t are the correct options.

(C)   When $\mu_2 = \mu_3$, the ray of light while coming out from the lens does not deviate from its path. Therefore p,r,t are the correct option.

(D) $\mu_2 > \mu_3$, the ray of light coming out of the lens deviates away from the normal. Therefore q,s are the correct options.

12.   A-(s); B-(q) ; C-(p); D-(r)

13.   A-(r, s, t); B-(p, q, t) ; C-(r, s); D-(r, s, t)

Solutions EXERCISE 3.5

1.   For the object O,

$$u = -(PO)$$
$$= -3 \text{ cm}$$

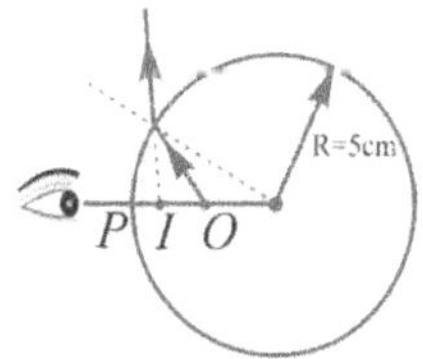

By refraction formula,

$$\frac{\mu_2}{v} - \frac{\mu_1}{u} = \frac{\mu_2 - \mu_1}{R}, \text{ we have}$$

$\mu_1 = 1.5$, $\mu_2 = 1$, and $R = -5$ cm

$\therefore \qquad \dfrac{1}{v} - \dfrac{1.5}{-3} = \dfrac{1 - 1.5}{-5}$

$\Rightarrow \qquad v = -2.5$ cm   **Ans.**

2.   For concave lens, $\quad u = +10$ cm (virtual object)

and $\qquad v = +15$ cm

We have $\qquad \dfrac{1}{+15} - \dfrac{1}{+10} = \dfrac{1}{f}$

$\therefore \qquad f = -30$ cm.   **Ans.**

3.   For the two positions of the lens, the image is formed on the same screen. So according to reversibility of path of light when object is at a distance u, its image will be at a distance v from the lens and vice versa (see figure.)

$\therefore \qquad |v| - |u| = 36 \qquad \ldots (i)$

and $\qquad \left|\dfrac{v}{u}\right| = 2 \qquad \ldots (ii)$

On solving above equations, we get

$$|u| = 36 \text{ cm and } |v| = 72 \text{ cm}$$

Now from lens formula, $\dfrac{1}{v} - \dfrac{1}{u} = \dfrac{1}{f}$, we have

$$\frac{1}{72} - \frac{1}{-36} = \frac{1}{f}$$

$\therefore \qquad f = 24$ cm   **Ans.**

4.   For convex lens, $u = -15$ cm, $f = +30$ cm.

By lens formula $\qquad \dfrac{1}{v} - \dfrac{1}{u} = \dfrac{1}{f}$, we have

$$\frac{1}{v} - \frac{1}{-15} = \frac{1}{+30}$$

$$\therefore \qquad v = -30 \text{ cm}.$$

Thus lens forms virtual image B of the object A. The image B becomes object for plane mirror, which is at a distance $30 + 15 = 45$ cm. Plane mirror forms the image C and finally lens forms the image D(see figure). The image C formed by mirror (becomes object for lens, so

$$u = -60, f = +30 \text{ cm}$$

$$\therefore \qquad \frac{1}{v} - \frac{1}{-60} = \frac{1}{30}$$

$$\text{or} \qquad v = 60 \text{ cm}$$

Thus final image D is formed at a distance 60 cm from the lens.

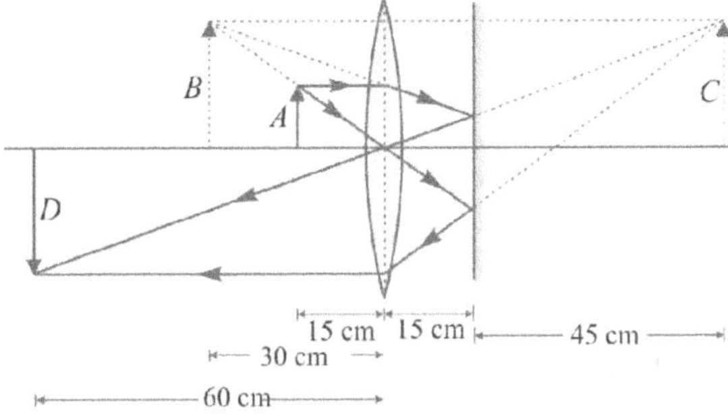

5. For convex lens, $u = -40$ cm $f = +20$ cm

$$\therefore \qquad \frac{1}{v} - \frac{1}{-40} = \frac{1}{+20}$$

$$\text{or} \qquad v = +40 \text{ cm}$$

The image I_1 formed by lens behaves as virtual object for the mirror and so for concave mirror,

$$\text{or} \qquad v = +(40 - 30) = 10 \text{ cm},$$

$$f = -10 \text{ cm}$$

By mirror formula, $\dfrac{1}{v} + \dfrac{1}{u} = \dfrac{1}{f}$

$$\frac{1}{v} + \frac{1}{+10} = \frac{1}{-10}$$

$$\therefore \qquad v = -5 \text{ cm}$$

This image I_2 (on being real) again becomes object for the lens, and so for convex lens.

$$u = -(30 - 5) = -25$$

$$f = +20 \text{ cm}$$

we have $\qquad \dfrac{1}{v} - \dfrac{1}{-25} = \dfrac{1}{20}$

$$\therefore \qquad v = +100 \text{ cm}$$

Thus a real image I_3 will form at a distance of 100 cm from the lens (see figure).

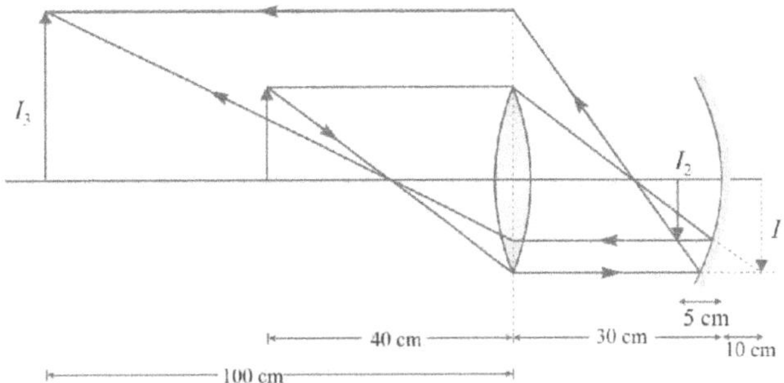

6. The object (ground) is very large distance from the lens, so its image will form at focus of the lens. If x is the length of ground photographed then by similar triangles, we have

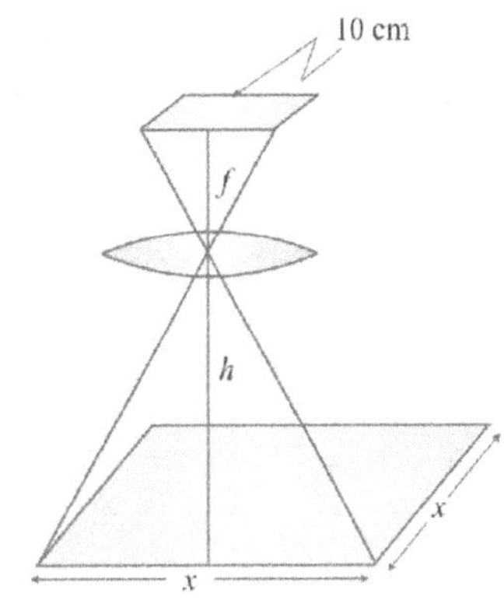

$$\frac{x}{h} = \frac{0.1}{f}$$

$$\therefore \qquad x = h\frac{0.1}{f}$$

$$= 10 \times 10^3 \times \frac{0.1}{1}$$

$$= 1000 \text{ m} = 1 \text{ km}$$

Thus area of the ground to be photographed will be $= x \times x = 1 \times 1 \text{ km}^2 = 1 \text{ km}^2$ ***Ans.***

1. The apparent position of the object O from the surface of water is

$$AD = \frac{RD}{\mu} = \frac{0.4}{4/3}$$

$$= 0.3 \ (AO')$$

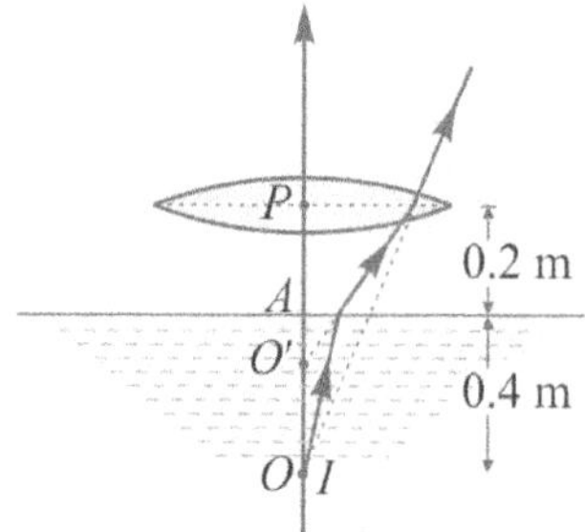

The distance $\quad PI' = 0.3 + 0.2 = 0.5$ m

For convex lens, $\quad u = -0.5$ m, $f = +3$ m

By lens formula, $\quad \dfrac{1}{v} - \dfrac{1}{u} = \dfrac{1}{f}$, we have

$$\frac{1}{v} - \frac{1}{-0.5} = \frac{1}{3}$$

$$\therefore \qquad v = -0.6 \text{ m } \textbf{\textit{Ans.}}$$

Thus image will form at the position of object.

2. For convex lens, $u = -15$ cm, $f = +10$ cm.

By lens formula, $\quad \dfrac{1}{v} - \dfrac{1}{u} = \dfrac{1}{f}$, we have

$$\frac{1}{v} - \frac{1}{-15} = \frac{1}{10}$$

$$\therefore \qquad v = 30 \text{ cm}$$

If we place a diverging mirror on the same principal axis to get the image on the object itself, then the image formed by the lens must lie on the coc of the mirror (see figure). Thus the distance between lens and mirror $= 30 - 24 = 6$ cm

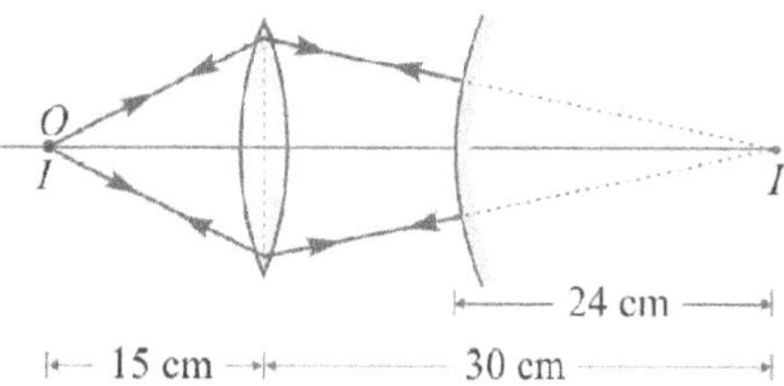

3. If y is the distance falls by the ball in time t, then $y = \dfrac{1}{2}gt^2$. The distance of the ball from the point P of the sphere,

$$u = -\left(y_0 - \frac{1}{2}gt^2\right) \text{ and velocity of ball, } v_0 = gt .$$

By refraction formula

$$\frac{\mu}{v} - \frac{1}{u} = \frac{\mu - 1}{R} \qquad \text{... (i)}$$

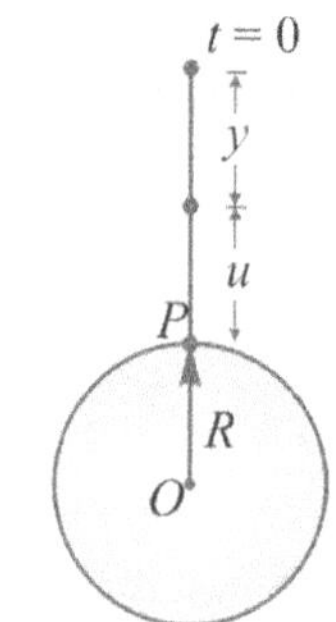

$$\frac{\mu}{v} - \frac{1}{-\left(y_0 - \dfrac{1}{2}gt^2\right)} = \frac{\mu - 1}{+R}$$

$$\therefore \qquad v = \left[\frac{(\mu-1)\left(y_0 - \dfrac{1}{2}gt^2\right) - R}{R\left(y_0 - \dfrac{1}{2}gt^2\right)}\right]$$

Differentiating equation (i) , we have

$$\mu\left(-\frac{1}{v^2}\right)\frac{dv}{dt} - \left(\frac{-1}{u^2}\right)\frac{du}{dt} = 0$$

$$\therefore \qquad \frac{dv}{dt} = \frac{1}{\mu}\frac{v^2}{u^2}\left(\frac{du}{dt}\right)$$

Or image velocity $v_i = \dfrac{1}{\mu}\dfrac{v^2}{u^2}v_0$.

After substituting the values of u, v and v_0, we get

$$v_i = \frac{\mu R^2 gt}{\left[(\mu-1)\left(y_0 - \dfrac{1}{2}gt^2\right) - R\right]^2}$$

$$\textbf{\textit{Ans.}}$$

4. For convex lens, $u = -0.4$ m, $f = +0.3$ m.

By lens formula, $\quad \dfrac{1}{v} - \dfrac{1}{u} = \dfrac{1}{f}$, we have

$$\frac{1}{v} - \frac{1}{-0.4} = \frac{1}{0.3}$$

$$\therefore \qquad v = 1.2 \text{ m}$$

The rate of change of position of the image can be calculated as;

$$v_i = \frac{v^2}{u^2}v_0$$

$$= \left(\frac{1.2}{0.4}\right)^2 \times (0.01)$$

$$= 0.09 \text{ m/s} \qquad \textbf{\textit{Ans.}}$$

The lateral magnification is given by

$$m = \frac{v}{u}$$

$$\therefore \qquad \frac{dm}{dt} = \left[\frac{u\dfrac{dv}{dt} - v\dfrac{du}{dt}}{u^2}\right]$$

$$= \frac{-0.4(0.09) - 1.2(0.01)}{(-0.4)^2}$$

$$= -0.3 \text{ per second. } \textbf{\textit{Ans.}}$$

5. The image of sun will form at the focus of the lens. Thus by geometry for small angle

$$\theta = \frac{d}{f}$$

or $$d = f\theta$$

$$\therefore \qquad d = 0.5 \times \left(\frac{32}{60} \times \frac{\pi}{180}\right) = 4\pi \times 10^{-3}\text{m} .$$

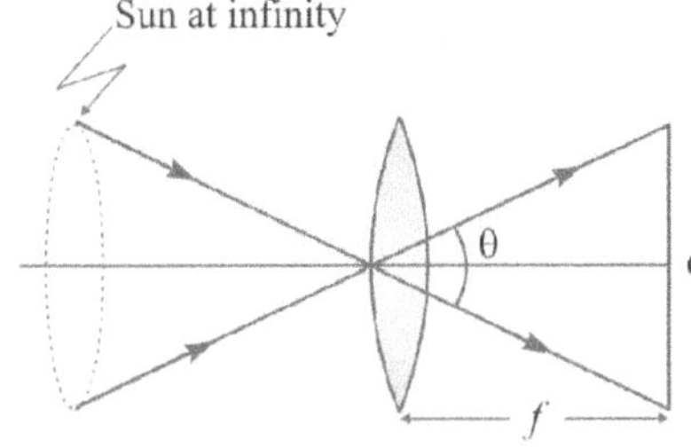

6. (a) When paperweight is placed with plane face on the printed page, the refraction takes place from spherical surface. Thus from refraction formula,

$$\frac{\mu_2}{v} - \frac{\mu_1}{u} = \frac{\mu_2 - \mu_1}{R}$$

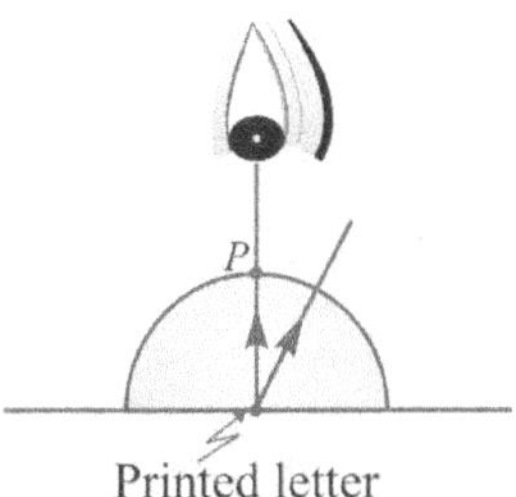

Here $\mu_2 = 1$, $\mu_1 = \mu = \dfrac{3}{2}$

$$u = -R$$
[Distances are measured from P]

Now $$\frac{1}{v} - \frac{\mu}{-R} = \frac{1-\mu}{R}$$

$$\therefore \qquad v = R$$
$$= 3.0 \text{ cm} \qquad \textbf{\textit{Ans.}}$$

(b) When paper weight is inverted, the refraction will occur from plane face.

$$\therefore \qquad v = \frac{u}{\mu} = \frac{3.0}{3/2} = 2.0 \text{ cm} \qquad \textbf{\textit{Ans.}}$$

7. The situation is shown in figure.

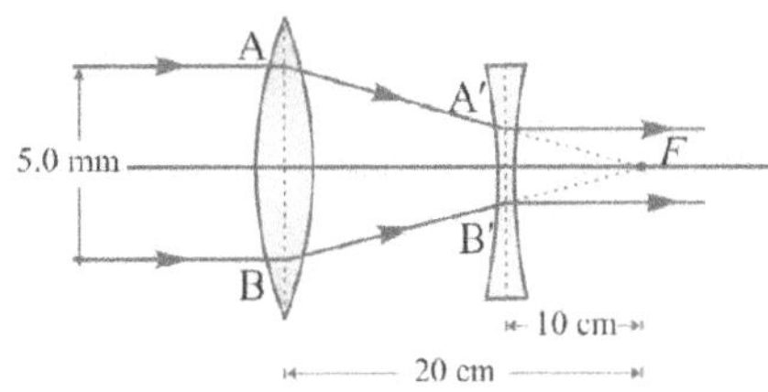

Rays incident parallel to principal axis of the convex lens will converge at focus F. As F also be the focus of the concave lens, so the rays become parallel after emerging from the concave lens. From similar triangles ABF and $A'B'F$, we have

$$\frac{AB}{20} = \frac{A'B'}{10}$$

$$\therefore \qquad A'B' = \frac{AB}{2} = \frac{5.0}{2} = 2.50 \text{ mm} \quad Ans$$

8. The observer must be at one of the points in the area BAC.

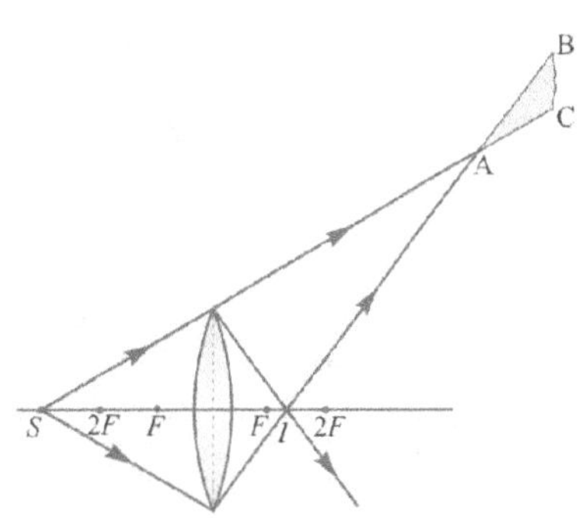

9.

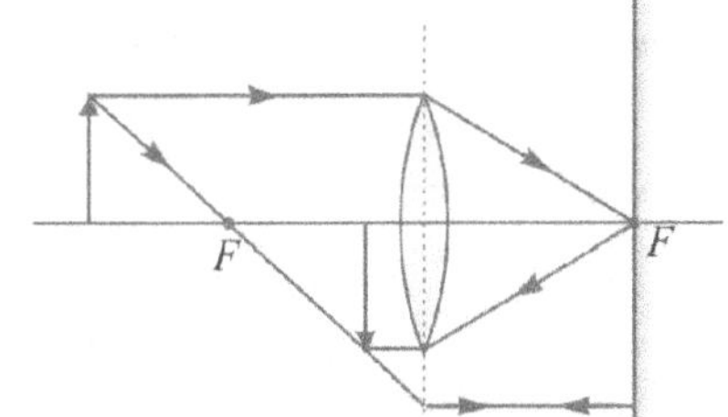

10. See ray diagrams.

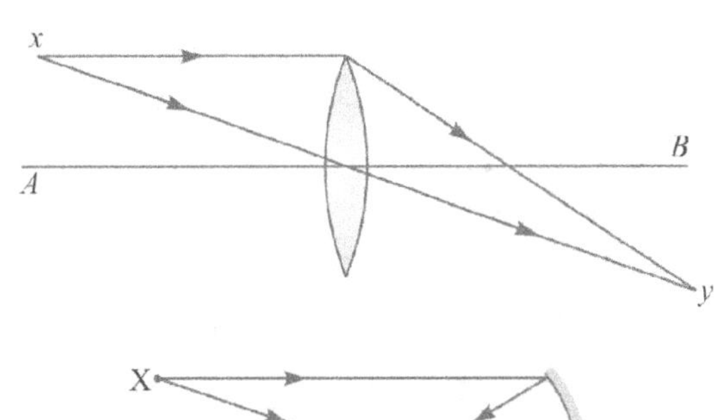

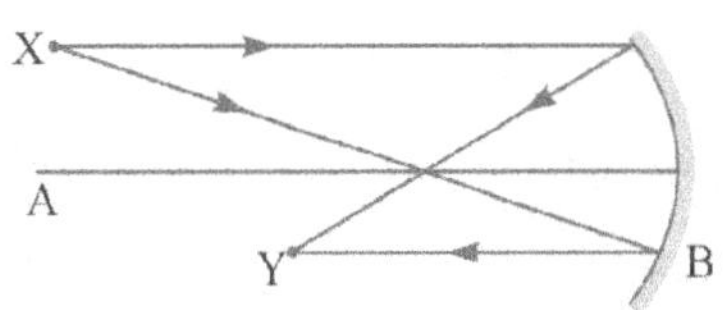

11. Convex lens will form the image I_1 of the object O. The image I_1 becomes the object for plane mirror. The final image I_2 is formed after two refractions and one reflection from the mirror, so we can write,

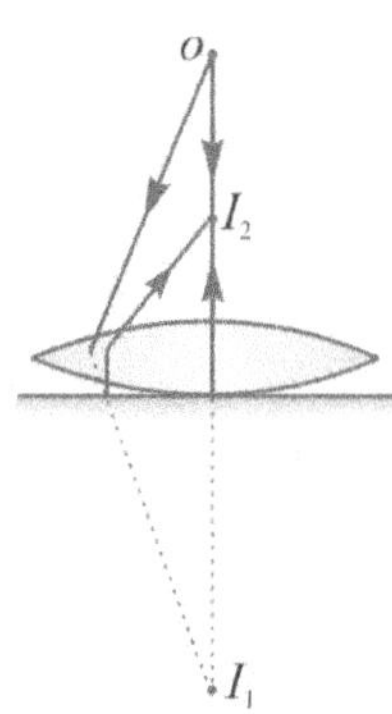

$$\frac{1}{f_e} = \frac{2}{f_\ell} + \frac{1}{f_m}$$

$$= \frac{2}{10} + \frac{1}{\infty}$$

$$\therefore \quad f_e = 5 \text{ cm}$$

The system behaves like a concave mirror, so we can use mirror formula,

$$\frac{1}{v} + \frac{1}{u} = \frac{1}{f}$$

or $$\frac{1}{v} + \frac{1}{-15} = \frac{1}{-5}$$

$$\therefore \quad v = -7.5 \text{ cm.} \qquad \textbf{\textit{Ans.}}$$

12. For eyepiece, $v_e = -25$ cm, $f_e = +5$ cm.

By lens formula, $\dfrac{1}{v} - \dfrac{1}{u} = \dfrac{1}{f}$, we have

$$\frac{1}{-25} - \frac{1}{u_e} = \frac{1}{+5}$$

$$\therefore \quad u_e = -\frac{25}{6} \text{cm}$$

For the objective lens,

$$v_O = L - |u_e|$$

$$= 20 - \frac{25}{6} = \frac{95}{6} \text{ cm}$$

Now $$\frac{1}{+\frac{95}{6}} - \frac{1}{u_o} = \frac{1}{+0.95}$$

$$\therefore \quad u_0 = -\frac{95}{94} \text{cm}$$

Total magnification, $$M = -\frac{v_o}{u_o}\left(1 + \frac{D}{f_e}\right)$$

$$= -\frac{(95/6)}{(-95/94)}\left(1 + \frac{25}{5}\right)$$

$$= -94 \qquad \textbf{\textit{Ans.}}$$

13. If f_1 and f_2 be the focal lengths of corrective lenses of left and right eyes respectively, then

$$\frac{1}{f_1} = \frac{1}{-40} - \frac{1}{-25} \text{ and } \frac{1}{f_2} = \frac{1}{-100} - \frac{1}{-25}$$

After solving, we get, $f_1 = \dfrac{200}{3}$ cm and $f_2 = \dfrac{100}{3}$ cm.

For making a telescope, eyepiece should be of smaller focal length. Thus right eye corrective lens can be used for the purpose. For relaxed eye magnification is given by

$$|M| = \frac{f_o}{f_e} = \frac{f_1}{f_2} = \frac{200/3}{100/3}$$

$$= 2 \qquad \textbf{\textit{Ans.}}$$

14. (i) For objective lens,

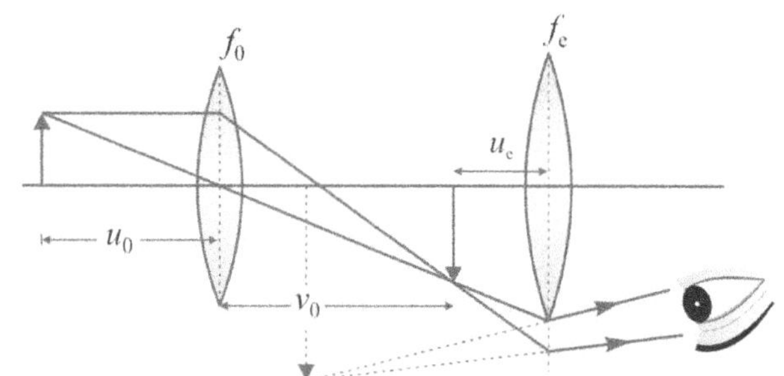

$$\frac{1}{v_o} - \frac{1}{-200} = \frac{1}{+50}$$

$$\therefore \quad v_o = \frac{200}{3} \text{cm}$$

For eyepiece,

$$\frac{1}{-25} - \frac{1}{u_e} = \frac{1}{+5}$$

$$\therefore \quad u_e = \frac{-25}{6} \text{ cm}$$

The separation between the objective and eyepiece

$$L = v_o + |u_e| = \frac{200}{3} + \frac{25}{6} = 70.8 \text{ cm}$$

(ii) The required magnification is calculated as

$$M = M_o \times M_e,$$

where $$|M_o| = \frac{v_o}{u_o} = \frac{200/3}{200} = \frac{1}{3}$$

and $$|M_e| = \frac{v_e}{u_e} = \frac{25}{25/6} = 6$$

$$\therefore \quad M = \frac{1}{3} \times 6 = 2. \qquad \textbf{\textit{Ans.}}$$

★ ★ ★

Chapter 4

Wave Optics

(183- 244)

4.1 WAVE OPTICS : AN INTRODUCTION

In geometrical optics, we have represented light as rays which travel in straight lines in a homogeneous medium. By doing this, we have studied a variety of phenomenon involving mirrors and lenses. The phenomenon like interference and diffraction can not be explained on the bases of particle nature of light. These phenomenon can only be explained on the basis of wave nature of light. This part of optics is called **physical optics**.

The wave theory of light was presented by Christiaan Huygens in 1678. During that period Newton's corpuscular theory had satisfactorily explained the phenomenon of reflection, refraction and rectilinear propagation of light. So scientist believed in the corpuscular theory; no one really believed in Huygen's wave theory. The wave characteristics of light was not really accepted until the interference experiments of Young in 1801. It should be pointed out that Huygens did not know whether the light waves were longitudinal or transverse and also how they propagate through vacuum. It was then explained by Maxwell by introducing electromagnetic wave theory in nineteenth century.

4.2 HUYGENS' PRINCIPLE

Huygens principle provides a geometrical method which allows us to determine the shape of the wavefront at any time, if the shape of the wavefront at an earlier time is known. A wave front is the locus of the points which are in the same phase. Huygens' principle can be stated as follows :

(i)   Each point of a given wavefront is a source of new disturbance which is called secondary disturbance. The wavelets originated from these points spread out in all directions with the speed of light.

(ii)   The envelope of these wavelets in the forward direction gives the shape and position of the new wavefront at any subsequent time.

To understand this consider a spherical wave front AB as shown in figure. Every point such as 1, 2, . etc. on AB becomes the source of secondary spherical wavelets. After time t the radius of each wavelet will be ct, where c is the speed of the light. Thus from the points 1, 2, 3,.... etc draw spheres of radii equal to ct. These spheres represent the secondary wavelets. According to Huygens the common envelope A_1B_1 in forward direction gives the position of new wavefront (see *fig.* 4.1).

Proof of law of reflection

Let xy be a reflecting surface. AMB is a plane wavefront incident at an angle i. All the particles on AB vibrate in same phase.

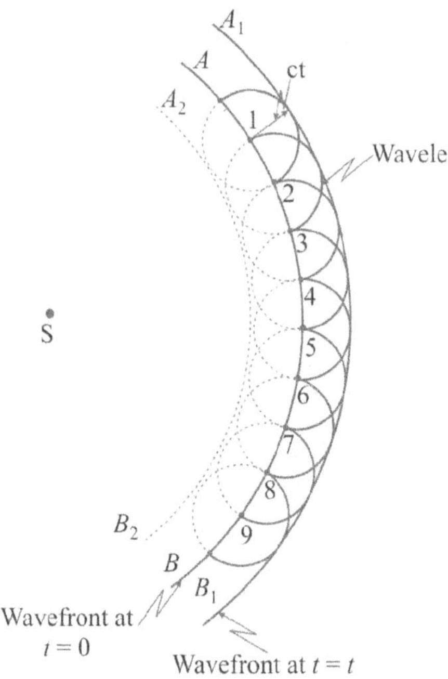

(a) Spherical wavefront.

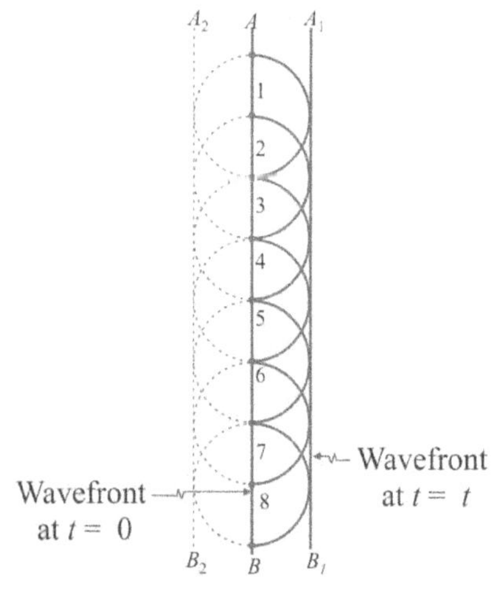

(b) Plane wavefront.

Fig. **4.1**

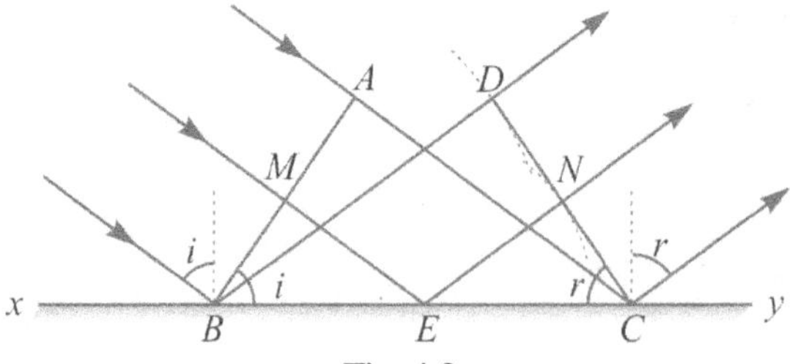

Fig. **4.2**

In the time the disturbance at A reaches C, the secondary waves from B will travel a distance BD such that $BD = AC$. With the point B as centre and radius equal to AC draw an arc. From the point C, draw the tangent CD.

In triangles BAC and BDC; BC is common and $BD = AC$

$$\angle BAC \;=\; \angle BDC = 90°$$

∴   The two triangles are congruent, and so

$$\angle ABC \;=\; \angle BCD$$

or $\qquad\qquad\qquad\qquad\qquad i \;=\; r.$

Thus angle of incidence is equal to angle of reflection. This proves the law of reflection.

Proof of law of refraction

Let xy is the interface between two media 1 and 2 of refractive indexes μ_1 and μ_2 respectively. Suppose v_1 and v_2 are the velocities of light in two media. The second medium is optically denser than first and so $v_2 < v_1$. AMB is the plane wavefront incident at an angle i. In the time disturbance at B reaches C, the secondary waves from A will travel a distance $AD = v_2 t$, where t is the time taken by the waves to travel the distance BC. Thus

$$BC = v_1 t$$
and
$$AD = v_2 t.$$

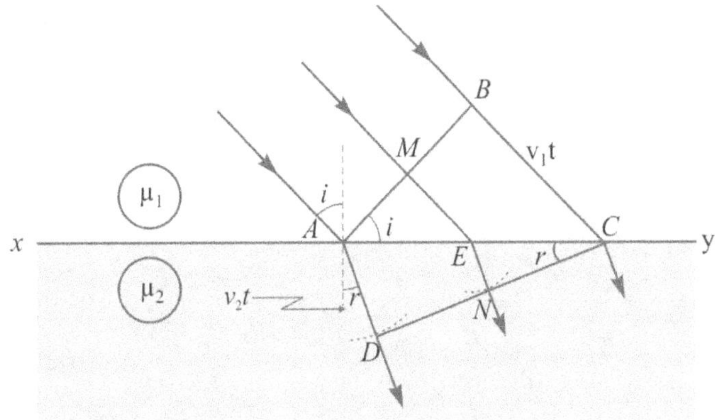

Fig. 4.3

With A as the centre and radius AD draw an arc. Then draw a tangent CD to the arc. CD represents the refracted wavefront. r be the angle of refraction. We have

$$\frac{BC}{AD} = \frac{v_1 t}{v_2 t} = \frac{v_1}{v_2}. \qquad \ldots(i)$$

In triangles ABC and ACD, we have

$$\frac{\sin i}{\sin r} = \frac{BC/AC}{AD/AC}$$

$$= \frac{BC}{AD}. \qquad \ldots(ii)$$

From equations (i) and (ii), we have

$$\frac{\sin i}{\sin r} = \frac{v_1}{v_2}$$

Since
$$\frac{v_1}{v_2} = \frac{\mu_2}{\mu_1},$$

$\therefore$
$$\frac{\sin i}{\sin r} = \frac{\mu_2}{\mu_1}$$

or
$$\mu_1 \sin i = \mu_2 \sin r.$$

This proves the law of refraction, which is called **Snell's law.**

4.3 INTERFERENCE

When two or more coherent waves superimpose, the resultant intensity in the region of superposition is different from the intensity of individual waves. This modification in the distribution of intensity in the region of superposition is called interference.

Young's double slit experiment (YDSE)

Thomas Young in 1801 devised an ingenious method of producing coherent sources. In this method a single wavefront is divided into two; these two split wavefronts act as if they originated from two sources having a constant phase relationship and therefore, when they were allowed to interfere, a stationary interference pattern was obtained. In the experiment light from a source S fell on a cardboard which contained two pinholes (or slits) S_1 and S_2 which were very close to one another. The spherical waves originating from S_1 and S_2 were coherent and so beautiful interference fringes or bands were obtained on the screen.

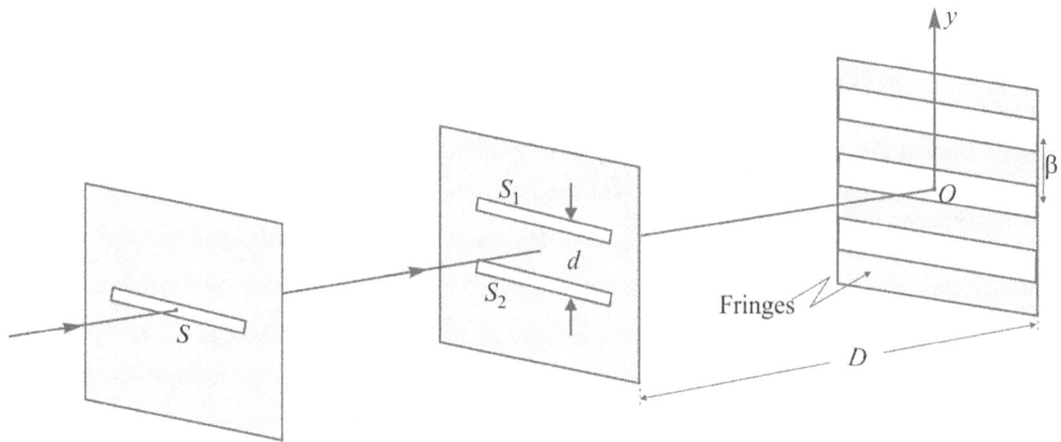

Fig. 4.4. Young's double slits arrangement.

Coherent sources

Two sources of light are said to be coherent if they emit light waves of same frequency and having constant phase difference (may be zero). It means the two sources must emit waves of the same wavelength. In practice it is not possible to have two independent sources which are coherent and so for practical purposes, two virtual sources formed from a single source can act as coherent sources. Young's double slits arrangement, Fresnel's biprism method, Llyod's mirror arrangement are the methods of producing two coherent sources from a single source.

> ***Note :***
>
> 1. Two independent laser sources of equal wavelengths can be coherent. Because they can maintained the constant phase difference for long time.
> 2. Two ordinary sources can not maintain the constant phase difference so they can not be coherent and hence will not interfere.

Analytical treatment of interference

Consider a monochromatic source of light S emitting light waves of wavelength λ and two narrow slits S_1 and S_2. S_1 and S_2 are separated a distance d and equidistance from S. S_1 and S_2 then becomes two virtual coherent sources of light waves. Let ϕ is the phase difference between the two waves reaching at point P. The equation of wave for any fixed position (say screen at $x = 0$) can be written as : $y = a \sin(\omega t - kx)$, where $x = 0$ and so, we get $y = a \sin \omega t$. Thus for two coherent waves, we can write

$$y_1 = a_1 \sin \omega t$$

and

$$y_2 = a_2 \sin(\omega t + \phi).$$

By principle of superposition, we have

$$y = y_1 + y_2$$

$$= a_1 \sin \omega t + a_2 \sin(\omega t + \phi)$$

$$= a_1 \sin \omega t + a_2[\sin \omega t \cos \phi + \cos \omega t \sin \phi]$$

$$= (a_1 + a_2 \cos \phi) \sin \omega t + a_2 \sin \phi \cos \omega t$$

Substituting

$$a_1 + a_2 \cos \phi = R \cos \theta \qquad ...(i)$$

and

$$a_2 \sin \phi = R \sin \theta, \text{ we get} \qquad ...(ii)$$

$$y = R \cos \theta \sin \omega t + R \sin \theta \cos \omega t$$

or
$$y = R\sin(\omega t + \theta). \qquad \ldots(1)$$

This shows that the resultant wave at any point P is simple harmonic of amplitude R. The amplitude R can be obtained as : Squaring equations (i) and (ii), we have

$$R^2 = a_1^2 + a_2^2 + 2a_1 a_2 \cos\phi. \qquad \ldots(2)$$

As intensity I of wave is proportional to square of the amplitude, and so

$$I = I_1 + I_2 + 2\sqrt{I_1 I_2}\,\cos\phi. \qquad \ldots(3)$$

Also dividing equation (ii) by (i), we get

$$\tan\theta = \frac{a_2 \sin\phi}{a_1 + a_2 \cos\phi}. \qquad \ldots(4)$$

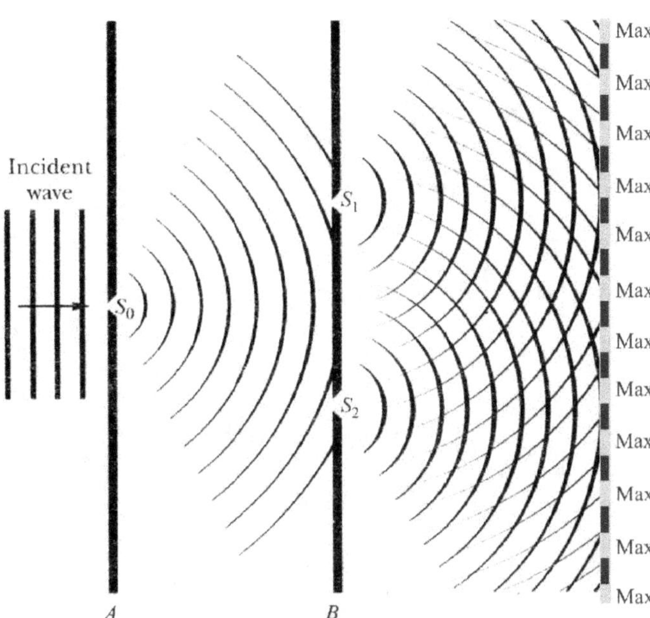

Fig. 4.5

In Young's interference experiment, incident monochromatic light is diffracted by slit S_0, which then acts as a point source of light that emits semicircular wavefronts. As that light reaches screen B, it is diffracted by slits S_1 and S_2, which then act as two point sources of light. The light waves traveling from slits S_1 and S_2 overlap and undergo interference, forming an interference pattern of maxima and minima on viewing screen C.

Depending on the phase difference ϕ between the two waves, the intensity of resulting wave may be minimum or maximum. Accordingly there are two types of interference. These are :

(i) Constructive interference (bright point)

The intensity I will be maximum, when

$$\cos\phi = +1,$$

or
$$\phi = 2\pi n, \qquad n = 0, 1, 2, \ldots$$

As path difference
$$\Delta x = \frac{\lambda}{2\pi}\phi;$$

$\therefore$
$$\Delta x = n\lambda$$

Now
$$I_{max} = R_{max}^2 = a_1^2 + a_2^2 + 2a_1 a_2$$

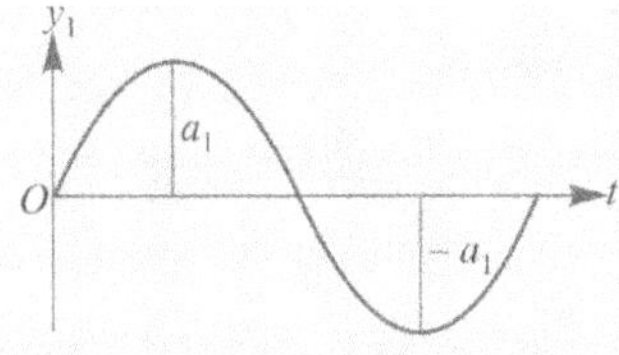

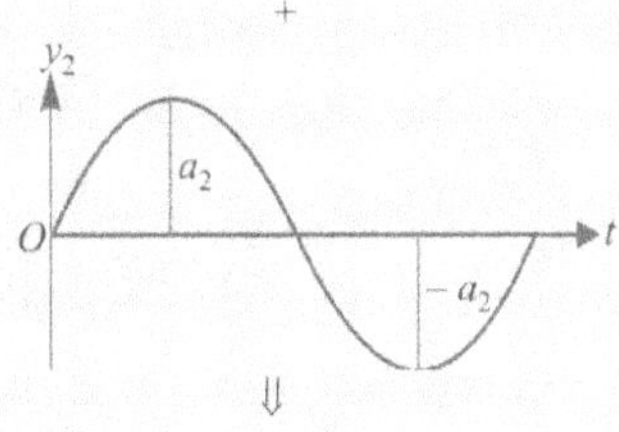

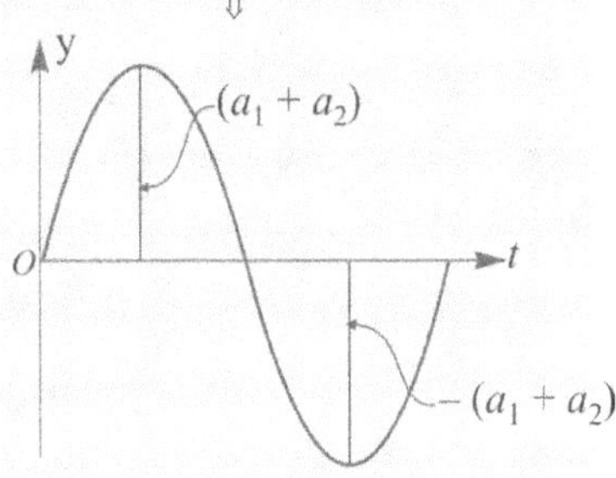

Interference between
two waves with $\phi = 0$.

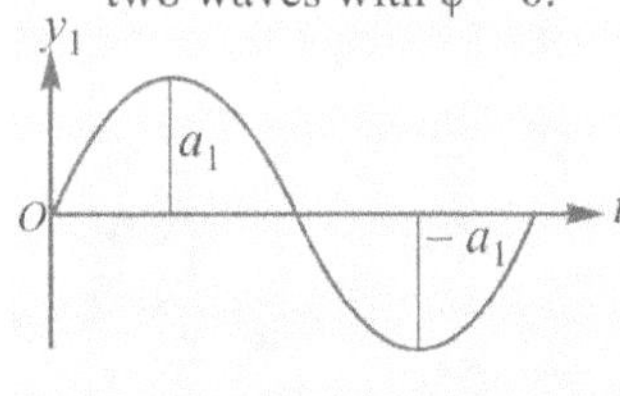

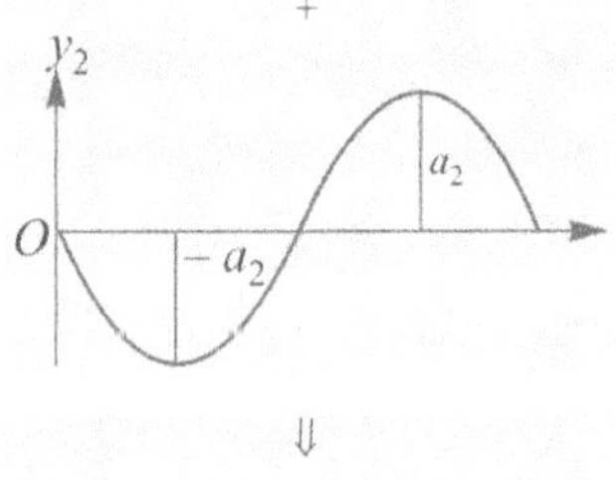

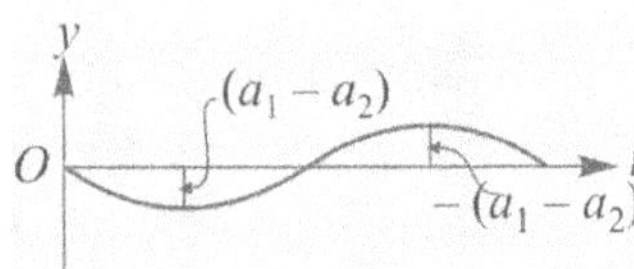

Interference between
two waves with $\phi = \pi$.

Fig. 4.6

or
$$I_{max} = R^2_{max} = (a_1 + a_2)^2 . \qquad ...(5)$$

(ii) Destructive interference (dark point)

The intensity I will be minimum, when
$$\cos\phi = -1$$

or
$$\phi = (2n-1)\pi, \quad n = 1, 2, 3, ...$$

Also
$$\Delta x = (2n-1)\frac{\lambda}{2}$$

Now
$$I_{min} = R^2_{min} = a_1^2 + a_2^2 - 2a_1 a_2$$

or
$$I_{min} = R^2_{min} = (a_1 - a_2)^2 \qquad ...(6)$$

Thus
$$\frac{I_{max}}{I_{min}} = \frac{R^2_{max}}{R^2_{min}} = \frac{(a_1 + a_2)^2}{(a_1 - a_2)^2} . \qquad ...(7)$$

Special cases : When two identical waves interfere,
$$a_1 = a_2 = a$$

$\therefore$
$$I_{max} = 4a^2 \text{ and } I_{min} = 0.$$

Also
$$I = a^2 + a^2 + 2\, aa \cos \phi$$
$$= 2a^2 (1 + \cos\phi)$$
$$= 2a^2 \times 2\cos^2 \frac{\phi}{2}$$
$$= 4a^2 \cos^2 \frac{\phi}{2}$$

or
$$I = I_{max} \cos^2 \frac{\phi}{2} . \qquad ...(8)$$

Intensity distribution

It has been obtained that intensity at bright points is $4a^2$ and at dark points is zero. According to law of conservation of energy, the energy of the intefering waves as a whole remains constant. Thus the energy from points of minimum intensity transfers to the points of maximum intensity. The intensity variation with phase difference is shown in *fig. 4.7*.

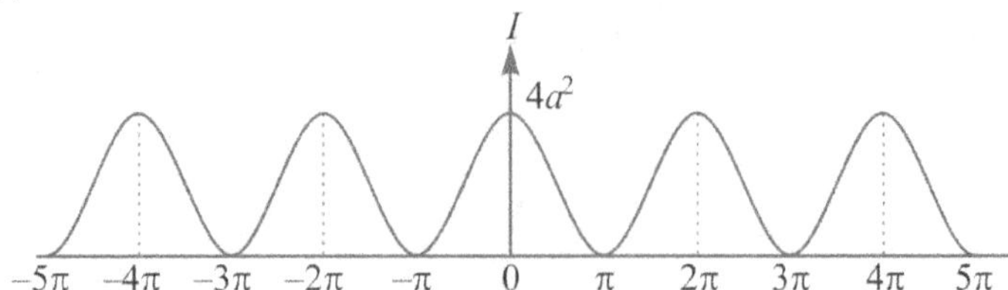

Variation of I with ϕ.

Fig. 4.7

Fringe width

Consider two sources S_1 and S_2 emitting monochromatic light of wavelength λ. The separation between them is d. The interference fringes are obtained on a screen placed at a distance D from the sources. The fringes are of equal width and alternatively bright and dark. The centre to centre distance between two consecutive bright or dark fringes is called **fringe width β.**

Consicer a point P on the screen at a distance y_n from the centre of the screen O. The angular position of the point P is θ from the centre of the sources (see *fig.* 4.8).

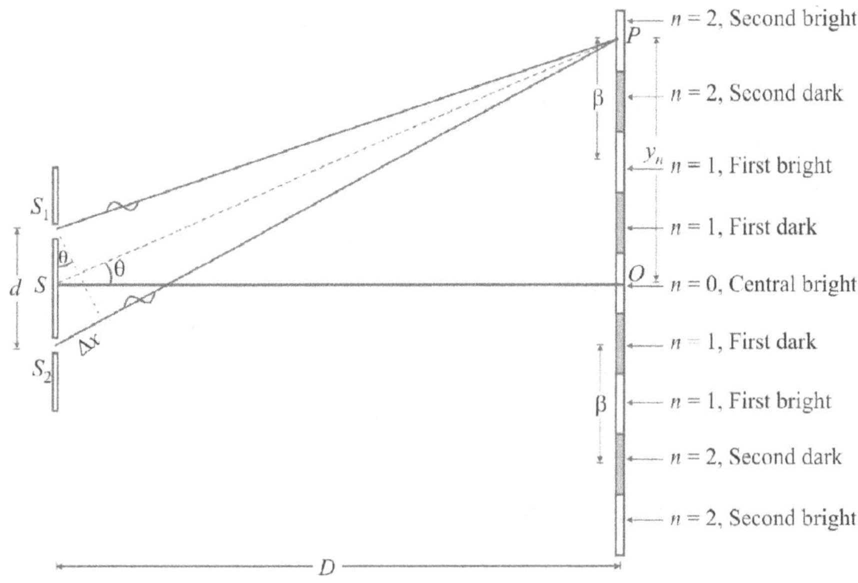

Fig. **4.8** Diagram showing fringe width.

The path difference between the waves on arriving at point P, is $S_2P - S_1P$, which is equal to Δx. From the figure $\Delta x = d \sin\theta$. For small θ, we can write $\sin\theta \simeq \tan\theta$. Thus

$$\Delta x \simeq d\tan\theta.$$

From the triangle SOP, $\quad \tan\theta = \dfrac{y_n}{D},$

$$\therefore \qquad \Delta x = \dfrac{d\,y_n}{D} \qquad \ldots(i)$$

(i) Bright fringes

There will be bright fringe at P, when $\Delta x = n\lambda$. Thus path difference

$$\dfrac{d y_n}{D} = n\lambda$$

or $\qquad y_n = \dfrac{n\,D\lambda}{d}; \quad n = 0, 1, 2, \ldots\ldots \qquad \ldots(9)$

Equation (9) represents the position of nth bright fringe. The $(n-1)^{\text{th}}$ fringe will be at a distance

$$y_{n-1} = (n-1)\dfrac{D\lambda}{d}$$

$\therefore \qquad$ Fringe width $\quad \beta = y_n - y_{n-1}$

$$= \dfrac{n\,D\lambda}{d} - (n-1)\dfrac{D\lambda}{d}$$

or $\qquad \beta = \dfrac{D\lambda}{d}. \qquad \ldots(10)$

(ii) **Dark fringes**

There will be dark fringe at P, when $\Delta x = (2n-1)\dfrac{\lambda}{2}$. Thus

$$\frac{d\,y_n}{D} = (2n-1)\frac{\lambda}{2}$$

or $$y_n = \frac{(2n-1)}{2}\frac{D\lambda}{d}; \quad n = 1, 2, \ldots \quad \ldots(11)$$

Equation (11) represents the position of nth dark fringe. The $(n-1)^{th}$ fringe will be at a distance

$$y_{n-1} = \left[\frac{2(n-1)-1}{2}\right]\frac{D\lambda}{d}$$

$\therefore$ Fringe width $\qquad \beta = y_n - y_{n-1}$

$$= \left[\frac{2n-1}{2}\right]\frac{D\lambda}{d} - \left[\frac{2(n-1)-1}{2}\right]\frac{D\lambda}{d}$$

or $$\beta = \frac{D\lambda}{d}.$$

It shows that the fringe width is equal for bright and dark fringe.

Note:

The maximum path difference $\Delta x_{max} = d$, when $\sin\theta = 1$. If n are the number of brights fringes on one side of the central bright, then $d = n\lambda$ or $n = \dfrac{d}{\lambda}$. Thus total number of fringes that can be on the screen are $= 2n+1$, including central central fringe.

Angular fringe width

Sometime it is required to represent fringe width in terms of angle subtended at the centre of the sources. If α is the angular fringe width, then

$$\alpha = \frac{\beta}{D}$$

$$= \frac{D\lambda/d}{D}$$

or $$\alpha = \frac{\lambda}{d} \text{ radian.}$$

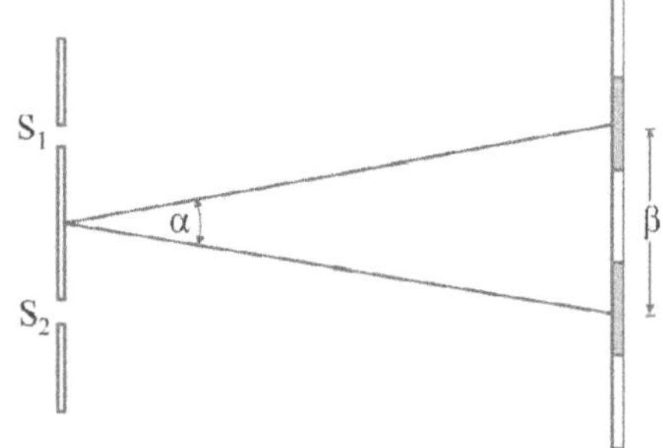

Fig. 4.9

Special case : If YDSE is performed in water, and observer is in air, then fringe width

$$\beta_{water} = \frac{D\,\lambda_{water}}{d}.$$

As $$\lambda_{water} = \frac{\lambda_{air}}{\mu_\omega},$$

$\therefore$ $$\beta_{water} = \frac{1}{\mu_\omega}\left[\frac{D\,\lambda_{air}}{d}\right] = \frac{\beta_{air}}{\mu_\omega}.$$

Important points :

1. In YDSE, the central fringe is bright, and all the bright fringes are of same intensity. Colour of bright fringes are of the colour of incident light.

2. If slits are of equal size, the intensity of all the dark frings are zero.

3. If slits are of unequal size, then the intensity of dark fringe is not zero.

4. All the fringes are of equal width.

5. If sources have random phase difference, then there will be no interference. The intensity at any point will be $I = a^2 + a^2 = 2a^2$.

6. If white light is used in the experiment, then the central fringe will be white, and other fringes are overlapped colour fringes.

Condition of obserable interference

1. The sources must be coherent.

2. The separation between the slits should be small (order of mm), so that size of fringe is large enough to observe.

3. The amplitudes of interfering waves are equal or nearly equal, otherwise the intensities of bright and dark fringes are not differentiable.

Ex. 1 Consider interference between two sources of intensities I and $4I$. Obtain intensities at points where the phase difference is (i) $\pi/2$ and (ii) π.

Sol. We know that resultant intensity

$$I_R = I_1 + I_2 + 2\sqrt{I_1 I_2}\cos\phi$$

(i) For $\phi = \pi/2$;

$$I_R = I + 4I + 2\sqrt{I \times 4I}\cos\frac{\pi}{2}$$

$$= 5I \qquad Ans.$$

(ii) For $\phi = \pi$;

$$I_R = I + 4I + 2\sqrt{I \times 4I}\cos\pi$$

$$= 5I - 4I = I \ Ans.$$

Ex. 2 A parallel wavefront of monochromatic light is incident on double slit arrangement at an angle α as shown in *fig. 4.10*. Find the position of zero order maxima from the centre of the screen. The distance of screen from the slits is D $(d << D)$.

Sol.

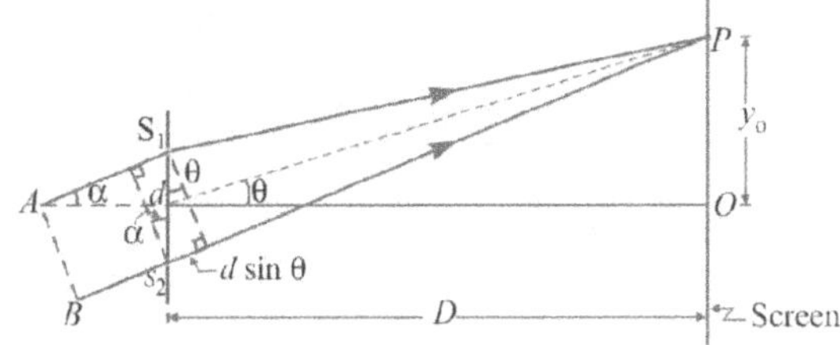

Fig. 4.10

Suppose the position of zero order maxima is at P at a distance y_0 from O. The path difference between two waves at P is

$$\Delta x = (BS_2 + S_2 P) - (AS_1 + S_1 P)$$

$$= (S_2 P - S_1 P) - (AS_1 - BS_2)$$

$$= d\sin\alpha - d\sin\theta$$

For small and $\sin\theta \simeq \tan\theta = \dfrac{y_0}{D}$ and for zero order maxima, $\Delta x = 0$.

or

$$0 = d\sin\alpha - d\frac{y_0}{D}$$

$$\therefore \quad y_0 = D\sin\alpha. \qquad Ans.$$

Ex. 3 The two coherent sources of monochromatic light of wavelength λ are located at a separation λ. The two sources are placed on a horizontal line and screen is placed perpendicular to the line joining the sources (see figure). Find position of the farthest minima from the centre of the sources.

Sol.

Suppose at P the farthest minima will occur. Let it subtends an angle θ at the centre of the sources.

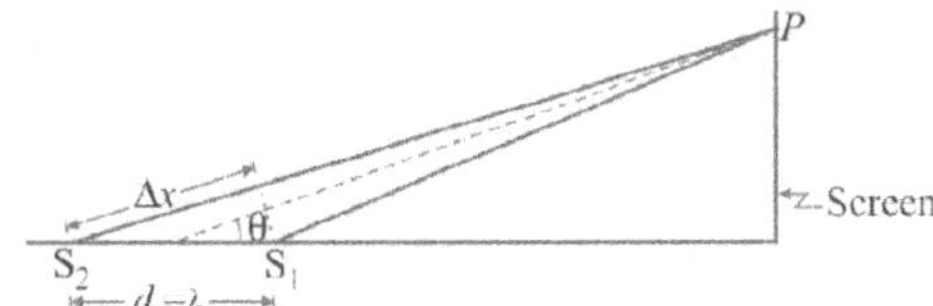

Fig. 4.11

The path difference

$$\Delta x = S_2 P - S_1 P$$

$$\simeq d\cos\theta$$

$$= \lambda\cos\theta$$

The maximum path difference can be

$$\Delta x_{max} = \lambda; \quad \text{when } \cos\theta = 1 \ or \ \theta = 0°$$

and minimum path difference

$$\Delta x_m = 0 \ ; \quad \text{when } \cos\theta = 0 \ or \ \theta = 90°$$

Thus in between these two positions there is only one minima for which

$$\Delta x = \frac{\lambda}{2}. \ \text{Thus}$$

$$\frac{\lambda}{2} = \lambda \cos\theta$$

or

$$\cos\theta = \frac{1}{2}$$

$$\therefore \quad \theta = 60°. \qquad \textit{Ans.}$$

Ex. 4
Two slits in Young's interference experiment have width in the ratio 1 : 4. Find the ratio of intensity at the maxima and minima in their interference.

Sol. The intensity of the wave is proportional to the area of the slit. Thus $\dfrac{I_1}{I_2} = \dfrac{b_1\ell}{b_2\ell} = \dfrac{b_1}{b_2} = \dfrac{1}{4}.$

If a_1 and a_2 are the amplitudes of the waves, then

$$\frac{I_1}{I_2} = \frac{a_1^{\,2}}{a_2^{\,2}} = \frac{1}{4}$$

$$\therefore \quad \frac{a_1}{a_2} = \frac{1}{2}.$$

The ratio

$$\frac{I_{max}}{I_{min}} = \frac{(a_1 + a_2)^2}{(a_1 - a_2)^2}$$

$$= \frac{(1+2)^2}{(1-2)^2} = \frac{9}{1}. \qquad \textit{Ans.}$$

Ex. 5
In double slit arrangement, the source S is not symmetrically placed from the slits. It is located as shown in the figure. Find the position of the zero order maxima from the centre of the screen. The separation between slits and screen is D ($d << D$).

Sol.

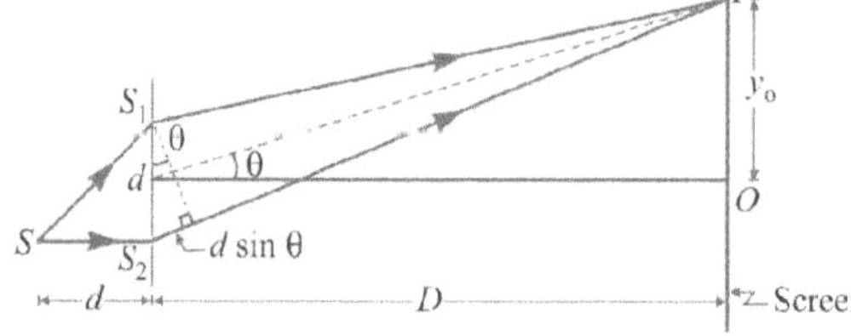

Fig. **4.12**

Suppose the position of zero order maxima is at P at a distance y_o from O. The path difference between two waves at P is

$$\Delta x = (SS_2 + S_2P) - (SS_1 + S_1P)$$

$$= -(SS_1 - SS_2) + (S_2P - S_1P)$$

$$= -\left(\sqrt{2}d - d\right) + d\sin\theta$$

For small θ, $\quad \sin\theta \simeq \tan\theta = \dfrac{y_o}{D}.$

$$\therefore \quad \Delta x = -\left(\sqrt{2}d - d\right) + \frac{d\,y_o}{D}$$

For zero order maxima, $\quad \Delta x = 0$

or

$$0 = -\left(\sqrt{2}d - d\right) + \frac{d\,y_o}{D}$$

$$\therefore \quad y_o = \left(\sqrt{2} - 1\right)D. \qquad \textit{Ans.}$$

Ex. 6
In an interference arrangement similar to Young's double slit experiment, slits S_1 and S_2 are illuminated with coherent microwave sources each of frequency 1 MHz. The sources are synchronized to have zero phase difference. The slits are separated by distance d = 150 m. The intensity I_θ is measured as a function of θ where θ is defined as shown in figure. If I_0 is the maximum intensity, calculate I_θ for (a) $\theta = 0°$ (b) $\theta = 30°$ and (c) = $90°$.

Sol.

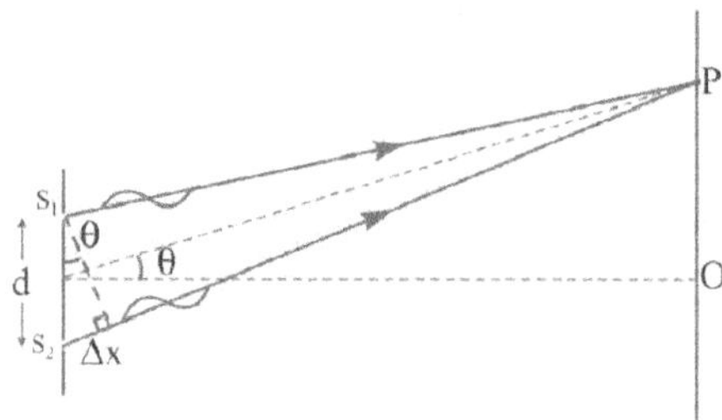

Fig. **4.13**

The wavelength of microwave

$$\lambda = \frac{c}{f} = \frac{3 \times 10^8}{10^6} = 300 \text{ m}$$

The path difference

$$\Delta x = d\sin\theta.$$

The corresponding phase difference

$$\phi = \frac{2\pi}{\lambda}\Delta x = \frac{2\pi}{300}(d\sin\theta)$$

$$= \frac{2\pi}{300}(150\sin\theta)$$

$$= \pi\sin\theta.$$

The resultant intensity in interference is given by

$$I_R = I_1 + I_2 + 2\sqrt{I_1 I_2}\cos\phi$$

$$= I_1 + I_2 + 2\sqrt{I_1 I_2}\cos(\pi\sin\theta).$$

For $I_1 = I_2 = I.$ $\quad I_R = 2I + 2I\cos(\pi\sin\theta).$

(a) For $\theta = 0°$, $I_R = 2I + 2I\cos 0° = 4I$

Given $I_0 = 4I; \therefore I = \dfrac{I_0}{4}.$ $\qquad \textit{Ans.}$

(b) For $\theta = 30°$

$$I_R = 2I + 2I\cos(\pi\sin 30°)$$

$$= 2I + 2I\cos\frac{\pi}{2} = 2I$$

$$= 2\frac{I_0}{4} = \frac{I_0}{2} \qquad \textit{Ans.}$$

(c) For $\theta = 90°$

$$I_R = 2I + 2I\cos(\pi\sin 90°)$$

$$= 2I - 2I = 0. \qquad \textit{Ans.}$$

4.4 DISPLACEMENT OF FRINGES

Suppose a transparent sheet of thickness t and refractive index μ is introduced in front of one of the slits of YDSE. The optical path of the light waves emerging from slit will increase by an amount $(\mu - 1)t$. In the arrangement shown the optical path of S_1P becomes $S_1P + (\mu-1)t$. Thus path difference between waves at P

$$\Delta x = S_2P - \left[S_1P + (\mu-1)t \right]$$

$$= (S_2P - S_1P) - (\mu-1)t$$

From the geometry of the figure

$$S_2P - S_1P = d\sin\theta$$

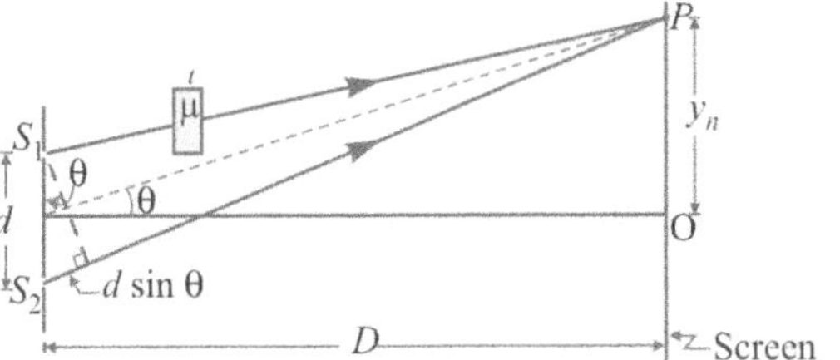

Fig. 4.14

For small angle θ, $\quad \sin\theta \simeq \tan\theta = \dfrac{y_n}{D}.$

$$\therefore \qquad \Delta x = \frac{dy_n}{D} - (\mu-1)t.$$

For bright fringes the path difference $\Delta x = n\lambda$. Thus

$$\frac{d\,y_n}{D} - (\mu-1)t = n\lambda; \qquad n = 0, 1, 2, ...$$

or

$$y_n = \frac{n\,D\lambda}{d} + \frac{D(\mu-1)t}{d}. \qquad ...(1)$$

In the absence of the sheet, the position of nth bright, $y_n = n\dfrac{D\lambda}{d}$. Thus displacement of fringes

$$\Delta = \frac{D(\mu-1)t}{d} \qquad (2)$$

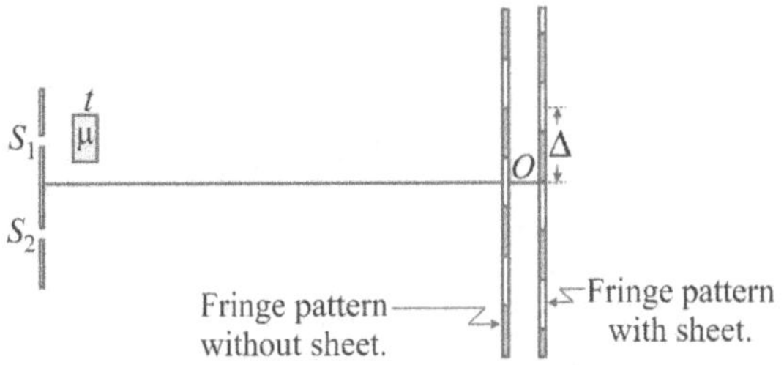

The position of $(n-1)^{th}$ order bright fringe

$$y_{n-1} = \frac{(n-1)\,D\lambda}{d} + \frac{D(\mu-1)t}{d}$$

The fringe width $\qquad \beta = y_n - y_{n-1}$

or $\qquad \beta = \dfrac{D\lambda}{d}.$

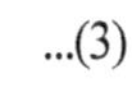

Fringe pattern without sheet.

Fringe pattern with sheet.

Fig. 4.15. Displacement of the fringes.

This shows that when a transparent sheet is introduced in the path of the slit, the entire fringe pattern will shift towards that side but fringe width remains same.

The number of fringe shifted

$$N = \frac{\Delta}{\beta} = \frac{D(\mu-1)t/d}{\left(\dfrac{D\lambda}{d}\right)}$$

or

$$N = \frac{(\mu-1)t}{\lambda}. \qquad ...(3)$$

Ex. 7 Two transparent sheets of thickness t_1 and t_2 and refractive indexes μ_1 and μ_2 are placed infront of the slits as shown in *fig. 4.16*. If D is the distance of the screen from the slits, then find the distance of zero order maxima from the centre of the screen. What is the condition that zero order maxima is formed at the centre O ?

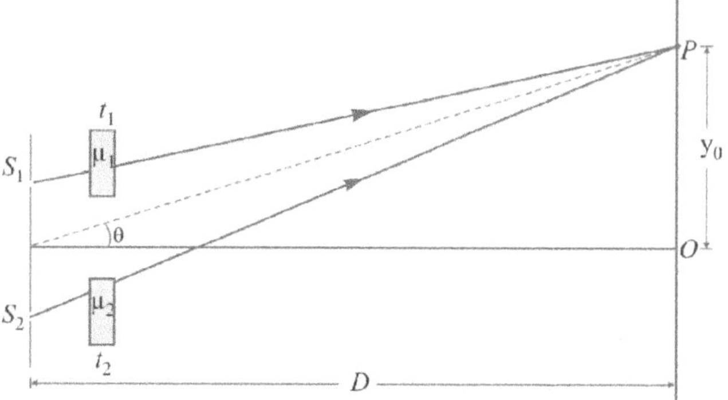

Fig. 4.16

Sol. Suppose P is the position of zero order maxima. The distance of P from the centre O of the screen is y_0.

The optical path of light waves from source S_1

$$x_1 = S_1P + (\mu_1 - 1)t_1$$

The optical path of light waves from source S_2

$$x_2 = S_2P + (\mu_2 - 1)t_2$$

The path difference

$$\Delta x = x_2 - x_1$$
$$= (S_2P - S_1P) + (\mu_2 - 1)t_2 - (\mu_1 - 1)t_1$$

From the geometry,

$$S_2P - S_1P = d\sin\theta \simeq d\tan\theta = \frac{d\,y_0}{D}.$$

$$\therefore \quad \Delta x = \frac{dy_0}{D} + (\mu_2 - 1)t_2 - (\mu_1 - 1)t_1$$

For zero order maxima, $\Delta x = 0$.

$$\therefore \quad 0 = \frac{d\,y_0}{D} + (\mu_2 - 1)t_2 - (\mu_1 - 1)t_1$$

or $$y_0 = \frac{D\left[(\mu_1 - 1)t_1 - (\mu_2 - 1)t_2\right]}{d} \quad Ans.$$

For zero order maxima at the centre O, $y_0 = 0$

$$\therefore \quad 0 = \frac{D\left[(\mu_1 - 1)t_1 - (\mu_2 - 1)t_2\right]}{d}$$

or $$(\mu_1 - 1)t_1 = (\mu_2 - 1)t_2. \qquad Ans.$$

4.5 FRESNEL'S BIPRISM

Fresnel developed another arrangement to get interference phenomenon. He used two small angled prisms (prism angle about $0.5°$) placed base to base. With this arrangement he produced two coherent sources by using a single source. *Fig. 4.17* shows a source S of monochromatic light and biprism arrangement. S_1 and S_2 are the virtual images of S as formed by two prisms. These sources are originated from the same source, and so they are coherent. If λ is the wavelength of light used, then fringe width is

$$\beta = \frac{D\lambda}{d}.$$

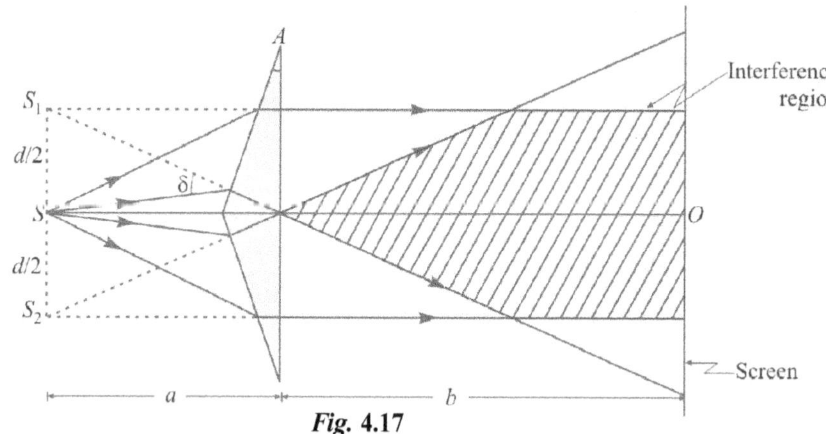

Fig. 4.17

In the arrangement $D = (a + b)$. The value of d can be determined by two methods. These are :

(i) **By displacement method**

In this method a convex lens is used to form real images of the sources. If d_1 and d_2 are the separations between images in two positions of the lenses, then

$$d = \sqrt{d_1 d_2}.$$

(ii) If A is the angle of prism, then angle of deviation produced by any prism
$$\delta = (\mu - 1)A.$$

From the geometry of the figure, for small angle

$$\delta = \frac{d/2}{a}$$

or $\qquad (\mu-1)A = \dfrac{d}{2a}$

$\therefore \qquad d = 2a(\mu-1)A$

4.6 LLOYD'S MIRROR ARRANGEMENT

In Lloyd's mirror arrangement, a plane mirror is used to produce another source, which together with real source constitutes two coherent sources. This set-up was developed by Lloyd in 1834. In this arrangement the interference pattern similar to Young's double slit experiment is obtained on the screen. But the central fringe is dark instead of being bright. It means there is destructive interference at the centre O. If we assume that mirror is perfectly reflecting, then the intensity of light waves from S_1 and S_2 is equal, let it is I. Then for destructive interference (zero resultant intensity)

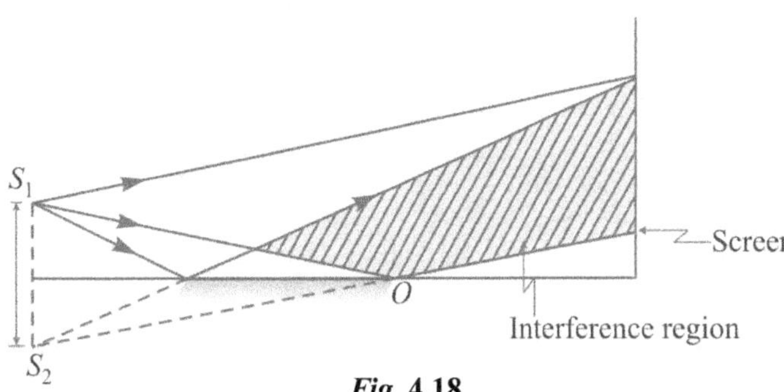

Fig. 4.18

$$0 = I+I+2\sqrt{II}\,\cos\phi$$

$\therefore \qquad \phi = \pi\text{ rad.}$

It shows that the wave after reflecting from mirror undergone a phase change of π rad. This experiment proves, that a light wave after reflection from an optically denser medium undergoes a phase change of π rad.

Ex. 8　A beam of light consisting of two wavelengths 6500 Å and 5200 Å is used to obtain interference fringes in a Young's double slit experiment :

(i)　Find the distance of the third bright fringe on the screen from the central maximum for the wavelength 6500 Å.

(ii)　What is the least distance from the central maximum where the bright fringes due to both the wavelengths coincide ? The distance between the slits is 2 mm and the distance between the plane of the slits and the screen is 120 cm.

Sol.

(i)　For bright fringe,

$$y_n = \dfrac{n\,D\lambda}{d}.$$

For third bright, $n = 3$

$\therefore \qquad y_3 = \dfrac{3\,D\lambda}{d}$

$$= \dfrac{3\times\left(120\times10^{-2}\right)\times6500\times10^{-10}}{2\times10^{-3}}$$

$$= 1.17\times10^{-3}\,m \qquad\qquad \textbf{\textit{Ans.}}$$

(ii)　Let n_1^{th} bright of 6500 Å concides with the n_2^{th} bright of 5200 Å, then

$$n_1\dfrac{D\lambda_1}{d} = n_2\dfrac{D\lambda_2}{d}$$

or $\qquad \dfrac{n_1}{n_2} = \dfrac{\lambda_2}{\lambda_1}$

$$= \dfrac{5200}{6500}$$

$$= \dfrac{4}{5}$$

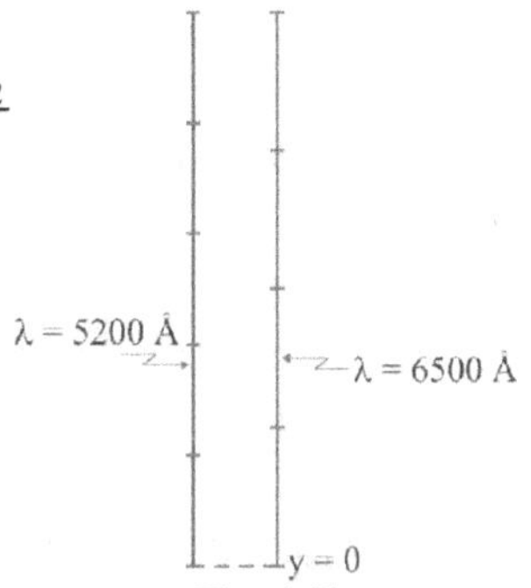

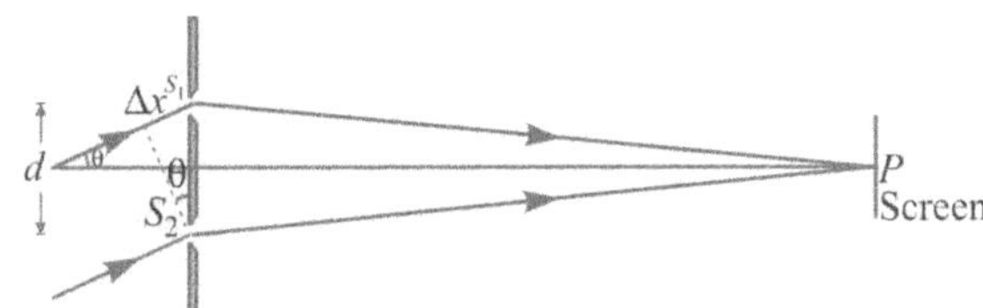

Fig. 4.19

The minimum of value of n_1 and n_2 are 4 and 5 respectively.

Therefore $\quad y_4 = \dfrac{4\,D\lambda_1}{d}$

$$= \dfrac{4\times\left(120\times10^{-2}\right)\times\left(6500\times10^{-10}\right)}{2\times10^{-3}}$$

$$= 1.56\times10^{-3}\,m. \qquad\qquad \textbf{\textit{Ans.}}$$

Ex. 9　A parallel beam of monochromatic light is used in a Young's double slit experiment. The slits are separated by a distance d and the screen is placed parallel to the plane of the slits. The light is incident an angle θ with the normal to the plane of slits. Find the value of θ so that, there will be dark fringe at the centre P of the pattern.

Sol.

Fig. 4.20

The path difference between two wavefronts at P

$$\Delta x = d\sin\theta$$

For dark fringe at P, $\qquad \Delta x = \dfrac{\lambda}{2}$

Therefore $\qquad d\sin\theta = \dfrac{\lambda}{2}$

or $\qquad \theta = \sin^{-1}\left(\dfrac{\lambda}{2d}\right). \qquad \textbf{\textit{Ans.}}$

Ex. 10 A narrow slit S transmitting light of wavelength λ is placed a distance d above a large plane mirror as shown in *fig. 4.21*. The light coming directly from the slit and that coming after reflection interfere at a screen Σ placed at a distance D from the slit. (a) What will be the intensity at a point just above the mirror, i.e., just above O ? (b) At what distance from O does the first maximum will occur ?

Sol.

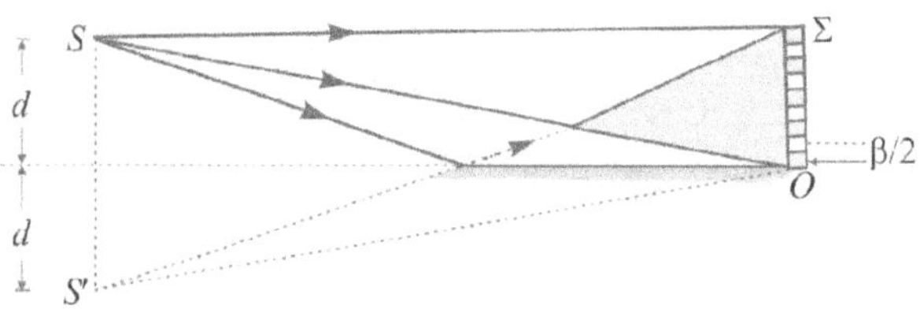

Fig. 4.21

(a) There will be dark fringe at O, therefore intensity of light at O will be zero.

(b) It is clear from the figure, that the distance of first maximum from O

$$y = \frac{\beta}{2} = \left(\frac{D\lambda/2d}{2}\right)$$

$$= \frac{D\lambda}{4d}. \qquad Ans.$$

Ex. 11 Two plane mirrors M_1 and M_2 are inclined to each other at an angle θ and an illuminated slit S is placed infront of them at a distance of 12 cm away from and parallel to the line of intersection of the mirror. An eye piece is mounted at a distance of 60 cm from the line of intersection of the mirrors. If the band-width obtained is 0.16 mm and wavelength of light used is 5460 Å. Find the value of θ.

Sol.

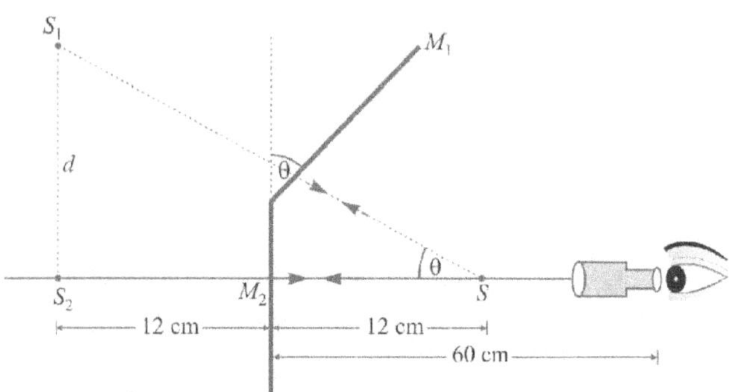

Fig. 4.22

From the figure $\qquad D = 60 + 12 = 72$ cm

Let separation between the sources formed by mirrors is d. We have

$$\beta = \frac{D\lambda}{d}$$

or $\qquad 0.16 \times 10^{-3} = \dfrac{\left(72 \times 10^{-2}\right) \times \left(5460 \times 10^{-10}\right)}{d}$

$\therefore \qquad d = 2.46 \times 10^{-3}\ m$.

For small angle $\qquad \tan\theta \simeq \theta = \dfrac{d}{0.24}$

or $\qquad \theta = \dfrac{2.46 \times 10^{-3}}{0.24}$

$\qquad = 10.25 \times 10^{-3}$ rad. $\qquad Ans.$

Ex. 12 S is a monochromatic point source emitting light of wavelength $\lambda = 500$ nm. A thin lens of circular shape and focal length 0.10 m is cut into two identical halves L_1 and L_2 by a plane passing through a diameter. The two halves are placed symmetrically about the central axis 50 with a gap of 0.5 mm. The distance along the axis from S to L_1 and L_2 is 0.15 m while that from L_1 and L_2 to O is 1.30 m. The screen at O is normal to SO.

(i) If the third intensity maximum occurs at the point A on the screen, find the distance OA.

(ii) If the gap between L_1 and L_2 is reduced from its original value of 0.5 mm, will the distance OA increase decrease, or remains the same ?

Sol.

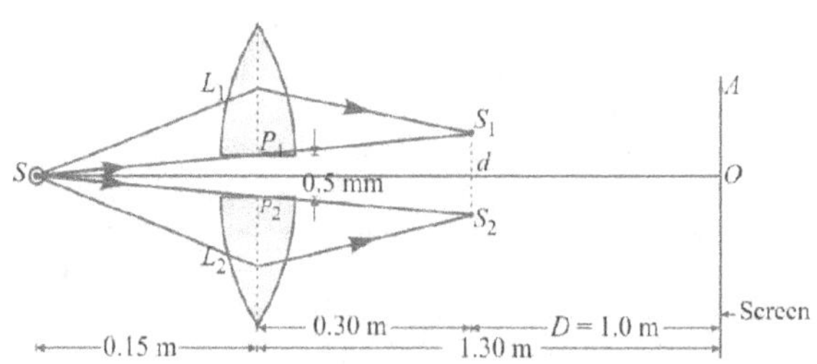

Fig. 4.23

Each half forms separate image of S. Let images formed are S_1 and S_2. These two be the coherent sources. They interfere and produce maxima and minima on the screen.

For any half

$$u = -0.15\ m$$
$$f = 0.10\ m$$

We have, $\qquad \dfrac{1}{v} - \dfrac{1}{u} = \dfrac{1}{f}$

or $\qquad \dfrac{1}{v} - \dfrac{1}{-0.15} = \dfrac{1}{0.10}$

$\therefore \qquad v = 0.30$ m.

Now from similar triangles $S\,S_1\,S_2$ and $S\,P_1\,P_2$ we have

$$\frac{d}{0.5 \times 10^{-3}} = \frac{(0.30 + 0.15)}{0.15}$$

or $\qquad d = 1.5 \times 10^{-3}$ m

(i) For third maximum $OA = y_3 = 3\dfrac{D\lambda}{d}$

$$= \frac{3 \times 1.0 \times 500 \times 10^{-9}}{1.5 \times 10^{-3}}$$

$$= 1 \times 10^{-3} \text{ m} \qquad \textbf{\textit{Ans.}}$$

(ii) As we have seen d is proportional to $P_1 P_2$, that is gap between L_1 and L_2, therefore with decrease in gap, d decreases and hence

OA increases, because $y \propto \dfrac{1}{d}$.

Ex. 13 Consider the arrangement shown in *fig.* 4.24. The distance D is large compared to the separation d between the slits.

(a) Find the minimum value of d so that there is a dark fringe at O.

(b) Suppose d has this value. Find the distance x at which the next bright fringe is formed. (c) Find the fringe width.

Sol.

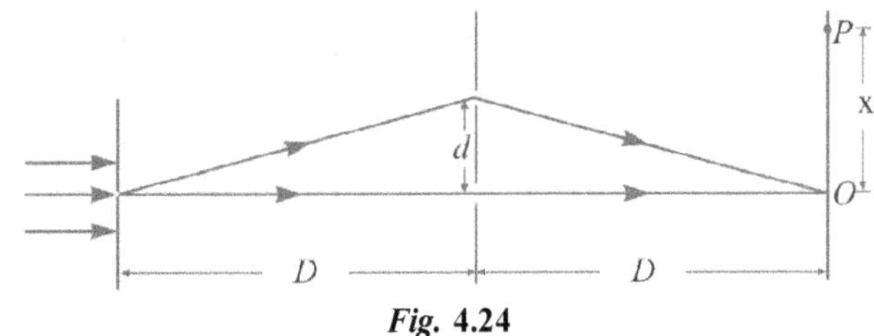

Fig. 4.24

(a) The path difference at O, $\Delta x = 2\sqrt{D^2 + d^2} - 2D$

For the dark fringe at O, $\Delta x = \dfrac{\lambda}{2}, \dfrac{3\lambda}{2},$

For minimum value of d,

$$2\sqrt{D^2 + d^2} - 2D = \frac{\lambda}{2}$$

or $\left(D^2 + d^2\right)^{1/2} - D = \dfrac{\lambda}{4}$

or $D\left(1 + \dfrac{d^2}{D^2}\right)^{1/2} - D = \dfrac{\lambda}{4}$

or $D\left(1 + \dfrac{d^2}{2D^2}\right) - D = \dfrac{\lambda}{4}$

or $D + \dfrac{d^2}{2D} - D = \dfrac{\lambda}{4}$

or $d = \sqrt{\dfrac{D\lambda}{2}}$. \qquad **_Ans._**

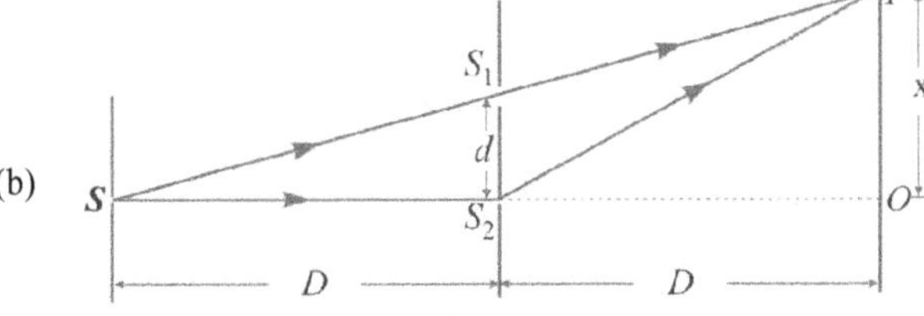

Fig. 4.25

Here the path difference $\Delta x = \left(SS_1 + S_1P\right) - \left(SS_2 + S_2P\right)$

$$= \left[\sqrt{\left(D^2 + d^2\right)} + \sqrt{\left(x - d\right)^2 + D^2}\right] - \left[D + \sqrt{D^2 + x^2}\right]$$

For the next bright fringe after first dark fringe, $\Delta x = \lambda$

$$\therefore \left[\sqrt{D^2 + d^2} + \sqrt{\left(x - d\right)^2 + D^2}\right] - \left[D + \sqrt{D^2 + x^2}\right] = \lambda$$

or $D\left(1 + \dfrac{d^2}{D^2}\right)^{1/2} + D\left(1 + \dfrac{\left(x - d\right)^2}{D^2}\right)^{1/2} - \left[D + D\left(1 + \dfrac{x^2}{D^2}\right)^{1/2}\right] = \lambda$

or $\left(D + \dfrac{d^2}{2D}\right) + D + \dfrac{\left(x - d\right)^2}{2D} - \left(D + D + \dfrac{x^2}{2D}\right) = \lambda$

or $\dfrac{d^2 + \left(x - d\right)^2 - x^2}{2D} = \lambda$

or $d^2 + x^2 + d^2 - 2xd - x^2 = 2\lambda D$

or $2d^2 - 2xd = 2\lambda D$

For $d = \sqrt{\dfrac{D\lambda}{2}}$, we get

$$2\left(\sqrt{\frac{D\lambda}{2}}\right)^2 - 2x\sqrt{\frac{D\lambda}{2}} = 2\lambda D$$

or $2\dfrac{D\lambda}{2} - 2x\sqrt{\dfrac{D\lambda}{2}} = 2\lambda D$

or $2x\sqrt{\dfrac{D\lambda}{2}} = -D\lambda$

or $\left(2x\sqrt{\dfrac{D\lambda}{2}}\right)^2 = \left(-D\lambda\right)^2$

which gives $x = \sqrt{\dfrac{D\lambda}{2}} = d$ \qquad **_Ans._**

(c) Fringe width $\beta = \dfrac{D\lambda}{d}$.

Ex. 14 Two coherent point sources S_1 and S_2 vibrating in phase emit light of wavelength λ. The separation between the sources is 2λ. Consider a line passing through S_2 and perpendicular to the line $S_1 S_2$. What is the smallest distance S_2 where a minimum of intensity occurs?

Sol. Path difference at P, $\Delta x = \sqrt{d^2 + x^2} - x$

$\Delta x_{\min} = 0$, when $x \to \infty$, and maxima will occur.
$\Delta x_{\max} = 2\lambda$, when $x = 0$, again maxima will occur.

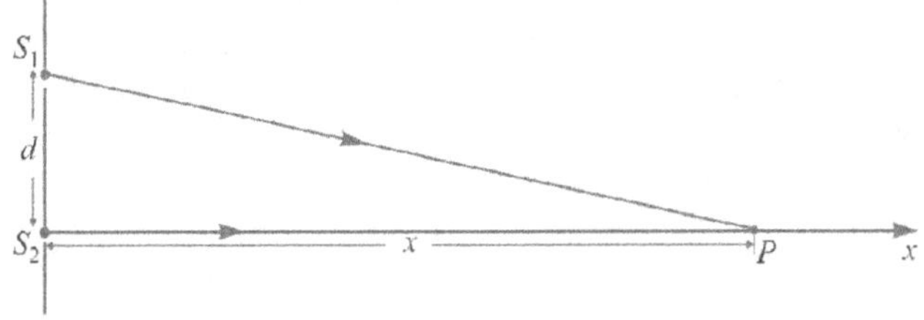

Fig. 4.26

$$\begin{array}{ccccc}
\underset{\text{Maxima}}{\Delta x = 2\lambda} & \underset{\text{Minima}}{\Delta x = 3\lambda/2} & \underset{\text{Maxima}}{\Delta x = \lambda} & \underset{\text{Minima}}{\Delta x = \lambda/2} & \underset{\text{Maxima}}{\Delta x = 0}
\end{array}$$

For nearest minima $\qquad \Delta x = \dfrac{3\lambda}{2}$

or $\qquad \sqrt{d^2 + x^2} - x = \dfrac{3\lambda}{2}$

or $\qquad d^2 + x^2 = \left(\dfrac{3\lambda}{2} + x\right)^2$

or $\qquad d^2 + x^2 = \dfrac{9\lambda^2}{4} + x^2 + 3\lambda x$

or $\qquad x = \dfrac{\left[d^2 - \dfrac{9\lambda^2}{4}\right]}{3\lambda}$

$$= \dfrac{(2\lambda)^2 - \dfrac{9\lambda^2}{4}}{3\lambda}$$

or $\qquad x = \dfrac{7\lambda}{12}.$ *Ans.*

Ex. 15 Consider the situation shown in *fig.* 4.27. The two slits S_1 and S_2 placed symmetrically around the central line are illuminated by a monochromatic light of wavelength λ. The separation between the slits is d. The light transmitted by the slits falls on a screen E_1 placed at a distance D from the slits. The slit S_3 is at the central line and the slit S_4 is at a distance z from S_3. Another screen E_2 is placed a further distance D away from E_1. Find the ratio of the maximum to minimum intensity observed on E_2 if z is equal to

(a) $\dfrac{\lambda D}{2d}$ $\qquad$ (b) $\dfrac{\lambda D}{d}$ $\qquad$ (c) $\dfrac{\lambda D}{4d}.$

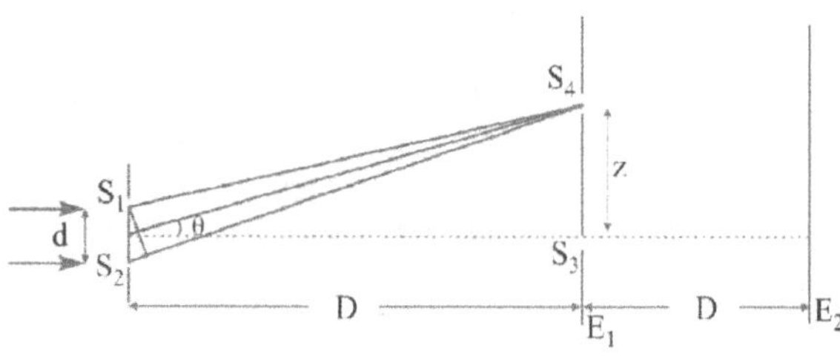

Fig. 4.27

Sol.

Light from sources S_1 and S_2 get interfered and thereafter S_3 and S_4 become new sources. At S_3 the path difference between the lights coming from S_1 and S_2 is zero. Therefore they interfere constructively and so $a_3 = (a + a) = 2a$

(a)   At S_4 the path difference

$$\Delta x = d\sin\theta \approx d\tan\theta$$

$$= d\dfrac{z}{D} = \dfrac{d \times \dfrac{\lambda D}{2d}}{D}$$

$$= \dfrac{\lambda}{2}$$

Corresponding phase difference $= \pi$ radian

$\therefore \qquad a_4 = 0$

The ratio $\qquad \dfrac{I_{\max}}{I_{\min}} = \dfrac{(a_3 + a_4)^2}{(a_3 - a_4)^2} = \dfrac{(2a + 0)^2}{2a - 0} = 1$

Ans.

(b) $\qquad \Delta x = \dfrac{d\,z}{D} = \dfrac{d\left(\dfrac{\lambda D}{d}\right)}{D} = \lambda$

Corresponding phase difference $= 2\pi$ radian

Now $\qquad a_4 = a + a = 2a$

and $\qquad \dfrac{I_{\max}}{I_{\min}} = \dfrac{(2a + 2a)^2}{(2a - 2a)^2} = \infty$ $\qquad$ *Ans.*

(c) $\qquad \Delta x = \dfrac{dz}{D} = \dfrac{d\left(\dfrac{\lambda D}{4d}\right)}{D} = \dfrac{\lambda}{4}$

Corresponding phase difference $= \dfrac{\lambda}{2}$ radian

$$A_4^2 = a^2 + a^2 + 2aa\cos\dfrac{\pi}{2} = 2a^2$$

or $\qquad A_4 = \sqrt{2}a$

$$\dfrac{I_{\max}}{I_{\min}} = \dfrac{(2a + \sqrt{2}a)^2}{(2a - \sqrt{2}a)^2} = \dfrac{(3.414)^2}{(0.586)^2}$$

$$= 34.$$ *Ans.*

Ex. 16 In a modified Young's double slit experiment, a monochromatic uniform and parallel beam of light of wavelength 6000Å and intensity $\dfrac{10}{\pi}$ W/m^2 is incident normally on two circular apertune A and B of radii 0.001 m and 0.002 m respectively. A perfect transparent film of thickness 2000 Å and refractive index 1.5 for the wavelength of 6000Å is placed infront of apertune A, see *fig.* 4.28.

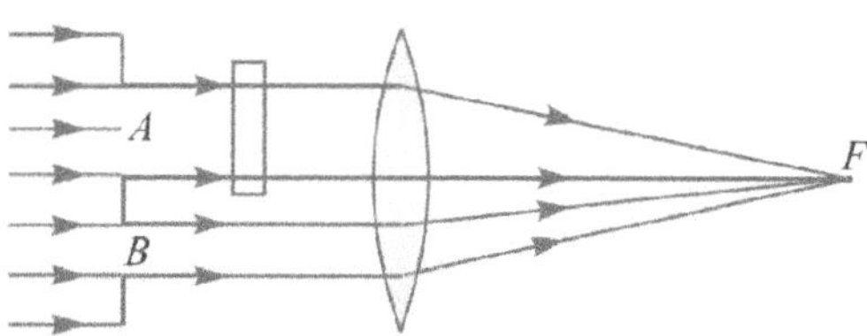

Fig. 4.28

Calculate the power (in watts) received at the focal spot F of the lens. The lens is symmetrically placed with respect to the aperture. Assume that 10% of the power received by each aperture goes in the original direction and is brought to the focus spot.

Sol.

The intensities of light of sources S_1 and S_2 are

$$I_1 = \left(\frac{10}{\pi}\right) \times \pi (0.01)^2 = 10^{-5} \ W$$

$$I_2 = \left(\frac{10}{\pi}\right) \times \pi (0.02)^2 = 4 \times 10^{-5} \ W.$$

The intensities of sources after emerging from the lenses are

$$I_A = 0.10 \times 10^{-5} \ W = 10^{-6} \ W$$
$$I_B = 0.10 \times 4 \times 10^{-5} \ W = 4 \times 10^{-6} \ W.$$

The path difference produced due to film

$$\Delta x = (\mu - 1)\, t = (1.5 - 1) \times 2000 \times 10^{-10} = 10^{-7} \ m$$

and

$$\phi = \frac{2\pi}{\lambda} \times \Delta x = \frac{2\pi}{6000 \times 10^{-10}} \times 10^{-7} = \frac{\pi}{3} \text{ radian}$$

Now power received at F

$$
\begin{aligned}
I &= I_A + I_B + 2\sqrt{I_A I_B}\,\cos\phi \\[2mm]
&= 10^{-6} + 4 \times 10^{-6} + 2\sqrt{10^{-6} \times 4 \times 10^{-6}}\,\cos\frac{\pi}{3} \\[2mm]
&= 7 \times 10^{-6} \ W \qquad \textbf{\textit{Ans.}}
\end{aligned}
$$

4.7 INTERFERENCE IN THIN FILMS

Thin film may be an oil film spread over water, paint on glass, or air film between two glass plates etc. The phenomenon of interference was first explained by Young. It has been observed that interference in the case of thin film takes place due to (1) reflected light (2) and transmitted light.

(1)   Interference in reflected light

Consider a thin film of transparent material of thickness t and refractive index μ is situated in air. A ray incident at A on the upper surface of the film is partly reflected and partly refracted along AB. At B it is partly reflected along BC and finally emerges out along BG. This process of reflection and refraction goes continuously at several points on the film (theoretically infinity).

To get the path difference between the light waves from points A and C, drop a perpendicular at D on the reflected ray from A and at E on the ray BC. Thus optical path difference,

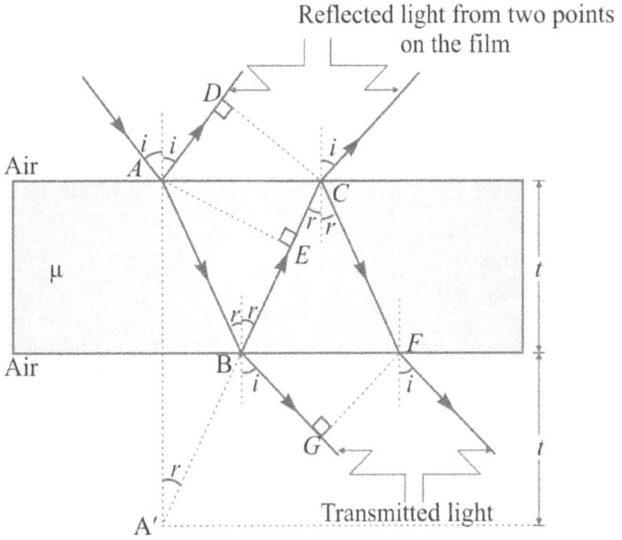

Reflected light from two points on the film

Air — D — A — C — E — B — F — G — A' — μ — t — i — r — Transmitted light

Fig. **4.29**

$$
\begin{aligned}
\Delta x &= (AB + BC)\text{ in medium} - AD \text{ in air} \\
&= (AB + BE + EC)\text{ in medium} - AD \text{ in air}
\end{aligned}
$$

We know that AB distance travels in medium of refractive index μ becomes equal to μAB in air, and so for BE and EC. Therefore

$$\Delta x = (AB + BE + EC)\,\mu \text{ in air} - AD \text{ in air} \qquad ...(i)$$

By Snell's law;

$$\mu = \frac{\sin i}{\sin r}$$

$$= \frac{AD/AC}{EC/AC} = \frac{AD}{EC}$$

$$\therefore \qquad AD = \mu\, EC. \qquad\qquad ...(ii)$$

Substituting this value in equation (i), we get

$$\Delta x = (AB + BE)\,\mu$$

As $\qquad AB = A'B,$

$$\therefore \qquad \Delta x = (A'B + BE)\mu$$
$$= (A'E)\mu.$$

From the triangle $AA'E$, $A'E = 2t \cos r$, and so

$$\Delta x = 2\mu t \cos r. \qquad\qquad ...(iii)$$

The path difference in equation (iii) is the optical path difference. It has been proved that when light is reflected from optical denser medium (upper surface of the film), it undergoes an abrupt phase change of π rad; an equivalent path difference $\lambda/2$. Therefore the effective path difference becomes,

$$\Delta x_e = 2\mu t \cos r \pm \frac{\lambda}{2} \qquad \ldots(1)$$

(i) The maxima will occur when $\Delta x = n\lambda$.

$$\therefore \qquad 2\mu t \cos r \pm \frac{\lambda}{2} = n\lambda$$

or $\qquad 2\mu t \cos r = (2n-1)\dfrac{\lambda}{2}; \qquad n = 1, 2, \ldots$

If we take $\qquad 2\mu t \cos r = (2n+1)\dfrac{\lambda}{2}$, then n will be 0, 1, 2, ...(2)

(ii) The minima will occur when $\Delta x = (2n-1)\lambda/2$.

$$\therefore \qquad 2\mu t \cos r \pm \frac{\lambda}{2} = (2n-1)\frac{\lambda}{2}$$

or $\qquad 2\mu t \cos r = n\lambda; \qquad n = 1, 2, \ldots \qquad \ldots(3)$

Here $n = 0$ is discarded because path difference $2\mu t \cos r$ can not be zero.

When this condition is fulfilled the film will appear dark in reflected light.

For normal incidence, angle of incidence i and hence r become zero and so $\cos r = 1$, then $2\mu t \cos r \rightarrow 2\mu t$.

(2) **Interference in transmitted light**

The optical path difference between the light waves originated from B and F can be calculated as in the case of reflected light. Thus

$$\Delta x = 2\mu t \cos r.$$

In this case the light rays emerge from B and F has no phase change because light emerges from F has gone two reflections, each with a phase change of π rad. Thus

$$\Delta x_e = 2\mu t \cos r + 0 = 2\mu t \cos r.$$

(i) The maxima will occur when $\Delta x = n\lambda$.

$$\therefore \qquad 2\mu t \cos r = n\lambda; \qquad n = 1, 2, \qquad \ldots(4)$$

(ii) The minima will occur when $\Delta x = (2n-1)\lambda/2$.

$$\therefore \qquad 2\mu t \cos r = (2n-1)\lambda/2; \quad n = 1, 2, \qquad \ldots(5)$$

Conclusion : The condition of maxima and minima for interference in reflected and transmitted light are opposite to each other. It means, if any colour is strongly reflected, then it will be absent in transmitted light.

Colours of thin film

When white light is incident on thin film, beautiful colours are observed. The incident light will split up due to reflection at the top and bottom of the film. The splitted rays interfere and gives bright colours. The interfering rays of only certain wavelengths will have a path difference satisfying the conditions of bright fringe. Hence only such wavelengths will be present there. Other wavelengths will be present with diminished intensity.

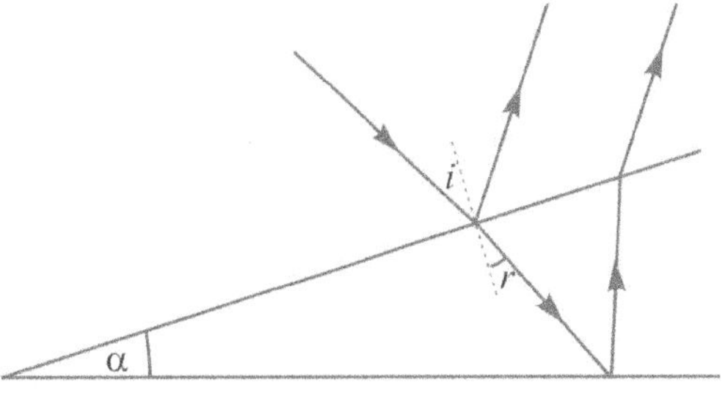

Fig. **4.30**

Interference in wedge shaped film

Consider a thin film of refractive index μ is enclosed between the two surfaces inclined at an angle α. For small angle α, the effective path difference between two light waves originated from upper surface can be taken equal to $2\,\mu t \cos r$. Thus for minima

$$2\,\mu t \cos r = n\lambda.$$

For normal incidence $r \to 0$, $\cos r = 1$.

$$2\,\mu t = n\lambda \qquad ...(i)$$

where t is the thickness of the film at the position of nth minima

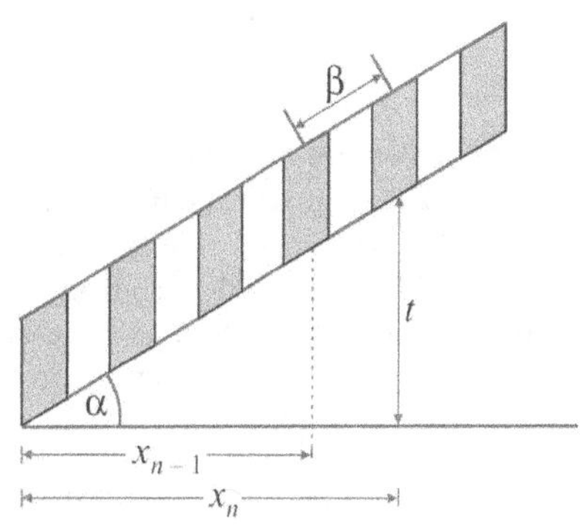

Fig. **4.31**

From the figure
$$\tan \alpha = \frac{t}{x_n}$$

or
$$t = x_n \tan \alpha$$

From equation (i), $2\,\mu(x_n \tan \alpha) = n\lambda$

or
$$x_n = \frac{n\lambda}{2\mu \tan \alpha} \qquad ...(ii)$$

and
$$x_{n-1} = \frac{(n-1)\lambda}{2\,\mu \tan \alpha} \qquad ...(iii)$$

$$\therefore \quad \beta = x_n - x_{n-1} = \frac{\lambda}{2\,\mu \tan \alpha}.$$

Newton's rings : Newton's rings are formed due to interference between the waves reflected from the top and bottom surfaces of the air film enclosed between the lens and the plate.

From the property of circle, we have

$$r \times r = t \times (2R - t)$$

or
$$r^2 = 2Rt - t^2$$
$$\simeq 2Rt \qquad [\text{Since } t << R]$$

$$\therefore \quad t = \frac{r^2}{2R}$$

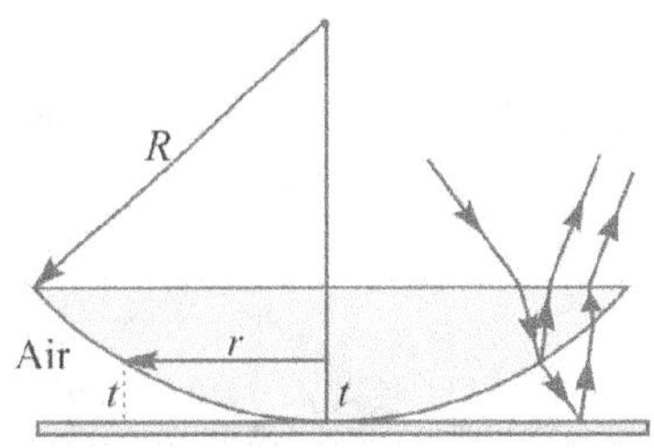

Air

Newton's ring by reflected light

For bright ring :
$$2\mu t = (2n-1)\lambda/2 \qquad n = 1, 2, 3, ...$$

or
$$2\mu \frac{r^2}{2R} = (2n-1)\frac{\lambda}{2}$$

or
$$r^2 = \frac{(2n-1)\lambda R}{2\mu}$$

or
$$\frac{D^2}{4} = \frac{(2n-1)\lambda R}{2\mu}$$

or
$$D_n^2 = \frac{2(2n-1)\lambda R}{\mu} \qquad ...(i)$$

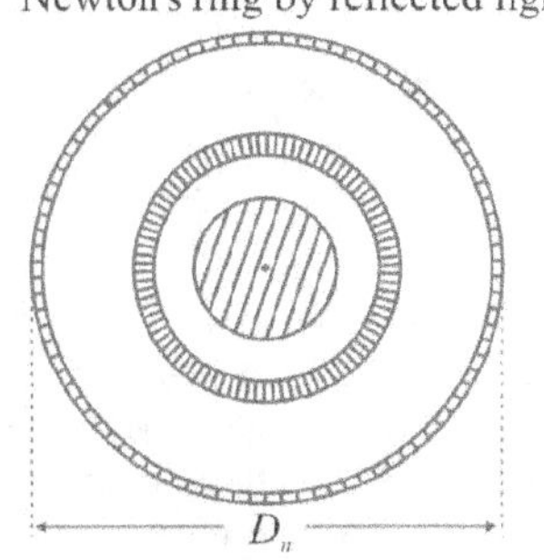

Fig. **4.32**

Similarly for dark ring

$$2\mu t = n\lambda, \quad n = 1, 2, 3$$

or

$$2\mu \frac{r^2}{2R} = n\lambda$$

or

$$r^2 = \frac{n\lambda R}{\mu}$$

or

$$\frac{D_n^2}{4} = \frac{n\lambda R}{\mu}$$

or

$$D_n^2 = \frac{4n\lambda R}{\mu}.$$

Ex. 17 A narrow monochromatic beam of light of intensity I is incident on a glass plate as shown in *fig. 4.33*. Another identical glass plate is kept close to the first one and parallel to it. Each glass plate reflects 25% of the incident on it and transmits the remaining. Find the ratio of the minimum and the maximum intensities in the interference pattern formed by the two beams obtained after one reflection at each plate.

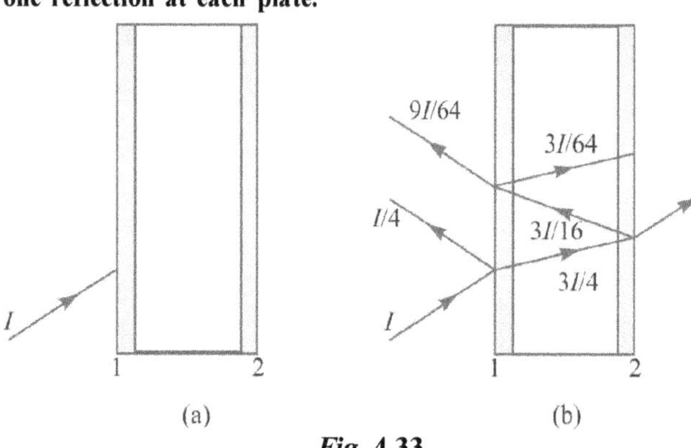

Fig. 4.33

Sol. The intensities of reflected beams at two points on the first plates are shown in figure. From which

$$I_1 = \frac{I}{4} \text{ and } I_2 = \frac{9I}{64}.$$

The intensities of maxima and minima after their interference are :

$$I_{max} = I_1 + I_2 + 2\sqrt{I_1 I_2}$$

and

$$I_{min} = I_1 + I_2 - 2\sqrt{I_1 I_2}$$

$$\therefore \quad \frac{I_{min}}{I_{max}} = \frac{I_1 + I_2 - 2\sqrt{I_1 I_2}}{I_1 + I_2 + 2\sqrt{I_1 I_2}}$$

After substituting the values of I_1 and I_2 and simplifying, we get

$$\frac{I_{min}}{I_{max}} = 1/49. \qquad Ans.$$

Ex. 18 In Young's double slit experiment using monochromatic light, the fringe pattern shifts by a certain distance on the screen when a mica sheet of refractive index 1.6 and thickness 1.964 micron is introduced in the path of one of interfering waves. The mica-sheet is then removed and the distance between the slits and the screen is doubled. It is found that the distance between successive maxima (or minima) now is the same as the observed fringe shift on the introduction of mica-sheet. Calculate the wavelength of the monochromatic light used in the experiment.

Sol. The shift produced in the fringes is

$$\Delta = \frac{D}{d}(\mu - 1)t.$$

When distance between slits and screen is doubled, the fringe width

$$\beta = \frac{(2D)\lambda}{d}.$$

According to the given condition

$$\frac{D}{d}(\mu - 1)t = \frac{(2D)\lambda}{d}$$

$$\therefore \quad \lambda = \frac{(\mu - 1)t}{2}$$

$$= \frac{(1.6 - 1) \times 1.964 \times 10^{-6}}{2}$$

$$= 5892 \text{ Å}. \qquad Ans.$$

Ex. 19 A glass plate of refractive index 1.5 is coated with a thin layer of thickness of t and refractive index 1.8. Light of wavelength λ travelling in air is incident normally on the layer. It is partly reflected at the upper and the lower surfaces of the layer and the two reflected rays interfere. Write the condition for their constructive interference. If the $\lambda = 648$ nm. Obtain the least value of t for which the rays interfere constructively.

Sol.

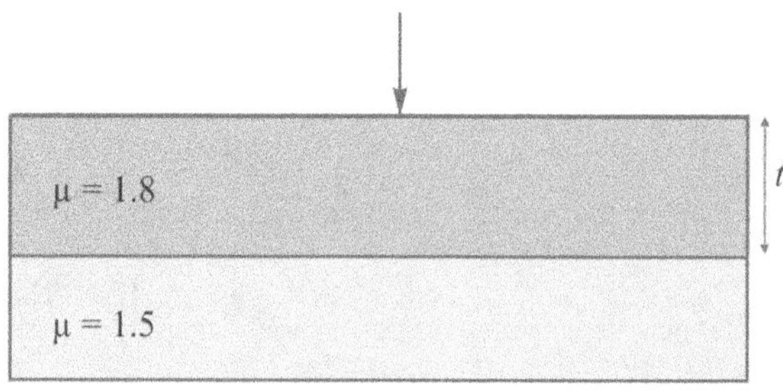

Fig. 4.34

Condition of constructive interference in the situation shown in figure is

$$2\mu t = (2n - 1)\lambda/2, \, n = 1, 2, 3,$$

$$\therefore \quad t = (2n - 1)\frac{\lambda}{4\mu}$$

For least value of t, $n = 1$

$$\therefore \quad t_{min} = (2 \times 1 - 1)\frac{\lambda}{4\mu} = \frac{\lambda}{4\mu}$$

$$= \frac{648 \times 10^{-9}}{4 \times 1.8} = 90 \times 10^{-9} \text{ m.} \quad \textit{Ans.}$$

Ex. 20 A vessel $ABCD$ of 10 cm width has two small slits S_1 and S_2 sealed with identical glass plates of equal thickness. The distance between the slits is 0.8 mm. POQ is the line perpendicular to the plane AB and passing through O, the middle point of S_1 and S_2. A monochromatic light source is kept at S, 40 cm below P and 2m from the vessel, to illuminate the slits as shown in figure. Calculate the position of the central fringe on the other wall CD with respect to the line OQ. Now, a liquid is poured into the vessel and filled upto OQ. The central bright fringe is found to be at Q. Calculate the refractive index of the liquid.

Sol.

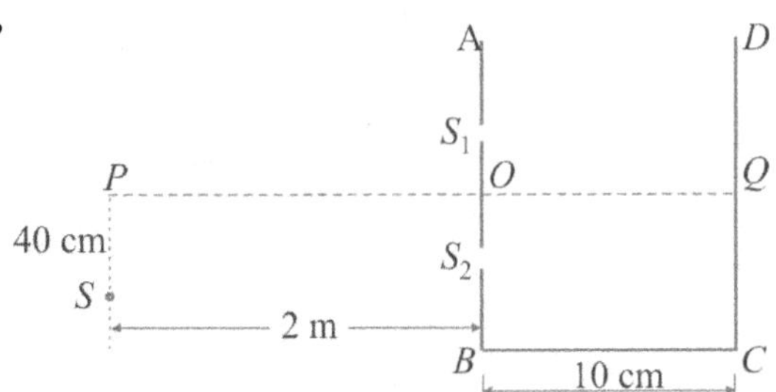

Fig. 4.35

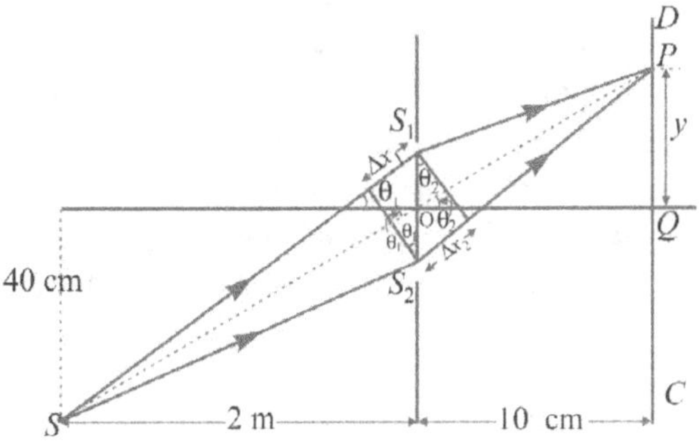

Fig. 4.36

The path difference,

$$\Delta x = (SS_1 + S_1P) - (SS_2 + S_2P)$$

$$= (SS_1 - SS_2) - (S_2P - S_1P)$$

$$= \Delta x_1 - \Delta x_2$$

For central bright $\Delta x = 0$

or $\quad 0 = \Delta x_1 - \Delta x_2$

or $\quad \Delta x_1 = \Delta x_2$

or $\quad d\sin\theta_1 = d\sin\theta_2$

or $\quad \sin\theta_1 = \sin\theta_2$

or $\quad \dfrac{0.4}{\sqrt{0.4^2 + 2^2}} = \dfrac{y}{\sqrt{0.1^2 + y^2}}$

After solving, we get $\quad y = 0.02$ m

$$= 2 \text{ cm.} \quad \textit{Ans.}$$

When water is filled in the vessel, it causes shift in position of fringe

$$\Delta = 2 \text{ cm}$$

or $\quad \dfrac{D}{d}(\mu - 1)t = 0.02$

$$\dfrac{0.10}{0.8 \times 10^{-3}}(\mu - 1) \times 0.1 = 0.02$$

which gives $\quad \mu = 1.002.$ $\quad$ *Ans.*

Ex. 21 In a modified YDSE the region between screen and slits is immersed in a liquid whose refractive index varies with time as $\mu_\ell = \left(\dfrac{5}{2}\right) - \dfrac{T}{4}$ until it reaches a steady state value of $\dfrac{5}{4}$.

A glass plate of thickness 36 μm and refractive index $\dfrac{3}{2}$ is introduced infront of one of the slits.

(a) Find the position of central maxima as a function of time and the time when it is at point O, located symmetrically on the x-axis.

(b) What is the speed of the central maxima when it is at O?

Sol.

(a)

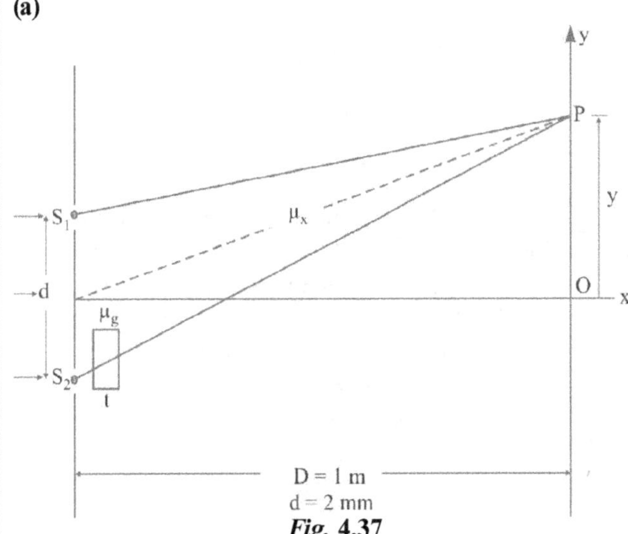

Fig. 4.37

The optical path difference between lights start from S_1 and S_2

$$\Delta x = \left[S_{2\,liquid}P + (\mu_g - \mu_\ell)t \right] - (S_1P)_{liquid}$$

$$= (S_2P - S_1P)_{liquid} + (\mu_g - \mu_\ell)t$$

$$= \mu_l(S_2P - S_1P)_{air} + (\mu_g - \mu_\ell)t$$

or $\quad \Delta x = \mu_l\, d\dfrac{y}{D} + (\mu_g - \mu_\ell)t$

For central maxima, $\Delta x = 0$

or $\qquad 0 = \mu_\ell\, d\dfrac{y}{D} + \left(\mu_g - \mu_\ell\right)t$

which gives $y = \dfrac{-D\left(\mu_g - \mu_\ell\right)t}{d\,\mu_\ell}$

$$= \dfrac{-D\left[\dfrac{3}{2} - \left(\dfrac{5}{2} - \dfrac{T}{4}\right)\right]t}{d\left[\dfrac{5}{2} - \dfrac{T}{4}\right]}$$

$$= \dfrac{D\left[1 - \dfrac{T}{4}\right]t}{d\left(\dfrac{5}{2} - \dfrac{T}{4}\right)} = \dfrac{D(4-T)t}{d(10-T)}$$

The time when y becomes zero,

$$0 = \dfrac{D\left(1 - \dfrac{T}{4}\right)t}{d\left(\dfrac{5}{2} - \dfrac{T}{4}\right)} \Rightarrow T = 4\,s. \qquad \textbf{Ans.}$$

(b) Speed of central maxima

$$v = \dfrac{dy}{dt} = \dfrac{6\,Dt}{(10-T)^2\,d}$$

Central maxima is at O at $T = 4\,s$

Thus $\qquad v = \dfrac{6\,Dt}{(10-4)^2\,d} = \dfrac{6\,Dt}{36d} = \dfrac{Dt}{6d}$

$$= \dfrac{1\times\left(36\times10^{-6}\right)}{6\times\left(2\times10^{-3}\right)} = 3\times10^{-3}\ m/s\ .\textbf{Ans.}$$

Ex. 22 A glass surface is coated by an oil film of uniform thickness 1.00×10^{-4} cm. The index of refraction of the oil is 1.25 and that of the glass is 1.50. Find the wavelengths of light in the visible region (400 nm - 750nm) which are completely transmitted by the oil film under normal incidence.

Sol.   Optical path difference for the light transmitted through oil is $= 2\mu t \cos r$ for normal incidence

$$r = 0, \cos r \to 1.$$

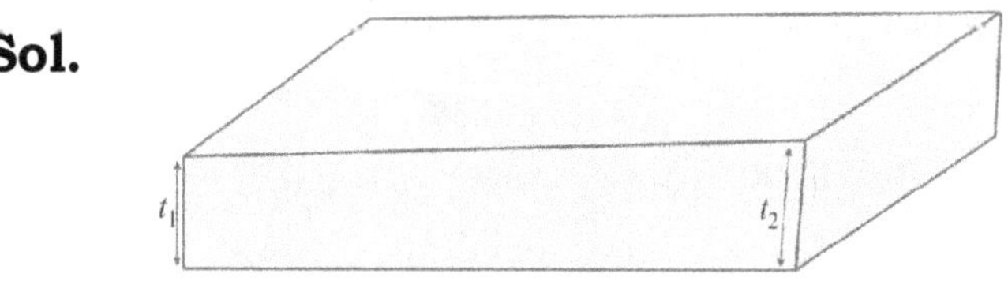

Fig. **4.38**

$\therefore \qquad \Delta x = 2\mu t$

But at the interface between oil and glass will produce an additional path difference of $\lambda/2$. Therefore effective path difference

$$\Delta x = 2\mu t + \lambda/2$$

For constructive interference in transmitted light

$$2\mu t + \dfrac{\lambda}{2} = n\lambda, n = 1, 2, ...$$

or $\qquad 2\mu t = (2n-1)\lambda/2$

or $\qquad \lambda = \dfrac{4\,\mu t}{(2n-1)}$

$$= \dfrac{4\times1.25\times1\times10^{-6}}{2n-1}$$

$$= \dfrac{5\times10^{-6}}{(2n-1)}$$

For $n = 1,\qquad \lambda = 5\times10^{-6}$ m $= 5000$ nm

$\quad n = 2,\qquad \lambda = \dfrac{5\times10^{-6}}{3}$ m $= 1666.67$ nm

$\quad n = 3,\qquad \lambda = \dfrac{5\times10^{-6}}{5}$ m $= 1000$ nm

$\quad n = 4,\qquad \lambda = \dfrac{5\times10^{-6}}{7}$ m $= 714.29$ nm

$\quad n = 5,\qquad \lambda = \dfrac{5\times10^{-6}}{9}$ m $= 555.55$ nm

$\quad n = 6,\qquad \lambda = \dfrac{5\times10^{-6}}{11}$ m $= 454.54$ nm

The wavelength which are strongly transmitted in visible range are : 714.29 nm, 555.55 nm and 454.54 nm

Ex. 23 Two square surfaces of a transparent plastic block having a shape of as shown in *fig.* 4.39 have thickness t_1 at one edge and t_2 at the other. The refractive index of the material is 1.6. When viewed at normal incidence, using a light of wavelength 5000 Å, 20 fringes are observed. Find the difference $(t_2 - t_1)$.

Sol.

Fig. **4.39**

Let, at the thickness t_1, n^{th} number of fringe is formed, then at thickness t_2, $(n+20)^{th}$ number of fringe will form. For reflected light

$$2\mu t_1 = n\lambda \qquad\qquad ...(i)$$
and $\qquad 2\mu t_2 = (n+20)\lambda \qquad\qquad ...(ii)$

Subtracting (i) from (ii), we get

$$2\mu\left(t_2 - t_1\right) = 20\lambda$$

$\therefore \qquad \left(t_2 - t_1\right) = \dfrac{10\lambda}{\mu}$

$$= \dfrac{10\times\left(5000\times10^{-10}\right)}{1.6}$$

$$= 3.125\times10^{-6}\ m. \qquad \textbf{Ans.}$$

4.8 DIFFRACTION

The bending of waves around the edges of an obstacle or aperture is called **diffraction**. This phenomenon was discovered by Grimaldi. The theorical explanation was first given by Fresnel. According to him diffraction results from the superposition of secondary wavelets originating from the different parts of the same wavefront. For diffraction to occur, the size of the aperture should be small enough. It should be comparable to the wavelength of wave. In case when size of aperture is very large in comparison to the wavelength, then there is no appreciable diffraction will occur, and so infront of the aperture, there is uniform illumination on the screen (see *fig.* 4.40).

If an obstacle with a small gap is placed in almost like a point source. If the gap is large however, the diffraction is much more limited. Small, in this context, means that the size of the obstacle is comparable to the wavelength of the waves.

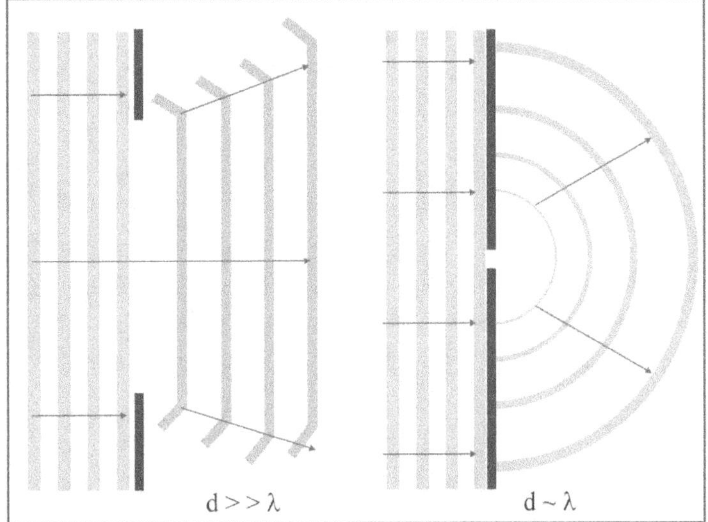

Fig. **4.40**

Difference between interference and diffraction

1. Interference takes place between two or more wavefronts originating from coherent sources. While in diffraction superposition takes place between the secondary wavelets originating from the same wavefront.
2. In the interference pattern the regions of minimum intensity are usually almost perfectly dark. While it is not so in diffraction pattern.
3. The fringe width in interference may or may not be equal, while in diffraction pattern fringe widths are never equal.
4. In interference all the maxima are of same intensity but in diffraction they are of varying intensity.

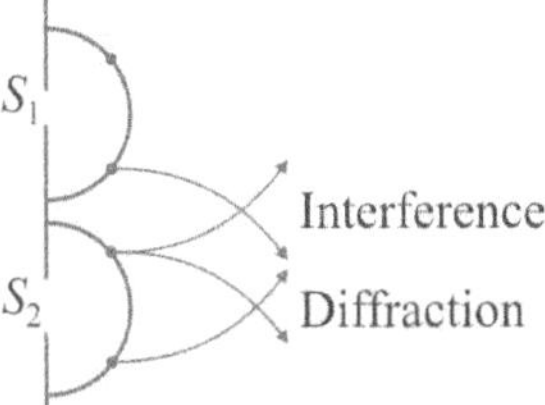

Fig. **4.41**

4.9 FRAUNHOFFER DIFFRACTION AT SINGLE SLIT

In this type of diffraction a plane wavefront falls on a slit and its response is seen on a plane screen placed at very large distance from the slit.

Suppose a plane wavefront falls on a slit of width d. Every point of the exposed part of the wavefront acts as a source of secondary wavelets. These wavelets superpose (interfere) and produce diffraction.

Intensity distribution

If the intensity of the principal maxima is I_0, then the intensity of the first maxima and second order maxima are found to be $\dfrac{I_0}{22}$

and $\dfrac{I_0}{61}$ respectively. The diffraction fringes are of decreasing width and decreasing intensity. In general for any angular position θ, the intensity I is given by

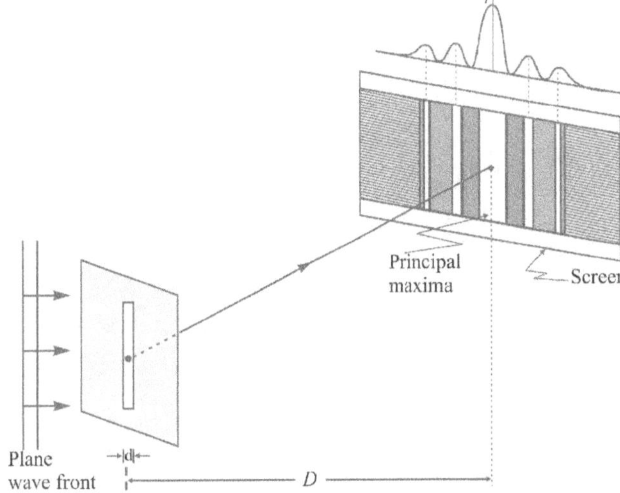

Fig. 4.42 Diffraction at single slit.

$$I_{(\theta)} = I_0 \left(\frac{\sin \alpha}{\alpha}\right)^2, \text{ where } \alpha = \frac{\pi a}{\lambda} \sin \theta.$$

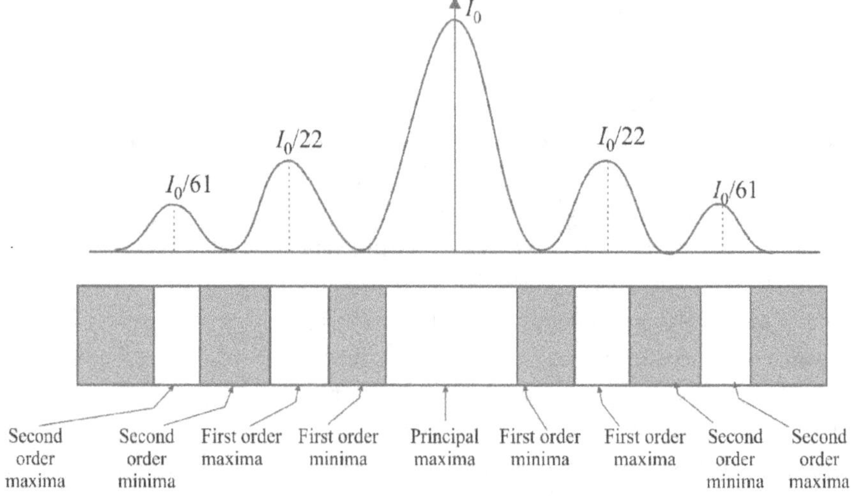

Fig **4.43. Intensity distribution in diffraction**

Diffraction maximas and minimas
Principal maxima :

When wavefront strikes the slit, the secondary wavelets from all point in the slit travel about the same distance to reach the centre of the diffraction pattern and thus are in same phase there. So they interfere constructively and produce principal maxima.

To understand higher order maximas, we can use a clever technique and the slit can be divided hypothetically into odd number of zones; three zones for first order maxima and five zones for second order maxima and so on.

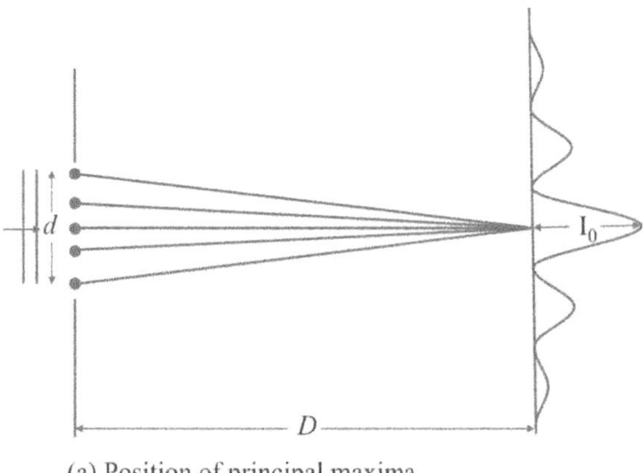

(a) Position of principal maxima.

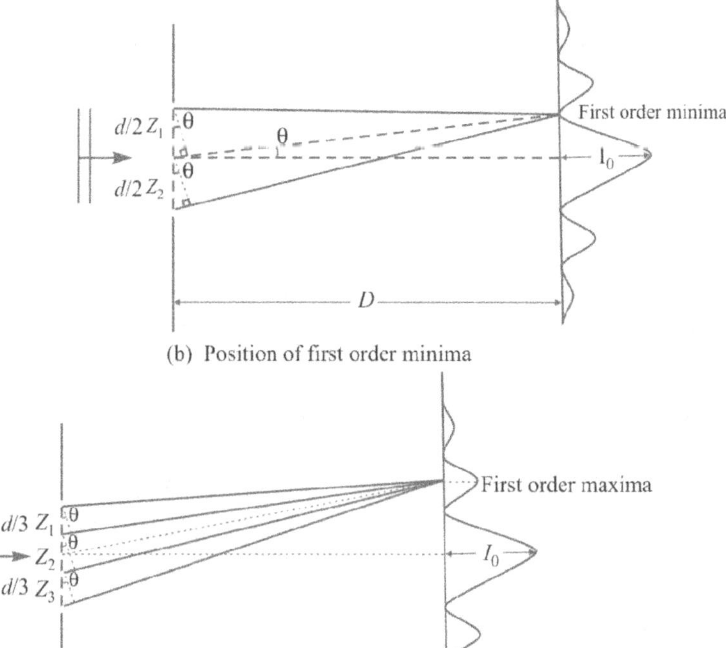

(b) Position of first order minima

(c) Position of first order maxima

Fig. **4.44**

Positions of first and higher order minimas

To understand first order minima, we can divide the slit hypothetically into two identical zones Z_1 and Z_2 each of width $d/2$. Take a wavelet from top of the zone Z_1 and other from the top of the zone Z_2. The path difference between them is $d/2\sin\theta$. All other similar pairs will have the same path difference.

If these wavelets interfere destructively, then they will produce minima. This will happen when $d/2\sin\theta$ is equal to $\lambda/2$. Thus for first order minima

$$d/2\sin\theta \;=\; \lambda/2$$

$$\text{or}\qquad d\sin\theta \;=\; \lambda \qquad\qquad ...(1)$$

The position of first order minima,

$$\sin\theta \;=\; \frac{\lambda}{d}.$$

The principal maxima spread symmetrically about central line in angle 2θ. Thus angular width of principal maxima is

$$2\theta \;=\; 2\sin^{-1}\!\left(\frac{\lambda}{d}\right). \qquad\qquad ...(2)$$

Linear width of principal maxima; $\beta = (2\theta D) = 2D\sin^{-1}\!\left(\dfrac{\lambda}{d}\right)$.

For second order minima, we can divide the slit hypothetically into four zones. The wavelets of nearest two zones interfere destructively and again produce minima. Thus for second order minima, we have

$$\frac{d}{4}\sin\theta \;=\; \frac{\lambda}{2},$$

$$\text{or}\qquad d\sin\theta \;=\; 2\lambda.$$

In general the positions of minimas can be obtained as :

$$d\sin\theta \;=\; n\lambda; \qquad n=1,2, \qquad\qquad ...(3)$$

Positions of first and higher order maximas

To understand first order maxima, we can divide the slit hypothetically into three identical zones Z_1, Z_2, Z_3 each of width $d/3$. The wavelets of two neighbouring zones Z_1 and Z_2 interfere destructively and cancel their mutual effect. The wavelets of remaining third zone will cause first order maxima. Thus for first order maxima the path difference between two wavelets, one from top of the zone Z_1 and other from top of zone the Z_2 is $d/3\sin\theta$. For destructive interference between them

$$\frac{d}{3}\sin\theta \;=\; \frac{\lambda}{2}$$

$$\text{or}\qquad d\sin\theta \;=\; \frac{3\lambda}{2}. \qquad\qquad ...(4)$$

Similarly for second order maxima, we can get

$$d\sin\theta \;=\; \frac{5\lambda}{2}.$$

In general, for higher order maxima, we can write;

$$d\sin\theta \;=\; (2n+1)\frac{\lambda}{2}; \qquad n=1,2, \;...(5)$$

Note:

The technique used to explain the positions of minima and maxima can not be used to get the intensity of maxima.

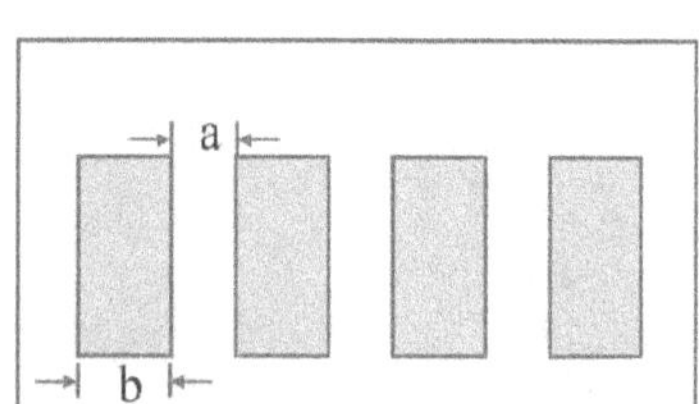

Fig. **4.45** Diffraction grating.

4.10   DIFFRACTION GRATING

A diffraction grating consists of equally spaced, parallel slits. If a is the width of the slit and b is the width of the opaque portion between two adjacent slits, then $(a + b)$ is the distance between the adjacent slits. This is known as **grating element.** If there are N parallel slits (rulings) in each centrimetre, then grating element is given by

$$(a+b) \; = \; \frac{1}{N} \text{ cm.}$$

The grating equation can be written as :

$$(a+b)\sin\theta \; = \; n\lambda; \; n = 1, 2, ...$$

The above equation gives the position of nth maxima.

Diffraction by a circular aperture

When a plane wavefront falls on a circular hole, it is diffracted by the hole. The response, if received on a screen at a large distance, the pattern is a bright disc surrounded by alternate dark and bright rings of decreasing intensity as shown in *fig.* **4.46.** The position of first dark ring from the hole at an angle θ with the axis

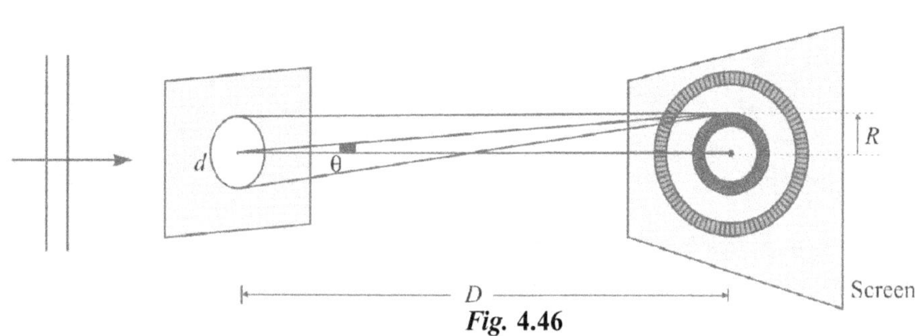

Fig. **4.46**

$$\sin\theta \; = \; \frac{1.22\lambda}{d},$$

where $\lambda \rightarrow$ wavelength of the light used.

The radius of first dark ring $\qquad R \; = \; D\theta = \dfrac{1.22\,\lambda D}{d}$ (for small θ).

Most of the light coming from the hole is concentrated within the first dark ring, this radius is also called radius of the **diffraction disc.**

Ex. 24 Plane microwaves are incident on a long slit having a width of 5.0 cm. Calculate the wavelength of the microwaves if the first diffraction minimum is formed at $\theta = 30°$.

Sol.   For first diffraction minima,

$$\sin\theta \; = \; \frac{\lambda}{d}$$

Given, $\qquad\qquad \theta \; = \; 30°$

$\therefore \qquad\qquad \sin 30° \; = \; \dfrac{\lambda}{5}$

or $\qquad\qquad \lambda \; = \; 5 \times \dfrac{1}{2}$

$$= \; 2.5 \text{ cm.} \qquad\qquad \textbf{\textit{Ans.}}$$

Ex. 25 Light of wavelength 560 nm goes through a pinhole of diameter 0.20 mm and falls on a wall at a distance of 2.00 m. What will be the radius of the central bright spot formed on the wall?

Sol. The radius of central dark can be obtained as

$$R \; = \; 1.22 \frac{\lambda D}{d}$$

$$= \frac{1.22 \times \left(560 \times 10^{-9}\right) \times 2}{0.20 \times 10^{-3}} = 0.68 \text{ cm.} \qquad \textbf{\textit{Ans.}}$$

Ex. 26 Angular width of central maximum in the Fraunhoffer diffraction pattern of a slit is measured. The slit is illuminated by light of wavelength 6000 Å. When the slit is illuminated by light of another wavelength, the angular width is decreases by 30%. Calculate the wavelength of this light. The same decrease in the angular width of central maximum is obtained when the original apparatus is immersed in a liquid. Find refractive index of the liquid.

Sol. Angular width of central maxima $= \dfrac{2\lambda}{d}$.

For the other light it is $= \dfrac{2\lambda'}{d}$

According to given condition, we have

$$\frac{2\lambda'}{d} \; = \; (0.70)\frac{2\lambda}{d}$$

$$\Rightarrow \qquad \lambda' \; = \; 0.7\,\lambda = 0.7 \times 6000 \text{ Å}$$

$$= \; 4200 \text{ Å.}$$

When the apparatus is immersed in liquid, the same decrease is observed in the angular width.

Angular width in liquid $\qquad = \; 2\dfrac{\lambda_\ell}{d} = \dfrac{\left(2\,\lambda_{air}\right)/\mu_\ell}{d}$

or $\qquad\qquad \mu_\ell \; = \; \dfrac{1}{0.7} = 1.43 . \qquad \textbf{\textit{Ans.}}$

Ex. 27 A convex lens of diameter 8.0 cm is used to focus a parallel beam of light of wavelength 620 nm. If the light be focused at a distance of 20 cm from the lens, what would be the radius of the central bright spot formed ?

Sol. The angular spread of central bright is given by

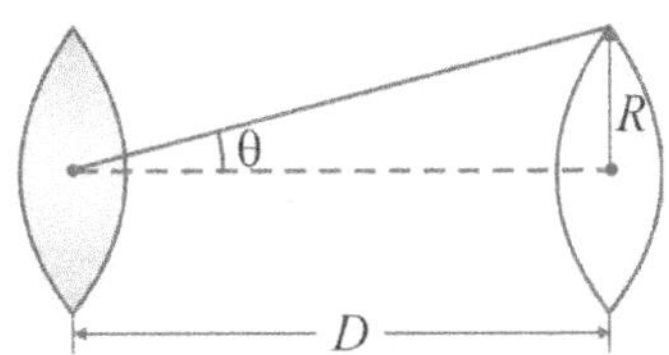

Fig. **4.47**

$$\sin\theta = \frac{1.22\lambda}{d}$$

$$= \frac{1.22 \times 620 \times 10^{-9}}{0.08}$$

$$= 9.455 \times 10^{-6} \; rad.$$

Since θ is small, so we can take

$$\tan\theta \simeq \sin\theta = 9.455 \times 10^{-6} \text{ rad}$$

By geometry, we have, $\tan\theta = \dfrac{R}{D}$

$$\therefore \qquad \frac{R}{D} = 9.45 \times 10^{-6}$$

or $\qquad R = 9.45 \times 10^{-6} \times 0.20$

$$= 1.89 \times 10^{-6} \, \text{m}. \qquad \textit{Ans.}$$

Ex. 28 A wedge of angle 0.5° is illuminated with sodium light whose two lines corresponds to the wavelengths 5890 Å and 5896 Å. Find the distance from the apex at which the maxima due to the two wavelengths first coincide when observed in the reflected light. (The wedge contains air).

Sol. Let the thickness of the wedge at the point where the maximums of both coincides be t. For constructive interference in reflected light, we have

$$2\mu t \cos r = (2n+1)\frac{\lambda}{2}$$

Fig. **4.48**

For normal incidence and $\mu_{air} = 1$, we have

$$2t = (2n+1)\frac{\lambda_1}{2}$$

and $\qquad 2t = (2n+3)\dfrac{\lambda_2}{2}$

According to given condition, we can write

$$\frac{(2n+1)\lambda_1}{2} = \frac{(2n+3)\lambda_2}{2}$$

or $\qquad (2n + 1) (5896) = (2n + 3) (5890)$

$$\therefore \qquad n = (1499) \text{ whole number}$$

and $\qquad t = (2n+1)\dfrac{\lambda_1}{4}$

$$= \frac{(2 \times 1499 + 1)}{4} \times 5896 \times 10^{-10}$$

$$= 0.004 \text{ cm}$$

Let x be the required distance from the apex, then

$$\frac{t}{x} = \tan\theta \simeq \theta$$

$$\therefore \qquad x = \frac{t}{\theta}$$

$$= \frac{0.004}{0.5 \times \dfrac{\pi}{180}} = 4.58 \text{ cm}. \quad \textit{Ans.}$$

Resolution limit and resolving power

When we decrease the separation between the two point objects, a limit is reached when our eyes can not differentiate them separately, even they are not in contact. The minimum separation between two closely placed objects, the eyes can distinguish them separately is known as **resolution limit** (*RL*). The reciprocal of resolution limit is known as **resolving power** (*RP*). Thus

$$RP = \frac{1}{RL} .$$

Rayleigh criteria

According to Rayligh, two images of two objects are said to be just resolved when central maxima of one diffraction pattern falls on first minima of other (see figure).

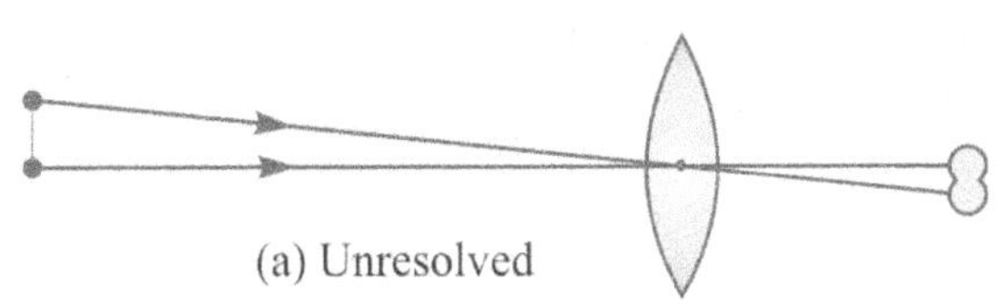

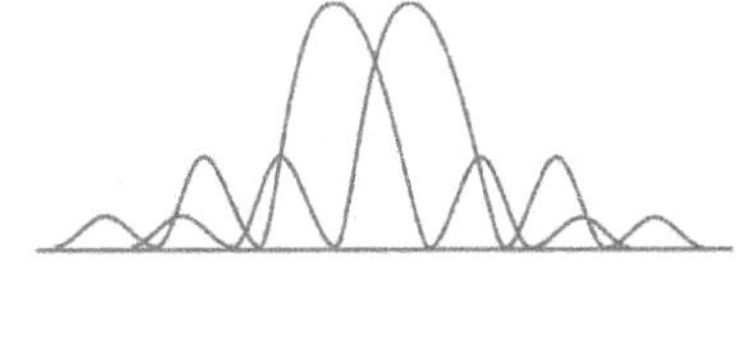

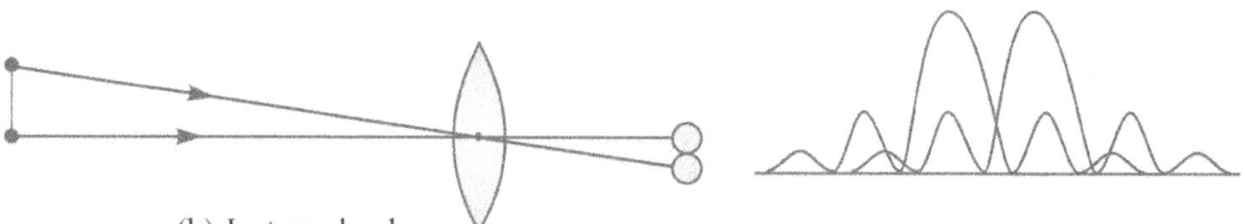

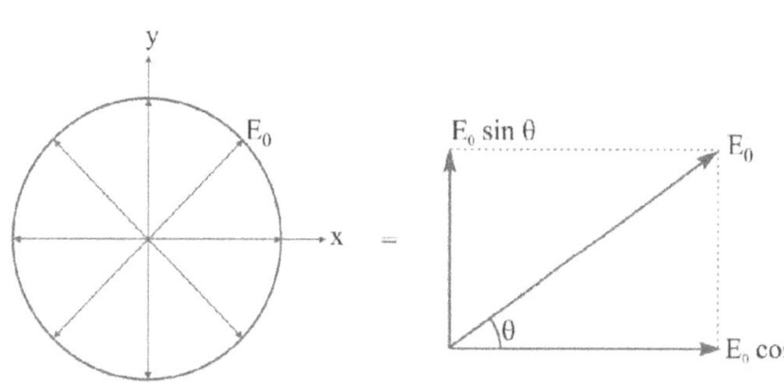

(b) Just resolved

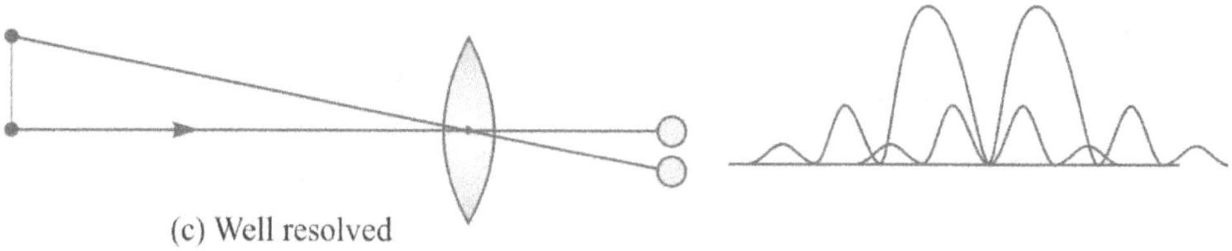

(c) Well resolved

Fig. 4.49

(i)   The resolution limit of normal human eye is one minute (1′).

(ii)   The resolution limit of a telescope is given by angle θ, where

$$\theta = \frac{1.22\,\lambda}{d}\ \text{rad.}$$

Here λ is the wavelength of light used and d is the diameter of objective lens of the telescope.

(iii)   The resolution limit of a microscope is given by

$$x = \left[\frac{1.22\,\lambda}{2\mu\,\sin\theta}\right]\text{metre,}$$

where μ is the refractive index of medium between objects and lens; θ is the angle subtended by the objects at objective lens of the microscope. $\mu\,\sin\theta$ is called **numerical aperture** of the lens.

4.11   TRANSVERSE NATURE OF LIGHT

Interference and diffraction phenomenon prove the wave character of the light. These phenomenon do not give any idea; whether light waves are transverse or longitudinal. Polarisation proves the transverse character of light waves. Transverse character of light waves was known in the early nineteenth century; however the association of electric and magnetic vectors with light wave was known only after **Maxwell**. The electric field in a light wave propagating in free space is perpendicular to the direction of propagation. Natural light consists of many pulses emitted by different atoms; in general have electric field in different directions. Hence the resultant electric field at a point changes continuously and randomly. Such a light is called **unpolarised light**. If E_0 is the amplitude of the resultant of all the waves, then it can be resolved into two components; E_x and E_y, where $E_x = E_0 \cos\theta$ and $E_y = E_0 \sin\theta$.

The intensity of light due to x-component is given by $I_x = E_x^2 = E_o^2 \cos^2\theta$, and due to y-component.

$I_y = E_o^2 \sin^2\theta$. To get the average intensity of light, we have to find the average of $\cos^2\theta$ and $\sin^2\theta$ over one complete cycle; which is

Fig. **4.50**

$$\frac{1}{2\pi}\int_0^{2\pi}\cos^2\theta\,d\theta = \frac{1}{2}\ \text{and}\ \frac{1}{2\pi}\int_0^{2\pi}\sin^2\theta\,d\theta = \frac{1}{2}.$$

Thus resultant intensity of the light I_0 can be written as :

$$I_0 = I_x + I_y = E_0^2 \cos^2 \theta + E_0^2 \sin^2 \theta$$

or

$$I_0 = \frac{E_0^2}{2} + \frac{E_0^2}{2} = E_0^2.$$

Thus unpolarised light can be assumed of two components; each of intensity $\dfrac{I_0}{2}$.

4.12 POLARISATION

When electric field vector (or magnetic) vibrates only along one direction perpendicular to the direction of propagation, the light is said to be linearly polarised light and the phenomenon associated is called **polarisation**. Thus when unpolarised light is incident on a polariser, the emerging light becomes linearly polarised of intensity $\dfrac{I_0}{2}$.

Plane of polarisation

The plane which passes through direction of propagation and perpendicular to the plane of vibration is known as plane of polarisation.

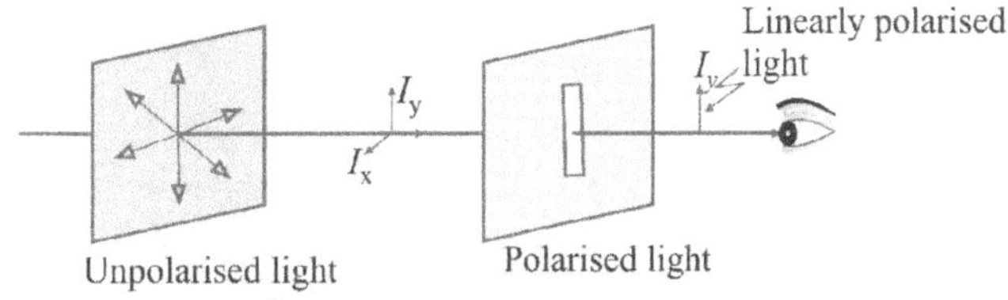

Fig. **4.51** Linearly polarised light.

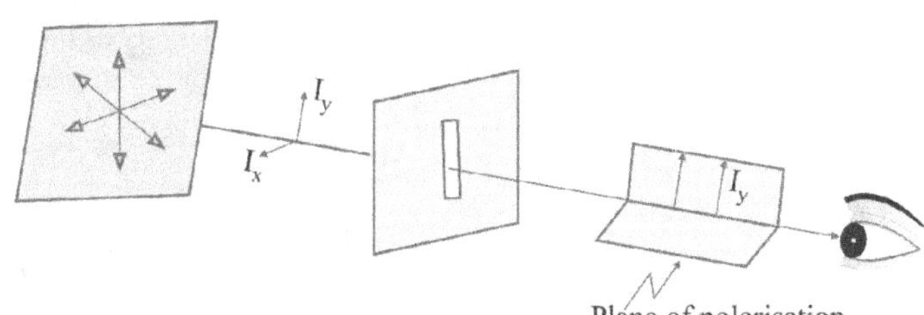

Fig. **4.52**

4.13 POLARISATION BY REFLECTION : BREWSTER'S LAW

In 1808 Malus found that when natural light is incident of a glass slab, the reflected light becomes partially polarised. Brewter forwarded his study and found that when light is incident on glass slab at certain angle, called polarising angle, the reflected light becomes linearly polarised. This happens when reflected and refracted rays are perpendicular to each other.

Consider a beam of natural light is incident on a glass slab at an angle i_p as shown in *fig.* 4.55. A part of it is reflected and a part is refracted. If r is the angle of refraction, then

$$r + i_P = 90°$$
$$\therefore \qquad r = 90° - i_P.$$

By Snell's law;
$$\mu = \frac{\sin i}{\sin r}$$

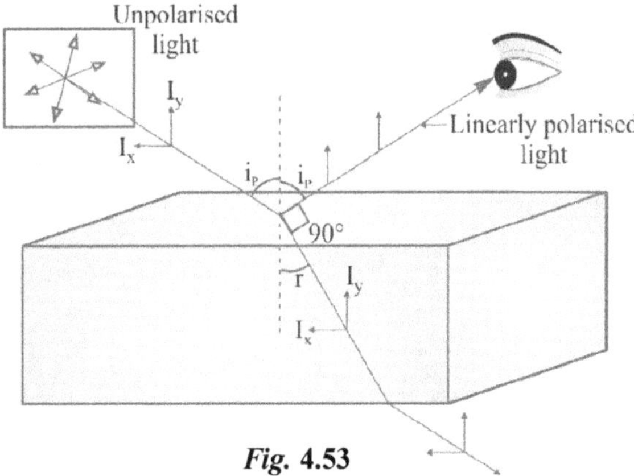

Fig. **4.53**

$$= \frac{\sin i_P}{\sin(90° - i_P)}$$

$$= \frac{\sin i_P}{\cos i_P}$$

$$\therefore \qquad \mu = \tan i_P. \qquad \text{Brewster's law}$$

The above relation is known as **Brewster's law.**
For ordinary glass
$$\mu = 1.5,$$

$$\therefore \qquad i_P = \tan^{-1}(\mu) = \tan^{-1}(1.5)$$
$$\approx 57°.$$

Thus when natural light is incident on glass slab, the reflected light becomes linearly polarised and refracted light becomes partially polarised.

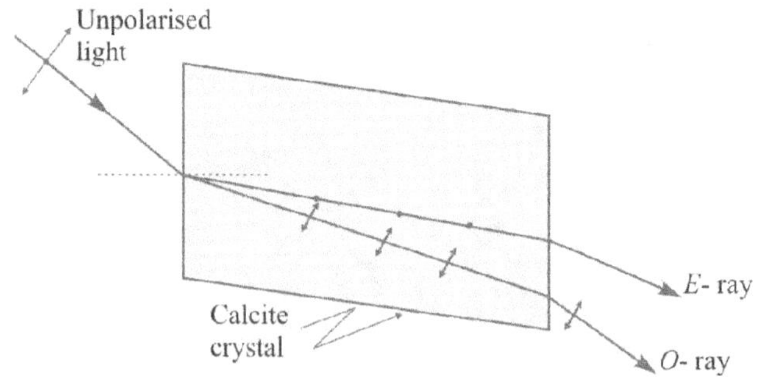

Fig. 4.54

Polarisation by double refraction

When unpolarised light (natural light) is incident on a calcite crystal, it splits into two rays; O-ray (ordinary ray) and E-ray (extra-ordinary ray). O-ray has same speed in all directions and hence obeys law of refraction. While E-ray has different speed in different directions in a medium and so does not obey law of refraction. These two rays are plane polarised and their planes of vibrations are mutually perpendicular.

4.14   MALUS' LAW

Consider a polariser and a analyser placed at an angle θ. If E is the amplitude of the incident wave, then the amplitude of the wave emerging from analyser will be $E\cos\theta$ and thus the intensity of the emerging beam will be given by;

$$
\begin{aligned}
I_\theta &= (E\cos\theta)^2 \\
&= E^2\cos^2\theta \\
I_\theta &= I\cos^2\theta. \qquad \textbf{Malus' law}
\end{aligned}
$$

Thus when plane polarised light is incident on an analyser, which is placed at an angle θ with the polariser, the intensity of emerging light from analyser becomes $I\cos^2\theta$.

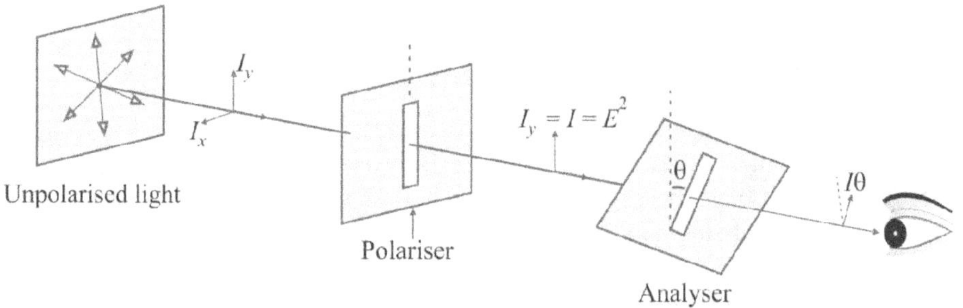

Fig. 4.55

In complete rotation of analyser, we will see two maximum and two zero intensities.

$$
\begin{aligned}
\text{For} \quad \theta &= 0°, \; I_\theta = I\cos^2 0° = I \\
\theta &= 90°, \; I_\theta = I\cos^2 90° = 0 \\
\theta &= 180°, \; I_\theta = I\cos^2 180° = I \\
\theta &= 270°, \; I_\theta = I\cos^2 270° = 0.
\end{aligned}
$$

Ex. 29 Two polaroids are placed at 90° to each other and the transmitted intensity zero. What happens when one more polaroid is placed between these two bisecting the angle between them ?

Sol.

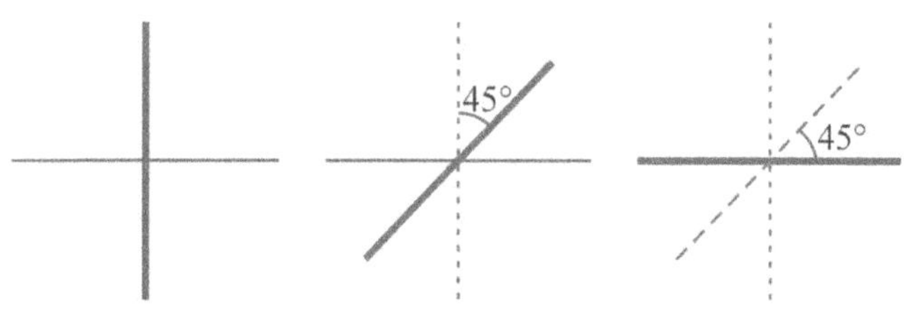

Fig. 4.56

Figure shows the orientation of the polaroids.

If I is the intensity of the light emerging from the first polaroid, then intensity of emerging light from second and third are $I\cos^2 45°$ and $(I\cos^2 45°)\sin^2 45°$. These are : $I/2$ and $I/4$ respectively.

Ex. 30 Three nicols prisms are placed such that, first and third are mutually perpendicular. Unpolarised light is incident on first nicol's prism, the intensity of light emerges from third nicol's prism is 1/16 the intensity of incident light. Find the angle between first and second nicol's prisms.

Sol. Suppose angle between first and second nicol's prisms is θ. Then the angle between second and third nicol's prisms becomes $90° - \theta$. If I_0 is the intensity of the incident light on the first prism, then intensity of emerging light from this will be $I = \dfrac{I_0}{2}$. The intensity of light emerging from second and third nicol's prisms be $\left(\dfrac{I_0}{2}\right)\cos^2\theta$ and

$\left[\left(\dfrac{I_0}{2}\right)\cos^2\theta\right]\sin^2\theta$ respectively.

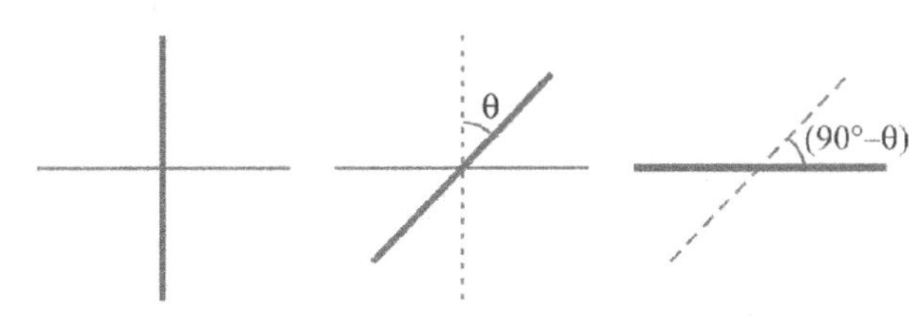

Fig. 4.57

Thus according to the given condition

$$\dfrac{I_0}{2}\cos^2\theta\,\sin^2\theta = \dfrac{I_0}{16}$$

$$(\sin\theta\,\cos\theta)^2 = \dfrac{1}{8}$$

$$\text{or}\qquad (2\sin\theta\,\cos\theta)^2 = \dfrac{1}{2}$$

$$\text{or}\qquad \sin^2(2\theta) = \dfrac{1}{2}$$

$$\text{or}\qquad \sin2\theta = \dfrac{1}{\sqrt{2}}$$

$$\therefore\qquad 2\theta = 45°$$

$$\text{or}\qquad \theta = 22.5°. \qquad \textbf{\textit{Ans.}}$$

Review of Formulae & Important Points

1. **Interference :** When two or more coherent waves travels in same direction, nearly in a line , they and superpose gives interference.

 * Interference is the phenomenon of conservation of energy. For two waves of amplitudes a_1 and a_2

$$y_1 = a_1\sin\omega t\,.$$
$$y_2 = a_2\sin(\omega t + \varphi)$$
$$y = y_1 + y_2 = A\sin(\omega t + \theta)\,.$$

The resultant wave

where
$$A^2 = a_1^2 + a_2^2 + 2a_1a_2\cos\varphi$$

or
$$I = I_1 + I_2 + 2\sqrt{I_1 I_2}\,\cos\varphi$$

and
$$\tan\theta = \dfrac{a_2\sin\varphi}{a_1 + a_2\cos\varphi}$$

(i) **Constructive interference :**
$$A_{max} = a_1 + a_2$$
for
$$\varphi = 2n\pi,\ n = 0, 1, 2, \ldots\ldots\ldots$$
or
$$\Delta x = n\lambda$$

(ii) **Destructive interference :**
$$A_{min} = a_1 \sim a_2$$
for
$$\varphi = (2n-1)\pi,\ n = 0, 1, 2, \ldots$$
or
$$x = (2n-1)\lambda/2$$

$$\dfrac{I_{max}}{I_{min}} = \dfrac{(a_1 + a_2)^2}{(a_1 - a_2)^2}$$

(iii) For $a_1 = a_2$

$$I_{max} = 4a^2$$
$$I_{min} = 0$$
$$I = I_{max}\cos^2(\varphi/2)$$

 * If waves are incoherent, they will not interfere, then
$$I_{max} = a^2 + a^2 = 2a^2$$

2. **Young's double slits experiment :**

$$\Delta x = d\sin\theta \approx d\tan\theta$$
$$= \dfrac{d\,y_n}{D}\,.$$

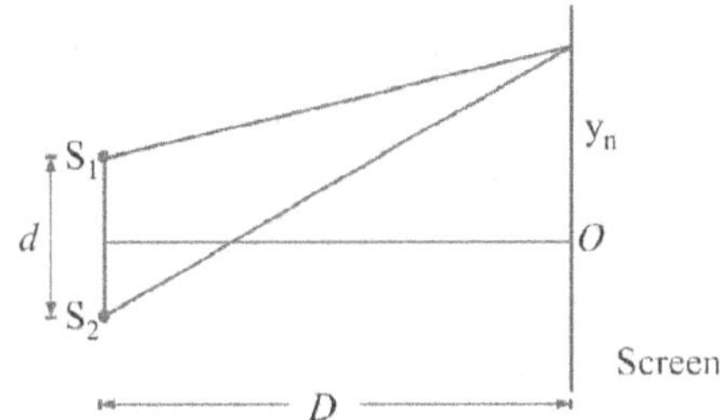

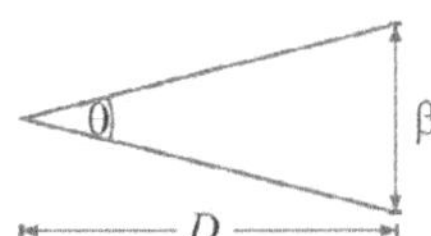

(i) For constructive interference

$$y_n = n\dfrac{D\lambda}{d}$$

$$\beta = \dfrac{D\lambda}{d}$$

(ii) For destructive interference

$$y_n = \dfrac{(2n-1)}{2}\dfrac{D\lambda}{d}$$

$$\beta = \dfrac{D\lambda}{d}\,.$$

Angular fringe width :

$$\theta = \dfrac{\beta}{D} = \dfrac{\lambda}{d}\,.$$

3. **Fresnel's biprism :**

$$d = 2Aa(\mu - 1)$$

$$\beta = \frac{(a+b)\lambda}{d}$$

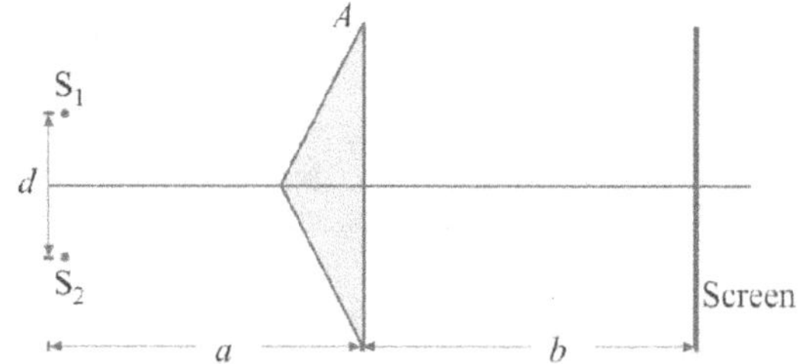

* Central fringe bright

* In Lioyd's mirror central fringe is dark.

4. **Displacement of fringes :**

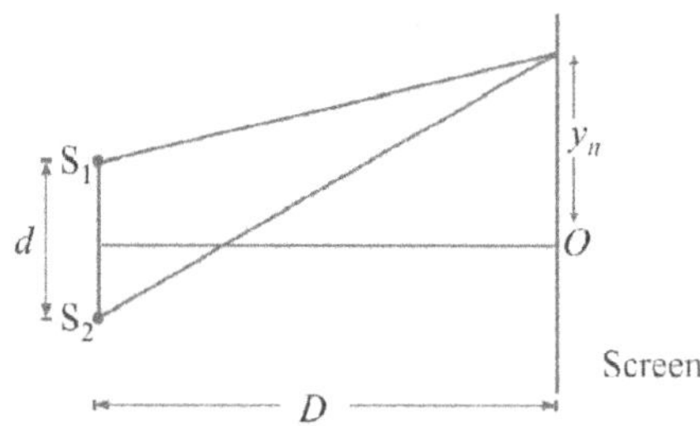

If a transparent plate is introduced in path of the light wave, the path of wave is increased by $(\mu - 1)t$.

Displacement of fringes : Entire fringe pattern shift towards side of plate. Fringe width remains same.

The displacement of the fringe

$$\Delta = \frac{D(\mu - 1)t}{d}$$

5. **Interference in thin films :**

(a) In reflected light :

$$2\mu t \cos r = (2n-1)\frac{\lambda}{2}, \quad n = 1, 2, \ldots \text{ for constructive}$$

interference

and $2\mu t \cos r = n\lambda$, $n = 0, 1, 2, \ldots\ldots\ldots$ for destructive interference

(b) In transmitted light :

$$2\mu t \cos r = n\lambda, \quad n = 0, 1, 2, \ldots\ldots\ldots \text{ for constructive}$$

interference

and $2\mu t \cos r = (2n-1)\dfrac{\lambda}{2}$, $n = 1, 2, \ldots\ldots\ldots$ for

destructive interference

6. **Interference in wedge shaped film :**

$$\beta = \frac{\lambda}{2\mu \tan \alpha}.$$

7. **Fraunhoffer diffraction at single slit :** Diffraction occurs due to super position between the wavelets originated from same wave front. For diffraction, size of aperture is order of wave length of wave.

$$a \sin \theta = \lambda, \text{ for first order minima}$$

Width of principal maxima $= 2\theta = 2\sin^{-1}(\lambda/a)$

8. **Polarization :** Symmetry to asymmetry of vibrations of optic vector is called polarisation.

* When natural light falls on polariser, its intensity become half the incident.

Malus Law : $I_\theta = I_0 \cos^2 \theta$

Brewster's law : $\mu = \tan i_p$.

★ ★ ★

Optics MCQ Type 1 *Exercise 4.1*

LEVEL - 1

Only one option correct

1. The figure shows a monochromatic rays of light traveling across parallel interfaces, from an original material I, through layers of material II and III, and then back into material I. The Materials according to the speed of light in them, greatest first are ;

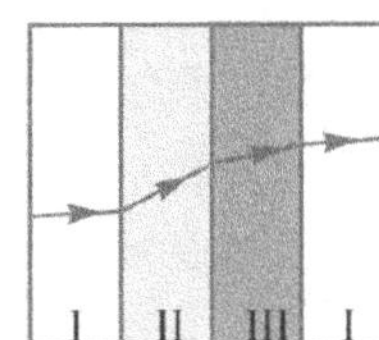

(a) II, III, I
(b) III, II, I
(c) I, II, III
(d) none of these

2. Each of the four pairs of light waves arrives at a certain point on a screen. The waves have the same wavelength. At the arrival point, their amplitudes and phase differences are :

(I) $2a_0$, $6a_0$ and π rad
(II) $3a_0$, $5a_0$ and π rad
(III) $9a_0$, $7a_0$, and 3π rad
(IV) $2a_0$, $2a_0$ and 0.

The pair/s which has greatest intensity is /are :

(a) I
(b) II
(c) II, III
(d) I, IV

3. Figure shows two light rays that are initially exactly in phase and that reflect from several glass surfaces. Neglect the slight slant in the path of the light in the second arrangement. The path length difference in terms of wavelength λ is :

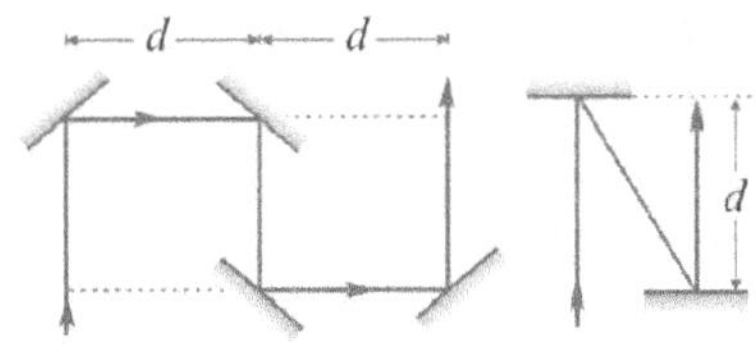

(a) $2d$
(b) $(d + \lambda)$
(c) $(2d + \lambda)$
(d) none of these

4. Figure shows two rays of light encountering interfaces, where they reflect and refract. Which of the resulting waves are shifted in phase at the interface ?

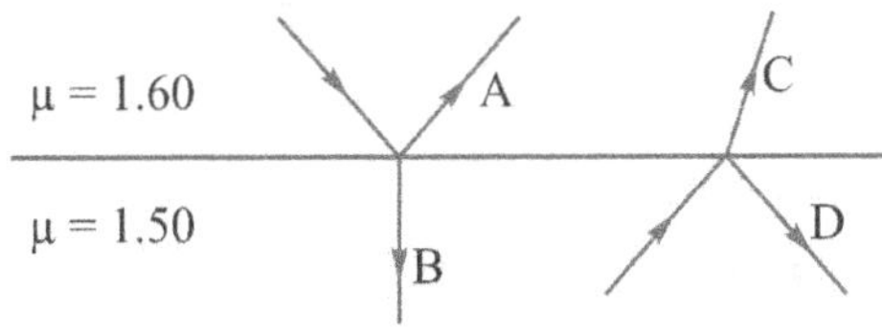

(a) A
(b) B
(c) C
(d) D

5. The magnetic field equation for an electromagnetic wave in vacuum is $B_x = B \sin(ky + \omega t)$, then electric field equation is ;

(a) $E_x = E \sin(kz + \omega t)$
(b) $E_y = E \sin(ky + \omega t)$
(c) $E_z = E \sin(ky + \omega t)$
(d) none of these

6. Two coherent monochromatic light beams of intensities I and 4I are superposed. The maximum and minimum possible intensities in the resulting beam are

(a) $5I$ and I
(b) $5\,I$ and $3I$
(c) $9\,I$ and I
(d) $9\,I$ and $3I$

7. Light appears to travel in straight lines since

(a) it is not absorbed by the atmosphere
(b) it is reflected by the atmosphere
(c) its wavelength is very small
(d) its velocity is very large

8. The ratio of intensities of two waves is 9 : 1. They are producing interference. The ratio of maximum and minimum intensities will be

(a) 10 : 8
(b) 9 : 1
(c) 4 : 1
(d) 2 : 1

9. Colours of thin films result from

or

On a rainy day, a small oil film on water show brilliant colours. This is due to

(a) dispersion of light
(b) interference of light
(c) absorption of light
(d) scattering of light

10. Two sources of waves are called coherent if

(a) both have the same amplitude of vibrations
(b) both produce waves of the same wavelength
(c) both produce waves of the same wavelength having constant phase difference
(d) both produce waves having the same velocity

Answer Key	1	(a)	2	(d)	3	(c)	4	(d)	5	(c)
Sol. from page 231	6	(c)	7	(c)	8	(c)	9	(b)	10	(c)

11. The dual nature of light is exhibited by
    (a) photoelectric effect
    (b) refraction and interference
    (c) diffraction and reflection
    (d) diffraction and photoelectric effect

12. To demonstrate the phenomenon of interference, we require two sources which emit radiation
    (a) of the same frequency and having a define phase relationship
    (b) of nearly the same frequency
    (c) of the same frequency
    (d) of different wavelengths

13. In Young's experiment, the distance between the slits is reduced to half and the distance between the slit and screen is doubled, then the fringe width
    (a) will not change
    (b) will become half
    (c) will be doubled
    (d) will become four times

14. The maximum intensity of fringes in Young's experiment is I. If one of the slit is closed, then the intensity at that place becomes I_0. Which of the following relation is true ?
    (a) $I = I_0$
    (b) $I = 2I_0$
    (c) $I = 4I_0$
    (d) there is no relation between I and I_0

15. In a double slit experiment, instead of taking slits of equal widths, one slit is made twice as wide as the other. Then in the interference pattern
    (a) the intensities of both the maxima and the minima
    (b) the intensity of maxima decreases and that of the minima increases
    (c) the intensity of maxima decreases and that of the minima increases
    (d) the intensity of maxima decreases and the minima has zero intensity

16. In a Young's double slit experiment, the separation of the two slits is doubled. To keep the same spacing of fringes, the distance D of the screen from the slits should be made
    (a) $\dfrac{D}{2}$
    (b) $\dfrac{D}{\sqrt{2}}$
    (c) $2D$
    (d) $4D$

17. Yellow light is used in single slit diffraction experiment with slit width 0.6 mm. If yellow light is replaced by X-rays then the pattern will reveal
    (a) that the central maxima is narrower
    (b) no diffraction pattern
    (c) more number of fringes
    (d) less number of fringes

18. Light waves can be polarised as they are
    (a) transverse
    (b) of high frequency
    (c) longitudinal
    (d) reflected

19. Figure represents a glass plate placed vertically on a horizontal table with a beam of unpolarised light falling on its surface at the polarising angle of 57° with the normal. The electric vector in the reflected light on screen S will vibrate with respect to the plane of incidence in a

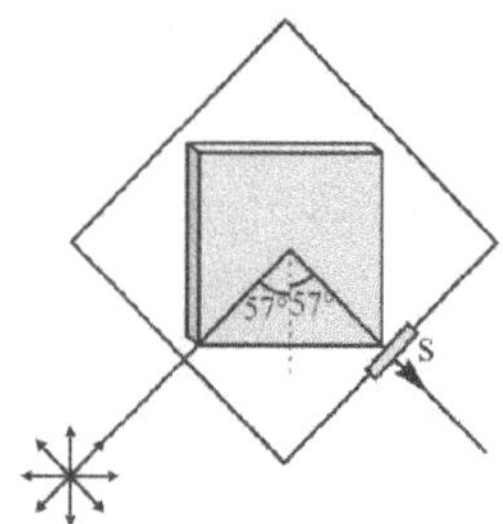

    (a) vertical plane
    (b) horizontal plane
    (c) plane making an angle of 45° with the vertical
    (d) plane making an angle of 57° with the horizontal

20. When an unpolarized light of intensity I_0 is incident on a polarizing sheet, the intensity of the light which does not get transmitted is
    (a) zero
    (b) I_0
    (c) $\dfrac{1}{2}I_0$
    (d) $\dfrac{1}{4}I_0$

21. A thin slice is cut out of a glass cylinder along a plane parallel to its axis. The slice is placed on a flat glass plate as shown. The observed interference fringes from this combination shall be

    (a) straight
    (b) circular
    (c) equally spaced
    (d) having fringe spacing which increases as we go outwards

22. Two coherent point sources S_1 and S_2 are separated by a small distance d as shown. The fringes obtained on the vertical screen will be :

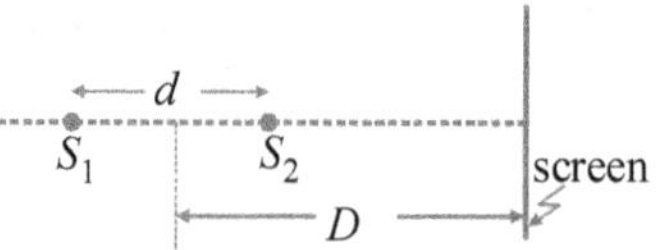

    (a) points
    (b) straight bands
    (c) concentric circles
    (d) semicircles

23. A beam with wavelength λ falls on a stack of partially reflecting planes with separation d. The angle θ that the beam should make with the planes so that the beams reflected from successive planes may interfere constructively is (where n, = 1, 2, ...)

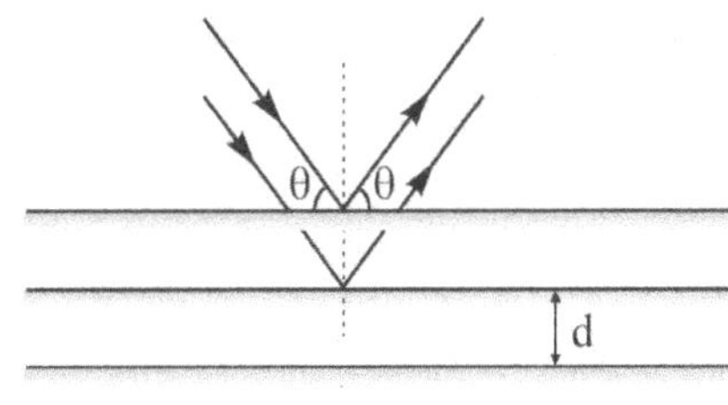

(a) $\sin^{-1}\left(\dfrac{n\lambda}{d}\right)$

(b) $\tan^{-1}\left(\dfrac{n\lambda}{d}\right)$

(c) $\sin^{-1}\left(\dfrac{n\lambda}{2d}\right)$

(d) $\cos^{-1}\left(\dfrac{n\lambda}{2d}\right)$

24. The maximum number of possible interference maxima for slit-separation equal to twice the wavelength in Young's double-slit experiment is
(a) infinite
(b) five
(c) three
(d) zero

25. A Young's double slit experiment uses a monochromatic source. The shape of the interference fringes formed on a screen is
(a) straight line
(b) parabola
(c) hyperbola
(d) circle

26. If I_0 is the intensity of the principal maximum in the single slit diffraction pattern, then what will be its intensity when the slit width is doubled
(a) I_0
(b) $\dfrac{I_0}{2}$
(c) $2I_0$
(d) $4I_0$

27. White light falls normally on a film of soapy water whose thickness is 5×10^{-5} cm and refractive index is 1.40. The wavelengths in the visible region that are reflected the most strongly are :
(a) 5600 Å and 4000 Å
(b) 5400 Å and 4000 Å
(c) 6000 Å and 5000 Å
(d) 4500 Å only

28. The radiation pressure (in N/m^2) of the visible light is of the order of
(a) 10^{-2}
(b) 10^{-4}
(c) 10^{-6}
(d) 10^{-8}

29. Laser beams are used to measure long distance because
(a) they are monochromatic
(b) they are highly polarised
(c) they are coherent
(d) they have high degree of parallelism

30. A mixture of light, consisting of wavelength 590 nm and an unknown wavelength, illuminates Young's double slit and gives rise to two overlapping interference patterns on the screen. The central maximum of both lights coincide. Further, it is observed that the third bright fringe of known light coincides with the 4th bright fringe of the unknown light. From this data, the wavelength of the unknown light is
(a) 393.4 nm
(b) 885.0 nm
(c) 442.5 nm
(d) 776.8 nm

31. In a Young's double slit experiment, 12 fringes are observed to be formed in a certain segment of the screen when light of wavelength 600 nm is used. If the wavelength of light is changed to 400 nm, number of fringes observed in the same segment of the screen is given by
(a) 12
(b) 18
(c) 24
(d) 30

32. When a thin transparent plate of thickness t and refractive index μ is placed in the path of one of the two interfering waves of light, then the path difference changes by
(a) $(\mu + 1)t$
(b) $(\mu - 1)t$
(c) $\dfrac{(\mu + 1)}{t}$
(d) $\dfrac{(\mu - 1)}{t}$

33. In a Young's double-slit experiment the fringe width is 0.2 mm. If the wavelength of light used is increased by 10% and the separation between the slits is also increased by 10%, the fringe width will be
(a) 0.20 mm
(b) 0.401 mm
(c) 0.242 mm
(d) 0.165 mm

34. The velocity of light emitted by a source S observed by an observer O, who is at rest with respect to S is c. If the observer moves towards S with velocity v, the velocity of light as observed will be
(a) $c + v$
(b) $c - v$
(c) c
(d) $\sqrt{1 - \dfrac{v^2}{c^2}}$

35. If a star is moving towards the earth, then the lines are shifted towards
(a) red
(b) infrared
(c) blue
(d) green

36. Conditions of diffraction is
(a) $\dfrac{a}{\lambda} = 1$
(b) $\dfrac{a}{\lambda} \gg 1$
(c) $\dfrac{a}{\lambda} \ll 1$
(d) None of these

37. Diffraction and interference of light suggest
(a) nature of light is electro-magnetic
(b) wave nature
(c) nature is quantum
(d) nature of light is transverse

Answer Key	23	(c)	24	(b)	25	(a)	26	(d)	27	(a)	28	(c)	29	(d)	30	(c)
Sol. from page 231	31	(b)	32	(a)	33	(c)	34	(c)	35	(a)	36	(b)	37	(b)		

38. Consider the following statements, in case of Young's double-slit experiment:

1. Initial slit is necessary if we use an ordinary extended source of light.

2. Initial slit is not needed if we use an ordinary but well collimated beam of light.

3. Initial slit is not needed if we use a spatially coherent source of light.

Which of the above statements are correct?

(a) 1, 2 and 3   (b) 1 and 2

(c) 2 and 3   (d) 1 and 3

39. A beam of electron is used in an YDSE experiment. The slit width is d. When the velocity of electron is increased, then

(a) no interference is observed

(b) fringe width increases

(c) fringe width decreases

(d) fringe width remains same

40. Three light waves combine at a certain point where their electric field components are

$$y_1 = a\sin\omega t,\ y_2 = a\sin(\omega t + 60°),\ y_3 = a\sin(\omega t - 120°)$$

Their resultant at that point is :

(a) a (b) $2a$

(c) $3a$ (d) none of these

41. Ocean waves moving at a speed of 4.0 m/s are approaching a beach at an angle of 30° to the normal, as shown in figure. Suppose the water depth changes abruptly at a certain distance from the beach and the wave speed there drops to 3.0 m/s. Close to the angle θ is :

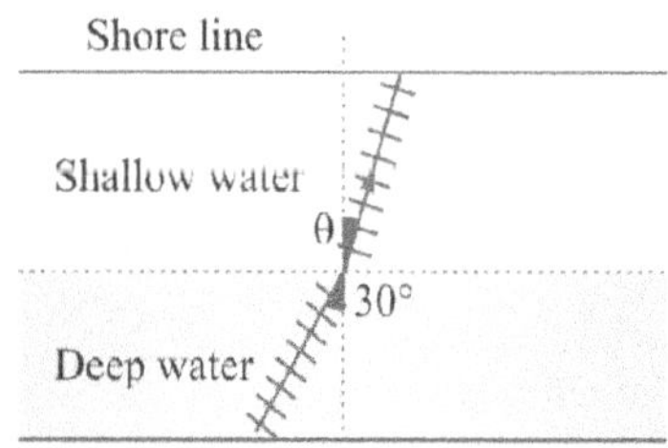

(a) $\sin^{-1}(3/4)$ (b) $\sin^{-1}(1/4)$

(c) $\sin^{-1}(3/8)$ (d) none of these

42. Two beams of light having intensities I and $4I$ interfere to produce a fringe pattern on a screen. The phase difference between the beams is $\dfrac{\pi}{2}$ at point A and π at point B. Then the difference between the resulting intensities at A and B is

(a) $2I$ (b) $4I$

(c) $5I$ (d) $7I$

43. The observed wavelength of light coming from a distant galaxy is found to be increased by 0.5% as compared with that coming from a terrestrial source. The galaxy is

(a) stationary with respect to the earth

(b) approaching the earth with velocity of light

(c) receding from the earth with the velocity of light

(d) receding from the earth with a velocity equal to 1.5×10^6 m/s.

44. In YDSE, how many maximas can be obtained on a screen including central maxima in both sides of the central fringe if λ = 3000Å, $d = 5000$Å

(a) 2   (b) 5

(c) 3   (d) 1

45. In hydrogen spectrum the wavelength of H_α line is 656 nm whereas in the spectrum of a distant galaxy, H_α line wavelength is 706 nm. Estimated speed of the galaxy with respect to earth is

(a) 2×10^8 m/s   (b) 2×10^7 m/s

(c) 2×10^6 m/s   (d) 2×10^5 m/s

46. In the figure is shown Young's double slit experiment. Q is the position of the first bright fringe on the right side of O, P is the 11th fringe on the other side, as measured from Q. If the wavelength of the light used is 6000×10^{-10}m, then S_1B will be equal to

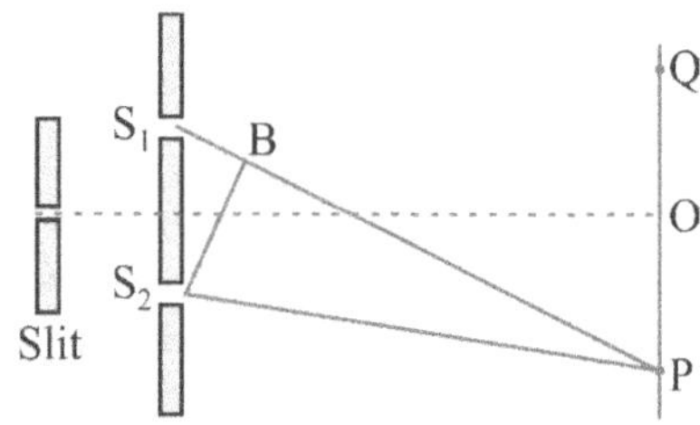

(a) 6×10^{-6} m   (b) 6.6×10^{-6}m

(c) 3.138×10^{-7} m   (d) 3.144×10^{-7} m

47. In Young's double slit experiment, the two slits act as coherent sources of equal amplitude A and wavelength λ. In another experiment with the same set up the two slits are of equal amplitude A and wavelength λ but are incoherent. The ratio of the intensity of light at the mid-point of the screen in the first case to that in the second case is

(a) $1 : 2$ (b) $2 : 1$

(c) $4 : 1$ (d) $1 : 1$

48. A monochromatic beam of light falls on YDSE apparatus at some angle (say θ) as shown in figure. A thin sheet of glass is inserted in front of the lower slit S_2. The central bright fringe (path difference = 0) will be obtained

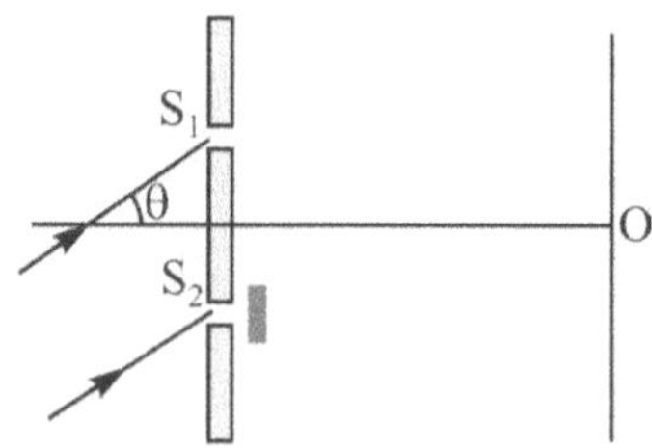

(a) at O   (b) above O

(c) blow O

(d) anywhere depending on angle θ, thickness of plate t and refractive index of glass μ.

Answer Key	**38**	(c)	**39**	(c)	**40**	(a)	**41**	(c)	**42**	(b)	**43**	(d)	**44**	(c)	**45**	(b)
Sol. from page 231	**46**	(a)	**47**	(b)	**48**	(d)										

49. In a Young's double slit experiment, the separation between the two slits is d and the wavelength of the light is λ. The intensity of light falling on slit 1 is four times the intensity of light falling on slit 2. Choose the correct choice(s)

(a) if $d = \lambda$, the screen will contain only one maximum

(b) if $\lambda < d < 2\lambda$, at least one more maximum (besides the central maximum) will be observed on the screen

(c) if the intensity of light falling on slit 1 is reduced so that it becomes equal to that of slit 2, the intensities of the observed dark and bright fringes will increase

(d) if the intensity of light falling on slit 2 is reduced so that it becomes equal to that of slit 1, the intensities of the observed dark and bright fringes will increase.

50. Light from a source emitting two wavelengths λ_1 and λ_2 is allowed to fall on a Young's double slit apparatus after one of the wavelengths is filtered. The position of interference maxima is noted. When the filter is removed i.e. both the wavelengths are now incident on the slits, it is found that the maximum intensity is now produced where the fourth maxima occurred previously. If the other wavelength is filtered, the third maxima is found at the same location. The ratio of the two wavelengths is :

(a) $\dfrac{3}{4}$

(b) $\dfrac{4}{5}$

(c) $\dfrac{3}{5}$

(d) $\dfrac{4}{7}$

51. Optical path for yellow light is same if it passes through 4 cm of glass or 6 cm of water. If the refractive index of water is $\dfrac{4}{3}$, what is the refractive index of glass ?

(a) 2

(b) 1.5

(c) $\dfrac{16}{9}$

(d) $\dfrac{3}{4}$

52. Two beams A and B of plane polarised light with mutually perpendicular planes of polarisation are seen through a polaroid. From the position when the beam A has maximum intensity (and the beam B has zero intensity) the polaroid is rotated through 30° to make A and B appear equally bright. If I_A and I_B are the initial intensities of A and B respectively, then what is the ratio of I_A to I_B?

(a) 1

(b) 1/3

(c) 3

(d) 3/2

53. A beam of unpolarized light of intensity I_0 passes through a combination of an ideal polarizer and an ideal analyzer with their transmission axes at 60°. What is the intensity of the beam coming out at the other end?

(a) I_0

(b) $I_0/2$

(c) $I_0/4$

(d) $I_0/8$

Answer Key	49	(b)	50	(a)	51	(a)	52	(b)
Sol. from page 231	53	(d)						

LEVEL -2

1. A beam of light of wavelength 600 nm from a distant source falls on a single slit 1 mm wide and the resulting diffraction pattern is observed on a screen 2 m away. The distance between the first dark fringes one other side of the central bright fringe is

(a) 1.2 mm

(b) 1.2 cm

(c) 2.4 cm

(d) 2.4 mm

2. Consider the three waves represented by

$$y_1 = 3\sin(kx - \omega t)$$

$$y_2 = 3\sin\left(kx - \omega t + \dfrac{2\pi}{3}\right)$$

$$y_3 = 3\sin\left(kx - \omega t + \dfrac{4\pi}{3}\right)$$

The amplitude of resultant of waves at $x = 0$ is

(a) 0

(b) 9

(c) 6

(d) 7

3. A single slit of width a is illuminated by violet light of wavelength 400 nm and the width of the diffraction pattern is measured as y. When half of the slit width is covered and illuminated by yellow light of wavelength 600 nm, the width of the diffraction pattern is

(a) the pattern vanishes and the width is zero

(b) $y / 3$

(c) $3y$

(d) none of these

4. In the ideal double-slit experiment, when a glass-plate (refractive index 1.5) of thickness t is introduced in the path of one of the interfering beams (wavelength λ), the intensity at the position where the central maximum occurred previously remains unchanged. The minimum thickness of the glass-plate is

(a) 2λ

(b) $\dfrac{2\lambda}{3}$

(c) $\dfrac{\lambda}{3}$

(d) λ

Answer Key	1	(a)	2	(a)	3	(c)	4	(a)
Sol. from page 232								

5. In a two slit experiment with monochromatic light fringes are obtained on a screen placed at some distance from the sits. If the screen is moved by 5×10^{-2} m towards the slits, the change in fringe width is 3×10^{-5} m/s. If separation between the slits is 10^{-3} m, the wavelength of light used is

(a) 6000 Å (b) 5000 Å

(c) 3000 Å (d) 4500 Å

6. Two ideal slits S_1 and S_2 are at a distance d apart, and illuminated by light of wavelength λ passing through an ideal source slit S placed on the line through S_2 as shown. The distance between the planes of slits and the source slit is D. A screen is held at a distance D from the plane of the slits. The minimum value of d for which there is darkness at O is

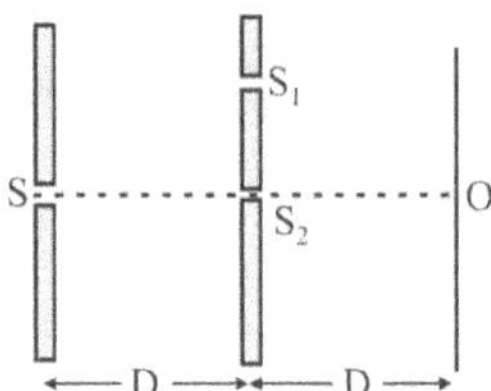

(a) $\sqrt{\dfrac{3\lambda D}{2}}$ (b) $\sqrt{\lambda D}$

(c) $\sqrt{\dfrac{\lambda D}{2}}$ (d) $\sqrt{3\lambda D}$

7. In a YDSE bi-chromatic light of wavelengths 400 nm and 560 nm are used. The distance between the slits is 0.1 mm and the distance between the plane of the slits and the screen is 1m. The minimum distance between two successive regions of complete darkness is

(a) 4 mm (b) 5.6 mm

(c) 14 mm (d) 28 mm

8. In Young's double slit experiment intensity at a point is (1/4) of the maximum intensity. Angular position of this point is (separation between slits is d)

(a) $\sin^{-1}\left(\lambda / d\right)$ (b) $\sin^{-1}\left(\lambda / 2d\right)$

(c) $\sin^{-1}\left(\lambda / 3d\right)$ (d) $\sin^{-1}\left(\lambda / 4d\right)$

9. Two glass slides A and B each of length L are placed with one end in contact and the other separated by a spacer of thickness h. Monochromatic light of wavelength λ falls normaly on the plate A and interference fringes are observed by the eye E through a microscope. The spacing between the successive resulting dark fringes is :

(a) $\dfrac{2h}{L\lambda}$

(b) $\dfrac{L\lambda}{2h}$

(c) $\dfrac{\lambda L}{h}$

(d) $\dfrac{2\,L\lambda}{h}$

10. The angle substanded by the first diffraction minimum for a point source viewed in the hydrogen line at 1420 MHz with a radio telescope having an aperture of 25 m is :

(a) 0.8° (b) 0.64°

(c) 1.2° (d) 2.2°

11. A glass plate 0.40 micron thick is illuminated by a beam of white light normal to the plate. The refractive index of glass is 1.50 and the limits of the visible spectrum are $\lambda_V = 4000$ Å and $\lambda_R = 7000$ Å. The wavelengths that get intensified in the reflected beam are

(a) 4800 Å and 5200 Å (b) 4800 Å and 6700 Å

(c) 4800 Å only (d) 5200 Å only

12. In an experiment, sodium light ($\lambda = 5890$ A°) is employed and interference fringes are obtained in which 20 fringes equally spaced occupy 2.30 cm on the screen. When sodium light is replaced by blue light, the setup remaining the same otherwise, 30 fringes occupy 2.80 cm. The wavelength of blue light is :

(a) 4780 Å (b) 5220 Å

(c) 4250 Å (d) 4000 Å

13. A wedged shaped air film having an angle of 40 second is illuminated by a monochromatic light and the fringes are observed vertically down through a microscope. The fringe separation between two consecutive bright fringes is 0.12 cm. The wavelength of light is :

(a) 5545 Å (b) 6025 Å

(c) 4925 Å (d) 4655 Å

14. Two rectangular glass plates are in contact at one edge while the other edges are separated by a space of some suitable thickness so as to form a low angle wedge. The spacer is placed parallel to the line of contact and is at a distance of 10 cm from it. When viewed normally in light of wavelength 5500 Å, a series of evenly spaced dark bands 0.5 mm apart are seen. The thickness of the spacer is :

(a) 0.0425 cm (b) 0.0036 cm

(c) 0.0055 cm (d) 0.0254 cm

Answer Key	5	(a)	6	(c)	7	(d)	8	(c)	9	(b)
Sol. from page 232	10	(c)	11	(c)	12	(a)	13	(d)	14	(c)

15. The maximum number of possible interference maxima for slit separation equal to twice the wavelength in YDSE is :

(a) 2   (b) 4

(c) 5   (d) 8

16. In an ideal YDSE when a glass plate ($\mu = 1.5$) of thickness t is introduced in the path of one of the interfering beams the intensity at the position where the central maximum occured previously remains unchanged. The maximum thickness of the glass plate is:

(a) λ (b) $\lambda / 3$

(c) $\dfrac{2\lambda}{3}$ (d) 2λ

17. In a Young's double slit experiment, if the incident light consists of two wavelengths λ_1 and λ_2, the slit separation is d, and the distance between the slit and the screen is D, the maxima due to the two wavelengths will coincide at a distance from the central maxima, given by :

(a) $\dfrac{\lambda_1 \lambda_2}{2\,Dd}$

(b) $(\lambda_1 - \lambda_2) \cdot \dfrac{2d}{D}$

(c) LCM of $\lambda_1 \cdot \dfrac{D}{d}$ and $\lambda_2 \cdot \dfrac{D}{d}$

(d) HCF of $\dfrac{\lambda_1 D}{d}$ and $\dfrac{\lambda_2 D}{d}$

18. When the diffraction pattern from a certain slit illuminated with laser light ($\lambda = 6330$ A°) is projected on a screen 150 cm from the slit, the second minima on each side are separated by 8 cm. This tells us that :

(a) the slit is approximately 0.005 cm wide

(b) the slit is approximately 0.05 cm wide

(c) a / λ is approximately 7.5 (a is the slit width)

(d) a / λ is approximately 750

19. There are two sources kept at distances 2λ. A large screen is perpendicular to line joining the sources. Number of maximas on the screen in this case is ($\lambda =$ wavelength of light)

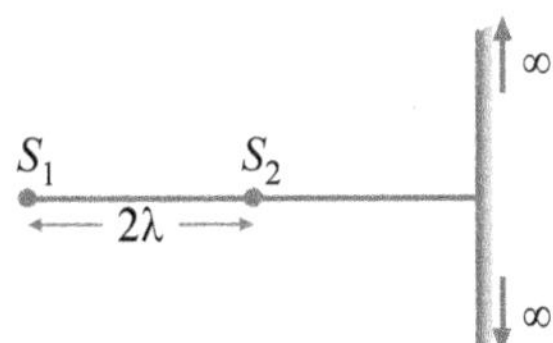

(a) 1   (b) 3

(c) 5   (d) 7

20. In YSDE, both slits are covered by transparent slab. Upper slit is covered by slab of R.I. 1.5 and thickness t and lower is covered by R.I. $\dfrac{4}{3}$ and thickness $2t$, then central maxima

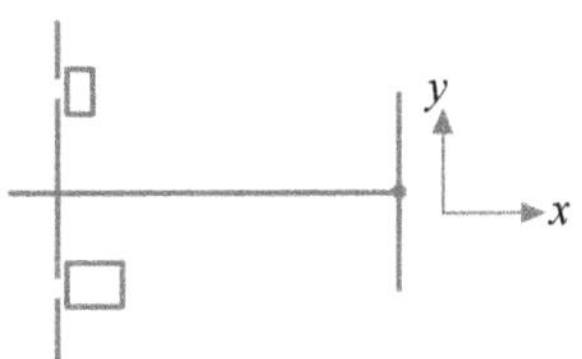

(a) shifts in +ve y-axis direction

(b) shifts in −ve y-axis direction

(c) remains at same position

(d) may shift in upward or downward depending upon wavelength of light

21. For the two parallel rays AB and DE shown here, BD is the wavefront. For what value of wavelength of rays destructive interference takes place between ray DE and reflected ray CD ?

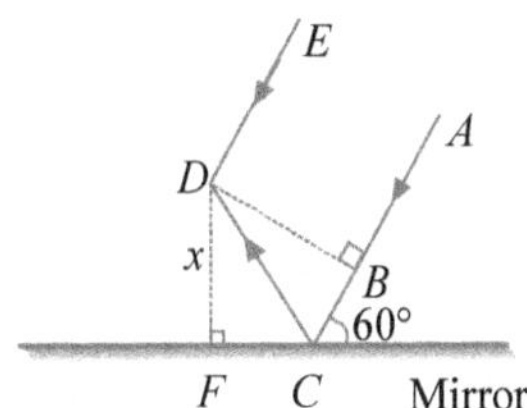

(a) $\sqrt{3}\,x$ (b) $\sqrt{2}\,x$

(c) x (d) $2\,x$

22. In the adjacent diagram, CP represents a wavefront and AO & BP, the corresponding two rays. Find the condition on θ for constructive interference at P between the ray BP and reflected ray OP

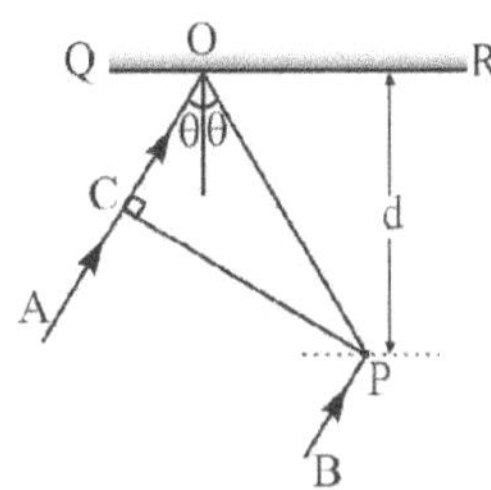

(a) $\cos\theta = 3\lambda/2d$ (b) $\cos\theta = \lambda/4d$

(c) $\sec\theta - \cos\theta = \lambda/d$ (d) $\sec\theta - \cos\theta = 4\lambda/d$

Answer Key	**15**	(c)	**16**	(d)	**17**	(c)	**18**	(a)
Sol. from page 232	**19**	(b)	**20**	(b)	**21**	(a)	**22**	(b)

23. Figure here shows P and Q as two equally intense coherent sources emitting radiations of wavelength 20 m. The separation PQ is 5.0 m and phase of P is ahead of the phase of Q by 90°. A, B and C are three distant points of observation equidistant from the mid-point of PQ. The intensity of radiations at A, B, C will bear the ratio

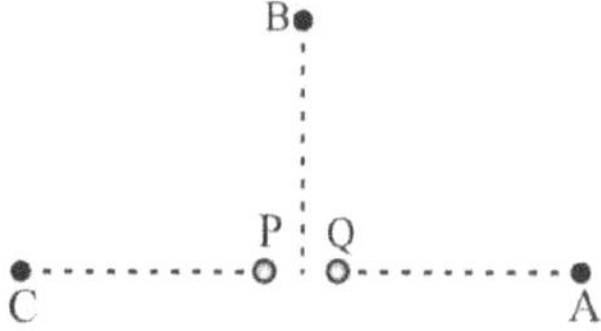

(a) $0 : 1 : 4$
(b) $4 : 1 : 0$
(c) $0 : 1 : 2$
(d) $2 : 1 : 0$

24. In Fresnel's biprism ($\mu = 1.5$) experiment the distance between source and biprism is 0.3 m and that between biprism and screen is 0.7 m and angle of prism is 1°. The fringe width with light of wavelength 6000Å will be

(a) 3 mm
(b) 0.11 mm
(c) 2 mm
(d) 4 mm

25. Two coherent sources separated by distance d are radiating in phase having wavelength λ. A detector moves in a big circle around the two sources in the plane of the two sources. The angular position of $n = 4$ interference maxima is given as

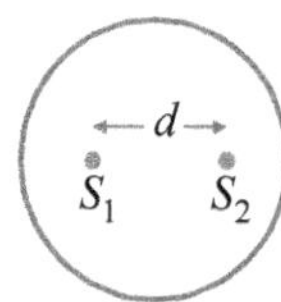

(a) $\sin^{-1}\dfrac{n\lambda}{d}$
(b) $\cos^{-1}\dfrac{4\lambda}{d}$
(c) $\tan^{-1}\dfrac{d}{4\lambda}$
(d) $\cos^{-1}\dfrac{\lambda}{4d}$

26. There are two plane mirrors. They are mutually inclined as shown in figure. S is a source of monochromatic light of wavelength λ. The reflected beam interfere and fringe pattern is obtained on the screen. If θ is small, the fringe width will be :

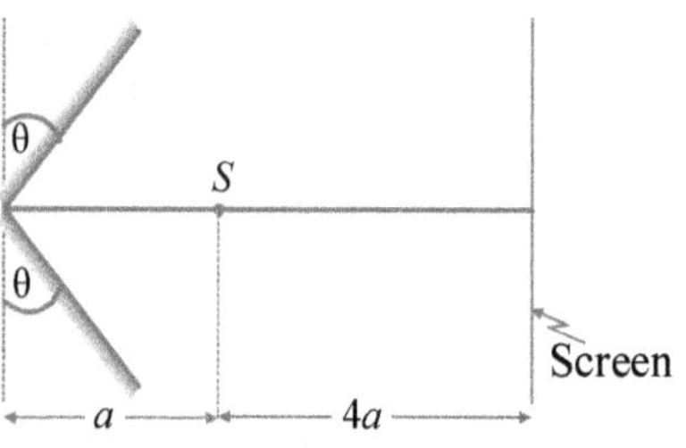

(a) λ/θ
(b) $3\lambda/2\theta$
(c) $2\lambda/3\theta$
(d) none of these

27. A YDSE is conducted in water (μ_1) as shown in figure. A glass plate of thickness t and refractive index μ_2 is placed in the path of S_2. The optical path difference at O is

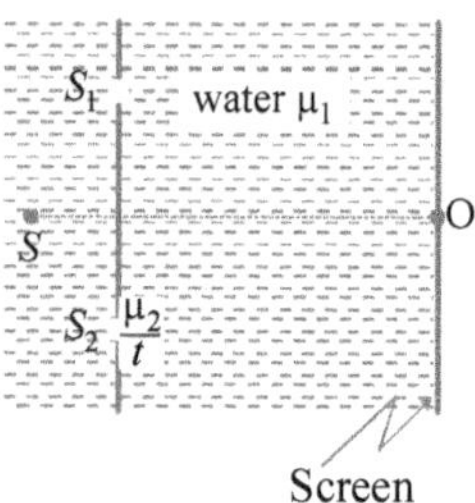

(a) $(\mu_2 - 1)t$
(b) $(\mu_1 - 1)t$
(c) $\left(\dfrac{\mu_2}{\mu_1} - 1\right)t$
(d) $(\mu_2 - \mu_1)t$

28. Two polaroids are placed in the path of unpolarized beam of intensity I_0 such that no light is emitted from the second polaroid. If a third polaroid whose polarization axis makes an angle θ with the polarization axis of first polaroid, is placed between these polaroids then the intensity of light emerging from the last polaroid will be

(a) $\left(\dfrac{I_0}{8}\right)\sin^2 2\theta$
(b) $\left(\dfrac{I_0}{4}\right)\sin^2 2\theta$
(c) $\left(\dfrac{I_0}{2}\right)\cos^4 \theta$
(d) $I_0 \cos^4 \theta$

Answer Key	23	(c)	24	(b)	25	(b)	26	(b)
Sol. from page 232	27	(d)	28	(a)				

Optics | **MCQ Type 2** | *Exercise 4.2*

Multiple correct options

1. In the Young's double slit experiment, the ratio of intensities of bright and dark fringes is 9. This means that
   (a) the intensities of individual sources are 5 and 4 units respectively
   (b) the intensities of individual sources are 4 and 1 units respectively
   (c) the ratio of their amplitudes is 3
   (d) the ratio of their amplitudes is 2

2. In Young's double slit experiment, white light is used. The separation between the slits is b. The screen is at a distance d (d >> b) from the slits. Some wavelengths are missing exactly in front of one slit. These wavelengths are
   (a) $\lambda = \dfrac{b^2}{d}$
   (b) $\lambda = \dfrac{2b^2}{d}$
   (c) $\lambda = \dfrac{b^2}{3d}$
   (d) $\lambda = \dfrac{2b^2}{3d}$

3. In an interference arrangement similar to Young's double slit experiment, the slits S_1 and S_2 are illuminated with coherent microwave sources each of frequency 10^6 Hz. The sources are synchronized to have zero phase difference. The slits are separated by distance $d = 150$ m. The intensity $I(\theta)$ is measured as a function of θ, where θ is defined as shown. If I_0 is maximum intensity, then $I(\theta)$ for $0 \le \theta \le 90°$ is given by

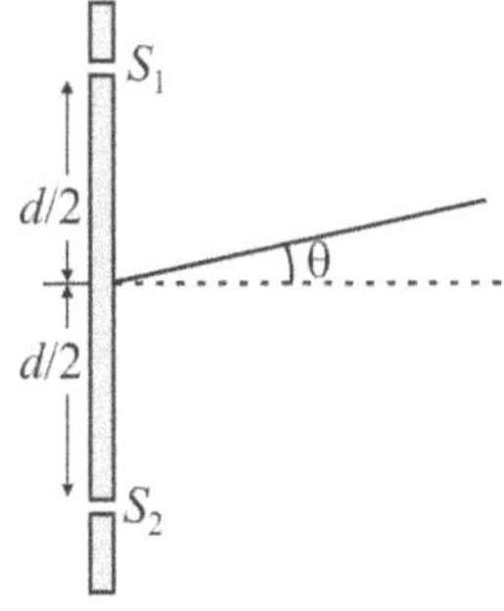

   (a) $I(\theta) = I_0 \ for \ \theta = 0°$
   (b) $I(\theta) = I_0 / 2 \ for \ \theta = 30°$
   (c) $I(\theta) = I_0 / 4 \ for \ \theta = 90°$
   (d) $I(\theta)$ is constant for all values of θ

4. If screen is shifted in x direction away from source, then which of the following is incorrect?

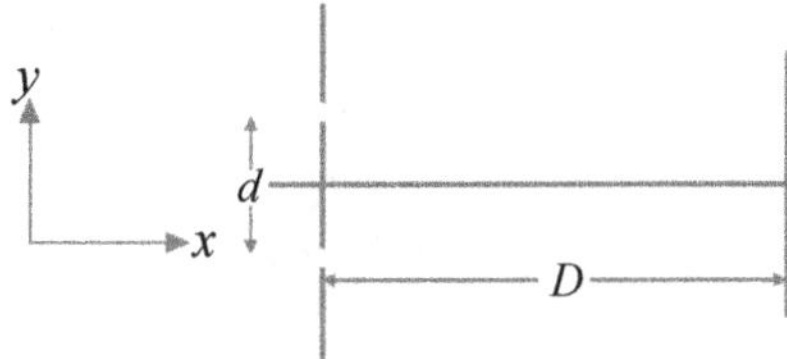

   (a) Central maxima is shifted along y-axis
   (b) Position of all maximas except the central maxima change
   (c) Fringe width remains constant
   (d) Angular width changes due to shifting

5. A parallel beam of light ($\lambda = 5000$Å) is incident at an angle $\alpha = 30°$ with the normal to the slit plane in YDSE. Assume that the intensity due to each slit at any point on the screen is I_0. Point O is equidistant from S_1 and S_2. The distance between slit is 1 mm, then

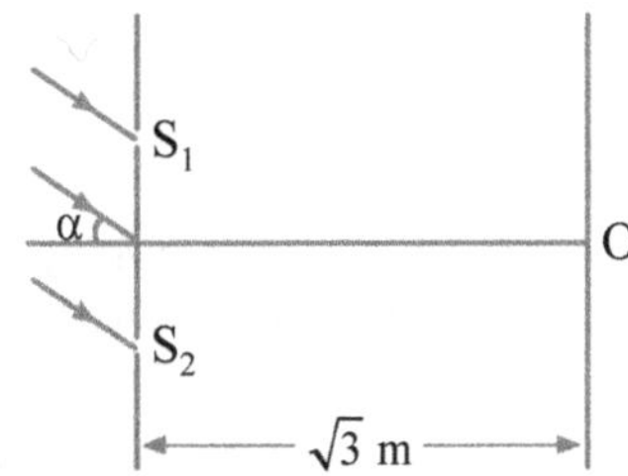

   (a) the intensity at O is 4 I_0.
   (b) the intensity at O is zero.
   (c) the intensity at a point 1 m below 0 is 4 I_0.
   (d) the intensity at a point on the screen 1 m below O is zero

6. Figure shows two point sources which emit light of wavelength λ in phase with each other and are at a distance d = 5.5 λ apart along a line which is perpendicualr to a large screen at a distance L from centre of the sources assume that d << L.

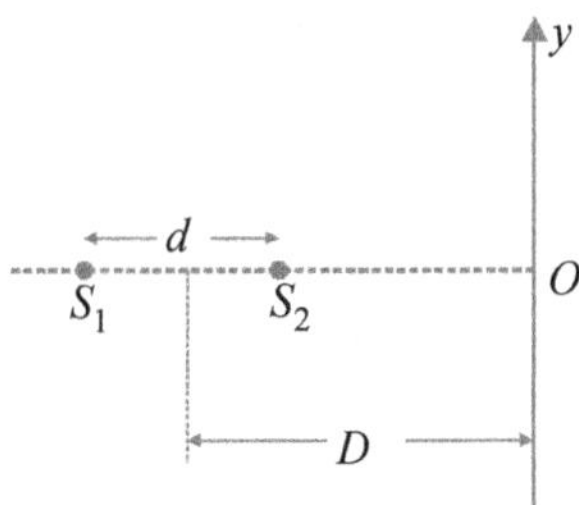

   (a) only five bright fringes appear on the screen
   (b) only six bright fringes apper on the screen
   (c) point $y = 0$ corresponds to bright fringe
   (d) point $y = 0$ corresponds to dark fringe.

Answer Key	1	(b, d)	2	(a, c)	3	(a, b)	4	(a, c)
Sol. from page 235	5	(a, c)	6	(a, d)				

Optics | **Statement Questions** | *Exercise 4.3*

Read the two statements carefully to mark the correct option out of the options given below. Select the right choice.

(a) If both the statements are true and the **Statement - 2** is the correct explanation of **Statement - 1**.

(b) If both the statements are true but **Statement - 2** is not the correct explanation of the **Statement - 1**.

(c) If **Statement - 1** true but **Statement - 2** is false.

(d) If **Statement - 1** is false but **Statement - 2** is true.

1. **Statement -1** : Corpuscular theory fails in explaining the velocity of light in air and water.

   Statement -2 : According to corpuscular theory, light should travel faster in denser medium than in rarer medium.

2. **Statement -1** : In everyday life the Doppler's effect is observed readily for sound waves than light waves.

   Statement -2 : The wavelengths of light waves are shorter than sound waves.

3. **Statement -1** : Coloured spectrum is seen when we look through a muslin cloth.

   Statement -2 : It is due the diffraction of white light on passing through fine slits.

4. **Statement -1** : Interference pattern is made by using yellow light instead of red light, the fringes becomes narrower.

   Statement -2 : In YDSE, fringe width is given by $\beta = \dfrac{D\lambda}{d}$.

5. **Statement -1** : Thin film such as soap bubble or a thin layer of oil on water show beautiful colours when illuminated by white light.

   Statement -2 : It happens due to the interference of light reflected from upper and lower face of the thin film.

6. **Statement -1** : No interference pattern is detected when two coherent sources are infinitely close to each other.

   Statement -2 : The fringe width is inversely proportional to the distance between the two sources.

7. **Statement -1** : It is necessary to have two waves of equal intensity to study interference pattern.

   Statement -2 : There will be an effect on clarity if the waves are of unequal intensity.

8. **Statement -1** : White light falls on a double slit with one slit is covered by a green filter. The bright fringes observed are of green colour.

   Statement -2 : The fringes observed are coloured.

9. **Statement -1** : Radio waves can be polarised.

   Statement -2 : Sound waves in air are longitudinal in nature.

10. **Statement -1** : Microwave communication is preferred over optical communication

    Statement -2 : Microwave provide large number of channels and band width compared to optical signals.

Answer Key	**1**	(a)	**2**	(a)	**3**	(a)	**4**	(a)	**5**	(a)	**6**	(a)
Sol. from page 136	**7**	(d)	**8**	(c)	**9**	(b)	**10**	(c)				

PASSAGES

Passage for (Qs. 1 - 3):

In YDSE experiment two slits S_1 and S_2 are kept at $\left(0, \dfrac{d}{2}, 0\right)$ and $\left(0, -\dfrac{d}{2}, 0\right)$. A screen is kept in y-z plane at x = D and a source of light is placed at $\left(-\dfrac{D}{4}, 0, 0\right)$. The central bright fringe is found to be at a point with coordinate (D, 0, 0) on the screen.

1. A student fills the region $-\infty < x \le 0$ and $0 \le y < \infty$ with a medium of refraction index μ_1. He found that now the central bright fringe is formed at a point P whose coordinates are –
    (a) y = 0
    (b) y > 0
    (c) y < 0
    (d) none of these

2. Another student now fills the region $0 \le x \le D$, $-\infty < y, z < +\infty$ with another medium of refractive index $\mu_2 > \mu_1$. Now he found the central bright fringe is formed at point Q, where y coordinate of Q is –
    (a) same at that of P
    (b) less than that of P
    (c) more than that of P
    (d) zero

3. Another student now removes both the medium and rearrange them such that medium of refractive index μ_1 is kept in a region $-\dfrac{D}{8} \le x \le 0$ and $0 < y < \infty$ whereas medium of refractive index $\mu_2 > \mu_1$ is kept in a region $-\dfrac{D}{8} \le x \le 0$ and $-\infty < y \le 0$. He also kept a convex lens of focal length $f = \dfrac{D}{8}$ at point $\left(-\dfrac{D}{8}, 0, 0\right)$. Now when he repeated the experiment, he found the central bright fringe at a point R whose y coordinate is –
    (a) y < 0
    (b) y > 0
    (c) y = 0
    (d) $y = \dfrac{\mu_1 D}{\mu_2}$

Passage for (Qs. 4 - 6):
Two parallel beams of light P and Q (separation d) containing radiation of wavelength 4000 Å and 5000 Å (which are mutually coherent in each wavelength separately) are incident normally on a prism as shown in . The refractive index of prism as a function of wavelength is given by the relation

$$\mu(\lambda) = 1.20 + \frac{b}{\lambda^2}$$

where λ is in Å and b is a positive constant. The value of b is such that the condition for total reflection at the face AC is just satisfied for one wave and is not satisfied for the other.

4. The value of b is
    (a) 4×10^5
    (b) 8×10^5
    (c) 9×10^5
    (d) none of the these

5. The deviations of the beam transmitted through the face AC is nearly
    (a) 30°
    (b) 45°
    (c) 53°
    (d) 62°

6. A convergent lens is used to bring these transmitted beams into focus. If the intensities of the upper and lower beams immediately after transmission from the face AC are 4 I and I respectively, the resultant intensity at focus is

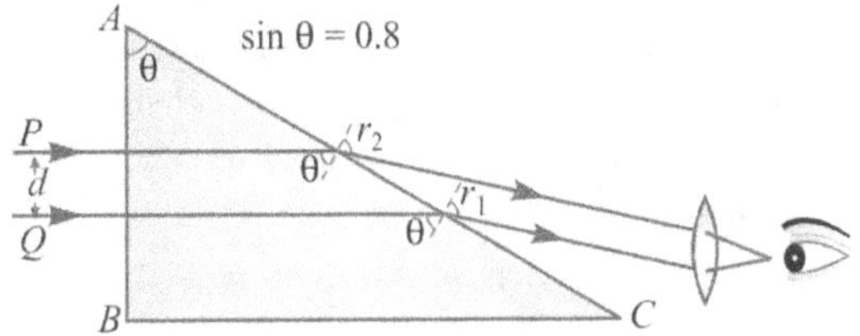

    (a) $9I$
    (b) $4I$
    (c) $5I$
    (d) zero

Passage for (Qs. 7 & 8):
A thin paper of thickness 0.02 mm having a refractive index 1.45 is pasted across one of the slits in a Young's double slit experiment. The paper transmits $\dfrac{4}{9}$ of the light energy falling on it.

7. The ratio of maximum to minimum intensity in the fringe pattern is :
    (a) 4
    (b) 9
    (c) 25
    (d) 36

8. How many fringes will cross through the centre if an identical paper price is pasted on the other slit also ? The wavelength of the light used is 6000 Å.
    (a) 15
    (b) 20
    (c) 25
    (d) 30

Answer Key	1	(b)	2	(b)	3	(b)	4	(b)	5	(c)
Sol. from page 237	6	(a)	7	(c)	8	(a)				

Paragraph for (Qs. 9 - 11)

Wave property of electrons implies that they will show diffraction effects. Davisson and Germer demonstrated this by diffracting electrons from crystals. The law covering the diffraction from a crystal is obtained by requiring that electron waves reflected from the planes of atoms in a crystal interfere constructively (see figure).

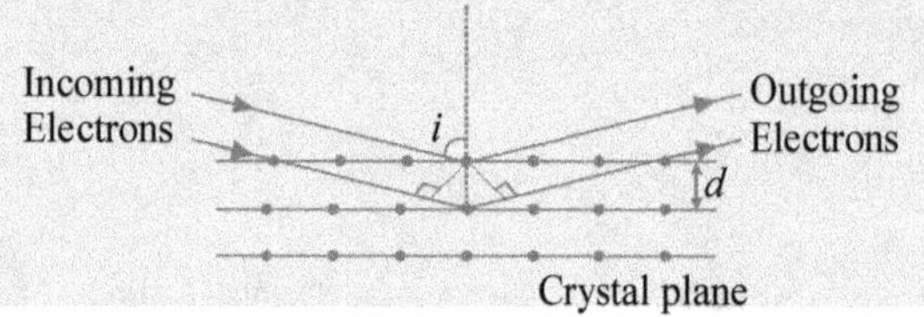

9. If a strong diffraction peak is observed when electrons are incident at an angle i from the normal to the crystal planes with distance 'd' between them (see figure), de Broglie wavelength λ_{dB} of electrons can be calculated by the relationship (n is an integer)

(a) $2d\cos i = n\lambda_{dB}$ (b) $2d\sin i = n\lambda_{dB}$

(c) $d\cos i = n\lambda_{dB}$ (d) $d\sin i = n\lambda_{dB}$

10. Electrons accelerated by potential V are diffracted from a crystal. If $d = 1$ Å and $i = 30°$, V should be about

$(h = 6.6 \times 10^{-34}\,\text{Js}, \quad m_e = 9.1 \times 10^{-31}\,\text{kg}, \quad e = 1.6 \times 10^{-19}\,\text{C})$

(a) 50 V (b) 500 V
(c) 1000 V (d) 2000 V

11. In an experiment, electrons are made to pass through a narrow slit of width 'd' comparable to their de Broglie wavelength. They are detected on a screen at a distance 'D' from the slit (see figure)

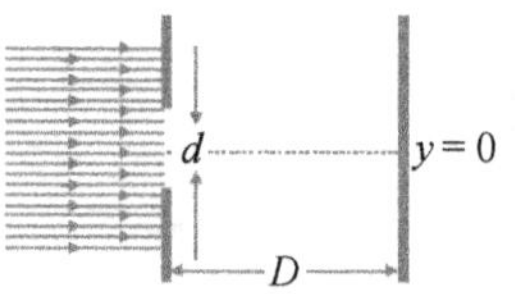

Which of the following graphs can be expected to represent the number of electrons 'N' detected as a function of the detector position 'y' ($y = 0$ corresponds to the middle of the slit)

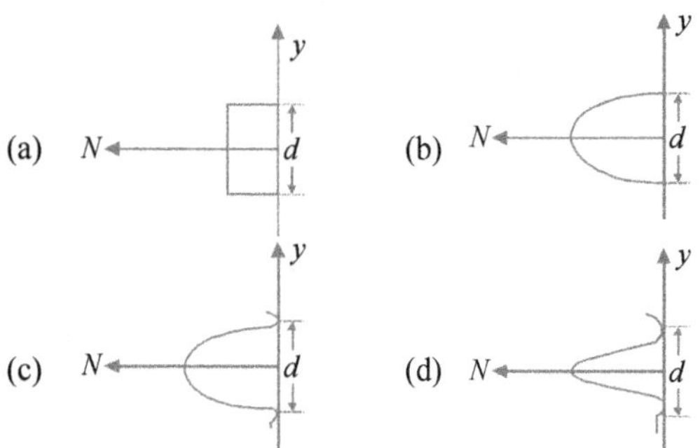

12. **Column I** shows four situation of standard Young's double slits arrangement with the screen placed far away from the slits S_1 and S_2. In each of these cases $S_1P_0 = S_2P_0$, $S_1P_1 - S_2P_1 = \lambda/4$ and $S_1P_2 - S_2P_2 = \lambda/3$. Where λ is the wavelength of the light used. In the case B, C and D, a transparent sheet of refractive index μ and thickness t is pasted on slit S_2. The thickness of the sheets are different in different cases. The phase difference between the light waves reaching a point P on the screen fromt he two slits is denoted by $\delta(P)$ and the intensity by $I(P)$. Match each situation given in **Column I** with the statement(s) in **Column- II** valid for that situation.

Column I

(A) 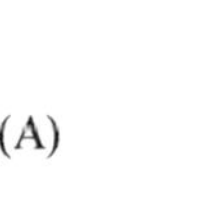

(B) $(\mu - 1)t = \lambda/4$ 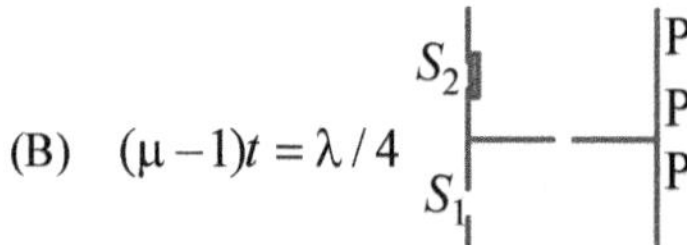

(C) $(\mu - 1)t = \lambda/2$ 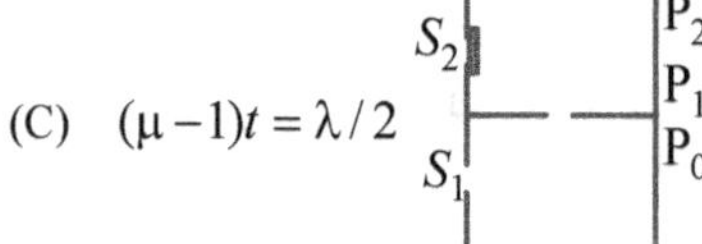

(D) $(\mu - 1)t = 3\lambda/4$ 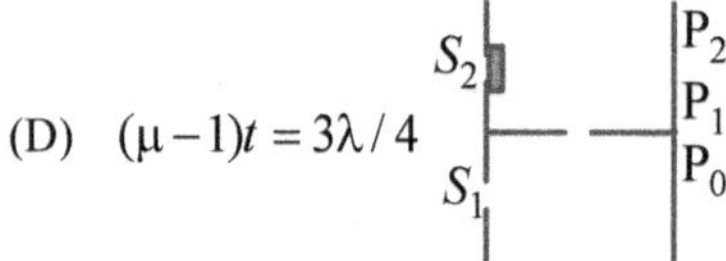

Column II

(p) $\delta(P_0) - 0$

(q) $\delta(P_1) = 0$

(r) $I(P_1) = 0$

(s) $I(P_0) > I(P_1)$

(t) $I(P_2) > I(P_1)$

Answer Key	9	(a)	10	(a)	11	(c)
Sol. from page 237	12	A-(p, s) ; B-(q) ; C-(t) ; D-(r, s, t)				

10. A parallel beam of monochromatic light of wavelength $\lambda = 100$ (Å) is incident on the slits separated by distance $d = 2$mm. There is a screen at a distance $D = 1$m from slit. If R.I. of the medium between slits and screen in varying with time as $\mu = 20 - 4t$ until it becomes 1. A glass slab of R.I. $\mu = 5$ and thickness 0.2 mm is placed in front of one of the slit S_1 as shown in figure. In figure y represent position of central maxima on the screen from its geometrical centre. Then match the **Column I** with **Column II** with suitable option (s)

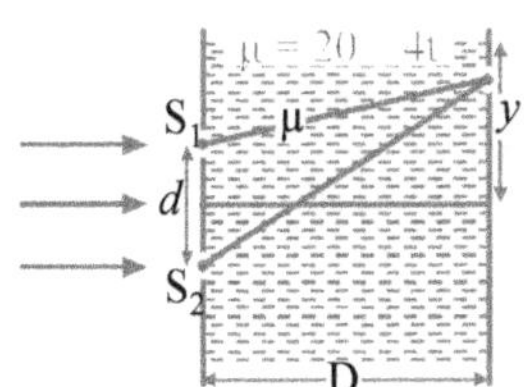

Column – I		Column – II	
A.	At $t = 0$, value of $\lvert y \rvert$ in (cm)	(p)	40
B.	At $t = 5$ s value of $\lvert y \rvert$ (in cm)	(q)	7.5
C.	Speed of central maxima when it is at geometrical centre of screen (in cm/s)	(r)	1
D.	Fringe width at time t = 3.75 sec (μm)	(s)	8
		(t)	12

11. Match the following S_1 and S_2 in column I represent coherent point sources, S represents a point source. λ = wavelength of light emitted by the sources.

Column I

(A)

(B)
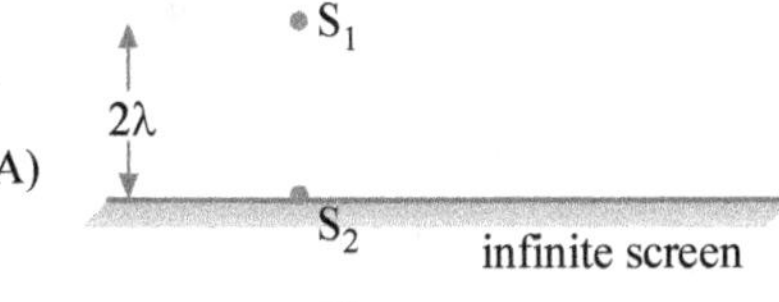

(C)
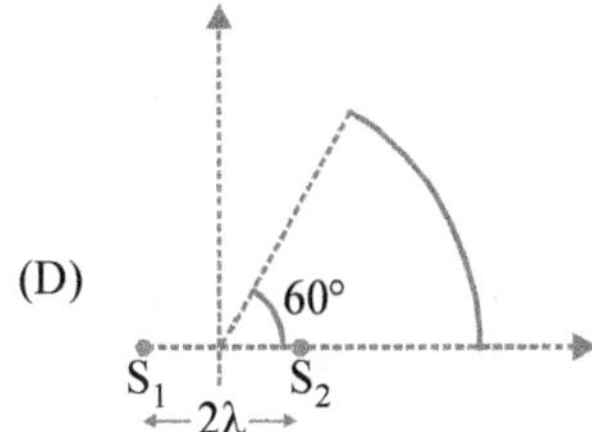

(D)

Column II

(p) Number of maximas = 2

(q) Number of minimas = 2

(r) Number of maximas = 4

(s) Number of minimas = 4

(t) Only hyperbolic fringes

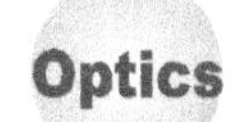 **Optics** | # Subjective Integer Type | *Exercise 4.5*

Solution from page 239

1. Two radio frequency point sources separated by 2.0 m are radiating in phase with $\lambda = 0.50$ m. A detector moves in a circular path around the two sources in a plane containing them. How many maxima it detects ? Do the problem by minimum calculations.

Ans. **16**

2. A double-slit arrangement produces interference fringes for sodium light ($\lambda = 589$ nm) that have an angular separation of 3.50×10^{-3} rad. For what wavelength would the angular separation be 10% greater ?

Ans. **648 nm.**

3. In figure, a broad beam of light of wavelength 683 nm is sent directly downward through the top plate of a pair of glass plates. The plates are 120 mm long. Tough at the left end, and are separately by a wire of diameter 0.048 mm at the right end. The air between the plates acts as a thin film. How many bright fringes will be seen by an observer looking down through the top plate?

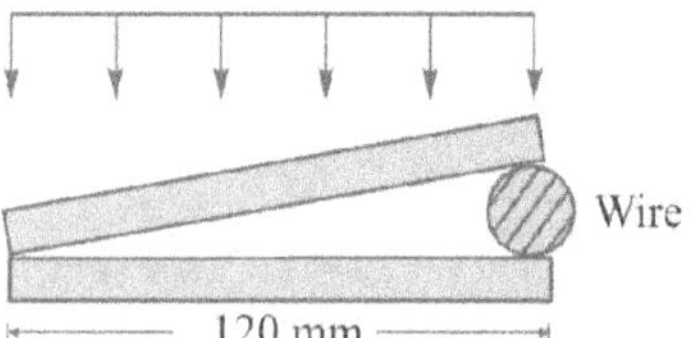

Ans. **140**

4. Two nicols are so oriented that the maximum amount of light is transmitted. To what fraction of its maximum value is the intensity of transmitted light reduced when the analyser is rotated through (a) 30° (b) 60° ?

Ans. **(a) 75% (b) 25%.**

Optics | # Subjective | *Exercise 4.6*

Solution from page 240

1. Two waves of the same frequency have amplitudes 2 and 4. They interfere at a point where their phase difference is 60°. Find their resultant amplitude.

Ans. $\sqrt{28}$

2. Find the sum y of the following quantities :

$y_1 = 8\sin\omega t$ and $y_2 = 10\sin(\omega t + 30°)$. *Ans.* **14.5**

3. What is the maximum intensity in case of interference of n identical waves each of intensity I_0, if the interference is (a) coherent (b) incoherent.

Ans. **(a) $n^2 I_0$ (b) nI_0.**

4. Show that in interference, energy is neither created nor destroyed but is conserved.

5. White light is used to illuminate the two slits is d are the screen is at a distance D (D >> d) from the slits. At a point on the screen directly in front of one of the slits find the missing wavelengths.

Ans. $\dfrac{d^2}{D}, \dfrac{d^2}{3D}, \dfrac{d^2}{5D}, \ldots$

6. In an interference pattern, at a point there observe 16th order maximum for $\lambda_1 = 6000\,\mathring{A}$. What order will be visible here if the source is replaced by light of wavelength $\lambda_2 = 4800$ Å?

Ans. **20**

7. Suppose that one of the slits of a YDSE is wider than the other, such that $I_1 = I$ and $I_2 = 4I$. Derive an expression for the light intensity I_R at the screen as a function of θ as shown in standard setup.

Ans. $I_R = \dfrac{I_0}{9}\left[1 + 8\cos^2\left(\dfrac{\pi d \sin\theta}{\lambda}\right)\right]$, I_0 **maximum intensity.**

8. In a double-slit arrangement the slits are separated by a distance equal to 100 times the wavelength of the light passing through the slits.

(a) What is the angular separation in radians between the central maximum and adjacent maximum ?

(b) What is the distance between these maxima on a screen 50.0 cm from the slits ?

Ans. **(a)** $\dfrac{1}{100} rad$ **(b) 0.5×10^{-2} cm.**

9. In figure, a microwave transmitter a height a above the water level of a wide lake transmits microwaves of wavelength λ towards a receiver on the opposite shore, a distance x above the water level. The microwaves reflecting from the water interfere with the microwaves arriving directly from the transmitter. Assuming that the lake width D is much greater than a and x, and that $\lambda >> a$, at what values of x is the signal at the receiver maximum?

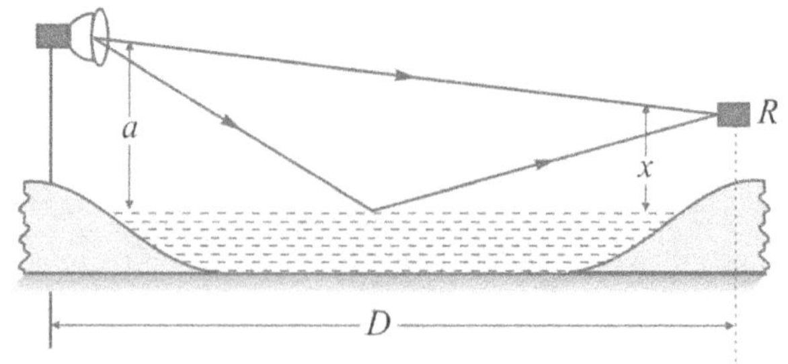

Ans. $x = \dfrac{D}{2a}\left(n + \dfrac{1}{2}\right)\lambda$, **n = 0, 1, 2, ...**

10. A two slit young's experiment is done with monochromatic light of wavelength 6000 Å. The slits are 2 mm apart and the fringes are observed on a screen placed 10 cm away from the slits. Now a transparent path of thickness 0.5 mm is placed in front of one of the slits and it is found that the interference pattern shifts by 5 mm. What is the refractive index of the transparent plate?

Ans. **1.2**

11. A monochromatic light of $\lambda = 5000$ Å is incident on two slits separated by a distance 5×10^{-4} m. The interference pattern is seen on a screen placed at a distance of 1m from the slits. A thin glass plate of thickness 1.5×10^{-6} m and refractive index $\mu = 1.5$ is placed between one of the slits and the screen. Find the intensity at the centre of the screen if the intensity is I_0 in the absence of plate. Also find the lateral shift of the central maximum.

Ans. $I_{centre} = 0$, $\Delta = 1.5$ mm.

12. A double slit S_1, S_2 is illuminated by a coherent light of wavelength λ. The slits are separated by a distance d. The experimental set up is modified by using plane mirrors as shown in figure. Find the fringe width of interference pattern on the screen.

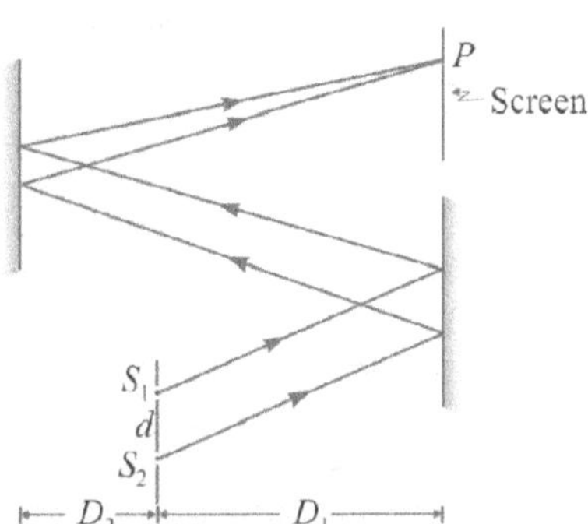

Ans. $\beta = \dfrac{(3D_1 + 2D_2)\lambda}{d}$

13. A young's double-slit arrangement produces interference fringes for sodium light ($\lambda = 5890$Å) that are 0.20° apart. What is the angular fringe separation if the entire arrangement is immersed in water (refractive index of water is 4/3).

Ans. **0.15°.**

14. Two coherent narrow slits emitting light of wavelength λ in the same phase are placed parallel to each other at a small separation of 2λ. The light is calculated on a screen S which is placed a distance (D >> λ) from the slit S_1 as shown in figure. Find the distance x such that the intensity at P is equal to the intensity at t → 0.

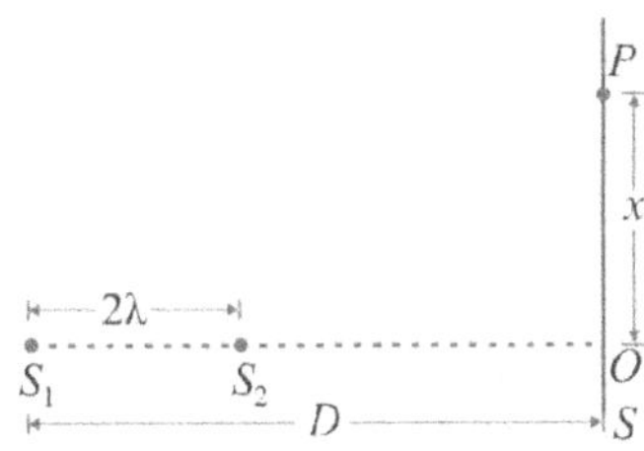

Ans. $\sqrt{3}D$.

15. In YDSE, $\lambda = 500$ nm, d = 1.0 mm and D = 1 m. Find the minimum distance from the central maximum for which the intensity is half the maximum intensity.

Ans. **1.25 × 10⁻⁴ m.**

16. Two small angled transparent prisms (each of refracting angle A = 1°) are so placed that their bases coincide, so that common base is

BC. This device is called Fresnel's biprism and is used to obtained coherent sources of a point source S illuminated by monochromatic light of wavelength 6000 Å placed at a distance a = 20 cm. Calculate the separation between coherent sources. If a screen is placed at a distance b = 80 cm from the device, what is the fringe width of fringes obtained (refractive index of material of prism $\mu = 1.5$)?

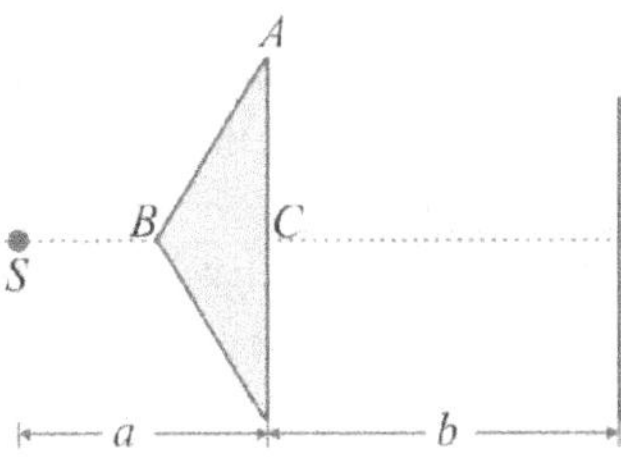

Ans. **3.48 × 10⁻³ m, 0.172 mm.**

17. In a double slit experiment the distance between slits is 5.0 mm and the slits are 1.0 m from the screen. Two interference patterns can be seen on the screen, one due to light of 4800 Å and the other 6000 Å. What is the separation on the screen, between the third order interference fringes of the two different pattern?

Ans. **0.0072 cm.**

18. The YDSE is done in a medium of refractive index 4/3. A light of wavelength 600 nm is falling on the slits having 0.45 mm separation. The lower slits S_2 is covered by a thin glass sheet of thickness 10.4 μm and refractive index 1.5. The interference pattern is observed on a screen placed 1.5 m from the slits as shown in figure.

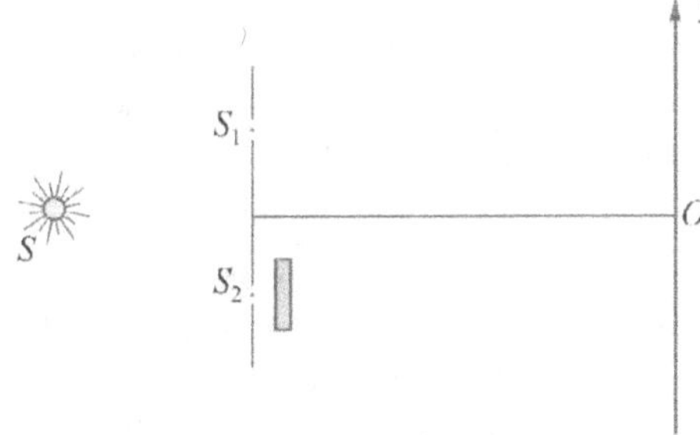

(a) Find the location of the central maximum on the y-axis.

(b) Find the light intensity at point O relative to the maximum fringe intensity.

(c) Now, if 600 nm light is replaced by white light of range 400 to 700 nm, find the wavelength of the light that form maxima exactly at O [All wavelengths in this problem are for the given medium of refractive index 4/3. Ignore dispersion.

Ans. **(a) 4.33 mm (b) I = 0.75 I_m (c) 650, 4333 mm**

19. If figure, S_1 and S_2 are identical radiators of waves that are in phase and of the same wavelengths λ. The radiations are separated by distance d = 3λ. Find the greatest distance from S_1, along x axis, for which fully destructive interference occurs.

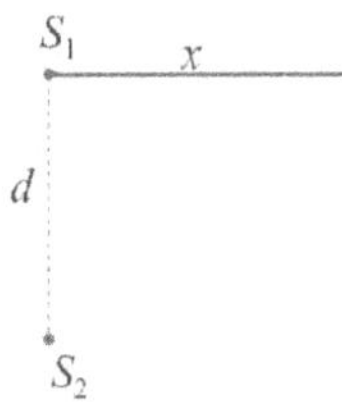

Ans. $x = \dfrac{35\lambda}{4}$.

20. Light of wavelength 624 nm is incident perpendicularly on a soap film (with $\mu = 1.33$) suspended in air. What are the least two thicknesses of the film for which the reflections from the film undergo fully constructive interference?

Ans. **0.117μm, 0.352 μm.**

21. In figure, a glass lens is coated on one side with a thin film of magnesium fluoride (MgF_2) to reduce reflection from the lens surface. The refractive index of MgF_2 is 1.38; that of glass is 1.50. What is the least coating thickness that eliminates. (via interference) the reflections at the middle of the visible spectrum ($\lambda = 550$ nm)? Assume that the light is approximately perpendicular to the lines surface.

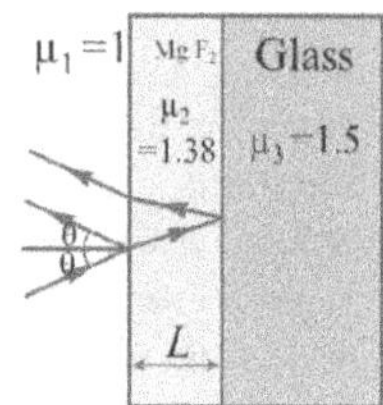

Ans. **99.6 nm.**

22. A slit of width d is illuminated by white light (which consists of all the wavelengths in the visible range).

(a) For what value of d will the first minimum for red light of wavelength $\lambda = 650$ nm appear at $\theta = 15°$?

(b) What is the wavelength λ' of the light whose first side diffraction maximum is at $15°$, thus coinciding with the first minimum for the red light ?

Ans. **(a) 2.5 μ m (b) 430 nm.**

23. Angular width of central maximum in the Fraunhoffer diffraction pattern of a slit is measured. The slit is illuminated by light of wavelength 6000Å. When the slit is illuminated by light of another wavelength, the angular width decreases by 30%. Calculate the wavelength of this light. The same decrease in the angular width of central maximum is obtained when the original apparatus is immersed in a liquid. Find refractive index of the liquid.

Ans. **4200Å, 1.43.**

24. A circular converging lens, with diameter $d = 32$mm and focal length $f = 24$, forms images of distance point objects in the focal plane of the lens. Light of wavelength $\lambda = 550$ nm is used .

(a) Considering diffraction by the lens, what angular separation must two distant point objects have to satisfy Rayleigh's criteria?

(b) What is the separation Δx of the centres of the images in the focal plane ? (That is, what is the separation of the central peaks in the two curves?)

Ans. **(a) 2.1×10^{-5} rad (b) 5.0 μm.**

25. An astronomical refracting telescope has an objective of diameter 1 m for light of wavelength 6000Å. Calculate the limit of resolution of the telescope. If the limit of resolution for the human eye be 2 minute of arc, find the useful magnifying power for the telescope.

Ans. **7.32×10^{-7} rad, 400.**

26. Two polaroides are placed at $90°$ to each other. What happens, when $(N - 1)$ more polaroids are inserted between them? Their axes are equally spaced. How does the transmitted intensity behave for large N.

Ans. $I = I_0[\cos(\pi/2N)]^{2N}, I_0$.

27. A beam of plane polarised light falls normally on a polariser (cross-sectional area 3×10^{-4}m²) which rotates about the axis of the ray with an angular velocity of 31.4 rad/s. Find the energy of light passing through the polariser per revolution and the intensity of the emergent beam if flux of energy of the incident ray is 10^{-3} W.

Ans. **10^{-4}J.**

28. A mixture of plane polarised and unpolarised light falls normally on a polarising sheet. On rotating the polarising sheet about the direction of the incident beam, the transmitted intensity varies by a factor 4. Find the ratio of the intensities I_p and I_0 respectively of the polarised and unpolarised components in the incident beam. Next the axis of polarising sheet is fixed at an angle of $45°$ with the direction when the transmitted intensity is maximum. Then obtain the total intensity of the transmitted beam in terms of I_0.

Ans. $\dfrac{3}{2}, \dfrac{5I_0}{4}$

Hints & Solutions

1. (a)

2. (d)
$$I_1 = (2a_0)^2 + (6a_0)^2 + 2 \times 2a_0 \times 6a_0 \cos\pi$$
$$= 16\,a_0^2$$
$$I_2 = (3a_0)^2 + (5a_0)^2 + 2 \times 3a_0 \times 5a_0 \cos\pi$$
$$= 4\,a_0^2$$
$$I_3 = (9a_0)^2 + (7a_0)^2 + 2 \times 9a_0 \times 7a_0 \cos3\pi$$
$$= 4\,a_0^2$$
$$I_4 = (2a_0)^2 + (2a_0)^2 + 2 \times 2a_0 \times 2a_0 \cos0°$$
$$= 16\,a_0^2$$
Clearly I and IV have greatest intensity.

3. (c)
$$x_1 = 5d + 4 \times \lambda/2 = 5d + 2\lambda$$
and
$$x_2 = 3d + 2 \times \frac{\lambda}{2} = 3d + \lambda$$
$$\therefore \quad \Delta x = x_1 \sim x_2 = (5d + 2\lambda) - (3d + \lambda)$$
$$= (2d + \lambda).$$

4. (d)

5. (c) The magnetic field vector must be perpendicular to both x and y-axis. So it is
$$E_z = E\sin(ky + \omega t).$$

6. (c)
$$I_{max} = I + 4I + 2\sqrt{I \times 4I} = 9I,$$
and $I_{min} = I + 4I - 2\sqrt{I \times 4I} = I.$

7. (c)

8. (c)
$$\frac{I_1}{I_2} = \frac{a_1^2}{a_2^2} = \frac{9}{1} \text{ or } \frac{a_1}{a_2} = \frac{3}{1}$$
$$\therefore \frac{I_{max}}{I_{min}} = \frac{(3+1)^2}{(3-1)^2} = \frac{16}{4} = \frac{4}{1}$$

9. (b)

10. (c)

11. (d) Diffraction phenomenon is related to wave nature of light and photoelectric effect is related to particle nature of light, so these to show dual nature of light.

12. (a)

13. (d)
$$\beta = \frac{D\lambda}{d} \text{ and } \beta' = \frac{(2D)\lambda}{(d/2)} = 4\beta$$

14. (c) If a is the amplitude of wave, then
$$I = 4a^2, \text{ then } I_0 = a^2 = \frac{I}{4}.$$

15. (c) For unequal width of slides, let $a_1 = a$, and $a_2 = 0.5\,a$
So $I_1 = (a_1 + a_2)^2 = (a + 0.5a)^2 = 2.25a^2 < 4a^2$
and $I_2 = (a_1 - a_2)^2 = (a - 0.5a)^2 = 0.25a^2 > 0.$

16. (c) $\beta = \beta'$

or $\dfrac{D\lambda}{d} = \dfrac{D'\lambda}{(2d)}$

$\therefore \quad D' = 2D$

17. (b) For diffraction to occur, $\lambda \sim d$. The wavelength of X-ray (~ 1 Å) is being much smaller than 0.6 mm.

18. (a)

19. (a)

20. (c)

21. (a)

22. (c)

23. (c) The path difference between reflected rays
$$\Delta x = 2x = 2d\sin\theta$$
For constructive interference
$$2d\sin\theta = n\lambda$$
or $\theta = \sin^{-1}\left(\dfrac{n\lambda}{2d}\right).$

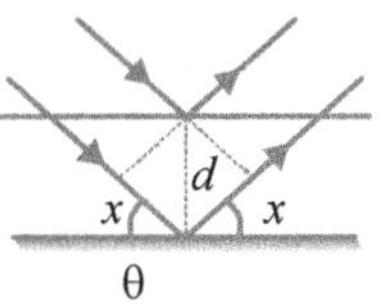

24. (b) $\Delta x_{max} = 2\lambda.$

So there are five maximums. These are for $\Delta x = 0, \pm\lambda, \pm2\lambda.$

25. (a) As shape of slits are rectangular and so fringes will be straight.

26. (d)

27. (a) For normal incidence,
$$2\mu t \cos0° = (2n-1)\frac{\lambda}{2}$$
or $\lambda = \dfrac{4\mu t}{(2n-1)} = \dfrac{4 \times 1.5 \times 5 \times 10^{-5}}{(2n-1)}$

For $n = 3, 4, \quad \lambda = 5000$ Å and 4000 Å

28. (c)

29. (d)

30. (c)
$$y_3 = y_4$$
or $\dfrac{3 \times D \times 590}{d} = \dfrac{4 \times D \times \lambda}{d}$
$\therefore \quad \lambda = 442.5$ nm.

31. (b) $n_1\beta_1 = n_2\beta_2$

or $n_1\lambda_1 = n_2\lambda_2$
or $12 \times 600 = n_2 \times 400$
$\therefore \quad n_2 = 18$

32. (b)

33. (a) $\beta = \dfrac{D\lambda}{d}$

and $\beta' = \dfrac{D \times 1.1\lambda}{1.1d} = \dfrac{D\lambda}{d} = \beta$

$= 0.2$ mm.

34. (c) Velocity of light does not depend on frame of reference.

35. (c) When star is moving towards earth, the wavelength coming from the star appears to decrease. So spectrum of light coming from the source shift towards blue.

36. (a)

37. (b)

38. (c)

39. (c) $\lambda = \dfrac{h}{P} = \dfrac{h}{mv}$, so with the increase in velocity of electron, wavelength decreases, and so fringe width decreases.

40. (a) The waves can be represented as :

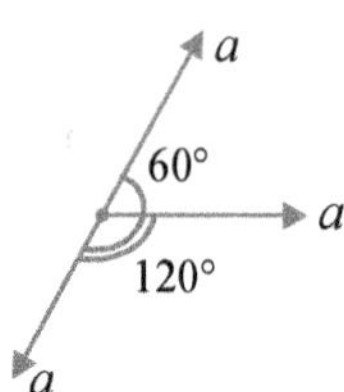

So resultant at the point of superposition $= a$.

41. (c) Using Snell's law, we have

$$\dfrac{\sin 30^\circ}{\sin \theta} = \dfrac{4}{3}$$

$$\therefore \sin \theta = \dfrac{3}{4} \times \dfrac{1}{2}$$

or $\theta = \sin^{-1}\left(\dfrac{3}{8}\right)$

42. (b) $I_A = I + 4I + 2\sqrt{I \times 4I}\cos \pi/2 = 5I$

and $I_B = I + 4I + 2\sqrt{I \times 4I}\cos \pi = I$

So $I_A - I_B = 5I - I = 4I$

43. (d) We can write

$$\dfrac{\Delta\lambda}{\lambda} = \dfrac{v}{c}$$

or $\dfrac{0.5}{100} = \dfrac{v}{3\times 10^8}$

$\therefore v = 1.5 \times 10^6$ m/s

44. (c) $\Delta x_{max} = d = 5000$ Å. Given $\lambda = 3000 \AA$

As $\lambda < d < 2\lambda$, $\therefore n = 3$.

45. (b) $\Delta\lambda = 706 - 656 = 50 nm$

We have, $\dfrac{\Delta\lambda}{\lambda} = \dfrac{v}{c}$

or $v = \dfrac{\Delta\lambda}{\lambda} \times c$

$= \dfrac{50}{656} \times 3 \times 10^8$

$= 2.28 \times 10^7$ m/s

46. (a) Path difference , $S_1 B = \Delta x = n\lambda$.

As P is the position of 11th fringe from Q, so from O it will be 10.

$\therefore \Delta x = n\lambda = 10\lambda$

$= 10 \times 6000 \times 10^{-10}$

$= 6 \times 10^{-6}$ m

47. (b) For coherent sources, $I_1 = (a + a)^2 = 4a^2$

For incoherent sources, $I_2 = a^2 + a^2 = 2a^2$

$\therefore \dfrac{I_1}{I_2} = \dfrac{4a^2}{2a^2} = 2$

48. (d)

49. (b)

50. (a) $y_n = \dfrac{4D\lambda_1}{d} = \dfrac{3D\lambda_2}{d}$

$\therefore \dfrac{\lambda_1}{\lambda_2} = \dfrac{3}{4}$.

51. (a) $\mu_g t_g = \mu_w t_w$

or $\mu_g = \dfrac{\mu_w t_w}{t_g}$

$= \dfrac{4/3 \times 6}{4} = 2$.

52. (b) $I_A \cos^2 30^\circ = I_B \cos^2 60^\circ$

$\therefore \dfrac{I_A}{I_B} = \dfrac{\cos^2 60^\circ}{\cos^2 30^\circ}$

$= \dfrac{1/4}{3/4} = \dfrac{1}{3}$

53. (d) $I = (I_0/2)\cos^2 60^\circ$

$= \dfrac{I_0}{2} \times \dfrac{1}{4} = \dfrac{I_0}{8}$.

1. (a) $\sin\theta = \dfrac{\lambda}{d}$

or $\theta \simeq \dfrac{600 \times 10^{-9}}{1 \times 10^{-3}}$

or $\theta = 6 \times 10^{-4}$ rad

$\therefore \beta = D\theta$

$= 2 \times 6 \times 10^{-4} = 1.2 \times 10^{-3}$ m

2. (a) The waves can be represented as follows :

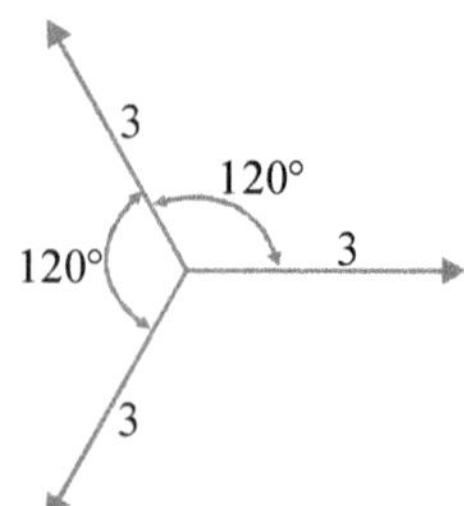

The resultant of three equal vectors (magnitude) each on 120° from other will be zero.

3. (c) $\sin\theta = \dfrac{\lambda}{d}$

   or $\theta \simeq \dfrac{\lambda}{d}$

   $\therefore \beta_1 = D\theta_1 = \dfrac{400}{d}D = y$

   and $\beta_2 = D\theta_2 = \dfrac{600D}{d/2} = 3y$.

4. (a) $\Delta = \beta$

   or $\dfrac{D(\mu-1)t}{d} = \dfrac{D\lambda}{d}$

   or $t = \dfrac{\lambda}{(\mu-1)} = \dfrac{\lambda}{(1.5-1)} = 2\lambda$.

5. (a) $\beta = \dfrac{D\lambda}{d}$

   or $\Delta\beta = \dfrac{(\Delta D)\lambda}{d}$

   or $3\times10^{-5} = \dfrac{(5\times10^{-2})\lambda}{10^{-3}}$

   $\therefore \lambda = 6000 \text{ Å}$.

6. (c) $\Delta x = (SS_1 + S_{10}) - (SS_2 + S_{20})$

   or $\dfrac{\lambda}{2} = 2\sqrt{D^2 + d^2} - 2D$

   $\therefore d = \sqrt{\dfrac{\lambda D}{2}}$

7. (d) For dark fringes of both waves at same place
   $$y_1 = y_2$$
   $$(n+1)\dfrac{D\lambda_1}{d} = n\dfrac{D\lambda_2}{d}$$
   or $(n+1)\times 400 = n\times 560$
   or $n = 2.5$, and $n+1 = 3.5$
   There integer value is 5 and 7.
   The distance between two regions of complete dark,
   $$\Delta x = 7\dfrac{D\lambda}{d} = \dfrac{7\times1\times400\times10^{-9}}{0.1\times10^{-3}}$$
   $$= 28 \text{ mm}.$$

8. (c) If a is the amplitude of the wave then

   $\dfrac{I_{max}}{4} = a^2 = a^2 + a^2 + 2aa\cos\phi$

   or $\cos\phi = -\dfrac{1}{2}$

   or $\phi = \dfrac{2\pi}{3}$.

   Corresponding path difference,

   $\Delta x = \dfrac{\phi\times\lambda}{2\pi}$

   $= \dfrac{(2\pi/3)\times\lambda}{2\pi} = \dfrac{\lambda}{3}$

So $d\sin\theta = \dfrac{\lambda}{3}$

or $\theta = \sin^{-1}\left(\dfrac{\lambda}{3d}\right)$.

9. (b) $\beta = \dfrac{\lambda}{2\mu\tan\alpha} = \dfrac{\lambda L}{2\times1\times h} = \dfrac{L\lambda}{2h}$.

10. (c) $\lambda = \dfrac{c}{f} = \dfrac{3\times10^8}{1420\times10^6} = 0.214 \text{ m}$

    $\sin\theta = \dfrac{1.22\lambda}{d} = \dfrac{1.22\times0.219}{25} = 0.010$

    or $\theta = 0.6°$, and $2\theta = 1.2°$

11. (c) For intensified reflected beam

    $2\mu t = (2n-1)\dfrac{\lambda}{2}$; $n = 1, 2, \ldots..$

    or $\lambda = \dfrac{4\mu t}{(2n-1)} = \dfrac{4\times1.5\times0.40\times10^{-6}}{(2n-1)}$

    $= \dfrac{2.4\times10^{-6}}{(2n-1)}$

    For $n = 3$,
    $\lambda = 4800$ Å (only wavelength between 4000 Å to 7000 Å)

12. (a) $\beta_1 = \dfrac{2.30}{20} = \dfrac{D\lambda_1}{d}$

    and $\beta_2 = \dfrac{2.80}{30} = \dfrac{D\lambda_2}{d}$

    or $\dfrac{\beta_1}{\beta_2} = \dfrac{2.30\times30}{20\times2.80} = \dfrac{\lambda_1}{\lambda_2}$

    $\therefore \lambda_2 = 0.81\,\lambda_1 = 0.81\times5890$
    $= 4780$ Å.

13. (d) $\beta = \dfrac{\lambda}{2\mu\tan\alpha} \simeq \dfrac{\lambda}{2\mu\alpha}$

    $\therefore \lambda = \beta\times 2\mu\alpha$

    $= 0.12\times10^{-2}\times2\times1\times\left(\dfrac{40}{60\times60}\times\dfrac{\pi}{180}\right)$

    $= 4655$ Å.

14. (c) $\beta = \dfrac{\lambda}{2\mu\alpha} = \dfrac{\lambda}{2\mu\left(\dfrac{t}{x}\right)}$

    $= \dfrac{\lambda x}{2\mu t}$

    or $t = \dfrac{\lambda x}{2\beta\mu}$

15. (c) The path difference,

$$d \sin\theta = n\lambda$$

$$\text{or } \sin\theta = \frac{n\lambda}{d}$$

$$= \frac{n\lambda}{2\lambda}$$

$$= \frac{n}{2}$$

For, $n = 0$, $\sin\theta = 0$, $\theta = 0°$

$n = 1$, $\sin\theta = \dfrac{1}{2}$, $\theta = 30°$

$n = 2$, $\sin\theta = 1$, $\theta = 90°$

Thus there is central maximum ($\theta = 0°$) and two for each $\theta = 30°$ and $90°$ and so total maximas are 5.

16. (d)

$$\Delta = \frac{D(\mu - 1)t}{d}$$

$$\text{Shift} = \frac{D\lambda}{d}$$

$$\therefore \quad \frac{D(\mu - 1)t}{d} = \frac{D\lambda}{d}$$

$$\text{or} \quad t = \frac{\lambda}{\mu - 1} = \frac{\lambda}{1.5 - 1} = 2\lambda$$

17. (c)

$$y_n = \frac{nD\lambda_1}{d} = \frac{(n+1)D\lambda_2}{d}$$

$$\text{or} \quad n = \left(\frac{\lambda_2}{\lambda_2 - \lambda_1}\right)$$

$$\text{and} \quad y_n = \left(\frac{\lambda_1\lambda_2}{\lambda_2 - \lambda_1}\right)\left(\frac{D}{d}\right).$$

18. (a)

$$\sin\theta_2 = \frac{2\lambda}{d}$$

$$\text{or} \quad \theta_2 = \sin^{-1}\left(\frac{2\lambda}{d}\right)$$

Given $y = D(2\theta_2) = 8 \times 10^{-2}$

$$\text{or } 1.5 \times 2 \times \sin^{-1}\left(\frac{2\lambda}{d}\right) = 8 \times 10^{-2}$$

$$\Rightarrow \quad d \simeq 0.005 \text{ cm}$$

19. (b) $\Delta x_{max} = 0$ and $\Delta x_{max} = 2\lambda$

Theortical maximas are $= 2n + 1 = 2 \times 2 + 1 = 5$
But on the screen there will be three maximas.

20. (b) $\quad \Delta x_1 = (\mu_1 - 1)t = (1.5 - 1)t = 0.5t$

$$\text{and } \Delta x_2 = (\mu_2 - 1) \times 2t = \left(\frac{4}{3} - 1\right) \times 2t = \frac{2}{3}t.$$

As $\Delta x_2 > \Delta x_1$, so shift will be along $-ve$ y-axis.

21. (a) Path difference,

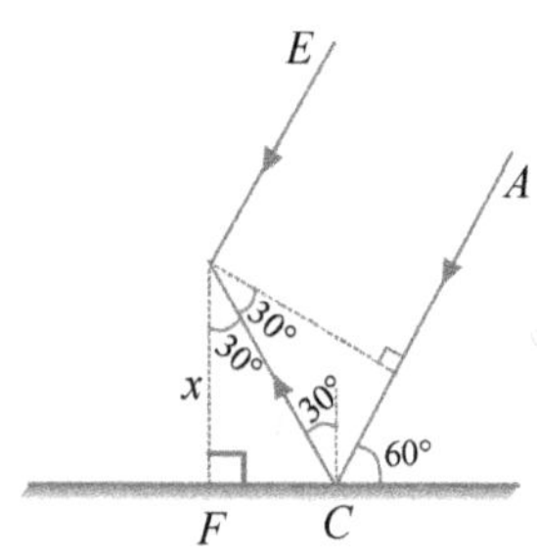

$$\Delta x = (BC + CD) + \frac{\lambda}{2}$$

Where $CD = \dfrac{x}{\cos 30°} = \dfrac{2x}{\sqrt{3}}$,

and $BC = CD \sin 30° = \dfrac{2x}{\sqrt{3}} \times \dfrac{1}{2} = \dfrac{x}{\sqrt{3}}$

Now $\Delta x = \left(\dfrac{x}{\sqrt{3}} + \dfrac{2x}{\sqrt{3}}\right) + \dfrac{\lambda}{2} = \sqrt{3}x + \dfrac{\lambda}{2}$

For destructive interference

$$\Delta x = \frac{3\lambda}{2} \text{ (here)}$$

$$\therefore \quad \sqrt{3}x + \frac{\lambda}{2} = \frac{3\lambda}{2}$$

$$\text{or} \quad \lambda = \sqrt{3}x$$

22. (b) $\quad PO = d \sec\theta$ and $CO = PO \cos 2\theta = d \sec\theta \cos 2\theta$

Path difference,

$$\Delta x = CO + PO$$
$$= (d \sec\theta + d \sec\theta \cos 2\theta)$$

Effective path difference

$$\Delta x_{eff} = d(\sec\theta + \sec\theta . \cos 2\theta) + \frac{\lambda}{2}$$

For constructive interference,

$$\Delta x_{eff} = \lambda$$

$$\text{or } d(\sec\theta + \sec\theta \cos 2\theta) + \frac{\lambda}{2} = \lambda$$

$$\text{or} \cos\theta = \frac{\lambda}{4d}.$$

23. (c) $\quad \lambda = 20 \text{ m}$; $PQ = 5\text{m} = \dfrac{\lambda}{4}$.

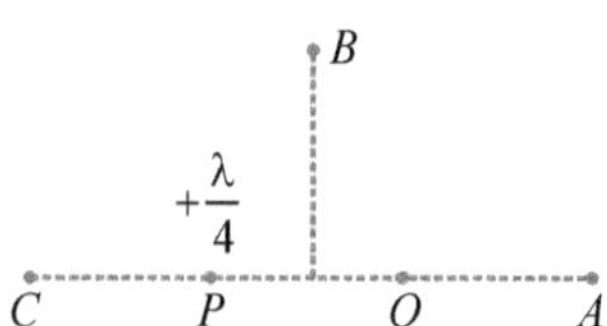

For A :

$$\Delta x = \left(PA + \frac{\lambda}{4}\right) - QA$$

$$= (PA - QA) + \frac{\lambda}{4}$$

$$= PQ + \frac{\lambda}{4}$$

$$= \frac{\lambda}{4} + \frac{\lambda}{4} = \frac{\lambda}{2}$$

or $\quad \phi = \pi$ rad .

Thus $I_A = I + I + 2\sqrt{II}\cos\pi = 0$.

For B :

$$\Delta x = \left(PB + \frac{\lambda}{4}\right) - QB$$

$$= (PB - QB) + \frac{\lambda}{4}$$

$$= 0 + \frac{\lambda}{4} = \frac{\lambda}{4}$$

or $\quad \phi = \dfrac{\pi}{2}$

Thus $I_B = I + I + 2\sqrt{II}\cos\pi/2$

$\qquad = 2I.$

For C :

$$\Delta x = QC - \left(PC + \frac{\lambda}{4}\right)$$

$$= (QC - PC) - \frac{\lambda}{4}$$

$$= \frac{\lambda}{4} - \frac{\lambda}{4} = 0 .$$

or $\quad \phi = 0$

Thus $I_C = I + I + 2\sqrt{II}\cos 0° = 4I.$

$\therefore I_A : I_B : I_C = 0 : 1 : 2.$

24.   (b) $a = 0.3$ m, $b = 0.7$ m. Angle of prism, A = 1°.

$\therefore D = a + b = 0.3 + 0.7 = 1$ m.

$$d = 2a(\mu - 1)A = 2 \times 0.3(1.5 - 1) \times \frac{\pi}{180}$$

$$= 0.0052 \text{ m}$$

Now $\beta = \dfrac{D\lambda}{d} = \dfrac{1 \times 6000 \times 10^{-10}}{0.0052}$

$\qquad = 1.15 \times 10^{-4}$ m

$\qquad = 0.115$ mm.

---

25.   (b)   Path difference,

$$\Delta x = S_1 P - S_2 P$$

$$= d\cos\theta .$$

$\therefore d\cos\theta = 4\lambda$

or $\quad \cos\theta = \left(\dfrac{4\lambda}{d}\right).$

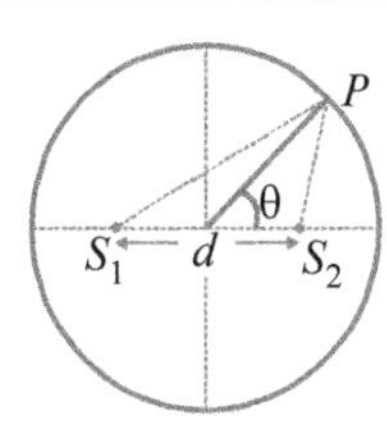

26.   (b)   Two images of the source are shown in figure.

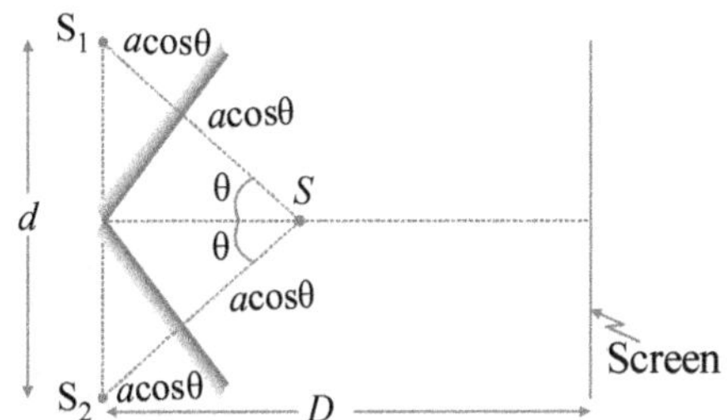

The separation between the two images,

$d = 2\,(2a\cos\theta\sin\theta)$

$\quad = 2a\sin 2\theta$

$D = (2a\cos\theta)\cos\theta + 4a$

$\quad = 2a\cos^2\theta + 4a$

For small θ, $\sin\theta \simeq \theta$ and $\cos\theta = 1$

$\therefore \qquad d = 2a \times 2\theta = 4a\theta$,

and $\qquad D = 6a.$

Now fringe width,

$$\beta = \frac{D\lambda}{d} = \frac{6a \times \lambda}{4a\theta}$$

$$= \frac{3\lambda}{2\theta}$$

27.   (d)   Optical path difference

$\Delta x = (\mu_2 - \mu_1)t .$

28.   (a) $I = \left[\left(\dfrac{I_0}{2}\right)\cos^2\theta\right]\cos^2(90° - \theta)$

$$= \frac{I_0}{2}\cos^2\theta\sin^2\theta$$

$$= \frac{I_0}{8}\sin^2 2\theta$$

---

1.   (b, d)   Given $\quad \dfrac{I_{\max}}{I_{\min}} = \dfrac{(a_1 + a_2)^2}{(a_1 - a_2)^2} = 9$

or $\quad \dfrac{(a_1 + a_2)}{(a_1 - a_2)} = 3$

or $\quad a_1 = 2a_2$

Also $\quad \dfrac{I_1}{I_2} = \dfrac{a_1^2}{a_2^2} = \dfrac{2^2}{1^2} = 4$

2.   (a, c)   For dark or missing wavelength,

$$y_n = \frac{(2n-1)}{2}\frac{d\lambda}{b}$$

or $\quad \dfrac{b}{2} = \left(\dfrac{2n-1}{2}\right)\dfrac{d}{b}\lambda$

or $\quad \lambda = \dfrac{b^2}{(2n-1)d}$

For $n = 1, 2 \quad \lambda = \dfrac{b^2}{d}, \dfrac{b^2}{3d} .$

3. (a, b) For $\theta = 0$, $\phi = 0$

$$\therefore \quad I = a^2 + a^2 + 2aa\cos 0° = 4a^2$$
$$= I_0$$

For $\theta = 30°$, $\quad \Delta x = d\sin\theta = d\sin 30° = \dfrac{d}{2}$;

$$\lambda = \frac{C}{f} = \frac{3\times 10^8}{10^6} = 3\times 10^2$$

Phase difference, $\quad \phi = \dfrac{2\pi}{\lambda}.\Delta x$

$$= \frac{2\pi}{300}\times\frac{d}{2} = \frac{2\pi}{300}\times\frac{150}{2} = \frac{\pi}{2}$$

Now $\quad I = a^2 + a^2 + 2aa\cos\dfrac{\pi}{2} = 2a^2$

$$= \frac{I_0}{2}$$

4. (a, c) Fringe width, $\beta = \dfrac{D\lambda}{d}$, and so with the increase in D, fringe width will increase. As angular fringe width $\alpha = \dfrac{\lambda}{d}$, and so it is independent of D.

5. (a, c)

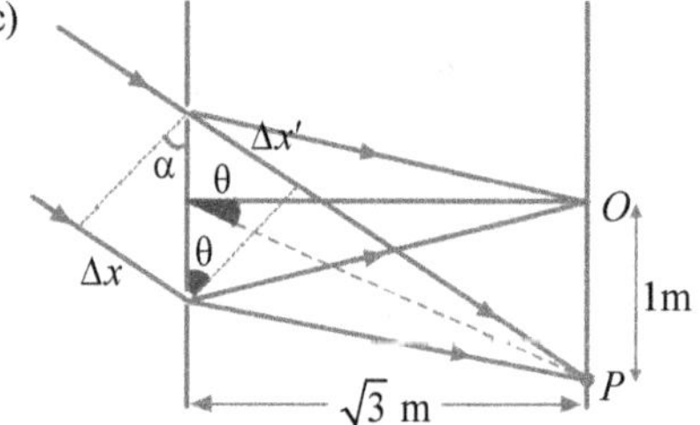

The path difference at 0,

$$\Delta x = d\sin\alpha = d\sin 30°$$
$$= \frac{10^{-3}}{2} \text{ m}$$

Now $\quad \phi = \dfrac{2\pi}{\lambda}.\Delta x = \dfrac{2\pi}{5000\times 10^{-10}}\times\dfrac{10^{-3}}{2}$

$$= 2\pi\times 10^3$$

So $\quad I = I_o + I_o + 2\sqrt{I_o I_o}\cos(2\pi\times 10^3)$

$$= 4I_o$$

The angular position of P, $\tan\theta = \dfrac{1}{\sqrt{3}}$; or $\theta = 30°$.

Now path difference $= \Delta x - \Delta x'$
$$= d\sin 30° - d\sin 30° = 0$$
So zero order fringe will form at P.

6. (a, d)

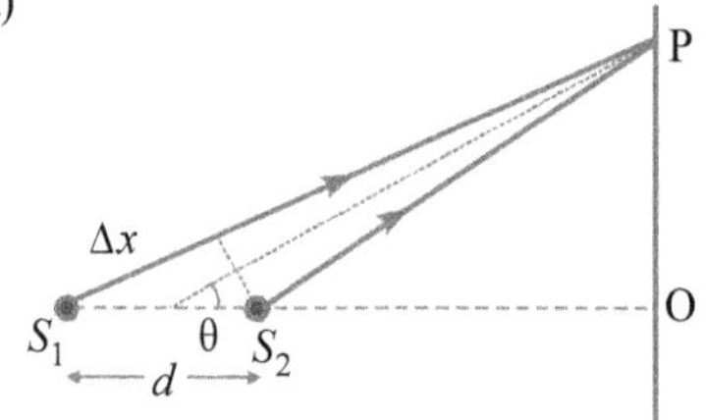

Path difference
$$\Delta x = d\cos\theta$$
$$\Delta x_{min} = 0$$
and $\quad \Delta x_{max} = d = 5.5\,\lambda$

So $\quad \Delta x = 0, \dfrac{\lambda}{2}, \lambda, \dfrac{3\lambda}{2}, 2\lambda, \dfrac{5\lambda}{2},$

$3\lambda, \dfrac{7\lambda}{2}, 4\lambda, \dfrac{9\lambda}{2}, 5\lambda, \dfrac{11\lambda}{2}$

Practically only five fringes will be on the screen, corresponding to $\Delta x = \lambda, 2\lambda, 3\lambda, 4\lambda$, and 5λ

Solutions **EXERCISE 4.3**

1. (a)
2. (a)
3. (a)
4. (a) As $\beta = \dfrac{D\lambda}{d}$ and wavelength of yellow light is shorter than red, so fringe width is narrower for yellow light.
5. (a)

6. (a) $\beta = \dfrac{D\lambda}{d}$. When $d \to 0$, $\beta \to \infty$, and so fringes will not be seen over the screen.
7. (d) For interference, the waves may be of unequal intensities.
8. (c) Interference will take place in green light only.
9. (b) Radio waves are transverse in nature, so they can be polarised.
10. (a)

Passage for Q no. 1 to 3

1. (b) Path difference will increase for upward ray hence $y > 0$.

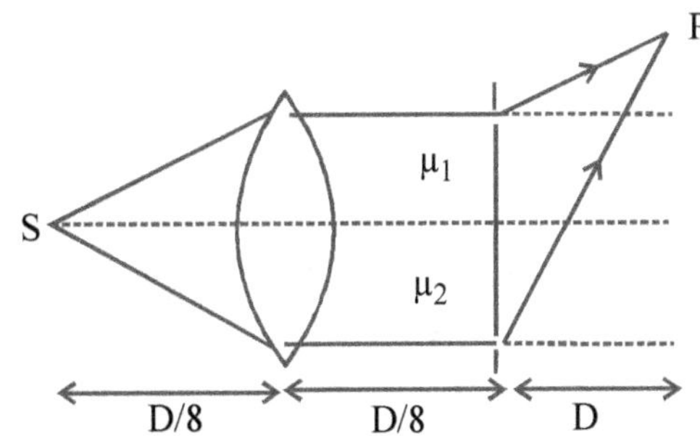

2. (b) Path difference will increase for the downward ray.

3. (a) Path difference will increase, hence $y > 0$.

Passage for Q no. 4 to 6

4. (b) The beams incident on face AB pass undeviated and incident on face AC at an angle θ.

For 4000 Å refractive index,

$$\mu_1 = 1.20 + \frac{b}{(4000)^2}$$

and for 5000 Å, $\mu_2 = 1.20 + \frac{b}{(5000)^2}$.

Critical angle in $C_1 = \frac{1}{\mu_1}$

and $\sin C_2 = \frac{1}{\mu_2}$

since $\mu_1 > \mu_2$

$\therefore \quad C_1 < C_2$.

Therefore total internal reflection can takes place for 4000 Å.

$$\therefore \quad \sin C_1 = \sin\theta$$

or $\frac{1}{\mu_1} = 0.8$

or $\left[1.20 + \dfrac{b}{(4000)^2} \right] = 0.8$

which gives $b = 8 \times 10^5 \left(\mathring{A} \right)^2$ **Ans.**

5 (c) Now $\mu_1 = 1.20 + \dfrac{8 \times 10^5}{(4000)^2} = 1.25$

and $\mu_2 = 1.20 + \dfrac{8 \times 10^5}{(5000)^2} = 1.232$.

The transmission of light takes place only of 5000 Å.

By Snell's Law

$$\mu_2 = \frac{\sin r_2}{\sin\theta}$$

or $\sin r_2 = 1.232 \times 0.8$

$= 0.9856$

and $r_2 \simeq 80.3°$

Angle of deviation $= r_2 - \theta = 80.3° - \sin^{-1}(0.8)$

$\simeq 53°$. **Ans.**

6. (a) The optical path difference between two waves

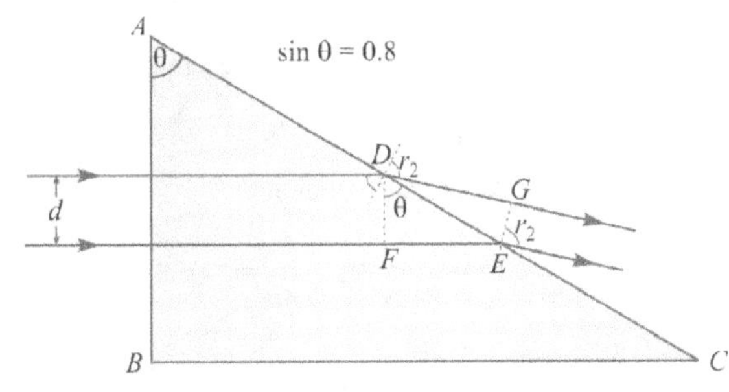

$\Delta x = $ DG in air $-$ EF in glass

$= $ DE $\sin r_2 - \mu\, d \tan\theta$

$= \dfrac{d \sin r_2}{\cos\theta} - \mu\, d \tan\theta$

$= \dfrac{d\,(\mu \sin\theta)}{\cos\theta} - \mu\, d \tan\theta$

Corresponding phase difference $\phi = 0$

$\therefore \quad I = I_1 + I_2 + 2\sqrt{I_1 I_2}\cos 0°$

$= 4I + I + 2\sqrt{4I \times I} = 9I$ **Ans.**

Passage for Q no. 7 to 8

7. (c) $I_1 = I$ and $I_2 = \dfrac{4I}{9}$.

$\dfrac{I_1}{I_2} = \dfrac{A_1^2}{A_2^2} = \dfrac{9}{4}$; or $\dfrac{A_1}{A_2} = \dfrac{3}{2}$

Thus $\dfrac{I_{max}}{I_{min}} = \dfrac{(A_1 + A_2)^2}{(A_1 - A_2)^2} = \dfrac{(3+2)^2}{(3-2)^2} = 25$.

8. (a) Displacement of fringes,

$$\Delta = \frac{D(\mu - 1)t}{d}, \text{ and}$$

fringe width, $\beta = \dfrac{D\lambda}{d}$

$\therefore \quad n = \dfrac{\Delta}{\beta} = \dfrac{D(\mu - 1)t/d}{(D\lambda/d)}$

$= \dfrac{(\mu - 1)t}{\lambda}$

$= \dfrac{(1.45 - 1) \times 0.02 \times 10^{-3}}{6000 \times 10^{-10}} = 15$.

Passage for Q no. 9 to 11

9. (a) $2d \cos i = n\lambda_{dB}$

10. (a) The path difference between the rays APB and CQD is
$$\Delta x = MQ + QN = d \cos i + d \cos i$$
$$\Delta x = 2d \cos i$$

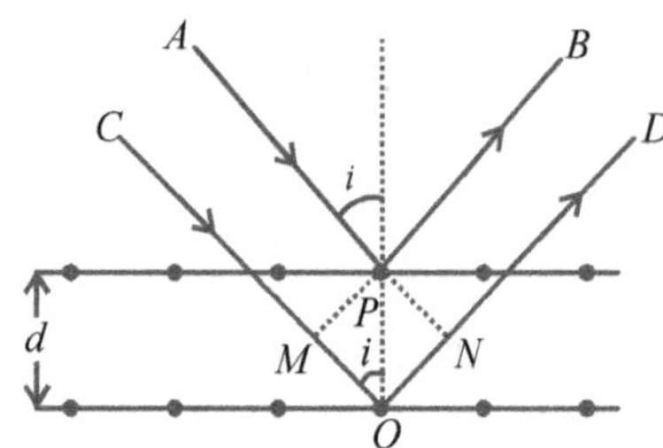

We know that for constructive interference the path difference is $n\lambda$

$\therefore$ $n\lambda = 2d \cos i$

Also by de-broglie concept

$$\lambda = \frac{h}{p} = \frac{h}{\sqrt{2mK.E}} = \frac{h}{\sqrt{2meV}}$$

$\therefore$ $\dfrac{nh}{\sqrt{2meV}} = 2d \cos i$

Here $n = 1 : V = \dfrac{h^2}{8med^2 \cos^2 i}$

$$= \frac{(6.6 \times 10^{-34})^2}{8 \times 9.1 \times 10^{-31} \times 1.6 \times 10^{-19} \times (10^{-10})^2 \times \cos^2 30}$$

$$= 50 \, \text{V}$$

11. (c)

12. **A-p, s; B-q; C-t; D-r, s, t**

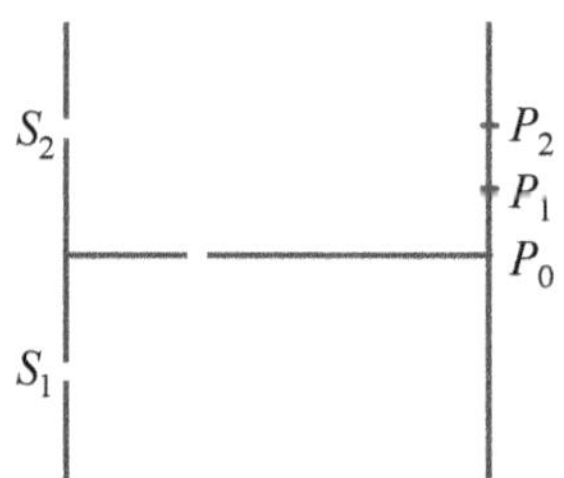

For path difference $\lambda/4$, phase difference is $\pi/2$.

For path difference $\lambda/3$, phase difference is $2\pi/3$.

Here, $S_1P_0 - S_2P_0 = 0$

$\therefore$ $\delta(P_0) = 0$

Therefore, (p) matches with (A).

The path difference for P_1 and P_2 will not be zero. The intensities at P_0 is maximum.

$$I(P_0) = I_1 + I_2 + 2\sqrt{I_1}\sqrt{I_2} \cos 0°$$

$$= (\sqrt{I_1} + \sqrt{I_2})^2 = (I_0 + I_0)^2 = 4I_0$$

$$I(P_1) = I_1 + I_2 + 2\sqrt{I_1}\sqrt{I_2} \cos \frac{\pi}{2}$$

$$= I_1 + I_2 = I_0 + I_0 = 2I_0$$

$$I(P_2) = I_1 + I_2 + 2\sqrt{I_1}\sqrt{I_2} \cos(2\pi/3)$$

$$= I_1 + I_2 - \sqrt{I_1}\sqrt{I_2} = I_0 + I_0 - I_0 = I_0$$

$\therefore$ $I(P_0) > I(P_1)$

Therefore, (s) matches with (A).

(B)

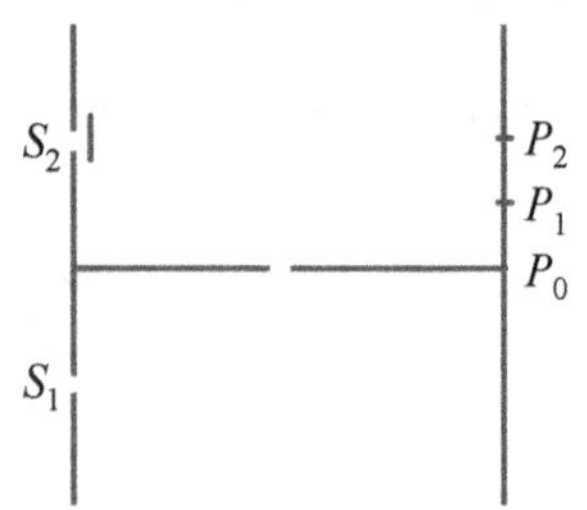

$$\delta P_0 = \frac{\lambda}{4}, \, \delta P_1 = 0, \, \delta P_2 = \frac{\lambda}{12}$$

$$I(P_0) = I_1 + I_2 + 2\sqrt{I_1}\sqrt{I_2} \cos \pi/2$$

$$= I_1 + I_2 = I_0 + I_0 = 2I_0$$

$$I(P_1) = I_1 + I_2 + 2\sqrt{I_1}\sqrt{I_2} = 4I_0$$

$$I(P_2) = I_1 + I_2 + 2\sqrt{I_1}\sqrt{I_2} \cos \pi/6$$

$$= I_1 + I_2 + \sqrt{3}\sqrt{I_1}\sqrt{I_2}$$

$$= I_0 + I_0 + \sqrt{3} \, I_0$$

$$= (2 + \sqrt{3})I_0$$

Therefore, q match with (B)

(C)

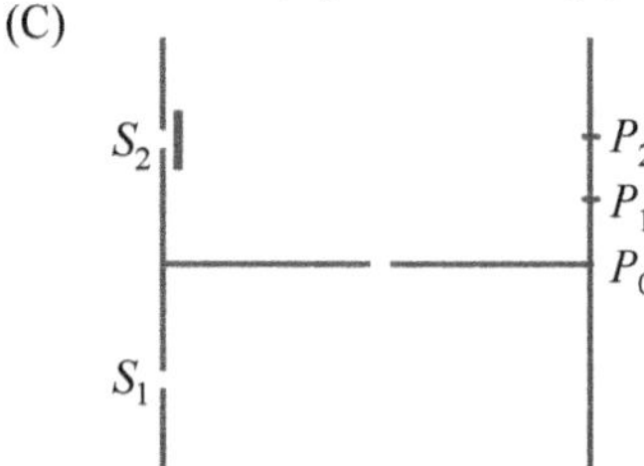

Here $\delta(P_0) = -\lambda/2; \, \delta(P_1) = -\lambda/4, \, \delta(P_2) = -\lambda/6$

$$I(P_0) = I_1 + I_2 + 2\sqrt{I_1}\sqrt{I_2} \cos(-\pi)$$

$$= I_1 + I_2 - 2\sqrt{I_1}\sqrt{I_2} = I_0 + I_0 - 2I_0 = 0$$

$$I(P_1) = I_1 + I_2 + 2\sqrt{I_1}\sqrt{I_2} \cos(-\pi/2)$$

$$= I_1 + I_2 = I_0 + I_0 = 2I_0$$

$$I(P_2) = I_1 + I_2 + 2\sqrt{I_1}\sqrt{I_2} \cos\left(-\frac{\pi}{3}\right)$$

$$= I_1 + I_2 + \sqrt{I_1}\sqrt{I_2} = I_0 + I_0 + I_0 = 3I_0$$

$\therefore$ $I(P_2) > I(P_1)$

(t) matches (C).

(D)

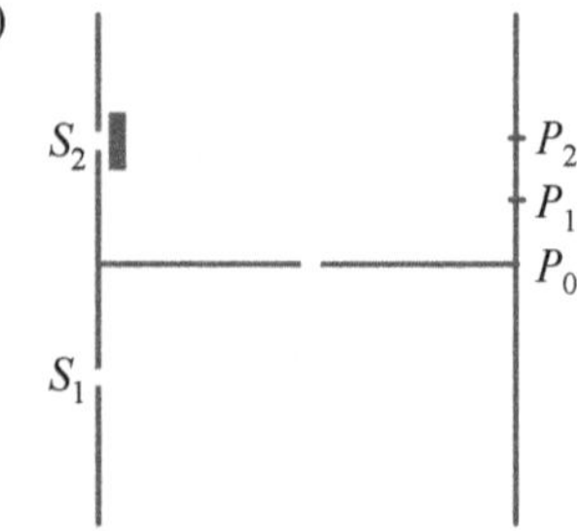

Here $\delta P_0 = 3\lambda/4; \delta P_1 = -\lambda/2; \delta P_2 = -5\lambda/12$

$$I(P_0) = I_1 + I_2 + 2\sqrt{I_1}\sqrt{I_2}\cos\left(\frac{-3\pi}{2}\right)$$

$$= I_1 + I_2 = I_0 + I_0 = 2I_0$$

$$I(P_1) = I_1 + I_2 + 2\sqrt{I_1}\sqrt{I_2}\cos(-\pi)$$

$$= I_1 + I_2 - 2\sqrt{I_1}\sqrt{I_2} = I_0 + I_0 - 2\sqrt{I_0}\sqrt{I_0} = 0$$

$$I(P_2) = I_1 + I_2 + 2\sqrt{I_1}\sqrt{I_2}\cos\left[-5\pi/6\right]$$

$$= I_1 + I_2 - \sqrt{3}\sqrt{I_1}\sqrt{I_2} = \left(2 - \sqrt{3}\right)I_0$$

(r), (s), (t) matches (D).

13.   **A-(q); B-(p) ; C-(s); D-(r)**

For central maxima, path diff $(\Delta x) = 0$ for any point P on the screen.

$$\Delta x = \mu_m(S_2P) - [\mu_m(S_1P - x) + \mu x]$$

masses $x = $ thickness of glass slab.

$$= \mu_m[S_2P - S_1P] - (\mu_m - \mu)x$$

$$= \mu_m\left(d.\frac{y}{D}\right) - (\mu_m - \mu)x = 0$$

Here,

$$y = \frac{D}{d}\left(\frac{\mu_m - \mu}{\mu_m}\right)x = \frac{Dx}{d}\left[\frac{20 - 4t - 5}{20 - 4t}\right]$$

$$= \frac{Dx}{d}\left[\frac{15 - 4t}{20 - 4t}\right] \quad \text{... (i)}$$

At time, t = 0

$$y = \frac{Dx}{d} \times \frac{15}{20} = \frac{1}{2} \times 0.2 \times \frac{15}{20} = \frac{15}{200} = \frac{3}{40}m = \frac{15}{2}cm = 7.5cm$$

R.I of medium cannot be less than 1 which become

At time $t = \frac{19}{4} = 4.755$. Here after this time R.I. of medium will

not change.

So position of central maxima at time $t = 5$ s will be same as at time $t = 4.75$ s

$$\therefore\ y = \frac{Dx}{d}\left[\frac{-4}{1}\right] = \frac{1}{2} \times 0.2 \times -4 = -0.4\,\text{m}$$

$|y| = 40$ cm.

For speed of central maxima, differentiating equation (i), w.r.t. time we get

$$\frac{dy}{dt} = \frac{Dx}{d}\left[\frac{-20}{(20 - 4t)^2}\right]$$

Central maxima will be at the centre of geometrical centre of screen when R.I. of medium is 5.

Hence at time $t = \frac{15}{4}$

$$\therefore\ \left.\frac{dy}{dt}\right)_{t=\frac{15}{4}} = \frac{Dx}{d}\left(-\frac{20}{25}\right) = \frac{1}{2} \times 0.2 \times -\frac{20}{25} = \frac{2}{25}\text{m/s} = 8\text{ cm/s}$$

Fringe width

$$\beta = \frac{D}{d}\frac{\lambda}{\mu} = \frac{1}{2\times10^{-3}} \times \frac{100\times10^{-10}}{5} = 10^{-6}\text{m} = 1\mu\text{m}$$

14.   **A - (p, q), B - (r, s), C - (r, t), D - (p)**

1.   The maximum path difference between the sources can be

$$\Delta x = 2.0\,\text{m}$$

$$= 4\times0.5 = 4\lambda$$

The maxima will be obtained for $\Delta x = 0$, λ, 2λ, 3λ and 4λ.

Thus in quarter rotation of a detector, there are four maximas. In full rotation there will be sixteen maximas (see figure).

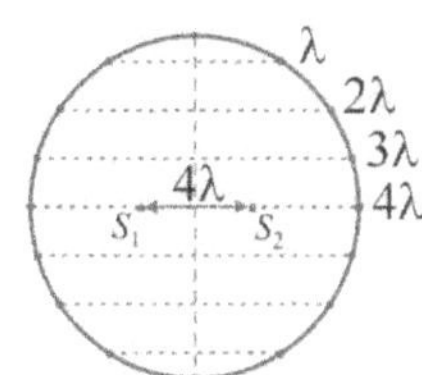

2.   The angular of fringes is given by, $\alpha = \frac{\lambda}{d}$. Thus for 10%

greater value of α, there need the wavelength 1.1 λ.

Therefore required wavelength = 1.1 × 589 = 648 nm.
Ans.

3.   The fringe wedge is given by

$$\beta = \frac{\lambda}{2\mu\tan\alpha}$$

Here $\tan\alpha = \frac{0.048}{120}$, $\mu = 1$ (air)

$$\therefore\ \beta = \frac{683\times10^{-9}}{2(1)\times\left(\dfrac{0.048}{120}\right)}$$

$$= 0.854 \times 10^{-3}\,\text{m.}$$

The number of fringes in total length of plate

$$= \frac{120\times10^{-3}}{0.854} \simeq 140 \quad \textit{Ans.}$$

4.   According to molus law, the intensity

$$I = I_0\cos^2\theta$$

(a) For $\theta = 30°$, $I = I_0\cos^2 30° = \frac{3I_0}{4} = 0.75\,I_0$

(b) For $\theta = 60°$, $I = I_0\cos^2 60° = \frac{I_0}{4} = 0.25 I_0$ \quad ***Ans.***

Solutions **EXERCISE 4.6**

1. The resultant amplitude is given by

$$R = (a_1^2 + a_2^2 + 2a_1a_2\cos\phi)^{1/2}$$
$$= (2^2 + 4^2 + 2\times 2\times 4\cos 60°)^{1/2}$$
$$= \sqrt{28} \,. \qquad \textbf{Ans.}$$

2. Given $a_1 = 8$, $a_2 = 10$ and $\phi = 30°$

$$\therefore \qquad R = (a_1^2 + a_2^2 + 2a_1a_2\cos\phi)^{1/2}$$
$$= (8^2 + 10^2 + 2\times 8\times 10\cos 30°)^{1/2}$$
$$= 14.5. \qquad \textbf{Ans.}$$

3. (a) The resulting intensity is given by

$$I = I_1 + I_2 + 2\sqrt{I_1 I_2}\cos\phi$$

and $\qquad I_{max} = (\sqrt{I_1} + \sqrt{I_2})^2$

For n identical waves, each of intensity I_0.

$$I_{max} = (\sqrt{I_0} + \sqrt{I_0} + ... n \text{ times})^2$$
$$= n^2 I_0 \qquad \textbf{Ans.}$$

(b) When interference is incoherent, then

$$I_{max} = I_1 + I_2$$

For n identical waves, each of intensity I_0m

$$I_{max} = I_0 + I_0 + ... n \text{ times}$$
$$= nI_0 \qquad \textbf{Ans.}$$

4. The intensity is given by

$$I = I_1 + I_2 + 2\sqrt{I_1 I_2}\cos\phi$$

The average intensity

$$I_{av} = \frac{\int_0^{2\pi} I d\phi}{\int_0^{2\pi} d\phi}$$

$$= \frac{1}{2\pi}\int (I_1 + I_2 + 2\sqrt{I_1 I_2}\cos\phi)d\phi$$

$$= I_1 + I_2 \,.$$

5. For missing wavelength

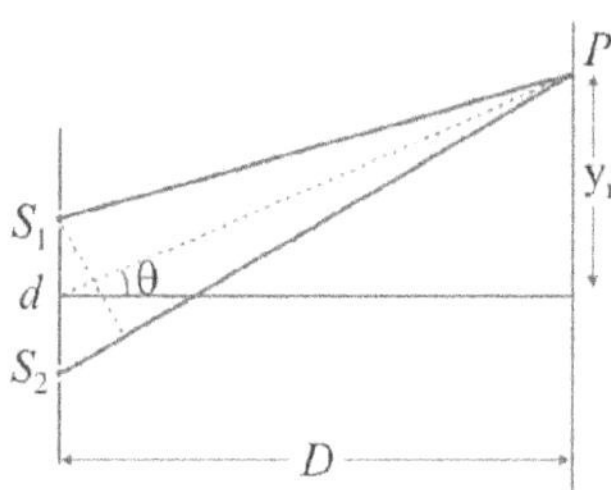

6. The distance of nth maxima from central maxima is given by

$$y_n = \frac{(2n-1)}{2}\frac{D\lambda}{d}$$

Given $\qquad y_n = \frac{d}{2}$,

$$\therefore \qquad \frac{d}{2} = \frac{(2n-1)}{2}\frac{D\lambda}{d}$$

or $\qquad \lambda = \frac{d^2}{(2n-1)D} \,.$

6. The distance of nth maxima from central maxima is given by

$$y_n = n\frac{D\lambda}{d},$$

For y_n to be constant, $n\lambda$ = constant. Thus

$$n_1\lambda_1 = n_2\lambda_2$$

$$\therefore \qquad n_2 = \frac{n_1\lambda_1}{\lambda_2} = \frac{16\times 6000}{4800} = 20 \quad \textbf{Ans.}$$

7. The path difference between the waves, arriving at P,

$$\Delta x = d\sin\theta,$$

the corresponding phase difference

$$\phi = \frac{2\pi}{\lambda}(d\sin\theta)$$

The intensity, $\quad I_R = I_1 + I_2 + 2\sqrt{I_1 I_2}\cos\phi$

$$= I + 4I + 2\sqrt{I\times 4I}\cos\left(\frac{2\pi}{\lambda}(d\sin\theta)\right)$$

$$= 5I + 4I\cos\left[\frac{2\pi}{\lambda}(d\sin\theta)\right] \quad ... \text{(i)}$$

The maximum intensity will occur, when

$\cos\phi = +1$, $\therefore$ $\quad I_0 = 9I$

On solving equations (i) and (ii), we get

$$I_R = \frac{I_0}{9}\left[1 + 8\cos^2\left(\frac{\pi d\sin\theta}{\lambda}\right)\right] \textit{Ans.}$$

8. If λ is the wavelength of light used, then

$$d = 100\,\lambda$$

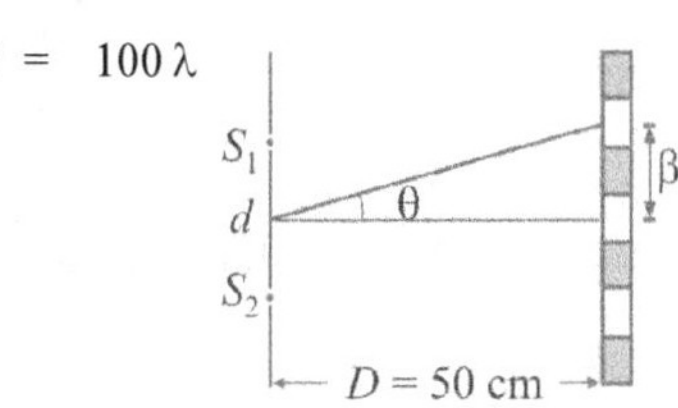

(a) The angular separation

$$\alpha = \frac{\beta}{D} = \frac{\lambda}{d} = \frac{\lambda}{100\lambda} = \frac{1}{100} \text{ radian} \qquad \textbf{\textit{Ans.}}$$

(b) $\beta = \dfrac{D\lambda}{d} = \dfrac{0.50 \times \lambda}{100\lambda} = 0.5 \times 10^{-2} \text{ cm} \qquad \textbf{\textit{Ans.}}$

9. The second wave gets reflected from the water surface suffers a phase changes of π rad or path difference of $\dfrac{\lambda}{2}$. The situation is shown in figure.

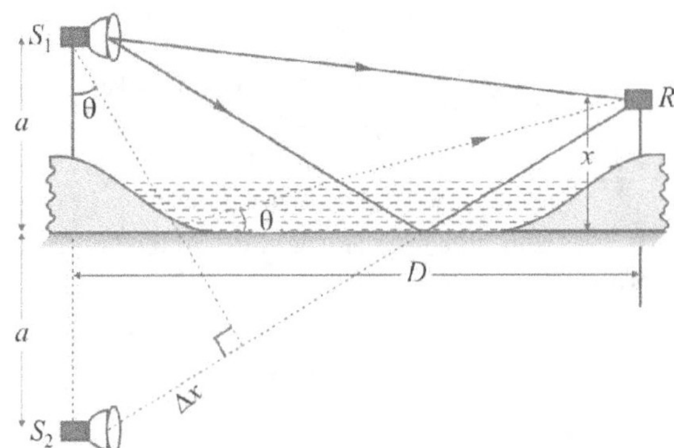

The path difference between the waves receiving at R is,

$$\Delta x = 2a\sin\theta$$
$$\simeq 2a\tan\theta$$
$$= 2a\frac{x}{D}$$

The effective path difference, $. \Delta x_e = 2a\dfrac{x}{D} \pm \dfrac{\lambda}{2}$.

For maxima, $\quad \Delta x_e = n\lambda$

or $\quad 2a\dfrac{x}{D} + \dfrac{\lambda}{2} = n\lambda$

$\therefore \qquad x = \dfrac{D}{2a}\left(\dfrac{2n+1}{2}\right)\lambda \;;\, n = 0, 1, 2. \quad \textbf{\textit{Ans.}}$

10. Given, $, d = 2 \times 10^{-3}$ m, $D = 10 \times 10^{-2}$ m, $D = 5 \times 10^{-3}$m.
The displacement of fringe pattern is given by

$$\Delta = \frac{D(\mu-1)t}{d}$$

or $\quad 5\times 10^{-3} = \dfrac{10\times 10^{-2}(\mu-1)\times 0.5\times 10^{-3}}{2\times 10^{-3}}$

$\therefore \qquad \mu = 1.2. \qquad \textbf{\textit{Ans.}}$

11. The path difference produced due to the introduction of the plate

$$\Delta x = (\mu-1)t$$
$$= (1.5 - 1)\times 1.5 \times 10^{-6}$$
$$= 0.75 \times 10^{-6} \text{ m}$$

The corresponding phase difference

$$\phi = \frac{2\pi}{\lambda}\Delta x$$
$$= \frac{2\pi}{5000\times 10^{-10}}\times 0.75\times 10^{-6}$$
$$= 3\pi .$$

If I is the intensity of each wave, then

$$I_{centre} = I + I + 2\sqrt{II}\cos 3\pi = 0 \qquad \textbf{\textit{Ans.}}$$

The lateral shift is given by

$$\Delta = \frac{D(\mu-1)t}{d} = \frac{1(1.5-1)\times 1.5\times 10^{-6}}{5\times 10^{-4}}$$
$$= 1.5 \times 10^{-3} \text{ m} \qquad \textbf{\textit{Ans.}}$$

12. The fringe width β is given by,

$$\beta = \frac{D\lambda}{d}$$

where $D = D_1 + (D_1 + D_2) + (D_1 + D_2) = 3D_1 + 2D_2$

$\therefore \qquad \beta = \dfrac{(3D_1 + 2D_2)\lambda}{d} . \qquad \textbf{\textit{Ans.}}$

13. If β be the fringe width in air, then in water

$$\beta_{water} = \frac{\beta}{\mu_w} = \frac{0.20°}{4/3} \qquad \textbf{\textit{Ans.}}$$

14. The path difference between the waves arriving at P

$$\Delta x = 2\lambda\cos\theta$$

The minimum path difference $\Delta x = 0$, when $\theta = 90°$, and maximum path difference, $\Delta x = 2\lambda$, when $\theta = 0$. Thus there must be one more maximum between these two .

For this $\quad \Delta x = \lambda$

or $\quad 2\lambda\cos\theta = \lambda$

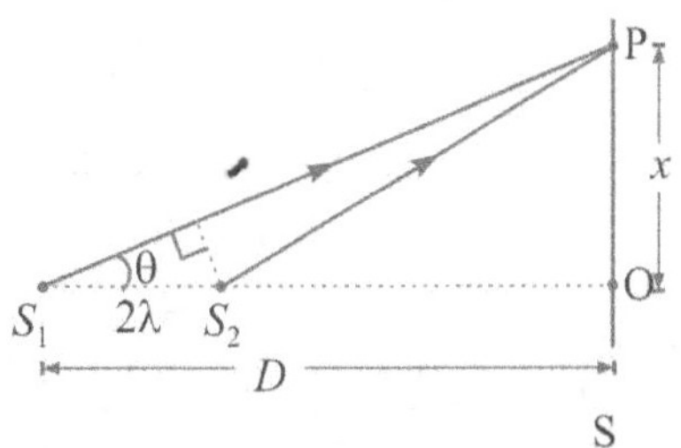

$\therefore \qquad \cos\theta = \dfrac{1}{2}$

From the geometry,

$$\cos\theta = \frac{D}{\sqrt{D^2 + x^2}}.$$

$$\therefore \qquad \frac{D}{\sqrt{D^2 + x^2}} = \frac{1}{2}$$

or $\qquad\qquad x = \sqrt{3}D.$ **Ans.**

15. If I is the intensity of each wave, then maximum intensity $I_{max} = 4I$. Suppose ϕ is the phase difference between the waves corresponding to $\dfrac{I_{max}}{2}$, then

$$\frac{I_{max}}{2} = I + I + 2\sqrt{II}\cos\phi$$

or $\qquad 2I = 2I + 2I\cos\phi$

$$\therefore \qquad \phi = \frac{\pi}{2}\ \text{rad}$$

The corresponding path difference

$$\Delta x = \phi \times \frac{\lambda}{2\pi} = \frac{\pi}{2} \times \frac{\lambda}{2\pi}$$

$$= \frac{\lambda}{4}.$$

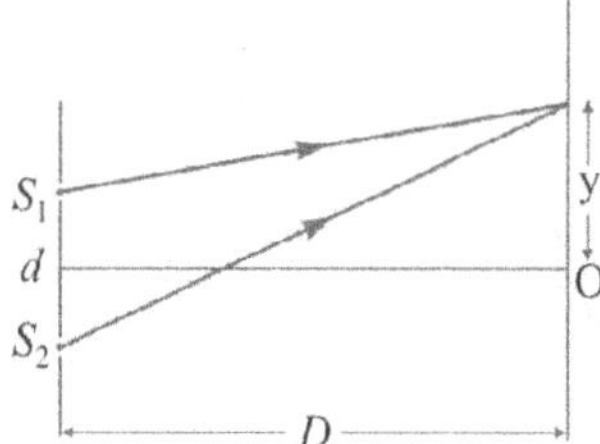

If y is the required distance, then

$$\Delta x = \frac{dy}{D}$$

or $\qquad\qquad \dfrac{dy}{D} = \dfrac{\lambda}{4}$

$$\therefore \qquad y = \frac{D\lambda}{4d}$$

$$= \frac{1 \times 500 \times 10^{-9}}{4 \times 1 \times 10^{-3}} = 1.25 \times 10^{-4}\,\text{m}.$$

16. The separation between the sources is given by

$$d = 2a(\mu - 1)A$$

$$= 2 \times 0.20(1.5 - 1) \times \left(1 \times \frac{\pi}{180}\right)$$

$$= 3.48 \times 10^{-3}\,\text{m} \qquad \textbf{Ans.}$$

The fringe width $\beta = \dfrac{D\lambda}{d}$

where $\qquad D = (a + b) = (20 + 80)\,\text{cm} = 1\,\text{m}$

$$\therefore \qquad \beta = \frac{1 \times 6000 \times 10^{-10}}{3.48 \times 10^{-3}} = 0.172\,\text{mm}.$$

Ans.

17. The distance of third bright fringe from central bright is given by

$$y = 3\frac{D\lambda}{d}.$$

Thus the separation between the fringes of two colour is

$$\Delta y = 3\frac{D}{d}(\Delta\lambda)$$

$$= 3 \times \frac{1}{5 \times 10^{-3}} \times (6000 - 4800) \times 10^{-10}$$

$$= 0.0072\,\text{cm}. \qquad \textbf{Ans.}$$

18. (a) The fringe displacement Δ is given by

$$\Delta = \frac{D(\mu - 1)t}{d} = \frac{D\left(\dfrac{\mu_g}{\mu_m} - 1\right)t}{d}$$

$$= \frac{1.5\left(\dfrac{1.5}{4/3} - 1\right) \times 10.4 \times 10^{-6}}{0.45 \times 10^{-3}}$$

$$= 4.33 \times 10^{-3}\,\text{m}.$$

(b) The path difference produced due to the introduction of glass sheet

$$\Delta x = (\mu - 1)t = \left(\frac{\mu_g}{\mu_m} - 1\right)t$$

$$= \left(\frac{1.5}{4/3} - 1\right) \times 10.4 \times 10^{-6}$$

$$= 1.3 \times 10^{-6}\,\text{m}.$$

The corresponding phase difference

$$\phi = \frac{2\pi}{\lambda}\Delta x$$

$$= \frac{2\pi}{600 \times 10^{-9}} \times 1.3 \times 10^{-6}$$

$$= \frac{13}{3}\pi$$

The intensity at O is given by

$$I = I_0 + I_0 + 2\sqrt{I_0 I_0}\cos\left(\frac{13\pi}{3}\right)$$

$$= 3I_0$$

Thus $\qquad \dfrac{I}{I_{max}} = \dfrac{3I_0}{4I_0} = \dfrac{3}{4}.$ **Ans.**

(c) The path difference at O is given by
$$\Delta x = 1.3 \times 10^{-6}\,\text{m}.$$

For maximum

$$\Delta x = n\lambda.$$

$$\therefore \quad n\lambda = 1.3 \times 10^{-6}$$

or

$$\lambda = \frac{1.3 \times 10^{-6}}{n} = \frac{1300 \times 10^{-9}}{n} = \frac{1300}{n}\,\text{nm}$$

For $n = 1, 2, 3, 4,$; $\lambda = 1300$ nm, 650 nm, 443.3 nm, 260 nm,..........
Thus the required wavelength range is 650 nm and 433.3 nm.

19. The minimum and maximum path difference between waves from S_1 and S_2 can be zero and 3λ corresponding to $x = \infty$ and $x = 0$. Thus for the farthest minima, $\Delta x = \lambda/2$.

If x is the required distance, then path difference

$$\Delta x = \sqrt{x^2 + d^2} - x$$

or

$$(\Delta x + x)^2 = x^2 + d^2$$

or $\Delta x^2 + x^2 + 2x\Delta x = x^2 + d^2$

or

$$\Delta x^2 + 2x\Delta x = d^2$$

Substituting, $d = 3\lambda$ and $\Delta x = \dfrac{\lambda}{2}$, we have

$$\left(\frac{\lambda}{2}\right)^2 + 2x\left(\frac{\lambda}{2}\right) = (3\lambda)^2$$

$$\therefore \quad x = \frac{35\lambda}{4}. \qquad \textbf{\textit{Ans.}}$$

20. If t is the thickness of soap film, then for constructive interference

$$2\mu t = (2n-1)\frac{\lambda}{2}$$

$$\therefore \quad t = (2n-1)\frac{\lambda}{4\mu}$$

For $n = 1$, $\quad t = \dfrac{\lambda}{4\mu} = \dfrac{624 \times 10^{-9}}{4 \times 1.33} = 0.117 \times 10^{-t}$

For $n = 2$, $\quad t = \dfrac{3\lambda}{4\mu} = 0.352 \times 10^{-6}$ m. **_Ans._**

21. In the situation given the air- MgF_2 and MgF_2 - glass both act as rigid boundary, and so for destructive interference in reflected light, we have.

$$2\mu_2 L = (2n-1)\frac{\lambda}{2}$$

or

$$L = (2n-1)\frac{\lambda}{4\mu_2}$$

For least value, $n = 1$, also $\mu_2 = 1.38$.

$$\therefore \quad \lambda = (2 \times 1 - 1) \times \frac{(550 \times 10^{-9})}{4 \times 1.38}$$

$$= 99.6 \text{ nm.} \qquad \textbf{\textit{Ans.}}$$

22. (a) For first minima, we have

$$d \sin\theta = \lambda$$

$$\therefore \quad d = \frac{\lambda}{\sin\theta}$$

$$= \frac{650\,\text{nm}}{\sin 15°} = 2511\,\text{nm}$$

$$\simeq 2.5 \ \mu\text{m}. \qquad \textbf{\textit{Ans.}}$$

(b) If λ' is the required wavelength, then for first order maximum

$$d \sin\theta = \frac{3}{2}\lambda'$$

$$\therefore \quad \lambda' = \frac{d \sin\theta}{1.5}$$

$$= \frac{2511 \times \sin 15°}{1.5}$$

$$= 430 \text{ nm.} \qquad \textbf{\textit{Ans.}}$$

23. The angular width of central maxima is,

$$\alpha \propto \lambda$$

For two wavelength λ_1 and λ_2, we have

$$\frac{\alpha_1}{\alpha_2} = \frac{\lambda_1}{\lambda_2}$$

$$\frac{\alpha}{0.70\alpha} = \frac{6000}{\lambda_2}$$

$$\therefore \quad \lambda_2 = 4200\text{Å.} \qquad \textbf{\textit{Ans.}}$$

For the same decrease in wavelength, if μ is the refractive index, then

$$\mu = \frac{\lambda_1}{\lambda_2}$$

$$= \frac{6000}{4200} = 1.43 . \qquad \textbf{\textit{Ans.}}$$

24. If θ_0 and θ_i are the angular separation between the objects and their images, then

$$\theta_0 = \theta_i = \frac{1.22\lambda}{d}$$

$$= \frac{1.22 \times (550 \times 10^{-9})}{32 \times 10^{-3}}$$

$$= 2.1 \times 10^{-5} \text{ rad.} \qquad \textbf{\textit{Ans.}}$$

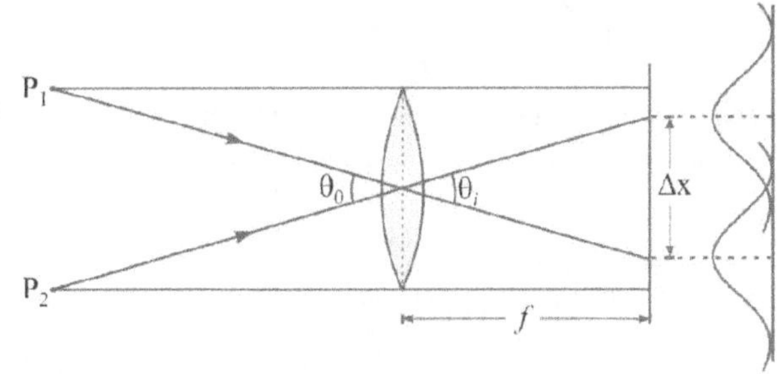

From the geometry, the separation

$$\Delta x = f\theta_i$$
$$= 0.24 \times 2.1 \times 10^{-5}$$
$$= 5.0 \ \mu m \qquad \textbf{\textit{Ans.}}$$

25. The resolution limit of the telescope is

$$\theta = \frac{1.22\lambda}{d} = \frac{1.22 \times 6000 \times 10^{-10}}{1}$$
$$= 7.32 \times 10^{-7} \ \text{rad}$$

The resolution limit of human eye

$$\theta = 2 \ \text{minute}$$
$$= \frac{2}{60} \times \frac{\pi}{180} = 2.91 \times 10^{-4} \ \text{rad}$$

The magnifying power of telescope is

$$M = \frac{RP \ \text{of telescope}}{RP \ \text{of eye}}$$
$$= \frac{\theta'}{\theta} = \frac{2.91 \times 10^{-4}}{7.32 \times 10^{-7}} \simeq 400 \ \textbf{\textit{Ans.}}$$

26. Total number of polaroids $= 2 + (N-1) = N+1$.

If θ is the angular between consecutive two polaroids, then

$$N\theta = \frac{\pi}{2}$$

or $\qquad \theta = \dfrac{\pi}{2N}.$

According to Malus, if I_0 is the intensity of the light incident on second polaroid (after emerging from first), then intensity of emerging light from it is given by

$$I_\theta = I_0 \cos^2\theta.$$

After emerging from N polaroid, it is

$$I = (I_0 \cos^2\theta)^N = I_0(\cos\theta)^{2N}$$
$$= \left[I_0 \cos\left(\frac{\pi}{2N}\right) \right]^{2N}. \qquad \textbf{\textit{Ans.}}$$

When N is very large ; $\dfrac{\pi}{2N} \to 0$,

$$\therefore \qquad I \to I_0.$$

27. If I_0 is the intensity of plane polarised light incident on the polariser, then intensity of emerging light is given by

$$I = I_0 \cos^2\theta$$

The average value of I over one revolution can be calculated as :

$$I_{av} = \frac{1}{2\pi} \int_0^{2\pi} I d\theta$$
$$= \frac{1}{2\pi} \int_0^{2\pi} I_0 \cos^2\theta \, d\theta$$
$$= \frac{I_0}{2}.$$

Intensity is given by

$$I_0 = \frac{\text{Power}}{\text{area}}$$
$$= \frac{10^{-3}}{3 \times 10^{-4}} = \frac{10}{3} \ \text{W/m}^2.$$
$$\therefore \qquad I_{av} = \frac{I_0}{2} = \frac{5}{3} \text{W/m}^2.$$

The energy of light passing through the polariser per revolution

$$E = I_{av} \times A \times T = I_{av} \times A \times \frac{2\pi}{\omega}$$
$$= \frac{5}{3} \times (3 \times 10^{-4}) \times \frac{2\pi}{31.4}$$
$$= 10^{-4} \ \text{J.} \qquad \textbf{\textit{Ans.}}$$

28. It should be remembered that the transmitted intensity of unpolarised light will be $I_0/2$ for all orientation of polariser sheet whereas the intensity of polarised light varies from zero to I_p. Thus intensity of emerging light from polarising sheet will be;

$$I_{min} = I_0/2,$$

and $\qquad I_{max} = \dfrac{I_0}{2} + I_p.$

According to given condition; $I_{max} = 4I_{min}$

or $\qquad \dfrac{I_0}{2} + I_p = 4\dfrac{I_0}{2}$

$$\therefore \qquad I_p = \frac{3I_0}{2}$$

or $\qquad \dfrac{I_p}{I_0} = \dfrac{3}{2}$

For $\theta = 45°$, $\qquad I = \dfrac{I_0}{2} + I_p \cos^2 45°$

$$= \frac{I_0}{2} + \frac{I_p}{2}$$
$$= \frac{I_0}{2} + \frac{3I_0/2}{2} = \frac{5I_0}{4}. \qquad \textbf{\textit{Ans.}}$$